DATE DUE

JUL 1 1 2003			
DEC 0 5 2011			

A Reference Guide to the Bible in Emily Dickinson's Poetry

FORDYCE R. BENNETT

The Scarecrow Press, Inc.
Lanham, Md., & London
1997

SCARECROW PRESS, INC.

Published in the United States of America
by Scarecrow Press, Inc.
4720 Boston Way
Lanham, Maryland 20706

4 Pleydell Gardens, Folkestone
Kent CT20 2DN, England

British Cataloguing-in-Publication Information Available

Library of Congress Cataloging-in-Publication Data

Bennett, Fordyce R.
    A reference guide to the Bible in Emily Dickinson's poetry / Fordyce R.
Bennett.
        p. cm.
    Includes bibliographical references and index.
    ISBN 0–8108–3247–X (alk. paper)
    1. Dickinson, Emily, 1830–1886—Religion—Indexes. 2. Religious poetry,
American—Indexes. 3. Bible—In literature—Indexes.
I. Title.
PS1541.Z5B435   1997
811'.4—dc20   96–42431
                                                 CIP

ISBN 0–8108–3247–X (cloth : alk.paper)

To my wife, Margie,
and my two daughters,
Kari and Kristi

CONTENTS

ACKNOWLEDGMENTS

Poetry is reprinted by permission of the publishers and the Trustees of Amherst College from *The Poems of Emily Dickinson*, Thomas H. Johnson, ed., Cambridge, Mass. : The Belknap Press of Harvard University Press, Copyright © 1951, 1955, 1979, 1983 by the President and Fellows of Harvard College and from *The Complete Poems of Emily Dickinson*, edited by Thomas H. Johnson. Copyright 1929, 1935 by Martha Dickinson Bianchi; Copyright © renewed 1957, 1963 by Mary L. Hampson: Little, Brown and Company, Boston.
Poetry is reprinted by permission of the publisher from *Life and Letters of Emily Dickinson*, edited by Martha Dickinson Bianchi. Copyright 1924 by Martha Dickinson Bianchi, © renewed in 1952 by Alfred Leete Hampson. Reprinted by permission of Houghton Mifflin Co. All rights reserved. Poetry is reprinted by permission of the publishers from *Emily Dickinson Face to Face*, edited by Martha Dickinson Bianchi. Copyright 1932 by Martha Dickinson Bianchi. Copyright © renewed 1960 by Alfred Leete Hampson. Reprinted by permission of Houghton Mifflin Co. All rights reserved.

Used by permission are references to *The Years and Hours of Emily Dickinson* by Jay Leyda, New Haven, Ct.; Yale University Press, copyright 1960.

Used by permission are references to *The Letters of Emily Dickinson*, Thomas H. Johnson, ed., Cambridge, Mass.: The Belknap Press of Harvard University Press, copyright 1958, 1986 by the President and Fellows of Harvard College.

Used by permission are references to *The Manuscript Books of Emily Dickinson*, R.W. Franklin, ed., Cambridge, Mass.: The Belknap Press of Harvard University Press, copyright 1981 by the President and Fellows of Harvard College.

Used by permission are references to *The Life of Emily Dickinson*, Richard Sewall, Cambridge, Mass.: The Belknap Press of Harvard University Press, copyright 1974, 1980, 1994 by the President and Fellows of Harvard College.

LIST OF ABBREVIATIONS

This reference guide uses the numbers and lines given in *The Poems of Emily Dickinson*, 3 volumes, edited by Thomas H. Johnson, Harvard University Press, 1955. The following shortened forms are used throughout:

Franklin *The Manuscript Books of Emily Dickinson*, edited by R.W. Franklin, 2 vols. Cambridge, Mass.: The Belknap Press of Harvard University Press, 1981.

Johnson *Emily Dickinson An Interpretive Biography*, by Thomas H. Johnson. New York: Macmillan Publishing Company, 1955.

Letters *The Letters of Emily Dickinson*, edited by Thomas H. Johnson, 3 vols. Cambridge, Mass.: The Belknap Press of Harvard University Press, 1958.

Leyda *The Years and Hours of Emily Dickinson*, edited by Jay Leyda, 2 vols. New Haven, Conn.: Yale University Press, 1960.

Poems *The Poems of Emily Dickinson*, edited by Thomas H. Johnson, 3 vols. Cambridge, Mass.: The Belknap Press of Harvard University Press, 1955.

Sewall *The Life of Emily Dickinson*, by Richard B. Sewall, one volume edition. Cambridge, Mass.: The Belknap Press of Harvard University Press, 1994.

The following abbreviations for the books of the Authorized King James Version of the Holy Bible have been used:

Ge	Genesis	Isa	Isaiah	Ro	Romans
Ex	Exodus	Jer	Jeremiah	ICo	ICorinthians
Le	Leviticus	La	Lamentations	IICo	IICorinthians
Nu	Numbers	Eze	Ezekiel	Ga	Galatians
De	Deuteronomy	Da	Daniel	Eph	Ephesians
Jos	Joshua	Ho	Hosea	Php	Phillipians
Jg	Judges	Joe	Joel	Col	Colossians
Ru	Ruth	Am	Amos	ITh	IThessalonians
ISa	ISamuel	Ob	Obadiah	IITh	IIThessalonians
IISa	IISamuel	Jon	Jonah	ITi	ITimothy
IKi	IKings	Mic	Micah	IITi	IITimothy
IIKi	IIKings	Na	Nahum	Tit	Titus
ICh	IChronicles	Hab	Habakkuk	Phm	Philemon
IICh	IIChronicles	Zep	Zephaniah	Heb	Hebrews
Ezr	Ezra	Hag	Haggai	Jas	James
Ne	Nehemiah	Zec	Zechariah	IPe	IPeter
Es	Esther	Mal	Malachi	IIPe	IIPeter
Job	Job	Mt	Matthew	IJo	IJohn
Ps	Psalms	Mr	Mark	IIJo	IIJohn
Pr	Proverbs	Lu	Luke	IIIJo	IIIJohn
Ec	Ecclesiastes	Joh	John	Jude	Jude
Ca	Canticles	Ac	Acts	Rev	Revelation

KJV King James Version

PREFACE

This *Reference Guide* contains a listing of words, phrases, and passages echoed or quoted from the Authorized Version of the Bible in the poems of Emily Dickinson. The relevant poems are treated seriatim beginning with the first poem of volume one of the Johnson edition. Cross-references to other poems, letters, and prose fragments as well as references to standard reference works are given. Where relevant, brief explanatory material is added. It is hoped that this work will serve the purpose of a handy reference to Bible backgrounds for the reader of Emily Dickinson's poetry.

Emily Dickinson found story and situation, syntax, symbolism and imagery, inspiration, and much more in the King James Bible. This reference guide attempts to identify all the verbatim quotes from the Authorized Version, which appear in the three-volume Johnson edition. Biblical backgrounds, characters, parallels, ideas, and echoes have been pointed out as well. Interpretation, though unavoidable, has been limited to brief parenthetical and terminal comments only where thought necessary. References to textual and biographical backgrounds have followed closely the primary Dickinson materials but with no attempt at exhaustiveness. The Leyda and Johnson editions furnish journal and correspondence contexts for individual poems without which the relevance of the King James is often missed. The letters of Emily Dickinson contain far more extensive and direct references to the Bible than do the poems. Her mind was saturated with the Authorized Version; to paraphrase Roethke, the Bible freed Emily Dickinson to hear her being from ear to ear.

For the benefit of the reader, the following sample entry is given:

62   **"Sown in dishonor"!**

> 1.1   " 'Sown...dishonor' ": ICo 15:43 ("It [the natural body] is sown in dishonour; it is raised in glory: it is sown in weakness; it is raised in power")
>
> 1.3   "May...be": ICo 15:43
>
> 1.6   " 'Sown...corruption' ": ICo 15:42 ("So also is the resurrection of the dead. It is sown in corruption; it is raised in incorruption")
>
> 1.8   "Apostle...askew": ICo 15:9 (St. Paul the Apostle," author of the Corinthian letters)
>
> 1.7   (variant) "By...means": Ro 6:15
>
> Comment: See *Poems*, I 47-48.

Entries follow the pattern of Johnson number and first line as title. Lines from the poems for which there are biblical quotations, word echoes, or background ideas are then treated seriatim. P62, "Sown in dishonor"!, uses quotations directly from the Authorized Version and also refers specifically to the Apostle Paul. For this entry, quotation has been given, although this will not always be the case for reasons of space. For example, P59 has as its immediate background the thirty-second chapter of Genesis as well as other chapters delineating the character of Jacob, complete quotation thus being unrealistic. Scripture verses should be studied as backgrounds and parallels and not simply as sources for verbatim use. Variant lines are so indicated and treated in like manner. Frequently, entries will end with comments giving explanatory notes and/or references to the basic works in the List of Abbreviations.

Throughout this volume are mentioned a number of literary personages and personal acquaintances of Emily Dickinson. Dates and biographical information relevant to identification may be found in *Poems*, III, 1189-1197; *Letters*, III, 933-958; and Leyda, I, xxvii-lxxxi. A brief list of selected persons mentioned in this reference guide is given in the appendix but is not intended as a substitute for the entries in Johnson or the lengthy discussions of grouped personages in Leyda.

Chapter 1

References and Notes on Poems 1 - 493
[1850 - 1862]

1   **Awake ye muses nine**

1.3   "Earth...made": Ge 2:4

1.4   "unity...twain": Ge 2:24 ("Therefore shall a man leave his father and his mother, and shall cleave unto his wife: and they shall be one flesh")

1.6   "God...single": Ge 1 (a reference to the binary nature of the creation account: heaven-earth, day-night, light-darkness, sea-dry land, and sun-moon)

1.7   "The...one": Ge 2:24; Joh 3:29; Rev 22:17 ("Into this holy estate these two persons present come now to be joined," "The Form of Solemnization of Holy Matrimony," *The Book of Common Prayer*)

1.8   "Adam...Eve": Ge 3:20

1.9   "The...be": Ge 3; Eph 5:22

1.12   "None...seeketh": Mt 7:7 ("Ask, and it shall be given you; seek, and ye shall find; knock, and it shall be opened unto you")

1.21   "The...bride": Ge 3:1-3, 19

1.28   "thou...sown": Lu 19:21; Ga 6:7 ("Whatsoever a man soweth, that shall he also reap")

1.33   "thou...see": ICo 13:12; Rev 3:18

1.40   "glory": Col 3:4; ITh 2:12; ITi 3:16; IPe 1:21, 5:1, 10; Jude 24; Rev 21:11, 23-26 (synecdochic of Heaven—here a witty hyperbole for the Paradise of united lovers)

Comment: See Leyda, I, 169.

2   There is another sky

ll.1-14 "There...come": Ge 2-3; Eze 28:13-14; 31:8-9, 16; 47:1-12; Rev 2:27; 22:1-5 (Paradise)

l. 14   "my garden": Ca 4:12, 16; 5:1; 6:2, 11 (the beloved as a garden)

Comment: See *Poems*, I, 2-3; *Letters*, I, 147-150; and Leyda, I, 219-220.

3   "Sic transit gloria mundi"

l.1   " 'Sic...mundi' ": ICo 7:31

l.17   "Put...Adam": Ge 3:1-12

ll.31-32 "That...tree": Ge 3

l.49   "The...them": ICo 15:52 ("the trumpet shall sound, and the dead shall be raised incorruptible")

Comment: See *Poems*, I, 3-6 and Leyda, I, 234-236.

4   On this wondrous sea

ll.4-6   "Knowest...o'er": Rev 21:1 (the New Jerusalem where there is no sea)

l.11   "Eternity": Isa 57:15

Comment: See *Poems*, I, 6-7; *Letters*, I, 226; and Leyda, I, 263.

5   I have a Bird in spring

ll.13-14 "Fast...Land": Rev 21-22 (Heaven)

ll.19-20 "In...light": Rev 21:23-24; 22:5

ll.22-24 "Each...removed": Rev 7:17; 21:4

ll.11,29 "Melody new," "Bright melody": Rev 5:9; 14:3

Comment: See *Poems*, I, 7-8; *Letters*, I, 305-307, 309-310; and Leyda, I, 317-318, 321.

7   The feet of people walking home

l.5   "The...Hallelujah": Rev 19:1, 6

l.11   "Seraph's": Isa 6:2, 6

ll.15-16 "Death...Immortality": ICo 15:50-55

l.19   "Angels": Rev 3:5; 5:11; 8:2, 6; 14:10; 15:1, 6-8; 21:9, 12

l.22   "My...adores": ICo 13:12

l.24   "resurrection": ICo 15:35-55

Comment: See *Poems*, I, 9-10.

8   There is a word

ll.1-3   "There...man": Heb 4:12; Rev 1:6; 19:15, 21 (the iconography is adapted for the uses of P8)

l.7   "Saved": Rev 21:24

l.8   "On...day": Joh 11:24 (the day of the resurrection)

10   My wheel is in the dark!

l.13   "gate": Rev 21:12-13, 15, 21, 25

13   Sleep is supposed to be

l.6   "The...stand": Heb 10:28

ll.10-15 "Morning...Day": Joe 2:31; Mal 3:2; 4:1; IIPe 3:7; Jude 6; Rev 6:17; 16:14 (the Judgment Morning or Day, the language here being apocalyptic)

ll.10,11,14 "Morning," "Aurora," "red array": Mal 4:2; Lu 1:78; IIPe 1:19; Rev 2:28; 22:16

l.12   "Eternity": Isa 57:15 (Heaven)

l.13   "banner": Ca 2:4

Comment: See *Poems*, I, 16-17; *Letters*, II, 344; and Leyda, I, 361-362. The context of P13 in the letters suggests the manner in which the apocalypticism of the poem is used for witty hyperbole.

15   The Guest is gold and crimson

ll.1,2,6 "Guest," "guest," "door": Rev 3:20

l.1   "gold," "crimson": Ex 26:29, 31-32, 37 (crimson, purple, blue, and gold are consistently used by the poet in nature epiphany poems—the colors being associated with the vail, with the tabernacle and its appurtenances, including the priestly garments, and, most importantly, with that ideal presence of face-to-face interview with God enjoyed by the patriarchs of the Old Testament and now only shared through the oblique and distant "Haunted House" of art, specifically its lexicon in poetry; see especially chapters 25 through 28 of Exodus)

         l.3   "Ermine": Rev 1:14; 3:4

        Comment: See *Poems*, I, 18-19.

18   The Gentian weaves her fringes

        l.8   "angels": see note, line nineteen, P7

        l.15   "Seraph": see note, line eleven, P7

        ll.17-19 "In...Amen": Mt 28:19-20 ("in the name of the Father, and of the Son, and of the Holy Ghost...Amen"); see also the "Ministration of Holy Baptism," *Book of Common Prayer* ("I baptize thee In the Name of the Father, and of the Son, and of the Holy Ghost. Amen.")

20   Distrustful of the Gentian

        l.15   "Heaven": Ge 1:1, 8

22   All these my banners be.

        l.8   "To...again": Mt 10:39

        l.10   "The...then": Mt 6:20

        l.19   " 'There...snow'": Rev 21:4

        l.20   "To...heart": Mt 5:8; Tit 1:15

23   I had a guinea golden

        l.18   "One...name": Job 9:9; 38:31

        l.31   "traitor": Ge 1:1, passim (P23 is a complaint regarding circuit world deprivation directed to God)

        ll.35-36 "And...find": Ec 2:11

24   There is a morn by man unseen

        l.1   "There...unseen": see note, lines ten-fifteen, P13 (for "unseen" see Isa 64:4; ICo 2:9: "Eye hath not seen, nor ear heard, neither have entered into the heart of man, the things which God hath prepared for them that love him")

l.3   "Seraphic": see note, line eleven, P7

l.17   "Chrysolite": Rev 21:20

l.20   "Mystic green": Rev 22:1-5 (this vision of paradise, as in P2, may owe something to the perpetual spring-summer in the New Jerusalem depicted by St. John the Divine)

l.24   "different dawn": Rev 2:28; 22:16 (suggesting the dawning of eternal morning, night being no more, Rev 22:5)

28   So has a Daisy vanished

l.4   "Paradise": see note, lines one-fourteen, P2

l.5   "crimson": see note, line one, P15

l.8   "Are...God": Rev 21:3

31   Summer for thee, grant I may be

ll.5-9   "For...forevermore": ICo 15:35-55 (the variant for "row" is "sow," the word "tomb" is a synonym for "grave," and the "I" is "gather[ed]" rather than raised; nevertheless, P31 might be described as a muted, Paulinian-resurrection poem)

32   When Roses cease to bloom, Sir,

ll.1,8   "When...pray": ICo 15:50-55 ("Sir" is Death and, by extension, God)

37   Before the ice is in the pools -

ll.6-8   "Before...me": Lu 2 (the poet here uses the Advent metaphorically; "wonder" echoes the frequent KJV doublet "signs and wonders," De 28:46; Ne 9:10; Jer 32:20; Da 6:27; Mt 24:24; Mr 13:22; Joh 4:48; Ac 2:22; Ro 15:19; IICo 12:12; Heb 2:4)

l.9   "What...of": Mt 14:36 ("And besought him that they might only touch the hem of his garment: and as many as touched were made perfectly whole"; see also Mt 9:20-21)

39   It did not surprise me -

1.8   "God's...vows": Ge 1-3; Ex 20:1-17 (the line may refer to the KJV in toto, suggesting God's revelation, which the more modern "story" transcends)

40   When I count the seeds

ll.1-6   "When...high": ICo 15:35-55 (the lexicon of P40 and its organic analogy are Paulinian)

1.7   "When...garden": Rev 22:1-5 (the poet may have in mind the Garden of Eden and paradise, Ge 2-3; Eze 28:13-14; 31:8-9, 16; 47:1-12; Rev 2:7)

1.8   "Mortal...see": ICo 15:50 ("Now this I say, brethren, that flesh and blood cannot inherit the kingdom of God; neither doth corruption inherit incorruption")

1.9   "Pick...blossom": Heb 11:1, 3

43   Could live - did live

1.4   "T[h]rough...not": Joh 20:29; Heb 11:1; IJo 4:12

ll.6-9   "Could...heart": ICo 15:50-55 (Death as the movement from the "scene familiar" of the circuit world)

46   I keep my pledge.

1.11   "Will...again": Joh 14:3

48   Once more, my now bewildered Dove

ll.1-8   "Once...Land": Ge 8:8-12 (Noah sent a dove from the ark three times, on the second flight the dove returning with an "oak leaf" suggesting "Land")

49   I never lost as much but twice,

1.4   "Before...God": Job 38:17; Ps 9:13; 107:18 (the gate or door of death)

1.5   "Angels...descending": Ge 28:12

1.7   "Burglar...Father": Mt 6:9 (God the "Father" is addressed in terms of domestic intimacy in the Lord's Prayer; prima facie the other terms for the Deity appear outrageous, but the KJV presents a jealous God [Ex 20:5; 34:14], a God of reckoning and counting [Nu 1, passim; Job 14:16; Lu 12:7], and, finally, a God in several places a "Burglar" or "thief" [ITh 5:2; IIPe 3:10; Rev 3:3; 16:15])

50   I hav'nt told my garden yet-

l.5   "I...street": Ec 12:4
l.15   "Riddle": ICo 15:51 (the "mystery" of death)

53   Taken from men - this morning -

l.7   "Eden": Ge 2-3; Eze 28:13; 36:35; Joe 2:3
l.9   "Far...Even": Ps 103:12
l.11   "Courtiers...Kingdoms": Rev 1:6; 11:15; 20:6; 22:5

54   If I should die,

l.1   "If...die": see notes for P1539 (the echo of the *New England Primer* sets the tone for P54)

57   To venerate the simple days

l.6   "mortality": IICo 5:4

58   Delayed till she had ceased to know -

ll.5,14 "Death," "Victory": ICo 15:54-55
l.18   "Doubtful...crowned": Rev 2:10; 3:11; 4:4, 10
Comment: See *Poems*, I, 43-44.

59   A little East of Jordan,

l.1   "A...Jordan": Ge 32:10 (the variant "over" appears in verse ten)
l.2   "Evangelist/Genesis": Ge 32 (the variant actually names the relevant book of the Old Testament)
l.3   "A...Angel": Ge 32:24-30 (the poet names Jacob both as "Gymnast" and "Wrestler"; the "Angel" is actually identified elsewhere, Ho 12:4)

l.5   "Till...mountain": Ge 32:24

ll.7-8   "The...return": Ge 32:26a ("And he [the "Angel"] said, Let me go, for the day breaketh")

l.9   "Not...Jacob": Ge 25:26 (Jacob, the heel-catcher, the supplanter, whose very name embodied "cunning" since he defrauded his brother Esau of his birthright and paternal blessing, was a prototypical confidence man)

ll.10-11   " 'I...me' ": Ge 32:26b ("And he [Jacob] said, I will not let thee go, except thou bless me")

l.11   "Stranger": Ge 32:29 (the "Angel" refuses to divulge an identity)

l.12   "The...to": Ge 32:29 (the "Angel" does, however, grant a new name to Jacob along with the requested blessing)

l.13   "Light...fleeces": Ge 32:31 (the sunrise)

l.14   " 'Peniel' ": Ge 32:30 (Jacob named the place Peniel, the location "East of Jordan" meaning literally "face of God")

l.16   "Found...God": Ge 32:30b ("for I have seen God face to face, and my life is preserved"); see also Ho 12:3-4 and the discussion of Ge 32 by Roland Barthes in *Image-Music-Text*

Comment: Although whimsical in tone, P59 veils a deep-seated anxiety of the poet regarding the absence of God, obliquely expressing an envy for that face-to-face ideal presence, shared for example by Jacob and Moses, which for her was "typic" of the beatific vision (Rev 22:4). See Poems, I, 44-45, which discusses and lists the extensive number of variants. It is also possible that P59 contains a subtle irony directed at an assertive maleness marked by the Deity as are the Spartans similarly by the State/Law in P1554. For the matter of self-marking see P508 and P1142.

60   Like her the Saints retire

ll.1-2   "Like...fire": IIKi 2:11 (Elijah ascended into Heaven in a chariot of fire)

l.5   "Purple...Cochineal": see note, line one, P15 (the gatherings and sunsets are both transitions occasioning epiphanies—the red and purple associated with the presence of God behind the vail of the tabernacle)

ll.7-9   " 'Departed'...found": Ge 5:24; IIKi 2:11; Heb 11:5 (Elijah and Enoch are the "Saints" "gathered away" or, as St. Paul says, speaking of Enoch, "translated")

Comment: See *Poems*, I, 45-46.

61   Papa above!

l.1   "Papa above": Mt 6:9 ("Our Father which art in heaven")

l.4   "Reserve...kingdom": Mt 6:10 ("Thy kingdom" also appears in The Lord's Prayer)

l.5   "A...Rat": Joh 14:2 ("In my Father's house are many mansions: if it were not so, I would have told you. I go to prepare a place for you")

ll.6-7   "Snug...day": Rev 7:16; 9:7-9; 22:1-2, 17 (the New Jerusalem promises the tree of life as well as the absence of hunger—oral gratification for the "Mouse" who wishes to eat rather than be eaten; an early expression of her dissatisfaction with the Beatitudes philosophy of poverty, mourning, and hunger below all for the delayed vision of God above, P61 is parodic of The Lord's Prayer which promises "daily bread" for her circuit world as well as the fulfillment of God's will here below as in Heaven—the latter conception she pokes fun at as "unsuspecting Cycles" unconcerned about the sublunary world of "Cat" and "Mouse")

62   "Sown in dishonor"!

l.1   " 'Sown...dishonor' " ICo 15:43 ("It [the natural body] is sown in dishonour; it is raised in glory: it is sown in weakness; it is raised in power")

l.3   "May...be": ICo 15:43

l.6   " 'Sown...corruption' ": ICo 15:42 ("So also is the resurrection of the dead. It is sown in corruption; it is raised in incorruption")

l.8   "Apostle...askew": ICo 15:9 (St. Paul the "Apostle," author of the Corinthian letters)

l.7   (variant) "By...means": Ro 6:15

Comment: See *Poems*, I, 47-48.

63   If pain for peace prepares

ll.1-2   "If...years": Lu 2:1 (see also Isa 9:6-7)

l.7   "If...noon": Ge 1:1-5 (the order of creation, first darkness, then light)

ll.8-9,12 "To...blaze": Rev 1:16; 10:1; 21:23-24; 22:5

l.11   "developed eyes": Rev 3:18 (the Emersonian and Blakean idea of apocalypse as vision: "Not 'Revelation'—'tis—that waits,/But our unfurnished eyes," P685; see also P574)

Comment: See *Poems*, I, 48-49.

64   Some Rainbow- coming from the Fair!

1.1   "Rainbow": Ge 13-16; Rev 4:3

1.1   "Fair": Ca 1:15; 4:1, 7; 7:6 (a favorite Canticles word here used as a synecdoche for God as creator of beauty manifested in nature, Ps 8; 19; 90)

1.4   "purple": see note, line one, P15

1.22   "Behold...these": Ge 1:26-31 ("Behold, I have given you...," Ge 1:29; this "Vision of the World Cashmere" is Edenic)

Comment: See *Poems*, I, 49-50.

65   I cant tell you- but you feel it-

1.1   "I...it": IICo 12:2-3

1.3   "Saints...pencil": IPe 1:8 (the "Saints" are the elect who have such inexpressible visions)

ll.5-6   "Sweeter...green": Ge 2-3 (the vision of April transcends any experience of prelapsarian Eden)

1.9   "Modest...it": Ge 3:8; Rev 3:4; 19:8

1.11   "Archangels": ITh 4:16; Jude 9 (neither KJV reference to archangels mentions vailed faces; the two instances most relevant—that of Rebekah, Ge 24:65, and Moses, Ex 34:33-35—do not fit the context of P65; nevertheless, the numerous KJV references to the vail— Ex 26:31-35; IICo 3:13-16; Heb 6:19; 9:3; 10:20— do suggest the presence of God of which the "April Day" is "typic")

1.13   "Not...it": IICo 12:4

1.19   "sublime Recitation": Rev 4:8-11; 5:9-13

Comment: See *Poems*, I, 50-52 and Leyda, I, 368.

66   So from the mould

1.2   "Scarlet...Gold": see note, line one, P15

ll.3, 6-8 "Many...gay": ICo 15:35-55 (P66 is a Hitchcockian poem, the "Bulb" and "Cocoon" emblematic of the resurrection—such metamorphosis making circuit world peasant poverty manifest)

67   Success is counted sweetest

l.4   "sorest need": Mt 5:3 (the poet's philosophy of circuit world poverty, deprivation, or destitution is based in the paradoxes of the Beatitudes, Mt 5:2-12); see also Mt 9:15; Lu 5:34-35)
l.8   "Victory": ICo 15:54-57 (a further KJV paradox that allowed the poet to transvalue circuit world notions of "Success")
Comment: See *Poems*, I, 53-54; *Letters*, II, 411-412, 625-627; and Leyda, II, 63-64, 302-303.

68   Ambition cannot find him

l.8   "Immortality": ICo 15:54-55

70   "Arcturus" is his other name-

l.1   " 'Arcturus' ": Job 9:9; 38:32
l.2   " 'Star' ": Ge 1:16
l.7   " 'Resurgam' ": Mt 27:63 ("After three days I will rise again")
l.8   " 'Oh...we' ": Ps 39:4
l.17   " 'Heaven' ": Ge 1:1, 8; Rev 3:12; 4:1-2; 19-22
l.20   "When...done": Rev 10:6 ("And sware by him that liveth for ever and ever, who created heaven,... that there should be time no longer")
ll. 26-27 "Perhaps...there": Mt 19:14 ("But Jesus said, Suffer little children, and forbid them not, to come unto me: for of such is the kingdom of heaven")
l.30   "Father...skies": Mt 6:9 ("Our father which art in heaven")
l.33   " 'Pearl' ": Rev 21:21
Comment: See *Poems*, I, 55-57.

73   Who never lost, are unprepared

ll.1-2   "lost," "find": Mt 16:25

l.2   "Coronet": Isa 62:3-4; ICo 9:25; ITi 4:8; Jas 1:12; IPe 5:4; Rev 2:9-10; 3:11; 4:4, 10 (the ideally circum-ferential diadem or crown)

l.3   "Who...thirsted": Mt 5:6 (see note, line four, P67)

l.7   "purple": see note, line one, P15

l.9   "overcome": Rev 2:7, 11, 17, 26; 3:5, 12, 21; 21:7 (line fifteen connects with line nine by Rev 3:12)

l.14   "Royal scar": Joh 19:2, 5, 34; 20; 25 (the wounds from the crucifixion; see Isa 53:3-5; the poet identified with the Passion Christ, P313)

l.15   "Angels...'Promoted' ": Rev 7:3-8; 22:4 (the name of God is written or sealed upon the foreheads of the "Promised"; see also Rev 3:12)

l.16   "Soldier's": IITi 2:3-4

Comment: See *Poems*, I, 58-59.

74   A Lady red- amid the Hill

l.3   "white": Rev 3:4-5, 18; 7:9; 19:8 (the poet's "Resurrection" and Revelation white)

l.15   "As...'Resurrection' ": ICo 15:50-55

l.16   "Were....strange": ICo 15:51 (St. Paul speaks of the resurrection as a "mystery")

Comment: See *Poems*, I, 59-60.

78   A poor- torn heart- a tattered heart-

ll.9-12 "The...God": Lu 16:22 (the poet has in mind Lazarus, a prototype of the destitute, hungry, circuit world beggar)

l.15   "blue": see note, line one, P15.

Comment: See *Poems*, I, 63-64 and Leyda, I, 377.

79   Going to Heaven!

l.1   "Going...Heaven": Rev 3:12; 4:1-2; 19-22

l.10   "Unto...arm": Ps 23:1; 80:1; Isa 40:11; Joh 10:11, 14; IPe 2:25; 5:4

l.16   "The...me": Rev 6:11; 19:8 (the dress of the sealed and crowned elect)

l.17   "And...'Crown' ": Rev 2:10; 3:11; 4:4, 10

Comment: See *Poems*, I, 64-65.

81   We should not mind so small a flower-

ll.9-10 "That...behold": Mt 6:28-38 ("And whoso shall receive one such little child in my name receiveth me," Mt 18:5)
ll.11-12 "The...gold": Rev 4:2-4; 8:2-3
Comment: See *Poems*, I, 66.

84   Her breast is fit for pearls,

ll.1,3,5 "breast," "brow," "heart": Ca 4 (appearing in other chapters of Canticles as well the taxonomy of the beloved gives to P84 at least its outline)
l.7   "Sweet": Ca 2:3, 14; 5:5, 13, 16; 7:9
Comment: See *Poems*, I, 68-69.

85   "They have not chosen me," he said

ll.1-2   " 'They...them' ": Joh 15:16 ("Ye have not chosen me, but I have chosen you, and ordained you, that ye should go and bring forth fruit, and that your fruit should remain: that whatsoever ye shall ask of the Father in my name, he may give it you")
l.4   "Bethleem": Joh 12:12 (the words of lines one and two were apparently "uttered" in Jerusalem)
ll.5-6   "I...dared": Isa 53; Mr 9:12-13
ll.3-8   "Brave...shared": Mt 12:17-21; Isa 42:1-4 (the poet has identified her own election, e.g., Mr 13:20, with that of Christ's being chosen by God as the "Suffering Servant," the prophecy of Isaiah concerning a "Brave—Broken hearted and dishonor[ed]" Jesus in a sense being "uttered" from all eternity "in Bethleem," the place of Christ's birth and the initiation point for His experience of the circuit world as Passion, an experience and role [Suffering Servant] with which the poet identifies)

89   Some things that fly there be-

l.5   "Grief...Eternity": Ps 18:7; 121:1; Ec 2:23; Isa 57:15
l.7   "There...rise": ICo 15:50-55

l.9   "How...lies": ICo 15:51 (the Paulinian "mystery" of the resurrection)

Comment: In the iconography of the poems, birds, bees, and butterflies are often emblems of the resurrection, thus needing "no Elegy."

90   Within my reach!

ll.1-2,8 "Within...fingers": Mt 14:36; Mr 6:56; Lu 6:19; Joh 20:27 (an instance of highly elliptical use of KJV echoes to intimate a missed opportunity for Emersonian vision)

92   My friend must be a Bird-

ll.1-2   "My...flies": Ps 90:10
ll.3-4   "Mortal...dies": ICo 15:53-54
l.5   "Barbs...Bee": ICo 15:55 ("O Death where is thy sting?")

Comment: The answer to the poet's riddle is the KJV "three-score years and ten"(Ps 90:10).

93   Went up a year this evening!

l.1   "Went up": Ac 1:10 (ascended into Heaven)
l.9   "Did...returning": Ec 12:7
ll.10-12 "Alluded...him": Mt 24:36-42
ll.17-18 "wonder," "wondrous": Ex 3:20; 4:21; 7:3; De 4:34; 6:22; Jos 3:5; Job 37:14, 16; Ps 77:14; 136:4; 145:5; Mt 24:24; Ac 2:19, 22; 7:31 (synecdochic for God)
l.22   "To...new": Rev 22:4 (the poem's terminal rhyme is apocalyptic for Revelation speaks of the New Jerusalem, a new name, a new song, a new heaven, and a new earth, Rev 3:12; 5:9; 14:3; 21:1-2; "Behold, I make all things new," Rev 21:5)
l.23   "Difference": ICo 15:51 ("...we shall all be changed"); see also IJo 3:2
l.24   "Is...knew": Rev 21:5

Comment: See *Poems*, I, 74. P93 echoes the epitaph of the poet: "Called Back."

94   Angels, in the early morning

l.1   "Angels": Ge 16:7-Rev 22:16 (in the KJV angels are spiritual beings who serve God in Heaven and are messengers of God below whose offices are to minister to and direct humans)

1.2   "Dews": Ge 27:28; Ex 16:13-14; Nu 11:9; Job 38:28; Ho 14:5; Mic 5:7; Zec 8:12 ("Dews" are visible signs of providential blessing connected with the heavens above)

1.6   "sands": e.g., Eze 37 (in the KJV desert places are ones of wandering, temptation, and sterility)

95   My nosegays are for Captives-

ll.1-2   "My...eyes": Ro 7:24; ICo 13:12; IICo 5:4; Php 3:21 ("Captives" are those in the body prison of the circuit world where postlapsarian vision has been darkened; the poems or "nosegays" of the poet have no other purpose or "errand" than to sustain those patiently awaiting "Paradise"—her poetry surrogate "prayer," a displacement given a circuit world whose essence is absence)

1.3   "Fingers...plucking": Ge 3:6, 22 (with the Fall, the fruit of "Paradise" or the tree of life is denied Adam and Eve); Rev 2:7; 22:2, 14 (in "Paradise" fingers are allowed to pluck the tree of life)

1.4   "Paradise": Rev 2:7, 21-22

1.6   "morning": Isa 58:8; Rev 2:28; 16:14; 22:16 ("morning" as apocalyptic promise)

96   Sexton! My Master's sleeping here.

ll.1-2,6 "Sexton...door": Joe 2:16; Ps 19:5 (the KJV marriage figuration is here applied to the spring as a bridegroom awakening and coming forth; the advent of spring is "typic" of the realization of paradise, Rev 19:7-9; 21:1-2; 22:1-5)

97   The rainbow never tells me

1.1   "rainbow": Ge 9:11-17; Rev 4:3; 10:1 (the rainbow is associated with the halcyon and heavenly; the wit of the poem turns on the contrast of the unconvincing partiality of Cato's Stoicism versus the convincing power of natural revelation even in its smiling aspects of "rainbow," "flowers," and "birds")

98   One dignity delays for all-

l.3   "purple": see note, line one, P15 (the color is also associated with the death of Christ, Mr 15:17, 20; Joh 19:2, 5)

l.4   "Crown": Job 29:14; Isa 28:5; 62:3-4; ICo 9:25; IITi 4:8; Jas 1:12; IPe 5:4; Rev 2:10; 3:11; 4:4, 10 (the "Crown" may be first, the divine favor and reward; second, the diadem of the Bride; third, a metonymy for the ideally circumferential face of God and for the name of God and the Lamb to be placed upon the forehead of the elect; see IICo 3:18; Rev 22:4)

l.13   "ermine": Rev 3:4-5, 18; 6:11; 7:9, 13-14; 19:8

l.15   "meek escutcheon": Mt 5:5; Rev 2:17; 3:12; 22:4 (an oxymoron based upon the poet's Beatitudes philosophy of circuit world poverty— "Blessed are the meek"— and her circuit world identity: "escutcheon" interchangeably metonymic for her face and name)

Comment: See *Poems*, I, 76.

99   New feet within my garden go-

ll.1-2,5-6 "New": Rev 2:17; 3:12; 5:9; 14:3; 21:1-2, 5 (the anaphora utilizes a pivotal apocalyptic term to achieve an understated structural irony)

l.6   "Weary": Job 3:17 (synecdochic of the dead)

100   A science- so the Savans say,

ll.8-12   "This...Butterfly": Mt 6:28-30; Lu 12:27-28 (echoing perhaps the "meanest flower" of Wordsworth's "Intimations Ode," "Comparative Anatomy," finding in the "meekest flower" of winter proof of the spirit)

101   Will there really be a "Morning"?

ll.1-2,12 "Will...lies": Mt 7:22; 10:15; 11:24; 12:36; 24:36, 50; 25:13; ICo 1:8; 5:5; 15:50-55; Eph 4:30; Php 1:6; IPe 1:19; IJo 4:17; Jude 6; Rev 6:17; 16:14 ("Morning" of the resurrection and the "Day" of judgment, the "great day of God Almighty"); see also note, line six, P95 l.10   "Wise Man": Mt 2:1-2 (the wise men were led to the birthplace of Christ by a star in the east)

102   Great Caesar! Condescend

ll.1-4   "Great...leave": Mt 22:17-21 (the wit of the poem depends upon the dramatic vignette in which Caesar is associated with money, circuit world imperium, and not the nature of a "Daisy," a gift from God; Caesar was an earthly ruler demanding a material tribute, not the spiritual emblem gathered by a frugal "Daughter" of Cato; see also Joh 19:15)

103   I have a King, who does not speak-

l.1   "I...speak": Ps 5:2; 10:16; 24:7-10; 29:10; 44:4; 47:2; 74:12; 84:3; 95:3; Rev 15:3; 17:14; 19:16 (the Deus absconditus)
l.2   "meek": Mt 5:5
l.16   " 'Father'...today": Mt 6:10; 26:42

104   Where I have lost, I softer tread-

l.14   "Who...snow": Rev 3:4-5, 18; 6:11; 7:9; 19:8

106   The Daisy follows soft the Sun-

l.1   "The...Sun": Ps 19:5; Mal 4:2; Lu 1:78; IIPe 1:19; Rev 2:28; 22:16 (the personified "Sun" as Bridegroom)
l.6   "love...sweet": Ca 2:1-4, 13-14; 5:5, 13, 16; 4:1; 7:6-9 (the language is that of Canticles where the beloved is frequently spoken of in relation to flowers or sun and moon, Ca 21-2, 16; 4:5; 5:13; 6:2-3, 10; 7:2)
l.11   "Amethyst": Rev 21:20
ll.10,12 "Enamored...possibility": Ca 2:17; 4:6 (the topoi of profane love are used in P106 to express a hoped-for apocalyptic consummation, Rev 19:7-9; 22:16-17)

110   Artists wrestled here!

l.1   "Artists...here": Ge 32:24-25 (an elliptical reference intended to underscore the fact that the sunset is a natural epiphany or theophany)

ll.2-3   "Lo": e.g., Mt 3:16-17; 24:23; Lu 2:9; Rev 14:1 (a distinctive KJV interjection used to express wonder)

l.3   "Rose": see note, line one, P15 (an epiphany color)

112   Where bells no more affright the morn-

l.6   "Thro'...noon": Rev 22:5

l.7   "Heaven": Rev 21-22

l.8   "Please...soon": Rev 22:20

ll.9-10   " 'Oh...o'er' ": De 34:1-4 (Moses viewed the promised land from the top of Mt. Nebo, an experience "typic" of a view of Heaven)

Comment: See *Poems*, I, 82-83.

113   Our share of night to bear-

l.8   "Day": see note, lines one-two, twelve, P101

114   Good night, because we must,

l.2   "dust": Ge 3:19; Ps 103:14

l.5   "Seraph": see note, line eleven, P7 (the "Seraph" enjoying the presence of God is "Incognito," the dead divulging no knowledge)

l.7   "Father": IJo 5:7 (God the Father)

115   What Inn is this

l.1   "Inn": Ge 1-3 (synecdochic of the created universe, the circuit world in which the poet experiences a Gnostic sense of dislocation, disaffection, and dispossession— a "Peculiar Traveller" amid "curious rooms" absent the amenities of hearth and home: "no ruddy fires" and "no brimming Tankards")

l.9   "Landlord": Ge 1:1, passim (God, the Deus absconditus or Absentee Landlord)

116   I had some things that I called mine-

ll.2,11,14 "And...law": Ge 18:25; Ps 19:7-8; 24:1; 89:14; Ac 3; 14; 7:52; 10:42; Ro 7:12; 12:2; IITi 4:8; Jas 5:9; Heb 12:23 (the wit of P116 turns on the KJV conception of an omnipotent God, who is Law, Justice, the Just, the Righteous, and the Judge, brought to trial in order that the poet might "vindicate the law")

Comment: See *Poems*, I, 85.

117   In rags mysterious as these

l.3   "purple": see note, line one, P15
l.4   "ermine": Rev 3:4-5, 18; 6:11; 7:9
l.8   "golden": see note, line one, P15

118   My friend attacks my friend!

l.8   "glory": Col 3:4; ITh 2:12; ITi 3:16; Rev 1:6; 4:9, 11; 5:12, 13; 7:12; 11:13; 19:1; 21:11, 23-26 (Heaven)

121   As Watchers hang upon the East,

ll.1,7   "As...East": Mt 24:27; Rev 2:28; 22:16 (perhaps apocalyptic in connotation)
l.8   "Amethyst": Rev 21:20
l.9   "morning": see note, line six, P95
l.10   "That...Guest": Rev 19:7-9
ll.6,12   "Heaven": Rev 7:16-17; 19:7-9; 22:1-3, 17 (Heaven imaged as compensation for circuit world oral deprivation; "Beggars" are circuit world espousers of the Beatitudes philosophy of destitution, Mt 5:2-12)

Comment: See *Poems*, I, 87.

122   A something in a summer's Day

l.5   "Azure": see note, line one, P15
l.5   "perfume": Ex 30:34-38
l.6   "extasy": Ge 15; Isa 1; 6; Ac 2; ICo 14; IICo 12 (numerous examples of ecstasy are mentioned in the KJV involving inspired sight or supernatural vision; frequently in the poems these occasions of heightened epiphanic awareness are transition times:

noon, sunset, dawn, spring, Indian summer; although the "transporting bright," 1.8, and the "shimmering grace," 1.11, have no specific KJV provenance, it is often the case that visionary experience is conveyed in images of fire and light, e.g., IKi 19:12; Eze 1:13; Mt 17:15; Ac 9:3; 10:30; Rev 1:14-16)

      1.10   "Then...face": Ex 26; 34:29-35; Le 16; IICo 3:13 (the vail was the barrier beyond which was the presence of God; the "summer's Day" yields an epiphanic vision, a "shimmering grace," which the poet wishes to approach obliquely, face-to-face contact with God the preserve of such Old Testament figures as Moses and Jacob)

      1.14   "purple": see note, line one, P15

      ll.16,18 "amber," "Red": see note, line one, P15

      1.21   "dews": Ge 27:28; Ex 16:13; De 33:28; Mic 5:7 (connected with the bounties of heaven, the unmerited favors of God)

      Comment: See *Poems*, I, 88-89.

125   For each extatic instant

      ll.1,4   "extatic instant," "extasy": see note, line six, P122; note, line fifteen, P783; and notes, lines five and eight, P1191

      1.5   "beloved": Ca 1:14, 16; 2:3, 8-10, 16-17; 4:16; 5:1-10; 6:1-3; 7:9-11

126   To fight aloud, is very brave-

      ll.9-12 "We...Snow": Rev 4:4; 5:11; 7:9-12; 15:6; 19:14

127   'Houses'- so the Wise Men tell me-

      ll.1-6   " 'Houses'...built": Joh 14:2 ("In my Father's house are many mansions: if it were not so, I would have told you. I go to prepare a place for you"; Philip then asks Jesus to be shown the Father: "Jesus saith unto him, Have I been so long time with you, and yet hast thou not known me, Philip? he that hath seen me hath seen the Father; and how sayest thou then, Shew us the Father?" Joh 14:9; see also Joh 14:7; the italic "I" is underlined in the fascicles, Franklin, I, 96—Jesus uses "I" eleven times in the first ten verses of the fourteenth chapter of John)

128   Bring me the sunset in a cup,

ll.3,12   "Dew," "Dews": see note, line twenty one, P122
l.6   "Who...blue": Ge 1:6-8; Ps 104:2
l.8   "extasy": see note, line six, P122
l.13   "Also...piers": Ge 9:13-14
ll.14,17 "Also...night": Ge 1:16
l.19   "Who...House": Ge 1:26-27
ll.20-21 "And...see": ICo 13:12
l.22   "Who'll...day": ICo 15
l.23   "With...away":   Rev1:1,   passim   (apparently   a reference to wings like those of the angels)
Comment: The KJV provenance of P128 is the first chapter of Genesis, the rhetorical questions of this whimsical theodicy less disturbing here than elsewhere in her poetry.

129   Cocoon above! Cocoon below!

ll.1,2,7,9 "Cocoon," "Chrysalis," "Butterfly": ICo 15:35-55 (the larva-pupa-imago metamorphosis is for the poet a Hitchcockian emblem of the resurrection)
ll.2-3   "Stealthy...suspect": ICo 15:51   (its   "secret"   is the "mystery" of its change typifying the resurrection)
l.5   "extasy": see note, line six, P122
l.6   "Defies imprisonment": Ro 7:24; IICo 5:4; Php 3:21 (the "Butterfly" transcends the "Cocoon," thus escaping the body prison)
l.12   "The...know": ICo 13:12

130   These are the days when Birds come back-

l.6   "blue...gold": see note, line one, P15
ll.8-9   "Almost...belief": Ac 26:28 ("Then Agrippa said unto Paul, Almost thou persuadest me to be a Christian")
l.10   "seeds": ICo 15:38
l.10   "bear witness": Ex 20:16; Joh 1:7-8; IJo 5:6
ll.13-18 "Oh...wine": Mt 26:26-30 (the language of the final two stanzas is Eucharistic)
l.18   "immortal": ICo 15:53-54
Comment: See *Poems*, I, 92-93.

131   Besides the Autumn poets sing

l.15   "Grant...Lord": Ps 85:7; 140:8; Ac 4:29; IITi 1:18 (KJV language for petitioning prayer)

l.16   "Thy...bear": Mt 26:42

Comment: See *Poems*, I, 93-94.

132   I bring an unaccustomed wine

l.14   "thirsty": Mt 25:35, 37, 42

ll.17-19 "And...slake": Mt 10:42

l.21   " 'Unto...me' ": Mt 10:42; 25:40 (the quotation is a conflation of parts of these two verses)

ll.20-22 "If...awake": Mt 25:31-46 (the reference is to the Last Judgment when the King separates those on the right hand from those on the left)

137   Flowers- Well- if anybody

l.1   "Flowers": Ca 2:1-2, 12, 16; 4:5; 5:13; 6:2-3; 7:2

ll.2-4   "Can...men": Ca 4:9; 8:6-7

ll.5-6   "Anybody...flow": Ca 4:12, 15

l.9   "Too...faces": Ca 1:8-15; 2:14; 4:1-7; 5:15; 6:4-9; 7:1-6

l.12   "Cruising...line": Ca 3:10; 7:5

Comment: The passionate attractiveness of "Flowers" to "men" is a "system of aesthetics" that overwhelms the "simple breast" of the speaker in P137. The poem apparently celebrates the mysterious intensity of profane love and its beauty, confessing at the same time some limit of imaginative sympathy.

138   Pigmy seraphs- gone astray-

l.1   "seraphs": see note, line eleven, P7

l.1   "gone astray": Ps 119:176; Isa 53:6; Mt 18:12; IIPe 2:15 (familiar KJV phrasing)

l.6   "Emerald": Rev 21:19

ll.12-14 "I...her": Ro 3:24; 5:21; 6:23; IITi 1:9 (grace is the unmerited favor of God, the guarantor of salvation and eternal life; in the religio-aesthetic lexicon of P138 the "grace" of the ideally circumferential rose is its beauty, acceding to the poet's wish to appropriate it as a substitute face with which she dwells in a state transcending that of royalty, a state "typic" of dwelling in eternity with God, Rev 21:3)

Comment: See *Poems*, I, 98-99.

139   Soul, Wilt thou toss again?

ll.1-4   "Soul...all": Mt 16:25-26 (the situation of the soul threatened by the adversary or enemy and in danger of the pit may most closely approximate the idea of the wager in the KJV, e.g., Job 33:28-30; Ps 30:3; 35:1-10; 143; Job and Psalms are the two KJV books in which the soul is frequently addressed in a dramatic fashion comparable to that of P139)

l.6   "Lingers...thee": Rev 2:17; 3:5; 21:7 ("tens have won" and their names are recorded in the Lamb's Book of Life)

ll.5-8   "Angels'...Soul": Rev 7, 9, 12 (wars in Heaven and earth between the "Angels" and "Imps")

Comment: Drama and dissonance are heightened by the poet's choice of the lexicon of politics and gambling—"toss," "hazard," "ballot," "Caucus," "Raffle"— to meditate upon the soul's eternal destiny. The wry wit of her vision of devils in a smoke-filled caucus room may have been her oblique gibe at male politics and theology.

140   An altered look about the hills-

l.5   "vermilion": see note, line one, P15
l.6   "purple": see note, line one, P15
l.13   "I cannot tell": IICo 12:2-3
l.15   "Nicodemus' Mystery": Joh 3:1-8; ICo 15:51 (April is viewed as the transition time of rebirth and/or resurrection)

Comment: See *Poems*, I, 99-100.

141   Some, too fragile for winter winds

l.11   "Sparrows...Father": Mt 10:29, 31; Lu 12:6-7
l.12   "Lambs...fold": Ps 23:1; 79:13; 80:1; 95:7; 100:3; Isa 40:11; Jer 23:1; 31:10; 50:6 Eze 34:12; Mt 9:36; 10:6; 12:1; 182-3; Mr 6:34; Lu 15:4-6; Joh 10:2, 11, 14, 16, 27; 21:15; Heb 13:20; IPe

2:25; 5:4 (Shepherd-sheep figuration is throughout the KJV, her favorite Old Testament character, Jacob, involved with its uses in Genesis, Ge 48:15; 49:24; the references to "Sparrows" raise questions about the solicitude of the "Father")

143   For every Bird a Nest

       l.1   "For...Nest": Mt 8:20; Lu 9:58
       ll.16-18 "Yet...rejoice": Rev 21:22-24; 22:5 (the final lines ask the question of Browning's "Andrea del Sarto": "Ah, but a man's reach should exceed his grasp,/Or what's a heaven for?")
       Comment: See *Poems*, I, 102-103

144   She bore it till the simple veins

       l.2   "azure": see note, line one, P15
       l.4   "purple": see note, line one, P15
       l.7   "I...seem": IICo 12:2-3
       l.8   "And...down": Rev 5:8; 8:3; 11:18; 13:10; 15:3; 19:8; 20:9 ("sat down" may be derived from Mt 8:11)
       l.13   "Crowns": Rev 2:10; 3:11; 4:4, 10; 6:2; 12:1; 14:14; 19:12
       l.13   "Courtiers": Rev 19:7-9; 21:2, 9; 22:17
       l.14   "fair": Ca 1:8, 15-16; 2:10, 13; 4:1, 7, 10; 5:9; 6:1, 10; 7:6 (it is the vision of the apotheosis of the beloved that grants the poet, by proxy as it were, a sense of presence)
       ll.14-15 "And...face": ICo 15:53-54; Rev 22:2-4

145   This heart that broke so long-

       l.3   "This...vain": Mt 2:1-10; Rev 2:28; 22:16

147   Bless God, he went as soldiers,

       ll.1-4   "Bless...blest": Eph 6:11-17; ITi 6:12; IITi 2:3; 4:7 (the first stanza speaks of the military metaphors and their application: those who go as soldiers need only bravery in the charge)
       ll.5-8   "Please...fight": Rev 19:11-21 (in these verses the Word of God appears leading an army clothed in white into battle; perhaps the poet has these verses in mind as offering a vision of the

apocalyptic—one of the "epauletted white" flattening the uncertainties of death and beyond into matters of "foe" and "fight"—competing with the more congenial one of the Marriage Supper of the Lamb, Rev 19:7-9, the dialectic being love conquers doubt, not bravery conquers fear)

148   All overgrown by cunning moss,

ll.14-15 "Gethsemane...anguish": Mt 26:36-46 (setting in part for the Passion of Christ and used by the poet as a metaphor for the essence of circuit world existence, a place of suffering, denial of the will, and "anguish")

l.17   "Soft...Eden": Ge 2-3
l.19   "Heaven": Rev 21-22
Comment: See *Poems*, I, 106.

150   She died- this was the way she died.

l.3   "simple wardrobe": ICo 15:53-54 (the "simple wardrobe" is that of incorruption and immortality)
l.4   "sun": Rev 21:23-24; 22:5
l.5   "Her...gate": Rev 21:21, 25; 22:14
l.6   "The...spied": Rev 21:12
l.8   "Upon...side": ICo 15:53-54
Comment: See *Poems*, I, 107.

151   Mute thy Coronation-

ll.1-2   "Mute...roi": Ca 1:4, 12; 3:9-11; ITi 1:17; 6:15; Heb 7:2; Rev 15:3; 17:14; 19:16
l.3   "Fold...courtier": Ca 1:1, passim; Rev 19:7-9 (the profane beloved of Canticles and/or the Bride of Christ)
l.4   "In...Sir": Rev 1:14; 7:9; 19:8; 20:11 ("Ermine" white is associated with the Bridegroom and Bride)
l.8   "Master...I": Mt 23:10; Eph 6:9; Col 4:1
Comment: Perhaps an early "White Election" poem that stands in striking contrast to the later work (P528).

153   Dust is the only Secret-

l.1   "Dust": Ge 2:7; 3:19; Ps 103:14
ll.1-2   "Dust...One": ICo 15:50-55
l.14   "Christ...nest": ICo 15:57
Comment: See *Poems*, I, 109-110.

154   Except to Heaven, she is nought

l.1   "Heaven": Rev 21-22
l.2   "Angels": see note, line nineteen, P7
l.4   "A...blown": Mt 6:28-29 (the line is a counterfactual, i.e., the "Housewife" is not a "flower superfluous" but one of the God-ordained lilies of the field)
l.5   "Except...provincial": Joh 3:8 (the "winds" of the Spirit; the "Except" comes from Joh 3:3, 5 and is being used to speak of a certain type of vision that transmogrifies the "smallest Housewife" into a substitute for the face of God in the circuit world, a world that only thereby becomes a "Home")
l.7   "dew": see note, line twenty one, P122
ll.9,11 "smallest Housewife," "face": Mt 6:28-29 (the "smallest Housewife" becomes emblematic within the spiritually saturated iconography of the landscape of P154: "Heaven," "Angels," "Bee," "flower," "winds," "Butterflies," and "dew": P154 may be a very sophisticated sympathy card intended to bolster the poet's sister-in-law)
Comment: See *Poems*, I, 110-111.

155   The murmur of a Bee

ll.1-5   "The...tell": IICo 12:1-5 (the "Witchcraft" in nature the poet cannot explain)
l.6   "Red": see note, line one, P15 (nature grants an epiphany, a sense of the presence of God)
ll.6,9,11 "The...Day": Mal 4:2; Lu 1:78; IIPe 1:19; Rev 2:28; 22:16 (solar imagery is used in speaking of the Deity)
l.13   "If...how": IICo 12:4
ll.14-15 "Artist...tell": Ge 1 (God is the Artist-Creator who has drawn His creation by "tell[ing]" or speaking)
Comment: See *Poems*, I, 111-112.

157   Musicians wrestle everywhere-

l.6   " 'New life' ": Rev 21:1-5 (the "New life" of Heaven, which includes a new song, Rev 5:9; 14:3; 15:3; but see also references to spiritual rebirth, Ro 6:4; IICo 5:17: Heb 10:20)

ll.11-12 "The...Afternoon": Job 38:7 ("When the morning stars sang together, and all the sons of God shouted for joy?")

ll.14-16 "Some...place": Rev 5:9-13; 7:9-12; 14:17; 15:3; 19:1-6

ll.17-18 "Where...Ascertain": ICo 13:12; 15:40, 49; IICo 3:18; Rev 22:4

Comment: See *Poems*, I, 113-114.

158   Dying! Dying in the night!

l.5   "And...gone": IPe 3:22 (the references to Jesus' absence may be ironic)

l.6   "They...came": Mr 28:20b

l.7   "Perhaps...House": Ec 12:3 (the "House" of death)

l.12   "Death...hurt": ICo 15:55

159   A little Bread- a crust- a crumb

l.1   "Bread": Mt 4:4; 6:11; 26:26; Joh 6:31-58 (deliberately chosen for its KJV reverberations in order to highlight circuit world destitution)

l.1   "crumb": Lu 16:21 (Lazarus, prototype for circuit world beggarliness)

l.2   "demijohn": Joh 13:23; 19:26; 20:2; 21:7, 20, 24; Rev 1:1-4, 9 (in addition to its obvious and fitting denotation, the word refers wittily to herself as half a St. John the Divine)

l.6   "Crown": Rev 2:10 (in addition to its witty double entendre, the word hints at eternal destiny)

l.8   "sting": ICo 15:55 (synecdochic, perhaps not simply of death but of the circuit world itself as a place of Passion, suffering)

l.8   "sweet": Ca 2:3, 14; 5:5, 13, 16; 7:9 (synecdochic of that half of the "Campaign" comprising love and affection)

l.12   "neighboring life": Rev 2:7, 10; 21:1-7, 27; 22:1-5, 12-17 (the "New life" of P157, line six; the life of the "new circumference," P313, or what the poet frequently termed Heaven, collapsing within it Eden, paradise, and the New Jerusalem)

Comment: See *Poems*, I, 115-116.

160   Just lost, when I was saved!

l.1   "saved": Mt 10:22; 24:13; Mr 13:13; 16:16; Lu 7:50; Joh 3:17; 10:9; Ac 2:21; Ro 8:24; ICo 1:18; 15:2; Eph 2:5, 8; Rev 21:24 (to be lost is to experience the return to the circuit world, P160 playing upon the paradox of Mt 16:25: "For whosoever will save his life shall lose it: and whosoever will lose his life for my sake shall find it")

l.3   "Eternity": Isa 57:15

l.4   "breath": Ge 2:7 (here synecdochic of the "living soul" in its self-conscious awareness of circuit world existence)

l.7   "Therefore...feel": Lu 16:30

l.10   "pale Reporter": Rev 1:17-19 ("And when I saw him, I fell at his feet as dead")

l.10   "awful doors": Rev 4:1 ("After this I looked, and, behold, a door was opened in heaven:")

l.11   "Seal": Rev 5:1; 6:3-9, 12; 7; 8:1; 9:4; 10:4; 20:2; 22:10 (seals clasp the book of Judgment and the Lamb's Book of Life and seals are upon the foreheads of the sealed elect; thus, the "Seal" is synecdochic of Judgment and ultimate destiny, as well as being a term denoting the coffin, grave, and death)

ll.13-15 "Next...Eye": ICo 2:9 ("Eye hath not seen, nor ear heard, neither have entered into the heart of man, the things which God hath prepared for them that love him"); Isa 64:4

Comment: See *Poems*, I, 116-117.

161   A feather from the Whippowill

l.2   "everlasting": Ps 90:2; 145:13; Isa 9:6; Da 45:3; Hab 1:12; IIPe 1:11 (the song of the "Whippowill" is of the everlasting kingdom of God or Heaven)

l.5   "Emerald": Rev 21:19

l.7   "Beryl": Rev 21:20

l.8   "Overhead": Rev 21-22 (Heaven or the New Jerusalem; the "everlasting" song of the Whippowill is "typic" of the new song of Moses and of the Lamb, Rev 5:9, 11-13; 14:3; 15:3)

Comment: See *Poems*, I, 117-118 and *Letters*, II, 364.

163   **Tho' my destiny be Fustian-**

ll.2-3   "damask," "silver": Ca 1:11; 3:10; 4:3; 5:10; 8:9, 121 (appearances associated with the beloved)

ll.5,8   "Gipsey," "Rosier": Ca 2:1 (the rose, perfection of beauty and ideal circumferentiality to the poet, was a token of love and affection)

l.9   "Frosts": Job 37:10

l.12   "Bloom Eternally": ICo 15:35-55

ll.13-14 "Roses...land": Rev 22:2 (the perpetual "summer" of that "steadfast land," the New Jerusalem; see also Isa 35:1)

l.16   "And...stand": Rev 14:14-20 (the image of the "Reapers" is apocalyptic)

Comment: See *Poems*, I, 119-120.

164   **Mama never forgets her birds,**

ll.7-8   "If...above": Mt 10:29, 31; Lu 12:6-7 (Lavinia Norcross, like the Father in Heaven, is solicitous over the welfare of two sparrows— her Louise and Frances Norcross)

Comment: See *Poems*, I, 20 and Leyda, II, 9.

165   **A Wounded Deer- leaps highest-**

l.1   "Wounded": Isa 53:5 (a Suffering Servant term fittingly used in a poem on the blood and agony of the circuit world)

l.3   "Extasy": see note, line six, P122 (death here induces the heightened awareness)

l.5   "The...gushes": Ex 17:6; Nu 20:7-11; Joh 19:34; ICo 10:4 (a Eucharistic reference connecting with the Christ of the Passion); see also Isa 53:4 ("smitten" is a Suffering Servant term as well)

l.8   "stings": ICo 15:55 (lines seven and eight may to some extent echo Joh 18:22-23)

ll.9,11 "Anguish," "blood": Lu 22:44 (terminology connecting the described experience with the Passion)

166   **I met a King this afternoon!**

l.1   "King": Rev 17:14; 19:16

l.2   "Crown": Rev 14:14; 19:12

l.5   "Ermine": Rev 1:14; 3:4; 4:4; 7:9; 14:14; 19:8, 14; 20:11

l.13   "Horse": Rev 6:2-8; 19:11, 19, 21

ll.17-20 "And...me": IIKi 2:11-12

l.27   "on high": Job 16:19; 31:2; Ps 113:5; Lu 1:78; Eph 4:8; Heb 1:3 (the dwelling place of God, Heaven)

Comment: The KJV resonances in the references add to the humorous hyperbole of P166.

167   To learn the Transport by the Pain-

ll.1-4   "To...run": Mt 5:2-12 (the Beatitudes philosophy of deprivation is the poet's essential cosmogony and theodicy: the raison d'etre for the circuit world is in order that humans "learn the Transport by the Pain")

ll.5-6   "To...shore": IICo 5:4-8 (disaffection and homesickness express the poet's Gnostic revulsion to the vile prison of the circuit world, Ro 7:24; Php 3:21)

l.8   "blue": see note, line one, P15

ll.9-10   "This...wo": Isa 53:3-5; Mt 26-27 (the identification here is with the Christ of the Passion; the "Sovreign Anguish" may be the sense of abandonment expressed by Christ on the cross, Mt 27:46, a species of cosmic "homesick[ness]" elsewhere identified with by the poet, P313)

l.16   "Mysterious Bard": Ge 1 (the "Bard"—God of creation who spoke worlds into existence is also the "Mysterious" Deus absconditus, Job 13:24; Ps 10:1; 44:24; 88:14; Isa 44:15; of the possible opacity of God's ways at least until time's end, Job 9:10; Ro 11:33; Rev 10:7)

Comment: See *Poems*, I, 122-123.

168   If the foolish, call them "flowers"-

ll.1-2   "If...tell": ICo 1:25-31 ("Because the foolishness of God is wiser than men...ye see...how that not many wise men after the flesh...are called: But God hath chosen the foolish things of the world to confound the wise... And base things of the world, and things which are despised, hath God chosen, yea, and things which are not, to bring to nought things that are:")

l.2 "*tell*": Joh 3:12 (the fascicles show the underlined "tell," Franklin, I, 134)

l.5 " 'Revelations' ": Rev 1:1, passim (the Book of Revelation of St. John the Divine; but see also the relevant mention of "visions and revelations" by St. Paul, IICo 12:1-7)

ll.5-8 "Those...Eyes": Isa 6:9-10; Eze 12:2; Mt 13:14-16; Mr 4:12; 6:52; 8:17-18; Lu 8:10; Joh 12:40; Ac 28:26-27; Ro 11:8; IICo 3:13-16 (the repetition of "read" may also echo the parallel structure in the words of Jesus: "Having eyes, see ye not? and having ears, hear ye not?" Mr 8:18; see also Rev 3:18)

ll.9-12 "Could...side": De 34:1-4

ll.17-20 "Low...'hand' ": Rev 4:1-10; 7:9-12; 14:1-7; 19:1-9; 21-22 (a Dantean vision of a heavenly flower composed of God and the Lamb on the throne surrounded by the heavenly hosts)

l.17 "glad Belles lettres": Rev 22:1-5 (the beatific vision as seeing for the first time in God's presence what was only typified by the experience of the beauty of "flowers" in the circuit world)

l.19 "*Stars...Galaxies*": ICo 15:41 ("...one star differeth from another in glory"; for other images from astronomy perhaps relevant here, Rev 1:16, 20; 2:1, 28; 3:1; 21:23; 22:5, 16)

Comment: See *Poems*, I, 123-124.

171 Wait till the Majesty of Death

l.1 "Wait...Death": ICo 15:50-55

l.2 "Invests...brow": Rev 2:10; 3:11; 4:4, 10; 7:3; 14:1; 22:4

ll.5-6 "Wait...dressed": Rev 3:4-5, 18; 6:11; 7:9

l.9 "Around...Courtier": Rev 18:23; 19:7-9; 21:2, 9; 22:17 (the marriage figuration into which "Courtier" fits)

l.10 "Obsequious...wait": Rev 7:1-2, 11; 14:1-7; 21:9, 12

l.11 "Full...Retinue": Rev 8:3-4; 11:18; 14:12; 15:3; 19:8; 20:9 (the saints of God)

l.12 "purple": see note, line one, P15 (the dead enjoys the presence of God)

l.14 "Modest Clay": Ge 2:7; Job 10:9; 13:12; 33:6; Ec 12:7; Isa 45:9; 64:8 (synecdochic of man's finitude—man fashioned by God from dust or clay)

l.15 " 'the Lord of Lords' ": De 10:17; ITi 6:15; Rev 17:14; 19:16

172   'Tis so much joy! 'Tis so much joy?

ll.1,13-18 " 'Tis...me": IPe 1:8

ll.2-12   "If...befall": Mt 5:2-12; 10:39; 16:25-26; Mr 8:35-36; Lu 9:24-25; Joh 12:25; IICo 6:10; 8:2, 9; Php 3:7-8 (the poet draws upon the paradoxes of St. Paul and Jesus, applying them in existential fashion to her circuit world condition where poor is rich, sad joy, loss gain, defeat victory, nothing all, and worst best)

l.4   "Have...throw": see note, lines one-four, P139 (again her version of Pascal's wager)

l.6   "Victory": Isa 25:8; ICo 15:54-55; IITi 4:7-8 (synecdochic of Heaven or perhaps of a consciousness wherein assurance of immortality and reward has stripped away the drama of P172's paradoxes; for all its euphoric talk of unspeakable joy, P172 hesitates before the assurance and finality of "Victory," thereby relishing its defeat-whets-victory, piquancy-of-the-pit energies)

Comment: See *Poems*, I, 126-127.

173   A fuzzy fellow, without feet,

ll.1-20   "A...Butterfly": ICo 15:50-55 (the butterfly's metamorphosis is a Hitchcockian emblem of the resurrection)

Comment: See *Poems*, I, 127.

174   At last, to be identified!

ll.1-3   "At...see": IJo 3:2 ("Beloved, now are we the sons of God, and it doth not yet appear what we.shall be: but we know that, when he shall appear, we shall be like him; for we shall see him as he is"); ICo 13:12 ("For now we see through a glass darkly; but then face to face: now I know in part; but then shall I know even as also I am known"); see also ICo 15:49; IICo 3:18; the components of the new identity would be as follows: the seal, Rev 7; 9:4; the crown, Rev 2:10; 3:11; 4:4, 10; bridal status, Rev 19:7-9; the new name, the culmination of being conformed to His image in preparation for the beatific vision, Rev 2:17; 3:12; 22:4)

l.4   "Past Midnight": Rev 21:25; 22:5 (there is no night in the New Jerusalem) l.4   "Past...Star": Rev 2:28; 22:16 (Christ is the "Morning Star")

ll.5-7   "Past...Day": Rev 21:23-25; 22:5 (the perpetual glory of God and the Lamb, an eternal "Day"; the poet may also refer here to the "great day of God Almighty," Rev 6:17; 16:14; or to resurrection morning, ICo 15:50-55)
        Comment: See *Poems*, I, 128.

175   I have never seen 'Volcanoes'-

l.17   "loving Antiquary": IJo 4:8 (God)
l.18   "On...Morn": ICo 15:50-55 (resurrection morning)
        Comment: Pain and anguish describe the "Volcanic" life in Passion imagery (Mt 26-27). It is remotely possible that the "palpitating Vineyard" is the chosen beloved (Ps 80:8-13; Ca 1:6; 8:12), the oxymoron more than likely simply yoking the irreconcilables, Pompeii and Vesuvius.

176   I'm the little "Heart's Ease"!

l.10   "Eden": Ge 2-3
l.11   "Birds...fellows": Ge 1:20
l.12   "Heaven": Ge 1:1, 8
l.12   "blue": see note, line one, P15

177   Ah, Necromancy Sweet!

ll.1-2   "Necromancy," "Wizard": De 18:11
l.4   "That...pain": see P258 ("Heavenly Hurt," "Seal Despair," and "imperial affliction")

178   I cautious, scanned my little life-

ll.2-3   "I...last": Ps 1:4; Jer 23:28; Mt 3:12; Lu 3:17 (winnowing the chaff from wheat)
l.5   "I...Barn": Lu 12:16-21 (P178 may be an ironic treatment of the parable of the rich man; see also Mt 6:19-21)
l.6   "The...away": Job 212:18; Da 2:35; Ho 13:3 (the chaff blown away by the wind)

ll.15,20 "Deity's," "Love": IJo 4:8, 16 (the poet brings into conflict the God of Love whose munificence supplies all needs [Mt 6:8, 32] with the parsimonious, frugal God of the "little Barn," of circuit world poverty and destitution)

179 If I could bribe them by a Rose

ll.1,7,13 "If...me": Mt 21:22 ("And all things, whatsoever ye shall ask in prayer, believing, ye shall receive")

ll.14-19 "Who...Hall": Lu 16:19-22; 18:1-8 (the roles of Lazarus and the Importunate Widow are here combined in a drama of expostulation and importunity; P179 is one of her many poems that might be labeled a *Putative*: a poem assuming an ideal presence—here a "them," "they," and "Hall"—before which the poet acts out in various roles the agonies of beggarliness, destitution, estrangement, dispossession, and a sense of absence)

180 As if some little Arctic flower

l.10 "Eden": Ge 2-3

184 A transport one cannot contain

l.4 "Extasy": see note, line six P122; note, line fifteen, P783; and note, lines five and eight, P1191

l.5 "Rapture": see note, line seven, P1468 and line four above (the poet uses "transport," "Extasy," and "Rapture" interchangeably)

l.7 "Holy Ghosts": Mt1:18; 28:19; Ac1:8; 2:4; IIPe1:21 (the third member of the Holy Trinity, the Holy Ghost is associated with the mysterious creative activity of God, which may reveal knowledge of divine things to individuals or inspire them to ecstatic utterance; in "Rapture" the spirit is in the grip of exalted passion, in "Extasy" an intermittent sense of presence, both of which keep the "Universe" from becoming the "inanimate cold world" of analysis and mechanism; the poet elsewhere writes of the operation of the Holy Ghost in the inspiration of the Bible, P1545)

l.7(variant) "Seraphim": see note, line eleven, P7

185 "Faith" is a fine invention

ll.1-2   " 'Faith'...*see*": Heb11:1 ("Now faith is the substance of things hoped for, the evidence of things not seen")

l.2   "*see*": ICo 2:9; 13:12; ITi 6:16; IJo 3:2; 4:12

Comment: See *Poems*, I, 134; *Letters*, II, 364; and Leyda, II, 7.

191   The Skies can't keep their secret!

l.13   "So...secret": De 29:29; Job 15:8; Ps 91:1

l.13   "Father": Rev 1:6; 2:27; 3:5, 21 (God the Father)

l.15   "Sapphire": Rev 21:19 (see also Ex 24:10; 28:18; 39:11; Eze 1:26; 10:1—the sapphire may not only be associated with the adornment of the beloved, Ca 5:14; Isa 54:11, but also with the mediated face of God)

l.16   "In...world": Rev 21:1, 5 ("And I saw a new heaven and a new earth: for the first heaven and the first earth were passed away; ...And he that sat upon the throne said, Behold, I make all things new")

193   I shall know why- when Time is over-

l.1   "Time is over": Rev 10:6

ll.1-2   "I...why": ICo 13:12

l.3   "Christ...anguish": Mt 26:69-75 (the poet may have in mind the denial of Christ by Peter or the sufferings of the Passion, Mt 26-27)

l.4   "In...sky": Rev 21-22

l.5   "He...promised": Mt 26:33-34; Mr 14:29; Lu 22:33-34; Joh 13:37-38 (Peter "promised" to lay down his life, to go to prison or death, for the Christ in whom he was not "offended")

l.6   "And...woe": Isa 53:3-5; Mt 26-27 (the poet identifies with the Suffering Servant, the Christ of the Passion)

l.7   "drop of Anguish": Lu 22:44 ("And being in agony he prayed more earnestly: and his sweat was as it were great drops of blood falling down to the ground")

l.8   "That...now": Mt 27:46; Mr 15:34 (see line eleven, P313)

194   On this long storm the Rainbow rose-

l.1   "Rainbow": Ge 9:13-16

ll.11-12 "The...her": ITh 4:16 ("For the Lord himself shall descend from heaven with a shout, with the voice of the archangel, and with the trump of God: and the dead in Christ shall rise first"); see also ICo 15:50-55

195   For this- accepted Breath-

l.1   "accepted Breath": Ge 2:7

l.2   "Through...Death": Ge 3:19 (dust and breath "compete" in the sense that their destinies differ, Ec 12:7; "Breath" may suggest inspiration and thereby poetic creation)

l.3   "this Crown": Rev 2:10; 3:11; 4:4, 10

l.4   "my title": Rev 2:17; 3:12; 22:4 (the apocalyptic figuration is religio-aesthetic; see also Ca 1:3; 2:4; and Rev 19:7-9)

l.7   "Wilderness": Ex; Nu; De (the "Wilderness" of the exodus of the Israelites from bondage in Egypt; the poet uses the term metaphorically to reinforce her sense of religio-aesthetic election)

l.10   "frost": Job 37:10

ll.11,12 "perennial bloom," "Certain June": Rev 22:1-3 (the paradisiacal vision of St. John the Divine of an eternal, "Certain June"; the "trance below" attending the poet is "typic" of the experience of ideal presence and the beatific vision in the New Jerusalem)

l.13   "Gabriel" Lu 1:19, 26-28 (the angel of the Annunciation who stands in the presence of God, Rev 8:2)

l.14   "Get...tongue": ICo 15:50-55; Rev 5:9; 14:3; 15:3; 22:5

l.15   "Most...show": Rev 1:6; 5:12-13; 7:12; 11:13; 19:1; 21:23-24; 22:5 (the "glory" of the "Saints" is praise, exalted song, beauty, light, and beatitude—products of ideal presence and of the beatific vision)

l.16   "Crown": see line three above

Comment: See *Poems*, I, 140.

196   We dont cry- Tim and I,

ll.13-14 "Cottages...high": Joh 14:2-3; IICo 5:1; Rev 21-22

l.17   "little Hymn": Mt 26:30; Eph 5:19; Col 3:16 (the reference may be ironic since the poem has a Blakean quality of unsuspecting innocence)

l.27   "Lord": Lu 2:11; Ac 11:17; Ro 1:7

197   Morning- is the place for Dew-

l.1   "Morning...Dew": Ex 16:13

198   An awful Tempest mashed the air-

l.4   "Heaven and Earth": Ge 1:1-Rev 21:1 (a frequent KJV pairing)

l.13   "Paradise": Ge 2-3; Eze 28:13-14; 31:8-9, 16; 47:1-12; IICo 12:4; Rev 2:7; 21-22

199   I'm "wife"- I've finished that-

l.1   " 'wife' ": Ge 2:24-25; 3:8, 17, 21; 4:1; Rev 19:7-9; 21:2, 9; 22:17

l.3   " 'Woman' ": Ge 2:22-23; 3:1-4, 6, 12-16 (a term frequently used to describe the New Eve, Rev 12)

l.8   "To...now": Rev 21-22

l.12   " 'Wife' ": see line one above

Comment: P199 uses apocalyptic bridal figuration to speak of the poet's new status. In Genesis the key words in order of appearance are "female," "woman," "wife," and "Eve," Ge 1:27; 2:22-23; 2:24-25; 3:20—important identity words in the poet's lexicon since she viewed as the recapturing of a paradisiacal, Edenic status her friends' marriages and, perhaps more importantly, as appropriating of Bride of Christ identity her own religio-aesthetic commitment.

201   Two swimmers wrestled on the spar-

ll.1-4   "Two...One": Mt 23:39-43 (Augustine found in this drama a caution versus the extremes either of despair or presumption, and perhaps the poet had in mind the arbitrariness of Calvinistic election with its precarious salvation by wrestling on a spar—what she elsewhere termed a "plank," P875—and the inexplicable outcome; the two-thieves situation nevertheless fascinated her, P1180 and P1305 both treating it; perhaps P201 has no KJV provenance, not treating of the saved or damned in any fashion; see the discussion in Sewall, 457-458)

Comment: See *Letters*, II, 363.

203   He forgot- and I- remembered-

ll.1-3   "He...Peter": Mt 26:33-34; Mr 14:29; Lu 22:33-34; Joh 13:37-38 (the example of Peter's promises to Christ as a model of trust and betrayal)

l.4   " 'Warmed'...'fire' ": Mr 14:54; Lu 22:55; Joh 18:18 (the fire was beneath the house or palace of the high priest, Caiaphas)

l.5   " 'Thou'...'Damsel' ": Mt 26:69; Mr 14:67; Lu 22:56; Joh 18:17

l.6   " 'No'...me": Mt 26:70; Mr 14:68; Lu 22:57; Joh 18:17

l.7   "Jesus...Peter": Lu 22:61 ("And the Lord turned, and looked upon Peter"); see also Ps 69:20

l.8   "Could...Thee": Mt 26:69-75; Mr 14:54, 66-72; Lu 22:54-61; Joh 18:15-18, 25-27 (inclusive references to the relevant KJV passages on Peter's betrayal or "forgetting")

204   A slash of Blue-

ll.1,3,5,6,7 "Blue," "scarlet," "purple," "Ruby," "Gold": see note, line one, P15

Comment: See *Poems*, I, 144-145.

207   Tho' I get home how late- how late-

l.3   "Extasy": see note, line six, P122; note, line fifteen, P783; and note, lines five and eight, P1191 (the experience anticipated is apparently that of face-to-face presence after years of Passion-"Agony," circuit world experience, ICo 13:12; Rev 22:5)

211   Come slowly- Eden!

l.1   "Eden": Ge 2-3
l.2   "Lips...Thee": Ca 4:3, 11; 5:13
l.3   "Bashful...Jessamines": Ca 5:1; 8:2

l.5   "Reaching...flower": Ca 2:1, 12, 16; 5:13; 6:2-3; 7:2
l.7   "Counts...nectars": Ca 4:11; 5:1
l.8   "Enters...Balms": Ca 2:16; 4:12, 16; 5:1, 13; 6:2-3,
11 (the chamber entered by the beloved, love analogized to oral
gratification, and the imagery of Eden: lips, flowers, and honey— all
suggest the Canticles provenance of P211)

213   Did the Harebell loose her girdle

l.5   " 'Paradise' ": Ge 2-3; Eze 28:13-14; 31:8-9, 16;
47:1-12; IICo 12:4; Rev 2:7; 21-22
l.6   "pearl": Rev 21:21
l.7   "Eden": Ge 2-3
Comment: The "Earl," the Courtier of Paradise (the
Bridegroom of Revelation), loses his Paradise status if the conditions
of stanza one are met. Thus, P213 is a Gnostic repudiation of the
physical, a dramatization of the mutual exclusivity of enjoyment of
bridal status in "Paradise" and an embrace of circuit world physicality.

214   I taste a liquor never brewed-

l.1   "I...brewed": Ps 36:9; Jer 2:13; Mt 26:26-30; Joh
3:5; 4:10-14; 6:31-58; 7:38; ICo 10:4; Rev 2:17; 7:17; 21:6; 22:1, 17
(the KJV contains numerous references to the heavenly manna or
spiritual bread and the spiritual wine or water, the most obvious in the
Eucharist but also central in the living bread and water discussions of
the Gospel of John, which point to the hidden manna and water of life
in Rev 2:17; 21:6; 22:1, 17); perhaps the most relevant KJV verses for
P214 are Mt 5:6: "Blessed are they which do hunger and thirst after
righteousness: for they shall be filled" and Mt 5:8: "Blessed are the
pure in heart: for they shall see God"; see Leyda, II, 20-21; P214 is a
poem of vision or what the poet termed "Extasy," for which see note,
line six, P122; note, line fifteen, P783; and note, lines five and eight,
P1191
l.2   "Pearl": Rev 21:21
l.6   "Dew": see note, line twenty one, P122
l.7   "endless summer": Rev 22:1-5
l.8   "Blue": see note, line one, P15
l.13   "Seraphs": see note, line eleven, P7

l.13   "snowy Hats": Rev 3:4-5; 6:11; 15:6; 19:14; (the color of heavenly dress)

l.14   "Saints": Rev 5:8; 8:3-4; 11:18; 14:12; 15:3; 19:8; 20:9

l.14   "windows": Mal 3:10b ("windows of heaven")

l.14(variant) "Sun": Mal 4:2; Lu 1:78; IIPe 1:19; Rev 1:16; 2:28; 21:23-24; 22:5, 16

Comment: See *Poems*, I, 149-150 and Leyda, II, 20-21, 27.

215   What is- "Paradise"-

l.1   " 'Paradise' ": Ge 2-3; Eze 28:13-14; 31:8-9, 16; 47:1-12; IICo 12:4; Rev 2:7; 21-22

l.7   "Do...'Eden' ": Ge 2:25; 3:7, 10-11 (Adam and Eve were naked in Eden; the poet may also humorously refer to the fact that in God's presence shoes were not worn, Ex 3:5; Ac 7:33; see also Rev 21:5)

l.8   "Is...there": Rev 21:4; 22:1-3

l.9   "Won't...hungry": Rev 7:16-17; 21:4

l.12   "As...sky": Mt 6:9 ("Our Father which art in heaven")

l.14   "O...'die' ": see line one, P54

l.15   " 'Jasper' " Rev 21:11, 18-19

l.16   "Ransomed folks": Rev 5:9; 6:11; 7; 14:3-4; 15:1-4; 19:1-9; 21:3, 7, 24; 22:14 (the saved or redeemed in Heaven; see also Isa 35:10; 51:10-11)

l.17   " 'Eden' ": Ge 2-3; Rev 21-22 ("Eden" is here the New Eden or New Jerusalem)

216   Safe in their Alabaster Chambers-

version of 1859

l.1   "Alabaster": Rev 1:14; 2:17; 3:4-5, 18; 4:4; 6:2, 11; 7:9, 13-14; 15:6; 19:8, 11, 14; 20:11 (the apocalyptic color is alabaster or white)

ll.2,3   "Untouched": Mt 22:31; Mr 12:26; Ac 24:21 (the echoes may be intentionally ironic)

ll.2,3   "Morning," "Noon": Joh 6:39-40, 44, 54; 11:24; ICo 15:50-55 (two transition times frequently intimating change of state; "Morning" would be associated also with the "last day" or resurrection morning)

l.4   "Sleep": ICo 15:41 ("We shall not all sleep, but we shall all be changed"); see also ICo 15:17-18 (the crux of P216)

l.4   "meek": Mt 5:5; 11:29

l.4   "Resurrection": ICo 15

l.6   "stone": Mt 27:60, 66

l.11   "Ah...here": Ec 9:10 ("...there is no work, nor device, nor knowledge, nor wisdom, in the grave, whither thou goest"); see also *Hamlet*, III, I, 150

version of 1861

l.6   "Years": Ge 1:14

ll.6,7   "Crescent," "Arcs": Ge 2:1, 4 (the heavens as seen by circuit world observers)

l.7   "Worlds": Heb 1:2; 11:3 (the cosmic, creation imagery is selected for hyperbolic effect)

l.8   "Firmaments": Ge 1:6-8, 14-20; Ps 19:1

l.9   "Diadems": Rev 2:10; 3:11; 4:4, 10 (crowns lost, not achieved)

l.9   "Doges": see, e.g., P213 (the "Doges" are failed dukes or earls, the inverse of Courtiers of Paradise)

l.10   "dots...Disc": Rev 7:2-8; 9:4; 14:1; 20:4 (the inverse of the seal and name of achieved identity, the "Disc" is a metonym for the forehead or face, which in Revelation, though not here, achieves ideal circumferentiality in the beatific vision, Rev 22:4; aurally and visually the final two lines create an unideal circumferentiality conveying the potential unmeaning of the apocalyptic, "Diadems," "Doges," and "dots" burying in a snow of anonymity the "Disc," which is both the grave and face of the dead)

l.10   "Snow": see line one, 1859 version above

Comment: See *Poems*, I, 151-155; *Letters*, II, 332, 379-380, 403; and Leyda, II, 42-43, 48, 52-54.

217   Savior! I've no one else to tell-

l.1   "Savior": Lu 2:11 (Jesus Christ)

l.3   "I...so": see the notes, P193 and P203 (the one who "forgot" the Savior was Peter) l.4   "Dost...me": Mt 26:75; Lu 22:61 (deliberately ironic given Peter's denial)

l.6   "imperial Heart": Mt 26:37-38; Mr 14:33-34 (the "heavy" "Heart" of the Passion Christ)

Comment: See *Poems*, I, 155-156.

219   She sweeps with many-colored Brooms-

l.5   "Purple": see note, line one, P15

l.6   "Amber": see note, line one, P15

l.8   "Emerald": Rev 21:19

Comment: See *Poems*, I, 157-158.

221   It cant be "Summer"!

l.8   "The...White": Rev 3:4; 6:11

l.10   "Chrysolite": Rev 21:20

Comment: See *Poems*, I, 158-159 and Leyda, II, 37.

223   I Came to buy a smile- today-

ll.1-8   "I...sell": Isa 53:3-4 (Jesus is the "man of sorrows" whose grace, His unmerited favor, comes to the poet in the form of a frown, the grief and anguish of the Passion that she experiences in the circuit world; see also Mt 26:37-38; Mr 14:33-34)

l.9   "Diamonds": Eze 28:13

l.12   "Topaz": Eze 28:13; Rev 21:20

l.13   "Jew": Mt 1:1-17 (the Jewish lineage of Jesus); Mt 2:2 (Jesus, King of the Jews)

Comment: The poems frequently deal with the Deus absconditus but here with the God who does not smile. See *Poems*, I, 160-161.

225   Jesus! thy Crucifix

l.1   "Jesus...Crucifix": Mt 27:26-37; Mr 15:12-26; Lu 23:20-38; Joh 19:16-19 (the anguished Passion Christ of the Crucifixion imaged on the "Crucifix")

l.4   "Jesus...face": Mt 26-27 (the "second face" of Jesus is that of the Suffering Servant, the Crucified Christ, whose human rather than divine nature enables Him to "guess/The smaller size" of those in the circuit world; on the divinity and humanity of Jesus see Joh 1:14; Ro 1:3-4; Php 2:6-7)

l.5   "Mind...Paradise": Lu 23:43; Rev 2:7; 21-22 (an expression of anxiety lest Christ forget in His glorified, exalted state in Heaven the sufferings of those below; the first face of Jesus would be His divine and glorified one, that of the exalted Christ who sits upon the throne at the right hand of God the Father in Heaven, Rev 21:1-7, 22-24; 22:1-5; see also Ps 110:1; Mt 22:44; 26:64; Mr 12:36; 14:62; 16:19; Lu 20:42-43; 22:69; Ac 2:33-34; Heb 1:13; IPe 3:22; the language may echo that of Christ to the thief: "Verily I say unto thee, Today shalt thou be with me in paradise," Lu 23:43)

Comment: See *Poems*, I, 161-162; *Letters*, II, 382-383; and Leyda, II, 38-39.

226   [Sh]ould you but fail [at]- Sea-

l.5   "rap...Paradise": Ps 78:23; Eze 47:1-2; Rev 4:1; 21:12-15, 21, 25; 22:14 (Heaven or Paradise with doors or gates)

ll.6-7   "I'd...in": Rev 3:20 (the poet reverses roles becoming an intercessor for Bowles)

Comment: See *Poems*, I, 162; *Letters*, II, 393; and Leyda, II, 43.

227   Teach Him- when He makes the names-

l.8   " 'Forbid...' ": Mt 19:14 ("But Jesus said, Suffer little children, and forbid them not, to come unto me: for of such is the kingdom of heaven"); see also Mr 10:14; Lu 18:16

228   Blazing in Gold and quenching in Purple

l.1   "Gold," "Purple": see note, line one, P15

ll.2,4   "Leopards," "spotted": Jer 13:23 (the unworthy "Face" of the day is effaced in the sunset; compare Ca 4:7; Eph 5:27; Rev 19:7-9)

Comment: See *Poems*, I, 163-165; *Letters*, II, 453-454; and Leyda, II, 114-115.

230   We- Bee and I- live by the quaffing-

ll.2-3   " 'Tis'nt...Life": Mt 6:25 ("Is not the life more than meat")

l.4   "Dim Burgundy": see note, line one, P214

l.14   "Vine": Joh 15:1, 5

l.15   "Cup": Mt 26:27; Mr 14:23; Lu 22:17-18

l.17   "humming Coroner": ICo 15:55-56 (death with its sting)

231   God permits industrious Angels-

ll.1,5   "Angels": Ge 16:11; 22:11; 32:24-30; Ex 3:2; Lu 2:8-14; Rev 4:9 (heavenly visitants and messengers here giving intimations of apocalyptic presence; see note, line nineteen, P7)

l.8   "Crown": Rev 2:10; 3:11; 4:4, 10

232   The Sun- just touched the Morning-

l.1   "Sun": Ps 19:5; Mal 4:2; Lu 1:78; IIPe 1:19; Rev 2:28; 21:23-24; 22:5, 16

l.2   "Morning": Ca 6:10

l.3   "He...dwell": Rev 3:20; 7:15; 21:3 (the motifs of God as heavenly visitant, the individual as His dwelling, temple, or habitation, and the need for preparation as host run throughout the KJV, the poet fusing these with bridal figuration; see also note, line one, P1142)

l.4   "Life...Spring": Rev 22:1-3 (the perennial "Spring" of "Paradise" or the New Jerusalem)

ll.5-6   "She...Thing": Ca 2:1-4, 10; 4; 7:10-13; 8:10; Rev 19:7-9; 21:9 (the elevation in status of the favored beloved)

l.8   "King": Rev 19:16 (a frequent term for the Deity)

l.11   "Hems": Mt 9:20; 14:36 (for the sacredness of Christ's vesture, Mt 27:35; Mr 15:24; Lu 23:34; Joh 19:24; the "spangled Hems" may owe something to the garments of the high priest who was allowed into the Holy of Holies, into the presence of God, Ex 28:33-34; 39:24-26)

ll.12,14 "Diadems," "Crown": Isa 28:5; 62:3-4; ICo 9:25; IITi 4:8; Jas 1:12; IPe 5:4; Rev 2:10; 3:11; 4:4, 10

l.15   "unannointed": Ex 28:41; 30:30; 40:13; Le 21:10; ISa 10:1; 16:3; Iki 1:39; 19:16; Ac 10:38 (the anointing by oil was an act of consecration performed upon kings, priests, and prophets; Christ meant the "Anointed," the Messiah; "unannointed" here suggests a failure to achieve or sustain the proffered espousal, a loss in terms both of identity and presence)

l.15   "forehead": Rev 3:12; 14:1; 22:4 (the signal mark of the name of the Lamb was upon the foreheads of the sealed and crowned elect, those conformed to the image of Christ, IICo 3:18, in preparation for the beatific vision—the consummation and subsumption of identity within the ideal presence of God)

234   You're right- "the way is narrow"-

l.1   " 'the narrow' ": Mt 7:14
l.2   " 'difficult...Gate' ": Mt 7:14
l.3   " 'few...be' ": Mt 7:14 ("Because strait is the gate, and narrow is the way, which leadeth unto life, and few there be that find it")

l.4   " 'enter...thereat' ": Mt 7:13 ("Enter ye in at the strait gate: for wide is the gate, and broad is the way, that leadeth to destruction, and many there be which go in thereat")

l.5   "Costly": Lu 14:28, 33
l.5   "*purples*": Rev 17:4; 18:12, 16 (symbolic of the city of this world, Babylon, made desolate in the Book of Revelation)
l.16   "*Breath*": Ge 2:7; Mt 16:25-26 (the destiny of the "living soul" is its payment of the "Costly" price)
ll.17-18 "With...'Death' ": ICo 15:50-55
l.9   "And...Heaven": Rev 21-22
ll.10-11 "The...Jail": Mt 25:31-46; Rev 20:12-15; 21:7-8 (the Last Judgment at which the "Good" and "Bad" are separated)

235   The Court is far away-

ll.1-4   "The...die": Job 1, passim (Job seeks an advocate to plead his case before God, his situation being archetypal: the Kingdom of Heaven is distant, a mediator is absent, the transcendent Deity is "offended" by fallen creatures, and mortals lack the righteousness to merit favor, "gain his grace"; the poet may not have Job in mind, but P235 dramatizes the necessity for an evolution beyond the stalemate of stanza one, and this is done by a revelation of the nature of intercession and grace)

l.5   "I'll...feet": e.g., Es 8:3 (the posture of the suppliant)

l.9   "Empire": Rev 21-22   (the Kingdom of Heaven; the parables of Jesus say much about the nature of intercession and grace, for example, the parables of the unmerciful servant, Mt 18:25-35, and of the creditor and two debtors, Lu 7:41-47)

l.11   "royalty": e.g., Ro 5 (grace as a free gift, not a matter of size or rank)

236   If He dissolve- then- there is nothing- more-

l.4   "Easter": Mt 28:1 (the day of Christ's resurrection, here associated with dawn and sunrise contrasted with "Sunset")

l.6   "Faint...Bethlehem": Nu 24:17; Mt 2:2; Lu 1:78; IIPe 1:19; Rev 2:28; 22:16 (the imagery of the star used in describing Christ, with Bethlehem His birthplace)

ll.12-13 "Say...red": Joh 19:34 (perhaps there is here an identification with the Christ of the Passion)

Comment: The almost cosmic extravagance of the KJV allusions accentuates the loss or threatened loss described.

237   I think just how my shape will rise-

ll.1-2   "I...'forgiven' ": Lu 5:23 (transmogrified, the episode is applied to the poet's desire for an acceptable face miraculously changed for that anticipated face-to-face presence in Heaven); see also Isa 33:24 for the "forgiven" in Zion, "typic" of Heaven

l.4   "Are...Heaven": Rev 22:4 (a witty paradox)

l.7   " 'Consider' ": Mt 6:28

l.8   " 'Sparrow' ": Mt 10:29, 31

ll.9,11 "I...broke": Ps 69:20; Isa 53:3-5 (the lexicon of the Passion)

l.13   " 'forgiven'' " see lines one-two above

Comment: See *Poems*, I, 171.

238   Kill your Balm- and it's Odors bless you-

l.1   "Balm": Jer 8:22; 46:11; 51:8 (the Balm of Gilead, a phrase used to describe Christ, was a healing agent; the proposition that embracing pain and death yields beauty and song is prima facie outrageous but actually frequent in the KJV in, for example, the sacrificial system of the Old Testament, the ideas of the Fortunate Fall and Atonement, and the paradoxes of the Beatitudes—see P165 and P861)

ll.1,2,3   "Odors," "Jessamine," "perfume": Ca 1:12; 2:13; 3:6; 4:6, 10-11, 14; 55, 13; 78, 13 (the provenance of the references is Canticles, an olfactory book; the references suggest that the odors are metaphors for the beautiful gifts produced out of sacrifice either as permanent achievements of the poet and/or as tokens of affection for the beloved)

l.7   " 'forgive' ": Lu 23:34
l.8   "Carol...gone": Joh 14:3, 26; 15:26; 16:7 (the poet identifies with Christ in the final two lines, leaving the "Carol" as her Comforter)

239   "Heaven"- is what I cannot reach!

ll.1,4   " 'Heaven' ": Rev 21-22
ll.2-3,6   "Apple...interdicted Land": Ge 3:22-24
l.6(variant) "ground": Ex 3:5; 19:12; Jos 5:15; Ac 7:33
l.8   "Paradise": Ge 2-3; Eze 28:13-14; 31:8-9, 16; 47:1-12; IICo 12:4; Rev 2:7; 21-22
l.9   "Purples": see note, line one, P15
l.11   "Conjuror": Ge 1:1
Comment: See *Poems*, I, 172-173.

240   Ah, Moon- and Star!

ll.1,6,13,16 "Moon," "Star," "Firmament": Ge 1:8, 14-17 (the poet's lexicon of Creation)
Comment: See *Poems*, I, 173-174.

241   I like a look of Agony,

l.1   "Agony": Lu 22:44
l.4   "Throe": Mt 27:46-50; Joh 19:28-30
ll.7-8   "The...strung": Lu 22:44 (the Passion Christ is perhaps in the background of this poem on the genuineness of "Anguish"; see also Isa 53; Mt 26-27)

242   When we stand on the top of Things-

l.1   "When..Things": Mal 3:2; Ro 14:10; Eph 6:13; Rev
6:7; 20:12 (standing in the presence of God at the judgment)
    ll.3-4   "The...scene": ICo 13:12
    ll.5-12   "Just...deeds": Rev 20:12-15 (the judgment of "small
and great" "according to their works")
    ll.5-6   "no...flaw": Rev 22:4 (the flawed souls "wink,"
failing to see God face-to-face)
    ll.7-8   "The...away": Rev 4:5; 11:19 (the "lightnings" in
Revelation before which, according to the poet, the "Sound" or
"Perfect" stand)
    ll.9-12   "The...deeds": Rev 2:10; 3:11-12; 4:4, 10: 7:2-8;
14:1; 21:23-24; 22:4-5 (the sealed and crowned perfected saints who
walk in the eternal "Noon" of the New Jerusalem)
    l.12   "Protected...deeds": Ro 2:6; Rev 2:23; 14:13; 20:12-
13; (Revelation stresses "deeds" or works, especially in chapters two
and three)
    l.14   "spotted": Jer 13:23; Jude 23
    Comment: See *Poems*, I, 174-175.

245   I held a Jewel in my fingers-

    l.1   "I...fingers": Isa 61:10 (see also Ca 1:10; 7:1; Mal
3:17)
    l.7   "Amethyst": Rev 21:20

246   Forever at His side to walk-

    ll.3-4   "Brain...Blood": Ge 2:23 ("And Adam said, This is
now bone of my bones, and flesh of my flesh: she shall be called
Woman, because she was taken out of Man")
    l.5   "Two...now": Ge 2:24
    ll.6-7   "Forever...part": Ge 3 (the poem owes more in
several of its lines to *Paradise Lost* than to the KJV)
    l.12   "Change": ICo 15:51
    l.13   "Heaven": Rev 21-22
    l.14   "Rapt...Men": Rev 5:9-13; 7:9-11; 14:1-5; 19:1-9

ll.15-16 "Just...lexicon": ICo 13:9-10, 12; Php 3:13; IJo 3:2 (collapse of the circuit world "lexicon" is a concomitant of the Presence and Vision of the New Jerusalem)

247   What would I give to see his face?

l.1   "What...face": Ca 2:14; 5:10-16; Rev 1:16; 19:7-9; 22:4 (the desire for presence, to see the face of the beloved)

l.12   "Blue": see note, line one, P15

l.17   "Dew": see note, line twenty one, P122

l.19   "firmamental seas": Ge 1:6-8; Ps 19:1; 150:1

l.20   "Purple": see note, line one, P15

l.22   " 'Shylock' ": see note, line thirteen, P223

l.26   " 'face' ": see line one above

l.27   "Extatic": see note, line six, P122

l.28   "Grace": see note, line six, P1068 (the unmerited favor of God here used ironically as a gibe at the niggardly beloved)

l.29   "Kingdom's": Mt 5:2-12 (perhaps an ironic swipe at her own Beatitudes philosophy of parsimony, which promises abundance above but deprivation in the circuit world); see also Mt 6:10; Lu 11:2 for the echo of The Lord's Prayer

248   Why- do they shut Me out of Heaven?

l.1   "Heaven": Rev 21-22

l.5   "Angels": Rev 1:1, 20; 2:1; 3:1, 5; 8:2-3; 21:12 (the references to the celestial beings in Heaven are too numerous to list: an angel sends and signifies St. John's Revelation, there are seven angels for the seven churches, Gabriel and other angels stand in God's presence in the eighth chapter, and angels stand at the twelve gates of the New Jerusalem)

l.8   "door": Rev 4:1 (the "door" of Heaven)

ll.9-10 "Oh...'Robe' ": Rev 1:13-18; 3:4-5 (the Son of man, the Alpha and the Omega)

l.11   "And...knocked": Rev 3:20

249   Wild Nights- Wild Nights!

l.3   "Wild Nights": Ca 2:16-17; 3:1-5; 4:6; 8:2-4

l.6   "To...port": Ca 2:1-4; 3:11; 4:9; 5:2; 8:6 (see also, in toto, Ps 107:23-30)

l.7   "Compass": Pr 8:27 (the circle inscribed upon chaos—the image of the circle or circuit versus that of the abyss or pit, the unbounded, a dialectic of closed, paradisiacal versus open-ended, bottomless infernal space at the heart of her sense of things; see, for example, P340)

l.9   "Eden": Ge 2-3

l.10   "Sea": Ge 1:2; Rev 21:1 (the primordial chaos is here connected with the wild, threatening disorder of the first line, "Wild Nights" synecdochic of a psychic turmoil needing the navigational helps of "Compass" and "Chart" for mere survival but, of course, desiring the haven of Edenic bliss)

Comment: See *Poems*, I, 179-180. P249 is an existential cry of desperation the source of which is in the absence of an external direction, control, norm, or value and the resolution of which is presented in terms of Canticles figuration. P249 might be compared with Stevens's "The Absence of an External Master of Knowledge." See also P368.

251   Over the fence-

ll.1-2   "Over...grow": Ge 2:17; 3:3

l.7   "God...scold": Ge 3:9-19

252   I can wade Grief-

l.1   "Grief": Isa 53:3-4

ll.6,8   "And...New Liquor": Ac 2:13

ll.10-12 "Power...hang": Ps 69:20; Isa 52-53; Mt 26-27; Mr 14:33 (the Suffering Servant, the Passion Christ, may be in the poet's mind as the prototype for all "Power" achieved through "Pain" and "Discipline")

ll.13-16 "Give...Him": Jg 13-16 (the example of Samson who succumbed to the blandishments of Delilah but in Gaza passed the test, the "Himmaleh")

253   You see I cannot see- your lifetime-

ll.13-14 "Like...want": ICo 13:12 ("Haunting" and "Teazing" comprise a circuit world lexicon for desire delayed and deferred, for sublunary experience as dispossession and absence; that the face-to-face ideal is not achieved necessitates the translations that haunt the "Heart")

l.15   "It...suffice": Rev 22:4 (the longed-for Vision and Presence)

254   **"Hope" is the thing with feathers-**

ll.1-2   " 'Hope' ": ICo 13:13; Heb 11:1; IPe 1:3 (see P1392)

256   **If I'm lost- now-**

ll.1-2   "If...found": Lu 15:3-10 (phrasing adapted from the parables of the lost sheep and lost piece of silver)

l.4   "Jasper": Rev 21:11, 18-19

l.4   "Gates": Rev 21:12-13, 15, 21, 25; 22:14

l.5   "Blazed open": Rev 3:8; 4:1 21:25; 22:14 (the open gate or door of the New Jerusalem, the Heavenly City, is a sign of acceptance, of welcome, of salvation; "Blazed" is used because of St. John the Divine's description of the holy city: "Having the glory of God: and her light was like unto a stone most precious, even like a jasper stone, clear as crystal...And the city had no need of the sun, neither of the moon, to shine in it: for the glory of God did lighten it, and the Lamb is the light thereof," Rev 21:11, 23; images of crystal and precious stones abound in the poet's favorite "Gem" chapter, Rev 21)

l.6   "awkward...face": Rev 1:12, 17; 4:1-2; 5:1-2, 6, 11; 6:1-2, 8-9, 12; 7:1-2, 9; 8:2, 13; 9:1, 17; 10:1, 5; 12:1, 3; 13:1-3, 11; 14:1, 6, 14; 15:1-2, 5; 17:1, 3, 6; 18:1; 19:11, 17, 19; 20:1, 4, 11-12; 21:1-2, 22; 22:1, 6, 8 (the pose of the poet before the "Angels" may be based upon that of St. John the Divine before the angel granting him the apocalyptic vision)

ll.7-8   "The...fleeces": Rev 3:4; 7:14; 10:1; 15:6; 19:14 (the garb of the "Angels," the "fleeces" of the Lamb)

l.12   "Savior's face": ICo 13:12; Rev 22:4 (the phrase denotes the sought-after beatific vision, the ideal presence suggested by the "Saviour's face" now turned away—"face" a cognate for "presence," Mt 18:10; IITh 1:9; the poet uses the title of "Savior," the one who makes whole, heals, saves, and delivers, in order to underscore the immensity of the banishment; for Jesus as "Savior" see Lu 2:11; Joh 4:42; Ac 5:31; Php 3:20; ITi 4:10)

257   Delight is as the flight-

ll.4,12,16 "Rainbow's," "Bent Stripe," "Rainbows": Ge 9:13-16; Eze 1:28; Rev 4:3; 10:1 (in the vision of Ezekiel the "Rainbow" suggests the "glory of the Lord"; God's presence in nature is made manifest in P257 by an emblematic reading of her phenomena, the "childish Firmament" of the "Bent Stripe" or "bow" promised Noah by God)

l.11   "East": IKi 4:30; Mt 2; 1-12 (in the KJV associated with wisdom)

l.14   "Firmament": Ge 1:6, 8; Ps 19:1

ll.20-21 "Butterflies...magic": ICo 15:50-55 ("Butterflies" as Hitchcockian emblems of the resurrection—the "magic" being in imaginative vision, the "childish Firmament," and not the "empty Skies")

l.24   "sudden morn": ICo 15:50-55 (resurrection morning; for "sudden" see also Mal 3:1-2; Mr 13:36)

258   There's a certain Slant of light,

l.1   "There's...light": Jas 1:17 ("Every good gift and every perfect gift is from above, and cometh down from the Father of lights, with whom is no variableness, neither shadow of turning"; in the KJV God is Light, Joh 1:7-9; 8:12; 9:5; the light experienced in P258 is ephemeral, a passing as well as geometrically partial or incomplete phenomenon that stands in contrast with the glory of God, the circumambient light suffusing the New Jerusalem, Rev 21:23-24; 22:5)

ll.3,5-6,10,11, 15-16 "oppresses," "Heft," "Hurt," "scar," "Despair," "affliction," "Distance," "Death": Isa 53:3-9; Mt 26-27; Mr 14:33; 15:34 (the lexicon of P258 is that of the Passion)

l.10   "Seal": Rev 7:2-8; 9:4 (in Revelation a sign of accession into the New Jerusalem, into the ideal presence of God, here used with almost oxymoronic effect with "Despair")

1.12   "Air": ITh 4:17 (synecdochic of Heaven, again suggesting the circumambient ideality of the heavenly experienced in the circuit world as a painful, fragmentary intermittence)

1.14   "Shadows...breath": Job 10:21-22; Ps 23:4 (in the KJV shadows are associated with death; here the encroachment of light is short-lived)

260   Read- Sweet- how others- strove-

l.1   "Sweet": Ca 2:3, 14; 5:5, 13, 16; 7:9 (the beloved)

l.1   "strove": Lu 13:24; ICo 9:25; IITi 2:5, 14, 24

ll.2,4,6   "Till": Eph 4:13; ITi 4:13 (used in Paulinian admonitions)

l.5   "How...witness": Lu 11:48; Joh 1:7-8; 3:28; 5:31, 36; 8:18; 10:25; 15:27; Ac 22:5; 23:11; IJo 1:2; 5:8 ("bear witness" is a frequent KJV phrase)

l.5   "faithful witness": Rev 1:5; 3:14; 20:4

l.7   "Kingdom": Mt 5:3, 10; 6:10, 13, 33; 25:34; ICo 6:9-10; 15:50; Ga 5:21; Eph 5:5; Col 1:13; 4:11; IITh 1:5; IIPe 1:11 (the "Kingdom" of God)

ll.8-13   "Read...Women": Rev 2:13; 17:6 (the martyrs); Heb 12:1 ("Wherefore seeing we also are compassed about with so great a cloud of witnesses")

l.15   "Renown": Ge 6:4 (perhaps synecdochic of Heaven, the word chosen for reverberations of distinction; nevertheless, the poet may here deliberately choose the Old Testament word in order to temporalize the reward of "Renown," to suggest that *Acts and Monuments* is really intended for her fellow martyrs like the beloved, "Sweet," or Christ the Sufferer—those who live out circuit world existence in the face of "Kingdom" unconcern)

262   The lonesome for they know not What-

l.2   "Eastern Exiles": Ge 3:24 (Adam and Eve, driven east from Eden, suggest by their "Fall" that the origin of religio-aesthetic, creative striving is a paradisiacal ache, a yearning to recapture that prelapsarian "strain" heard upon that "Transatlantic Morn," the morning of creation)

l.3   "Amber": see note, line one, P15

l.4   "madder Holiday": Ge 2-3 (the first "Holiday" is here the loss of paradise in the third chapter of Genesis)

l.5   "purple": see note, line one, P15

ll.9-12   "The...upon": Ge 1-2 (the "Blessed Ether" is the inimitable "strain" of the creation of God, the music of Heaven-Paradise)

Comment: See *Poems*, I, 187-188.

263   A single Screw of Flesh

l.1   "Flesh": Ge 2:23-24; ICo 15:50

l.2   "Soul": Ge 2:7; ICo 15:45

l.3   "That...Deity": Ge 1:27 ("So God created man in his own image, in the image of God created he him; male and female created he them"); Rev 19:7-9 (the "Soul," in terms of bridal figuration, "stands for" the Lamb or Groom)

l.4   "Upon...Vail": Ex 26:31-33; Ru 3:15; Ca 5:7 (first, the "Vail" may be that of the betrothed: Adam and Eve, Ruth and Boaz, Solomon and his beloved, and Christ and His bride; second, the "Vail" may be that of the tabernacle, a barrier walling out all but the high priest from the presence of God; the "Vail" may be that "Amber line" or "purple Moat" of P262, which stands as an insuperable obstacle to any return to Paradise or the sea and reefs of P313 blocking achievement of the "shore beyond," "new circumference," or Heaven)

l.6   "name": Ge 2:23-24; Rev 19:7-9; 21:1-2, 9; 22:17 ("wife" or Bride of Christ, metaphorical for a sense of assurance about the paternity, identity, and destiny of the "Soul")

l.9   "In...Alphabet": Mt 19:5-6; Mr 10:6-9; Eph 5:31 (the language of the marriage ceremony; it is possible that the poet here glances at the Alpha and Omega, the "Alphabet"—see Rev 1:11-12)

l.12   "Eternity": Isa 57:15; Rev 21-22 (Heaven)

l.18   "Clay": Ge 2:7; 3:19; Job 10:9; 13:12; 33:6

l.19   "Heaven": Rev 21-22

l.20   "Keepsake": Rev 19:7-9; 21:1-2, 9; 22:17 (the "Keepsake" is the memory of the experience of stanzas two and three, which is here rehearsed as a reminder of the conditions of flesh/soul dualism and of circuit world separations and distances this "side the Vail")

Comment: See *Poems*, I, 188-189.

264   **A Weight with Needles on the pounds-**

ll.1-4,7 "A...Anguish": Ps 22:16; Isa 52-53; Zec 12:10; Mt 26-27; Mr 14:33; Joh 19:34, 37; Rev 1:7 (the lexicon of the poem is that of the Passion)

l.6   "Frame": Ps 103:14 ("For he knoweth our frame; he remembereth that we are dust")

l.8   "As...name": Ge 2:19-20

265   **Where Ships of Purple- gently toss-**

l.1   "Purple": see note, line one, P15

266   **This- is the land- the Sunset washes-**

ll.2,6   "Yellow," "purple": see note, line one, P15

l.3   "Where...rushes": Joh 3:8 ("whence it cometh, and whither it goeth")

l.4   "Western Mystery": Job 38:19-20

l.5   "Night...Night": Ps 19:1-2

l.7   "Opal": Rev 21:19-21

Comment: See *Poems*, I, 189-190.

267   **Did we disobey Him?**

ll.1-8   "Did...you": Ge 2-3; Joh 3:16 (a witty retelling of the Christian story of man's disobedience and Divine love, which in its intentional presumption of consensus reveals that the story's rational consistency is anything but self-evident, the mind behind design being irreverently labeled "Dunce")

268   **Me, change! Me, alter!**

l.2   "Everlasting Hill": Ge 49:26; Hab 3:6 (the poet may here refer to the holy hill of Zion, the dwelling place of God, Ps 2:6; 48; 50:1-2; 87:2-3; 102:16, 21; Isa 31:4; 33:20; 40:9; 60:14; Joe 2:32; 3:16-17, 21; Rev 14:1)

l.3   "Purple": see note, line one, P15

l.6   "At...close": Rev 10:6 (the poet refers to the cessation of time when sun and sunsets will be no more, Rev 21:23; 22:5)

269   Bound- a trouble-

ll.3-4   "Limit...scarlet": Lu 22:44; Joh 19:34
Comment: See *Poems*, I, 191-192.

270   One Life of so much Consequence!

ll.1-4   "*One...salary*": Mt 6:25, 33; 24-26
ll.5-8   "*One...Life*": Mt 13:44-46 (the parables of the pearl of great price and of the treasure in the field convey the same idea of total "cost," the price of her religio-aesthetic commitment)
l.10   "*Gem*": Isa 61:10; Mal 3:17; Mt 13:45-46; Rev 21:2, 10-11, 18-21 (the poet is acceptably adorned by her "Gem")
l.12   "*Diadem*": Isa 62:3-4; Rev 2:10; 3:11; 4:4, 10
l.15   "*Monarchs*": Rev 1:5-6; 5:10; 15:3; 17:14; 19:6-9, 16 (the apocalyptic imagery of P270 emphasizes the significance of the poet's accession to royal status)

271   A solemn thing- it was- I said-

ll.2-3   "A...wear": Rev 3:4-5, 18; 6:11; 9:7-9; 21:2, 9; 22:17
l.3   "if...fit": IITh 1:11; Col 3:18
l.4   "Her...mystery": ICo 1:8; IIPe 3:14
ll.5-8   "A...until": Joh 4:6-14
ll.9-12   "I...fog": ICo 13:12 (the poet contemplates the future versus present value of her status as "Woman white")
l.13   "And...life": Job 7:7; Ps 90:10; Ec 2:17; Mt 5:2-12; 6:19-21, 25, 33; 7:13-14; Joh 12:25 (in Old Testament wisdom literature and in New Testament preachments of Jesus the "size" of the circuit world would be depicted as "small," a depiction unacceptable to the poet of P271, who sheds a reverent, timorous compliance in the first stanzas for a sneering temerity in the fourth)
Comment: See *Poems*, I, 193.0.

272   I breathed enough to take the Trick-

l.3   "Breath": Ge 2:7 (God breathed into man the "breath of life and man became a living soul"; P272 intentionally parodies the Genesis account with the poet's description of her death-in-life, her simulation of the "Trick")

273   He put the Belt around my life-

ll.3,5,6,8 "imperial," "Duke," "Title Deed," "Member": Rev 1:6; 5:10; 17:14; 19:7-9; 20:6; 22:1-5 (accession to Heaven as an inheritance of the Kingdom and an eternal reign with God is here given metaphorical adaptation in the poet's own rite of entail, coronation, or investiture)
l.6   "Kingdom's": Mt 5:3, 10; ICo 15:50; IIPe 1:11; Rev 1:9; 12:10 (the Kingdom of God)
l.8   "Cloud": Rev 1:7; 10:1; 14:14-16 (synecdochic of Heaven)
l. 10   "Toils": Ge 5:29 (synecdochic of the circuit world to which the poet here condescends because of her regal stature)
Comment: See *Poems*, I, 194-195.

274   The only Ghost I ever saw-

l.7   "Mosaic": Ex; Le; Nu; De (the poet may refer to Moses as an example of the antique in "fashions"; she may also be thinking of Moses as a "Ghost" at the Transfiguration, Mt 17:3)
l.15   "And...behind": Ge 19:17, 26 (God forbade Lot and his family to "look behind")
Comment: See *Poems*, I, 195.

275   Doubt Me! My Dim Companion!

l.1   "Dim Companion": ICo 13:12; Rev 19:7-9 (Christ, the Bridegroom)
l.8   "Delight": Ca 2:3; 7:6
ll.9-10 "It...before": Ge 2:7; Ec 12:7; Joh 3:3-8; Ro 8:16; ICo 15:45-46; Rev 22:17
l.11   "Dust": Ge 2:7; 3:19; Ps 103:14
l.13   "freckled Maiden": Jer 13:23 (an expression of unworthiness in contrast to the ideal, Ca 4:7; Eph 5:27; Rev 21)

ll.16-17 "Some...thee": Rev 19:7-9; 21-22

ll.18-25 "Sift...you": Ps 51:7; Isa 1:18; Mal 3:3; 4:1; Mt 3:12; 13:30; Lu 3:17 (the lines contain two apocalyptic preparationist motifs: first, the separation of chaff from wheat by sifting and winnowing, the chaff to be burned by the "refiner's fire"; second, the purification from spot—"freckled Maiden"—in order to be made "whiter than snow," Ps 51:7; the imagery of these lines may also owe a debt to St. John the Divine's description of the Alpha and Omega, the Son: "His head and his hairs were white like wool, as white as snow; and his eyes were as a flame of fire," Rev 1:14)

Comment: See *Poems*, I, 196-197.

276   Many a phrase has the English language-

ll.1-16   "Many...me": Ps 19:1-3 (an Emersonian poem in praise of the language of nature)

Comment: See *Poems*, I, 197.

277   What if I say I shall not wait!

l.2   "What...Gate": Ge 2:23-24; ICo 15:50 (the body is here viewed as a prison, Ro 7:24; IICo 5:3-4; Php 3:21)

l.4   "What...off": ICo 15:53-54

Comment: See *Poems*, I, 198.

278   A Shady friend- for Torrid days-

ll.9-12 "Who...made": Ge 1:26-27; 2:7, 18, 21-24; Ps 139:14 ("Paradise" is here Eden where God the "Weaver" placed the first humans or "Tapestries")

279   Tie the Strings to my Life, My Lord,

l.1   "My Lord": ICo 15:47, 54-57; Rev 1:8; 4:8, 11; 19:1, 6

l.7   "Judgment": Rev 6; 20

l.11   "Everlasting Race": ICo 9:24; Heb 12:1

l.13   "Goodbye...live": Ga 2:20

Comment: See *Poems*, I, 199.

280   **I felt a Funeral, in my Brain,**

l.2   "Mourners": Ec 12:5

l.10   "Soul": Ge 2:7; ICo 15:45 ("Soul" replaces "Brain," which the poet emphatically eliminated with five heavy lines, Franklin, I, 341; the revision reveals more a certainty of sense and sound than any concern for a KJV resonance)

l.13   "Heavens": Ge 2:1, 4

l.19   "World": Heb 1:2; 11:3

l.20   "And...then": ICo 13:12 (the poet's irony directed at the traditional view of death as yielding the ultimate in knowledge)

Comment: See *Poems*, I, 199-200.

281   **'Tis so appalling- it exhilirates-**

ll.15-16 "Looking...Breath": Ac 17:25; ICo 15:50-55 (to look at "Death" as terminus is to "let go the Breath," to accept life as dust devoid of spirit)

l.22   "It...liberty": Lu 4:18; Ro 8:21

l.23   "And...free": Ro 5:15; Ga 5:1 (the Paulinian ideas of the free gift of grace and the liberty gained from sin and death are here transmogrified into the figures of "Fright" and "Terror" whose *danse macabre* celebrates a bleak holy day, which is the obverse of Easter)

Comment: See *Poems*, I, 200-201.

282   **How noteless Men, and Pleiads, stand,**

l.1   "Pleiads": Job 9:9; 38:31

ll.3-4   "Reveals...Eye": IIKi 2:12

l.5   "Invincible": Col 1:15; ITi 1:17; Heb 11:27 (the "noteless Men" are joined with the "Invisible" God in the world of spirit)

l.10   "Heavens": Ge 1:1, 8; 2:1, 4

Comment: See *Poems*, I, 201-202.

283   **A Mien to move a Queen**

ll.2,5,10-11,13-14,16,22: "child," "humbler," "Wren's," "shy," "slight," "Sprite," "Low," "small": Mt 5:2-12; 18:3; 19:13-14; Mr 10:13-14 (the Lilliputian persona based upon the Beatitudes philosophy of diminution and the preachments of Jesus regarding children as symbolic of the kingdom)

ll.1-3,9, 19-21,23: "Queen," "Heroine," "Orleans," "Duke," "supreme," "Realm," "Diadem," "distant": Rev 1:5-6; 5:10; 15:3; 17:14; 19:6-9, 16; 20:4-6; 22:5 (the lexicon of heavenly coronation entailing as well the bridal figuration)

l.21   "Diadem": Isa 62:3-4; Rev 2:10; 3:11; 4:4, 10; 19:6-9

Comment: See *Poems*, I, 202-203.

284   The Drop, that wrestles in the Sea-

l.1   "The...Sea": Ge 32:24-30 (the poet may have had in mind Jacob who wrestled with an angel before receiving confirmation of identity)

l.4   "incense small": e.g., Ex 30:7-10 (offerings and incense were part of the proscribed worship of God)

l.5   "All...All": ICo 12:6; 15:28; Eph 1:23 (plenitude allows no additions, the poet here playing with the paradoxes of the Divine nature and of the One and the many)

ll.7-9   "The...'Me' ": Rev 19:7-9 (the poet pleads for her identity as Bride of Christ)

Comment: See *Poems*, I, 203-204.

285   The Robin's my Criterion for Tune-

l.12   "The...flit:" Ec 3:1

Comment: See *Poems*, I, 204.

286   That after Horror- that 'twas us-

ll.9-10   "The...Bell": Lu 22:42-43 (the thief on the cross may have been in the poet's thoughts here since the "Thief's Request" is mentioned in the letter to Higginson,which quotes the third paragraph of P286, the poet signing the letter "Barabbas," Mt 27:16-26; Joh 18:40)

ll.9-16   "The...in": ICo 13:12; 15:50-55; IJo 3:2; Rev 22:5 (conjecture involves death and its aftermath: will the beatific vision with its ideal presence result or will "possibility" terminate with a

"Face of Steel," the latter face of "Thought" the forbidding "profile" of the unachieved apocalyptic)

    l.10   "Moment's Bell": ICo 15:52

    l.16   "drills/nails": Joh 20:25 (another echo of the Crucifixion adding to the nightmarish landscape of P286)

    Comment: See *Poems*, I, 204-205; *Letters*, II, 425-426; and Leyda, II, 82.

287   A Clock stopped-

    ll.6-9   "An...Noon": Mt 27:46-50; Mr 15:34-37

    l.9   "Degreeless Noon": Rev 21:23-24; 22:5 (the perpetual "Noon" of Heaven)

    ll.17-18 "The...Him": Rev 10:6 (a Heaven without time supersedes the circuit world "Dial life")

289   I know some lonely Houses off the Road

    ll.11-12 "Old...surprise": Mt 13:11-17 (P289 concerns types of vision suggested by the answers to Chanticleer's question given by the "Trains" and the "old Couple": one, the sunrise is a thing to be observed in time and space, "Where"; two, the sunrise is a thing gone, a thing of the past, the concern of "Almanac[s]"; an "old Couple," whose "pain of Spectacles" parallels the "Windows hanging low" of the "lonely Houses," lays up treasure upon earth, Mt 6:19-21, while the sunrise comes as a thief in the night, IIPe 3:10, and misses the "surprise" of the dawn—dawn coming to those who are imaginatively awake, as Thoreau's *Walden* insists, or to those spiritually attuned to its figurative significance, Mal 4:2; Lu 1:78; IIPe 1:19; Rev 2:28; 22:16)

    Comment: See *Poems*, I, 207-208.

290   Of Bronze- and Blaze-

    l.1   "Of...Blaze": Ge 1:14-18

    ll.8,12   "Infects...Oxygen": Ge 1:27; 2:7

    l.18   "dishonored Grass": Ge 3:17 ("cursed is the ground for thy sake")

    Comment: See *Poems*, I, 209.

291   How the old Mountains drip with Sunset

l.1   "old Mountains": Ge 49:26; Job 15:7; Pr 8:25 (proverbially antique)

ll.5,24   "Scarlet," "Gold": see note, line one, P15

l.8   "That...tell": see line twenty-two below

l.11   "Sapphire": Rev 21:19 (see also note, line fifteen, P191)

l.15   "And...carry": Ex 3:2; Na 2:3; Ac 2:3; Rev 1:14; 2:18; 10:1; 19:12; 20:9 (fire or flame is associated with theophanies)

l.21   "Visions": Ge 12:7; Nu 24:4; Isa 1:1; IICo 12:1 (the experience of "Sunset" yields heightened, epiphanic awareness; see, on the parallel "Extasy," note, line six, P122; note, line fifteen, P783; and note, lines five and eight, P1191)

l.22   "never told": IICo 12:1-4 ("It is not expedient for me doubtless to glory. I will come to visions and revelations of the Lord. I knew a man in Christ above fourteen years ago, (whether in the body, I cannot tell; or whether out of the body, I cannot tell: God knoweth;) such an one caught up to the third heaven. And I knew such a man, (whether in the body, or out of the body, I cannot tell: God knoweth;) How that he was caught up into paradise, and heard unspeakable words, which it is not lawful for a man to utter")

l.24(variant) "Powerless...unfold": IICo 12:1-4

Comment: See *Poems*, I, 210-211.

292   If your Nerve, deny you–

ll.1-2,9-10   "If...door": Mt 5:29-30 (the syntax and the draconian response to weakness are both imitated)

ll.9-10   "If...door": Ge 2:7, 23; Mt 26:41 (a sardonic attack upon the pusillanimity of her own spirit with an ironic inversion of the hegemony of the "Soul" in traditional Platonic-Christian thinking by equating it with the scientific element, "Oxygen")

Comment: See *Poems*, I, 211.

293   I got so I could hear his name–

l.1(variant) "take...name": Ex 20:7

l.4   "Thunder": Ex 19:16; 20:18; Rev 4:5; 11:19; 14:2; 19:6

ll.13-15 "Could...Extremity": Ps 84:11; Ro 3:24; 5:2, 20; IPe 3:7; Heb 4:16; Eph 3:7 (grace, as the unmerited favor of God, is here "renowned" for meeting every need, including the poet's sense of loss)

l.18   "Petition's way": Ps 20:5; IJo 5:15 (in the attitude of petitionary prayer)

ll.19-20 "Tho'...utters": Ro 8:26

l.21   "Cloud": Ex 16; 10; 19:9, 16; 24:15-16; 34:5; 40:34-38; Ps 78:14; Mt 24:30; 26:64; Mr 13:26; 14:62; Rev 1:7; 14:14-16 (the "Cloud" is associated with manifestations of God's presence and power)

l.22   "Power": Mt 6:13

l.24   "It...way": IPe 5:7

Comment: In her tradition, profane love was a stepping-stone to divine love ("Cupid taught Jehovah to an untutored mind"), romantic love serving as a paradigm by which to clarify relations with the heavenly beloved. Yet P293, with its requisite hyperboles, love sites, and love tokens, charts the reverse process leading not to intimacy of presence and communication but rather to silence and separation, "Business with the Cloud." See *Poems*, I, 211-213.

295   Unto like Story- Trouble has enticed me-

l.1   "Unto...me": see P260 (stories of martyrs like those in *Acts and Monuments*)

l.3   "preferred...Glory": IICo 4:17-18

l.5   "Dungeons...chanted": Ac 16:25

l.6   "Till...time": Lu 1:57; Gal 4:4; Eph 1:10

ll.9-10,11 "Unto...these": ICo 9:25; IITi 4:8; Jas 1:12; IPe 5:4; Rev 2:10; 3:11; 4:4, 10

ll.8,11,15 "Shame," "rejected," "Crucifixion": Isa 50:6; 53:3-6; Mt 21:42; 26-27 (the lexicon of the Passion)

l.10   "fair": Ca 1:15-16; 2:10, 13; 4:1, 7, 10; 7:6

l.16   "As...rolled": ICo 15:52; Rev 1:10; 4:1; 8:2, 6, 13; 9:14 (though "martial," the "Trumpets" have apocalyptic resonance)

l.24   "Light": Rev 21:23-24; 22:5 (the "Light" of the New Jerusalem, the glory of God)

Comment: See *Poems*, I, 214.

296   One Year ago- jots what?

ll.6-8   "Such...Wo": Mt 22:30

ll.10-11 "In...real": Rev 2:7; 7:16; 19:7-9; 21:6; 22:2, 14 (the tree and water of life and the Marriage Supper of the Lamb may not be "Banquet's real" in the circuit world sense, the absence of hunger suggesting a change from the "flesh and blood" of the "natural body," 1Co 15:42-55)

l.13   "Wine": Mt 26:26-29

l.14   "Come...World": Mt 26:29

l.16   "Thirst": Ps 69:21; Joh 19:28   (other possible P296 words in the lexicon of the Passion: "Wo," "hurt," "bore," "pain," Isa 53:4; Ac 2:24)

Comment: See *Poems*, I, 215-216.

297   It's like the Light-

l.1   "It's...Light": Ge 1:3 (God is "Light," Joh 1:5, 8-9, 14; 1Jo 1:5; living in "Light," Ex 24:10; 1Ti 6:16; and "Light" in the KJV is associated with the sacred, holy, and spiritual)

ll.3-8   "It's...Trees": Joh 3:8

ll.9-10   "It's...done": Rev 7:1

ll.11-12 "And...Noon": Rev 10:6; Rev 21:23-24; 22:5 (the "Clocks" are those of eternity where time has collapsed into eternal "Noon"; the wind in P297 grants an epiphany conveyed in a muted apocalyptic lexicon)

298   Alone, I cannot be-

l.1   "Alone...be": Joh 8:16; 16:32

l.2   "Hosts": Isa 47:4 ("Lord of Hosts," the frequent KJV designation for God in the Old Testament); Lu 2:13 (the heavenly "Hosts," the angels; the poet may here use the KJV term as vehicle to speak metaphorically of her imagination)

299   Your Riches- taught me- Poverty.

ll.1,5   "Riches," "Dominions": Ps 103:22; 104:24; 145:13; Rev 1:6; 5:12

l.1   "Poverty": Mt 5:2-12

ll.7-8   "And...you": Php 3:8 ("I count all things but loss for the excellency of the knowledge of Christ Jesus my Lord: for whom I have suffered the loss of all things")

l.10   "But...Gems": Rev 21

l.12   "And...Diadems": Isa 62:3-4; Rev 2:10; 3:11; 4:4, 10

ll.13-14 "So...know": Rev 19:7-9; 21 (the Bride of Christ, the "Queen," and the Heavenly City, the New Jerusalem adorned with the "Gems," Rev 21:2)

ll.18-20 "To...Jew": Rev 22:4 (the "Jew" is the Deity, the poet here envious of properly adorned ideal presence, the beatific vision)

l.26   "Gold": Ca 5:11, 14-15 (the idealized beloved); Rev 21:18, 21 ("Gold" suggests the New Jerusalem but also the acceptably purified, circumferential diadem, Rev 3:18; 4:4, and the God whose "Riches" are Vision and Presence, Rev 21-22)

ll.29-30 "It's...Pearl": Mt 13:44-46; Rev 21:21

Comment: See *Poems*, I, 218-221; *Letters*, II, 400-402, 405, 411-412; and Leyda, II, 63-64.

300   "Morning"- means "Milking"- to the Farmer-

l.5   "Just...revelation": IPe 1:13; Rev 1:1

l.5   "Beloved": Ca 1:14, 16; 2:3, 8-10, 16-17; 4:16; 5:1-2, 4-6, 8-10, 16; 6:1-3; 7:9, 11, 13; 8:5, 14; Rev 20:9 (the New Jerusalem is metaphorically the "Beloved" and "Bride," Rev 21:2, 9)

l.7   "Brides...Apocalypse": ICo 15:50-55; Rev 19:7-9; 21:2, 9; 22:17 (resurrection morning brings bridal status to the "Beloved")

l.9   "Faint...Lives/Eyes": ICo 13:12; Rev 22:4 (for relevant references to "Faint" not concerned with vision see Lu 18:1; IICo 4:1, 16; Ga 6:9; Eph 3:13)

l.9   "Their...Sighing": Isa 35:10; Rev 7:17; 21:4

l.10   "Faith": Heb 11:1 ("Faith" is here a type of seeing, a willingness to view "Morning" as "typic" of apocalyptic day, and adding to the wit is the corroboration of such seeing by "Experiment," a proof by the death and resurrection of "Our Lord")

l.10   "The...Lord": Mt 26-28 (the Passion and Resurrection of Christ; the Lord is also associated with the "Morning," Rev 2:28; 22:16)

Comment: See *Poems*, I, 221-222.

301   I reason, Earth is short-

l.1   "I...short": Ps 89:47
ll.2-3   "And...hurt": Mt 26-27 (the lexicon of the Passion)
ll.5-7   "I...Decay": Ge 3:19
l.11   "new": Rev 21:5 ("Behold, I make all things new")
ll.9-11   "I...given": Mt 5:2-12 (the poet's philosophy of deprivation is the "Equation" of the circuit world; since the Passion-circuit world of "Anguish," the Genesis-guaranteed "Decay," and the "even" of "Heaven" are "given[s]" not amenable to "reason," P301 uses with irony "Equation," a word from that Platonic model of rational intelligibility, the lexicon of mathematics)
Comment: See *Poems*, I, 222-223.

302   Like Some Old fashioned Miracle

l.1   "Like...Miracle": see note, line six, P122; note, line fifteen, P783; and note, lines five and eighteen, P1191 (the "Miracle" is one of the ecstasy or enchantment achieved by memory of summer)
Comment: See *Poems*, I, 223-234.

303   The Soul selects her own Society-

ll.1-2   "The...Door": Rev 3:20 (having been selected, the poet "selects," her commitment a religio-aesthetic one to "Present" herself through words and then only to the "One"—such a commitment perhaps a corroboration of election, IIPe 1:10)
l.5   "Unmoved": ICo 15:58
l.10   "One": Ca 2:10, 13; 6:9; 8:10; Rev 19:7-9 (the beloved or the Groom, Christ)
l.12   "Stone": IPe 2:5 (the dynamic of P303 is the very real withdrawal and absence suffered for an anticipated apocalyptic of ideal presence, Rev 21-22—a dynamic most closely approximated in verses of St. Paul, IICo 5:6-9)
Comment: See *Poems*, I, 225.

304   The Day came slow- till Five o'clock-

l.3   "Rubies": see note, line one, P15

l.3   "Light": see note, line one, P297

l.5   "Purple": see note, line one, P15 (the "Purple" of the vail is associated with the experience of the dawn as epiphany, revelation, but other KJV echoes of "Purple" relate to the "Prince" and "Lady" and to the "Jew," Ca 3:10; 7:5; Mr 15:17, 20; Joh 19:2, 5)

l.5   "East": Mt 28 (as the place of the dawn, the "East" is "typic" of the resurrection)

l.6   "Sunrise": Lu 1:78; IIPe 1:19

l.7   "Topaz": Rev 21:20

ll.9,12   "Winds," "Wind": Joh 3:8; Ac 2:2

l.9   "Timbrels": Ps 81:2; 149:3; 150:4

ll.11,12   "Prince": Isa 9:6; Ac 5:31; Rev 1:5

ll.10-11   "The...Prince": Rev 4:2-10; 5:6, 8, 11-13; 7:9-17

l.13   "Orchard": Ge 2-3; Eze 28:13-14; 31:8-9, 16; Rev 21-22 (the vision of the dawn combines Eden, Paradise, and the New Jerusalem)

l.13   "Jew": Ge 1:1; Mt 2:2 (the Deity)

ll.14-15   "How...place": Ge 28:16-19; 32:30-31

l.16   "The...Day": Ge 1:5, 8, 13-19, 23, 31; 2:2-3 ("Day" is synecdochic of God and His creation, His habitation, Ps 24:1; the "Parlor" or dawn may be metaphorically the anteroom or holy place before the vail, Ex 26:33—the experience in P304 is "typic" of or a metonym for the beatific vision, Rev 22:4)

Comment: See *Poems*, I, 226.

305   The difference between Despair

ll.6-8   "Contented...see": Rev 22:4 (imagery from the terminus of apocalyptic striving is here used to delineate the stasis of spiritual "Despair")

Comment: See *Poems*, I, 226-227.

306   The Soul's Superior instants

l.2   "alone": Ex 24:2; Da 10:7-8; Heb 9:7 (a frequent condition for theophanies, for being in the presence of God)

ll.3-4   "friend...withdrawn": Lu 22:41

ll.5-6   "ascended...Hight": Isa 14:14

l.8   "Omnipotent": Rev 19:6

l.9   "This Mortal": ICo 15:53-54

l.10   "fair": Ca 1:15-16; 2:10, 13; 4:1, 7, 10; 6:10; 7:6

ll.11-12 "Apparition...Air": Joh 3:8 (as God dictates, the "Air" comes and goes, the intimations of immortality for the "Apparition" or Spirit likewise)

ll.13-14 "Eternity's...few": Isa 42:1; 65:9; Mr 13:20, 27; Ro 8:29-33; IITi 2:10; Tit1:1; IPe 1:2; 2:5-6; 5:13; IIPe 1:10 ("favorites" may signify the elect; the poet may also have in mind those of her KJV "favorites" who received "Eternity's disclosure" in "Superior instants": Enoch, Ge 5:24; Heb 11:5; Elijah, IIKi 2:11; Moses, Ex 3; 19:3; 24:18; 32:11; 34:2; Mt 17:3; Jacob, Ge 28:10-22; 32:24-32; though never mentioned by name, the high priest Aaron, Ex 28; Heb 9:7; St. Paul, IICo 12; and Christ, Mt 17; 26-28)

l.15   "substance": Heb 10:34; 11:1

l.16   "Immortality": ICo 15:53-54; ITi 6:16

Comment: See *Poems*, I, 227-228.

307   The One who could repeat the Summer day-

l.2   "greater than": Mt 11:11; 12:41-42; Lu 11:31-32; Joh 4:12; 8:53

ll.2-3   "Were...be": Lu 7:28 (a religio-aesthetic adaptation stressing Art over Nature, the triumph of imagination over circuit world evanescence)

Comment: See *Poems*, I, 228-229.

308   I send Two Sunsets-

l.2   "Day": Ge 1:5, 8, 13-19, 23, 31; 2:2-3 (synecdochic of the God of creation)

Comment: See *Poems*, I, 229-230.

310   Give little Anguish-

ll.1,3   "Give": Mt 6:11 (an oblique, sardonic request for the proper measure of pain)

ll.6-7   "Death...Disc": see note, line ten, version 1861, P216

Comment: See *Poems*, I, 230-231.

311   It sifts from Leaden Sieves-

l.3   "Alabaster Wool": Rev 1:14

ll.5,7   "Face," "Forehead": Rev 22:4 (Perhaps the initial version associated the white of Revelation with the snow as a type of God's face, underscoring its circumferential "Unbroken Forehead"; the later, 1864 version's "Baseless Arc" is a more fitting geometrical figure given the poem's conclusion, title [given by the poet], and overall conception—"Baseless Arc," fittingly, owing more to *The Tempest* than to Revelation)

l.11   "Fleeces": Rev 1:7, 14; 10:1; 14:14-16

l.12   "Celestial": ICo 15:40 (heavenly)

l.12(variant) "Crystal": Rev 4:6; 21:11; 22:1

l.12   "Vail": Ex 26:31-35; Mt 27:51; IICo 3:13-16; Heb 6:19; 10:20 (beyond the Biblical vail was the unmediated presence of God, the snow here a "Vail" comparable to that in the Old Testament tabernacle; this and other KJV images were excised in the 1864 version, making it a more coherent and unified poem stressing the natural magic of the snow)

Comment: See *Poems*, I, 231-234; *Letters*, III, 699, 768; and Leyda, II, 307.

312   Her- "last Poems"-

ll.13-14 "Crown," "Diadem": Isa 62:3; Rev 2:10; 3:11; 4:4, 10

l.15   "Be...sign": ICo 15:54-55 (the "Grave" a sign of immortality)

l.18   "What...Bridegroom": Rev 19:7-9

Comment: See *Poems*, I, 234-236.

313   I should have been too glad, I see-

l.1   "glad": Ca 1:4; Rev 19:7 (the KJV term for calmly happy, well-off)

ll.1,7,13 "I see": Joh 9:25 ("one thing I know, that, whereas I was blind, now I see")

l.3   "Of...Round": Ec 3

l.4   "little Circuit": Job 22:14; Ps 19:6; Ec 1:6 (the circuits of God are in the heavens, the "little Circuit" the sublunary world of the poet) l.5   "new Circumference": Rev 21-22 (Heaven; circumferential imagery abounds in Revelation: the seal, crown, faces of the elect, the circled throne, and the walled New Jerusalem—St. John the Divine's images of idealized, paradisiacal, bounded space working a profound attraction upon the poet; see Rev 2:7, 10; 3:11; 4:1-10; 5:6, 11; 6:2, 4; 7; 9:7; 12:1, 3; 14:14; 19:12; 20:11-13; 22; St. John places the excluded in the unbounded space of the "bottomless pit," Rev 20:3; such imagery of the unbounded is also used for effect by the poet, e.g., stanza five, P280)

l.6   "homelier time": Ec 3

l.7   "saved": Rev 21"24

l.8   "Fear": Rev 11:18; 14:7; 15:4; 19:5; (P313 contends that justification is by "Fear" not faith; the "Fear" experienced is linked with the Crucifixion)

ll.9-11   "That...Sabachthani": Mt 27:46 ("And about the ninth hour Jesus cried with a loud voice, saying, *Eli, Eli, lama sabachthani*? that is to say, My God, my God, why hast thou forsaken me?"); see also Ps 22:1-11

ll.15-16   "I...justify": Mt 26-27; 28:8; Lu 24:41, 52 (the "Joy" is experienced after the Resurrection; the "Fear" is that of the Passion)

l.17   "Palm": Joh 12:12-13 (the palms of Palm Sunday, occasion of Christ's triumphal entry into Jerusalem)

l.17   "Calvary": Lu 23:33 (Golgotha, the site of Christ's Crucifixion)

l.18   "Savior": Lu 1:47; 2:11; Joh 4:42; Ac 5:31 (the Crucified is asked to "Crucify")

l.18   "Crucify": Mt 27:31, 35; Mr 15:13-14, 24-25; Joh 19:16, 18

l.20   "Gethsemane": Mt 26:36; Mr 14:32 (the garden in which Christ agonized over His "cup" or destiny, His anguish paradigmatic for the poet's circuit world experience)

l.21   "Shore": Rev 21-22 (Heaven)

l.22   "Beggars": Mt 5:6; Lu 16:19-21

l.22   "Banquets": Rev 19:7-9 (Heaven as a "Banquet," the Marriage Supper of the Lamb; for Heaven in terms of oral gratification see Rev 2:7; 7:16-17; 21:6; 22:14)

l.23   "Thirsting": Mt 5:6; Joh 19:28

l.23   "Wine": Mt 26:27-29 ("Wine" has apocalyptic reverberations since it is associated with judgment, Rev 14:10, 19-20; 16:19; 19:15; in Biblical iconography "Wine" would be associated

with the abundance of the promised land, Nu 13:21-27, and thus
suggestive of Heaven)

1.24   "Faith": Heb 11:1
1.24   "bleats": Isa 53:7; Ac 8:32 (apparently again
identifying with the Christ of the Passion, the poet differentiates her
"bleat[ing] to understand" from Him who "opened not his mouth,"
that is, said "thine be done" to the will of Heaven in contrast to P313's
insistence upon an intelligible theodicy, a raison d'etre for circuit
world existence)

Comment: See *Poems*, I, 236-237.

314   Nature- sometimes sears a Sapling-

1.7   "Souls": Ge 2:7
1.8   "Die oftener": ICo 15:31
Comment: See Poems, I, 237-238.

315   He fumbles at your Soul

1.1   "He...Soul": Ca 2:1-7; 4:7; 8:2-4; Rev 19:7-9; 21-22
(the idealized depiction of the beloved is the point of contrast for the
fumbling Smithy-God Whose handling of the "Soul" is as awkward as
the blacksmith's attempting the piano's "Keys")

11.4-5   "He...Nature": Mal 3:2 (the "Soul" is by heating
prepared, later "bubbl[ing] Cool")

1.6   "Etherial Blow": Ro 4:6 (imputed righteousness)
1.11   "imperial Thunderbolt": Ro 4:6
1.12   "That...Soul": Isa 40:3; 61:10; 62:3-4; Mt 3:3; 22:2-
14; Eph 5; Rev 3:18; 19:7-9; 21-22 (the poet may here mock her own
proclivity toward preparationist and bridal figuration, her desire for a
verse to adorn her when such would be incommensurate given the
context, since "He" ignores etiquette and form, aesthetic and
otherwise, with his staccato "Hammers" and unpredictable
"Thunderbolt"; the "naked Soul," Ge 2:25, is innocent and unadorned,
"scalp[ed]" in order to receive the necessitated substitute face, IICo
3:18; Rev 22:4)

1.13   "Winds": Ge 1:2; Joh 3:8; Ac 2:2 (Divine "Winds"
are mighty forces superior to mere "Nature," unsentimental as
manifested in "fumbl[ing]" and "Paw[ing]" and resistant to those
conventional and genteel fictions used to domesticate them)

l.14   "Universe/Firmaments": Ge 1:6-8, 14-17, 20
l.14   "is still": Zec 2:13 ("Be silent, O all flesh, before the Lord: for he is raised up out of his holy habitation")
Comment: See *Poems*, I, 238-239. P315 is apparently a critique of conventional preparationist etiquette.

317   Just so- Jesus- raps-

ll.1-11   "Just...thee": Ca 5:2; Rev 3:20 (Jesus as the solicitous beloved; for the metaphor as counsel of persistence see Mt 7:7-8; Lu 11:9-10)
Comment: See *Poems*, I, 241-242. The variant "mat" for line ten may suggest a link between P317 and P303.

318   I'll tell you how the Sun rose-

ll.1,8   "I'll...'Sun' ": Mal 4:2; Lu 1:78; IIPe 1:19; Rev 2:28; 22:16
l.3   "Amethyst": Rev 21:20
l.10   "purple": see note, line one, P15
l.14   "Dominie": Mt 23:8, 10; Joh 1:38; 13:13-14; Eph 6:9; Col 4:1 (the Lord is Master and Shepherd)
l.16   "And...away": Ps 23; Isa 40:11; Lu 12:32; Joh 10; Ac 20:28; Heb 13:20; IPe 5:2 (the "flock" may have apocalyptic resonance here as well, Mt 25:32-33)
Comment: See *Poems*, I, 242-243; *Letters*, II, 403; and Leyda, II, 52-54.

319   The nearest Dream recedes- unrealized-

l.2   "The...chase": Josh 1:1-6 (the later reference to honey may suggest that the promised land was the paradise of romantic fulfillment here thought of)
l.11   "steadfast Honey": Ex 3:8, 17; 23:31; Nu 14:8; De 6:3; 11:9 ("Honey" is the food of Canaan, the promised land; "Honey" is also associated with the beloved, Ca 4:11; 5:1)
Comment: See *Poems*, I, 243-244; *Letters*, II, 403; and Leyda, II, 52-54.

320   We play at Paste-

l.2   "Till...Pearl": Rev 21:21

l.6   "And...Hands": Rev 21:5

l.7   "Learned...Tactics": Rev 21 (the "Gem" chapter describes the Heaven achieved after the religio-aesthetic practice of P320)

Comment: See *Poems*, I, 245; *Letters*, II, 403; and Leyda, II, 52-54.

321   Of all the Sounds despatched abroad,

l.5   "Wind": Ge 2:7; Joh 3:8; Ac 2:2 (the "Wind" is associated with breath or spirit as the "fleshless Chant" of line twenty-seven suggests)

ll.9,11 "Inheritance...away": IPe 1:4

ll.10,25 "Beyond...Boughs": Eph 2:8-9

ll.12-13 "By...fingers": Mt 6:19-20

l.13   "not...fingers": Eph 2:8-9 ("For by grace are ye saved through faith; and that not of yourselves: it is the gift of God: Not of works, lest any man should boast")

l.15   "golden": see note, line one, P15

l.17   "Dust": Ge 2:7; 3:19; Ps 103:14

ll.18-24 "Do...Orchestra": ICo 15:50-55 (perhaps the poet's playful view of the resurrection, which Higginson found sacrilegious)

l.27   "fleshless Chant": Ge 2:23-24; ICo 15:50 (again, the "Wind" is distinguished from the "Dust" or flesh)

Comment: See *Poems*, I, 245-249; *Letters*, II, 404-405; and Leyda, II, 56-57.

322   There came a Day at Summer's full,

l.1   "There...full": Rev 6:17; 16:14 (the summer solstice of June is "typic" here of resurrection morning, the "great day of God Almighty")

l.3   "I...Saints": Rev 11:18; 14:12; 15:3; 19:8; 20:9 (the "Saints" may also be those, like St. John the Divine and St. Paul, granted revelations)

l.4   "Resurrections": ICo 15:35-55; 20:5-6

l.4(variant) "Revelations": IICo 12:1; Rev 1:1, passim

l.7   "soul": Ge 2:7; ICo 15:45

l.7   "solstice": Mal 4:2; Lu 1:78; IIPe 1:19; Rev 1:16; 2:28; 22:16 (the play is upon the Sun-Son, the light of Heaven where the sun has reached its final stop, Rev 21:23-24; 22:5)

l.8   "That...new": Rev 21:5 ("And he that sat upon the throne said, Behold, I make all things new")

l.9   "The...speech": Rev 8:1

l.10   "The...world": Joh 1:1 (ideal presence eliminates the need of "symbol" or metaphor)

ll.11-12 "Was...Lord": Mt 26:26-29

l.13   "Sealed Church": Rev 7 (the seal, crown, and white raiment necessary preparations for the Marriage Supper of the Lamb and beatific vision, Rev 2:10; 3:5, 18; 7:3; 9:4; 14:1; 19:8; 22:4)

l.16   "Supper...Lamb": Rev 19:7-9

l.23   "Each...Crucifix": Mt 26-27 (the image of the Passion Christ is the basis of the troth pledged, of "Calvaries of Love")

ll.25-26 "rise...Grave": ICo 15:50-55

l.27   "new Marriage": REv 19:7-9; 21:2, 9; 22:4, 17

l.28   "Justified": Ro 3:20-28; 8:29-30 (as in P313 justification is here by suffering)

l.28   "Calvaries...Love": Lu 23:33 (Calvary, the site of the Crucifixion)

Comment: See *Poems*, I, 249-253; *Letters*, II, 389-390, 404-405; and Leyda, II, 44, 56-57.

323   As if I asked a common Alms,

ll.1-8   "As...Dawn": Ac 3:1-11 (Peter and John offer the lame man, who has asked alms, not "Silver and gold" but the miraculous, the ability to walk; the lame man experiences this miracle at the "gate of the temple which is called Beautiful" or "Beautiful gate of the temple"; P323 uses this incident metaphorically to convey a Wordsworthian, Simplon Pass, surprised-by-joy experience of epiphany)

l.3   "Kingdom": Mt 5:3

l.7   "purple": see note, line one, P15

l.8   "Dawn": Mt 28:1; IIPe 1:19 (L964 may suggest that the poet views the "Dawn" as "typic" of the resurrection, ICo 15:50-55)

Comment: See *Poems*, I, 253-254; *Letters*, II, 408-409; III, 857-858; and Leyda, II, 60-61.

324   **Some keep the Sabbath going to Church-**

l.1   "Some...Church": Ex 20:8
l.6   "I...Wings": Isa 40:31
l.9   "God...Clergyman": Ro 1:20
l.11   "at last": Joh 6:39-40, 44, 54; 11:24; 12:48; ICo 15:26, 52; IPe 1:5, 20; Jude 18 (obeisant to Emerson, P324 complements the conventional view of Heaven as object of eschatological hope with the notion that it can be possessed "all along")

Comment: See *Poems*, I, 254; *Letters*, II, 411-412; and Leyda, II, 63-64.

325   **Of Tribulation- these are They,**

ll.1-2   "Of...White": Rev 7:14 ("These are they which came out of great tribulation, and have washed their robes, and made them white in the blood of the Lamb"); 14:1-5
l.3   "Spangled Gowns": Isa 61:10; Rev 21:2 (the "Brides" adorned for the Groom are also "saved" but of "lesser Rank" than her "Tribulation"—Passion saints, the wise virgins, ll.12-16 below)
ll.5-6   "All...times": Rev 2:17; 3:5, 12, 21; 21:7
ll.7-8   "Wear...Palms": Rev 7:9 ("After this I beheld, and, lo, a great multitude...before the Lamb, clothed with white robes, and palms in their hands")
l.11   "Outgrown Anguish": Isa 53:3
ll.12-16 "Remembered...said": Mt 25:1-13 (the preparationist motif and the discussion of the tribulation and Parousia in the preceding chapter may suggest the parable of the wise and foolish virgins was in the poet's mind; see also Mt 24:29-31; Mr 13:24-27)
l.15   "House": Joh 14:2
l.16   "SAVED": Rev 21:24
Comment: See *Poems*, I, 256-257; *Letters*, II, 411-412; and Leyda, II, 63-64.

327   **Before I got my eye put out**

ll.1-17   "Before...dead": Ge 3:5-7; Pr 27:20; Ec 1:8 ("finite eyes" may be those of a corporeal, possessive vision occasioned by the Fall; Sewall, 559, suggests that seeing God in nature face-to-face is connected with the Old Testament prohibition, Ge 32:30; Ex 33:20, 23; Jg 6:22-23; 13:22)

ll.18-19   "So...pane": Mt 5:8; 13:9-17; ICo 13:12; Rev 3:18

ll.3,20   "Creatures": Ro 1:25 (see also Ro 8:19-25; IICo 5:7)

Comment: See *Poems*, I, 259-260; *Letters*, II, 414-415; and Leyda, II, 65-66.

329   So glad we are- a Stranger'd deem

l.1   "glad": Ca 1:4; Mt 5:12; Rev 19:7
l.5   "justified": Ro 3:24; 5:1
l.6   "Grief": Isa 53:3-4
l.6   "Joy": Mt 28:8; Lu 24:41, 52
Comment: See *Poems*, I, 263.

331   White Asters

l.1   "Asters": see note, line one, P15 (purple)
ll.2-3   "On...Everlasting": Ge 49:26
ll.3-4   "Everlasting...Covenant": Ge 9:16; 17:7, 13, 19; Le 24:8; IISa 23:5; ICh 16:17; Ps 105:10; Isa 55:3; 61:8; Jer 32:40; Eze 16:60; 37:26; Heb 13:20
l.4   "Gentians": see note, line one, P15 (blue)

332   There are two Ripenings- one- of sight-

ll.1-8   "There...Air": Rev 14 (the "Ripenings" have apocalyptic overtones, Joe 3:13; Rev 14:15, 18; the elect, virginal, "Tribulation" saints of P325 are those whose "Ripening" has been in the "Bur," Rev 14:4—for these, the "firstfruits," see Ex 22:29; Ro 8:23; Jas 1:18)
l.7   "That...disclose": Job 37:10
Comment: See *Poems*, I, 264-265.

333   The Grass so little has to do-

l.1   "The...do": Ge 1:11-12; Mt 6:25-33

l.9   "Dews": Pr 19:12 (see note, line twenty-one, P122)
l.9   "Pearls": Rev 21:21
ll.10-11 "And...common": Rev 19:8
l.13   "And...pass": Ps 103:15; IPe 1:24
l.14   "Odors...divine": Ec 6:10; Da 2:46; Php 4:18; Rev 5:8

l.15   "spices...sleep": Joh 19:40-42; ICo 15:51
ll.14-16 "The...perishing": Ca 1:12; 2:13; 4:10-11, 13-14, 16; 5:1, 13; 6:2; 7:8, 13; 8:14 (for "Spikenards" see also Mr 14:3; Joh 12:3; smells and spices are repeatedly associated with the beloved)
l.17   "And...dwell": Rev 21:3
l.19   "The...do": see line one above
l.20   "Hay": Pr 27:23
Comment: See *Poems*, I, 265-267.

334   All the letters I can write

ll.1-2   "All...this": Ca 2:1; 4:1, 3 (Canticles furnishes metaphors of the beloved as flower, the "fair," comely one whose speech is more beautiful than letters or poetry)
l.2   "fair": Ca 1:8, 15-16; 2:10, 13; 4:1, 7, 10; 5:9; 6:1, 10; 7:6

ll.5-6   "Depths...Thee": Ca 4:3, 11; 5:1, 13 (the "Ruby" lips of the beloved and the idea of drinking, "undrained" and the "sipped" of the final line; Canticles frequently uses the oral imagery of feeding and drinking)
Comment: See *Poems*, I, 267-268; *Letters*, II, 414; and Leyda, II, 64.

335   "Tis not that Dying hurts us so-

l.1   " 'Tis...so": ICo 15:54-55
l.4   "A...Door": Mt 27:60; 28:2; Rev 3:20
l.10   "For...Crumb": Lu 16:21
l.11   "pitying Snows": Rev 1:14
l.12   "Home": Rev 21-22
Comment: See *Poems*, I, 268; *Letters*, II, 420-421; and Leyda, II, 73-74. The poet's words to the Norcross cousins prefacing P335 were: "Let Emily sing for you because she cannot pray."

336   The face I carry with me- last-

l.1   "The...last": Ro 8:29; ICo 15:49; IICo 3:18; Col 3:10; IJo 3:2 (the "face" is that of Christ, the poet having been conformed to His image)

l.2   "When...Time": Rev 10:6

l.3   "To...West": Rev 7; 14:4; 19:7-9; 21:1-7, 23-27; 22:1-5

l.4   "That...thine": see line one above

ll.5,11   "Angel," "Gabriel":Da 8:16; 9:21; Lu 1:19, 26; Rev 8:2

ll.6-7   "Degree...Kingdoms": Mt 5:3, 10, 19-20; 6:33; 7; 13; Col 1:13; IIPe 1:11 (the poet's "Degree" is in the kingdom of heaven, references to which are too numerous to list)

l.7   "the Raised": ICo 15:15-20 (Jesus Christ)

l.10   "crown": ICo 9:25; IITi 4:8; Jas 1:12; IPe 5:4; Rev 2:10; 3:11; 4:4, 10

l.15   "bore": Lu 14:27; ICo 15:49

l.15   "Master's": Mt 23:8, 10

l.15   "name": Rev 2:13; 3:8; 22:4

l.16   "Sufficient": IICo 3:5; 12:9

l.16   "Royalty": Isa 62:3-4; IPe 2:9 (the sufficiency or adequacy involves the face that has prepared the poet for accession into Heaven and for the beatific vision, Rev 22:4)

337   I know a place where Summer strives

l.2   "With...Frost": Job 37:10

ll.3-4   "She...'Lost' ": Lu 15:6

l.5   "But...Pools": Ca 4:16

l.7   "Her Vow": Lu 15:4

l.7   "Heart": Ca 3:11; 4:9; 8:6

l.8   "And...Refrains": Ca 1:1

l.9   "Into...Adamant": Eze 28:13; Zec 7:12; Rev 4:6; 15:2; 21:11, 18, 21; 22:1 (metaphorically the poem concerns fire and ice, the "Adamant" an image of ice along with "Frost" and "Quartz")

l.10   "spices": Ca 4:10, 14, 16; 5:1, 13; 6:2; 8:14

l.10   "Dew": Ca 5:2 (see note, line twenty-one, P122)

l.11   "That...Quartz": Rev 4:6; 15:2; 21:11, 18, 21; 22:1 (for the significance of crystallization in P337 and its source in Rev.

Wadsworth, see Sewall, 456; as in Dante and Eliot the "fire" world of passion, suffering, desire, and loss is enveloped by the apocalyptic "ice" world, the fundamental oppositions of P337 those of Canticles versus the "Gem" chapter)

1.12   "Amber": Eze 1:4, 27; 8:2 (the associations of "Amber" with "Summer" fire)

338   I know that He exists.

1.1   "I...exists": Job 19:25-26
1.2   "Somewhere...Silence": Ge 3:23-24; Ex 33:20; De 4:12; Isa 45:15; Joh 1:18; ITi 1:17; 6:16; IJo 4:12, 20 (the God of exclusion, distances, and separation, the unapproachable, invisible Deus absconditus)
1.3   "He...life": Isa 45:15 ("Verily thou art a God that hidest thyself, O God of Israel, the Saviour")
1.3   "rare life": Joh 4:24; Col 1:15; ITi 1:17; Heb 11:27 (God is invisible, a Spirit)
1.4   "From...eyes": Isa 64:4; ICo 2:9; 13:12; IJo 3:2; Rev 3:18 (deficiencies in the sight of the "finite eyes"; the poet may also have in mind the Paulinian idea that "flesh and blood cannot inherit," ICo 15:50)
1.4   "gross": Mt 13:15; Ac 28:27
ll.5-8   " 'Tis...surprise": Ge 2-3 (the "play" and "Ambush" —the construction P338 places upon the Fall after which "Bliss" must earn its Paradise within a circuit world circumscribed by a "Death" which may turn out a nihilistic "surprise")
ll.10-12 "Prove...stare": Ps 22:15-18 (the references to the Passion Christ; for other uses of "piercing," Joh 19:34, 37; Rev 1:7)
1.14   "Look...expensive": Mt 20:28; ICo 6:20; 7:23; ITi 2:6 (again the references are to the Passion Christ, ones used to describe her experiences of "play," "fun," and "jest" as "piercing earnest")
ll.12,16 "In...far": Ge 3; ICo 15:35-55 ("Death" here takes on the face given it by the first Adam, that of the serpent, instead of the face of the second Adam, as in her favorite Paulinian Resurrection chapter; the facelessness of God in stanza one and the stiff stare of "Death" in stanza three suggest the potential unmeaning of the apocalyptic)
Comment: See Poems, I, 270.

339   I tend my flowers for thee-

l.1   "I...thee": Isa 40:3; Mal 3:1; Mt 3:3; Mr 1:3; Lu 1:76 (a preparationist [P339 is also a "Putative," for which see note, lines fourteen-nineteen, P179] poem; the flowers are associated with the beloved, Ca 2:1-2, 12, 16; 4:5; 5:13; 6:2-3; 7:2)

l.2   "Bright Absentee": Rev 1:18; 2:28; 21:16

l.4   "Sower": Mt 13:3-8, 37; ICo 15:35-45; Rev 14:14-20

l.5   "spot": Ca 4:7; Eph 5:27 (the word reveals anxiety about being fittingly adorned)

l.9   "spice": Ca 4:10, 14, 16; 5:1, 13; 6:2; 8:14

l.13   "odors": Ca 1:12; 2:13; 3:6; 4:10-11; 7:8, 13

l.17   "Garden": Ca 4:12, 15-16; 5:1; 6:2, 11; 8:13

l.20   "Crimson": Isa 53:3-5; Mt 26:28; 27:28; Mr 15:17, 20; Lu 22:44; Joh 19:2, 5, 34; 20:25 (crimson and purple are associated with the Passion Christ and the beloved, Ca 3:10; 4:3; 7:5; "Fuschzia's," "Geraniums," "Carnations," "Hyacinth," and "Roses" all suggest a purple and red achieved through suffering or at least a process of violence since such is reflected in the verbs: "Rip," "spot," "split," and "break"—the production of such profusion of color and beauty a metaphor for a religio-aesthetic regimen, the writing of poems, in order to adorn herself for her "Lord-away"; the purple and crimson, along with the yellow of the "Daisies," suggest the longed-for presence of the beloved—see note, line one, P15)

l.22   "Lord": Rev 19:1, 6

l.23   "It...me": ITi 2:9-10 ("In like manner also, that women adorn themselves in modest apparel, with shamefacedness and sobriety; not with broided hair, or gold, or pearls, or costly array; But [which becometh women professing godliness] with good works")

ll.24,27 "I'll...thee": ITi 2:9-10; IPe 3:3-5; Rev 19:7-9 (perhaps the "Gray" garb anticipates the white raiment of the sealed and crowned elect, Rev 3:5, 18; 6:11; 7:9, 13-14; 19:8; the "Calyx" may refer to the body prison—Ro 7:24; IICo 5:4; Php 3:21—whose compensatory beauties do not attract because of their unworthiness or because, as the ironic final line implies, the "Absentee" is aesthetically unresponsive)

l.25   "How...alway": ITi 2:9-10

l.27   "Draped...thee": Isa 61:10; ITi 2:9-10; IPe 3:3-5; Rev 3:4-5, 18; 6:11; 7:9; 19:7-9

Comment: See *Poems*, I, 270-271.

340   Is Bliss then, such Abyss,

l.1   "Bliss": Ge 2-3; Eze 28:13-14; 31:8-9, 16; 47:1-12; Rev 21-22 (Paradise or Heaven)

l.1   "Abyss": Ge 1:2; Job 38:30; 41:31-32; Ps 42:7; Pr 8:28; Rev 9:1-2, 11; 11:7; 17:8; 20:1, 3 (the deep or bottomless pit is the unbounded, infernal space of the abyss)

ll.2-8   "I...store": Ge 2-3; Ex 3:5; Ac 7:33 (the "foot" is the innocent, inexperienced, and unshod prelapsarian soul that enjoys the paradisiacal presence of God; the "Boot," the timorous, corporified, and commodified postlapsarian self; since a decision of moment is involved see also Mt 16:24-26)

ll.9-11   "But...more": Joh 3:16-17; ICo 6:20; 7:23; Heb 9:12; IPe 1:18-19; Rev 5:9 (the poet may refer to the purchase of "Bliss" through the Atonement, not to be bought since a matter of grace and faith, Eph 2:8; the "Patent," lost through the Fall, forces the momentous decision upon the "foot"; on the other hand these lines may simply suggest that "Bliss" was sold once in Eden, and in the postlapsarian world "Bliss" has become "Abyss," a situation terrifying the "Lady" with its irrevocable finality)

l.14   "Verdict...Boot": Ro 7:24; IICo 5:4; Php 3:21 (not a choice but a sentence of condemnation to the vile body prison with all its implications of frustration for the religio-aesthetic aspirations associated with the "foot")

Comment: See Poems, I, 271-272.

341   After great pain, a formal feeling comes-

l.1   "pain": Rev 21:4

ll.3-4   "The...before": Isa 53:3-5 (the question arises whether this pain parallels that of the Passion Christ, Mt 26-27)

l.8   "Regardless grown": Job 3:4; 30:20; Ps 106:44; Ec 5:8

l.9   "Quartz": Rev 4:6; 21:11; 22:1 (the use of crystallization here is negative and ironic)

l.10   "Hour": Mt 26:45; Mr 14:41; Joh 2:4; 12:23

l.12   "Snow": Rev 1:14 (the echoes of Revelation in P341 are ironic; the poem in its rhymes, repetitions, parallelisms, and

ceremonious open and close creates as it were a circuit, the unideally circumferential, the face of the false apocalyptic, its potential unmeaning in stark contrast to the desired beatific vision, Rev 22:4; instead here there is no regard for the self rent into fragments: "Nerves," "Heart," and "Feet")
Comment: See *Poems*, I, 272-273 and Franklin, I, 395.

342   It will be Summer- eventually.

1.1   "It...eventually": Ge 8:22; Rev 22:1-3 (the promise of summer's return is "typic" of that perpetual apocalyptic "Summer")
1.7   "Tho'...Parian": Rev 1:14; 2:17; 3:4; 4:4; 6:11; 7:9; 15:6; 19:8; 20:11 (apocalyptic white as part of the priestly, Eucharistic symbolism of the poem)
1.10   "purple": Mt 26:26-29 (as with the white of line seven, the purple and red of the poem are Eucharistic; see also note, line one, P15, since the poem is one of epiphany via nature)
ll.11-12 "will...Forefathers": Pr 15:5 (because of the proverbial wisdom of the "Bees"); Jer 31:29 (because the "Bees" are part of the poet's paradisiacal iconography); De 32; Rev 15:3 (because the "Bees" sing the new version of "Their Forefathers'" song)
1.13   "Rose...redden": see line ten above and note, line one, P15
ll.14-16 "The...frill": see notes, P331
ll.17-18 " 'Till...Gown": Heb 1:10-12 ("And, Thou, Lord, in the beginning hast laid the foundation of the earth; and the heavens are the works of thine hands: They shall perish; but thou remainest; and they all shall wax old as doth a garment; And as a vesture shalt thou fold them up, and they shall be changed: but thou art the same, and thy years shall not fail")
ll.19-20 "Or...done": Mt 26:26-29
Comment: See *Poems*, I, 273-274.

343   My Reward for Being, was This.

1.1   "Being": Ac 17:28
1.1   "This": Ca 5:16 (the beloved)
1.6   "Thrones": Rev 1:4; 3:21; 4:2-10; 5:1, 6-7, 11-13; 6:16; 7:9-17; 8:3; 12:5; 14:3, 5; 19:4-5; 20:4, 11; 21:5; 22:1-3 (a metonym for God)

l.7　　　"With...'Me' ": Rev 22:4

l.8　　　"Thee": Ca 1:3-4, 9, 11; 4:7; 7:12-13; 8:1-2, 5 (the beloved)

l.9　　　"Dominions": Da 7:27 (the hyperbole may have its roots in Genesis 1:26, 28, since a variant line echoes the first chapters of Genesis: " Creation...powerless")

l.9　　　"Grace": Eph 2:4-8 (a metonym for Christ the Beloved, her pattern for sacrifice of happiness or "Bliss" to a higher religio-aesthetic commitment)

l.10　　　"Election": Ro 9:11; ITh 1:4; IPe 1:2; IIPe 1:10

l.11　　　"Ballots...Eternity": Rev 2:17

Comment: See *Poems*, I, 274-275.

344　　　'Twas the old- road- through pain-

l.1　　　" 'Twas...pain": Isa 53:3-5; Mt 26-27 (the way of the Passion)

l.3　　　"thorn": Mt 27:29; Mr 15:17; Joh 19:2, 5

l.4　　　"That...Heaven": Mt 7:14; Rev 21-22

l.13　　　"The...back": Ca 1:2-4, 9; 2:2-7, 10, 13; 3:5, 10; 4:1, 7, 10; 5:2, 8; 6:4; 7:6

ll.17-18 "Another...tonight": Rev 22:5

l.19　　　"Chambers bright": Rev 21:23-24; 22:5

Comment: See *Poems*, I, 275-276.

345　　　Funny- to be a Century-

ll.1-4　　　"Funny...He": Job 34:21; Pr 15:3 (the omniscient Sentry-God is the "staid," distant observer)

l.5　　　"He...very": De 29:29; Job 15:8 (secrets belong to God); Ps 44:21 (God knows the secrets of the hearts of all)

l.6　　　"Were...tell": Lu 8:17

l.8　　　"So...Publicity": Ge 3:8-11

346　　　Not probable- The barest Chance-

l.3　　　"And...Rest": Rev 20:5, 15; 21:8 (the damned)

l.4　　　"The...Paradise": Rev 19:7-9; 21:23-24; 22:1-5

l.5　　　"Bird": Rev 19:7-9 (the Lamb or Groom seeking His bride)

l.6   "Sweets": Ca 2:3, 14; 5:5, 13, 16; 7:9
l.6   "Mortals": ICo 15:53-54
l.7   "Forget...wing": see line five above ("His wing" is a synecdoche for the Groom's mission in search of the "Queen"; it is remotely possible the poet may have adapted the one metaphorical use of the bird as deliverer, Isa 31:5; loss and search, separation and return are part of the topoi of profane love, Ca 3:1-4; 5:6-8; 6:1, 13)
l.10   "Oh...Queen": Ca 6:8-9; Rev 19:7-9; 21:2, 9; 22:17 (the Bride, but here a "Phantom" because apocalyptic fulfillment is not achieved)

347   When Night is almost done-

l.1   "When...done": Job 7:4; 30:17; Ec 2:23

348   I dreaded that first Robin, so,

l.6   "Till...by": Mt 27:29; Mr 15:18; Joh 19:3
ll.7-8   "Not...me": Joh 19:10-11
l.11   "pierce": Ps 22:16; Zec 12:10; Joh 19:34, 37; Rev 1:7
ll.14-16 "So...me": Ps 22:17; Zec 12:10; Joh 19:37; Rev 1:7 ("And again another scripture saith, They shall look on him whom they pierced,"Joh 19:37)
ll.17-21 "I...though": Ps 22:16; 88:17; 118:12 ("They compassed me about like bees," Ps 118:12)
ll.21-23 "not...me": Ro 8:18-25 (the interest of "Blossom" and "creature" in the "Queen" and the source of her dread are explained by these verses from St. Paul—verses also showing the connection between the anguish of P348 and that expressed in the opening lines of Eliot's *The Waste Land*)
l.24   "Calvary": Lu 23:33
l.25   "Each...goes": Mt 27:29; Mr 15:18; Joh 19:3 ("And began to salute him, Hail, King of the Jews!," Mr 15:18)
l.26   "childish Plumes": Mt 27:29 ("reed in his right hand")
ll.27-28 "Lift...Drums": Lu 23:34
Comment: See *Poems*, I, 278-279.

349   I had the Glory-that will do-

ll.1-2   "I...Honor": Isa 62:3-4; Mal 3:17; Rev 4:9, 11; 5:12-13; 19:1, 7; 21:11, 23-26

ll.3-4   "When...'Nay' ": Mt 19:29-30 (the path of renunciation)

ll.2,5   "Thought...shape": Ca 2:14; 5:15; Rev 19:7-9; 22:4 (the "shape" of "Bliss" is the disembodied, idealized face of the beloved; in "Thought," which like her letter is the "Mind alone without corporeal friend," the poet through imagination "can turn" without the anxiety that the beloved may "turn" from her presence—see Ca 2:17; 6:1 and *Letters*, II, 386; the apparent renunciation of P349 is at once a profession and possession acceptably disembodied)

ll.6-7   "Gulphing...possibility": ICo 15:53-54; IICo 54 (perhaps there is an adaptation from St. Paul here)

350   They leave us with the Infinite.

l.1   "Infinite": Ge 17:1; 35:11; Ps 147:5; Rev 21:22
l.2   "But...man": Nu 23:19 ("God is not a man")
ll.3-4   "His...men": Ps 8:3; Pr 30:4
l.5   "And...Arm": Job 40:9
ll.6-7   "As...Shoe": Ge 49:26; De 33:15; Job 15:7; Ps 65:6; Hab 3:6
l.9   "So...Comrade": IISa 22:3; Ps 18:2; 91:2
l.11   "Eternity...ample": Isa 57:15
l.12   "quick enough": Nu 16:30; Ps 55:15
Comment: See *Poems*, I, 279-280.

351   I felt my life with both my hands

ll.1-2   "I...there": ICo 15:49-55; Rev 21:5 (P351 is written from the postresurrection, changed point of view, which forces adjustments to the "image of the heavenly")

ll.3-8   "I...Sound": ICo 15:49; IICo 3:18; IJo 3:2; Rev 22:4 (the metaphors attempt to explain the experience of new name and new face at the beatific vision)

ll.12,14 "Conviction...time": ICo 15:47-50 (the "me" is that of "flesh and blood," the "image of the earthy")

l.15   "But...Heaven": Rev 21-22

l. 16   "As...Home": IICo 5:6

352   Perhaps I asked too large-

l.1   "Perhaps...large": Mt 7:7; 21:22; Joh 14:13-14; 15:7, 16; 16:23; IJo 3:22; 5:14

l.2   "skies": ICo 15:40, 48-49

l.3   "Earths": Ge 1:10; ICo 15:47-49 (a metonym for the spiritually stunted)

l.5   "My...Firmaments": Ge 1:6-8, 14-17, 20; Ps 19:1

354   From Cocoon forth a Butterfly

ll.13-15 "Cloud...go": Ex 16:10; 24:15; 34:5; 40:34-38; Job 22:14; Ps 104:3; 147:8; Isa 19:1; Da 7:13; Mt 24:30; 26:64; Ac 1:9; ICo 10:2; ITh 4:17; Rev 1:7; 10:1; 11:12; 14:14-16 (the mysterious, almost impalpable beauty of the butterfly is associated with the world of "Cloud" and "Phantom," its leisurely irrelevance salient in a landscape of Puritan-ethic-enslaved hay harvesters and "Bees" and "Flowers"; in P354 metamorphosis and flight become metaphors for pure products of the imagination not to be reduced to design, adaptation, utility, or emblem—the poem anticipating Stevens's "Sunday Morning" in seeing evanescence as the mother of beauty)

l.16   "In ...Circumference": Ps 19:6; Isa 40:22

l.19   "zealous": Ac 21:20; 22:3; ICo 14:12; Tit 2:14; Rev 3:19

l.20   "Idleness": Pr 31:27

355   'Tis Opposites- entice-

l.9   "Thee": see line eight, P343 (her desire is to "enamor" the putative Other, the God of Plenitude who demands "lack" as essence of circuit world existence, Mt 5:2-12; see also, note lines fourteen-nineteen, P179)

ll.4,10-12 "The...Me": Rev 19:7-9; 22:4 (P355 wishes to make the banal truism of line one a basis for apocalyptic hope only to concede that its ironic outcome may be a solipsistic apotheosis, the "Me" as "Divinity")

Comment: See Leyda, II, 42.

356   The Day that I was crowned

l.1   "The...crowned": Ca 6:8-9; Isa 61:10; 62:3-4; Rev 2:10; 3:11; 4:4, 10; 19:7-9; 21:2, 9; 22:17
l.3   "Until...came": Rev 1:6; 5:10; 20:4, 6; 22:5
l.5   "Carbon...Coal": Ge 2:7; 3:19; ICo 15:47-51
l.6   "And...Gem": Eze 28:13; Ca 1:10; 7:1; Isa 61:10; Mal 3:17; ICo 15:47-51; Rev 21
l.8   "Diadem": Isa 62:3-4; Rev 2:10; 3:11; 4:4, 10
l.10   "Day": Rev 6:17; 16:14
l.11   "Myself...Majesty": Job 40:10; Ps 93:1; 104:1; Heb 1:3; 8:1
l.12   "Were...adorned": Isa 61:10; Rev 21:2
l.13   "The...chose": Ro 8:29-33; 9:11; 11:5; Eph 1:4-6; IPe 1:2; 2:3-9; IIPe 1:10; Rev 7; 14:4; 17:14 (the chosen are the elect by "Grace")
l.14   "Crown": Rev 2:10; 3:11; 4:4, 10
ll.15-16 "That...Mine": Rev 1:5; 3:14 (the "Witness" and Guarantor of "Grace" is Christ, but the poet states that "Witness" and election were hers—" 'twas Mine")
Comment: The religio-aesthetic experience of P356 uses regal imagery and bridal figuration to speak of a metamorphosis, a crystallization (Sewall, 456), a new state or status, the "Grace" of which may be self-imputed—see P528.

357   God is a distant- stately Lover-

l.1   "God...Lover": Joh 3:16; IJo 4:8 (for God as the Deus absconditus see note, line two, P338)
l.2   "Woos...Son": Joh 3:16; Ro 5:8; IJo 4:9-10 (the tradition of Christ as Lover is based in Canticles and Revelation, especially chapters nineteen and twenty-two)
l.5   "lest...Soul": Ca 1:7; 3:1-4; Isa 61:10
l.6   "Envoy": Mt 1:1 (Jesus Christ, the Chosen One or "Envoy," e.g., Heb 3:2; IPe 2:4)
l.6   "Groom": Mt 6:9 (God the Father)
l.8   " 'Miles'...Synonyme": Joh 10:30 ("I and my Father are one")
Comment: See *Poems*, I, 284-285.

358   If any sink, assure that this, now standing-

ll.1-2   "If...Failed": Ps 69:2-3, 14
l.5   "Tell...Moment": IICo 4:17 ("affliction, which is but for a moment")
l.8   "Dying...kill": Lu 12:5; ICo 15:50-55

359   I gained it so-

l.4   "Bliss": see note, line one, P340
l.11   "Lest...fall": Ac 27:17; ICo 10:11; ITi 3:7; 4:11; Heb 12:15
l.13   "Grace": Eph 2:8 (the "instant's Grace" may be an assurance of election or a vision of "Bliss," the experience presented metaphorically as ascent of a tree in order to gain what "hung so high" and afterward to "clutch it"—perhaps the fruit of the tree of life, Rev 3:7; 22:2)
l.14   "Beggar's face": Lu 16:19-21 (the face of the circuit world destitute, Mt 5:2-12)
Comment: The uncertainty of the antecedents of "This" and "it" (used five times) leaves open the possibility that P359 concerns a reentry into an Eden of the beloved, Ca 2:3; 3:6; 4:13, 16; 5:16; 6:11; 7:13; 8:7, 11-13.

360   Death sets a Thing significant

l.3   "perished": ICo 15:18
l.5   "little Workmanships": Eph 2:10

361   What I can do- I will-

l.1   "What...will": Ec 9:10

364   The Morning after Wo-

l.1   "The...Wo": Mt 26-28 (the Passion and Resurrection are here used as metaphors)
l.3   "Surpasses...before": Mt 28 (the unfeeling profusion of nature is an ironic Resurrection)

l.4 "Jubilee": Le 25:9-15, 28-33, 40, 50, 52, 54; 27:17-24 (associations of the joys of freedom, release, and forgiveness with "Jubilee" are obviously ironic here)

l.15 "Crucifixal": Mt 27:35; Mr 15:24-25; Lu 23:33; Joh 19:18-20

l.16 "Calvary": Lu 23:33

Comment: See *Poems*, I, 289.

365   Dare you see a Soul *at the White Heat?*

l.1 "White": Rev 2:17; 3:4-5, 18; 6:11; 7:9, 13-14; 14:3-4; 19:8 (the "White" of the elect "Soul" still not released from circuit world purgatorial "Heat")

l.1 "Heat": Rev 7:16

l.3 "Red...tint": Isa 48:10; Zec 13:9; Mal 3:2-3 (the imagery of the refiner's fire)

l.4(variant) "quickened": Joh 5:21; 6:63; Ro 4:17; 8:11; ICo 15:36, 45; Eph 2:1, 5; Col 2:13; IPe 3:18

l.8 "unannointed": Ps 2:2; 20:6; Isa 45:1; IICo 1:21; IJo 2:27 (the anointed are God's chosen)

ll.9-10 "Least...ring": Isa 44:12; 54:16 (the KJV use of the "Blacksmith" metaphor)

l.13 "Refining...Ores": Mal 3:2-3

l.15 "Designated": Rev 2:10; 3:11; 4:4, 10; (the crown); Rev 7 (the seal); Rev 2:17 (the white stone); Rev 3:4-5, 18; 6:11; 7:9; 19:8 (white raiment); Rev 19:7-8 (bridal status); Rev 3:12; 22:4 (the new name—all the marks of election)

l.15 "Light": Joh 1:9 (the "true Light, which lighteth every man"); Eph 5:8; Col 1:12; ITh 5:5 (the elect as "children of light"); Rev 21:23-24; Rev 22:5 (the "Light" of the New Jerusalem); (in preparationist, religio-aesthetic terms, the "Designated Light" may be that disembodied, idealized face that her poetry hammers and refines for a world of pure vision and presence)

l.16 "Repudiate...Forge": Ro 7:24; IICo 5:4; Php 3:21 (P365 may usurp the prerogatives of purgatorial refinement in order to vanquish and repudiate the implied dross and limitation of the "Forge" —prison of the circuit world in the process of achieving self-apotheosis through a commitment to art; that the poet termed P365 "Cupid's Sermon" is ample warning, nevertheless, that the religious and aesthetic are not here mutually exclusive)

Comment: See *Poems*, I, 289-291 and *Letters*, III, 681.

366   Although I put away his life-

l.1   "put...life": Le 21:7; De 22:19, 29; Ezr 10:3, 19; Isa 50:1; Mt 1:19; 5:31-32; 19:3, 7-9; Mr 10:2, 4, 11-12; Lu 16:18; ICo 7:11-12 (the language is connected with husband-wife relationships, including an addendum to the Ten Commandments, Mt 19:8-9; P366 is an ironic treatment of Mt 19:4-6 since the poet has "put asunder" her bond with the deity only to then rehearse the dutiful obedience He has missed—all with tongue-in-cheek wit)

1.2   "Ornament": Rev 3:12; 22:4 (the name of the Deity upon the forehead, a confirmation of bridal status and achieved identity)

1.3   "Forehead": Rev 7:3; 14:1; 22:4

1.4   "Hand": Ge 3:22 (a synecdoche deliberately chosen to express wifely submission and not rebellion)

1.11   "delighted": Ca 2:3; 7:6

1.12   "I...go": Ca 3:4

1.17   "weariest Commandment": Ex 20:1-17 (obliquely this line refers to the first and second of the Ten Commandments, in particular for it is the jealousy—"avarice"—of God concerning "other gods," earthly beloveds, that has led to her circuit world isolation)

1.18   "sweeter": Ca 2:3, 14; 5:5, 13, 16; 7:9

1.19   "obey": Ex 19:5; De 11:27-28; 13:3-4 (the echoes of the Ten Commandments, of the jealousy of God and of His admonitions regarding idolatry, are all part of the ironic play of P366)

1.20   "Than...'Seek' ": see P703 (the imputation is that the Deity has relinquished the domestic compensations for games such as "Hide and Seek")

1.24   "Dust": Ge 2:7; 3:19; Ps 103:14 (this line of P366 prima facie reads as a sobering philosophical truth, Ec 3:20, but it is a rhetorical question in the form of the declarative: does "Dust" give glory to such a cold and distant "Fame"?)

1.30   "Paradise": Ge 2-3; Eze 28:13-14; 31:8-9, 16; 47:1-12; Rev 21-22 (the New Jerusalem or Heaven, but with the specific promise of paradise, bridal consummation)

ll.29,31-32 "That...me": Ex 20:3-6; Isa 61:10; 62:3-4; Mal 3:17; Rev 14:3-4; 19:7-9; 21:2, 9; 22:17 (bittersweet for the betrothed of the Deity, the "promise" whose essence is "avarice" is at once marriage vow for the Bride of Christ and motive power for a creation that yields as its theodicy the inscrutable personality and conduct of the jealous lover)

Comment: See *Poems*, I, 291-292.

367   Over and over, like a Tune-

1.4   "Cornets...Paradise": Rev 1:10; 4:1; 8:2, 6, 13; 9:14
ll.5-6   "Snatches...grand": Rev 7:14-15; 14:3-4
1.7   "Justified": Ro 3:24, 28; 5:1, 9; 8:30, 33; Ga 2:16; Tit 3:7 (the "Justified" include the saved, the sealed and crowned elect, Rev 2:10; 3:11; 4:4, 10; 7; 14:3-4; 21:7, 24)
1.7   "Processions": Rev 5:11-13; 7; 14:1-5; 19:5-9
1.8   "At...hand": Mt 25:31-34; Rev 21:7

368   How sick- to wait- in any place- but thine-

1.1   "How...thine": Ca 2:5, 14; 4:9-10; 5:8; 6:5; 7:4-5; 8:6 (the language of "thine," "thee," and "thou" is that of Canticles)
1.3   "Thinking...alone": Ca 3:1; 6:1 (absence and reunion compose the rhythm of Canticles)
1.5   "ducal": Ca 1:4, 12; 3:9, 11; 6:8-9; 7:5 (the regal imagery of Canticles entails as one of the profane love topoi accession to royal status)
1.6   "thine": Ca 4:9-10; 6:5; 7:4-5; 8:6
ll.6-7   "That...mine": Ca 2:4, 16; 4:8-16; 6:1-3, 9; 7:10-13; 8:6-7 (another of the profane love topoi—an absolute, all-encompassing exclusivity)
1.9   "thee": Ca 1:3-4, 9, 11; 4:7; 6:1, 13; 7:5, 12-13; 8:1-2, 5

ll.8-12   "Our's...there": Ca 3-7 (again, the rhythm of profane love in Canticles: agony-ecstasy, approach-withdrawal, absence-presence)
1.10   "unladen": Mt 11:28
1.11   "spicy": Ca 4:10, 14, 16; 5:1, 13; 6:2; 8:2, 14 (the "spicy isles" would be the Canticles garden, an enclosed Edenic-paradisiacal space with the beloved)
1.12   "thou": Ca 1:7-8, 15-16; 2:17; 4:1, 7, 9, 16; 5:9; 6:1, 4; 7:6; 8:1, 12-14

370   Heaven is so far of the Mind

ll.1-2   "Heaven...dissolved": IICo 5:1 ("For we know that if our earthly house of this tabernacle were dissolved, we have a building of God, an house not made with hands, eternal in the heavens")

ll.5-6   " 'Tis...idea": ICo 2:9 ("Eye hath not seen, nor ear heard, neither have entered into the heart of man, the things which God hath prepared for them that love him")

ll.6,7   "fair," "desire": Ca 1:15-16; 2:10, 13; 4:1, 7, 10; 6:10; 7:6, 10

l.7   "To...desire": Rev 2:7, 17; 3:12, 21

l.8   "No...Here": Lu 17:21("the kingdom of God is within you"); (the thought of P370 may echo Browne or Milton: "The mind is its own place" and the "Paradise within thee happier far")

371   A precious- mouldering pleasure- 'tis-

l.2   "Antique Book": see P1545 (although the Bible is not mentioned, the words "Dreams" and "presence" suggest her favorite character Jacob)

ll.22-24 "As...born": Ge 28:11-17; 31:10-16 (Jacob as a dreamer from that Old Testament world where "Dreams" were realities, where God was seen face-to-face, and where the "Literature of Man" had not to strain to be a "Haunted House"; see Leyda, I. 351-352)

l.25   "His...Enchantment": Ec 10:11-12

l.26   "You...go": Ge 32:26

Comment: See *Poems*, I, 295-296.

373   I'm saying every day

l.2   " 'If...tomorrow' ": Ca 6:8-9; Isa 61:10; 62:3-4; Rev 14:3-4; 19:7-9; 21:2, 9; 22:17 (the "Queen" is the Bride of Christ)

l.4   "deck": Isa 61:10; Eze 16:10-12

l.5   "wake": ICo 15:50-55

l.5   "Bourbon": Rev 1:6; 5:10; 20:4, 6; 22:5 (accession to Heaven as accession to royal status)

l.8   "Begged": Lu 16:20, 22 (the Lazarus persona of the beggar associated with the "Market place" of the circuit world and its philosophy of deprivation based in the Beatitudes, Mt 5:2-12; in the

KJV the "Market place" is associated with the ostentatious display of power and wealth, Mr 12:38; Lu 11:43; 20:46)

ll.12-15 "So...me": Mt 22:1-14; IICo 5:3; Eph 4:24; Col 3:10, 12; Rev 3:4, 18; 16:15; 19:8 (the preparationist motif)

l.26 "Better...ready": Mt 22:4, 8; 24:44; Lu 12:40; Rev 19:7

ll.27-29 "Than...on": see lines twelve-fifteen above

l.32 "Summoned...unexpectedly": Mt 24:44; 25:13; Lu 12:39; ITh 5:2, 6; Rev 3:3; 16:15

l.33 "Exeter": Rev 21-22 (Heaven; see line two above for "Exeter"—Heaven is the place of her coronation-wedding)

Comment: See *Poems*, I, 296-297.

374   I went to Heaven-

l.1 "I...Heaven": Rev 21

l.2 " 'Twas...Town": Rev 21:15-17 (the physical measurements of the New Jerusalem)

l.3 "Lit...Ruby": Rev 21:18-21

l.4 "Lathed...Down": Rev 21:21 (the pearl gates and transparent glass streets)

l.8 "No Man": Rev 2:17; 3:7-8, 11; 5:3-4; 7:9; 13:17; 14:3; 15:8; 19:12

ll.9-12 "People...names": Rev 1:4, 14; 2:17; 3:1, 4-5, 18; 4:4-5; 5:6; 6:2, 9, 11; 7:9, 13-14; 14:14; 15:6; 16:3; 19:8, 14; 20:4; 21:10; 22:17 (the imagery suggests the white appearance and spiritual state of the "People" in the New Jerusalem)

l.12 "Eider names": Rev 3:12; 22:4 (specifically that "New name" suggesting accession to the celestial, to the world of spirit)

ll.13-14 "Almost...be": Ac 26:28

ll.15-16 " 'Mong...Society": Rev 14:1-5

375   The Angle of a Landscape-

l.7 "Bough...Apples": Ge 3; Ca 2:3, 5; 7:8; 8:5 (the "Angle" of this "Landscape" is that of a desire for which nature and its seasons are "typic"; the KJV apple-of-the-eye idiom refers to the most precious chosen such as Moses, David, the Israelites, De 32:10; Ps 17:8; Pr 7:2; La 2:18; Zec 2:8) ll.14,15 "Emerald," "Emeralds": Ex 28:17-21; 39:10-14; Eze 28:13; Rev 21:19-20

    l.16   "Diamonds": Ex 28:18; 39:11; Eze 28:13

    l.16   "Snow": Rev 1:14

    l.17   "Polar Caskets": Ca 1:10; 7:1; Isa 61:10; 62:3-5; Eze 16:10-12; Mal 3:17 (the jewels that adorn the beloved or chosen, the Merchant of Venice imagery reinforcing the muted marital figuration of choice and adornment)

    l.20   "never stir": Ca 2:7; 3:5; 8:5 (an ironic echo)

376   Of Course- I prayed-

ll.1-2   "Of...Care": see note, line two, P338 ("Verily thou art a God that hidest thyself, O God of Israel, the Saviour," Isa 45:15)

    l.5   " 'Give me' ": Mt 6:11; 7:7-11

    l.6   "Life": Ge 2:7

    l.9   "Atom's Tomb": Ge 2:21-22 (homophonous for Adam's Tomb, the body of Adam from which came the rib for the creation of "Woman"); Ge 2:7; 3:19; Ps 103:14 (the dust the "Life" of which has been cursed with death)

    l.11   "Than...Misery": Mt 26-27 (the "Misery" of the circuit world as Passion, as suffering unredeemed by an intelligible raison d'etre for "Life"; the body prison may also be intended, Ro 7:24; IICo 5:4; Php 3:21)

377   To lose one's faith-surpass

ll.1,4   "faith": Heb 11 ("faith" is here seen as co-existensive with the course of "Life," Ro 11:20; ITi 6:12; IITi 4:7; Heb 12:1-2)

ll.5-6   "Inherited...Belief": Eph 1:3-23; ITh 1:4; IITh 2:13; ITi 1:16; IPe 1:2-9 (the poet may also have in mind the Old Testament basis of faith rooted in the Creation of cosmos and man, Ge 1-2, or perhaps the New Testament idea of a new creation in Christ through faith, IICo 5:17)

378   I saw no Way- The Heavens were stitched-

    l.1   "I...stitched": Isa 64:1 (for the Deus absconditus,see note, line two, P338) ll.3,6,7,8 "Hemispheres," "Speck," "Ball," "Circumference," "Bell": Rev 22:4 (P378 concerns the potential unmeaning of the apocalyptic: the solitude and silence of a pathless "Way" whose circumferential imagery—"Hemispheres," "Speck," "Ball," "Circumference," and "Bell"—yields not vision or presence but an unillusioned isolation)

379   Rehearsal to Ourselves

l.2   "Delight": Ca 2:3; 7:6 (in the absence of the beloved, the poems become displacements, "faint Rehearsals," P503, for an anticipated presence)

l.4   "Omnipotent": Rev 19:6 (the poet arrogates to herself the prerogative of the deity to murder and create; the only KJV use of the word is in the Marriage Supper of the Lamb passage)

ll.5-8   "We...died": ICo 11:23-26 (the Eucharistic echoes are ironic)

380   There is a flower that Bees prefer-

l.1   "flower": Ca 2:1-2, 12, 16; 4:5; 5:5, 13; 6:2-3; 7:2;
l.3   "Purple": see note, line one, P15
l.6   "Honey": Ca 4:11; 5:1
l.9   "Her...Moon": Ca 6:10
l.10   "And...Gown": Ca 5:10
l.14   "Green": Ca 1:16; 2:13
l.15   "Countenance": Ca 2:14; 5:15
l.16   "Wind": Ca 4:16
l.20   "Sweet": Ca 2:3, 14; 5:5, 13, 16; 7:9
l.23   "spice": Ca 3:6; 4:6, 10, 14, 16; 5:1, 13; 6:2; 8:14
l.24   "For...jealousy": Ca 8:6 (the contrast here is with the Deity, Ex 20:5; 34:14)
l.32   "When...Frost": Job 37:10

Comment: The innocent license of the Edenic landscape of P380 is experienced by an indirection similar to the disembodied enjoyment of marriage in a removed Heaven in numerous other poems. See *Poems*, I, 301-302.

381   A Secret told-

ll.1-7   "A...bride": Pr 25:9-10

382   For Death- or rather

l.4   "Opportunity": Heb 11:15
l.6   "Room": Joh 14:2 (each of "Death's Gifts" can be read simply as effects of physical death with grave and marker or as fulfillments of apocalyptic hopes)
l.7   "Escape...Circumstances": Ro 7:24; IICo 5:4; Php 3:21 (extrication from the body prison)
l.8   "Name": Rev 2:17; 3:12; 22:4
ll.9-10   "With...compare": Jas 1:17 (the "Gifts" spoken of in P382 are those of "Life" and "Death," the latter not conventionally so considered yet inextricably linked with life in Genesis, Ge 2:7; 3:19)
l.10   "compare": Ro 8:18
l.11   "We...not": Ec 9:5
l.12   "Here": Heb 13:14
Comment: See *Poems*, I, 302-303.

383   Exhiliration- is within-

ll.1-12   "Exhilaration...offering": see note, line one, P214

384   No Rack can torture me-

l.2   "Soul": Ge 2:7
l.2   "mortal": ICo 15:53-54
l.2   "Bone": Ge 2:23
ll.5-6   "You...Cimitar": Heb 11:37
l.7   "Two Bodies": ICo 15:44
l.8   "Bind...fly": Ps 90:10
ll.9-10   "The...divest": Ex 19:4; De 32:11; Job 39:27; Isa 40:31; Jer 49:16; Rev 12:14
ll.12-14   "Thou...Enemy": ISa 28:15-16 (verbal echoes)
ll.15-16   "Captivity...Liberty": Ro 7:23-24 ("Captivity"); Ro 8 ("Liberty")
Comment: See *Poems*, I, 304.

385   Smiling back from Coronation

ll.1-2 "Smiling...Luxury": Ca 6:8-9; Isa 61:10; 62:3-4; Mal 3:17; Rev 2:10; 3:11; 4:4, 10; 7; 14:3-4; 19:7-9; 21:2, 9; 22:17 (the "Coronation" metaphor suggests accession to Bride of Christ status—a metaphor here used to indicate election, Ro 8:29-33; Eph 1:4; IPe 1:2-9; 2:5)

l.7 "dusty": Ge 2:7; 3:19; Ps 103:14

387   The Sweetest Heresy recieved

l.1 "Sweetest": Ca 2:3, 14; 5:5, 13, 16; 7:9
l.1 "Heresy": Wx 20:3-5 (the "Heresy" is the idolatrous commitment to a church of "Two")
l.2 "Man...Woman": Ge 2:7-8, 15-25
l.3 "Convert": Mt 18:3; Ac 3:19
l.4 "Faith": Ro 1:17; Ga 3:11; Heb 10:38
l.4 "Two": Mt 18:18-20
l.5 "Churches": Col 1:18 (Christ is foundation and head of "Churches")
l.6 "Ritual": Ex, Le, Nu, De (the poet's "small" contrasts with the elaborate rites, ceremonies, offerings, and sacrifices outlined in the Pentateuch)
l.7 "Grace...unavoidable": Ro 4:4-24 (in the language of amor, imputed righteousness becomes the inevitability of their love)
l.8 "fail": ICo 13:8
l.8 "Infidel": IICo 6:15; ITi 5:8

388   Take Your Heaven further on-

l.1 "Take...on": Rev 3:20 (the proffered "Heaven" is at once resented because it demands such dramatizations as P388 concerning the putative beloved but at the same time valued—or, re-valued upon her own terms as follows: "You" are a bungling, inattentive courtier whose sky "Courtesies" touch not my circuit-world, Passion existence although I have dressed in bridal-apocalyptic "White" in adherence to preparationist etiquette; see note, lines fourteen-nineteen, P179)
l.2 "Heaven divine": Rev 21-22 (P388, thus, concerns the death-in-life of her heavenly bridal status)
l.5 "An...on": ICo 15:53-54
ll.6-7 "Now...Hand": Rev 3:20

l.10   "Sufferer": Mt 17:12; Mr 8:31; 9:12; Lu 9:22; 17:25; 22:15; 24:26, 46; Ac 3:18; 17:3; 26:23; IICo 1:5-7; Php 3:10; IPe 4:13 (the identification here is with the Passion Christ)

ll.11-12 "Dressed...White": Rev 7:13-14; 19:8

389   There's been a Death, in the Opposite House,

ll.1-4   "There's...along": Ec 12:3-4
l.7   "A...Pod": ICo 15:36-38
l.15   "Mourners": Ec 12:5

390   It's Coming- the postponeless Creature-

l.1   "Creature": Ro 8; 21
l.6   "Enemy": ICo 15:26
l.8   "And...God": Ec 12:7

391   A Visitor in Marl-

l.1   "A...Marl": Job 37:10 ("Marl" suggests the dust of mortality-death, Ge 2:7; 3:19; Ps 103:14; and the white of the apocalyptic, Rev 2:17; 3:4-5, 18; 4:4; 6:11; 7:9)

l.2   "Flowers": Ca 2:1-2, 12, 16; 4:5; 5:13; 6:2-3; 7:2

ll.2-4   "Who...Glass": Isa 61:10; Eze 16:10-12; Mal 3:17; Rev 21 (the "Flowers" are bejewelled by the "Visitor," the crystallization process not unambiguous since organic beauty is frozen into the order and elegance of "Glass")

ll.5-7   "Who...interview": Ca 2:17; 4:6 (the "visits" of the beloved parallel those of the "Visitor")

l.8   "Caresses...gone": Ca 5:6

ll.9-10   "But...run": Ca 5:5, 14; 7:1

l.11   "And...kissed": Ca 1:2; 5:16; 7:9

l.12   "Is...been": Ca 2:17; 4-6; 8:14 (in Canticles it is the presence, not absence of the beloved that is predominant; the contrast is instructive since P391 is a lover's complaint, an expression of anxiety and dread that Christ the Courtier of apocalyptic desire may be indistinguishable from the nighttime aggressor whose inexplicable absences follow unsought attentions—with the resultant conflation in the poem of loving and dying)

392   Through the Dark Sod- as Education-

l. 1   "Through...Education": ICo 15:36-38, 42-46 (the "Dark Sod" is the circuit world as the vale of soul making for the sown seed of the "Lily")

l.2   "Lily": Mt 6:28

l.3   "White": Rev 2:17; 3:4-5, 18; 6:11; 19:8

ll.2-4   "The...fear": Ro 8:28-30; IPe 1:2-9; 2:5 (in religio-aesthetic terms, the "Lily" is the elect: a certain fearless, bold flower of faith, the equivalent of the artist's poetry)

l.5   "Afterward...Meadow": Ge 2-3; Eze 28:13-14; 31:8-9, 16; 47:1-12; Rev 21-22 (Paradise)

l.6   "Beryl": Eze 28:13; Rev 21:20

l.6   "Bell": Ex 28:34-35 (associated with God's presence, the music of stanza two is paradisiacal in contrast to that of the Passion beauty produced through the "Dark Sod" of stanza one)

l.7   "The...now": Rev 7:16-17; 21:4

l.8   "Extasy": see note, line fifteen, P783; notes, lines five and eight, P1191; and note, line seven, P1468

393   Did Our Best Moment last-

l. 1   "Best Moment": see note, line fifteen, P783; notes, lines five and eight, P1191; and note, line seven, P1468 (rapture, ecstasy, assurance of grace, intimations of immortality, and visionary awareness may be suggested by "Best Moment"; the "Moment" like noon, Indian summer, and other transition times may pivot back into the circuit world or "last," ICo 15:52)

l.2   "Heaven": Rev 21-22

l.3   "A...procure": Ge 5:24; IIKi 2:11; Mt 26-28 (the "few" would include Enoch, Elijah, and Christ)

l.8   "Heavenly": ICo 15:48-49; Heb 11:16

l.9   "A...Divine": Eph 2:8; Jas 1:17-18

l.11   "dazzled": Ac 9:3-7; 22:6-11

l.12   "unfurnished": ICo 13:12; Php 3:12-13; IJo 3:2 (a deficiency of vision may be hinted at; see P574 and P685); Mt 5:2-12 (the beggarly destitution of the quotidian circuit world may also be intended)

l.12   "Rooms": see note, line one, P725; note, line one, P674; and note, line one, P1142 (for the metaphor of the individual as dwelling or habitation; the preparationist motif may here be relevant as well, Rev 3:18-20)

394   'Twas Love- not me-

l.2   "punish": Mt 25:46; IITh 1:9; IIPe 2:9 (the poet imagines the judgment at which she pleads that her only baseness was to have loved as Jesus loved, making the two look "so alike"—a bold co-option of the mediatorial function of Christ by claiming an identity in "Love")

ll.3-4   "The...me": Joh 3:16-17 (the "Real one" is Christ who died in fulfillment of God's plan—"for Thee")

l.5   "Such...most": Ex 20:3-5; Mt 22:37 (the only "Guilt" of Christ was to have fulfilled the commandment "most")

l.7   "Forgive": Mt 6:12; Mr 2:7; Lu 5:21; IJo 1:9 (God is forgiver of sins; P394 is a bold repudiation of any sense of sin and an accusation of injustice against God)

l.8   " 'Twas...most": see line two above (her "Love" was as "base" as Jesus' "Love" was "most")

l.9   "Justice": Ge 18:25; Rev 15:3; 16:7; 19:2 (God who metes out rewards and punishments)

ll.10-12 "We...Strike": see line two above (the poet and Christ have only been "Guilty" for "Love's" "Sake," a fit basis neither for sin nor punishment)

Comment: See *Poems*, I, 309-310.

395   Reverse cannot befall

ll.1-3   "Reverse...interior": Ps 91:1-10
l.5   "Diamond": Ex 28:18; Eze 28:13; Rev 21

396   There is a Languour of the Life

ll.1-4   "There...can": Mt 26-27 (the poem questions whether after a Passion life of suffering the "Successor" will be only a comalike languishing; thus, P396 is among numerous poems treating the potential unmeaning of the apocalyptic)

ll.14-15 "A...Him": Mt 3:11-12; Mr 1:7-8; Lu 3:16-17 (John the Baptist, who ministered as the forerunner of Christ his successor, termed Him "mightier"; through a complex application and

adaptation, including subtle substitutions, the poet uses the KJV analogue to emphasize the extremity of a "Languour" beyond "skill")
Comment: See Poems, I, 310-311.

397   When Diamonds are a Legend,

l.1   "Diamonds": Ex 28:18; Eze 28:13; Rev 21

l.2   "Diadems": Isa 62:3-4; Rev 2:10; 3:11; 4:4, 10

ll.3-4   "I...sale": Isa 61:10; Eze 16:10-12; Mal 3:17; Rev 21 (in stanza one there is a religio-aesthetic self coronation and bedecking with jewels in preparation for the "Summer Day" or Heaven of "Art")

l.4   "sow...Raise": ICo 15:35-38, 42-44 (the language is deliberately used to point out the potency of the artist and art—the "I" of the poem the seed, grain, or merely natural)

ll.5-6   "And...Patrons": Ro 4:3; 9:8; Ga 3:6; Heb 3:3; 11:18-19 (the language—"sale" and "accounted"—is not so much that of commerce as of election and imputed righteousness, metaphorical for an "Art" self-chosen and chosen by "Patrons")

l.7   "Queen": Ca 6:8-9; Isa 61:10; 62:3-4; Eze 16:10-12; Rev 19:6-9; 20:6; 22:5

l.8   "Butterfly": ICo 15:50-55 (metaphorical for the flight of "Art" beyond its conditions)

398   I had not minded- Walls-

ll.7-8   "Then...Eyes": Ca 4:9; 5:12; 6:5; ICo 13:12; Rev 22:4 (stanzas one and two give the story of the poet, a quest-romance that climaxes with vision and presence; she is here creator of conditions and controller of destiny, her representation becoming the desired reality—a recapitulation of the Fall)

l.11   "Cobweb": Job 8:14 (proverbially insubstantial)

ll.9-12   "But...Straw": Ex 20:3-5 (because of His jealousy, God will not allow the construction of competing stories, of romances intelligible within the "Vail" of the circuit world but instead hedges His virgin lover about with psychic "filament[s]" and "Cobweb[s]" of "Adamant," a "Citadel" complete with "Dragons")

l.13   "Vail": Ex 26:31-35 (the barrier separating the "Lady's face" from presence and vision)

l.16   "Dragons": Ps 74:12-14; Isa 27:1; Jer 10:22; Rev 20:2-3 (evil leviathans or sinful serpents, the "Dragons" suggest the

Devil or Satan, adversaries of God; the final line may suggest that the strength of the "Mesh" is the stigma of sin placed upon circuit world love)

Comment: See *Poems*, I, 312.

399   A House upon the Hight-

1.1   "A...Hight": Isa 57:15; Joh 14:2 (P399 may not concern the ultimate destiny of the poet—a heavenly mansion—but rather the fate of the poet's art, the haunted house it aspires to be and its ultimate, lofty ascension above circuit world converse to stand in an isolation that divulges no secrets)

400   A Tongue- to tell Him I am true!

1.1   "A...true": Rev 3:7, 14; 19:11; 21:5; 22:6 (the words of St. John describe an ideal pattern of "faithful and true" love of Christ for the Bride, which is here appropriated for other purposes; in addition, Revelation imagery is used to charge the pledge with added value)

1.2   "It's...Gold": Rev 3:18; 21:18, 21

1.8   "Truth...True": Joh 14:6; IICo 1:18 (language generally describing the Deity whose self-referentiality suggests that the pledging of her troth may itself be the object of P400—a poem then on the eternizing powers of art)

ll.10-11 "Beginning...begun": Ge 1:1-5 (P400 has the cosmic sweep of all time, Genesis to Revelation)

ll.18-20 "Thy...Rubies": Ex 28:18; Isa 61:10; Eze 16:10-13; 28:13; Mal 3:17; Rev 21

ll.23-24 "That...Plain": Isa 40:4 ("Every valley shall be exalted, and every mountain and hill shall be made low: and the crooked shall be made straight, and the rough places plain")

ll.26-27 "And...conclude": Rev 21-22 (the poet refers to a point beyond apocalypse)

1.29   "Least...Road": Isa 40:3 (the poet claims for her art a permanence beyond that given in the apocalyptic vision of Isaiah—P400 a self-referential, covenant poem in which commitment to art takes the poet beyond Heaven and God)

Comment: The desire of P400 may parallel that of Job (Job 19:23) whose wish is for an idealized shape of language (a Redeemer to plead the case of his righteousness) that will stand before God after the worms have destroyed his body with its anguished sense of absence. From a similar anguish the poet builds an immortal "Message" from a foundation in the topoi of profane love.

401   What Soft- Cherubic Creatures-

l.1   "Soft": Mt 11:8 ("they that wear soft clothing are in kings' houses")

l.1   "Cherubic": Ge 3:24; Ps 80:1; 99:1; Isa 37:16; Eze 10

l.1   "Creatures": Mr 16:15; Ro 1:25; 8:19-21; IICo 5:17; Jas 1:18

l.7   "freckled": Le 13:39

l.8   "Of...ashamed": Mr 8:38 ("Whosoever shall be ashamed of me and of my words in this adulterous and sinful generation; of him also shall the Son of man be ashamed, when he cometh in the glory of his Father with the holy angels"); see also Lu 9:26; Ro 1:16; Heb 11:16; IPe 4:16

l.9   "common...Glory": Joh 3:16-17; Tit 2:11; ITi 2:4; IIPe 3:9 (salvation is for all; nevertheless, the poet intends an oxymoron because of the KJV associations with "Glory," Mt 25:31; Ac 7:2; Ro 8:18; IICo 3:18; Col 1:27; 3:4; ITi 3:16; IPe 5:1, 4, 10)

l.10   "A...Degree": Mt 4:18-19 (Simon Peter and Andrew were fishermen called by Jesus to be His disciples, "fishers of men")

l.11   "Redemption": Eph 1:7; Col 1:14; Heb 9:12

l.12   "Be...Thee": see line eight above

403   The Winters are so short-

l.4   "And...Pod": Ge 7:16 (Noah's entering and exiting the ark parallel the actions of the poet "moving into Pod" only to later "strike [her] Tent")

ll.7-8   "strike...again": Ge 8:13-18

l.11   "Winter": Ge 7-8 (the "Deluge" is the KJV equivalent to the season of "Winter"—in the economy of the spirit, rainbows of "Summer" are spoiled by memories of "Deluge" —"Winter," the "Legend" status of the "Deluge" and "Noah" not diminishing metaphorical truth: the "Ararat"—"Summer" cannot erase the "Deluge"—"Winter" as an authentic, ineradicable state of the soul)

    l.12   "And...starved": Ge 7:21-23 ("all flesh died")

    ll.13-14 "And...away": Ge 7-8 (the destruction of the "World" by the Flood)

    l.15   "But...now": Ge 8:4

    l.16   "And...Noah": Ge 5-10 (the poet "credits" Noah as father of the race, author of a new covenant, object of modern skepticism, and symbol in the soul's iconography)

404   How many Flowers fail in Wood-

    l.1   "Flowers": Ca 2:1-2, 12, 16; 4:5; 5:13; 6:2-3; 7:2

    l.4   "Beautiful": Ca 1:8, 15-16; 2:10, 13; 4:1, 7, 10; 6:1, 4, 10; 7:1, 6

    l.7   "Scarlet": see note, line one, P15

    l.8   "It...Eyes": Ca 4:9; 8:10 (P404 speaks of poetic creations using Canticles imagery)

405   It might be lonelier

    l.3   "I'm...Fate": Mt 26-27 (her experience of the circuit world as Passion)

    l.4   "Perhaps...Peace": Isa 9:6; Eph 2:14 (Christ is the beloved "Other"; "Peace" is also the condition opposite "Suffering" and a basis of apocalyptic hope, Ps 85:8; Isa 26:12)

    l.5   "Dark": ICo 13:12; IIPe 1:19 (the condition of the circuit world)

    l.7   "Too...contain": Ex 26-27; Rev 21:17 (the two ideal spaces containing the Presence of God were measured in "Cubits": the Holy of Holies and the New Jerusalem)

    l.8   "Sacrament": Mt 26:26-28 (here a metonym for Christ's Presence within the circuit world, her "little Room" or "scant degree/Of Life's penurious Round," P313)

    l.9   "I...Hope": ICo 13:7

    l.11   "sweet": Ca 2:3, 14; 5:5, 13, 16; 7:9

    l.11   "blaspheme": IKi 21:10, 13; Isa 37:6; 65:7; Jas 2:7; Rev 13:6; 16:9, 11, 21 (the logical impossibility here is a piece of ironic wit)

    l.12   "Ordained": Isa 26:12 (see line four above)

l.12   "Suffering": Mt 16:21; 17:12; Mr 8:31; 9:12; Lu 9:22; 24:26; Ac 3:18; 17:3; 26:23; IPe 3:18; 4:1 (the circuit world has been foreordained as a place of Passion "Suffering")

l.15   "Blue": see note, line one, P15

l.15   "Peninsula": Ge 2-3; Eze 28:13-14; 31:8-9, 16; 47:1-12; Rev 21-22 (Eden, Paradise, or Heaven)

ll.15-16 "gain," "perish": Mt 16:26; Mr 8:36; Lu 9:25; Joh 3:15-16; 6:27; Php 1:21; 3:7; Jas 1:11; IPe 1:7; IIPe 3:9 (the calculus of "gain" is used paradoxically to attempt to grasp hold of the intractable problem of the many and the one, mortal and immortal, time and eternity, circuit world and Heaven, and "Suffering" and "Delight")

l.16   "Delight": Ca 2:3; 7:6
Comment: See *Poems*, I, 316.

406   Some- Work for Immortality-

l.1   "Immortality": ICo 15:53-54

l.5   "Slow Gold": Rev 3:18

l.5   "Everlasting": Ge 21:33; Ps 41:13; 90:2; 145:13; Isa 9:6; 40:28; 61:7; 63:16; Da 4:3; Hab 1:12; Mt 19:29; Lu 16:9; Joh 3:16; ITi 1:16; IIPe 1:11

l.6   "The...Today": Mt 6:19-20 ("Lay not up for yourselves treasures upon earth, where moth and rust doth corrupt, and where thieves break through and steal: But lay up for yourselves treasures in heaven, where neither moth nor rust doth corrupt, and where thieves do not break through nor steal"); see also Jas 5:3

l.8   "Immortality": ICo 15:53-54

l.9   "Beggar": Mt 5:2-12; Lu 16:20 (a Lazarus whose philosophy of destitution allows an appreciation of the distinction between the "Mine" and the "Money")

l.10   "Is...discern": ICo 2:14
Comment: See *Poems*, I, 316-317.

407   If What we Could- were what we would-

l.1   "If...would": Ro 7:15 (an adaptation of struggles with intention versus outcome as applied to the recalcitrant medium of language)

ll.3-4   "It...Tell": Pr 14:23

408   Unit, like Death, for Whom?

l.1   "Unit...Whom": Ec 9:4-5, 10
ll.2-5   "True...strict": Job 14:13 (in addition, for the fifth line see Job 14:14; ICo 15:55)
ll.7-8   "Bearer," "Borne": ICo 15:49 (verbal echoes)
ll.10-11 "The...Syllable": Ec 9:4-5, 10
ll.15-16 'Fear...tremor": Job 4:14; Ps 2:11; 55:5; Mr 5:33; ICo 2:3; IICo 7:15; Eph 6:5; Php 2:12
l.16   "All's...sure": Ro 8:28; ICo 15:51

409   They dropped like Flakes-

l.7   "No...place": Mt 10:29-30
l.8   "But...face": Rev 20:12-13; 22:12
l.9   'On...List": Rev 3:5; 17:8; 20:12, 15; 21:27 (the "Repealless List" is the "Lamb's book of life")
Comment: See *Poems*, I, 318.

410   The first Day's Night had come-

ll.1-4   "The...sing": Job 35:10
Comment: See *Poems*, I, 319.

411   The Color of the Grave is Green-

l.1   'Green": Ca 1:16; 2:11-13 ('Green" is associated with the beloved and with the renewal of life)
l.6   "infinite asleep": ICo 15:6, 18, 51
l.19   'Not...white": Ps 51:7; Isa 1:18; Rev 1:14 (the Biblical imagery draws attention to the separation of nature from supernature and reinforces the hyperbole: no miracle could transmute the black inner death—the 'Duplicate Grave within" created by the loss of the beloved—into 'white"; apocalyptic white and ICo 15 'Grave" echo throughout the poem, adding poignance to the sense of irretrievable loss)
l.20   "Not...Green": see line one above
Comment: See *Poems*, I, 320.

412   I read my sentence- steadily-

ll.1-5   "I...shame": Ge 3:19; IICo 1:9-10
ll.6-7   'Pious...'mercy' ": Ps 4:1; 6:2; 9:13; 30:10; 31:9; 51:1; 123:3; Ro 9:15-18 (the 'Pious Form" appears a number of times in the KJV and repeatedly in the litanies of the Prayer Book)
ll.7-8   'Soul...Him": Ge 2:7 (legalese for the creation of the "Soul" by God)
l.10   "Agony": Lu 22:44 (the soul is familiarized with life in the circuit world as like the Passion)
l.11   'But...Hint": ICo 15:25-55 ('Death" is transmogrified from "sentence" to "friend")
l.12   'Matter": Ge 2:7; 3:19; Ps 103:14 (a piece of Biblical wit as the poet puns on 'Matter" to suggest the ultimate triumph of the soul over the body)

413   I never felt at Home- Below-

ll.1,3   "at Home": Ec 12:5; IICo 5:6
l.2   'Handsome Skies": Ge 1:6-8; Ps 19:1 (the firmament, Heaven)
l.4   'Paradise": Ge 2-3; Eze 28:13-14; 31:8-9, 16; 47:1-12; Rev 21-22
l.5   'Because...time": Ex 20:8-11 (the poet envisions an eternal sabbath of stasis in Heaven)
l.7   'Eden'll...lonesome": Ge 2:8, 10, 15; 3:23-24 (Adam and Eve were not alone but marriage is nonexistent in Heaven, Mt 22:30; Mr 12:25; Lu 20:35)
l.11-13   'So...us": De 11:12; IICh 2:9; Job 28:24; 34:21; Ps 11:4; 33:13; Pr 5:21; 15:3 (the final two stanzas of P413 deal with the atemporal omnipresence of a God whose very nature makes the plan to 'run away" absurd; for God's omnipresence see Job 28; the poet may be repeating here the obverse of her frequent complaint that God's omnipresence is an absence for no one sees God, Joh 1:18)
l.14   "Myself...away": Ge 3:8; Rev 6:16
l.15   "From...All": IJo 5:7
l.16   'But...'Day' ": Mt 11:22, 24; 12:36; Mr 6:11; IICo 5:10; IIPe 2:9; 3:7; IJo 4:17; Jude 6; Rev 6:17; 14:7; 16:14; 20:4

414   'Twas like a Maelstrom, with a notch,

ll.1-3   " 'Twas...Wheel": Ge 1:2; Ro 10:7; Rev 9:1-2, 11; 11:7; 17:8; 20:1 (like the deep, abyss, or pit the "Maelstrom" is a fathomless, unbounded depth—a metaphor for her psychic anguish)

l.4   "Agony": Lu 22:44

l.6   "Hem": Mt 9:20; 14:36 (used with irony since the "Hem" is associated with miraculous extrication but also with the unideal circumferentiality of the circuit world)

ll.10-17 "As...go": IPe 5:8 (the poet uses a simile to suggest that the "Maelstrom" is like the devouring adversary)

l.17   "Overcome": Joh 16:33; IJo 2:13-14; 5:4-5; Rev 2:7, 11, 17, 26; 3:5, 12, 21; 12:11; 21:7 (in addition to its ambiguity, "Overcome" has the KJV suggestion of spiritual victory—used with irony since the renewal is to a death-in-life)

l.23   "Creature": Ro 8:19-21; IICo 5:17; Col 1:15; Jas 1:18

ll.18-25 "As...live": Ro 7:24; IICo 5:4; Php 3:21 (the death-in-life described is that of the body prison of the circuit world)

l.25   "To...live": Joh 3:15-17 (the echo here is again ironic since P414 parodies notions of predestination and regeneration; P414 is the mock relation of a "Reprieve[d]" adult who insists that before and after are distinctions without a difference, "Dungeons" to "Gibbets" and "Agony" to "Anguish," the final blindness and confinement succeeding a benumbing experience of dream, threat, and doubt over the "Maelstrom")

415   Sunset at Night- is natural-

l.3   "Master": Mt 8:19; 12:38; 19:16; 22:16; 23:8; Mr 10:17; 12:14; Lu 5:5; 8:24, 45; 9:33, 49; 17:13; Joh 13:13; 20:16; Eph 6:9 (a term frequently used of Jesus as lord and teacher and in a context suggesting His control of nature, Mr 4:38; Lu 8:24; the order of nature contravened in P415 was created through the Word, Joh 1:1-3, which may suggest irony in the poet's addressing herself to "Master"; also the term may be metaphorical suggesting the desired presence of a "Master" of trustworthy knowledge and experience)

ll.5,7   "Eclipses...suddenly": Ps 44:24; Isa 45:15 (the "Eclipse" may be God as the Deus absconditus or perhaps the unexpected loss of a beloved through death—darkness frequently metaphorical in the KJV for separation from God, e.g., IIPe 2:17; the experience of the eclipse is the opposite of the desired face-to-face experience of the beloved or of God in the beatific vision, Ca 2:14; 5:15; Rev 22:4-5)

    l.8   "Jehovah's": Ex 3:14; 6:3; Ps 83:18; Isa 12:2; 26:4 (as the covenant name of God, "Jehovah" would denote that changelessness of the "I Am" here impugned)

416   A Murmur in the Trees- to note-

    l.3   "A...seek": Mt 2:1-15
    ll.6-8   "A...Sweet": Isa 52:7; Na 1:15; Ro 10:15
    ll.9-10   "A...unperceived": IICo 5:1
    ll.11-12 "All...believed": Joh 3:12
    ll.17-18 "But...Word": Lu 8:10-15 (the key KJV verses behind P416, a poem that deals with two types of vision: one believing only what is perceived, the other responsive to intimations)
    ll.19-20 "So...Road": Mt 7:13-14

417   It is dead- Find it-

    l.1   "It...it": ICo 15:42-44
    l.8   "This": ICo 15:53-54 (the pronouns are used for ironic effect)
    l.10   "dumb": Isa 35:6
    Comment: See *Poems*, I. 324.

418   Not in this World to see his face-

    l.1   "Not...face": ICo 13:12; Rev 22:4 (the poet may refer to an earthly beloved or to Christ the Bridegroom)
    ll.2-4   "until...Primer": ICo 15:19-55; Heb 11; Rev 1-3; 20-22 (of course the sentiment is expressed innumerable times in the KJV—"promise of the life that now is, and of that which is to come," ITi 4:8b)
    ll.4-6   "to...yet": Rev 3:5; 13:8; 17:8; 20:12; 21:27 (the Lamb's Book of Life contains the "life Unopened rare"; this book and the New England Primer are apparently here being referred to)
    l.8   "Book": see lines four-six above
    l.9   "sweeter": Ca 2:3, 14; 5:5, 13, 16; 7:9

l.11   "A-B-C": Rev 1:8, 11; 21:6; 22:13 (the alphabet of the Primer is a metaphor for an earthly beloved or circuit world attachments; on the other hand, the Alpha and Omega is Christ the Bridegroom, the Alphabet of Heaven—the Biblical wit of the poem turning on the two alphabets and the notion of life-as-book and book-as-life)

l.12   'Himself...Skies": Ge 1:6-8, 14-20; De 33:26; Job 37:18; Ps 19:1 ('Himself" is the Heavenly Lover here rejected since "Skies" is a metonym for Heaven, Rev 21-22)

419   We grow accustomed to the Dark-

l.1   "We...Dark": Ge 1:2; ICo 13:12 (the condition of the circuit world is one of the "Dark" absent "Light")

ll.2-3   'Light," 'Lamp": Ge 1:3-4; Ex 27:20; IISa 22:29; Ps 119:105; Joh 1:4-9; IJo 1:5

l.12   "Or...within": IIPe 1:19

l.16   "But...see": Mt 13:16

l.20   "And...straight": Isa 40:3; Mt 3:3; Mr 1:3; Lu 3:4; Joh 1:23; Heb 12:13 (the preparationist motif is fitting since the poet with no little irony describes that minimalist accommodation of sight to 'Darknesses" and 'Evenings of the Brain," which is her metaphor for the efficacy of grace—an indeterminate 'Either"-'Or" within which if it yields not perfect straightness at least encourages bravery in the "steps" of "Life")

420   You'll know it- as you know 'tis Noon-

l.1   "You'll...Noon": IPe 1:8 ('it" is the assurance of election: "joy unspeakable and full of glory")

ll.2-6   'By...Son": Rev 2:28; 21:11, 23-26; 22:4, 16 (the Father and Son are the glory, light, and sun of 'Heaven" or the New Jerusalem, comprising that ideal presence-vision known in unmediated fashion, "not by terms")

l.11   'Omnipotence": Rev 19:6 (God, here specifically the God of Creation)

l.11   'had...Tongue": Ge 1-2 (God speaks the universe and man into existence but His Creation is unmediated by spoken "terms" of the "Tongue")

l.12   "His...Sun": Ge 1:16; Job 37:3; 38:7, 19, 25; Ps 19:4

l.13   "His...Sea": Ge 1:2; Job 38:8, 16; Rev 21:1

ll.14-15 " 'How'...Eye": Ro 8:24-30 (the knowledge of election, the assurance of grace, comes by hope and faith, the 'Eye' of the final line, which is not the small 'eye' of sense experience; the poem argues by metaphor that God's revelation within the individual is given by an intuition of 'it' unmediated 'by terms," a relationship analogous to that of God in the Creation of 'Mightiest Things," one of God creating realities not of a "Tongue" speaking "terms")

421   A Charm invests a face

ll.1-2   "A...beheld": ICo 13:12; Rev 22:4 (the experience of Jacob in Genesis would also be relevant, Ge 32:30; the poem plays with the paradox that an 'Image" of circuit world face-to-face 'satisfies" in a way that beholding with 'Vail" lifted would not—the poet inverting the KJV's giving precedence to heavenly over earthly, divine pattern over images and shadows, ICo 15:49; Heb 8:5; 10:1)

l.3   "The...Vail": Ex 26:31-35; 34:33-35; IICo 3:13-16 (the KJV associates the lifting of the "Vail" with the presence of God, the poet, paradoxically, associating an imagined satisfaction behind "Vail" or 'mesh" as superior since it allows faceless anonymity and power/control: 'wishes and denies"; ostensibly about the 'Charm" of imperfect beholding and action at a distance, P421 obliquely expresses ambivalence over the apocalyptic in which all wishing and denying are dispelled by perfect beholding, Rev 22:4)

l.7   'Interview": Ge 5:4; 32:24-30; 33:9; Ex 34:29-35; De 5:4-6 (examples of patriarchal interviews in God's presence, adumbrations of the apocalyptic; among other uses of 'Interview," see especially P1556 and P1721)

l.8   "That...satisfies": ICo 15:49; Heb 8:5; 10:1 (see lines one-two above; the poet is ironically aware that the 'Charm" of the "Image" is in its potency as an idolatrous and self-deceiving substitute)

422   More Life- went out- when He went

ll.1-2   'More...Breath": Ca 3; 6 (this lover's complaint may owe some debt to the topos of separation from the beloved in Canticles)

l.4   "Requiring...Quench": Ca 8:7

Comment: See *Poems*, I, 327-328, for the indebtedness to Ik Marvell and for a similarity of metaphor, Ca 8:6-7.

423   The Months have ends- the Years- a knot-

ll.1-2   "The...untie": Rev 10:6 (the poem takes its force from the ineluctable, inescapable time of the circuit world)

ll.9-12   "The...away": ICo 13:11 (in the delineation of human finitude of P754, the poet makes a similar point)

424   Removed from Accident of Loss

ll.1-2   "Removed...Gain": Mt 16:26; Mr 8:36; Lu 9:25; Php 3:7 (the poet may be defining the plenitude of the Deity, Jas 1:17, a state of abundance beyond "Accident," devoid of imagination— "power to dream"—since the latter is the essence of circuit world deprivation)

l.4   "Myself...earn": Ro 1:17

l.5   "Riches": e.g., Eph 3:8 (to be removed from "Accident" and "Loss," to possess "Riches" in perpetual "Holiday," is the circumstance of the Bridegroom whose niggardliness of "dream" will be rewarded accordingly with a lesser dowry; in the more complex lexicons of commerce, theology, marriage, and aesthetics, P424 contains the message of P67)

ll.11-12 "That...Him": Rev 19:7-9 (the poet implies that a full dowry comes only through the religio-aesthetic regimen of the imagination)

425   Good Morning- Midnight-

l.10   "When...Red": see line one, P15

l.13   "fair":Ca 1:8, 15-16; 2:10, 13; 4:1, 7, 10; 5:9; 6:1, 10; 7:6

ll.3,5,7,8,14 "Day," "Sunshine", "Morn," "Day": Mal 4:2; Lu 1:78; IIPe 1:19; Rev 2:28; 21:25; 22:16 ("Day" may be a metonym for the Bridegroom)

426   It dont sound so terrible- quite- as it did-

l.6   "A...bitterest": Heb 12:15 (verbal echoes only)

l.12   "new Things": IICo 5:17; Rev 2:17; 3:12; 5:9; 21:1-2, 5 (the associations are with metamorphoses and the apocalyptic adding resonance to the more obvious quotidian suggestions of the unfamiliar)

Comment: See *Poems*, I, 330 and Leyda, II, 50.

427   I'll clutch- and clutch-

ll.1-24   "I'll...me": Rev 3:18; 19:7-9; 21:2

Comment: P427 concerns her religio-aesthetic regimen whereby she will create an acceptably ornamented bride for the Groom—the "meek array" of death complemented by the rich "display" of her art. The lexicon of the poem—"golden," "Diamonds," "Hem," "Diadem," "Ornament," "array," and "rich"   —is derived from the preparationist, adornment metaphors in the KJV associated with the Presence of God, the adornment of the chosen, and the ornamentation of the bride (Ex 28; 39; Isa 61:10; 62:3-4; Eze 16:10-12; Mal 3:17; Rev 3:18; 19:7-9; 21).

428   Taking up the fair Ideal,

l.1   "fair": Ca 1:8, 15-16; 2:10, 13; 4:1, 7, 10; 5:9; 6:1, 10; 7:6 (the Canticles adjective suggests a personification of the "Ideal" as beloved)

l.4   "Crown": Isa 62:3; ICo 9:25; IITi 4:8; IPe 5:4; Rev 2:10; 3:11 (the apocalyptic, otherworldly associations of the word are used in conjunction with "splintered" to create a synecdoche for the circuit world)

ll.5-6   "Makes...lie": Tit 1:2; Heb 6:18; IJo 5:10 (the Incarnation, not the Platonic Idea, is the metaphor for the "fair Ideal")

ll.7-8   "Doubtless...perjury": Ge 3:12 (the Biblical wit is in Adam's "perjury" as only a prima facie truth: he blames Eve for the Fall, for not being a "fair Ideal"—which the poet insists is a postlapsarian contradiction in terms)

l.9   "poor": IICo 6:10; 8:9 (the "Ideal" of P428 is spoken of as Christ)

l.10   "purer dress": ICo 15:53-54 ("incorruption" and "immortality" but also the white of Heaven, Rev 3:4-5, 18; 4:4; 6:11; 7:13-14; 15:6; 19:8)

l.11   "glorified": Joh 13:31-38; 17

l.13   "broken": ICo 11:24

ll.13-14 "creatures...whole": Ro 1:25 ("Who changed the truth of God into a lie, and worshipped and served the creature more then the Creator, who is blessed for ever")

l.15   "Stains...washed": Isa 1:18; 63:3; Rev 1:5; 7:14

l.16   "Transfigured": Mt 17:2; Mr 9:2; Lu 9:31-32

429   The Moon is distant from the Sea-

ll.2,9   "Amber": Eze 1:4, 27; 8:1-3 ("Amber" is associated with theophanies)

l.4   "Along...Sands": Job 14:5; Ps 104:19

l.9   "Hand": Ps 139:10; Lu 1:66 (synecdochic for the power of God)

l.11   "Obedient...command": ICo 14:34

l.12   "eye": De 11:12; Ps 34:15; IPe 3:12

430   It would never be Common- more- I said-

ll.18,28 "Gold," "Golden": Ge 2:11-12; Eze 28:13; Rev 3:18; 4:4; 21 (the golden is associated with the paradisiacal)

l.22   "Dew": Ex 16:13-14; Nu 11:9 (suggestive of special grace)

l.27   "Wilderness": Ex 14; 16:1; 17:1; Nu 10:12; 13:3, 21; 20; 27:14; 33:11-12, 36; 34:3-4; De 1:19; 8:2; 32:10, 51 (the place of the wanderings of the children of Israel here used as a metaphor for that loss of a "moment of Brocade" in which special grace was her common lot)

l.28   "lines": Ps 16:6 ("The lines are fallen unto me in pleasant places")

l.29   "Sackcloth": Ge 37:34; IISa 3:31; IKi 20:31; IIKi 6:30; Job 16:15; La 2:10; Eze 7:18 (a dark clothing suggesting mourning over death, defeat, or loss)

Comment: See *Poems*, I, 333-334. Like Donne's "Canonization," Drayton's "Since there's no help, come let us kiss and part," Sidney's "Leave me, O love which reachest but to dust," and a number of Browning's monologues, P430 begins with a bold, exclamatory, self-dramatization, the poet sardonically subverting Puritan ideas of common and special grace as applied to her own condition and art and mixing complaint with haughty disdain regarding the ambiguous "Common" of the first line.

431   Me- come! My dazzled face

 l.1 "come": ICo 15:35; Rev 3:20; 4:1; 11:12; 12:10; 14:7, 15; 15:4; 17:1; 19:7; 21:9; 22:17, 20 (Sewall, 456-457, places P431 in the context of a response to Rev. Wadsworth, Rev 22:17)

 l.1 "dazzled face": ICo 13:12; Rev 22:4 (apparently "dazzled" by the countenance of the Alpha and Omega, Rev 1:16)

 l.2 "shining place": Rev 21 (the New Jerusalem)

 l.3 "Me...Ear": Rev 2:7, 11, 17, 29; 3:6, 13, 22; 13:9

 l.4 "The...these": Rev 8-9 (the sounds of the trumpet signifying the completion of God's judgment)

 l.5 "Saints": Rev 5:8; 8:3-4; 11:18; 14:12; 15:3; 19:8; 20:9

 ll.8-9 "remember...Paradise": Lu 23:42-43 (the language appears again in P1180)

 l.10 "That...name": Rev 2:17; 3:5, 12; 5:4; 13:8; 17:8; 22:4

432   Do People moulder equally,

 l.2 "Grave": ICo 15:54-55

 ll.9-11 "I...Death": Mt 16:28 ("Verily I say unto you, There be some standing here, which shall not taste death, till they see the Son of man coming in his kingdom")

 l.20 "He...dead": Mt 16:28 (see also: Isa 25:8; Joh 8:51-52; ICo 15:26, 54-55; IITi 1:10; Rev 21:4)

433   Knows how to forget!

 l.23 (later version) "Rabbi...Book": Joh 1:38, 49; 3:2; 6:25 (Christ was addressed as "Rabbi," or teacher; the "Wise Book" is the Bible)

 Comment: See *Poems*, I, 335-337.

435   Much Madness is divinest Sense-

 l.1 "Much...Sense": Joh 10:20

ll.2-3   'To...Madness": ICo 2:14 ('But the natural man receiveth not the things of the Spirit of God: for they are foolishness unto him: neither can he know *them,* because they are spiritually discerned")

436   The Wind- tapped like a tired Man-

l.1   "Wind": Joh 3:8 (see note, line one, P824)
ll.1-3   "tapped...then": Rev 3:20

437   Prayer is the little implement

l.1   'Prayer": Isa 55:6; Mt 7:7; 21:22; Lu 21:36; Col 4:2; ITh 5:17; Jas 5:16 (P437 is written with these positive pronouncements regarding prayer as a background—pronouncements making the irony of the poem's ineffectual gestures and mechanical imagery more obvious)
l.3   'Presence": Ge 32:30; Ex 33:11 (Jacob and Moses encountered that 'Presence" for which 'Prayer" has become a substitute; for Dickinson her poetry was the displaced 'Speech" of "Prayer" reaching from absence toward "Presence")
ll.5-6   'God's...hear": IISa 22:7; Ps 18:6; 34:15; IPe 3:12 (the hearing 'Ear" of God, frequently affirmed in the KJV, is here tentatively placed in the subjunctive)

438   Forget! The lady with the Amulet

l.8   "Lord": Rev 19:7-9
l.16   'thy Will": Mt 6:10; 25:42; Lu 22:42 (like Chaucer's 'Retraction," P438 speaks of lesser and greater commitments, apologizing for a love of art and nature, of a haunted house and one that tried to be haunted)
Comment: See *Poems*, I, 339.

439   Undue Significance a starving man attaches

ll.1-2   "Undue...Food": Mt 6:25 (see P67)
l.3   "For...sighs": La 1:11

ll.7-8   'Distance...Savory": Ge 8:21; Ex 29:18, 25, 41; Le 1:9; 2:2; Nu 15:3; 28:2; 29:2 (the essence or spiritual significance is not the edible but that which is sensed and savored at a distance)

441   This is my letter to the World

l.1   'This...World": Ge-Rev (the poet has in mind the analogy of her own poetic production to that of God's revelation, in the KJV and "Nature")

ll.3-4   'The...Majesty": Ge 1-2; Ps 104 (the 'simple News" told by 'Nature" is that this haunted house is in its essence meaning, a tender "Message" directed to an ideal audience)

ll.4,7-8 'tender," 'love," 'Sweet," 'tenderly": Ca 1:2-4, 9, 15; 2:2-7, 10, 13-15; 3:5, 10; 4:1, 7, 10; 5:2, 5, 8, 13, 16; 6:4; 7:6, 9, 12; 8:4-7

Comment: See *Poems*, I, 340.

442   God made a little Gentian-

l.5   "Purple Creature": Mr 15:17; Joh 19:2, 5

ll.5,10 'Purple," 'Tyrian": IICh 2:14 (since the purple Gentian is here a Hitchcockian emblem, see as well note, line one, P15)

l.8   "Mockery": Mt 27:29, 31; Lu 23:11

l.9   "The...condition": Job 37:10

l.12   "Creator": Ec 12:1; Isa 40:28; Ro 1:25; IPe 4:19

ll.11-12 'Until...bloom": Ro 4:6, 22; IICo 5:19; Jas 2:23 (the Gentian, which 'tried," 'failed," and was then 'invoke[d]," is emblematic of imputed righteousness)

Comment: See *Poems*, I, 341.

443   I tie my Hat- I crease my Shawl-

ll.2-4   "Life's...me": Lu 16:10-11

ll.11-13 "And...away": IICo 4:7-5:17 (dying to the flesh—a death-in-life and life-in-death—is at the heart of the Gospel)

l.14   "As...Man": Eph 4:13

ll.17-19 "There...work": Ro 8:13 (mortifying the deeds of the body, the simulation of meaningful "Action") ll.20-23 'To...unshaded": Ex 33:20-23 (the Biblical wit depends upon the KJV idea that no "unshaded" eyes could see God; paradoxically, "Science" and "Surgery" are blind to "what we are" even though having "Telescopic Eyes")

ll.30-31 "Therefore...done": ICo 3:8; IICo 5:8-9

Comment: See *Poems*, I, 341-343 and Franklin, I, 537-538, 553-555.

444   It feels a shame to be Alive-

l.3   "Dust": Ge 3:19; Ps 103:14

l.12   "Before...obtain": ICo 9:24

ll.9-14 "The...Pearl": Mt 13:44-46 (these lines adapt the Biblical purchase of the pearl to the purchase of "Liberty" by the "Enormous Pearl" of the soldiers' lives; a "price" paid for others suggests Christ, ICo 6:20)

l.13   "Are...worth": Mt 25:14-30 (the fear expressed is that of becoming like the "slothful servant" of the Parable of the Talents; the language echoes Milton's "When I consider how my light is spent": "They also serve who only stand and wait")

l.15   "As...Us": Mt 20:28; Joh 3:16; 10:28; Ro 5:10; Col 3:4 (the atoning function of the "Spartan" dead again echoes Christ)

l.19   "Saviors": Joh 4:42 (the title given Christ)

l.20   "Present Divinity": Joh 15:13

Comment: See *Poems*, I, 343-344.

445   'Twas just this time last year, I died.

l.2   "I...Corn": Ho 2:22 (see Johnson, 152)

ll.23-24 'How...me": Isa 61:2; ITh 4:16; IITh 1:7; Jude 14; Rev 14:13 (the "perfect year" is the "acceptable year of the Lord" or the "fulness of times," Eph 1:10; also, the "perfect year" may here be thought of metaphorically as the final harvest since P445 uses a local color version of KJV apocalyptic, Joe 3:13; Mt 9:37-38; 13:30, 39; Joh 4:35; Rev 14:15)

Comment: See *Poems*, I, 344-345.

446   I showed her Hights she never saw-

l.1   "Hights": Job 22:12; Ps 102:19; 148:1 (as the dwelling of God, here suggestive of spiritual aspiration)

ll.5-6   "I...across": Ge 1:5, 14 (the language of the poem may also echo Job 38:4-12)

l.7   "And...'Guest' ": Rev 3:20

ll.9-10   "And...glow": Mt 25-26; Joh 1:4-9; 3:19; 8:12; 9:5 (the poet identifies with the Passion Christ and Light of the world)

Comment: See *Poems*, I, 345-346.

448   This was a Poet- It is That

ll.1-16   "This...Time": Mt 26:6-13; Mr 14:3-9; Joh 12:1-8 (the "Fortune" of the beloved "Poet" in contrast to the "ceaseless Poverty" of the ordinary and familiar, the centrality of the spikenard, and the memorializing function of this symbolic distillation are all suggestive analogues; the final lines of P448 may echo Mt 26:13)

449   I died for Beauty- but was scarce

l.7   "Themself"...One": Ge 2:24; Eph 5:31 (significantly, the marriage is achieved with the dissolution of the body; the first line of the poem and the word "Kinsmen" may unconsciously echo the Book of Ruth, 1:17; 2:1, 20: 3:9-13; 4:1-3, 6-8, 14)

l.12   "And...names": Ec 6:4

450   Dreams- are well- but Waking's better,

ll.2,4,7-8 "Morn," "Dawn," "Day": IIPe 1:19; Rev 2:28; 6:17; 16:14; 22:16 (the language of apocalyptic hope is used to express the superiority of the imagination—Thoreau's "That day dawns to which we are awake")

l.5   "Sweeter": Ca 2:3, 14; 5:5, 13, 16; 7:9

451   The Outer- from the Inner

l.8   "dust": Ge 2:7; 3:19; Ps 103:14

ll.9-12   "The...Brand": Pr 27:19

452   The Malay- took the Pearl-

l.1   "Pearl": Mt 13:45-46; Rev 21:21

ll.8,10 "Jewel": Eze 16:10-12; Isa 61:10; Mal 3:17; Rev 21
(the "Pearl-Jewel" is metaphorical as the treasured goal of her religio-
aesthetic regimen and apocalyptic hope; in contrast to the "Malay,"
whose commercial acquisitiveness has as its basis a hearty, physically
courageous will devoid of fear or second thoughts, the timorous "I"
realizes that only to such an undivided consciousness can the Pearl's
loss or gain be approached as "One" and that to gain the Pearl for the
"Hut" is to lose it forever for the imagination—ever to be "wooed,"
never to be won, like the poetic truth emanating from the figures on
Keats's urn)

Comment: See *Poems*, I, 349.

453   Love- thou art high-

l.1   "Love...high": e.g., Ps 113:5; Heb 1:3 (the dwelling
of God, here imaged as the sought-after Beloved)

l.2   "I...thee": Ca 2:8; 4:6; 8:14 (mountains may be
associated with the desired Beloved)

l.6   "Ducal...thee": Rev 19:7-9; 20:12 (the "stand up"
may also connect with the admonition to St. John given by the angel,
Rev 19:10; 22:9)

l.12   "Sun": Mal 4:2; Lu 1:78; IIPe 1:19; Rev 1:16; 2:28;
21:23; 22:5, 16

l.13   "Love...Vailed": Ex 33:20; Isa 45:15

ll.14-15 "A...die": Ge 32:30; Ex 33:11 (a "few" such as Jacob
and Moses)

l.18   "Eternity": Isa 57:15 (the place of union with the
Beloved is "Bliss" or Heaven)

Comment: See *Poems*, I, 350.

454   It was given to me by the Gods-

ll.3-4   "They...small": Mt 2:11 (perhaps a parallel drawn
with the gift of gold to the Christ child)

ll.9,13   "Rich": Rev 3:18 (a suggestion that the gift is
spiritual not material)

ll.14-15 "Gold": Ge 2:11-12; Eze 28:13; Rev 21 ("Gold" is
associated with Eden and the New Jerusalem); Ca 1:10-11; 5:11, 14-
15 ("Gold" is associated with the beloved); Rev 4; 6 ("Gold" is part of

the heavenly wardrobe and thus associated with bridal status in accession to the New Jerusalem—its centrality in her identity, "name of Gold," connected with ideal vision and presence, Rev 22:4); IKi 9:28; 10:11; 22:48 (Ophir was the source of Biblical gold and is explicitly mentioned in P1366; here "Gold" is the religio-aesthetic equivalent of imputed righteousness)

455   Triumph- may be of several kinds-

ll.3-4   "When...overcome": ICo 15:54-55
l.5   "finer Mind": Ro 11:34; 12:2; Eph 4:17-24; Php 2:5; 3:15; IIPe 3:1 (the mind of Christ versus the fleshly, carnal, or reprobate mind, Ro 1:28; 8:7; ITi 6:5; IITi 3:8)
ll.6-8   "When...Throng": ICo 9:24-27; Ga 2:2; 5:7; Heb 12:1-2; Php 2:16; 3:13-14; Eph 6:14 (the military and athletic striving suggested by P455 is Paulinian as well as being connected to the "Severer Triumph" of the Passion Christ)
ll.14-16 "pass...Countenance": Mt 25:31-34; Rev 1:7; 20:12; 21:7 (in general, a reference to the Last Judgment)
l.15   "Naked": Ge 2:25; 3:7, 10-11; Heb 4:13
l.15   "Bar": Ro 14:10; IICo 5:10; Rev 1:4; 3:21; 4:2-10; 5:1-13; 7:9-17; 14:1-5; 19:4-5; 20:11; 21:5; 22:1-3 (the "Bar," seat, or throne of judgment)
l.16   "Jehovah's Countenance": ICo 13:12; IJo 3:2; Rev 22:4 ("Jehovah's Countenance" suggests ideal presence and vision experienced temporarily in the circuit world by such Old Testament figures as Adam and Eve, Jacob, and Moses and promised the "Acquitted" in the vision of St. John; in addition, "Jehovah's Countenance" is the face of an exclusive love proscribing all lesser loves as species of idolatry, thus the concomitant demand for circuit world renunciation, Ex 20:1-6; Mt 10:37-39; 16:24-28)
Comment: See *Poems*, I, 351-352.

456   So well that I can live without-

ll.1-6   "So...thee": Joh 3:16-17; IJo 3-4 (like the love of Shakespeare expressed in his Sonnets, the poet's love is unrequited and sacrificial but not possessive—not a greater or better but different love than that of Jesus for "Men")

457   Sweet- safe- Houses-

l.1   "Sweet": Ca 2:3, 14; 5:5, 13, 16; 7:9 (the Canticles-love word initiates the overall oxymoronic strategy in P457's treatment of death)

ll.1-2   "Houses": Ex 12:1-8 (the darkened house of mourning where "Sickness" and "Death" reign in P457 is treated with an aggressive gaiety dubiously supported by the metaphor of the stream with its conventional connotations providing a "whisper[ing]" subtext)

l.6   "Brooks": Job 6:15; Ps 124:4-5 (the domestic images create a countercurrent to that of the traditional stream)

458   Like Eyes that looked on Wastes-

ll.1-16   "Like...reign": Ro 8:29; ICo 13:12; 15:49; IICo 3:18; Jas 1:23; IJo 3:2; Rev 22:4 (conformity to any other image—be it that of the self or some circuit world beloved—than that of the Son would be a species of idolatry, perhaps treated with some optimism in P351 but approached here with a sense of desolation and loss; P458 is a face-in-the-mirror poem in which the poet confronts the terrifying void at the center of her disembodied self after having initiated the search for an existential core—the "Cause was Mine"; the imagery of suffering, isolation, and separation characterize a "divine reign" without hope, her final vision not a revelation but an evacuation of identity—the apocalyptic no guarantor of ideal unity and presence but a cruel vacancy, a final displacement in the triumph of a solipsistic void)

ll.3-4   "Wilderness...Night": Mt 8:12; 22:13; 25:30
Comment: See *Poems*, I, 353.

459   A Tooth upon Our Peace

ll.1,4   "Peace," "Grace": Ro 1:7; ICo 1:3; Ga 1:3; Eph 1:2; Php 1:2; Col 1:2; ITh 1:1; IITh 1:2; Phm 3; IIPe 1:2; Rev 1:4 (with irony, the poet jolts a platitudinous acceptance of the cause-effect linkage of "Grace" and "Peace" by suggesting that pain vitalizes grace just as "Thirsting vitalizes Wine" in P313—here a rather arch treatment of theodicy issues of evil and pain)

l.4   "Grace": Ro 3:24; Eph 2:8-9

l.5   'The...Hell": Rev 1:18; 21:1 (a Blakean paradox in her vision of the circuit world as a Passion-fraught "Hell")

l.7   'sign": Ge 9:12-13; Ps 65:8; Mr 13; Lu 16:30-31 (tokens or signs in the creation, the rainbow, the miracles of Jesus, and in the signs of the Second Coming are just examples of the Biblical use of 'sign," which frequently give a sense of direction, guidance, or assurance from 'Heaven"; that the poet was dissatisfied with 'signalize" might be explained by her desire for a more satisfactory rhyme as well as a word more attuned to the ambiguousness of a Biblical rather than technological "sign")

Comment: See *Poems*, I, 354 and Franklin, II, 776.

460   I know where Wells grow- Droughtless Wells-

l.1   'I...Wells": Rev 7:17 ('For the Lamb which is in the midst of the throne shall feed them, and shall lead them unto living fountains of waters: and God shall wipe away all tears from their eyes"; Rev 21:6 (the 'fountain of the water of life"; see also Rev 1:15; 19:6; 22:1, 17 and for figurative "Wells," Isa 12:3; Joh 4:6-14; 7:38)

l.3   "Where...away": Rev 22:2

ll.5-8   "Belt...on": Ex 28:15-21; Eze 28:13; Rev 21:18-21

l.13   'Old...Book": Rev 1-22 (the Book of Revelation or the KJV itself)

l.14   'That...'more' ": Rev 7:16 ('They shall hunger no more, neither thirst any more; neither shall the sun light on them, nor any heat"); see also Isa 49:10 ('They shall not hunger nor thirst; neither shall the heat nor sun smite them: for he that hath mercy on them shall lead them, even by the springs of water shall he guide them")

Comment: See *Poems*, I, 354-355.

461   A Wife- at Daybreak I shall be-

l.1   'Wife": Isa 61:10; 62:3-4; Rev 19:7-9; 21; 22:17 (the Bride of Christ)

l.1   'Daybreak": IIPe 1:19; Rev 16:14 (the poet may refer to the day of resurrection, ICo 15)

l.4   "Bride": Rev 19:7-9; 21: 22:17

l.5   "Then...thee": Rev 21:25; 22:5 (the suggestion may be of the exclusion of night in Heaven or of the triumph over death in the resurrection and accession to bridal status)

l.6   "Unto...Victory": ICo 15:54-57

ll.7-8   "Good...Hall": Rev 19:1-7

l.12   "Eternity": Isa 57:15

ll.12,13 "Sir," "Savior," "Master"(variant): Mr 4:38; Lu 1:47; 8:24; Joh 4:11-19, 42; 13:13; Ac 5:31 (all titles for Christ in the New Testament); the deleted line twelve may suggest Rev 3:20 for the "Vision" of His "face"

l.13   "seen...face": Rev 22:4

Comment: See *Poems*, I, 355-356.

462   Why make it doubt- it hurts it so-

l.7   "Sake": "Rev 2:3 (a metonym for the Deity here used for the sake of irony since its KJV associations are with a divine disclosure or revelation here withheld)

l.10   "Vision": Isa 1:1; Eze 1:1; Rev 9:17 (the KJV "Vision" is associated with the communications of profound mysteries here connected with the poet's desire for resolution of doubt—a "doubt" pictured as a dying patient whose "last They said" is not a source of apocalyptic hope)

l.11   "remember me": Lu 23:42 (see P217; P431; P1180; and P1502)

l.13   "Master": Mt 23:8; 26:18; Lu 8:24; Joh 13:13; 20:16; Eph 6:9

463   I live with Him- I see His face-

l.1   "I...face": Ca 2:14; 5:15; Rev 19:7-9; 22:4

l.5   "Only One": Ca 6:9

ll.6-8   "Right...Me": Ro 8:23-30; ICo 15:19-23; Jas 1:18; Rev 14:1-5 (as an elect Bride of Christ, there is a "Claim invisible" upon her)

l.9   "I...Voice": Ca 2:8, 14; 5:2; Rev 1:10, 12, 15; 3:20; 14:2

l.10   "I...Today": ICo 15:22

ll.11-12 "To...Immortality": ICo 15

1.15 "That...stopless": Joh 3:15-16, 36; 14:6; Ro 5:10, 17; 6:4, 22-23; IITi 1:1; IJo 5:11-12 (bridal status, accession to election, conveys an assurance of eternal life)

1.15 "stopless/endless": Heb 7:16

1.16 "Judgment": Rev 14:7; 20:4 (the strength of her love assures more than "Judgment" frightens, the profane equivalent in Canticles 7:6-7)

464 The power to be true to You,

ll.2-3 "Until...Picture": Rev 22:4 (the ideas of being like Christ, of being conformed to His image, and of receiving His name as a new identity are in these lines given poetic, if somewhat literal, expression—see Ro 8:29; ICo 13:12; 15:49; IICo 3:18; IJo 3:2; Rev 3:12; 14:1; the root KJV idea behind stanza one is that of the jealous God, Ex 20:1-5)

1.6 "Heaven": Rev 21-22 (a metonym for the Deity and the Vision and Presence offered in the New Jerusalem)

1.7 "invitation": Rev 3:20; 19:7-9

465 I heard a Fly buzz- when I died-

1.1 "Fly": IIKi 1:2-3, 6, 16; Mt 10:25; 12:24, 27; Mr 3:22; Lu 11:15-19 (added to more conventional associations of the fly with decay, death, and possibly evil is that connection with Beelzebub, the Prince of Devils)

1.7 "King": Rev 15:3; 17:14; 19:16 (Christ may here be thought of as "King" in His triumph over death, ICo 15:50-57)

1.8 "Room/his power": ICo 15:43; Eph 1:19; Php 3:10; Heb 2:14 (the "power" to be "witnessed" is that of the "King" over death)

1.13 "Blue": see note, line one, P15

1.13 "Buzz": see line one above (the onomatopoeia suggests Beelzebub, the snakes of Milton's Pandemonium, and death as cacophony and dissonance rather than resolution and harmony)

1.14 "light": Joh 1:4-9; IJo 1:5; Rev 21:23-24; 22:5

1.16 "I...see": ICo 13:12; IJo 3:2; Rev 1:7; 3:18; 22:4 (vision is of the essence of apocalyptic hope—to know as known, to see as seen; P465 inverts conventional views of death and Heaven, dealing as it does with the potential unmeaning of the apocalyptic)

Comment: See *Poems*, I, 358-359.

466   'Tis little I- could care for Pearls-

      l.1   "Pearls": Rev 21:19-21

      ll.3-4   "When...me": Isa 61:10; 62:3-4; Eze 16:10-12; Mal 3:17; Rev 21 (the poem uses the KJV metaphor of the adorning of the beloved)

      l.4   "Rubies": Pr 20:15; 31:10; Rev 21:19-21

      l.5   "Gold": Eze 28:13; Rev 21:18-21

      l.6   "Diamonds": Ex 28:18; Eze 28:13; Rev 21:19-21

      l.7   "Diadem": Isa 61:10; 62:3-4; Rev 2:10 (the metaphor of adornment is used to speak of circuit world treasures, friends or poems)

Comment: See *Poems*, I, 359.

467   We do not play on Graves-

      ll.1-2   "We...Room": Ec 9:10; 12:4-7 (the incompatibility of death with the music of the imagination is the subject of P467)

      l.10   "Enemies": ICo 15:26

468   The Manner of it's Death

      l.2   "When...die": Heb 9:27

      l.5   "When...past": ICo 1:27-28; Eph 1:4; IITh 2:13; IPe 2:4, 9 (within election the "Miracle" is having been chosen, thereby making "Babble of the styles" superfluous)

      l.6   "Love": IJo 4:8 (God is "Love" and stipulates the death of the body)

      l.7   "little Fate": ICo 15:44 (the death of the "natural body")

      l.8   "small": see lines six and seven above ("small" may refer to the stipulation of the "little Fate" or to the "Customs" of St. James, which miss the fundamental "Miracle"; as Johnson noted, the line is "clearly separated" from lines seven and nine, *Poems*, I, 360, and see also Franklin, I, 603)

469   The Red- Blaze- is the Morning-

ll.1-3   "Red," "Violet," "Yellow": see note, line one, P15
l.7   "Argent": Rev 3:4-5, 18; 6:11; 19:8; 20:11

470   I am alive- I guess-

ll.1,9,17 "I...alive": Rev 1:18
l.8   "Breath": Ge 2:7
l.16   "Immortality": ICo 15:53-54
ll.27-28 "Alive...Thee": Joh 3:3-8; ICo 15:22; IPe 1:23
(spiritual birth in stanza seven follows six stanzas of a death-in-life,
minimalist view of circuit world existence, P470 perhaps reflecting
gnostic stresses because of bodily circumscriptions: parlor-coffin-
name)

471   A Night- there lay the Days between-

l.8   "Till...more": Rev 21:25; 22:5

472   Except the Heaven had come so near-

ll.1-2   "Except...Door": Rev 3:20 ("Heaven" and the later
"Grace" may be metonyms for Christ since the first lines suggest His
knocking at the "Door"; nevertheless, it is "Distance" that haunts the
poet, suggesting that the language of election may simply be a vehicle
for expressing unillusioned feelings of loss); Ro 8:28-30; Eph 1:4;
IITh 2:13; IPe 2:4, 9 (among many, these references touch upon the
idea of being chosen)
l.5   "Grace": Joh 1:17; ICo 15:10; IICo 8:9; IITi 1:9
("Grace" may be a metonym for Christ or suggestive of a religio-
aesthetic experience involving imagination, its waxing and waning)

473   I am ashamed- I hide-

l.2   "Bride": Ca 1-8; Isa 61:10; 62:3-4; Eze 16:10-12;
Mal 3:17; Rev 14:1-5; 19:7-9; 21; 22:17 (a preparationist, bridal-
accession poem in which the poet gathers her ideal identity)
l.4   "dazzled Face": Rev 22:4
l.5   "No...Grace": Rev 2:17; 3:12; 19:7-9; 21:1-5
l.7   "Me...tell": Rev 21:2 (see line two above)
l.10   "Gown": Rev 19:8

l.11   "Raiment": Rev 3:5, 18

l.15   "Fair": Ca 1:8; 5:9; 6:1

l.16   "Brow": Rev 14:1; 22:4

l.16   'Earl': Rev 1:6; 5:10 (the regal status attendant upon accession into Heaven)

l.18   "Pearl": Rev 21:21

l.20   "Fashion...quaint": Php 3:21

l.20   "white": Rev 2:17; 3:4-5, 18; 6:11; 7:9, 13-14; 19:8

l.21   "Quick": ICo 15:36, 45

l.22   'Light': Joh 1:4-9; ITi 6:16; IJo 1:5; Rev 21:23-24; 22:5

l.27   'Baptized...Bride': Rev 2:17; 3:12; 14:1; 19:7-9; 21; 22:4 (the new name, the rechristening with an achieved identity as Bride of Christ)

Comment: See *Poems*, I, 363.

474   They put Us far apart-

l.3   'unsown Peninsula': ICo 15:42-44 (a metonym for the body that in P474 separates—the paradisiacal ideal being a reciprocal, disembodied vision face-to-face)

l.12   'Souls': Ge 2:7; Ca 1:7; 3:1-4; ICo 15:45 (the spiritual, disembodied nature of the experience is stressed)

l.14   "sweet": Ca 2:3, 14; 5:5, 13, 16; 7:9

l.15   'stapled feet': Mt 27:35; Mr 15:24-25; Lu 23:33; 24:39-40; Joh 19:18; 20:25 (the identification here and elsewhere in the poem is with the crucified Christ, with the sufferings of His Passion, including motifs of separation, descent into darkness, opportunity of recantation, and awareness of 'Paradise" in the face of death, Lu 23:43)

l.17   "Permission...recant": Mt 27:11-12

l.19   'Sun': Mal 4:2; Lu 1:78; IIPe 1:19; Rev 1:16; 2:28; 21:23; 22:5, 16 (the Deity; nevertheless, P474 may be read as a body-of-this-death poem in which the 'Sun" is synecdochic of the circuit world, bodily limitation, and separation from the Bridegroom)

l.21   'Death': Rev 21:4 (absent from the New Jerusalem is "Death" as well as the "Sun," Rev 21:23; 22:5)

l.22   'Paradise': Rev 22:4 ('Paradise" is here the beatific vision, the experience of ideal presence, or, if P474 is read as a poem concerned with the poet and a profane beloved, 'Paradise" is the

Heaven of a final, face-to-face, disembodied vision, albeit partial—"all the Disc"); Ge 2-3; Eze 28:13-14; 31:8-9, 16; 47:1-12; Rev 19; 21-22 ("Paradise" is associated with ideal marriage—marital figuration inseparable from her consciousness of ideal presence and vision)

      1.23   "Each...Face": Rev 22:4

475   Doom is the House without the Door-

      1.1   "Doom...Door": Ro 7:24; IICo 5:4; Php 3:21 (a reference to the body prison of the circuit world—P475 the poet's version of Plato's Myth of the Cave)

      1.2   "Sun": Mal 4:2 (the solar image suggests the world of spirit, the "new circumference")

      1.3   "Ladder's...away": Ge 28:12 (the glance at Jacob underscores the loss of connection and presence, his dream, taking place at Bethel, the "house of God" and "gate of heaven," Ge 28:17, emphasizing communion, presence, and possession—in contrast to the sense of dispossession and absence at the heart of P475)

      1.8   "Hemlock's/hundreds...God": Rev 7:14 (the variant "hundreds" may have originally given the poem an inappropriate apocalyptic ending, focusing as it does on worshipers around the throne of God in Heaven; "Hemlocks" reinforces the nature imagery and coincides with the metaphoric use of indoors and outdoors)

      Comment: See *Poems*, I, 365.

476   I meant to have but modest needs-

      1.1   "modest needs": Mt 6:8, 31-33; Lu 12:27-31 (that God "knoweth what things ye have need of, before ye ask him" is part of the delicious irony of P476)

      1.2   "Content": Php 4:11; ITi 6:6-8; Heb 13:5 (again, the KJV echo is ironic)

      1.2   "Heaven": Mt 6:9 (the irony of P476 pivots on the desire for a circuit world as "Heaven")

      1.8   "Grace": Ro 5:15; Eph 1:7 ("Grace" as a free gift, a request granted)

      1.11   "A...Your's": Rev 21-22

      1.13   "Jehovah's": Ex 6:3; Ps 83:18; Isa 26:4

      1.14   "Cherubim": Ge 3:24; Ex 25:18-20; 37:6-9; Ps 99:1; Isa 37:16; Eze 10:1-20 (the poet probably intends "Cherubim" as simply the angels and archangels surrounding the throne of God in the Book of Revelation)

l.15   "Grave Saints": Rev 11:18; 14:12; 15:3; 19:8; 20:9

l.20   "Judgment": Rev 14:7; 19:2 (the twinkling eye of Jehovah)

l.23   'That...'ask' ": Mt 21:22 ("And all things, whatsoever ye shall ask in prayer, believing, ye shall receive")

l.24   " 'Itself'...'You' ": Mt 7:7 ("Ask, and it shall be given you; seek, and ye shall find; knock, and it shall be opened unto you")

l.27   "As Children": Mt 7:7-11; 19:14 (again, the KJV echo is ironic)

Comment: See *Poems*, I, 365-366.

478   I had no time to Hate-

l.1   "time...Hate": Ec 3:8

l.7   "time...Love": Ec 3:8

l.9   "Some...be": Ge 3:19; Ec 9:10

l.10   "Toil": Mt 6:28; Lu 12:27

Comment: See *Poems*, I, 367.

479   She dealt her pretty words like Blades-

ll.1-4   'She...Bone": Heb 4:12 ("For the word of God is quick, and powerful, and sharper than any two-edged sword, piercing even to the dividing asunder of soul and spirit, and of the joints and marrow, and is a discerner of the thoughts and intents of the heart")

ll.7-8   "A...bear": Ro 8:1-21 (the Paulinian language of "Flesh" and "Creatures" reinforces the superciliousness)

ll.11-12 "Mortality's...Die": ICo 15:53-54; IICo 5:4

Comment: See *Poems*, I, 367-368.

480   "Why do I love" You, Sir?

l.3   'Wind": see note, line one, P824 ("Wind," "Lightning," and "Sunrise" are all associated with the Deity)

l.8   "And...not": Joh 3:8

l.11   'Lightning": Job 37:3; 38:35; Eze 1:13-14; Mt 24:27; Rev 4:5; 8:5; 11:19; 16:18

l.17   "Sunrise": Ps 84:11; 89:36; Mal 4:2; Lu 1:78; IIPe 1:19; Rev 1:16; 2:28; 21:23; 22:5, 16
Comment: See *Poems*, I, 368-369.

481   The Himmaleh was known to stoop

l.1   "Himmaleh": Ca 2:8, 17; 4:8; 8:14 (mountains are associated with the beloved)
l.3   "Compassion": Ps 86:15; 111:4; 112:4; 145:8; La 3:22 (characteristic of the Deity; the poet may have chosen the word for the suggestions of condescension and distance in New Testament usages, e.g., Mt 9:36; 14:14; 15:32; 18:27; 20:34)
ll.5-6   "Where...Snow": Job 26:7; Ps 104:2

482   We Cover Thee- Sweet Face-

ll.1-6,8,12 "Thee," "Thyself," "Thou": Ca 1:2-4, 7-11, 15-16; 2:14, 17; 4:1-5, 7, 9-11, 13, 16; 5:9; 6:1, 4-7, 13; 7:1-3, 5-9, 12-13; 8:1-2, 5, 12-14 (the mode of address is taken from Canticles)
l.1   "Sweet": Ca 2:3, 14; 5:5, 13, 16; 7:9
l.1   "Face": Ca 2:14; 5:15
l.2   "Not...Thee": Ca 2:5; 5:8 (P482 inverts the Canticles topos of the lover sated with the beloved)
l.4   "Remember": Ca 1:4 ("we will remember thy love more than wine")
l.7   "turn": Ca 1:7; 2:17; 6:5 (associated with the presence or absence of the beloved)
l.9   "love": Ca 1-8 (an impalpable, disembodied love knows only the limits of imagination, a fitting harbinger of the beatific vision, Rev 22:4)
l.11   "Sweet": see line one above
Comment: See *Poems*, I, 369-370.

483   A Solemn thing within the Soul

ll.1-2   "A...ripe": Rev 14:14-20 (the ripening of the golden apple has apocalyptic overtones)
l.3   "golden": Ge 2:11-12; Ca 1:10-11; 3:10; 5:11, 14-15; Eze 28:13; Rev 3:18; 4:4; 21:18, 21 (the Paradise-Heaven "golden," also associated with the beloved of Canticles)

l.3   "And...up": Ca 2:3, 5; 7:8; 8:5 (the ripened apple suggests the beloved); De 32:10; Ps 17:8; Zec 2:8 (the ripened fruit as suggestive of the chosen); Rev 14:4 (perhaps an echo of the virginal firstfruits)

l.4   "Maker's": Ps 95:6; Isa 54:5; Heb 11:10

l.4   "Ladders": Ge 28:12

l.5   "Orchard": Ca 4:12-16; 5:1; 6:2; 8:13 (the beloved as garden-orchard or the garden as dwelling of the beloved); Ge 2-3; Eze 28:13 (paradisiacal associations)

ll.7,15 "Sun": Ps 84:11; 89:36; Mal 4:2; Lu 1:78; IIPe 1:19; Rev 1:16; 2:28; 21:23; 22:5, 16

l.14   "Harvest": Mt 9:37-38; 13:30, 39; Mr 4:29; Lu 10:2; Rev 14:14-20

ll.15-16 "Every...lives": Ro 8:29-30; Eph 1:4; IPe 1:2; 2:5-6 (the "Sun" as "Single" suggests election)

484   My Garden- like the Beach-

l.1   "Garden": see note, line five, P483

l.3   "Summer": Rev 21:4; 22:1-5 (just as the existence of the "Beach" denotes a "Sea" as also does her "Garden" a Heaven-"Summer")

ll.4-5 "Pearls...Me": Rev 21:21 (just as the sea yields pearls so also she becomes a pearl associated with the adorned Bride of Revelation)

485   To make One's Toilette- after Death

ll.1-6 "To...gay": Mt 25:1-13 (the preparationist motif is here inverted); Ro 8:29; ICo 13:12; 15:49; IICo 3:18; IJo 3:2; Rev 3:12; 14:1; 22:4 (the preparation of an image for self and/or others rather than for God is the poet's expression of ambivalence regarding the attraction-repulsion of her own aggressively embraced religio-aesthetic identity)

l.7   "When...wrenched": Rev 22:4 (an inversion of the beatific vision, the fondling "eyes" suggesting those of the profane beloved, Ca 2:14; 3:3; 6:13)

l.8   "By...away": Ex 20:2-5 (the God of the Decalogue is a jealous God allowing worship of no lesser god, "graven image," or likeness)

Comment: See *Poems*, I, 371.

486   I was the slightest in the House-

l.1   "I...House": Mt 11:11; 19:30; 20:16; Mr 10:31; Lu 7:28; 13:30 (based upon the paradox that the least will be greater, the last first, and the Beatitudes' philosophy of deprivation, Mt 5:3-12)

l.2   "I...Room": Mt 23:6; Mr 12:39; Lu 14:8-10; 20:46 (again, the KJV paradox is adapted to the poet's religio-aesthetic concern for the grace of inspiration—'For whosoever exalteth himself shall be abased; and he that humbleth himself shall be exalted," Lu 14:11)

ll.5-7   "So...Basket": Ex 16:4-15; Mt 14:20; 15:37; Mr 6:43; 8:8; Lu 9:17; Joh 6:13 (a religio-aesthetic experience of inspiration is spoken of in terms adapted from KJV miraculous dispensations)

487   You love the Lord- you cannot see-

l.1   "You...see": I Jo 4:12 ('No man hath seen God at any time")

l.5   "Ample Letter": Joh 1:1; Rev 1:8; 11 (emulation of the Word is the poet's religio-aesthetic; the misplaced concreteness of conventional worship, in contrast, reduces spirit to the letter—a 'little note"—and "His House" to a mere "Step")

l.8   "And...see": IICo 5:1 ('For we know that if our earthly house of this tabernacle were dissolved, we have a building of God, an house not made with hands, eternal in the heavens")

Comment: The Biblical wit of P487 is directed at fleshly, unpoetic souls who "cannot see": 'But the natural man receiveth not the things of the Spirit of God: for they are foolishness unto him: neither can he know them, because they are spiritually discerned," ICo 2:14.

488   Myself was formed- a Carpenter-

l.1   "Myself...Carpenter": Mt 13:55; Mr 6:3 (the poet identifies herself with Christ)

l.12   "We...said": Ac 7:48; 17:24; IICo 5:1 (the "Art of Boards" is a sacrilege to the spiritual temple that is poetry, just as money changing had defiled the temple in Christ's time, Mt 21:12-13; the thought of P487 and P488 connects, both perhaps being directed at Higginson—see Johnson, 116-117)

489   We pray- to Heaven-

l.1   "We...Heaven": Mt 6:9 ("After this manner therefore pray you: Our Father which art in heaven, Hallowed be thy name")
l.6   "Is...Tree": Rev 21-22 (the notion that Heaven has "no Geography" is perhaps Miltonic, e.g., *Paradise Lost*, I, 252-253; XII, 462-465)
l.10   "But...Focus": Ca 1-8; Isa 61:10; 62:3-4; Eze 16:10-12; Mal 3:17; Rev 14:1-5; 19:7-9; 21; 22:17 (Heaven as bridal accession)
l.11   "Omnipresence": Ac 17:27-28
Comment: See *Poems*, I, 373.

490   To One denied to drink

ll.1-8   "To...lip": Lu 16:19-26 (the story of the rich man and Lazarus is adapted to this description of the human condition, a theodicy poem much like P313; the Biblical associations with well and water heighten the sardonic tone of the poem, Joh 4:10, 14; 7:38; Rev 7:17; 21:6; 22:1-2)

491   While it is alive

ll.4-5   "Dwell...Sacrament": Mt 26:26-28 (the communion of soul and body united in P491 by "Love")
ll.6-8   "Show...Grave": Ro 8:35-39 ("Who shall separate us from the love of Christ?...neither death, nor life,...nor things present, nor things to come...shall be able to separate us from the love of God, which is in Christ Jesus our Lord")
ll.7-8   "Love...'Live' ": Ge 2:7; ICo 15:50-57 (unifier of soul and body, life and death, circuit world and new circumference is not abstract "Love" but the Bridegroom, Guarantor of the resurrection)
Comment: See *Poems*, I, 374-375.

492   Civilization- spurns- the Leopard!

ll.1-9   "Civilization...frown":   Isa   11:6;   Jer   13:23
(excoriated in the present or placed in the future's peaceable kingdom,
the "Leopard's nature" with its potent demands and ineradicable
memories is out of place in a civilized present)

493   The World- stands- solemner- to me-

l.2   "Since...Him": Ca 1-8; Isa 61:10; 62:3-4; Eze 16:10-
12; Mal 3:17; Rev 14:1-5; 19:7-9; 21; 22:17 (a bridal accession poem)
l.4   "That...name": Rev 2:17; 3:12; 14:1; 22:4
l.6   "pearl": Rev 21:21 (probably used with the reference
in line ten to suggest Revelation white, Rev 2:17; 3:4-5, 18; 6:11; 7:9,
13-14; 19:8)

Chapter 2

References and Notes on Poems 495 —1176
[1862 —1870]

495   **It's thoughts- and just One Heart-**

ll.1,23   "One Heart," "two Heart": Ca 3:11; 4:9; 8:6
l.4   "two...three": Mt 18:20 ("For where two or three are gathered together in my name, there am I in the midst of them")
ll.5-6   "Upon...Crowded": Ps 42:4
l.6   "Sacrament": Mt 26:20-29
ll.23-25   "It's...Counterfeit": Rev 3:20 (the "Counterfeit" is the profane equivalent of entertainment of the Heavenly Guest; see also *Paradise Lost*, XII, 618-619)

496   **As far from pity, as complaint-**

ll.3,11   "Revelation,"   "Revelations":   Rev   (used metaphorically to suggest natural revelation, speech, her poetry, and, at once, apocalyptic hope and despair)
l.4   "As...Bone": Eze 37 (Biblical wit suggesting that her attempted speech to the dead equates to Ezekiel's attempts to prophesy to dry bones)
l.10   "How...lies": Ex 12:46 ("and all the daughters of musick shall be brought low")

497   **He strained my faith-**

l.3   "Shook...trust": Job 13:15 ("Though he slay me, yet will I trust in him: but I will maintain mine own ways before him")

l.9   "Wrong...Anguish": Job 7:11

ll.11-12 " 'Tho...say": Job 1-2 (the occasion for the trial of Job is never explained to him)

l.14   "sweet": Ca 2:3, 14; 5:5, 13, 16; 7:9 (the Canticles word reinforces the sense of her desire to know Jesus as beloved Bridegroom rather than exemplar of life as Passion)

l.15   "little": Mt 19:14 ("But Jesus said, Suffer little children, and forbid them not, to come unto me: for of such is the kingdom of heaven")

l.15   " 'John' ": Joh 13:23-24; 19:26-27

l.16(variant) "Slay...me": Job 13:15 (see line three above and Franklin, I, 386)

Comment: See *Poems*, II, 380-381.

498   I envy Seas, whereon He rides-

l.8   "Heaven/Eden": Ge 2-3; Eze 28:13-14; 31:8-9, 16; Rev 21-22

l.23   "Everlasting Night": Mt 22:13; 25:46

l.24   "Gabriel": Da 8:16-17; 9:21-22; Lu 1:11-20, 26-38; Rev 8:2

Comment: See Poems, II, 382-383. Heaven as seeing the beloved anticipates the beatific vision, Rev 22:4—Gabriel associated with that ideal presence of apocalyptic hope.

499   Those fair- fictitious People-

l.1   "fair": Ca 1:15-16; 2:10, 13; 4:1, 7, 10; 5:9; 6:1, 10

l.4   "Ivory": Rev 3:4-5, 18; 6:11; 7:9, 13-14 (the Eternity color)

l.9   "trust": IICo 1:10

l.9   "places perfecter": Joh 14:2-3

l.10   "Inheriting": Mt 19:29; 25:34; Rev 21:7

l.10   "Delight": Ca 2:3

l.14   "Blesseder": Mt 25:34; Rev 14:13; 19:9; 22:14

l.15   "Knowing": ICo 13:12

l.15   "where...hope": Tit 1:2; 3:7; Heb 6:18-19; (the hope of eternal life)

l.16   "Receiving/Beholding": IPe 1:9; Rev 22:4

l.17   "Expectation": Ro 8:19; Php 1:20

l.20　　"Except...Holiness": Heb 12:14

ll.23-24 "Through...come": ICo 15:50-55 (much of the lexicon of P499 is Johannine or Paulinian)

Comment: See *Poems*, II, 382-383.

501　　This World is not Conclusion

l.1　　"This World": Joh 18:36 ("Jesus answered, My kingdom is not of this world"); Rev 11:15

l.3　　"Invisible": Col 1:15; ITi 1:17; Heb 11:27

l.12　　"Crucifixion": Mt 27:35; Mr 15:24-25; Lu 23:33; Joh 19:18

ll.13-14 "Faith...see": Heb 11:1 ("Now faith is the substance of things hoped for, the evidence of things not seen")

l.18　　"Hallelujahs": Rev 19:1, 3-4, 6 (used with heavy irony since the word is only used in the Marriage Supper of the Lamb section of the KJV, thereby conveying a smug complacency on the part of the "Pulpit")

Comment: P501 speaks of a "Species beyond" as if it were an "Invisible Music" anticipating the song of Moses and the Lamb (Rev 14:3; 15:3), an impalpable essence in contrast to the bellowed assurances of the conventionally orthodox. See *Poems*, II, 384-385.

502　　At least- to pray- is left- is left-

l.2　　"Jesus...Air": ITh 4:17

l.3　　"thy chamber": Ps 19:5; Ca 1:4; Joe 2:16

l.4　　"I'm...everywhere": Lu 11:9 ("And I say unto you, Ask, and it shall be given you; seek, and ye shall find; knock, and it shall be opened unto you"; the unrewarded importunity is ironical)

l.6　　"And...Sea": Ps 107:24-25

l.7　　"Jesus...Nazareth": Ac 3:6; 4:10

l.8　　"Arm": Job 40:9; Joh 12:38 (a KJV usage suggesting the power of God: the reference to the stormy sea of line six may echo the rescue of Peter by Christ, Mt 14:30-31)

503　　Better- than Music! For I- who heard it-

l.3   "Translation": Col 1:13; Heb 11:5 (the KJV provenance of the word conveys a movement beyond the realm of the natural, of the circuit world)

ll.9,11,14-15 "Eden," "Eve's," "Eve,": Ge 2-3

l.24   "Drop...Throne": Rev 14:3-4 ("And they sung as it were a new song before the throne, and before the four beasts, and the elders: and no man could learn that song but the hundred and forty and four thousand, which were redeemed from the earth. These are they that were not defiled with women; for they are virgins. These are they that follow the Lamb whithersoever he goeth. These were redeemed from among men, being the firstfruits unto God and to the Lamb")

Comment: P503 reveals that her poems were "faint Rehearsal[s]" for the song of Moses and the Lamb of Revelation. See *Poems*, II, 386.

504   You know that Portrait in the Moon-

l.2   "So...like": Ca 2:9; 4:2-5; 5:13; 7:1-9 (the convention of the similitude for the beloved is one of the topoi of profane love in Canticles)

ll.3,5,12 "eyes," "Cheek," "Golden": Ca 5:10-13

l.7   "Ishmael": Ge 16:11, 15-16; 21:9-21 (the poet identifies with the pariah Ishmael)

l.9   " 'Tis Thou": Ca 1:7-8, 15-16; 4:1, 7, 9; 5:9; 6:1; 8:13 (the form of address is frequently repeated in Canticles)

505   I would not paint- a picture-

ll.1-8   "I...Despair": Ge 1-3; Rev 21-22 (P505 implicitly contrasts human with Divine Creation; the painting is the "bright impossibility" of a circuit world likeness)

l.9   "Cornets": IISa 6:5; ICh 15:28; Ps 98:6; Ho 5:8; Rev 1:10; 4:1; 8:2, 6, 13; 9:14 (the cornet or trumpet is a frequently mentioned KJV instrument; in Revelation the voice of the Alpha and Omega makes the sound of the trumpet)

ll.23-24 "Had...Melody": Rev 14:2-4 (see the ending of P503, the significance of which directly connects with that of P505; the "Bolts" and thunder about the throne of God are accompanied by the "Melody" of eternity for it is only the Divine Creator for whom process

and product are one, who is the Medium, the Word, who need not tell truth slant or by likeness or indirection; for God has no need—to paraphrase Yeats—to bruise body to pleasure soul since "Ether" is His oxygen and "Balloon"-"Melody" His unencumbered, bodiless essence)
Comment: See *Poems*, II, 387-388.

506   He touched me, so I live to know

l.1   "He...know": Ca 2:6; 5:4; 8:3 (the touch of intimacy, part of the topoi of profane love); Ge 24 (P506 mentions Rebekah, a virgin of the kindred of Abraham, the wife chosen for Isaac—an anticipation of Rev 14:1-5; 19:7-9; 21; Ca 1-8; Isa 61:10; 62:3-4; Eze 16:10-12; Mal 3:17; Rev 14:1-5; 19:7-9; 21; 22:17 (bridal accession is here suggested)
ll.3-4   "I...me": Lu 16:22-23 (the "bosom of Abraham" as a metaphor for the final destiny of the chosen)
l.6   "minor streams": Ca 4:15
l.9   "Royal Gown": Isa 61:10; Rev 3:18; 6:11; 7:9, 13-14; 19:8; 21
ll.11-12 "My...Renown": Ro 8:29; ICo 13:12; 15:49; IICo 3:18; IJo 3:2; Rev 3:12; 14:1; 22:4 (the achieved identity is spoken of in terms of the conformed image, the acceptable face transfigured for the beatific vision)
l.13   "Into..come": Heb 12:18-24 ("For ye are not come unto the mount that might be touched...But ye are come unto mount Sion, and unto the city of the living God, the heavenly Jerusalem,...To the general assembly and church of the firstborn, which are written in heaven...And to Jesus the mediator of the new covenant..."; the poet's use of profane love topoi domesticates the terror associated with the experience of the "voice of words" and "sight" of God, which made even Moses "quake")
l.14   "Rebecca": Ge 24 (see line one above)
l.14   "Jerusalem": Rev 19; 21-22 (a metonym for the Bridegroom since the New Jerusalem is intended)
l.15   "ravished": Ca 4:9 ("Thou hast ravished my heart, my sister, my spouse; thou hast ravished my heart with one of thine eyes, with one chin of thy neck")
l.17   "Crucifixal sign": Mt 26-27 (perhaps evidences of Passion experiences in her "Gipsy face")

l.18   "imperial Sun": Ps 84:11; 89:36; Mal 4:2; Lu 1:78; IIPe 1:19; Rev 1:16; 2:28; 21:23; 22:5, 16
Comment: See *Poems*, II, 388-389.

508   I'm ceded- I've stopped being Their's-

ll.1-4   "I'm...now": Rev 2:17; 3:12; 22:4 (the baptismal name of the circuit world is replaced by the "new name" of Revelation, sign of her achieved religio-aesthetic identity)
ll.5-6   "And...childhood": ICo 13:11 ("when I became a man, I put away childish things")
ll.8-10   "Baptized...name": Ga 3:27 ("For as many of you as have been baptized into Christ have put on Christ"); Php 2:9 ("God also hath highly exalted him, and given him a name which is above every name"); Rev 22:4
l.11   "Called": Rev 19:9
ll.11-13 "Called...Diadem": Isa 62:3; ICo 9:25; IITi 4:8; IPe 54; Rev 2:10; 3:11; 4:4, 10 (the ideally circumferential diadem or crown suggests accession to royal status)
l.12(variant) "Eye...filled": Ec 1:8 (see Franklin, I, 363)
l.16   "Queen": Ca 6:8-9; Rev 19:7-9; 21
l.19   "Crown/Throne": Rev 3:21; 14:3-5; 19:4-5; 20:11; 21:5; 22:1-3; see also note above, lines eleven-thirteen
Comment: See *Poems*, II, 389-390.

510   It was not Death, for I stood up,

l.9   "And...all": Job 34:3 ("For the ear trieth words, as the mouth tasteth meat")
l.14   "And...frame": Ps 103:14; Eph 2:21; 4:16 (nevertheless, the lines of the stanza convey the sense of the circuit world as body prison, Ro 7:24; IICo 5:4; Php 3:21)
l.19   "frosts": Job 37:10
l.24   "To...Despair": Ro 3:28; 5:1; Ga 2:16; 3:24 (the KJV connection of justification with faith makes the collocation with "Despair" pointedly ironic)
Comment: See *Poems*, II, 391-392.

511   If you were coming in the Fall,

l.13   "If...out": Mt 25:13; ICo 15:19

l.16   "Eternity": Isa 57:15 (the new circumference)

l.20   "That...sting": ICo 15:55 (the "Goblin Bee" is death whose uncertainties of time and effects trouble the poet)

Comment: See *Poems*, II, 392-393.

512   The Soul has Bandaged moments-

ll.3-7   "She...lips": Ca 1:6; 2:6, 9, 14; 3:3; 4:1, 3, 8, 11; 5:4-5, 13; 6:5, 9-11, 13; 7:5, 9; 8:3 (the "Fright-Goblin" is the false lover whose opposite is the Ideal Lover of the "Soul," the Bridegroom or the beloved of Canticles; the "thought so mean" is the "Bandaged" soul's realization of its own pusillanimity regarding faithfulness to its ideal vision)

l.8   "Lover": Ca 1-8 (the beloved of Canticles)

l.10   "fair": Ca 1:8, 15-16; 2:10, 13; 4:1, 7, 10; 5:9; 6:1, 10; 7:6 (the "Theme" is fidelity to the beloved of the soul)

ll.11-18 "The...Paradise": Ca 3-5, 7 (moments of idyllic freedom when "Bee" and "Rose" recapture paradise)

ll.19-22 "The...Song": Mt 26-27 (the retaken "Soul" as shackled and stapled "Felon" suggests the Passion Christ or perhaps the soul riveted to the body prison, Ro 7:24; IICo 5:4; Php 3:21; regardless, the "Horror" or false lover aborts the "Song," which is the Song of Songs of ideal love, Ca 1-8)

l.24   "brayed...Tongue": Job 6:5

Comment: See *Poems*, II, 393-394.

513   Like Flowers, that heard the news of Dews,

l.1   "Dews": Ge 27:28, 39; Ex 16:14; Nu 11:9; Zec 8:12 (the dew is associated with a special dispensation from God)

l.2   "prize": ICo 9:24; Php 3:14

l.3   "Brows": Rev 7:3; 9:4; 14:1; 22:4 (the mark of election)

l.10   "Or...Ear": Mt 11:15; 13:16; Joh 3:8 (the simile may suggest spiritual rebirth; for more on "wind" see note, line one, P824)

l.13   "The...come": Heb 12:18-24 (the experience suggests being surprised by the joy of her election, IPe 1:8-9); Mt 5:2-12 (the final stanza is also consonant with her philosophy of deprivation as expressed in the Beatitudes)

Comment: See Poems, II, 394-395.

515   No Crowd that has occurred

ll.1-4   "No...does": ICo 15 (St. Paul speaks of the general resurrection of the dead; the "Crowd" may have its resurrection counterpart in that "general assembly and church of the firstborn," Heb 12:23; Rev 14:1-5)

l.5   "Circumference...full": Rev 10:6 (Noon or Eternity when "there should be time no longer")

l.6   "restricted/subjected": Ro 8:20 ("For the creature was made subject to vanity, not willingly, but by reason of him who hath subjected the same in hope")

l.6   "Grave": ICo 15:55

l.7   "Privilege/Primogeniture": Ro 8:29-30; Col 1:13-22; Heb 12:23; ICo 15:20-23; Rev 14:1-5

ll.7-8   "Assert...live": ICo 15:50-55

l.8   "Dust": Ge 2:7; 3:19; Ps 103:14

l.9   "On...place": ICo 15:44 (the resurrected spiritual body has "features," ICo 13:12; Rev 7:3; 9:4; 14:1; 22:4)

ll.10-11 "All...Comparison": Rev 7:9 ("After this I beheld, and, lo, a great multitude, which no man could number, of all nations, and kindreds, and people...")

l.12   "As...star": IIPe 3:10-12 (the imagery of the simile is apocalyptic)

ll.13-16 "Solemnity...Numb": Rev 11:18; 14:7; 20:12-13 ("and they were judged every man according to their works")

ll.15,20 "each...Consciousness," "Me": Rev 3:20 (the momentousness of the Judgment for the individual)

Comment: See *Poems*, II, 395-396.

516   Beauty- be not caused- It Is-

l.1   "Beauty...Is": Ex 3:14 ("And God said unto Moses, I Am That I Am..."; the poet models beauty on this indefinable essence—see P988)

ll.4-8   "Overtake...it": Jer 10:12-13; 51:15-16 (the treasures of God-Beauty can be experienced but not possessed or overtaken, the religio-aesthetic equivalent for which: "No man hath seen God at any time," IJo 4:12)

Comment: See *Poems*, II, 396-397.

517   **He parts Himself- like Leaves-**

ll.1-12   "He...Moon": Ps 19:4-6 (the first lines suggest the benign albeit fragmentary theophanies of prelapsarian consciousness associated with the beneficent sun)

ll.13-20 "What...Cocoon":   Ge   3   (the   "Ignorance"   of postlapsarian "Night" and "Frost")

Comment: See *Poems*, II, 397-398.

518   **Her sweet Weight on my Heart a Night**

l.1   "sweet," "Heart," "Night": Ca 2:3, 14, 17; 3:8, 11; 4:6, 9; 5:2, 5, 13, 16; 7:9

l.2   "Had...lie": Ca 1:13 ("A bundle of myrrh is my well-beloved unto me; he shall lie all night betwixt my breasts")

ll.3-4   "When...away": Ca 2:17; 4:6; 5:6 (P518 uses the profane love topos of possession and loss as metaphor for religio-aesthetic certitude, the Borges motif of stanza two reminiscent of the final lines of Keats's "Ode to a Nightingale"; see Ca 5:6 : "I opened to my beloved; but my beloved had withdrawn himself, and was gone: my soul failed when he spake: I sought him, but I could not find him; I called him, but he gave me no answer")

l.6   "Heaven...confirm": Ca 5:2; Rev 3:20; 19:7-9; 21; 22:1-5 (the "Heaven" is that ideal presence that can be imagined but with ontological status only of a "Fiction superseding Faith")

l.11   "Fiction...Faith": Heb 11:1, 3 ("Now faith is the substance of things hoped for, the evidence of things not seen....Through faith we understand that the worlds were framed by the word of God, so that things which are seen were not made of things which do appear"; the modernist theme of P518 is the supersession of "Faith" by "Fiction," the products of language and metaphor "by so much" the remaining reality)

519   **'Twas warm- at first- like Us-**

ll.5,16   "Forehead...Adamant": Eze 3:9 ("As an adamant harder than flint have I made thy forehead")

520   I started Early- Took my Dog-

ll.2,24   "Sea": Ge 1:2; 21:1 (the sea, as a KJV symbol of the primordial abyss, of potency, of chaos needing cosmos, becomes in P520 a richly nondiscursive metaphor suggesting among other things sexuality, the unconscious, nature, death, and the circuit world as problematic matrix out of which poetry is born. In the face of this, the domestic, "Solid Town" child's creation of an ostensibly safe place for the play of fanciful language reveals the Gnostic sensibility's obdurate insistence upon the unreal, illusory, and ultimately threatening quality of such a limiting and riddling world of Experience)

Comment: See Poems, II, 399-400 and compare to Whitman's "Out of the Cradle Endlessly Rocking" and Stevens's "The Idea of Order at Key West."

522   Had I presumed to hope-

l.1   "hope": Ro 8:19-25
l.4   "As...away": Ge 6:4; Nu 13:33 (a simile suggesting the presence of God associated with an antique time of Eden and the promised land)
ll.5-7   "Had...Grace": Eph 2:8-9
ll.9-10   " 'Tis...Despair": Ro 3:24, 28 (justification by "Confident Despair," not faith and grace—see P313 for another expression of her oxymoronic and paradoxical manner of appropriating her Puritan heritage)
l.10   "Confident/diligent": Heb 11:6; IPe 1:10; IIPe 3:14
ll.11-12 "Celestial," "Terrestrial": ICo 15:40
l.13   " 'Tis...die": Php 1:21 ("For me to live is Christ, and to die is gain")
l.14   "For...obtain": Ro 8:24b ("So run, that ye may obtain")
l.15   "Till...Death": ICo 15:36 ("Thou fool, that which thou sowest is not quickened, except it die")
l.16   "Second Gain": Rev 2:11; 20:6, 14; 21:8 (the poet has in mind the "second death" of Revelation, which contrasts with the "Second Gain," the resurrection and eternal life, awaiting the elect)
Comment: See *Poems*, II, 401.

523   Sweet- You forgot- but I remembered

ll.1,12   "Sweet": Ca 2:3, 14; 5:5, 13, 16; 7:9

ll.3-4   "So...You": Ca 8:6 ("for love is strong as death")

l.3   "Sum/Love": Ca 1:2, 9, 15; 2:2, 4, 10; 4:1, 7; 6:4; 8:4-7

l.5   "Farthings": Mr 12:42-44 (the poor widow gave her all, a farthing; giving all for love is one of the topoi of profane love, Ca 8:7 : "Many waters cannot quench love, neither can the foods drown it: if a man would give all the substance of his house for love, it would utterly be contemned")

l.10   "Heart": Ca 4:9; 8:6

l.11   "Barefoot Vision": Ca 2:11; 6:13 (the desire for a vision of the beloved for which all would be sacrificed or surrendered is an obvious displacement revealing her desire for The Beloved, Guarantor of Presence and Vision; in some respects, "Barefoot Vision" describes the point of view of her work as an author)

Comment: See *Poems*, II, 401-402.

524   Departed- to the Judgment-

l.1   "Judgment": Rev 6:17; 14:7; 16:14; 20:4 (the "great day of God Almighty," the day of "Judgment")

l.3   "Great Clouds": Mt 24:30; 26:64; Mr 13:26; 14:62; Lu 21:27; Rev 1:7; 14:14-16

ll.5-6   "The...begun": Joh 3:6; Ro 8:1-21; Php 3:21 (St. Paul speaks of a celestial or spiritual as distinct from natural body, ICo 15:40, 44; IICo 5:6-8; here the poet speaks of the celestial as "Bodiless" since as St. Paul wrote: "Now this I say, brethren, that flesh and blood cannot inherit the kingdom of God; neither doth corruption inherit incorruption")

l.7   "Two Worlds": Mt 13:40; Heb 6:5 (the repeatedly spoken of "this world" and the "world to come")

l.8   "And...alone": IICo 5:10; Heb 9:27; Rev 20:12

525   I think the Hemlock likes to stand

ll.5-6   "That...cloy": Ex 19:2; 23:31; Nu 20:1; 27:14; 33:16; Mt 3:1-4; 4:1-11; Mr 1:1-8, 13; Lu 3:1-18; 4:1-13; Joh 1:15-34 ("Wilderness" and "Desert" are associated with that "Austerity" suggested by the temptation of Christ, the life and preaching of John the Baptist, and the wanderings in the deserts of the children of Israel—all aspects of an "awe" she elsewhere associates with the Deity, P1733)

Comment: See *Poems*, II, 403-404.

526   To hear an Oriole sing

ll.1-3   "To...divine": Mt 13:9-17 (for a similar view see P685)

527   To put this World down, like a Bundle-

l.1   "this World": Mt 12:32; 13:22, 40; Mr 4:19; Lu 16:8; 20:34; Joh 8:23; 9:39; 11:9; 12:25, 31; 13:1; 14:30; 16:11; 18:36; Ro 12:2; ICo 1:20; 2:6-7; 3:19; 7:31; IICo 4:4; Rev 11:15 ("I am not of this world," Joh 8:23; "My kingdom is not of this world," Joh 18:36; here used of the limited "little circuit")

ll.3-4   "Agony...way": Lu 22:44 ("And being in an agony he prayed more earnestly: and his sweat was as it were great drops of blood falling down to the ground")

l.5   "straight": Mt 7:13-14 ("Enter ye in at the strait gate...Because strait is the gate, and narrow is the way, which leadeth unto life, and few there be that find it")

ll.5-6   "Trodden...God": Mt 26-27 (the identification here is with the Christ of the Passion)

l.7   "faint Confederates": Mt 26:40-41 ("And he cometh unto the disciples, and findeth them asleep, and saith unto Peter, What, could ye not watch with me one hour?...the spirit indeed is willing, but the flesh is weak")

l.9   "Crucifixion": Mt 27:22-35; Mr 15:24-25; Lu 23:23, 33; Joh 19:18

l.10   "Filaments...sowed": Mt 27; Mr 15; Lu 23; Joh 19 (Pontius Pilate, governor of Judea, released to the crowd the criminal Barabbas and capitulated to demands for Christ's crucifixion)

l.11   "Barabbas' ": Mt 27:16-17, 20-21, 26; Mr 15:7, 11, 15; Lu 23:18; Joh 18:40

ll.10-11 "Filaments...Clusters": Nu 13:23-25; Joh 15:1-11 (the grapes of Eschol are a type of Christ, "Strong Clusters" yielding the drops of the sacrament)

l.12   "Sacrament...us": Mt 26:26-28

l.13   "Patent...drop": Mt 26:28; Lu 22:44

l.14   "Brand...Drinker": Mt 26-27 (the "Brand" is the Passion with its capstone in the Crucifixion); Mt 20:19; Mr 10:33; Lu 18:32 (the "Gentile Drinker" may be the Gentiles into whose hands Jesus was placed for crucifixion—perhaps more specifically Pontius Pilate—during the time of the Passover; the "Gentile Drinker" may also be God the Father who enforces the drinking of the cup of His Will, Mt 26:39; Mr 14:36; Lu 22:42; Joh 18:11)

l.15   "Who...Cup": Mt 26:26-28; Mr 14:22-24; Lu 22:15-20 (the "Cup" of the "Sacrament"); Mt 26:39; Mr 14:36; Lu 22:42; Joh 18:11 (the "Cup" of the will of God the Father necessitating the Crucifixion)

Comment: See *Poems*, II, 404-405.

528   Mine- by the Right of the White Election!

ll.1-3,5-6,9 "Mine": Ca 2:16; 6:3 ("My beloved is mine")

l.1   "White": Ca 5:10 (suggestive of the beloved); Isa 1:18; Rev 7:14 (suggestive of regenerative purification); Rev 2:17; 3:4-5, 18; 6:11; 7:9, 13-14; 19:8 (suggestive of apocalyptic, bridal accession)

l.1   "Election": Ro 8:29-33; 9:11; 11:5-7, 27-29; Col 3:12; Tit 1:1; IPe 1:2-9; 2:5-7; IIPe 1:10 (the KJV idea of election is here used to express possession of a religio-aesthetic identity and vocation: Poet, Firstfruits-Elect and Bride of Christ)

l.2   "Royal": Rev 1:6 ("And hath made us kings and priests unto God and his Father"); see also Rev 20:6; 22:5

l.2   "Seal": Rev 7:3-8; 9:4 (the stamp, signet, seal, or brand upon the crowned and white robed—an authenticating, identifying, circumferential mark signifying election)

l.3   "Sign": Rev 15:1 (a supernatural wonder confirming her "White Election" even while in the body in the circuit world)

l.3   "Scarlet prison": Isa 1:18 ("though your sins be as scarlet, they shall be as white as snow; though they be red as crimson, they shall be as wool"; scarlet is thus associated with sin, the body, and circuit world limitation); Mt 27:28; Lu 22:44; Joh 19:34 (scarlet is associated with the blood of the Passion, with the anguish and suffering of the circuit world); Ro 7:24; IICo 5:4; Php 3:21 (the prison of the body)

l.5   "Vision": IICo 12:1 (by "Vision" is meant an inspired appearance, here confirming her "White Election"; the other pole of circuit world dialectic is the "Veto" of doubt and rejection)

l.6   "Grave's Repeal": ICo 15:50-55 (the grave repeals what is given only via heightened awareness in the "Scarlet prison")

ll.7-8   "Titled...Charter": Rev 2:17; 3:12; 14:1; 22:4 (the title or confirmation as the new name of the Father written on the white stone or on the foreheads of the elect); Rev 19:7-9; 21; 22:17 ("Titled" as Bride of Christ)

l.8   "long...steal": Rev 2:25; 3:3, 11 ("Behold, I come quickly: hold that fast which thou hast, that no man take thy crown"; the apocalyptic "hold fast" motif may explain the repeated insistence upon possession)

Comment: See *Poems*, II, 405-406.

529   I'm sorry for the Dead- Today-

l.10   "noise/sound": Ec 12:4 (death's association with diminution of sound and cessation of activity may connect P529 With Ecclesiastes 12)

Comment: See *Poems*, II, 406-407.

530   You cannot put a Fire out-

ll.5-6   "You...Drawer": Ge 7; Jer 46:7; Da 9:26; Am 8:8; Na 1:8 (P530 connects directly the inscrutable, enigmatic, and uncontrollable forces within with her creative production—whether as loaded gun, volcano, fire, bomb, or "Flood")

531   We dream- it is good we are dreaming-

ll.1-2   "dream...awake": Isa 29:7-8
l.3   "it...us": Job 13:15
ll.5-6   "Men...Blood": Ge 2:23-24; 3:19; ICo 15:50
l.16   "prudenter...dream": Isa 29:9-14 (in the Ariel chapter of Isaiah sleep-dream conflicts with prudence whereas P531 prefers equivalence)

Comment: See *Poems*, II, 408.

532   I tried to think a lonelier Thing

ll.3-4   "Omen...Nearness": Ge 2:23; 3:19
l.11   "Heavenly Love": Mt 6:14, 26, 32; 15:13; 18:35; Lu 11:13; IJo 4:8 (God the Father)
l.11   "forgot": Mt 27:46 (see P313)
ll.18-19 "pity...me": Ps 69:20

533   Two Butterflies went out at Noon

l.1   "Butterflies": ICo 15:50-55 (Hitchcockian emblems of the resurrection, which may also suggest the religio-aesthetic quest for imaginative transcendence)
l.1   "Noon": see note, line one, P393; note, line one, P420; note, line fifteen, P783; note, line eight, P916; note, line eight, P1056; note, line five, P1634; and note, line six, P1649
l.3   "Firmament": Ge 1:6-8
l.4   "Beam": Ps 104:3
l.6   "shining Sea": Eze 1:22; Rev 4:6 (the imagery of both the 1862 poem and 1878 redaction has a cosmic sweep, visionary and apocalyptic)
l.9(1878) "Rapture": see note, line seven, P1468
l.12(1878) "hurled...noon": see line one above and *Paradise Lost*, I, 45
Comment: See *Poems*, II, 409-411. The final lines of the redaction suggest a Keatsian complexity absent from the 1862 ending.

534   We see- Comparatively-

l.1   "We...Comparatively": Ec 1:8 ("the eye is not satisfied with seeing, nor the ear filled with hearing"; the rhythms of Swiftian perspectival shifts, of gain and loss, hope and anguish, are the educative design in a circuit world characterized by possessive vision)
l.11   "Firmament": Ge 1:6-8 (a metonym for God's design for circuit world vision: unlimited imaginative hope-desire coupled to frustration of possession of the "Thing"; P534 is at once a theodicy poem and one explaining Heaven, albeit an austere and immaterial one—a post-Kantian poem since we never know the "Thing," for we see in a created time and space that if reduced to our possession, would make Heaven a mere "Gnat's embrace"; thus, God's discipline of

anguish instructs in His relation to "Firmament": "Through faith we understand that the worlds were framed by the word of God, so that things which are seen were not made of things which do appear," Heb 11:3)

l.14   "Morning...Chagrin": ICo 15:50-55 (resurrection morning upon which "Striding Spirits" or "shrinking natures," the Brobdingnagians or Lilliputians of perception, will be chagrined by their misapplication of circuit world categories to the "new circumference," Heaven)

Comment: See *Poems*, II, 411-412.

535   She's happy, with a new Content-

l.1   "Content": Php 4:11
l.2   "Sacrament": Mt 26:26-28
l.3   "Care": Mt 13:22 (the "care of this world" has altered to things more heavenly)
l.4   "As...Air": Ge 2:7; Joh 3:8 (the suggestion is of rebirth or commitment to things of the spirit)
l.7   "meek": Mt 5:5; IPe 3:4
l.8   "Minister": Ro 12:7 (the KJV lexicon of P535 is apparently used with irony in order to depict parodoxically the inverse of the process of sincere election)

Comment: See *Poems*, II, 412.

536   The Heart asks Pleasure- first-

l.1   "asks": Mt 21:22 (P536 glances at two prayers: The Lord's Prayer and *The New England Primer's* "Now I lay me down to sleep")
l.7   "The...Inquisitor": Mt 6:9-13 (the reference is to the God of surveillance whose telescopic eyes inquisitorially spy: see P413)

537   Me prove it now- Whoever doubt

l.3   "Make haste": Ca 8:14
l.5   "feet": Ca 7:1
l.6   "Heart": Ca 3:11; 4:9; 8:6
l.7   "Lover": Ca 1:14, 16; 2:3, 8-10, 16-17; 5:1-10; 6:1-3

ll.8,16   "Thee": Ca 1:3-4, 9-11; 4:7; 6:1, 13; 7:5, 12-13; 8:1-2 ("Thee" and "thou" are used throughout Canticles in addressing the beloved)

l.9   "breast": Ca 4:5; 7:3, 7-8

l.10   "Hands": Ca 2:6; 5:4; 8:3

l.13   "Mouth": Ca 1:2; 5:16; 7:9

l.14   "Remember": Ca 1:4

l.15   "eyes": Ca 1:15; 4:1, 9; 5:12; 7:4; 8:10 (the lexicon of Canticles is used in P537 for Ophelia-like self-dramatization; P537 is one of her many putative [see ll.14-19, P179] poems, that is a poem rehearsing the profane love topoi in hopes of recognition, in hopes that the absent beloved will somehow be bound or obligated; thus, P537 is a displacement for apocalyptic assurance of bridal accession and the presence and reciprocated recognition that are its concomitants, Rev 19:7-9; 21; 22:4)

Comment: See *Poems*, II, 413-414.

538   'Tis true- They shut me in the Cold-

ll.4,11   "Forget it," "Forgive Them": Lu 23:34 ("Then said Jesus, Father, forgive them; for they know not what they do")

l.4   "Lord/Christ": Rev 22:21 (titles for Jesus whose Passion and mediatorial function the speaker here imitates)

l.10   "bore": Isa 53:4 ("Surely he hath borne our griefs, and carried our sorrows: yet we did esteem him stricken, smitten of God, and afflicted")

ll.11-12   "Forgive...me": Ex 32:32 ("Yet now, if thou wilt forgive their sin-; and if not, blot me, I pray thee, out of thy book which thou hast written"); Ge 18 (in addition to Moses' intercession for his people, there are perhaps echoes of Abraham's pleading for Sodom and Gomorrah); Mt 6:12-15; Lu 6:27-38; 23:34

Comment: See *Poems*, II, 414.

539   The Province of the Saved

l.1   "the Saved": ICo 1:18; 15:2; Eph 2:5, 8; Rev 21:24

ll.2-12   "To...to": IICo 4:1-18

540   I took my Power in my Hand-

l.1   "Hand": ISa 17:40, 46, 49-50

ll.3-8   " 'Twas...small": ISa 17:4-54 (Goliath, a giant of Gath "whose height was six cubits and a span," was slain by the shepherd boy David, who used a sling and stone—here "Hand" and "Pebble;" "And David put his hand in his bag and took thence a stone, and slang it, and smote the Philistine in his forehead, that the stone sunk into his forehead; and he fell upon his face to the earth")

Comment: See *Poems*, II, 415.

541   Some such Butterfly be seen

l.3   "noon": see note, line one, P533

l.3   "Sweet": Ca 2:3, 14; 5:5, 13, 16; 7:9

l.5   "Spice/Rose": Ca 2:1; 4:10, 14, 16; 5:1, 13; 6:2; 8:14

Comment: See *Poems*, II, 415-416.

542   I had no Cause to be awake-

l.2   "My...sleep": ITh 4:13-17

ll.13-14   " 'Twas...Sigh": Isa 35:10; Rev 7:17; 21:4

l.15   "Sabbath": Ex 20:9-11

ll.17-20   "So...There": Rev 3:5, 18; 4:4; 19:5-9 (the speaker joins those clothed in white raiment who praise God for eternity)

545   'Tis One by One- the Father counts-

ll.1-4   " 'Tis...Ten": Ex 20:1-17 (the Ten Commandments function as a metonym for the Old Covenant)

l.6   "Quick": Ro 8:11; Eph 2:1, 5 (a quickening allows movement beyond the mere ciphering of "Slate and Pencil" to the New Covenant)

ll.7-8   "Then...Rule": Heb 8:6-13; 9-12 (dowering and adorning suggest the new math of the New Covenant with its "Rule" of love, grace, and forgiveness, Mt 5:38-48)

l.12   "Eternal Rule": see lines seven-eight above (by the end of stanza three, the God of P545 is no longer the distant schoolmaster of the opening lines but rather the solicitous shepherd of the Parable of the Lost Sheep, Mt 18:12-14)

ll.13-14 "Regards...Band": Lu 9:48 ("Whosoever shall receive this child in my name receiveth me...for he that is least among you all, the same shall be great")

ll.15-16 "And...hand": Mt 6:28-30; Ro 8:29-30; Eph 4:7; Rev 20:13; 22:12

Comment: See *Poems*, II, 418-419.

547   **I've seen a Dying Eye**

l.8   " 'Twere...seen": Joh 20:29b ("blessed are they that have not seen, and yet have believed")

548   **Death is potential to that Man**

ll.3-4   "unconspicuous...God": Mt 10:29-32

ll.5-8   "Of...God": Ps 103:14 ("For he knoweth our frame; he remembereth that we are dust")

l.8   "dissolved": IICo 5:1

549   **That I did always love**

ll.1,3,5,7 "love," "loved": Ca 1:2-4, 7, 9; 2:2, 4-5, 7; 3:1-5, 10; 4:1, 7, 10; 5:2, 8; 6:4; 7:6, 12; 8:4-7 (see also the language from "The Solemnization of Holy Matrimony," *Book of Common Prayer*: "love...so long as ye both shall live" and Adam to Eve in *Paradise Lost*, IX, 908-910: "How can I live without thee, how forgo/Thy sweet Converse and Love so dearly join'd,/To live again in these wild Woods forlorn?")

ll.2,6,9 "thee," "thou": see note, lines eight, sixteen, P537

l.8   "And...Immortality": ICo 15:53-54; IITi 1:10 (the language is adapted to the Shelleyan idea of *Prometheus Unbound* that "eternal Love" is beyond change and time)

l.9   "dost": Ca 5:9

l.9   "Sweet": Ca 2:3, 14; 5:5, 13, 16; 7:9

l.12   "Calvary": Lu 23:33 (the Hill of the Skull where Christ was crucified)

Comment: See *Poems*, II, 420.

550   **I cross till I am weary**

ll.1-5   "I...Desert": Heb 11:38 ("they wandered in deserts, and in mountains, and in dens and caves of the earth")

ll.4-17 "What...Gain": Php 1:21; 3:7, 14

ll.24-25 "Or...Victory": ICo 15:55 ("O death, where is thy sting? O grave, where is thy victory?")

Comment: See *Poems*, II, 421.

551   There is a Shame of Nobleness-

l.7   "One...told": Mt 25:34 ("Then shall the King say unto them on his right hand, Come, ye blessed of my Father, inherit the kingdom prepared for you from the foundation of the world")

552   An ignorance a Sunset

ll.1-2   "An...Eye": ICo 13:12; Rev 3:18 ("Sunset" occasions reminders that circuit world vision is limited and inferior: "Not 'Revelation'—'tis—that waits,/But our unfurnished eyes," P685)

l.4   "Circumference": Rev 21-22 (the "Sunset" is "typic" of Heaven)

l.5   "Amber": Eze 1:4, 27; 8:2 (a visionary color also associated with the vail and thus with the presence of God—see note, line one, P15)

l.5   "Revelation": Rev 1, passim (the "Sunset" is a harbinger of that apocalyptic presence that entails the beatific vision, that is "unfurnished eyes" face-to-face with "Omnipotence"; to the furnished eyes of the circuit world God only shows His "Revelation" mediated through the "Sunset"—the only face God reveals to the "inferior face" of man since "No man hath seen God at any time," IJo 4:12)

l.8   "inferior face": ICo 15:49-50 (the "inferior face" is the "image of the earthy," which must become the "image of the heavenly"— the sealed and crowned, named and robed elect who see God face-to-face, Rev 22:4—of course, the latter is a postresurrection event of which the "Sunset" is an intimation)

ll.10-12 "Victory...Immortality": ICo 15:50-55

Comment: See *Poems*, II, 422.

553   One Crucifixion is recorded- only-

ll.1,15 "Crucifixion": Mt 27:22-50; Mr 15:12-37; Joh 19:15-30

l.5 "Calvary": Lu 23:33 (the Hill of the Skull where Christ was crucified)

l.8 "Gethsemane": Mt 26:36; Mr 14:32 (the garden near Jerusalem in which Christ prayed that the cup pass from Him; Gethsemane and Christ's Passion symbolized for the poet the inescapable sorrow, separation, and anguish of circuit world existence)

l.10 "Judea": Mt 2:1; 23:37; Lu 3:1; 21:21; Joh 11:7 (a main division of Palestine containing both Bethlehem, the birthplace of Jesus Christ, and Jerusalem, its capital, the site of the crucifixion)

l.13 "Our Lord": Rev 22:21 (Christ)

l.13 "Compound Witness": Php 2:6-7 (the divinity and humanity of Christ, His dual nature); Mt 26-28 (the "Compound Witness" may also refer to the Passion and Resurrection, the latter, the poet felt, too eagerly embraced by her contemporaries as the only "Witness" of Jesus Christ)

554   The Black Berry- wears a Thorn in his side-

ll.1-2 "The...cry": IICo 12:7 (St. Paul's "thorn in the flesh"); Mt 27:29; Mr 15:17; Joh 19:2, 5 (Christ's "crown of thorns"); Joh 19:34

555   Trust in the Unexpected-

l.1 "Trust...Unexpected": Heb 11:1

ll.13-16 "The...believed": Joh 20:27, 29 ("Then saith he to Thomas, Reach hither thy finger, and behold my hands; and reach hither thy hand, and thrust it into my side: and be not faithless, but believing....Thomas, because thou hast seen me, thou hast believed: blessed are they that have not seen, and yet have believed"); the variant line fifteen echoes the twenty-ninth verse as well: " 'Twas blesseder—the seeing not-")

Comment: See *Poems*, II, 424-425.

557   She hideth Her the last-

l.1 "hideth": Isa 45:15 ("Verily thou art a God that hidest thyself, O God of Israel, the Saviour") l.4   "The...eyes": Isa 1:15 ("I will hide mine eyes from you"; like the face of "Omnipotence" in P552, sunset and sunrise give intermittent intimations of a higher life, of immortality)

l.5   "Purple": see note, line one, P15 (as a color of the vail, purple suggests an experience of God's presence, however fleeting)

l.9   "life": IITi 1:10 (sunset and sunrise are "typic" of death and resurrection)

l.11   "imperfect": Ps 139:16 ("Thine eyes did see my substance, yet being unperfect")

Comment: See *Poems*, II, 425-426.

558   But little Carmine hath her face-

l.1   "Carmine": Ca 4:3; 5:10
l.1   "face": Ca 2:14; 5:15
l.2   "Emerald": Eze 28:13; Rev 21:19
l.2   "Gown": Rev 3:5, 18; 6:11; 7:9, 13-14; 19:8 (see also Isa 61:10; 62:3-4; Eze 16:10-12; Mal 3:17; Rev 21; P558 uses the trope of adornment in speaking of the beloved, perhaps a beautiful flower)
l.3   "Beauty": Ca 6:4; 7:1
l.3   "love": Ca 1:2-8:7
l.4   "Mine": Ca 2:16; 6:3

559   It knew no Medicine-

l.1   "It": Ro 7:24; IICo 5:4; Php 3:21 (the Gnostic sensibility's revulsion at the body prison)

l.5   "Cheeks": Ca 1:10; 5:13

l.12   "Paradise": Ge 2-3 (the Fall as possible explanation for the attraction-repulsion regarding unparadised desire and its circumscription by inevitable death, Ge 3:19)

l.13(variant) "sweet": Ca 2:3, 14; 5:5, 13, 16; 7:9

Comment: See *Poems*, II, 426-427.

560   It knew no lapse, nor Diminution-

l.1   "It": Ge 2:7; ICo 15:45 (the soul that survives the "Dissolution" of line three); see *Letters*, II, 423-424, containing the last stanza of P560 (the poet included P683 in her letter to Colonel Higginson—a poem that, along with the letter itself, clarifies the references of "It" and "Planetary forces")

ll.3-4   "Dissolution...Men": Ec 12:7 ("Then shall the dust return to the earth as it was: and the spirit shall return unto God who gave it")

ll.7-8   "Exchange...World": Lu 18:30; Rev 21-22 (the lost beloveds or "Planetary forces" have exchanged this present world for the world to come or Heaven; the poet applies this loss to her separation from Higginson, a "Planetary force" at that time leading his regiment in South Carolina)

Comment: See *Poems*, II, 427-428; *Letters*, II, 423-424; and Leyda, II, 78.

561   I measure every Grief I meet

ll.1,5   "Grief," "bore": Isa 53:4 ("Surely he hath borne our griefs, and carried our sorrows: yet we did esteem him stricken, smitten of God, and afflicted")

ll.13-16 "I...Oil": Mt 25:1-13

l.27   "Death...once": Heb 9:27 ("And as it is appointed unto men once to die, but after this the judgment"); Rev 2:11; 20:6, 14; 21:8 (the second death awaits only the damned)

l.28   "nails": Joh 20:25; Col 2:14

l.35   "piercing": Joh 19:34, 37

l.35   "Comfort": Isa 40:1; 51:3; 66:13; Zec 1:17

l.36   "Calvary": Lu 23:33 (the Hill of the Skull where Christ was crucified)

l.37   "Cross": Mt 27:32, 40, 42; Mr 15:30, 32; Lu 23:26; Joh 19:17, 19, 25

Comment: See *Poems*, II, 428-429.

562   Conjecturing a Climate

ll.1-2   "Climate...Suns": Rev 21:23-25 ("And the city had no need of the sun, neither of the moon, to shine in it: for the glory of God did lighten it, and the Lamb is the light thereof....And the gates of it shall not be shut at all by day: for there shall be no night there"); see also Rev 10:6; 2:1-5 ("And there shall be no night there; and they need no candle, neither light of the sun; for the Lord God giveth them light: and they shall reign for ever and ever," Rev 21:5)

    l.5   "To...Country": Heb 11:16 ("But now they desire a better country, that is an heavenly: wherefore God is not ashamed to be called their God: for he hath prepared for them a city")

    ll.7-8   "Not...Latitude": Rev 10:6; 21-22 ("Degree" and "Latitude" characterize the "penurious round" of the circuit world with death, sorrow, tears, time, sea, and sun, all of which are absent from the New Jerusalem)

564   My period had come for Prayer-

    ll.1-2   "My...Art": Mt 6:9 ("After this manner therefore pray ye: Our Father which art in heaven, Hallowed be thy name")

    l.3   "My...rudiment": Ge 1:1 ("In the beginning God created the heaven and earth")

    l.4   "Creator": Ec 12:1; Isa 40:28; Ro 1:25; IPe 4:19

    l.5   "God...above": Job 3:4; Ps 8:1; Joh 3:31; Jas 1:17

    l.7   "And...North": Job 26:7

    ll.15-16 "Infinitude...Thee": Ex 33:20 ("And he said, Thou canst not see my face: for there shall no man see me, and live"); IJo 4:12 ("No man hath seen God at any time")

    l.16   "That...Thee": Ca 6:13 ("Return, return, O Shulamite; return, return, that we may look upon thee")

    l.17   "The...condescended": De 4:33 ("Did ever people hear the voice of God speaking out of the midst of the fire, as thou hast heard, and live?"); the God of P564 is without face or voice except to patriarchs such as Moses, and yet God does condescend to speak obliquely through His "Creation")

    l.18   "Creation stopped/Heavens paused": Ps 19:1-3 ("The heavens declare the glory of God; and the firmament sheweth his handywork. Day unto day uttereth speech, and night unto night sheweth knowledge. There is no speech nor language, where their voice is not heard"); Jos 10:12-13 (perhaps the poet had such contravention of the natural order in mind as "typic" of assurance of grace)

    Comment: Stanza one contains Biblical wit with its play upon multiple meanings of "Art" and "rudiment," the latter establishing a "rude" tone as well as connecting Creator-Creation with the notion of beginnings. Nevertheless, stanza five with Job-like solemnity speaks of the primacy of worship for the Emersonian sovereign soul in the universe of the Deus absconditus (P683, P1733). See *Poems*, II, 431.

566   A Dying Tiger- moaned for Drink-

ll.1-3   "A...Rock": De 32; Ps 69:21; Joh 19:28; ICo 10:4 (the unslaked thirst of the "Dying Tiger" is the unsated desire of Moses on Nebo and of Christ on the cross who receives vinegar mingled with hyssop—the paradigmatic situation of her poetry: a sense of absence sharpened by an unappeasable yearning for presence)
ll.5-12   "His...dead": Rev 22:4 (the circumferential eyes of the animal yield only a mirror image of desire, suggesting the potential unmeaning of the apocalyptic; P566, the song of the "Dying Tiger," is in implied contrast with the Song of Moses and of the Lamb, songs of deliverance and achieved presence, Ex 15; De 32; Rev 14:3; 15:3)

567   He gave away his Life-

l.1   "He...Life": Mt 20:28 ("Even as the Son of man came not to be ministered unto, but to minister, and to give his life a ransom for many")
l.13   "quickening": ICo 15:36
l.13   "sowed": ICo 15:36-37, 42-44
l.16   "Pod": ICo 15:38 (the seed or body); ICo 15:55 (the grave)
l.16   "Brake...Pod": Mt 28; ICo 15:50-55 (the Resurrection)
Comment: See *Poems*, II, 433.

568   We learned the Whole of Love-

l.1   "Whole...Love": Ro 8:39; Eph 3:18-19 (the Biblical references in stanza one treat in metaphorical fashion the KJV as the revelation of the religion of love learned by the would-be lovers)
l.2   "Alphabet": Rev 1:8, 11; 21:6; 22:13
l.2   "Words": Joh 1:1; IJo 4:8
l.3   "Chapter": ICo 13
l.3   "Book": Ge-Rev (the KJV itself as a revelation of love; the poet might also have in mind the Book of Canticles)

l.4   "Revelation": Rev 1-22 (the Book of Revelation, to share the knowledge of which is not to share its vision)

l.7   "Diviner...Childhood's": Mt 19:14 (a reference to Christ's equation of the child with the kingdom)

569   I reckon- when I count at all-

l.1   "I reckon": Ro 8:18

l.3   "Heaven...God": Rev 21-22

l.12   "Heaven": Rev 21-22

ll.13-14 "Be...Them": ICo 2:9 ("But as it is written, Eye hath not seen, nor ear heard, neither have entered into the heart of man, the things which God hath prepared for them that love him")

Comment: See *Poems*, II, 434-435.

571   Must be a Wo-

l.11   "price": ICo 6:20; 7:23

l.12   "Grace": Ro 5-6 (grace flows from the sacrifice of Christ on the Cross)

ll.13-15 "Our...Cross": Php 2:6-8 ("Who, being in the form of God, thought it not robbery to be equal with God:...And being found in fashion as a man, he humbled himself, and became obedient unto death, even the death of the cross")

572   Delight- becomes pictorial-

l.1   "Delight": Ca 2:3; 7:6

l.3   "fair": Ca 1:15-16; 2:10, 13; 4:1, 7, 10; 6:10; 7:6

ll.6,7   "Amber": Eze 1:4, 27; 8:2 (see also note, line one, P15; a color here associated with natural epiphanies)

573   The Test of Love- is Death-

ll.1-2   "The...saith": Joh 3:16 ("For God so loved the world, that he gave his only begotten Son, that whosoever believeth in him should not perish, but have everlasting life")

ll.3-4   "What...doth": Joh 15:9

l.10   "Dust": Ge 2:7; 3:19; Ps 103:14

l.11   "Last": Mt 19:30; 20:16; Mr 9:35; 10:31; Lu 13:30

L.11   "Least": Lu 9:48 ("Whosoever shall receive this child in my name receiveth me: and whosoever shall receive me receiveth him that sent me: for he that is least among you all, the same shall be great")

l.12   "The...Request": Lu 23:34 ("Father, forgive them; for they know not what they do")

574   My first well Day- since many ill-

ll.11,19-20 "Redder," "bright...Threads": see note, line one, P15 (the colors suggest the vail [as well as the coverings and curtains of the tabernacle, God's place], thus indicating that nature may be offering "Etherial Gain")

l.15   "Rainbows": Ge 9:16 (symbolic of life and hope)

l.16   "Sepulchre": Mt 27:60-66 (symbolic of death and defeat)

ll.23-24 "Put...eyes": Isa 45:15 ("Verily thou art a God that hidest thyself, O God of Israel, the Saviour"); see notes, lines one-two and line five, P552 and P685 (similarly, the God of P338 "has hid his rare life/From our gross eyes")

ll.25-26 "Loss," "Gain": Php 3:7-8

l.27   "Grave": Ec 9:10; ICo 15:55

l.28   "Sun": Ps 84:11; 89:36; Mal 4:2; Lu 1:78; IIPe 1:19; Rev 1:16; 2:28; 21:23; 22:5, 16

Comment: See *Poems*, II, 437-439; *Letters*, II, 418-419, 423-424; and Leyda, II, 69-70.

575   "Heaven" has different Signs- to me-

l.1   " 'Heaven' ": Rev 21-22

l.13   "Rapture": see note, line seven, P1468

l.16   " 'Paradise' " Lu 23:43; Rev 2:7; 21-22

l.17   "fairer": Ca 1:8, 15-16; 2:10, 13; 4:1, 7, 10; 5:9; 6:1; 7:6 (Heaven as an adorned beloved may be in the poet's mind in stanza five)

l.19   "Adorned...Grace": Isa 61:10; Rev 21:2 (the "Superior Grace" may be her bridal accession: Isa 61:10; 62:3-4; Eze 16:10-12; Mal 3:17; Rev 14:1-5; 19:7-9; 21; 22:17)

l.20   "Not...see": ICo 2:9; 13:12; IJo 3:2

576   I prayed, at first, a little Girl,

l.5   "If...around": Mt 10:29-31 (the conditional suggests her questioning of such special providences)

l.9   "And...today": Mt 6:11 ("Give us this day our daily bread")

ll.12-13 "The...Divinity": Ex 33:23 (since the Deity does not "look around," His "mingled side" only remains)

ll.18-21 "Till...stay": Pr 16:11 ("A just weight and balance are the Lord's: all the weights of the bag are his work")

Comment: See *Poems*, II, 440-441.

577   If I may have it, when it's dead,

l.3   "Breath...out": Ge 2:7

ll.7,9,13,14,20,27 "Thee": see note, lines eight, sixteen, P537

l.8   "Myself...key": Isa 22:22; Mt 16:19; Rev 1:18; 3:7 (it is the Alpha and Omega who holds the keys of hell and death; in the "Grave" with the profane beloved the poet has usurped the prerogatives of the Deity; among other uses of the key see especially stanza four of P510 and stanza two of P640 where the "Sexton" keeps the key)

l.9   "Lover": Ca 1:16; 2:3, 8-9, 16-17; 5:1-10; 6:1-3; 8:14

l.10   "Permitted...be": ICo 13:12; Rev 22:4 (the situation imitates that of the beatific vision)

l.11   "After...Death": Ro 7:24 (the poet imagines being extricated from that death-in-life that is the body prison)

l.25   "Calvary": Lu 23:33

l.27   "For...Thee": Ex 20:3-5, 10 (here and in line ten is an expressed awareness of the idolatry involved in this imagined rendezvous)

l.28   "frost": Job 37:10 (a metonym, specifically, for the imagined dead beloved who can now be possessed in the confines of the grave and, generally, for the Divine decree of death, Ge 3:19)

l.29   "Paradise": Lu 23:43; IICo 12:4; Rev 2:7; 21-22

Comment: See *Poems*, II, 441-442.

578   The Body grows without-

ll.1-8   "The...honesty": ICo 6:19-20 ("What? know ye not that your body is the temple of the Holy Ghost which is in you, which ye have of God, and ye are not your own? For ye are bought with a price: therefore glorify God in your body, and your spirit, which are God's"); see also ICo 3:16-17; IICo 6:16; Eph 2:19-22

579   I had been hungry, all the Years-

l.1   "I...Years": Mt 5:6
ll.2-9   "My...Bread": Mt 26:17-30; Rev 19:6-9 (the Last Supper and the Marriage Supper of the Lamb)
ll.7,19   "I...Windows": ICo 13:12
ll.10-12   " 'Twas...Room": Lu 16:20-21
l.13   "The...new": Rev 21:5 ("Behold, I make all things new")
ll.17-20   "Nor...away": Rev 7:16-17 ("They shall hunger no more, neither thirst any more; neither shall the sun light on them, nor any heat. For the Lamb which is in the midst of the throne shall feed them, and shall lead them unto living fountains of waters: and God shall wipe away all tears from their eyes")
l.20   "Entering": Mt 7:13; Rev 22:14 (see also Lu 13:24-30 where "Entering" begins the symbolism of the apocalyptic, heavenly banquet; that the apocalyptic might gratify in a way discontinuous with circuit world desire is one side of her treatment of its potential unmeaning)

580   I gave myself to Him-

ll.1-4   "I...way": Ca 1-8; Isa 61:10; 62:3-4; Eze 16:10-12; Mal 3:17; Eph 5:22-33; Rev 14:1-5; 19:7-9; 21; 22:17 (the religio-aesthetic commitment is here spoken of as marriage using the language of contract and commercial exchange; the Bridegroom is embraced as a promissory note, "Pay," toward fulfillment of the "Vision")
l.1   "I...Him": Ca 7:12
ll.3-4   "The...way": Mt 10:39 ("...he that loseth his life for my sake shall find it")
ll.7,10   "great Purchaser," "Merchant": Eph 5:22-33; Rev 14:1-5; 19:7-9; 21-22 (the Bridegroom whose "Pay" guarantees the final bridal accession of His virginal firstfruits)

l.11   "Spice": Ca 4:10, 14, 16; 5:1, 13; 6:2; 8:14

l.15   "Sweet": Ca 2:3, 14; 5:5, 13, 16; 7:9 (the double entendre of this line reveals the cunningly devised fable that is P580: a story of a disembodied lover whose transcendence of the world of contract, law, and debt guarantees His acceptance at "Noon" of "subtle Cargoes" rather than insistence upon some more palpable profit related to the "Daily Own—of Love")

581   I found the words to every thought

ll.1-2   "I...One": Joh 1:1-5 ("In the beginning was the Word, and the Word was with God, and the Word was God. The same was in the beginning with God. All things were made by him; and without him was not any thing made that was made. In him was life; and the life was the light of men. And the light shineth in darkness; and the darkness comprehended it not")

l.4   "Sun": Ps 84:11; 898:36; Mal 4:2; Lu 1:78; IIPe 1:19; Rev 1:16; 2:28; 21:23; 22:5, 16

l.6   "Blaze": Joh 1:7-9; ITi 6:16; IJo 1:5; Rev 21:23-24; 22:5

l.6   "Cochineal": see note, line one, P15 (the colors of the vail are associated with the presence of God; the final lines admit the inadequacy of thought by metaphor to show the primal unity, the initial conditions of the "One," ideal presence and being, or metaphorically speaking, the face of God)

582   Inconceivably solemn!

ll.8-15   "Flags...near": Ec 1:8; Isa 6:9-10; Eze 12:2; Mt 13:13-17; Mr 4:12; Lu 8:10; Joh 12:40; Ac 28:26-27

584   It ceased to hurt me, though so slow

ll.9,15   "But...Peace": Isa 53:3-5 (the identification is with the Passion Christ and the transition is from suffering in a trackless "Wilderness" to a state equated with eschatological hope)

l.14   "Wilderness": Ex 15:22; 16:1; 17:1; 19:1; Le 7:38; Nu 1:1; 3:4; 13:21; 20:1; 27:14; 33:11-12, 36; 34:3-4; De 32:51 (the wilderness sojourn of the Israelites is used as a metaphor for her past anguished condition)

Comment: See *Poems*, II, 446-447.

585   **I like to see it lap the Miles-**

l.14   "Boanerges": Mr 3:17 ("And James the son of Zebedee, and John the brother of James; and he surnamed them Boanerges, which is, The sons of thunder")

l.16   "omnipotent": Rev 19:6 ("And I heard as it were the voice of a great multitude, and as the voice of many waters, and as the voice of mighty thunderings, saying, Alleluia: for the Lord God omnipotent reigneth"; the word is used only once in the KJV)

Comment: See *Poems*, II, 447-448.

586   **We talked as Girls do-**

l.3   "fair": Ca 1:8, 15-16; 2:10, 13; 4:1, 7, 10; 5:9; 6:1, 10; 7:6 (the Canticles word associated with the profane beloved of the circuit world)

l.3   "Grave": ICo 15:55 (the matter of death to which the Divine Beloved holds the keys, Rev 1:18; 3:7)

ll.5-8   "We...Authority": Job 34:13; 37:14-16; Pr 16:33

ll.11-12 "When...Degree": Ca 1:8; 5:9; 6:1 ("Degree" may suggest the sealed and crowned white-robed Bride of Christ, Rev 19:7-9; 21; 22:17)

ll.13-16 "We...night":   see   the   "Solemnization   of Matrimony," *Book of Common Prayer* ("To have and to hold from this day forward, for better for worse, for richer for poorer, in sickness and in health, to love and to cherish, till death us do part")

Comment: See *Poems*, II, 448-449.

587   **Empty my Heart, of Thee-**

ll.1,3,10,11 "Thee": see note, line eight, sixteen, P537

l.1   "Heart": Ca 4:9 ("Thou hast ravished my heart, my sister, my spouse; thou hast ravished my heart with one of thine eyes, with one chain of thy neck")

588   **I cried at Pity- not at Pain-**

l.1   "I...Pity": Ps 69:20 ("Reproach hath broken my heart; and I am full of heaviness: and I looked for some to take pity, but there was none; and for comforters, but I found none")

ll.11-12 "Heaven...Gold": Rev 21:18, 21

l.16   "Had...differently": Eph 1:5

Comment: See *Poems*, II, 450-451.

589   The Night was wide, and furnished scant

l.20   "Thee": see note, lines eight, sixteen, P537

590   Did you ever stand in a Cavern's Mouth-

l.11   "Judgment": Heb 9:27; IJo 4:17; Rev 20

l.12   "The...'die' ": Heb 9:27 ("And as it is appointed unto men once to die, but after this the judgment")

591   To interrupt His Yellow Plan

ll.9-11 " 'Tis...place": Job 26:7-9 ("He stretcheth out the north over the empty place, and hangeth the earth upon nothing. He bindeth up the waters in his thick clouds; and the cloud is not rent under them. He holdeth back the face of his throne, and spreadeth his cloud upon it")

ll.15-16 "emits...justify": Job 26:14; 40:9

592   What care the Dead, for Chanticleer-

l.1   "Chanticleer": Ca 1:1; 2:12 (Chanticleer is a metonym for the Song of Songs, Canticles, and the profane beloved and love itself there celebrated)

l.2   "Day": Ca 3:11; 8:8

l.3   "Sunrise": Ca 2:17; 4:6

l.4   "Purple": see note, line one, P15

l.4   "Morning": Ca 6:10

l.9   "Summer": Ca 2:11-13

ll.12-16 "And...be": Ca 2:12 (the song of Chanticleer is at the reach of the circuit world imagination)

l.20   "As...Breeze": Ca 4:16

l.21   "Cinnamon": Ca 4:14

l.24　"Spices": Ca 4:10, 14, 16; 5:1, 13; 6:2; 8:2, 14
Comment: See *Poems*, II, 453-454.

593　I think I was enchanted

ll.4-8　"The...tell": Joh 1:1-18 (the impact of Elizabeth Barrett Browning is spoken of in terms of grace, conversion, sanctification, and the traditional imagery of dark and light)
l.7　"Light": Joh 1:9; IJo 1:5 (see also P435, "Much Madness is divinest Sense")
l.8　"I...tell": IICo 12:2 ("whether in the body, I cannot tell; or whether out of the body, I cannot tell: God knoweth")
l.19　"Jubilee": Le 25:8-17 ("Jubilee," inaugurated by silver trumpets in the "fiftieth year, and proclaim[ing] liberty throughout all the land," becomes a metaphor for personal redemption, for the emancipatory effects of Elizabeth Barrett Browning's poetry)
l.22　"Conversion": Mt 18:3; Ac 3:19; 15:3; Jas 5:19-20
l.22　"Mind": Ro 12:2; Php 2:5
l.23　"Like...Soul": Ac 20:32; 26:18; ICo 1:2; 6:11; IITi 2:21; IPe 1:1-5; 3:15 (accession to a religio-aesthetic status via a grace from without is spoken of metaphorically in terms of conversion and sanctification)
ll.25-26　" 'Twas...Sane": Joh 8:48-52; 10:20 (the charge of madness was directed against Jesus Christ; see note, line seven above)
l.29　"solid Witchcraft": Ex 22:18; ISa 15:23; 28:7-14; IIKi 9:22 (disreputable witchcraft exemplified by Jezebel and the Witch of Endor was familiar to the poet from the KJV; here the KJV itself and the poetry of Elizabeth Barrett Browning would qualify as "solid Witchcraft")
Comment: See *Poems*, II, 454-455.

594　The Battle fought between the Soul

l.1　"The...Soul": Ro 7:18-25; ICo 9:24-27; IICo 10:3-5; ITi 1:18; IITi 2:3-4; 4:7-8; Eph 6:10-18 (St. Paul frequently uses military metaphors for spiritual warfare)
l.2　"No Man": Eph 6:12 ("For we wrestle not against flesh and blood, but against principalities, against powers, against the rulers of the darkness of this world, against spiritual wickedness in high places"); ITi 6:16; IJo 4:12 (metaphorically, "No Man" may

suggest that "flesh and blood" that cannot inherit the kingdom of the invisible God, ICo 15:50; ITi 1:17; Heb 11:27—that is, by extension, the body prison of the circuit world with all its distractions, deprivations, attractions, and limitations)

ll.6-8   "It's...Unknown": IITi 4:7-8 ("I have fought a good fight, I have finished my course, I have kept the faith: Henceforth there is laid up for me a crown of righteousness, which the Lord, the righteous judge, shall give me at that day: and not to me only, but unto all them also that love his appearing")

l.10   "Legions": Mr 5:9; Lu 8:30 ("And Jesus asked him, saying, What is thy name? And he said, Legion: because many devils were entered into him")

595   Like Mighty Foot Lights- burned the Red

l.1   "Red": see note, line one, P15

ll.6-8   "While...God": Rev 22:4 (Sunset, as the terminus ad quem of life's penurious round and the terminus a quo for the new circumference of eternity, is a displacement for the face of God, ideal presence and vision)

596   When I was small, a Woman died-

l.4   "His...Victory": Isa 25:8; ICo 15:54-55
l.9   "Paradise": Lu 23:43; IICo 12:4; Rev 2:7
ll.17-19 "I'm...Braveries": Rev 19:1-6; 21:7
l.20   "Yonder/Scarlet": see note, line one, P15
Comment: See *Poems*, II, 457-458.

597   It always felt to me- a wrong

ll.1-24   "It...Thee": De 32:48-52 ("And the Lord spake unto Moses that selfsame day, saying, Get thee up into this mountain Abarim, unto mount Nebo, which is in the land of Moab, that is over against Jericho; and behold the land of Canaan, which I give unto the children of Israel for a possession: And die in the mount whither thou goest up, and be gathered unto thy people; as Aaron thy brother died in mount Hor, and was gathered unto his people: Because ye trespassed against me among the children of Israel at the waters of Meribah-Kadesh, in the wilderness of Zin; because ye sanctified me not in the midst of the children of Israel. Yet thou shalt see the land before thee; but thou shalt not go thither unto the land which I give the children of Israel")

l.2   "Moses": Ex 2-4 (the leader of the Israelites during the Exodus from Egyptian bondage and the sojourn in the Wilderness)

l3   "Canaan": Ge 12:5-7; 13:14-18; 17:8 (ancient Palestine, the promised land of the Israelites)

l.10   "Stephen": Ac 7:59; 8:2; 22:20 (the first Christian martyr who was stoned to death)

l.10   "Paul": Ac 7:58-28 (the Book of Acts connects St. Paul with Stephen and gives the bulk of information known about his life; according to tradition, St. Paul suffered martyrdom by beheading during persecutions of Christians by the Roman emperor, Claudius Caesar Nero)

l.18   "Tribes": Nu 26 (along the lines of these social organizations, Canaan was divided into twelve territories; see the entire Book of Joshua)

l.20   "Pentateuchal": Ge-De (the Pentateuch, or Five Books of Moses, is Genesis, Exodus, Leviticus, Numbers, and Deuteronomy)

l.20   "Robes": Ex 28:39 (the poet may have associated the robe spoken of in Exodus with the patriarchal enjoyment of God's presence, thus anticipating the robes of Revelation, Rev 6:11; 7:9, 13-14; 19:8)

l.23   "Nebo": Nu 32:38; 33:47 (one of the mountains of Abarim near the mouth of the Jordan River where Moses died after blessing his people and looking into the promised land)

Comment: See *Poems*, II, 458-459.

598   Three times- we parted-Breath- and I-

ll.1,2,5 "Three times": Mt 12:40 ("For as Jonas was three days and three nights in the whale's belly; so shall the Son of man be three days and three nights in the heart of the earth"); Mt 17:23; Mr 10:34; Lu 24:46; Ac 10:40

l.7   "Blue": see note, line one, P15

ll.15-16 "Then...lived": ICo 15:50-55 (a Hitchcockian emblem of the resurrection)

Comment: See *Poems*, II, 459.

599   There is a pain- so utter-

l.2   "It...up": IICo 5:4 ("For we that are in this tabernacle do groan, being burdened: not for that we would be unclothed, but clothed upon, that mortality might be swallowed up of life"); for verbal echoes see also Job 5:5

l.3   "Abyss": Ge 1:2

l.8   "Bone...Bone": Ge 2:23 ("Bone" is a synecdoche for the body, for circuit world consciousness imprisoned in flesh and dust, Ge 3:19; Ps 103:14)

600   It troubled me as once I was-

ll.1-2   "It...Child": ICo 13:11 ("When I was a child, I spake as a child, I understood as a child, I thought as a child: but when I became a man, I put away childish things")

ll.6,16   "Blue": see note, line one, P15

Comment: See *Poems*, II, 460-461.

601   A still- Volcano- Life-

ll.1-12   "A...away": IIPe 3:10; Rev 6:12-17; 8:5-12; 16:18-21; 18:21; 21:8 (the imagery of volcanic flickering, earthquake, hissing sea, and melting cities suggests the apocalyptic, its cataclysmic phenomena here adapted to give—along with the oxymorons—a portentous quality to "still Volcano life")

Comment: See *Poems*, II, 461.

603   He found my Being- set it up-

l.3   "Then...it": Rev 14:1

l.4   "And...East": Mt 24:27

l.5   "Be faithful": Rev 2:10

l.6   "And...again": Joh 14:2-3 ("In my Father's house are many mansions: if it were not so, I would have told you. I go to prepare a place for you. And if I go and prepare a place for you, I will come again, and receive you unto myself; that where I am, there ye may be also")

l.7 "With...Amber": Eze 1:4, 27-28; 8:2-4; Mt 25:31; Mr 13:26; Lu 21:27 ("Amber" is the visionary color associated with the glory of the Lord here manifested in the Parousia)

605 The Spider holds a Silver Ball

l.1 "The...Ball": Pr 30:28 ("The spider taketh hold with her hands, and is in kings' palaces")

l.2 "In...Hands": Job 10:8; Ps 8:3, 6; 102:25; 138:8

l.5 "He...Nought": Job 26:7 ("He stretcheth out the north over the empty place, and hangeth the earth upon nothing"); Heb 11:3 (ex nihilo creation is not explicitly spoken of in the canonical books of the KJV but is mentioned in the apocryphal II Maccabees 7:28, the heavens, earth, and man having been made by God not "out of things that existed")

l.10 "His...Light": Ge 1:3-4; Joh 1:1-9

ll.11-12 "dangle/perish...forgot": Job 34:13-15 ("Who hath given him a charge over the earth? or who hath disposed the whole world? If he set his heart upon man, if he gather unto himself his spirit and his breath; All flesh shall perish together, and man shall turn again unto dust"); Ps 104:24-32

Comment: See *Poems*, II, 464.

606 The Trees like Tassels- hit- and swung-

l.5 "Psalteries": 1Ch 25:1-6; IICh 5:11-14 (the psaltery is associated with songs of praise, celebration, and joy)

ll.6-7 "Ear...satisfy": Ec 1:8 ("the eye is not satisfied with seeing, nor the ear filled with hearing")

l.8 "fair": Ca 1:8, 15-16; 2:10, 13; 4:1, 7, 10; 5:9; 6:1, 10; 7:6

ll.10,14 "hid...view": Isa 45:15

ll.12-13 "Cloud...Him": Eze 1:4 ("a great cloud, and fire infolding itself, and a brightness was about it, and out of the midst thereof as the colour of amber, out of the midst of the fire"); Ex 16:10; 19:9; 34:5; 40:34-35; Job 22:14 (the clouds as coverings for the glory of God)

l.21 "Bright...Calyx": Ca 2:12

l.23 "Sweet": Ca 2:3, 14; 5:5, 13, 16; 7:9

l.24   "Spices": Ca 4:10, 14, 16; 5:13; 6:2; 8:2, 14 (the Canticles imagery has Edenic, paradisiacal connotations)

l.26   "to...see": Mt 13:13-17

Comment: See *Poems*, II, 464-465 and Franklin, I, 557-558.

607   Of nearness to her sundered Things

l.1   "sundered Things": Mt 19:6 ("Wherefore they are no more twain, but one flesh. What therefore God hath joined together, let not man put asunder"); see also the "Solemnization of Matrimony," *Book of Common Prayer* ("Those whom God hath joined together let no man put asunder")

ll.19-20 "they...mourned": Mt 5:4 ("Blessed are they that mourn: for they shall be comforted")

608   Afraid! Of whom am I afraid?

l.1   "Afraid...afraid": Ps 27:1 ("The Lord is my light and my salvation; whom shall I fear? The Lord is the strength of my life; of whom shall I be afraid?")

l.3   "The...Lodge": Mr 13:32-37

ll.7-8   "In...be/Deity decree": Rev 2:11; 20:5-6, 14; 21:8 (the first existence ends in death and resurrection; the second death is eternal damnation—eternal life apparently what the poet had in mind as the second existence)

l.8   "Just": Lu 14:14; Ac 3:14; 7:52; 22:14; Ro 3:26; Heb 2:2; Rev 15:3

l.9   "Of...East": ICo 15

ll.9-11   "East...forehead": Rev 14:1; 22:4 (the sunrise upon the face of "Morn" becomes a metaphor for the signature of God upon the forehead of the resurrected saint)

l.12   "As...Crown": Isa 62:3; ICo 9:25; IITi 4:8; IPe 5:4; Rev 2:10; 3:11; 4:4, 10

Comment: See *Poems*, II, 467.

609   I Years had been from Home

l.1   "I...Home": Lu 15:11-32 (the pariah situation parallels that of the prodigal son)

1.2 "Door": Rev 3:20 (the "Door" is, among other things, a metonym for the face of God and His judgment); Lu 23:39-43 (the "Door" is also the cross, the point of intersection between little circuit and new circumference where one thief is saved, one lost); Mt 25:1-13 (in the Parable of the Wise and Foolish Virgins, containing a situation in parallel to that of the two thieves on the cross, the foolish virgins have the door shut in their faces when the bridegroom insists, "I know you not")

ll.2-6 "And...there": Lu 13:25-28 (the unfamiliar "Face" of the Lord staring "stolid" is an expression of her trepidation regarding the potential unmeaning of the apocalyptic)

ll.7-8 " 'My'...'there' " Mt 25:11; Lu 23:42; Rev 3:20 (is there acceptance and recognition, that is, life or presence elsewhere, or is the door, like the whiteness of the whale in *Moby Dick,* a blank empty of content, a confirmation of absence at the heart of things?)

ll.23-24 "And...House": Lu 23:39-43 (acting the part of unworthy thief is here preferred to hearing a definite "Depart from me" or "Today shalt thou be with me in paradise"; compare P1180)

Comment: See *Poems,* II, 467-469 and Franklin, I, 457-458. See especially the redaction of a decade earlier.

610 You'll find- it when you try to die-

1.13 "fair": Ca 1:8, 15-16; 2:10, 13; 4:1, 7, 10; 5:9; 6:1, 10; 7:6

1.14 "Grace": Eph 2:8

611 I see thee better- in the Dark-

ll.1-4 "I...Violet": ICo 13:12; IICo 3:18 (the Divine Beloved is associated with light and the glass, the profane beloved with darkness and the prism)

ll.1,3,5,9,12 "Thee": see note, lines eight, sixteen, P537

1.2 "Light": Joh 1:7-9; IJo 1:5

1.3 "The...Thee": Ca 1:2-4, 9-10; 2; 4:1, 7, 10; 5; 6:3-4; 7:6

1.4 "Violet": see note, line one, P15 (the claim is hyperbolic since the color is associated with the presence of God)

1.12 "I...Thee": Ca 2:4

ll.13-16 "What...Meridian": Rev 21:23-25 (the "Dark" in the grave with the profane beloved surpasses the eternal "Day" of the New Jerusalem whose "Sun" is the Divine Beloved; in the grave the profane beloved is the sun at its zenith guaranteeing the perpetual day and ideal circumferentiality associated with the profane love spoken of)

l.14   "Sun": Ps 84:11; 89:36; Mal 4:2; Lu 1:78; IIPe 1:19; Rev 1:16; 2:28; 21:23; 22:5, 16

Comment: See *Poems*, II, 470 and P1666.

612   It would have starved a Gnat-

ll.1-5   "It...Claw": Mt 5:6 (the circuit world as epitomized by hunger-desire; see Rev 7:16)

l.8   "Dragon": Isa 27:1; Rev 20:2 (hunger is associated with the Fall, the loss of Eden, and the Devil or Satan)

613   They shut me up in Prose-

l.1   "They...Prose": Ro 7:24; IICo 5:4; Php 3:21 (the body prison is here the "Prose" of the circuit world and all the restrictions and limitations it entails)

l.3   "They...Closet": Joe 2:16

l.4   "Because...'still' ": ICo 14:34; ITi 2:11-12

l.11   "Captivity": Jg 5:12; Eph 4:8 (P613 is a Song of Deborah, a type of the Ascension)

614   In falling Timbers buried-

l.1   "In...buried": Ro 7:24; IICo 5:4; Php 3:21 (such premature burial is a metaphor for the body prison—that buried life or death-in-life—that is the circuit world)

l.11   "Oh": Ro 7:24

l.16   "Grace": Eph 2:8 (the rescue is a failure but the extrication from the circuit world is an unintended gift, here parallel to that of God's "Grace")

Comment: See Poems, II, 472-473.

615   Our journey had advanced-

l.7   "Cities": Rev 3:12; 21; 22:14, 19

l.11   "White": Rev 3:4-5, 18; 4:4; 6:11; 7:9, 13-14; 19:8, 14; 20:11 (the "White Flag" might be the pearl of which the twelve gates of the New Jerusalem are made, Rev 21:21)

l.12   "every Gate": Rev 21:12-15, 21, 25; 22:14

616   I rose- because he sank-

l.17   "Emperors": Rev 15:3; 17:14; 19:16

ll.18-19 "Who...true": Rev 2:10; 3:5, 12; 14:1-5, 12-13; 19:1-17

Comment: See *Poems*, II, 473-474.

617   Dont put up my Thread & Needle-

ll.5-6   "These...plain": Isa 40:4 ("Every valley shall be exalted, and every mountain and hill shall be made low: and the crooked shall be made straight, and the rough places plain")

ll.7-9   "I'll...tracing": Rev 3:18; 6:11; 7:9, 13-14; 19:8 (the perfected garment is the white raiment of the sealed and crowned elect, her uniform as Bride of Christ and synonymous with her perfected art; "sowing"—a metaphor for her religio-aesthetic commitment as artist—has preparationist echoes in P617, Isa 40:1-11; see P1138 and, for what Edward Taylor called the "Robe of Evangelicall Righteousness," Mt 22:11-12)

l.12   "Like...Dot": Mt 5:18 (the use of alphabet as metaphor here suggests that ideal circumferentiality anticipating Rev 22:4—that is, she is achieving identity by crowning herself via print)

ll.15-16 "zigzag...strong": Isa 40:4 (see above quotation, "Straight" in the KJV has moral and apocalyptic reverberations, Isa 40:3; Mt 3:3; Mr 1:3; Lu 3:4; Joh 1:23; Heb 12:13)

l.19   "at...sleeping": ICo 15:20, 51; ITh 4:13-17 (for those who "sleep in Jesus" the "sowing" done in springtime is preparation for resurrection; thus, the use of "Sow" in the poem may echo St. Paul's organic metaphors, ICo 15:36-37, 42-44—perhaps deliberate on the poet's part and not a mistake as Johnson suggests, *Poems*, II, 475)

620   It makes no difference abroad-

l.8   "Calvary": Lu 23:33

l.9   "Judgment": IICo 5:10; IIPe 3:7; IJo 4:17; Jude 6; Rev 14:7; 15:4; 18:10; 20

l.11   "Rose": Ca 2:1 (the beauty and ideal circumferentiality of the rose suggest the profane beloved perfectly adapted to the ministrations of the bee)

621   I asked no other thing-

ll.1-3   "I...it": Mr 8:36-37 ("For what shall it profit a man, if he shall gain the whole world, and lose his own soul? Or what shall a man give in exchange for his own soul?"; the speaker has given up this circuit world and all it entails for an assurance that dispossession, disaffiliation, loss, separation, and absence will no longer be suffered in the presence and possession of "Brazil")

l.4   "The...sneered": Mt 13:45 ("Again, the kingdom of heaven is like unto a merchant man, seeking goodly pearls: Who, when he had found one pearl of great price, went and sold all that he had, and bought it"; the speaker conceives of God as a Shylock hoarding treasure—see note, line thirteen, P223 and line twenty two, P247; for KJV commercial language see Mt 20:28; Mr 10:45; Ac 20:28; ICo 6:20; 7:23; 10:33; 12:7; 13:3; Eph 1:14; ITi 2:6; 4:8; Heb 12:10; IIPe 2:1; Rev 3:18)

l.5   "Brazil": Rev 21("Brazil" as metaphorically a gem may suggest the New Jerusalem and the allied idea of bridal accession, which is associated with gems and jewels: Isa 61:10; 62:3-4; Eze 16:10-12; Mal 3:17; Rev 21; see also note, line fifteen, P191)

622   To know just how He suffered- would be dear-

l.4   "Paradise": Lu 23:43; IICo 12:4; Rev 2:7
l.5   "patient...content": ITi 6:6-12
l.26   "Eternity": Isa 57:15; Rev 21-22

623   It was too late for Man-

l.3   "Creation...help": Isa 65:17; IIPe 3:13; Rev 21:1, 5 (as with Arnold in "Stanzas from the Grand Chartreuse," the speaker is "Wandering between two worlds, one dead,/The other powerless to be born")

ll.4-8 "But...God": Mt 6:9-13 (the speaker ironically echoes The Lord's Prayer, its words generally the only "hospitable face" God reveals, this latter only because of her bold insinuation of familiarity)

624   Forever- is composed of Nows-

ll.1-12 "Forever...Dominies": Rev 10:6 ("And sware by him that liveth for ever and ever, who created heaven, and the things that therein are, and the earth, and the things that therein are, and the sea, and the things which are therein, that there should be time no longer")
l.24   "Anno Dominies": Isa 61:2; Lu 4:19

625   'Twas a long Parting- but the time

l.3   "Before...God": Mt 27:19; Joh 19:13; Ro 14:10; IICo 5:10; Rev 20:4, 11-15
l.4   "The...time": Rev 20:6 ("on such the second death hath no power")
l.5   "Fleshless": ICo 15:50 ("Now this I say, brethren, that flesh and blood cannot inherit the kingdom of God; neither doth corruption inherit incorruption")
ll.6-12   "A...now": ICo 13:12; Rev 22:4 (the earthly lovers are now apotheosized by a reciprocated "Gaze" in language suggesting the beatific vision)
l.10   "Appareled...new": Rev 2:10; 3:4-5, 11-12, 18; 4:4, 10; 6:11; 7; 14:1-5; 19:7-9; 21 (the seal, white crown and white robe apparel the "new")
ll.11-12 "Unborn...born": Joh 3:3-8 (the language of spiritual rebirth is here adapted)
ll.13-16 "Was...Guest": Rev 19:7-9; 21-22 (the background of Bride of Christ and Bridegroom at the Marriage Supper of the Lamb heightens the significance of this "Bridal" with Heaven itself as host and angelic beings as guests)
l.15   "Cherubim," "Seraphim": Ge 3:24; Ex25:18-22; Isa 6:2, 6; Eze 28:14; Heb 9:5 (members of the celestial hierarchy present at the "Bridal"; as guests these angels and the "Host," along with the Bride and Groom, comprise counterparts to the dramatis personae in the Parable of the Marriage Feast, Mt 22:1-14, a "Bridal" typic of the Marriage Supper of the Lamb)

626   Only God- detect the Sorrow-

l.1   "Sorrow": Isa 53:3-4
l.3   "Jehovahs": Ex 6:3; Ps 83:18; Isa 12:2; 26:4 (there may here be Biblical wit either because of the permutations in the name in the KJV—Ge 22:14; Ex17:15; Jg 6:24—or because of the shortening of Jehovah to JAH, Ps 68:4)
ll.1,2,4,5,7 "God," "Son," "Spirit's": IJo 5:7 ("For there are three that bear record in heaven, the Father, the Word, and the Holy Ghost: and these three are one")

627   The Tint I cannot take- is best-

ll.7-8   "Like...sky": see note, line one, P15 (if the reference is to *Antony and Cleopatra*, II,ii, then the "impalpable Array" contains a refined distillation of the colors of the vail associated with God's presence as mediated through "Color" in nature)
l.9   "Moments...Dominion": Ps 145:13; Da 4:3, 34; 6:26; 7:13-14; IPe 5:11; Jude 25; Rev 1:6 (the everlasting dominion of the Deity contrasts with the momentary epiphanic awareness of "Dominion" in the circuit world)
l.16   "Chariots": IIKi 2:11 (a "chariot of fire" conveyed Elijah from the "little circuit" to the "new circumference," just as the tints of nature push the eye beyond natural facts); Ca 3:9-10 (see the variant "Columns—in the Breast")
ll.18-19 "Snow," "Tulle/Blonde": Rev 3:4-5, 18; 4:4; 6:11; 7:9, 13-14; 19:8, 14 (the natural fact of snow may signify the spiritual fact of Revelation white, the absence of color bespeaking the presence of God)
l.22   "Cheated Eye": Ec 1:8; ICo 13:12; Heb 11:3; IJo 3:2
Comment: See *Poems*, II, 482.

628   They called me to the Window, for

l.3   "Sapphire": Ex 28:18; 39:11; Ca 5:14; Isa 54:11; Eze 28:13; Rev 21:19 (see also note, line fifteen, P191 and for the variant "Amber" see note, line one, P15 and Eze 1:4, 27; 8:2)
ll.5-6   "Cattle...Hill": Ps 50:10 ("For every beast of the forest is mine, and the cattle upon a thousand hills")

l.13 "This...away": Ps 19:1-3 ("The heavens declare the glory of God; and the firmament sheweth his handywork. Day unto day uttereth speech, and night unto night sheweth knowledge. There is no speech nor language, where there voice is not heard")

629 I watched the Moon around the House

l.1 "I...House": Ca 6:10 (the moon is approached as the profane beloved, an attempt at domestication by the romantic imagination)

ll.4-8 "I...upon": Ca 6:13 ("Return, return, O Shulamite; return, return, that we may look upon thee")

ll.11-12 "Like...she": Ca 5:10-16; 7:1-6 (the speaker wishes to capture the moon in a Canticles inventory of the profane beloved, a "Formula")

l.13 "Head": Ca 2:6; 5:2, 11; 7:5; 8:3

l.15 "Amber": Eze 1:4, 27; 8:2 (see also the golden color associated with the vail, note, line one, P15; "Amber," as also "Blue" in the final line, gives testimony to the self-contained existence of the moon, an ideally circumferential, disembodied essence "engrossed to Absolute" and thus provoking the Gnostic envy of the speaker)

l.17 "Flower": Ca 2:1-2, 12, 16; 4:5; 5:13; 6:2-3; 7:2

l.21 "No Hunger": Ca 1:7; 2:16; 4:5; 6:2-3 (the disembodied moon transcends circuit world appetite as well as deprivation, Mt 5:6)

ll.24-26 "For...Nay": Ec 6:12

ll.27-28 "engrossed...shining": Rev 22:4 (the "Moon" in relationship to the "Absolute" or sun symbolizes the beatific vision)

l.36 "Or...Blue": see note, line one, P15 ("engrossed to Absolute," the "Moon," enjoying that ideal presence with bodiless self-possession, is a reminder of the circumscription of circuit world imagination, the distance between "around the House" and "superior Road")

630 The Lightning playeth- all the while-

ll.1-2 "The...then": Job 37:2-5 ("Hear attentively the noise of his voice, and the sound that goeth out of his mouth. He directeth it under the whole heaven, and his lightning unto the ends of the earth. After it a voice roareth: he thundereth with the voice of his excellency;

and he will not stay them when his voice is heard. God thundereth marvellously with his voice; great things doeth he, which we cannot comprehend")

     l.11   "Nor...speech": Job 37:14, 19-20

     l.12   "cross Ourselves": Joh 19:17, 19, 25, 31 (a cruciform gesture of obeisance, its form imitating the configuration of the cross of the Crucifixion)

631   Ourselves were wed one summer- dear-

     l.1   "Ourselves...dear": Ca 2:10-17

     l.8   "I...Sign": Ca 8:6 ("Set me as a seal upon thine heart, as a seal upon thine arm")

     l.13   " 'Tis...Bloom": Ca 4:12 ("A garden inclosed is my sister, my spouse"); Ca 5:1 ("I am come into my garden, my sister, my spouse")

     l.15   "Queens": Ca 6:8-9

     ll.15-16 "And...June": Ca 3:11 ("Go forth, O ye daughters of Zion, and behold king Solomon with the crown wherewith his mother crowned him in the day of his espousals, and in the day of the gladness of his heart"; there is in Canticles the equation of espousal and coronation)

633   When Bells stop ringing- Church- begins-

     ll.3-4   "Circumference...Wheels": Eze 1; 10 (the visions of Ezekiel use wheel imagery here adapted in Dante-like fashion to speak of eternity as the ideally circumferential); Da 7:9

634   You'll know Her- by Her Foot-

     l.26   "Threnodies/Extacies...Pearl": Rev 21:21 (for "Extasies" see note, line fifteen, P783 and notes, lines five and eight, P1191)

     Comment: See Poems, II, 487-488.

636   The Way I read a Letter's- this-

     l.16   "The...bestow": Rev 2:7; 21:1-7, 21-27; 22:1-5

637   **The Child's faith is new-**

1.1   "The...new": Mr 10:14-15 ("Suffer the little children to come unto me, and forbid them not: for of such is the kingdom of God. Verily I say unto you, Whosoever shall not receive the kingdom of God as a little child, he shall not enter therein"); Mt 18:3-4; Lu 18:16-17

1.8   "Paradise": Lu 23:43; IICo 12:4; Rev 2:7; 21-22

ll.10-16 "Deems...All": Mt 22:17-22; Joh 19:15

638   **To my small Hearth His fire came-**

ll.1-2   "To...aglow": see note, line one, P724 and note, line one, P1142 (the metaphor of the individual as the home or habitation of God is frequently used in the KJV)

1.3   "light": Joh 1:4-9; IJo 1:5

1.4   "Sunrise": Ps 84:11; 89:36; Mal 4:2; Lu 1:78; IIPe 1:19; Rev 1:16; 2:28; 21:23; 22:5, 16

ll.5-6   "Impanelled...Decay": Rev 21:4, 23-25; 22:1-5 (in the New Jerusalem there is no death nor seasonal change)

1.7   " 'Twas...Night": Rev 21:25 ("And the gates of it shall not be shut at all by day: for there shall be no night there"; for "Noon" see note, line one. P533)

1.8   "Nay...Day": Rev 21:5 (see also note, line nine, P830 and Ca 3:11 where the day of espousal is "typic" of the day of the advent of the Divine Beloved)

Comment: See *Poems*, II, 490-491.

640   **I cannot live with You-**

ll.1-2   "I...Life": Ro 7:24; IICo 5:4; Php 3:21 (the tortuous logic that hope is despair and despair hope, that life is death and death life, that presence is absence and absence presence is the rationalization—however paradox-riddled and anguished—for her post-"White Election" stalemate)

ll.3-4   "And...Shelf": Rev 2:7, 10; 21:6; 22:1-5 ("Life" is reserved for a fleshless, sexless, disembodied state)

1.5   "The...to": Rev 1:18; 3:7 (it is the Divine Beloved who holds the keys of heaven and hell, life and death)

l.7   "His Porcelain": Rev 3:4-5, 18; 6:11; 7; 14:1-5; 19:7-9 ("Porcelain" is a metonym for all the white of Revelation: the virginal firstfruits before the throne of God, the sealed elect of the seventh chapter, the Bride of Christ, and, generally speaking, all the sealed, crowned, white-robed saved)

ll.22-24 "Because...Grace": Rev 22:4

l.29   "They'd...How": Rev 20:13

l.30   "served...Heaven": Ex 20:3-6; Mt 4:10 (the speaker is self-consciously aware of the proscription regarding idolatry)

l.36   "Paradise": Rev 2:7; 21-22

l.37   "And...lost": Rev 20:15; 21:8

ll.38-40 "Though...fame": Rev 3:5; 13:8; 17:8; 21:27 (the names of the saved are written in the Lamb's Book of Life)

ll.41-44 "And...Me": Rev 21:7-8 (see *Paradise Lost*, IX.830-833; XII.617-618)

l.49   "White": Rev 2:17; 3:4-5, 18; 6:11; 7:9, 13-14; 19:8, 11, 14; 20:11 (the oxymoronic language describes graphically her actual condition—door ajar, dressed in white, despairing of the profane beloved—and yet the austere parameters of the apocalyptic mapped out in P640 are a "Sustenance" for her as palpable as manna in the Wilderness or the elements of the Eucharist)

643   I could suffice for Him, I knew-

l.5   " 'Would'...broached": Joh 5:5-6 ("And a certain man was there, which had an infirmity thirty and eight years. When Jesus saw him lie, and knew that he had been now a long time in that case, he saith unto him, Wilt thou be made whole?")

l.8   " 'Twas...God": Ge 32:30; Ex 33:11; ICo 13:12; Rev 22:4

644   You left me- Sire- two Legacies-

ll.1-4   "You...of": Mt 22:37-39; Joh 3:16; 15:8-14; Ro 5:8; IJo 4 (the Canticles "Sweet" is a variant for "Sire" suggesting Christ or the Divine Beloved whose legacies include love and Passion-Calvary)

ll.5-8   "You...Me": Isa 53:3-4 ("He is despised and rejected of men...Surely he hath borne our griefs, and carried our sorrows: yet we did esteem him stricken, smitten of God, and afflicted"); Mt 26-27

(the second legacy is that of the Passion Christ, a legacy of pain and anguish)

645   Bereavement in their death to feel

ll.6-7   "There...friends": ICo 15:54-55

646   I think To Live- may be a Bliss

l.1   "I...Bliss": Php 1:21 ("For me to live is Christ, and to die is gain"; again, as in P640, the speaker views life as elsewhere)
ll.13-16 "No...Doom": Rev 21:4
ll.17-18 "But...Mind": Rev 22:1-5 (interestingly enough, the vision of life with the beloved borrows from the New Jerusalem)
l.28   "Thee": see note, lines eight, sixteen, P537
Comment: See *Poems*, II, 497-498.

647   A little Road- not made of Man-

l.1   "A...Man": IICo 5:1 ("For we know that if our earthly house of this tabernacle were dissolved, we have a building of God, an house not made with hands, eternal in the heavens")
l.2   "Enabled...Eye": Isa 64:4; ICo 2:9
l.3   "Accessible...Bee": see P1254 ("Elijah's wagon knew no thill," IIKi 2:11)
l.6   " 'Tis...say": IICo 12:2-3 ("whether in the body, or out of the body, I cannot tell: God knoweth")
Comment: See *Poems*, II, 498.

648   Promise This- When You be Dying-

ll.3,4,9,17,25 "Mine": Ca 2:16; 6:3 ("My beloved is mine, and I am his: he feedeth among the lilies")
l.4   "Mine...Eye": Ca 4:9; 8:10
l.7   "Be...Buckle": Ca 4:3, 11; 5:13; 7:9
ll.18-20 "To...Morn": Ca 4:16; 5:2; 6:10
l.21   "To...favor": Ca 8:10
ll.22-24 "Lest...face": Ca 8:6 ("for love is strong as death; jealousy is cruel as the grave")

ll.25-26 "Mine...be": Isa 7:14; Mt 1:18, 23 (the Virgin Mary, Mother of Jesus)

l.29   "Just...feature": Ca 2:14 ("let me see thy countenance...for sweet is thy voice, and thy countenance is comely")

ll.31-33 "For...been/glories...denied/gained": Php 3:7; Mt 25:31; Mr 13:26; Lu 21:27; 24:26; Joh 1:14; Ac 7:55-56; Col 3:4; ITh 2:12; ITi 3:16; IPe 5:1, 4; Jude 24-25; Rev 1:6 (the gain of Heaven is the Divine Beloved, its chief glory, all of which the poet inverts in favor of the profane beloved)

Comment: See *Poems*, II, 498-500 and Franklin, II, 821-823. Johnson pointed out the unfinished state of the text, "beyond editorial reconstruction." The present line twenty-nine may be a variant for line twenty-seven, thus regularizing the stanzaic pattern—the final lines of such a reconstructed stanza seven being a request that she be substituted for Christ in beholding the countenance of the beloved in obvious imitation of the beatific vision, Rev 22:4.

649   Her Sweet turn to leave the Homestead

l.1   "Sweet": Ca 2:3, 14; 5:5, 13, 16; 7:9 (the Canticles term is here applied to death)

l.3   "Guests-True": Mt 22:10 (the funeral is spoken of in bridal terms)

ll.9-12 "Never...indeed": Isa 61:10; 62:3-4; Rev 19:7-9; 21; 22:4 (the kinsmen, the dead, and the farewell salute with garland are displacements suggesting bridal accession with seal and crown, the name of the Groom upon the forehead, and, finally, the beatific vision itself)

l.11   "fair": Ca 1:8, 15-16; 2:10, 13; 4:1, 7, 10; 5:9; 6:1, 10; 7:6

l.13   "Fitter...us": Ca 7:1

l.15   "Lily": Ca 2:1-2 16; 4:5; 5:13; 6:2-3; 7:2

l.17   "Of...Her": "The Solemnization of Matrimony," *Book of Common Prayer* (the bride is given to the groom by the father, the latter here a displacement for the Heavenly Father)

l.19   "Palm": Ca 7:7-8

l.25   "Crystal Angle": ICo 13:12 (a metonym for circuit world vision, its glass or lens enabled by refracted light; it is also possible that the "Crystal Angle," or its variant "limit," is a specific reference to the crystal river of life before the throne of God in the

New Jerusalem, a "Crystal limit" that must be passed to achieve the beatific vision, Rev 22:1-4)

ll.25,27 "He": Isa 61:10; 62:5; Mt 22:2; 25:1, 5-6, 10; Joh 3:29; Rev 19:7-9; 21:2, 9 (the Bridegroom who has asked for her of "Her Father")

l.28   "Paradise": Lu 23:43; IICo 12:4; Rev 2:7; 21-22 (the "Equal Paradise" may be the beatific vision, Rev 22:4)

Comment: See *Poems*, II, 500-501 and Franklin, II, 817-819.

650   Pain- has an Element of Blank-

ll.3-4   "When...not": Pr 8:22-30; Joh 1:1-3; 17:5; IJo 1:1-2 (like wisdom or the Word itself, "Pain" is conceived as coeternal with God)

651   So much Summer

l.8   "Look...know": Ca 2:9; 4:8; 6:10, 13 (the request is for a "Look" from the beloved)

l.9   "Crumb": Mt 15:27; Mr 7:28; Lu 16:21 (the image is associated with her beggar persona and her Beatitudes philosophy of deprivation)

652   A Prison gets to be a friend-

l.1   "A...friend": Ro 7:24; IICo 5:4; Php 3:21 (the body prison; for the circuit world as entombment, premature burial, or imprisonment see P470, P510, and P640 and for the One who holds the keys of heaven and hell, life and death: Isa 22:22; Mt 16:19; Rev 1:18; 3:7; 20:1)

l.6   "appointed": ICo 4:9; IITi 1:11; Heb 1:2; 3:2; 9:27; IPe 2:8 (the word is used to suggest an inescapable, ineluctable destiny; the appointed measure of light and food as proscriptions of the "shaven" life of the circuit world indicate that the "Ponderous face" of the "Prison" is God's face revealed piecemeal, through apertures as it were, since "no man hath seen God at any time," IJo 4:12)

ll.7-8   "It...same": Mt 5:6 (the regnant condition of the circuit world is that deprivation or destitution spoken of in the Beatitudes, translated into the unabated imaginative desire of her religio-aesthetic discipline)

l.12   "sweet": Ca 2:3, 14; 5:5, 13, 16; 7:9 (the Canticles word is used for its Edenic connotations)

l.17   "Posture...Key": see note, line one above (what Blake termed "mind forg'd manacles," the translation of the "Prison" into the heart, mind, and soul)

ll.26-27 "Hope," "Content": Ro 8:24-25; ICo 13:7, 13; Php 4:11; ITi 6:6; Heb 6:18; 13:5 (the Paulinian lexicon may here be used sardonically)

Comment: See *Poems*, II, 503-504 and Franklin, I, 483-485.

654   A long- long Sleep- A famous- Sleep-

l.1   "A...Sleep": ICo 15:51; ITh 4:14-18
l.8   "Nor...Noon": Lu 21:28; Ro 8:19, 23
l.8   "Noon": Rev 4:8; 7:15; 21:25; 22:5 (the Biblical wit of P654 may rest upon the fact of the absence of night or sleep in the New Jerusalem and the insouciance of the "independent One"; see note, line one, P533)

655   Without this- there is nought-

ll.1-2   "nought...Riches": Rev 18:17 (the echoes are verbal)
l.5   "I...care": Mt 13:22 ("He also that received seed among the thorns is he that heareth the word; and the care of this world, and the deceitfulness of riches, choke the word, and he becometh unfruitful"); Mr 4:19; Lu 8:14
ll.5-6   "gain...Whole": Mt 16:26 ("For what is a man profited, if he shall gain the whole world, and lose his own soul? or what shall a man give in exchange for his soul?"); Mr 8:36; Lu 9:25 (the commitment to the kingdom is total costing family, possessions, and, finally, this circuit world life itself; thus, the "this" of line one is her religio-aesthetic equivalent: the total commitment to her art)

656   The name- of it- is "Autumn"-

ll.2,8.10,11 "Blood," "Scarlet," "ruddy," "Rose," "Vermillion": see note, line one P15 (as a nature epiphany poem, P656 uses the colors of the vail to suggest mediated presence)
l.12   "Wheels": Eze 1; 10; Da 7:9 (the associations are with visionary transcendence—loosely speaking, the glory of the Lord

is mediated by nature, an epiphany eddying away upon the ideally circumferential "Wheels")
Comment: See *Poems*, II, 506.

657   I dwell in Possibility

l.1   "I...Possibility": IISa 7:2; ICh 17:1 ("I dwell in an house of cedar"; these words of David to Nathan are echoed in the poet's contention that "Nature" is a haunted house, but art a house that tries to be haunted")
ll.2,9   "fairer," "fairest": Ca 1:8, 15-16; 2:10, 13; 4:1, 7, 10; 5:9; 6:1, 10; 7:6
l.2   "House": Ca 1:17; 2:4; 3:4; 8:2, 7 (the house of poetry is that of the profane beloved, the circuit world surrogate for the House of God constructed by King David)
l.5   "Chambers": Ca 1:4; 3:4
l.5   "Cedars": Ca 1:17; 8:9
l.12   "gather": Ca 5:1; 6:2
l.12   "Paradise": Lu 23:43; IICo 12:4; Rev 2:7; 21-22 (see also IICo 5:1:"For we know that if our earthly house of this tabernacle were dissolved, we have a building of God, an house not made with hands, eternal in the heavens")

658   Whole Gulfs- of Red, and Fleets- of Red-

ll.1-2   "Red," "Blood": see note, line one, P15 and P656, a cognate nature epiphany poem
l.4   "As...Ground": Ex 3:5
l.5   "appointed Creatures": Ge 1:20-21, 24; 2:19; Ps 104:19; Pr 8:29; Ro 1:25 (the KJV language underscores the decreed display of the sunset by the Creator)
l.6   "Arrays": Mt 6:29; Lu 12:27 (again the language is intended to underscore the sunset as the garment of God, in the Carlylean sense, a signal of the invasion of the circuit world by the transcendent)
l.7   "Due...Drama": Le 16 (it is perhaps remotely possible that the poet had in mind the ritual sacrifice of the Old Testament—the sunset associated with the transition from day to night "typic" of death; a sacramental reading of sunset would then have as background Old and New Testament resonances: the animal sacrifice

undertaken by the high priest in the holy place of the tabernacle would connect with the vicarious atonement affirmed through the crucifixion and resurrection of Christ, Heb 9:24: "For Christ is not entered into the holy places made with hands, which are the figures of the true; but into heaven itself, now to appear in the presence of God for us")

659   That first Day, when you praised Me, Sweet,

l.1   "first Day": Ca 3:11; 8:8 (the day of espousal, of bridal accession, Isa 61:10; 62:3-4; Mal 3:17; Rev 19:7-9; 21)
l.1   "Sweet": Ca 2:3, 14; 5:5, 13, 16; 7:9
ll.2-3   "And...mighty": Ps 24:8 ("Who is this King of glory? The Lord strong and mighty, the Lord mighty in battle")
ll.5-6   "Glows...Golds": Ca 1:10-11; 3:10; 5:11, 14-15; Isa 61:10; 62:3-4; Eze 16:10-13; Mal 3:17; Rev 19:7-9; 21 (the language of jewels and gold is associated with bridal accession, metaphorical for her religio-aesthetic commitment)

660   'Tis good- the looking back on Grief-

l.1   " 'Tis good": Ge 1:4, 10, 12, 18, 21, 25, 31 ("it was good" is the Creation refrain, here used with the tense fittingly changed and with sardonic boldness; the language of P660 is elemental: "Day," "Grass," "Summer," "Sea," and "Water"—all from Genesis, chapter one; such a world "conceived by Joy" is remembered in "Grief" and "Wo" by Ge 3:19, the "Mighty Funeral-/Of All")
l.2   "Day": Ge 1:5, 8, 13, 19, 23, 31 (the days of Creation, associated with Edenic joy)
l.3   "Mighty Funeral": Ge 3:19
l.5   "Grass": Ge 1:11-12
l.7   "Summer": Ge 1:14
l.8   "stone": Ge 2:12
l.9   "Wo": see *Paradise Lost*, I.1-4 ("Of Man's First Disobedience, and the Fruit/Of that Forbidden Tree, whose mortal taste/Brought Death into the World, and all our woe,/With loss of Eden,")
l.10   "Sea": Ge 1:2, 10, 22, 26, 28
l.12   "Water": Ge 1:2, 6-7, 9-10, 20-22; 2:10
Comment: See *Poems*, II, 508.

662   **Embarrassment of one another**

ll.1-2   "Embarrassment...God": Ge 3:8-24 ("and Adam and his wife hid themselves from the presence of the Lord God amongst the trees of the garden," Ge 3:8b)

ll.3-7   "Is...seal": Isa 45:15 ("Verily thou art a God that hidest thyself, O God of Israel, the Saviour"); see also note, line two, P338; Rev 5:1-9; 6:1-8:6 (it is possible that "Divinity under seal" refers to the book of destinies with seven seals that, along with the Lamb's Book of Life, Rev 21:27, contained God's complete revelation "under seal"; see also Da 12:4, 9; Rev 10:4-10; the poet's own religio-aesthetic regimen may imitate the divine reticence)

l.5   "chief": Ca 5:10 ("the chiefest among ten thousand;" the word is here used with all the KJV force of privileged exclusivity)

663   **Again- his voice is at the door-**

ll.1-29   "Again...stain": Ca 2-7 (the poem rehearses the Canticles topoi of profane love: anticipation, announcement, meeting, and separation)

l.1   "Again...door": Ca 2:8 ("The voice of my beloved!"); Rev 3:20 ("Behold, I stand at the door and knock")

ll.5-6   "I...justify": Ro 5 (for justification by faith, P663 substitutes justification by profane love, for which the "flower" is a metonym: Ca 2:1-2, 12, 16; 4:5; 5:13; 6:2-3; 7:2)

ll.11-12   "I...more": Ca 2:14; 4:8-12; 5:9-16; 7 (the ravishing presence of the beloved as "all this world contains")

l.21   "And...alone": Ca 3:1 ("I sought him, but I found him not"); 6:1 ("Whither is thy beloved gone")

l.25   "We...High": Rev 7:9 ("After this I beheld, and, lo, a great multitude, which no man could number, of all nations, and kindreds, and people, and tongues, stood before the throne, and before the Lamb, clothed with white robes, and palms in their hands")

l.27   "purple": see note, line one, P15 (as one of the colors of the vail, purple is associated with the enjoyment of presence however fleeting); Ca 3:10; 7:5 (purple is associated with the beloved and with the concomitant regal and bridal accession; for KJV associations of purple with regality, e.g., Jg 8:26; Eze 27:7, 16); Mr 15:17, 20; Joh 19:2, 5 (purple is associated with the Passion Christ with whom there is apparently an identification in the closing lines of

P663); Nu 13:23-24; Mt 26:28 (the imagery may be eucharistic, suggesting that the blood of the Divine Beloved is her blood); all of these associations may be relevant since P663 is a memory poem, a rehearsal of an occasion of enhanced status—"old Degree"

     l.28   "He...count": Ro 4:1-5 (the speaker deals with a Divine Beloved who counts and thus feels justified by her "flower" love and "drops" of Passion suffering)

     l.28   "drops": Lu 22:44 (an identification with the suffering Christ of the Passion)

     l.29   "price": Mt 27:6; ICo 6:20

     l.29   "stain": Isa 63:3 (the price she pays for every stain is her circuit world deprivation, her Passion suffering, which becomes her path to the spotlessness of the Beloved, Ca 4:7; Eph 5:27; IPe 1:19)

     Comment: See *Poems*, II, 510-511.

664   Of all the Souls that stand create-

     l.1   "Of...create": Ge 2:7 ("And the Lord God formed man of the dust of the ground, and breathed into his nostrils the breath of life; and man became a living soul")

     l.2   "I...One": Ro 8:29-33; Eph 1:3-14 (the selection of a beloved is spoken of in terms of divine predestination)

     l.3   "When...away": ICo 15:54

     l.5   "When...was": ICo 15:46 ("Howbeit that was not first which is spiritual, but that which is natural; and afterward that which is spiritual"); Rev 1:4 ("from him which is, and which was, and which is to come"; the phrasing, here adapted, appears as a formula throughout Revelation, Rev 1:8; 4:8; 11:17; 16:5)

     l.6   "Apart...stand": Rev 20:12 ("And I saw the dead, small and great, stand before God")

     l.7   "Tragedy...Flesh": Ro 7:24; IICo 5:4; Php 3:21 (the body prison); Ro 7-8 (St. Paul discusses the "Flesh," or *sarx*, human nature with its frailties and passions, technically separate from *soma* or the body; the "Tragedy of Flesh" may be the entrance of sin into time, Ge 2-3, which causes what St. Paul terms a "warring in his members," Ro 7:23)

     l.9   "royal Front": Rev 2:10; 3:4-5, 11, 18; 4:4, 10; 6:11; 7; 19:8 (the seal, crown, and white robe—the regal array fit for ideal presence and vision, Rev 22:4; the "royal Front" may also be the "incorruption" and "immortality" of the resurrected, ICo 15:50-55)

l.11   "Behold": Joh 19:5 ("Behold the man!")

l.11   "Atom": ICo 15:45 (the homophonous link of "Atom" with Adam allows her to state wittily her preference for the second over the first)

l.12   "Clay": Ge 2:7 ("And the Lord God formed man of the dust of the ground"); Job 10:9; 33:6 (the "Clay" is both the first Adam and all mankind)

665   Dropped into the Ether Acre-

ll.2-4   "Wearing...Broach": Isa 61:10; Eze 16:10-13; Mal 3:17; Rev 19:7-9; 21

l.5   "Horses...Blonde": Rev 6:2, 8

l.5   "Coach...Silver": Ca 3:10

l.6   "Pearl": Rev 21:21

l.7   "Down": Rev 3:4-5, 18; 6:11; 19:8

l.7   "Diamond": Ex 28:18; 39:11; Eze 28:13; Rev 21

l.8   "Riding...Earl": Rev 19:16 ("And he hath on his vesture and on his thigh a name written, KING OF KINGS, AND LORD OF LORDS")

Comment: See *Poems*, II, 512.

666   Ah, Teneriffe!

ll.3,5   "Purples," "Red": see note, line one, P15

l.4   "Sapphire": Ex 28:18; 39:11; Ca 5:14; Isa 54:11; Eze 28:13; Rev 21:19 (see also note, line fifteen, P191)

Comment: See *Poems*, II, 512-513.

667   Bloom upon the Mountain- stated-

l.2   "Blameless...Name": Ge 32:29 (like the angel with whom Jacob wrestled, the "Bloom-Efflorescence" remains without a name)

ll.5-20   "Seed...Experience": ICo 15:35-55 (the "Sunset" is an emblem, or "typic," of the resurrection)

l.5   "Purple": see note, line one, P15

l.6   "Day": see note, line nine, P830

l.12   "Witness...here": Rev 1:15; 3:14 (the "true and faithful witness" for the reality or essence of what is typified is elsewhere; as is frequently the case, in P667 reality or presence is displaced, the poem itself an extended metonym or Hitchcockian emblem attempting to witness to the resurrection as had the apostles, Ac 1:22; 4:33)

ll.17-18 "And...Countenance"; ICo 15:49; IICo 3:18 (briefly conformed to the heavenly image, the mountain reverts to its circuit world, earthy one)

Comment: See *Poems*, II, 513-515 and P258.

668   "Nature" is what we see-

ll.1,5,9 " 'Nature' ": Ge 1 (the created world; in *The Manuscript Books* the nature in quotation marks is kept clearly distinct from the nature described as "Heaven" and "Harmony," Franklin, II, 845)

ll.4,8   "Nature": Heb 11:3; Joh 1:1-3; IIPe 3:2-11 (the "Simplicity/Sincerity" of the essential world is only captured by The Word, The Logos, a Divine Expression beyond circuit world "art to say" or metaphor, direct not slant, essential not phenomenal)

ll.9-10 "Nature...say": Job 38-42 ("Who is this that darkeneth counsel by words without knowledge?" Job 38:2; the actual wording is a post-Kantian and post-Emersonian adaptation of lines from Pope's *Essay on Criticism*: "True wit is Nature to advantage dress'd,/What oft was thought, but ne'er so well express'd")

Comment: See *Poems*, II, 515-516 and Franklin, II, 845.

671   She dwelleth in the Ground-

l.1   "dwelleth": Ca 8:13

l.3   "Maker": Job 36:3; Ps 95:6; Isa 17:7 (the God of Creation)

l.5   "To...Grace": Ca 5:1; 6:2 (the gathering of spices and flowers is an action symbolic of love)

l.5   "Here": Ca 5:10

l.6   "Fairness": Ca 1:8, 15-16; 2:10, 13; 4:1, 7, 10; 5:9; 6:1, 10; 7:6

l.7   "Firmament's": Ge 1:6-8

l.8   "Thee": see note, line eight, sixteen, P537

l.8   "mine": Ca 2:16; 6:3 (the Canticles lexicon is used in poems involving the profane beloved)

Comment: See *Poems*, II, 518-519.

672   The Future- never spoke-

l.1   "Future": Mt 24 (the future is conceived in terms suggesting the Parousia or Second Coming)

l.3   "Reveal...sign": Mt 24:36 ("But of that day and hour knoweth no man, no, not the angels of heaven, but my Father only"); see also Mt 16:4; Mr 8:12 ("Why doth this generation seek after a sign? verily I say unto you, There shall no sign be given unto this generation")

l.4   "Of...Come": Rev 1:4, 8; 4:8; 11:17 ("I am Alpha and Omega, the beginning and the ending, saith the Lord, which is, and which was, and which is to come, the Almighty," Rev 1:8)

ll.5-8   "But...Substitute": Rev 16:15 ("Behold, I come as a thief. Blessed is he that watcheth, and keepeth his garments, lest he walk naked, and they see his shame"); Mt 24:43; Lu 12:39; ITh 5:2-4; IIPe 3:10; Rev 3:3 (the word "escape" appears in ITh 5:3)

l.10   "Dower...Doom": Mt 24:40-42; 25:31-46; Rev 20; 21:7-8 (salvation or damnation)

l.11   "His...execute": Jude 14-15 ("Behold, the Lord cometh with ten thousand of his saints, To execute judgment upon all"); see also Isa 22:22; Mt 16:19; Rev 1:18; 3:7; 20:1

l.12   "Fate's-Telegram": Rev 5-8 (the book of destinies, of the seven seals); Rev 20:12-15; 21:27 (the Lamb's Book of Life)

Comment: See *Poems*, II, 519-520.

673   The Love a Life can show Below

l.1   "The...Below": Ca 1:2-8:7 (the profane love of the circuit world, an image or shadow of divine love)

l.2   "I...know": ICo 15:49; Col 2:17; Heb 10:1 (the "filament" is an image or shadow of the "diviner thing")

l.3   "Of...thing": Joh 3:16; IJo 4:8-10; Rev 1:5 (the divine love)

l.6   "Gabriel's Wing": Da 8:16-17; 9:20-23; Lu 1:11-20, 26-38; Rev 8 (the angel Gabriel is associated with impartation of heavenly knowledge to Daniel, with the announcement of the births of

John and Jesus, and, finally, according to tradition, with the enjoyment of God's presence as one of the seven angels, Rev 8:2)

l.12   "Iodine": see note, line one, P15

l.16   "Paradise": Lu 23:43; IICo 12:4; Rev 2:7; 21-22 (the poet tended to conflate the Biblical Eden and Heaven, Paradise and the New Jerusalem—see *Letters*, III, 796)

Comment: See *Poems*, II, 520-521 and *Letters*, II, 402.

674   The Soul that hath a Guest

l.1   "The...Guest": Rev 3:20 ("Behold, I stand at the door and knock: if any man hear my voice and open the door, I will come in to him, and will sup with him, and he with me"; the metaphors of God as Heavenly Visitant or Guest and of the individual as His habitation—for the latter see note, line one, P1142)

l.8   "Emperor...Men": Isa 9:6; Rev 11:15; 17:14; 19:16

Comment: See *Poems*, II, 521-522.

675   Essential Oils- are wrung-

ll.1,2,8   "Oils," "Attar," "Ceaseless/Spiceless Rosemary": Ca 1:3, 12-14; 2:13; 3:6; 4:6, 10-11, 13-14, 16; 5:1, 5, 13; 7:8, 13 (the olfactory imagery has its provenance in Canticles where it is associated with the profane beloved)

l.3   "Be": Ge 1:3 ("And God said, Let there be light: and there was light"); Ge 1:6, 14

l.3   "expressed...alone": Ge 1:14-18 (the implicit contrast is with the divine creation of Genesis)

ll.2,5   "Rose": Ca 2:1 (the ideally circumferential rose, symbol of the profane beloved, is subject to that decay to which "Essential Oils," the poems of the poet, are not)

l.4   "gift...Screws": Mt 26-27; Joh 20:25 (generally the Passion but more specifically the nails of the crucifixion symbolizing the sacrifice of her religio-aesthetic "wrung," the price paid for the eternizing power of art)

Comment: See *Poems*, II, 522-523.

676   Least Bee that brew-

l.1   "Least": Mt 13:31-32; Mr 4:30-32 (the parable of the mustard seed is here adapted to her own account of the creative activity of the Bee-artist in Arnoldian sweetness-and-light terms—the apocalyptic burden of the mustard seed parable temporalized as justification of her "smallest fraction," her religio-aesthetic output)

l.5   "Amber": Eze 1:4, 27; 8:2 (the visionary color is also associated with the vail, see note, line one, P15; metaphorically speaking, the products of art from the bee's activity must await an achieved presence elsewhere—for example, see her account of the "Doom of Fruit without the Bloom" in the life of George Eliot, *Letters*, III, 769-770)

677   To be alive- is Power-

l.2   "Existence...itself": ITi 6:16 (an attribute of the Deity only; see Ge 3:22-23)

l.4   "Omnipotence": Rev 19:6 (an attribute of the Deity, "Enough" making the line oxymoronic in an arch way)

ll.5-6   "To...God": Mt 6:10 ("Thy will be done in earth, as it is in heaven"; the will of God cannot be resisted, Da 4:35; Eph 1:5, let alone imitated by "Finitude")

ll.7-8   "The...Finitude": Ge 1:26 ("And God said, Let us make man in our image, after our likeness"; the Biblical wit of P677 is in its implied question: has man made God in his image or vice versa?)

Comment: See *Poems*, II, 523-524.

679   Conscious am I in my Chamber,

l.19   "esteem Him": Isa 53:3-4 (verbal echoes)

l.20   "Immortality": ICo 15:53-54; IITi 1:8-14 (the latter quote connects "Immortality" with the "shapeless friend" of line two, adapted of course to her religio-aesthetic commitment—the Holy Ghost as Muse)

Comment: See Poems, II, 525-526.

680   Each Life Converges to some Centre-

ll.1-20   "Each...Again": Php 3:13-14 ("Brethren, I count not myself to have apprehended: but this one thing I do, forgetting those things which are behind, and reaching forth unto those things which are before, I press toward the mark for the prize of the high calling of God in Christ Jesus")

ll.4,10,13,14,15,16,17,19 "goal," "reach," "persevered," "high," "Saints," "diligence," "Ungained," "enable," "endeavouring": IICo 8:7, 22; Eph 4:4, 12; 6:18; Php 1:1, 21; 3:7, 13-14; 4:22; Col 1:12; ITh 2:17; ITi 1:12; 5:10; Heb 6:11 (the references could be multiplied to support the contention that P680, concerned with pressing toward a "Goal," has a Paulinian lexicon as its basis)

Comment: See *Poems*, II, 526-527.

681   Soil of Flint, if steady tilled-

1.1   "Soil...tilled": Pr 28:19 ("He that tilleth his land shall have plenty of bread"; for the oil or water from the "Flint" see De 8:15; 32:13; Ps 114:8—a symbolical fructification equivalent to that of the corn and wine)

ll.1-8 (semi-final draft) "On...Sand": Isa 51:3 ("For the Lord shall comfort Zion: he will make her wilderness like Eden, and her desert like the garden of the Lord; joy and gladness shall be found therein, thanksgiving, and the voice of melody"); Eze 36:29-36 ("And the desolate land shall be tilled, whereas it lay desolate...This land that was desolate is become like the garden of Eden," Eze 36:34-35)

1.4 (semi-final draft) "Yielded...Maise": De 33:28 ("Israel then shall dwell in safety alone: the fountain of Jacob shall be upon a land of corn and wine; also his heavens shall drop down dew"; KJV corn and wine, translated into New England "Grape" and "Maize," remain firstfruits evidences of God's special blessing and election, of His promise to turn wilderness into promised land, desert into Eden; thus, P681 is not simply Poor Richard talk of the importance of New England salt and grit but an expression of election optimism, of the conviction that God "is a rewarder of them that diligently seek him," Heb 11:6—the enduring basis of her religio-aesthetic perseverance in contradistinction to what she also well knew along the pulse as the curse of Cain, Ge 4:11-12: "And now art thou cursed from the earth...When thou tillest the ground, it shall not henceforth yield unto thee her strength; a fugitive and a vagabond shalt thou be in the earth")

Comment: See *Poems*, II, 528.

682   **'Twould ease- a Butterfly-**

ll.3,4,7 "Thou'rt," "Thee":Ca 1:2-4, 7-8, 10; 2:14; 4:1-5, 9-
11, 13; 5:9; 6:1, 5-7; 7:1-4, 7-9; 8:5, 13 (see also note, lines eight,
sixteen, P537; the pronouns are those used in addressing the profane
beloved)

l.5   "Blossom": Ca 2:1-2, 12, 16; 4:5; 5:13; 6:2-3; 7:2
(the "Butterfly" and "Bee" are Edenic creatures also associated with
profane love, along with "Blossom")

ll.9-11 "Content...Divinity": Isa 40:8; ICo 15:31; IPe 1:24
(the KJV echoes are part of the calculated hyperbole of P682's claim
of the superiority of "moment" to "Eternity")

ll.13-14 "Eye...me": Ca 2:14 ("O my dove, that art in the
clefts of the rock, in the secret places of the stairs, let me see thy
countenance, let me hear thy voice; for sweet is thy voice, and thy
countenance is comely"); Ca 4:9 ("Thou hast ravished my heart, my
sister, my spouse; thou hast ravished my heart with one of thine
eyes"); Ca 6:13; 8:10

Comment: P682 attempts the spiritualizing of sense by
apotheosizing the moment of face-to-face recognition by the profane
beloved—much to be preferred to an "Eternity" of "Bee" feeding upon
"Blossom." Thus, the commas of line five indicate syntactical
inversion, not direct address as Johnson suggested. See *Poems*, II, 528-
529.

683   **The Soul unto itself**

ll.1-3   "The...Spy": Ge 1:26, 28; 2:7; 3:7-24 (created with
"dominion," the "Soul" falls into the internal divisions of a post-
lapsarian consciousness circumscribed by death)

Comment: See *Poems*, II, 529-530; *Letters*, II, 423-424; and
Leyda, II, 78.

684   **Best Gains- must have the Losses' Test-**

ll.1-2   "Best...Gains": Mt 16:26 ("For what is a man
profited, if he shall gain the whole world, and lose his own soul?");
Php 3:7 ("But what things were gain to me, those I counted loss for
Christ"; the KJV paradox becomes the basis for her idea of the
compensatory value of circuit world deprivation)

Comment: See *Poems*, II, 530 and *Letters*, II, 423-424.

685   Not "Revelation"- 'tis- that waits,

l.1   "Not...waits": Rev 1, passim (the Book of Revelation is used as a metonym for the apocalyptic, which P685 insists is not a something disclosed or manifested but a new, postresurrection type of seeing freed from the dross of the body and circuit world limitation)

l.2   "unfurnished eyes": ICo 13:12; IJo 3:2; Rev 3:18; 22:4 (see the second stanza of P694); the poet may also have in mind IICo 5:4 ("For we that are in this tabernacle do groan, being burdened: not for that we would be unclothed, but clothed upon, that mortality might be swallowed up of life")

Comment: See *Poems*, II, 530 and *Letters*, II, 423-424.

686   They say that "Time assuages"-

l.2   "Time...assuage": Job 16:6 ("Though I speak, my grief is not assuaged: and though I forbear, what am I eased?")

l.4   "As...age": Job 30:16-17

l.5   "Time...Trouble": IIKi 19:3; Ne 9:27; Ps 20:1; 27:5; 37:39; 41:1; 50:15; 59:16; 77:2; 86:7; Pr 25:19; Isa 22:5; 33:2; 37:3; Jer 2:27-28; 11:12; 14:8; 51:2; Hab 3:16 (a "day" or "time of trouble" appears frequently in the KJV, often with God as strength, rest, salvation, or deliverer)

l.6   "But...Remedy": Jer 14:19 ("we looked for peace, and there is no good; and for the time of healing, and behold trouble!")

Comment: See *Poems*, II, 530-531 and *Letters*, II, 453-454.

687   I'll send the feather from my Hat!

l.1   "I'll...Hat": Ge 37:31-35 (the motif is adapted from the story of Joseph)

l.6   "Adamant": Zec 7:12

690   Victory comes late-

l.1   "Victory...late": ICo 15:54-55, 57 ("O grave, where is thy victory?")

ll.2-6   "And...Drop": Ca 2:3, 14; 4:11; 5:2, 5, 13, 16; 7:9 (the lexicon of "lips," "sweet," "tasted," and "Drop" echoes Canticles—the metaphor of love as a banquet described in oral imagery)

l.7   "Was...economical": Mt 5:3-12 (the God of the Beatitudes, of the circuit world philosophy of deprivation; the Divine economy of penury and niggardliness is here treated with asperity)

l.8   "His...Us": Ca 1:12; 2:4 (the banqueting metaphor of love as feeding extends throughout Canticles); Lu 16:19-31 (the story of the rich man who "fared sumptuously" contains the "Crumbs" image and the Lazarus-beggar/child persona used in P690); Rev 19:7-9 (the Marriage Supper of the Lamb)

l.10   "Crumbs": Mt 15:27; Mr 7:28; Lu 16:21 (the persona of P690 is the circuit-world-bound beggar/child)

l.12   "Golden Breakfast": Rev 19:7-9

l.13   "God...Sparrows": Mt 10:29-31; Lu 12:6-7 ("Are not five sparrows sold for two fathings, and not one of them is forgotten before God? But even the very hairs of your head are all numbered. Fear not therefore: ye are of more value than many sparrows")

Comment: See *Poems*, II, 533-534 and *Letters*, II, 399-400, especially Johnson's explanation of the relationship of P690 to the death of Frazar Stearns during a Union victory in Newbern, North Carolina. Nevertheless, P690 has a more universal significance as an attempt to make rationally intelligible, from the circuit world point of view, the meaning of apocalyptic "Victory," and her conclusion that a surfeiting "Golden Breakfast" comes only in a world of no hunger (Rev 7:16) is testimony to her unflinching candor regarding the incommensurability of "life's penurious round" and the "new circumference" and of the considerable obstacles to a reconciliation of conventional theodicy and eschatology.

691   Would you like summer? Taste of ours.

l.1   "Would...summer": Ge 1-2; Ca 2:8-13; Eze 28:13-14; Rev 22:1-5 (the poet equated the New Jerusalem and Eden, places of perpetual summer, to her imagination, *Letters*, III, 796 [see also note, line sixteen, P673]; for the paradisiacal associations with the beloved, see the context in *Letters*, II, 371-372)

l.1   "Taste...ours": Ca 1:7; 2:3, 16; 4:5; 6:2-3 (the oral imagery of tasting and feeding runs throughout Canticles)

l.2   "Spices...here": Ca 4:10, 14, 16; 5:1; 7:9; 8:2, 14
l.3   "I'll...parching": Ca 1:2, 4; 4:10; 5:1; 7:9; 8:2
l.4   "Weary...down": Ca 1:16; 3:1, 7, 10; 6:2
ll.5-6   "Perplexed...roses": Ca 2:1-2, 12, 16; 4:5; 5:13; 6:2-3; 7:2 (flower imagery abounds in Canticles; of course, the garden is associated with Eden and Paradise, Ge 2:8-10, 15-16; 3:1-3; Ca 4:16; 5:1; 6:2, 11; Eze 28:13; Rev 22:1-2)
l.8   "Even...medicine": Ge 1-2; Rev 21:4 (death is excluded from that Paradise which the poet equated with wedded bliss)
Comment: See *Poems*, II, 534 and *Letters*, II, 371-372.

693   Shells from the Coast mistaking-

ll.4,7-8   "To...begin": Mt 13:45-46 ("Again, the kingdom of heaven is like unto a merchant man, seeking goodly pearls: Who, when he had found one pearl of great price, went and sold all that he had, and bought it"); Rev 21:21 (the "Pearl" is associated with a new period of religio-aesthetic commitment, perhaps with a concomitant self-conscious identification of herself with the heavenly city, the New Jerusalem, the Bride of Christ; see also P320)
Comment: See *Poems*, II, 535.

694   The Heaven vests for Each

l.2   "small Deity": Joh 1:14 ("And the Word was made flesh, and dwelt among us, [and we beheld his glory, the glory as of the only begotten of the Father,] full of grace and truth")
ll.5-6   "Half...see": Ex 33:18-23 ("And he [Moses] said, I beseech thee, shew me thy glory....And he [God] said, Thou canst not see my face: for there shall no man see me, and live....while my glory passeth by...my face shall not be seen")
ll.7-8   "Till...Eternity": IICo 5:1 ("For we know that if our earthly house of this tabernacle were dissolved, we have a building of God, an house not made with hands, eternal in the heavens"); see also IIPe 1:13-14 (the tabernacle is the body, the residence of the soul while in the circuit world; in "Eternity," the "tabernacle of God is with man," Rev 21:3-5, the state the poet described as "unfurnished eyes," P685, the state of beatitude, Rev 22:4)
l.10   "Star": Nu 24:17; Mt 2:2; IIPe 1:19; Rev 22:16 (Christ is the "Star")

ll.9-12 "How...Despair": Php 2:6-8 ("Who, being in the form of God, thought it not robbery to be equal with God: But made himself of no reputation, and took upon him the form of a servant, and was made in the likeness of men: And being found in fashion as a man, he humbled himself, and became obedient unto death, even the death of the cross")

l.13 "A...common": Joh 3:14-21; ITi 4:10; Tit 1:4; IIPe 3:9; Jude 3 (salvation is common to all, termed a "fisherman's degree" in P401)

l.14 "We...fear": Ro 8:15

ll.15-16 "Enabling...adore": Rev 19:1, 5-6

695 As if the Sea should part

l.1 "As...part": Ex 14:15-31 (the Old Testament story of Moses and the parting of the Red Sea is one of exodus and quest—a journey to the promised land, reward of wilderness longing; "typic" of Redemption, it is her applied to the poet's apparent longing for salvific vision: an infinitely repeatable questing of the individual soul for heightened awareness; in P313, for example, the quest is for the "shores beyond," emblematic of Eternity, but in contrast, P695 defines Eternity not as stasis or arrival but as "Verge" or threshold—as if Heaven were to become in the imagination of P695's Ulysses-like speaker a distillation of all circuit world brinks: Indian summer, dawn, sunset, and so forth and also as if the much-envied divine presence and vision were conceived as an infinite set of Chinese boxes)

696 Their Hight in Heaven comforts not-

ll.3-4 " 'Twas...see": ICo 13:9-10, 12 ("For we know in part, and we prophesy in part. But when that which is perfect is come, then that which is in part shall be done away....For now we see through a glass darkly; but then face to face: now I know in part; but then I shall know even as also I am known")

l.15 "This...Evidence": Heb 11:1 ("Now faith is the substance of things hoped for, the evidence of things not seen")

697 I could bring You Jewels- had I a mind to-

l.1 "Jewels": Ca 1:10; 7:1

l.3   "Odors": Ca 1:12; 2:13; 3:6; 4:6, 10-11, 14; 5:5, 13; 7:8, 13

l.9   "Topaz": Ex 28:17; 39:10; Eze 28:13; Rev 21:10

l.10   "Emerald": Ex 28:18; 39:11; Eze 28:13; Rev 21:19

l.11   "Dower": Isa 61:10; Eze 16:10-12; Mal 3:17; Rev 21 (the idea of adornment of the beloved or bride is the unifying trope of P697)

698   Life- is what we make it-

ll.1-16   "Life...now": Isa 53; ICo 15

l.12   "Paradise": Lu 23:43; Rev 2:7; 21-22 (see also note, line sixteen, P673)

l.14   "Tender": Mt 11:29; Jas 5:11

699   The Judge is like the Owl-

l.1   "The Judge": Ge 18:25; Heb 12:23 (if the poem contains no such KJV provenance but reflects solely regional lore, then its Blakean quality is lost and it becomes a jeu d'esprit)

l.4   "Amber": Eze 1:4, 27; 8:2 (the visionary color also associated with the vail, see note, line one, P15; the associations with epiphanic intimations and with light are obviously ironic given the judge-like appearance of the owl—proverbially black—and his nocturnal, predatory habits: in the KJV the owl is associated with destruction and desolation, Isa 34:11-15)

ll.11-12 "Owl...Refrain": Mic 1:8 (the doleful, mournful "Tune" of the owl is here stressed)

Comment: The owl, a secretive nocturnal bird of prey with large head and eyes and with a signature, cacophonous hoot, could only be a candidate for nightingale to the mind of a child—the persona used by the poet in P699. The ingenuous invitation with its unintended contradictions hardly flatters "The Judge" whose "favorite Refrain," the screech of the hunt, reflects a universe "Red in tooth and claw" contrasting with the small-prices, favorite-tune world of childish imagination.

700   You've seen Balloons set- Hav'nt You?

l.4   "Diamond": Eze 28:13, 15-21

l.18   "Dust": Ge 2:7; 3:14, 19; Ps 103:14

702   A first Mute Coming-

l.1   "A...Coming": Ge 19:1-2 (Johnson makes this identification of the background story, *Poems*, II, 541)
l.3   "A...Going": Ge 19:16, 29 (if Johnson is correct, then this is a reference to the escape from Sodom and Gomorrah by Lot)
l.5   "first Exchange": Ge 18:22-32 (the bargain struck by Abraham with God)
l.6   "What...been": Ge 17:1-19 (the righteous of the covenant mixing with those of Sodom and Gomorrah)
ll.7-8   "For...alone": Lu 17:28-29; IIPe 2:1-9 (the experience of Noah and his generation becomes a type of the Last Judgment, Mt 25:32; Rev 20, "exhibited" to Lot by "Faith alone")

703   Out of sight? What of that?

l.8   "Blue": Ex 26; 28; 35-36; 38-39; Nu 4 (the coverings, cloths, and garments of the tabernacle and priests were blue); Ex 26:31-33; 36:35 (the vail beyond which was the holy of holies was, among other colors, blue; thus, blue was associated with the glory and presence of God and was a color repeatedly used in nature epiphany and intimations poems; see also note, line one, P15)
l.9   "Amber": see note, line fifteen, P629 and note, line four, P699
l.10   "Seek...see": Mt 7:7 (the arc swept by the bird in the "Steep Air" becomes emblematic of aspiration and ascent, of the desire for vision)
l.11   "Heaven...all": Isa 45:15 (for the Deus absconditus see note, line two, P338)

704   No matter- now- Sweet-

ll.1,14   "Sweet":Ca 2:3, 14; 5:5, 13, 16; 7:9 (the profane beloved)
ll.2,8   "When...Earl": Rev 1:6; 5:10; 19:7-9; 20:6; 21; 22:5 (accession to royal status, perhaps as Bride of Christ)

l.10   "Crests": Rev 2:10 (the crown of life; the seal may also be intended, Rev 7; 14:1-5)

l.13   "Ermine...Gown":Rev 3:4-5, 18; 6:11; 7:9, 13-14; 19:8 (the white garb of the sealed and crowned elect)

705   Suspense- is Hostiler than Death-

l.5   "But...anew": Joh 3:16 ("For God so loved the world, that he gave his only begotten Son, that whosoever believeth in him should not perish, but have everlasting life"; the echo here, and in line eight of I Corinthians, reinforces the notion of the imperishability of "Suspense")

l.8   "With Immortality": ICo 15:50-55

706   Life, and Death, and Giants-

ll.1-3   "Life...Minor": Ro 8:38-39

707   The Grace- Myself- might not obtain-

ll.1-4   "The...Her": Ca 2:1 (one convention used by P707 is that of the beloved as flower; another is that of the desire for the grace or favor of the beloved, Ca 2:16; 6:3; 8:10; also, the longing for the gracious, responsive countenance: "O my dove, that art in the clefts of the rock, in the secret places of the stairs, let me see thy countenance, let me hear thy voice; for sweet is thy voice, and thy countenance is comely," Ca 2:14; of course, her desire for a substitute or translated face—in the context of the Divine Beloved rather than the profane—may have apocalyptic overtones: Ro 8:29; ICo 13:12; 15:49; IICo 3:18; IJo 3:2; Rev 22:4)

708   I sometimes drop it, for a Quick-

l.5   "Wo so monstrous": Ro 7:24; IICo 5:4; Php 3:21 (her Gnostic bodily prison in the circuit world)

l.12   "Paradise": see note, line sixteen, P673

709   Publication- is the Auction

l.7 "White": Rev 2:7; 4:4; 6:2, 11; 7:9, 13-14; 19:8, 11, 14; 20:11 (the color of the apocalypse is white: the robes of the sealed Elect, the raiment of the elders, the horses, and the great white throne)

l.7 "White Creator": Rev 1:14

ll.9-11 "Thought...illustration": Joh 1:1-5 (God is "Thought" and gave the ultimate expression of the incorporeal in Jesus Christ, the "Corporeal illustration" and, therefore, model for all subsequent artistic incarnation)

l.12 "Royal Air": Joh 1:1-5 (the "Royal Air" is, again, Christ, the Incarnate Word, Royal Heir, and exemplar for all others who would incarnate the Word as artists, becoming heirs also, not auctioneers)

l.13 "Parcel": Joh 1:1 ("Parcel" may be the Word and by extension poetic words, instantiations of the "Heavenly Grace")

l.14 "Heavenly Grace": Ro 5:15-18; Eph 3:7; Heb 6:4; IPe 4:10 (the "Heavenly Grace" is a free gift of God)

Comment: See *Poems*, II, 544-545 and Leyda, II, 47-48. P709 develops an incarnational poetics based upon the first chapter of the Gospel of John, a metaphor of poetry ("Snow" and "Grace") as a gift comparable to the free gift of God's grace.

710   The Sunrise runs for Both-

ll.2,4,11 "Purple," "Blue," "Iodine": note, line one, P15 (the colors of the vail are frequently used in nature epiphany poems)

711   Strong Draughts of Their Refreshing Minds

l.3 "Desert": Ex 19:2; Nu 27:14; 33:16; Isa 48:21; Joh 6:31; Heb 11:38

l.3 "Wilderness": Ex 14; Nu 10:12; 13:3; 20; 33; De 1:19; 8:2; 32:10; Mt 4 (in the KJV the desert and wilderness have symbolic significance as places of testing and temptation, transition and maturation)

l.4 "Sealed": Joh 6:27; IICo 1:22; Eph 1:13; 4:30; Rev 7

l.4 "Wine": Mt 26:27-28 (the Sealed Church of the Gnostic "Mind" is able in "Desert" and "Wilderness" to find the Eucharistic sustenance from within)

712   Because I could not stop for Death-

l.1   "Death": Ge 2:17; 3:19; Ca 8:6; Rev 1:18; 6:8; 19:7-9 (personified, "Death" may represent one of the Four Horsemen of the Apocalypse, Death, associated with destruction, or the Lamb, the Son of Man, holding the keys of Death and, also, as Groom of all the elect, offering marriage)

l.3   "Carriage": IIKi 2:11-12; Ca 3:9-10

l.4   "Immortality": ICo 15:50-55

ll.6-8   "And...Civility": Mt 11:28-30

ll.15-16 "Gossamer...Tulle": Rev 19:8, 11, 14 (the fine linen bridal dress of Revelation)

ll.23-24 "Horse...Eternity": Zec 6; Rev 6; 19:11, 14 (apocalyptic horses)

Comment: See *Poems*, II, 546-547.

713   Fame of Myself, to justify,

l.8   "Diadem": Isa 62:3; Rev 2:10 (symbolic of accession to status and degree)

714   Rests at Night

l.3   "Rest...Men": Rev 14:13

715   The World- feels Dusty

ll.1-2,10 "The...comes": Joh 19:28

l.1   "Dusty": Ge 2:7; 3:19

l.3   "Dew": see note, line one, P513

716   The Day undressed- Herself-

ll.1,4-5 "The...World": Ge 1:5 ("And God called the light Day")

ll.2-3   "Gold," "Purple": see note, line one, P15 (the colors associated with the vail are frequently used in nature epiphany poems; the colors are associated with the profane beloved, Ca 1:10-11; 3:10; 5:11, 14-15; 7:5)

ll.6-8   "And...Hemisphere/Firmament...Her": Ge 1:7-17 ("And God made the firmament...And God said, Let there be lights in the firmament...he made the stars also. And God set them in the firmament of the heaven to give light upon the earth")

ll.9-10 "Too...fear": Mt 6:9 ("Our Father which art in heaven")

Comment: See *Poems*, II, 548 and Franklin, I, 529.

717 The Beggar Lad- dies early-

l.7 "Nor...'Bread'": Mt 7:9 ("Or what man is there of you, whom if his son ask bread, will he give him a stone?")

l.9 "Redeemed Children": Mt 19:14; Lu 18:16; Ro 8:16-17, 21; Ga 3:7, 26

719 A South Wind- has a pathos

ll.4-6 "An...understood": Joh 3:8 ("The wind bloweth where it listeth, and thou hearest the sound thereof, but canst not tell whence it cometh, and whither it goeth: so is every one that is born of the Spirit")

720 No Prisoner be-

l.1 "Prisoner": Eph 3:1; 4:1; IITi 1:8 (a Paulinian metaphor; see also the idea of the body prison, Ro 7:24; Php 3:21)

ll.1-3 "No...Thee": IICo 3:17 ("where the Spirit of the Lord is there is liberty")

721 Behind Me- dips Eternity-

l.2 "Before...Immortality": ICo 15:50-55

ll.7-8 " 'Tis...Monarchy": Rev 11:15 ("The kingdoms of this world are become the kingdoms of our Lord, and of his Christ; and he shall reign for ever and ever"); Rev 22:5 ("And there shall be no night there; and they need no candle, neither light of the sun; for the Lord God giveth them light: and they shall reign for ever and ever")

l.9 "Prince": Rev 1:5 ("Jesus Christ, who is the faithful witness, and the first begotten of the dead, and the prince of the kings of the earth"); Rev 17:14; 19:16

l.9   "Son...None": Rev 1:8 (" 'I am Alpha and Omega, the beginning and the ending, saith the Lord,' which is, and which was, and which is to come, the Almighty"); see also, Isa 41:4; 44:6; 48:12; Rev 21:6; 22:13 (it is also possible that the poet here glances at an Old Testament type of Christ, Joshua, son of Non or Nun, whose name meant "Jehovah" and whose father's name meant "noon" or "perpetuity," Jos 1:1)

ll.11-12 "Himself...divine": Ro 8:29; ICo 15:49; IICo 3:18; IJo 3:2 (the redeemed, conformed to His image, become Divine duplicates; the reference may be to the sealed elect, Rev 7, or to the virginal firstfruits, Rev 14:1-5, or to the beatific vision, Rev 22:4, at which, to use the poet's language, the face of Jesus puts out the faces of the redeemed for ever and ever, the achievement of ideal circumferentiality and authentic identity—"and his name shall be in their foreheads")

Comment: See *Poems*, II, 552-553.

722   Sweet Mountains- Ye tell Me no lie-

l.1   "Sweet": Ca 2:3, 14; 5:5, 13, 16 (the Canticles term of endearment for the beloved)

l.1   "Mountains": Ca 2:8, 17; 4:6, 8; 8:14 (although not personified in Canticles as here, the mountains are associated with the beloved)

l.2   "Never...Never": Heb 13:5 ("I will never leave thee, nor forsake thee")

ll.3-4   "Those...Me": Ca 2:14 ("let me see thy countenance...thy countenance is comely")

l.5   "Or...vain": Ex 20:7 ("Thou shalt not take the name of the Lord thy God in vain")

l.6   "Violet": see note, line one, P15

l.7   "Madonnas": Mt 1:18; Lu 2 (the Madonna is Mary, mother of Jesus)

l.12   "To...You": Ps 121:1-2 ("I will lift up mine eyes unto the hills, from whence cometh my help. My help cometh from the Lord, which made heaven and earth")

724   It's easy to invent a Life-

l.1   "It's...Life": Ge 2:7 ("And the Lord God formed man of the dust of the ground, and breathed into his nostrils the breath of life; and man became a living soul")

ll.3-4   "Creation...Authority": Ge 2-3 (the creation of man was a "Gambol" of God's creative freedom or "Spontaneity")

l.9   "The...murmur": Ge 2-3 (Adam and Eve are the "Patterns" bringing death with the Fall, "murmur" here an echo of Ro 8:22: "For we know that the whole creation groaneth and travaileth in pain together until now")

ll.11-12 "Proceed...Man": Mt 1:18; Joh 1:1-9 (the "Sun" is the Incarnate Word, the Son—"Sun" of Righteousness, Mal 4:2; Lu 1:78; IIPe 1:19; Rev 1:16; 2:28; 21:23; 22:5, 16, and also the Second Adam, ICo 15:45; the "Man" is the first Adam, Ge 1:26-27; 3:19; ICo 15:21, 45-47)

725   Where Thou art- that- is Home-

ll.1,11   "Thou art": Ca 1:15-16; 2:14; 4:1, 7; 6:4; 7:6

l.1   "Home": Ca 1:4, 17; 2:4; 3:4; 4:12, 16; 5:1; 6:2, 11; 8:2, 7, 13 (the dwelling of the beloved as garden, chamber, or house)

l.2   "Calvary": Lu 23:33

l.3   "Shame": Heb 12:2 ("Looking unto Jesus ...who...endured the cross, despising the shame")

l.5   "So...Come": Ca 2:10, 12-13; 4:8, 16; 5:1; 7:11

ll.6,13 "Thou dost": Ca 5:9

l.6   "What...Delight": Ca 2:3 ("I sat down under his shadow with great delight, and his fruit was sweet to my taste"); Ca 7:6

l.11   "Where...Wo": Ca 3:1; 5:6 ("I opened to my beloved; but my beloved had withdrawn himself, and was gone: my soul failed when he spake: I sought him, but I could not find him; I called him, but he gave me no answer")

l.12   "Tho'...row/blow": Ca 4:16 ("blow upon my garden, that the spices thereof may flow out"); Ca 4:10, 14; 5:1, 13; 6:2; 8:2, 14

l.14   "Gabriel": Da 8:16-26; 9:20-27 (the angel Gabriel is associated with divine revelation); Lu 1:11-21, 26-38 (the angel Gabriel announces the births of John and Jesus); Rev 8:2 (the angel Gabriel is one of the "seven angels which stood before God; and to them were given seven trumpets")

Comment: See *Poems*, II, 554-555.

726   We thirst at first- 'tis Nature's Act-

l.1   "We...Act": Mt 5:6 (the deprivation characteristic of the circuit world)

ll.2-4   "And...by": Joh 19:28-29 ("After this, Jesus...saith, I thirst"; there may here also be a glance at the rich man of Lu 16:24)

ll.5-8   "It...Immortality": Rev 21:6; 22:17 ("And the Spirit and the bride say, Come. And let him that heareth say, Come. And let him that is athirst come. And whosoever will, let him take the water of life freely")

728   Let Us play Yesterday-

l.4   "Untold tale": Ps 90:9 ("we spend our years as a tale that is told")

l.5   "Easing...famine": Mt 5:6 (again the unassuageable hunger of the circuit world is based in the paradoxes of the Beatitudes)

l.8   " 'Twas...Wine": Ca 1:4; 4:10; 5:1; 7:9; 8:2 (the wine is associated with physical enjoyment of the profane beloved)

l.11   "Reds": see note, line one, P15 (the vail color is associated with presence and heightened awareness)

l.12   "Make...leap": Mt 15:31; Lu 7:22 ("the lame...walk, and the blind...see"; there may here be glances at specific miracles, Mr 10:46-52; Ac 14:10, since "Miracle" and "Light" are connected in stanza six; also, the verb "leap" may have relevance with regard to the nature of the freedom offered, Ca 2:8)

729   Alter! When the Hills do-

l.1   "Hills": Ge 49:26; IKi 20:28; Ps 121:1-3

l.2   "Sun": Ps 84:11; 89:36; Mal 4:2

730   Defrauded I a Butterfly-

ll.1-2   "Defrauded...Thee": Ro 4:13-16; 8:17; Ga 3:29; 4:1, 7 ("For the promise, that he should be the heir of the world, was not to Abraham, or to his seed, through the law, but through the righteousness of faith. For if they which are of the law be heirs, faith is made void, and the promise made of none effect:...Therefore it is of faith, that it might be by grace; to the end the promise might be sure to all the seed; not to that only which is of the law, but to that also which is of the faith of Abraham; who is the father of us all," Ro 4:13-14, 16)

Comment: P730 is a poem sent with a flower as an affection token. By law (that of nature), the butterfly has been defrauded of an "Heir," and the "Heir" is now given as confirmation of love in the realm of supernature. The Biblical wit here pivots on the Paulinian notion that the promise of Abraham was not through his seed (that of nature) but by his faith—by faith we are made joint-heirs of Christ with God(Ro 8:17). The bestowal of the love token is a gracious act comparable to Biblical faith and confirming the lovers' joint-heirship.

732   She rose to His Requirement- dropt

l.1   "She...dropt": Ca 2:10 ("My beloved spake, and said unto me, Rise up, my love, my fair one, and come away")

l.5   "If...Day": Ca 3:11 (the day of espousal, of bridal accession—see also Rev 19:7-9)

ll.7,10   "Gold," "Pearl": Ge 2:11-12; Ca 1:10-11; 3:10; 5:11, 14-15; Eze 16:10-13; 28:13; Rev 3:18; 4:4; 21:18, 21 (gold and pearl would be associated with the Edenic and paradisiacal and with her bridal accession)

Comment: See *Poems*, II, 558-559.

733   The Spirit is the Conscious Ear.

ll.1-8   "Spirit...Hear": Mt 13:9-17 (spiritual discernment is inaudible and placeless, a "Hear" rather than a "Here': "Sound" is a matter of the aural, of physical awareness through the "smaller Ear," always associated with the body and a "Here," and the only "Hear" most achieve—"this people's heart is waxed gross, and their ears are dull of hearing")

Comment: P733 privileges the "Conscious Ear" of the "Castle/Centre/City" over the "smaller/minor Ear" of the body—the former gains admittance and credence, the latter hangs its fleshly ear outside the "City" where it is relegated to performance of menial "Services/purposes." A Gnostic withdrawal into the citadel of Spirit, P733 at least obliquely repudiates the physical world of bodily limitation through imagery of diminution—"smaller," "minor" and "only." See *Poems*, II, 559.

735   Upon Concluded Lives

l.3   "sweet": Ca 2:3, 14; 5:5, 13, 16 (the Canticles word is selected to intimate bridal accession at death; for the variant "new" see Rev 21:1-2, 5)

l.7   "Coronal": Ca 3:11; Isa 62:3-4; Eze 16:12; ICo 9:25; IITi 4:8; Jas 1:12; IPe 5:4; Rev 2:10 (the crown is part of that wedding dress associated with accession to status or degree: the "sweet" and "Bells" side of death)

Comment: See *Poems*, II, 560.

737   The Moon was but a Chin of Gold

l.1   "The...Gold": Ca 5:11 ("His head is as the most fine gold"); Rev 21:18, 21 (the moon's turning apparently from gibbous to full gives the poet an epiphany of the ideally circumferential, of the crown-like "perfect Face," described in the imagery of the beloved in Canticles and of the Old Testament vail but also using the apocalyptic colors, gems, and metals); Ex 26:31-33; 28:6 (the high priestly ephod and the vail of the tabernacle contained gold—the vail covered the holy of holies into which only the high priest could enter; the gems of the high priestly breastplate were repeated in the poet's favorite "Gem Chapter" of Revelation, see Ex 28:15-21; Rev 21)

l.5   "Blonde": Rev 3:4, 5, 18; 7:9, 13-14; 19:8 (the appearance of the moon is apocalyptic white; because of the repeated use of "forehead" in Revelation, including the climactic Rev 22:4, the "perfect Face" of the moon may be a displacement for the face of God)

l.6   "Beryl": Ex 28:20; 39:13; Ca 5:14; Eze 28:13; Rev 21:20

ll.9,20   "Amber," "Blue": Ex 26:31-33; 28:6, 15-21 (gold and blue would be associated with the vail, breastplate, and ephod—all directly connected to the presence and glory of God; amber is also associated with the visionary imagery of Ezekiel, Eze 1:4, 27; 8:2; see also note, line one, P15)

Comment: See *Poems*, II, 562.

738   You said that I "was Great"- one Day-

ll.1-3   "Great," "Small": Rev 19:5; 20:12
ll.2,4,12,14,18 "Thee": see note, lines eight, sixteen, P537
l.13   "Queen": Ca 6:8-9; Rev 19:7-9
Comment: See *Poems*, II, 562-563 and Leyda, II, 42.

740   You taught me Waiting with Myself-

l.9   "The...understand": ICo 13:9-10, 12; IJo 3:2
l.10   "That...ashamed": IJo 2:28 ("And now, little
children, abide in him; that, when he shall appear, we may have
confidence, and not be ashamed before him at his comimg")
l.11   "Upon...Hand": Mt 26:64; Mr 16:19; Lu 22:69; Ac
2:33; 7:55-56; Ro 8:34; Col 3:1; Heb 1:3; 8:1; 10:12; 12:2; IPe 3:22
(Christ sits at the right hand of God in Heaven)
Comment: See *Poems*, II, 564.

743   The Birds reported from the South-

ll.1-2   "Birds...Me": Ca 2:12-13 ("The flowers appear on
the earth; the time of the singing of birds is come, and the voice of the
turtle is heard in our land; The fig tree putteth forth her green figs,
and the vines with the tender grape give a good smell. Arise, my love,
my fair one, and come away"); see also Ca 4:16
l.3   "spicy": Ca 1:13; 3:6; 4:6, 10, 14, 16; 5:1, 5, 13; 6:2;
8:14
l.3   "Charge": Ca 2:7; 3:5; 5:8-9; 8:4
l.5   "Flowers": Ca 2:1, 2, 12, 16; 4:5; 5:5, 13, 33; 6:2-3;
7:2 (the birds and flowers offer a present associated with possession of
the profane beloved)
l.6   "I...Door": Ca 5:4-5 ("I rose up to open to my
beloved"; also, in contrast, the variant for line sixteen reads: "rose to
comfort"; P743 shuts out a summer of possession—"Go blossom to the
Bees"—for a sympathy of frost, suffering, and death)
l.13   "At...Myself": Ec 12:5 (comfort for those who mourn
is stressed in the variant line sixteen, for which see Mt 5:4)
Comment: See *Poems*, II, 566-567 and Franklin, II, 906-906.

744   Remorse- is Memory- awake-

l.1   "Remorse": Ps 69:20 ("Reproach hath broken my heart, and I am full of heaviness: and I looked for some to take pity, but there was none; and for comforters, but I found none"; Dickinson identifies with the Passion Christ whose "reproach" she applies in psychological and individual terms as the universal and inescapable condition of self-reproach or remorse; this disease which God cannot heal is without comfort or remission, Isa 59:16; 63:5)

l.3   "A...Acts": Ge 2-3 (the biting again which is remorse—the equivalent of eating from the forbidden tree—is in P744 a central paradox, that of the unfortunate Fall, "His institution")

ll.9-12   "Remorse...Hell": Rev 20:12-15; 21:8 (Hell, the place of eternal damnation and the second death, is the complement of "Remorse," that post-lapsarian consciousness which makes the life of the circuit world a "Disease")

Comment: See *Poems*, II, 567-568.

745   Renunciation- is a piercing Virtue-

l.3   "A...Expectation": Ro 8:19 ("For the earnest expectation of the creature waiteth for the manifestation of the sons of God")

l.8   "Day's...Progenitor": Ge 1:3-5 ("And God said, Let there be light...And God called the light Day")

l.12   "Itself...justify": Ro 3:24, 28; 8:30, 33 (justification by grace is here redefined in terms of the needs of the speaker for an intelligible theodicy: one explaining the circumscription of the circuit world and the enhancement of Heaven vis-a-vis presence vs. absence and blindness vs. sight)

748   Autumn- overlooked my Knitting-

ll.5-6   "Cochineal...Thee": Ca 5:10 ("My beloved is white and ruddy, the chiefest among ten thousand"; for "Thee" see note, lines eight, sixteen, P537)

Comment: See *Poems*, II, 570.

749   All but Death, can be Adjusted-

l.1   "Death": ICo 15:54-55
l.8   "Change": ICo 15:51-52

750   **Growth of Man- like Growth of Nature-**

ll.9-12 "Effort...Belief": ITh 1:3; IITh 1:4; ITi 6:11; IITi 3:10; 4:7; Heb 6:12; 12:1; 13:21 (stanza three reads like a catalogue of the Paulinian virtues)

751   **My Worthiness is all my Doubt-**

l.1   "My...Doubt": Rev 3:4 (the worthy are those who walk in white)

l.5   "Lest...prove": Rev 16:15 ("Behold, I come as a thief. Blessed is he that watcheth, and keepeth his garments, lest he walk naked, and they see his shame")

l.6   "For...Need": Ca 7:10 ("I am my beloved's, and his desire is toward me")

ll.9-10 " 'Tis...incline": Ge 1-3; Joh 1:1-14; Php 2:5-8 (the poet may have in mind the Creation and Incarnation)

ll.13-15 "So...Soul": Ro 8:29 ("For whom he did foreknow, he also did predestinate to be conformed to the image of his Son, that he might be the firstborn among many brethren"); see also IICo 3:18; IPe 2:3-9

ll.15-16 "as...Sacrament": Eph 5:22-32; Rev 19:7-9; 21 ("Husbands, love your wives, even as Christ also loved the church, and gave himself for it; That he might sanctify and cleanse it with the washing of water by the word, That he might present it to himself a glorious church, not having spot, or wrinkle, or any such thing; but that it should be holy and without blemish," Eph 5:25-27; the apocalyptic bridal figuration points back to Canticles through St. Paul)

Comment: See *Poems*, II, 572.

754   **My Life had stood- a Loaded Gun-**

l.1   "My...Gun": Ge 2:7 ("And the Lord God formed man of the dust of the ground and breathed into his nostrils the breath of life; and man became a living soul")

l.3   "The...identified": Ge 1:26-27 ("So God created man in his own image, in the image of God created he him; male and female created he them")

ll.4,5-7,9,13 "And": Ge 1-3 (the use of anaphoric "And" suggests the Creation account) l.5   "And...Woods": Ge 2:8-9

l.7   "And...Him": Ge 2:19 (the function of speaking is aligned with the remainder of P754's revisionist presentation of the "Owner" and His story of origins)

l.9   "And...light": Ge 1:3 ("And God said, Let there be light: and there was light")

l.13   "And...done": Ge 2:2 ("And on the seventh day God...rested...from all his work which he had made"; "it was good" is the Creation refrain, Ge 1:4, 10, 12, 18, 21, 25, 31)

l.18   "second time": Rev 2:11; 20:6, 14; 21:8

ll.23-24 "For...die": Ge 3:19; Rev 1:18; 3:7; 20:1 (the final circumscription, paradoxically enough, is a withholding of the "power to die" to one whose essence has been described as destructiveness; P754 rewrites the story of origins in order to explain how potentialities within expressed in the actualizations of "emphatic Thumb," "Yellow Eye," and "Vesuvian face" pleasure the Master-Owner—an outrageously blasphemous theodicy); Rev 1:18 ("I am he that liveth and was dead; and, behold, I am alive for evermore, Amen; and have the keys of hell and of death")

Comment: See *Poems*, II, 574.

756   One Blessing had I than the rest

l.1   "One...rest": see note, line fifteen, P783 and notes, lines five and eight, P1191 (the "Blessing" is elsewhere termed "Extasy")

l.9   "I...Cold": Rev 21:4 ("And God shall wipe away all tears from their eyes; and there shall be no more death, neither sorrow, nor crying, neither shall there be any more pain: for the former things are passed away")

l.13   "Heaven above": Rev 21-22

l.14   "ruddier Blue": Ex 26:31-33; 28:6, 15-21 (the red and blue are associated with the high priestly ephod and breastplate, the vail, and the appurtenances of the tabernacle—curtains, coverings, and hangings for which see Ex 26; gold, crimson, blue, and purple were associated with the glory and presence of God—see note, line one, P15 and P737; the colors frequently appear in nature epiphany or ectasy poems and may be metaphorically considered as substitutes for the face of God; ruddy is used to describe the profane beloved, Ca 5:10)

l.18   "Paradise": Lu 23:43; Rev 2:7; 21-22
l.19   "Why...Bowls": Ge 6:17; 7:6-10; Job 28:11 (the God of "Floods" is here accused of niggardliness or parsimoniousness)
Comment: See *Poems*, II, 575-576.

757   The Mountains- grow unnoticed-

ll.2,7   "Purple," "golden": see note, line one, P15
l.6   "Sun": Ps 84:11; 89:36; Mal 4:2; Lu 1:78; IIPe 1:19; Rev 1:16; 2:28; 21:23; 22:5, 16 (the face of the Sun-Son looking upon the mountains' "Eternal Faces" is a displacement for the beatific vision, Rev 22:4)

758   These- saw Visions-

l.1   "These [eyes]": Ca 1:15; 4:1, 9; 5:12; 6:5; 7:4; 8:10
l.3   "These [cheeks]": Ca 1:10; 5:13
l.3   "Dimples": compare with line ten, P351
l.5   "This [voice]": Ca 2:8, 12, 14; 5:2; 8:13
l.6   "Sweet Mouth": Ca 1:2; 2:14; 4:3, 11; 5:13, 16; 7:9
l.7   "This [hair]": Ca 4:1; 6:5; 7:5
l.9   "These [hands]": Ca 2:6; 5:4, 5, 14; 7:1; 8:3
l.10   "Fingers": Ca 5:5
l.10   "Slim Aurora": Ca 2:17; 3:11; 4:6; 8:8 (oxymoronic language used to describe the slenderness of the fingers but also the tenuity of that natural dawn associated with enjoyment of the beloved's presence)
l.12   "These [feet]": Ca 5:3; 7:1
l.13   "Shoe": Ca 7:1
ll.13-14   "Pearl...Paradise": Rev 21:21 ("And the twelve gates were twelve pearls; every several gate was of one pearl")
l.14   "Palace": Ca 1:17; 2:4; 3:4; 8:2; Rev 21-22 (the house of the profane beloved is exchanged for the palace of the New Jerusalem)
Comment: See *Poems*, II, 577.

760   Most she touched me by her muteness-

ll.5, 10, 11 "Crumb," "Beggar": Lu 16:20-21 ("And there was a certain beggar named Lazarus...desiring to be fed with the crumbs which fell from the rich man's table")

l.6 "Were...land": Ge 12:10; 26:1; 42:5; 43:1; Ru 1:1 (the words occur frequently in the Old Testament)

l.12 "On High": Ps 7:7; 68:15; 93:4; 107:41; 113:5; Isa 33:5, 16; Jer 25:30; Eph 4:8 (the reference is to God's dwelling place)

ll.13-15 "I...singing": Rev 5:9-13; 14:1-5 (the final two stanzas of P760 may adapt such sections of Revelation; see also Rev 19:5: "Praise our God, all ye his servants, and ye that fear him, both small and great")

Comment: See *Poems*, II, 578-579 and Franklin, I,. 514-515.

763   He told a homely tale

l.11 "Or...Firmament": Mt 6:9 ("Our Father which art in heaven")

l.16 "ransomed/found...alive": Lu 15:4-7 ("I have found my sheep which was lost," Lu 15:6)

Comment: See *Poems*, II, 580-581.

765   You constituted Time-

ll.1-8 "You...idolatry": Ex 20:1-5 ("Cupid taught Jehovah to many an untutored Mind," the poet wrote, *Letters*, II, 617, and P765 speaks of being conformed to a Higher Image, "Himself," as "slow idolatry"—see IICo 3:18; IJo 3:2)

766   My Faith is larger than the Hills-

l.1 "My...Hills": Heb 11:1 ("Now faith is the substance of things hoped for, the evidence of things not seen"; in P766 the "thing not seen" is the face of God of which the diurnal round of the sun is typic)

ll.3,8 "Purple," "Golden": see note, line one, P15 and P737 and P756 (the colors are associated with the glory and presence of God as mediated by natural phenomena, here the diurnal round of the sun)

l.3 "Wheel": Eze 1; 10; Da 7:9 (the ascent of God in the wheeled throne-chariot is part of the majestic vision of God's glory by the prophet Ezekiel; "Faith" takes the "Wheel," the circumferential route of the sun from golden to purple, as an emblem of the face of God, the experience of which in nature betokens the beatific vision, Rev 22:4)

l.4 "Sun": Mal 4:2; Rev 1:16; 2:28; 21:23; 22:5, 16

l.12 "Paradise": Lu 23:43; Rev 2:7; 21-22 (the imagery of stanza three suggests a parallel between the return of the "Sun" and the advent of the profane beloved, Ca 2:8-13)

l.15 "Lest...me": Ge 1:6-8, 14-18 (the "Firmament" is a metonym for the beloved, the "greater light" or Sun-Son whose return her "Faith" necessitates)

Comment: See *Poems*, II, 582.

769 One and One- are One-

l.6 "Everlasting": Isa 9:6 (the Deity); Ro 6:22 (everlasting life); Ps 145:13; Da 4:3; IIPe 1:11 (the everlasting kingdom of God)

771 None can experience stint

ll.7-8 "Poverty...Indigence": Mt 5:3-12 ("Blessed are the poor in spirit: for theirs is the kingdom of heaven...Blessed are they which do hunger and thirst after righteousness: for they shall be filled"; the philosophy of deprivation has been honed upon the paradoxes of the Beatitudes which oppose physical and spiritual, temporal and eternal, literal and figurative)

Comment: See *Poems*, II, 585.

772 The hallowing of Pain

ll.3-4 "Obtains...given": Lu 14:26-33 ("For which of you, intending to build a tower, sitteth not down first, and counteth the cost, whether he have sufficient to finish it?" Lu 14:28)

ll.7-8 "But...All": Lu 14:33 ("So likewise, whosoever he be of you that forsaketh not all that he hath, he cannot be my disciple"; see also IITi 4:7-8: "I have fought a good fight, I have finished my course, I have kept the faith: Henceforth there is laid up for me a crown of righteousness, which the Lord, the righteous judge, shall give me at that day: and not to me only, but unto all them also that love his appearing")

773   Deprived of other Banquet,

l.1   "Deprived...Banquet": Ca 2:4 ("He brought me to the banqueting house, and his banner over me was love"; there may be here a glance at the banquet of divine love as well, Rev 19:7-9: "Blessed are they which are called to the marriage supper of the Lamb")

ll.1-12   "Deprived...charity": Mt 5:3-12 (the Beatitudes' philosophy of "sumptuous" deprivation is behind the poem); Lu 16:19-21 (the persona of P773 may be based on the beggar Lazarus who seeks a "Berry from our table," a crumb from the banquet of the rich man clothed in purple and fine linen)

Comment: See *Poems*, II, 586

774   It is a lonesome Glee-

ll.1,6   "It...Cause": IPe 1:8 ("Whom having not seen, ye love; in whom, though now ye see him not, yet believing, ye rejoice with joy unspeakable and full of glory")

l.2   "Yet...Mind": Ro 12:2 ("be ye transformed by the renewing of your mind"; see also IPe 1:2; 3:15)

Comment: P774 shows the positive, smiling aspects of the isolated, imperial self, its purified, rectified "Mind" luxuriating in "joy unspeakable and full of glory"(IPe 1:8), transcending "Cause" and "Arrest" and identifying with "Bird" song and "Wind"—"matter[s] of the Skies." The "Mind" has here become its own heavenly tabernacle (Rev 21:3) experiencing a foretaste of glory divine, a taste of the heavenly gift.

776   The Color of a Queen, is this-

ll.4,9   "Purple," "Amber," "Iodine": see note, line one, P15 and P737 and P756 (purple, gold, and red are colors frequently used in nature epiphany poems, colors associated with the vail, the high priestly accoutrements, and the appurtenances of the tabernacle); Eze 1:4, 27; 8:2 ("Amber" is a visionary color in Ezekiel as well); Jg 8:26; Es 8:15; Ca 3:10; 7:5; Mr 15:17; Joh 19:2, 5 (fine linen and purple had regal associations in the KJV, perhaps to her mind linked with Rev 19:7-9)

       l.4   "Beryl": Ex 28:20; 39:13; Ca 5:14; Eze 28:13; Da 10:6; Rev 21:20

       Comment: See *Poems*, II, 587 and Franklin, II, 955 for the variant, "Nature has respect to," lines seven and eight.

777   The Loneliness One dare not sound-

       ll.10-11 "But...suspended": ICo 13:12 ("For now we see through a glass darkly; but then face to face; now I know in part; but then shall I know even as also I am known"; the tentativeness, the suspension of circuit world "Consciousness," is associated with anxiety over the failure of the bodily image to coalesce, at least with any meaningful finality other than extinction)

       l.12   "And...Lock": Isa 22:22; Rev 1:18; 3:7 (the keys of heaven and hell, life and death are possessed by the Lamb, the Alpha and Omega, the Son of God)

       l.14   "The...soul": Ge 2:7 ("And the Lord God formed man of the dust of the ground, and breathed into his nostrils the breath of life; and man became a living soul"); Isa 54:5 ("For thy Maker is thine husband; the Lord of hosts is his name; and thy Redeemer the Holy One of Israel")

       l.16(variant) "[Make] manifest": ICo 3:13; 4:5; 11:19; 14:25; IICo 2:14; 4:10-11; 5:11; Eph 5:13; Col 1:26; IITi 1:10 (the phrasing is frequently used by St. Paul especially for the revelation of God through Jesus Christ)

       Comment: See *Poems*, II, 588 and Franklin, II, 957-958.

778   This that would greet—an hour ago-

       l.3   "Had...Paradise": Rev 3:20 ("Behold, I stand at the door, and knock: if any man hear my voice, and open the door, I will come in to him, and will sup with him, and he with me")

779   The Service without Hope-

       l.1   "Service": Ro 12:1 ("I beseech you therefore, brethren, by the mercies of God, that ye present your bodies a living sacrifice, holy, acceptable unto God, which is your reasonable service"); Eph 6:7-8 ("With good will doing service...Knowing that whatsoever good thing any man doeth, the same shall he receive of the Lord")

l. 1   "Hope": Ro 4:13-18; 8:24-25; ICo 13:7; Heb 11:1

l. 4   "Rewarded Work": ICo 3:8 ("every man shall receive his own reward according to his own labour")

l. 5   "Has...Gain": Php 1:21; 3:7; ITi 6:6 (again the poet has in mind the loss-gain lexicon of St. Paul)

l. 6   "And...Goal": ICo 9:24 ("Know ye not that they which run in a race run all, but one receiveth the prize? So run, that ye may obtain"); Php 3:14 ("I press toward the mark for the prize"); IITi 4:7-8 ("I have fought a good fight, I have finished my course, I have kept the faith: Henceforth there is laid up for me a crown of righteousness")

l. 7   "Diligence": Heb 11:6 ("he is a rewarder of them that diligently seek him")

l. 8   "Until": ICo 4:5; Eph 1:14; Php 1:6; ITi 6:14; Heb 1:13 ("Being confident of this very thing, that he which hath begun a good work in you will perform it until the day of Jesus Christ"; the "Until" is basis for apocalyptic hope, here eschewed along with the other key words from the Paulinian lexicon)

Comment: See *Poems*, II, 589 and Franklin, II, 960.

780   The Truth- is stirless-

ll. 7-8   "Body...Bone": Ge 2:23

781   To wait an Hour- is long-

ll. 3-4   "To...end": Rev 19:7-9; 21-22 (the apocalyptic is palatable when conceived as "Love")

782   There is an arid Pleasure-

l. 1   "There...Pleasure": Ca 7:10 ("I am my beloved's, and his desire is toward me"; "arid Pleasure" is just such circuit world desire without reciprocation)

l. 3   "Frost": Job 37:10 ("By the breath of God frost is given"; frost is the arid, postlapsarian manifestation of the "element") l.3   "Dew": Ex 16:14 (associated with the nurturing, fructifying manifestation of God and with the profane beloved, Ca 5:2; dew is the prelapsarian manifestation of the "element" associated with the Edenic-paradisiacal trope for possession of the profane beloved: the bee extracting nectar from rejoicing flowers)

ll.5,6   "Flowers": Ca 2:1-2, 12, 16; 4:5; 5:13; 6:2-3; 7:2 (associated with the profane beloved)

l.7   "Honey": Ca 4:11; 5:1 (associated with the profane beloved but also with another romantic image of possession, the promised land, Ex 3:8, 17)

783   The Birds begun at Four o'clock-

l.2   "Dawn": Job 3:9; 38:12; 41:18; Mt 28:1; Lu 1:78-79; IIPe 1:19 (dawn is associated with resurrection and revelation; see also P1002)

l.15   "Extasy": Ge 15; 28; 32; Ex 3; Nu 11:25ff.; 12; IKi 19:9-18; IIKi 3:15; Isa 1:1; 6; Jer 4:23-26; Eze 1-3; 8:3; 11:1, 5; 40-48; Am 1:1; 7-9; Ob 1:1; Lu 1:41ff.; 4:1-12; Ac 2; 9; 10:9-16; ICo 14; IICo 12; Rev, passim (references to ecstasy in the Bible are too numerous to mention as are the many figures who became empowered by God's Spirit to speak His Words, such as Abraham, Moses, Jacob, Isaiah, Elijah, Jeremiah, Amos, St. Paul, and St. John the Divine; Dickinson tailors the Biblical ecstasy to her own religio-aesthetic needs emphasizing first, a sense of transport, exultation, of heightened epiphanic awareness; second, a setting that is a highly symbolic, natural landscape often, though not in P783, of visionary colors and props such as "Birds," "Music," "Noon," "Dawn," "Sun," and "East"; third, a pressure toward exclusion of bodily limitation and temporal conditions—here "Universe" and "Men" are blanked out by the "independent" and "measureless" heavenly "Music"; fourth, that like Biblical prayer, religio-aesthetic song is of the private closet; fifth, an awareness of the intermittent, fleeting character of visionary communion with God)

l.21   "Sun": Ps 84:11; 89:36; Mal 4:2; Rev 21:23; 22:5

Comment: Contrasted with the mundane, sublunary "Day," associated with the "World" and the "homely industry" of men, is the transition time of "Dawn"—a time of vision, of possible translation into Eternity—associated with the "measureless Musick" of the "Birds." P783 aspires to that disembodied, "independent Extasy" of pure vision typified in the heavenly "Music." Heard by few and appreciated by none, the song of the "Birds" becomes "typic" of the song of Moses and the Lamb (Rev 15:3) and P783 in toto becomes an extended, metonymic displacement for ideal presence, for the beatific vision (Rev 22:4)—an aspiring to see God's face in the "Dawn"(P1002) by creating the religio-aesthetic equivalent of prayer in poetic birdsong. See *Poems*, II, 591.

785   They have a little Odor- that to me

    l.1   "Odor": Ca 1:12; 3:6; 4:6, 10-11, 14; 5:5, 13, 16; 7:8 (odors would be associated with not only profane love but also sacred love since a sweet-smelling odor pleasing to God is a form of prayer analogous to poetry—see Ex 30:7-8; Php 4:18; Rev 5:8)
    l.2   "metre/Poesy...melody": Ca 1:1
    l.3   "spiciest": Ca 4:10, 14, 16; 5:1, 13; 6:2; 8:2, 14
    Comment: See *Poems*, II, 592 and Franklin, II, 968.

788   Joy to have merited the Pain-

    l.4   "Paradise": Rev 2:7; 21-22
    ll.5-8   "Pardon...Paradise": ICo 13:12; 15:49; IICo 3:18; IJo 3:2; Rev 3:18; 22:4 (the face-to-face vision of Paradise is here contrasted with the earthly one associated with the profane beloved; the verb "buy" is used in Rev 3:18 and the word "new," Rev 21:5)
    ll.9-10   "Because...them": Ca 4:9 ("Thou hast ravished my heart, my sister, my spouse; thou hast ravished my heart with one of thine eyes"); see also Ca 1:15; 4:1; 5:12; 6:5; 7:4; 8:10
    ll.17-19   "Hight...Depth": Eph 3:17-19 ("That Christ may dwell in your hearts by faith; that ye, being...grounded in love, May be able to comprehend...[the] depth, and height; And to know the love of Christ")
    Comment: See *Poems*, II, 594-595 and Franklin, II, 872-873.

789   On a Columnar Self-

    ll.9-12   "Suffice...God": Mt 18:20 ("For where two or three are gathered together in my name, there am I in the midst of them")
    l.11   "And...Assembly": Heb 12:23 ("the general assembly of the firstborn")

Comment: See *Poems*, II, 595-596 and Franklin, II, 875.

791   God gave a Loaf to every Bird-

l.1   "God...Bird": Mt 6:26 ("Behold the fowls of the air: for they sow not, neither do they reap, nor gather into barns; yet your heavenly Father feedeth them. Are ye not much better than they?")

ll.2,15   "Crumb": Lu 16:20-21 ("a certain beggar named Lazarus...desiring to be fed with the crumbs which fell from the rich man's table")

l.4   "My...luxury": Mt 5:6 ("Blessed are they which do hunger and thirst")

l.7   "Sparrow's chance": Mt 10:29-31 (her state is providentially ordained as is the sparrow's)

l.8   "Ampler Coveting": Ex 20:17 (an ironic glance at the truth commandment in fittingly oxymoronic language)

ll.9-11   "It...Plenty": Ge 41:1-36 ("Famine," "Plenty," and "Ear" are taken from the Genesis account of Pharaoh's dream and Joseph's interpretation—the poet apparently using "Ear" as a synecdoche for oral abundance)

l.12   "My...fair": Ps 144:13 ("That our garners may be full, affording all manner of store")

Comment: See *Poems*, II, 597-598 and Franklin, II, 884.

792   Through the strait pass of suffering-

ll.1-12   "Through...Air": Rev 14:1-7 (the "Martyrs" stand on Mt. Sion with the Father's name upon their foreheads singing the song of Moses and the Lamb: "These are they which were not defiled with women; for they are virgins. These are they which follow the Lamb whithersoever he goeth. These were redeemed from among men, being the firstfruits unto God and to the Lamb. And in their mouth was found no guile; for they are without fault before the throne of God," Rev 14:4-5)

Comment: For the letter to Bowles and the semifinal draft see *Poems*, II, 598-599; *Letters*, II, 394-395; Franklin, II, 887; and Leyda, II, 47-48.

796   Who Giants know, with lesser Men

l.1   "Giants": Ge 6:4; Nu 13:33; De 2:11; ISa 17:1-18:5 (see P641 and P706)

Comment: See *Poems*, II, 602-603 and Franklin, II, 796. Mere mortals (for the Giants were offspring of the sons of God and daughters of men) are as gnats to the "Giants" whose size makes them anomalies ("Accident" she calls it in P706) among "minor Company." Seemingly indestructible, except by miraculous intervention aiding a David or Elhanan (ICh 20:5), these primitive inhabitants of the promised land terrified all but the likes of Caleb and Joshua. In possession of the promised land, beyond death and struggle, the troglodytes are irrelevant. Which consciousness, she seems to ask in P796, is most adaptive, Brobdingnagian or Lilliputian? To know Giants is to be foredoomed to maladjustment—out of place in God's creation where infinite is otherworldly gift of finite, and "Greatness" the heavenly prize for painful smallness. To know the world as a Lilliputian is adaptive although achieved by somewhat grandiose delusions of significance. Nevertheless, better a "Gnat" using the art of P706 and "room" of P641 for achievement within the circuit world—a curious theodicy in justification of God-created finitude.

797   By my Window have I for Scenery

l.12   "Of...borne": Ca 1:12-13; 3:6; 4:6, 10-11, 14, 16; 5:1, 5, 13, 16; 6:2; 7:8; 8:14   ("Spice" and "Odors" are here synecdochic of love, perhaps the circuit world essence of the "Pine")

l.13   "Of...within": IKi 19:11-12

l.14   "Can...Divine": Mt 13:9-16 ("Therefore speak I to them in parables: because they seeing see not; and hearing they hear not, neither do they understand....For this people's heart is waxed gross, and their ears are dull of hearing...But blessed are your eyes, for they see: and your ears, for they hear")

l.15   "Melody": see note, line one, P988

ll.17-18 "It...Sight": IICo 5:7 ("For we know in part...But when that which is perfect is come, then that which is in part shall be done away....when I became a man, I put away childish things. For now we see through a glass darkly; but then face to face: now I know in part; but then shall I know even as also I am known")

ll.21-23 "That...Infinity": ICo 15:49-54 (by "Apprehensions" the "image of the earthy" becomes a harbinger of the "image of the heavenly") l.23   " 'Royal' Infinity": Rev 1:6; 5:10; 17:14; 19:16; 20:6; 22:5

Comment: See *Poems*, II, 603-604 and Franklin, II, 927-929.

798   She staked her Feathers- Gained an Arc-

l.2   "Rose again": ICo 15:4; IICo 5:15; ITh 4:14

l.5   "And...Circumference": Job 22:14; Ps 19:6; Isa 40:22 (God's habitation as a circuit or circle; circumferential imagery with apocalyptic significance would include the seal and crown: Rev 2:10; 3:11; 4:4, 10; 6:2; 7; 9:4, 7; 12:1, 3; 13:1; 14:14; 19:12)

Comment: See *Poems*, II, 604.

799   Despair's advantage is achieved

ll.2,5   "Suffering": Mt 17:12; Mr 8:31; 9:12; Lu 9:22; 17:25; 22:15; 24:26, 46; Ac 3:18; 5:41; 17:3; 26:23; IICo 1:5-7; Php 3:10; Heb 2:10; IPe 2:21; 3:18; 4:13; 5:1 ("the sufferings of Christ abound in us...knowing, that as ye are partakers of the sufferings, so shall ye be also of the consolation," IICo 1:5-7; the lexicon of P799, of suffering, affliction, and death, is that of the Passion)

ll.7-8   "The...tasting": Heb 2:9 ("But we see Jesus, who was made a little lower than the angels for the suffering of death, crowned with glory and honour; that he by the grace of God should taste death for every man")

ll.10-11 "As...Affliction": IITi 1:8 ("be thou partaker of the afflictions"); see also IICo 1:7; for the Passion associations of "Affliction": Isa 53:4, 7 ("Surely he hath borne our griefs, and carried our sorrows: yet we did esteem him stricken, smitten of God, and afflicted....He was oppressed, and he was afflicted, yet he opened not his mouth"); Isa 63:9 ("In all their affliction he was afflicted"); Col 1:24

Comment: See *Poems*, II, 604-605 and Franklin, II, 933.

800   Two- were immortal twice-

l.1   "Two...twice": Ge 5:24; IIKi 2; Heb 11:5 (the two were Enoch and Elijah) l.1   "immortal twice": ICo 15:53-54 (Enoch and Elijah were "immortal twice" because they escaped the first and second deaths, Rev 2:11; 20:5-6, 14; 21:8)

l.4   "Reversed Divinity": Php 2:6-8 (Christ Jesus "took upon him the form of a servant, and was made in the likeness of men: And being found in fashion as a man, he humbled himself, and became obedient unto death, even the death of the cross"; the translation of Enoch and Elijah reverses the descent and death of the Incarnate God, "Reversed Divinity")

l.5   "ignoble Eyes": ICo 13:12; IJo 3:2; Rev 3:18 (the "unfurnished eyes," P685, of circuit world perception)

l.7   "Paradise": Lu 23:43; IICo 12:4; Rev 2:7; 21-22

802   Time feels so vast that were it not

l.2   "Eternity": Isa 57:15

l.3   "Circumference": see note, line five, P798 ("Circumference" is here a word for a type of sublime, a feeling of vastness, of an ideal circumferentiality which so engrosses her "Finity" that it endangers the Brobdingnagian-Lilliputian dialectic of God's theodicy)

ll.5-8   "To...Diameters": ICo 2:9-10 ("Eye hath not seen, nor ear heard, neither have entered into the heart of man, the things which God hath prepared for them that love him. But God hath revealed them unto us by his Spirit: for the Spirit searcheth all things, yea, the deep things of God")

l.6   "Processes...Size": Mr 10:15 ("Verily I say unto you, Whosoever shall not receive the kingdom of God as a little child, he shall not enter therein"); Mt 5:3-12 (the Beatitudes philosophy of diminution would also be relevant)

ll.7-8   "For...Diameters": Rev 21-22 (the "Stupendous Vision" may refer specifically to Rev 22:4)

Comment: See *Poems*, II, 607 and Franklin, II, 938.

803   Who Court obtain within Himself

l.7   "can add": Mt 6:27 ("Which of you by taking thought can add one cubit unto his stature?")

l.7 "Crown": Rev 2:10; 3:11 (coronation is a trope for accession to spiritual status or degree and the diadem is an external confirmation of election)

Comment: See *Poems*, II, 607-608 and Franklin, II, 939.

804 No Notice gave She, but a Change-

l.1 "No...Change": ICo 15:51-52 ("we shall be changed")

ll.13-15 "And...Spring": ICo 15:35-38, 42-44, 50-55 ("But some man will say, How are the dead raised up? and with what body do they come?...But God giveth it a body as it hath pleased him, and to every seed his own body...It is sown a natural body; it is raised a spiritual body...For this corruptible must put on incorruption and this mortal must put on immortality")

l.20 "As...knew": Mt 7:23 ("And then will I profess unto them, I never knew you")

Comment: See *Poems*, II, 608 and Franklin, II, 940-941.

805 This Bauble was preferred of Bees-

l.1 "preferred": Ro 8:33
l.4 "justified": Ro 8:33
l.8 "created": Ge 1:1

Comment: An emblematic nature poem in which a trifling flower hopelessly distanced from heaven, the "Bauble," is elected by Bees and Butterflies, justified by Birds, and embellished with the beauty of Eternity by Noon and Summer.

807 Expectation is Contentment-

l.1 "Expectation": Ro 8:19; Php 1:20 (the Paulinian lexicon is given a Yankee twist in stanza two)

ll.1-2 "Contentment-Gain": ITi 6:6 ("But godliness with contentment is great gain")

Comment: P807 is a Paulinian homily on the dangers of "Satiety," "established Fortune," "secure Possession," and "Contented Measure."

809 Unable are the Loved to die

ll.2-3   "For...Deity": IJo 4:8 ("God is love")

ll.5-6   "For...Divinity": ICo 15:35-55 (the reforming of "Vitality/Into Divinity" is the change spoken of by St. Paul: earthy becomes heavenly, the corruptible incorruptible, the natural spiritual, and the mortal immortal)

Comment: See *Poems*, II, 611; Franklin, II, 1171; *Letters*, II, 441; and Leyda, II, 97.

810   Her Grace is all she has-

l.1   "Grace": Eph 2:8 ("For by grace are ye saved through faith; and that not of yourselves: it is the gift of God"; the beauty of the flower is the equivalent in nature of theological "Grace," the free gift of nature wittily played off against the poet's "Art")

Comment: See *Poems*, II, 611-612 and Franklin, II, 1173.

812   A Light exists in Spring

l.1   "Light": Joh 1:4-9; IJo 1:5; Rev 21:23; 22:5 (light at transitional spring is typic of The Light)

l.20   "Sacrament": Mt 26:26-29 (not a KJV word but the symbolical approach to the natural becomes in P812 the sacramental or emblematical way of responding to that nature epiphany which is the antithesis of "Trade")

Comment: See *Poems*, II, 613-614 and Franklin, II, 1179-1180.

813   This quiet Dust was Gentlemen and Ladies

l.1   "Dust": Ge 2:7; 3:19; Ps 103:14

815   The Luxury to apprehend

l.3   "To...time": Ca 6:13 ("Return, return, O Shulamite; return, return, that we may look upon thee")

l.4   "An...Me": Ca 8:10 ("then was I in his eyes as one that found favour")

l.11   "bouquet": Ca 2:4 (the bouquet trope and love as feeding run throughout Canticles) l.11   "To...Countenance": Ca 2:14 ("O my dove, that art in the clefts of the rock, in the secret places of the stairs, let me see thy countenance, let me hear thy voice; for sweet is thy voice, and thy countenance is comely")

l.12   "Sumptuousness": see line fifteen below

l.13   "Table": Ca 1:12

l.15   "Crumb": Lu 16:20-21 (the "Crumb" is the badge of her Lazarus-beggar destitution, a consciousness structured on absence, separation, and inescapable desire; by contrast, the "certain rich man" of the parable "fared sumptuously every day," Lu 16:19, "sumptuously" appearing only once in the KJV)

l.16   "Thee": see note, lines eight and sixteen, P537

Comment: See *Poems*, II, 616-617; *Letters*, II, 457; Franklin, II, 1078-1079; and Leyda, II, 122.

816   A Death blow is a Life blow to Some

ll.2-3   "Who...lived": Mt 10:39 ("He that findeth his life shall lose it: and he that loseth his life for my sake shall find it")

Comment: See *Poems*, II, 617-618; Franklin, II, 1183; and *Letters*, II, 451.

817   Given in Marriage unto Thee

l.1   "Given...Marriage": Mt 22:30 ("For in the resurrection they neither marry, nor are given in marriage, but are as the angels of God in heaven")

ll.1-4   "Given...Ghost": Rev 19:7-9 (bridal figuration is used to celebrate accession to heavenly status)

ll.3-4   "Father," "Son," "Holy Ghost": IJo 5:7

ll.3-4   "Bride": Rev 19:7-9; 21:2, 9; 22:17 (the Bride of Christ)

l.5   "Other...dissolve": see line one above and Mr 12:25; Lu 20:35

l.7   "Ring/Seal": Joh 6:27; IICo 1:22; Eph 4:30; Rev 7 (the ring is the seal of her election here typified by bridal accession)

l.8   "Conquer Mortality": ICo 15:53-54; IICo 5:4

Comment: See *Poems*, II, 618-619.

818   I could not drink it, Sweet,

l.1   "Sweet": Ca 2:3, 14; 5:5, 13, 16; 7:9

l.2   "Till...first": Ca 5:1 ("I have drunk my wine with my milk: eat, O friends; drink, yea, drink abundantly, O beloved"); see also Ca 2:3; 8:2

Comment: See *Poems*, II, 619 and *Letters*, II, 429.

820   All Circumstances are the Frame

l.1   "All...Frame": Heb 11:3 ("Through faith we understand that the worlds were framed by the word of God, so that things which are seen were not made of things which do appear")

ll.1,3   "All Circumstances," "All Latitudes": Ro 11:36 ("For of him, and through him, and to him, are all things: to whom be glory for ever. Amen"; see also the repetition of "All" in the Genesis creation chapters, Ge 1:26, 29; 2:1-3, 20; 3:14, 17, 20 and of the word "Face," Ge 1:2, 29; 2:6—in a sense, the imprint of God's "Face" is upon created nature)

l.5   "The...Dark": Ge 1:3-5 ("And God said, Let there be light...And God called the light Day, and the darkness he called Night"); see also Joh 1:1-5

l.6   "The...Will": Ge 1:1-31; 2:1-3 (the reference is to the leisurely pace of God's creative activity)

l.7   "In...set": Ac 17:28 ("For in him we live, and move, and have our being"); Rev 1:8 ("I am Alpha and Omega, the beginning and the ending")

l.8   "A...illegible": Isa 45:15 ("Verily thou art a God that hidest thyself"); Ro 11:33 ("O the depth of the riches both of the wisdom and knowledge of God! how unsearchable are his judgments, and his ways past finding out"; for the Deus absconditus see note, line two, P338; it is remotely possible that the poet views the Creation as an alphabet—created by the Word, the Alpha and Omega, Joh 1:1-14; Rev 1:8, 11; 21:6; 22:13—now "illegible")

Comment: See *Poems*, II, 620.

822   This Consciousness that is aware

l.3   "Will...Death": Ge 3:19 (physical death since the point of the poem is the persistence of identity via the "Soul") l.8   "Appointed unto Men": Heb 9:27 ("And as it is appointed unto men once to die, but after this the judgment")

ll.13-16 "Adventure...identity": Rev 20:11-13 ("every man" faces the "Adventure" of death and judgment)

Comment: See *Poems*, II, 622-623.

823   Not what We did, shall be the test

ll.1-4   "Not...been": Eph 2:8-9 ("For by grace are ye saved through faith; and that not of yourselves: it is the gift of God: Not of works, lest any man should boast"; P823 turns on the faith-works antithesis and the idea that righteousness is imputed—"Now to him that worketh is the reward not reckoned of grace but of debt. But to him that worketh not, but believeth on him that justifieth the ungodly, his faith is counted for righteousness," Ro 4:4-5)

Comment: See *Poems*, II, 623.

824   The Wind begun to knead/rock the Grass-

ll.1-20 "The...Tree" (first version), "The...Tree" (second version): Job 37; Eze 1 (simply examples of storms as theophanies; the association of lightning with "Doom" in P1593 may suggest that the storm here has apocalyptic overtones, Mt 24:27; Rev 6:1; 8:5; 11:19; 16:18; the anthropomorphic "Hand" and "Hands" of both versions appear frequently in the KJV as metonymic for God's agency, e.g., Job 28:9; Ps 10:12; Isa 41:20)

l.19   "my Father's House": Joh 14:2 ("In my Father's house are many mansions: if it were not so, I would have told you. I go to prepare a place for you"; the poet frequently used this phrasing of the Homestead, "Father's House" being typic of Heaven for which see IICo 5:1: "For we know that if our earthly house of this tabernacle were dissolved, we have a building of God, an house not made with hands, eternal in the heavens")

Comment: See *Poems*, II, 624-625; *Letters*, II, 519; II, 770; and Leyda, II, 214, 396.

825   An Hour is a Sea

l.2   "Between...me": Ge 31:49 ("The Lord watch between me and thee, when we are absent one from another")

Comment: See *Letters*, II, 445-446 and Leyda, II, 104.

826   Love reckons by itself- alone

1.1   "Love...alone": Joh 3:16; IJo 4:8 ("God is love," and P826 may be speaking of divine love)

1.2   "Sun": Ps 84:11; 89:36; Mal 4:2; Lu 1:78; IIPe 1:19; Rev 1:16; 2:28; 21:23; 22:5, 16 (the "Sun" may here be typic of the celestial Bridegroom and thus a metonym for "Love")

1.4   "Itself...has": Ex 3:14 (the poet may have in mind the "I Am" which resists similitude or the Divine proscription of lesser likenesses, Ex 20:4)

Comment: In P826, God as Love defeats metaphor; the quintessentially non-quantitative is yoked with the language of quantification: "reckons," "as large as." and "all the like." The Biblical wit of line two—a *sui generis* God frustrates all analogizing—underscores the fact that "Love" is a matter of experience not definition or concept (the centripetal, linguistic reflexiveness of the poem dramatizing the resistance of "Love" to formal definition).

827   The Only News I know

1.1   "The...know": Pr 25:25 ("As cold waters to a thirsty soul, so is good news from a far country")

1.3   "Immortality": ICo 15:53-54; IITi 1:10 (the word is perhaps selected to suggest circumference)

ll.5-6   "Tomorrow...Eternity": Heb 13:8 ("Jesus Christ the same yesterday, and to day, and for ever")

ll.7-8   "The...God": Mt 4:10 ("Thou shalt worship the Lord thy God, and him only shalt thou serve")

1.12   "tell/testify...You": Rev 22:16, 18 (the model for "News" from "Immortality" is the Book of Revelation, the poet testifying as had St. John the Divine)

Comment: See *Poems*, II, 626-627; Franklin, II, 975; *Letters*, II, 431; and Leyda, II, 90.

828   The Robin is the One

ll.11-12 "Submit...best": Tit 2:3-5 ("The aged woman...teach the young women to be sober...discreet, chaste, keepers at home, good, obedient")

Comment: The Paulinian Robin—a bird of sanctity, faith, and submissiveness—perhaps represents three states of the soul in March, April, and the after time. Ecstasy of April is followed by domesticity, or gathering of consciousness in recollection. See *Poems*, II, 627-628 and Franklin, II, 1133.

829 Ample make this Bed-

l.3 "wait": ITh 1:10 ("to wait for his Son from heaven"; see also Lu 12:36-40; ICo 1:7)

l.3 "Judgment": Rev 14:7 ("the hour of his judgment is come"); Rev 20:13 ("they were judged every man according to his works"; P829 refers to Judgment Day)

ll.3-4 "break...Fair": IIPe 1:19 ("until the day dawn, and the day star arise in your hearts"; see also Rev 2:28); Rev 6:17; 16:14 (in P829 the "great day of God Almighty" is spoken of metaphorically as an "Excellent" and "Fair" daybreak which parallels as well the "true and righteous" judgments of God, Rev 16:7; 19:2)

Comment: See *Poems*, II, 628-629; Franklin, II, 1088; *Letters*, II, 454; III, 770; and Leyda, II, 115, 396.

830 To this World she returned.

ll.1-2 "this World," "that": Mt 12:32 (the references are to the circuit world and the "world to come")

l.3 "Compound manner": ICo 15 (the flesh and blood, the corruptible, the terrestrial compounded temporarily with that which in the resurrection will be changed in the "twinkling of an eye" into the celestial, incorruptible, and immortal)

l.5 "Violet": see note, line one, P15 (the color of the flower associates it with the "Skies")

l.8 "half of Dust": Ge 1:27; 2:7, 20-25 (the "Bride" of "Dust" is Eve)

l.9 "half of Day": Rev 19:7-9 (the "Bride" of "Day" is the wife of the Lamb; "Day" may refer to the eternal day in the presence of the Lamb, Rev 21:25, or to the great day of God Almighty spoken of numerous times, e.g., Isa 49:26; Ro 2:18; ICo 1:8; 5:5; IICo 1:14; Php 1:6; IIPe 3:10, 12; Jude 6; Rev 6:17; 16:14)

Comment: See *Poems*, II, 629-630; Franklin, II, 1188; and Leyda, II, 92.

831   Dying! To be afraid of thee

l.7   "Dust": Ge 2:7; 3:19; Ps 103:14

l.8   "enemy": ICo 15:26 ("The last enemy that shall be destroyed is death")

l.8   "Beloved": Ca 1:14, 16; 2:3, 8-10, 16-17; 4:16; 5:1-6, 8-10, 16; 6:1-3; 7:9-13; 8:5, 14

ll.11-12 "Two...Reverse": Ca 1-8; Rev 19:7-9; 21-22 (the certain, profane love clashes with that uncertain opposite associated with apocalyptic hope as Bride of Christ)

Comment: See *Poems*, II, 630-631; Franklin, II, 1167-1168; and Leyda, II, 120-121.

833   Perhaps you think me stooping

l.1   "stooping": Joh 19:17 (Christ bearing the cross in a stooping position; there may also be a reference here to the washing of the disciples' feet, Joh 13:4-17, or to the position of prayer assumed by Christ in Gethsemane, Mt 26:36-56; in a more figurative sense, "stooping" may refer to the crucifixion itself during which the Infinite God stoops to die on the cross)

l.2   "not ashamed": Ro 1:16 ("For I am not ashamed of the gospel of Christ")

l.3   "Christ...Grave": Mt 26-27 (the Passion of Jesus Christ with which Dickinson identifies; P833 is telling Bowles that she identifies as much with the Passion chapters of Matthew, the presumed penultimate ones, as with the supposed, climactic final chapter dealing with the resurrection; the poem becomes a rhetorical question regarding whether the Eucharist commemorates only the resurrected and glorified Christ)

l.4   "Sacrament": Mt 26:26 (the Eucharist)

l.5   "Dishonor": Ps 69:19 ("Thou hast known my reproach, and my shame, and my dishonor"; see also Ps 22:6-7; Isa 53:3; Heb 12:2) ll.6-7   "Or...Death": Php 2:6-9 ("Who, being in the form of God...made himself of no reputation...being found in fashion as a man, he humbled himself, and became obedient unto death, even the death of the cross")

l.8   "Redignified/Re-royalized, above": Ps 68:18 ("Thou hast ascended on high"; see also Joh 3:13; Ac 1:9; Eph 4:8-10; and Col 3:1: "If ye then be risen with Christ, seek those things which are above, where Christ sitteth on the right hand of God"); Rev1:5 ("And from Jesus Christ...the prince of the kings of the earth"; Christ is also spoken of as "Lord of lords, and King of kings," Rev 17:14; 19:16)

Comment: See *Poems*, II, 631-632 and Franklin, II, 1040.

835   Nature and God- I neither knew

l.1   "God...knew": Isa 45:15 ("Verily thou art a God that hidest thyself"; IJo 4:12:"No man hath seen God at any time"; for the Deus absconditus, note, line two, P338; see also Ro 11:33)

l.2   "Yet...me": Ps 103:14; ICo 13:12

l.6   "My...secure": De 29:29 ("The secret things belong unto the Lord our God")

Comment: See *Poems*, II, 633.

836   Truth- is as old as God-

ll.1-4   "Truth...Co-Eternity": Joh 1:1-14 ("In the beginning was the Word, and the Word was with God, and the Word was God. The same was in the beginning with God. All things were made by him...And the Word was made flesh and dwelt among us, (and we beheld his glory, the glory as of the only begotten of the Father,) full of grace and truth"; Christ, the Word, is truth:"I am the way, the truth, and the life," Joh 14:6; the KJV speaks of the Spirit or Comforter as the truth, Joh 15:26; IJo 5:6—also associated with "Co-Eternity," Ge 1:2)

l.7   "From...Universe": Joh 14:2

Comment: See *Poems*, II, 633-634.

837   How well I knew Her not

l.1   "I...not": Ge 28:16 ("Surely the Lord is in this place; and I knew it not")

Comment: See *Poems*, II, 634; Franklin, II, 1054; and Leyda, II, 91.

838   Impossibility, like Wine

ll.1-3   "Wine...it": Ps 104:15 ("And wine that maketh glad the heart of man")

839   Always Mine!

l.1   "Always Mine": Ca 2:16 ("My beloved is mine, and I am his: he feedeth among the lilies"); Ca 6:2 ("I am my beloved's, and my beloved is mine"); Mal 4:2; IIPe 1:19; Rev 1:16; 2:28; 21:23; 22:5, 16 (the dawn brings possession of the day star, an experience typic of marriage to the Sun-Son-Bridegroom in an eternal day)
l.2   "No...Vacation": Rev 4:8; 14:11 ("they rest not"); Rev 21:25; 22:5 ("there shall be no night there")
ll.3-5   "Term...Sun": Rev 21:23; 22:5 ("And there shall be no night there; and they need no candle, neither light of the sun; for the Lord God giveth them light: and they shall reign for ever and ever"; the diurnal round, "fair rotation," is typic of eternal day—"fair" being the Canticles term for the beloved, Ca 1:15-16; 2:10, 13; 4:1, 7, 10; 7:6)
ll.6-7   "Old...East": Rev 22:5 ("Behold, I make all things new"; the "Old" is that "Grace" of necessity mediated through nature)
l.8   "Purple": see note, line one, P15 (the color is associated both with the profane, Ca 3:10; 7:5, and divine beloved— the purple of the sunrise typifies the yearned for Divine Presence)
l.9   "Dawn": IIPe 1:19 (see line one above)

842   Good to hide, and hear'em hunt!

ll.6-8   "Best...dull": Mt 13:13-15
Comment: P842 concerns the poet and her desired, ideal audience. Using Jesus' explanation of the use of parables as a background, the poem anticipates those of "rare Ear." "Tell all the truth but tell it slant"(P1129) since "Best, to know and tell" even if the general audience be gross and dull of hearing. Thus, the "Fox" poet indeed "fits the Hound."

843   I made slow Riches but my Gain

l.1   "slow Riches": Mt 6:19-20 ("Lay not up for yourselves treasures upon earth...But lay up for yourselves treasures in heaven")

ll.1,6   "Gain": Mt 16:26 ("For what is a man profited, if he shall gain the whole world, and lose his own soul?")

844   Spring is the Period

ll.1-2   "Spring...God": Ac 14:17 ("Nevertheless he left not himself without witness, in that he did good, and gave us rain from heaven, and fruitful seasons, filling our hearts with food and gladness")

ll.7-8   "Without...God": Ge 3:8 (the poet may here glance at this "interview")

846   Twice had Summer her fair Verdure

l.8   "wandering Bird": Isa 16:2

847   Finite- to fail, but infinite to Venture-

ll.2-3   "For...Creature": Ps 124:2-4 ("If it had not been the Lord who was on our side...the waters had overwhelmed us")

848   Just as He spoke it from his Hands

l.1   "He Spoke": Ge 1:3, 6, 9, 11, 14, 20, 24, 26, 28-29 ("God said, Let there be"—God "spoke" the "Edifice" of the world into existence; see also Ps 33:6; Joh 1:1-14; IIPe 3:5)

l.1   "Hands": Heb 1:10 ("And, Thou, Lord, in the beginning hast laid the foundation of the earth; and the heavens are the works of thine hands"; see also Ps 102:25)

l.2   "remain": Isa 66:22

ll.5-7   "According...ornament": Ps 102:25-26 ("Of old hast thou laid the foundation of the earth: and the heavens are the work of thy hands. They shall perish, but thou shalt endure: yea, all of them shall wax old like a garment; as a vesture shalt thou change them, and they shall be changed"); IIPe 3:5-11

l.8   "His...character": Isa 45:15 (for the Deus absconditus see also note, line two, P338; the use of "absent' may echo IICo 5:6-9; see also Ro 1:20)

849   "The good Will of a Flower"

l.5   "minted Holiness": Ro 4:6; 6:22-23; 8:29-30; Eph 4:24

Comment: Numerous references could be given on "Holiness" as a "minted" or manufactured gift, certified or imputed. Thus, the Biblical wit of P849 involves the contrast of the artificial "good Will" of "Man" with the natural "good Will of a Flower," with verbal play upon "mint" suggesting conformity to the image of nature as certification for possession—the legal, organic, and theological lexicons clashing in humorous dissonance.

850   I sing to use the Waiting

l.1   "Waiting": ICo 1:7 ("waiting for the coming of our Lord Jesus Christ"); Ro 8:19, 23, 25; ITh 1:10; IITh 3:5

ll.3,5   "And...approaching": Rev 3:20 ("Behold, I stand at the door and knock")

l.6   "Day": see note, line nine, P830 (see also Heb 10:25: "as ye see the day approaching")

851   When the Astronomer stops seeking

l.2   "Face": Ca 2:14; 5:15; Rev 22:4 (the "Face" of the seventh star not visible to the naked eye is "typic" of the face of the beloved, profane or divine)

l.5   "Covenant": Ge 2-3; Ex 19-20; Mt 26:28; Ac 3:25; Ro 9:4; IICo 3:6; Ga 3:16-17; 4:21-28; Eph 2:12-13; Heb 7:1-22; 8-9; 13:20 (the Old Covenant of Works and the New Covenant of Grace; the "Covenant" may also be that of marriage, Ge 2; Mt 19; Rev 19)

Comment: P851 states conditions contrary to fact in order to hold the lover to his word—not to forsake (Heb 13:5), to marry (Rev 19:7-9), and to reveal his long-sought-for face (Rev 22:4). Thus, P851 is a "Putative"[see note, lines fourteen-nineteen, P179; note line one, P339; and Comment, P961].

854   **Banish Air from Air-**

l.2   "Divide...dare": Mt 19:6 ("What therefore God hath joined together, let not man put asunder"); ICo 6:17 ("But he that is joined unto the Lord is one spirit")

l.7   "cannot annul": Ga 3:15 ("Brethren, I speak after the manner of men; Though it be but a man's covenant, yet if it be confirmed, no man disannulleth, or addeth thereto")

l.8   "Odors": Ex 29:25, 41; 40:27; Rev 8:3-4 (the product of combustion is the accepted, sweet-smelling odor)

ll.9-12   "Force...Steam": Rev 3:4 ("they shall walk with me in white"); Rev 19:8 ("arrayed in fine linen, clean and white"; using a conceited, metaphysical style, P854 contends as does P528 for the indissoluble essence of her religio-aesthetic commitment, her "White Election," her marriage to "Air," "Light," and "Steam" whose perdurability through metamorphosis or chemical change echoes Paulinian hope, ICo 15:51-53)

855   **To own the Art within the Soul**

l.2   "Soul": Ge 2:7; ICo 15:45 (P855 is a "mind alone without corporeal friend" poem)

856   **There is a finished feeling**

l.1   "finished": Ac 20:24 ("I might finish my work with joy"); IITi 4:7 ("I have finished my course, I have kept the faith")

l.2   "Experienced...Graves": ICo 15:55 ("O death, where is thy sting? O grave, where is thy victory?")

l.7   "Eternal function": Ro 6:23 ("the gift of God is eternal life through Jesus Christ our Lord")

857   **Uncertain lease- developes lustre**

ll.3-4   "Uncertain...Sum": ICo 13:12 ("now I know in part")

l.5   "The...chiefest":   Mr   10:44-45   ("And whosoever...will be chiefest...even the Son of man came...to give his life a ransom for many")

l.7   "Inheritors...tenure": Col 3:24 ("Knowing that of the Lord ye shall receive the reward of the inheritance"); IPe 1:4 ("To an inheritance incorruptible, and undefiled, and that fadeth not away, reserved in heaven for you")

l.8   "Prize": Php 3:14 ("I press toward the mark for the prize of the high calling of God in Christ Jesus")

858   This Chasm, Sweet, upon my life

ll.1,10   "Sweet," "Darling": Ca 1:9, 14-16; 2:2-3, 7-10, 13-14, 16-17; 3:5; 4:1, 7, 10, 16; 5:1-10, 13, 16; 6:1-4; 7:6, 9-13; 8:5, 14

ll.5-6   "it's...Tomb": Joh 20:27

l.8   "Favorite": Ca 8:10

ll.17-18 "bear...Burial": IICo 4:10 ("Always bearing about in the body the dying of the Lord Jesus, that the life also of Jesus might be made manifest in our body")

l.19   "A...depart": Php 1:23 ("For I am in a strait betwixt two, having a desire to depart, and to be with Christ; which is far better")

Comment: In profane love terms, P858 rehearses the turbulent, desperate isolation of that Gnostic sensibility imprisoned in "Life," distanced from the presence of the beloved, and granted only a vision of "Tomb," "Doom," and "Burial."

860   Absence disembodies- so does Death

l.1   "Absence...Death": IICo 5:6, 8 ("whilst we are at home in the body, we are absent from the Lord...We are...willing rather to be absent from the body, and to be present with the Lord"); ICo 15:35 ("How are the dead raised up? and with what body do they come?"; St. Paul goes on at length about how "Death" through resurrection "disembodies," ICo 15:42-55)

861   Split the Lark- and you'll find the Music-

l.7   "Scarlet...Thomas": Joh 20:24-31 (Thomas refused to believe—"Except I shall see in his hands the print of the nails, and put my finger into the print of the nails, and thrust my hand into his side, I will not believe"; the "Scarlet Experiment" is Thomas's touching the wounds of Christ with his hands, Joh 20:27, Christ admonishing "Sceptic Thomas" at the same time to "be not faithless but believing")

l.8   "Bird...true": Rev 14:3, 5 ("they sung as it were a new song...And in their mouth was found no guile")

Comment: The identification with Christ in line seven may suggest a link between splitting the "Lark" and smiting the "Rock," ICo 10:4, and Old Testament type, Ex 17:6; Ps 78:15, 20; 105:41; Isa 48:21—the language of violent loosing of the flood which "gushed out." See *Poems*, II, 644.

864   The Robin for the Crumb

l.1   "Crumb": Lu 16:21 ("desiring to be fed with the crumbs which fell from the rich man's table"; synecdochic of circuit world destitution, the "Crumb" can never qualify as efficient or final cause of song)

Comment: See *Letters*, III, 908 and Leyda, II, 95.

865   He outstripped Time with but a Bout,

l.1   "He...Bout": Mt 26-28 (the Passion and Resurrection of Jesus Christ)

ll.3-4   "And...Throne": Heb 9:24; 12:2 ("Looking unto Jesus the author and finisher of our faith; who for the joy that was set before him endured the cross, despising the shame, and is set down at the right hand of the throne of God"; see also Ro 8:34; Eph 1:20-22; Heb 1:3-13; 8:1; IPe 3:22)

l.5   "And...List": Col 3:1; Heb 7:25 (the intercession of Christ is viewed as a battle, perhaps derived from the idea of the "battle of that great day of God Almighty," Rev 16:14); Heb 8 (Christ in his eternal intercession is the "mediator of a better covenant")

l.7   "Glory": Jude 24; Rev 21-22 (the presence of God is spoken of as one of "Glory")

ll.7-8   "larger Glory...less...Ring": Rev 22:1 (the "larger Glory" and the "less" are God and the Lamb; among others, two possible readings of these final two lines might be as follows: God's "Glory" is the ideally circumferential arena, the "Ring," in which for all eternity Christ the Intercessor runs His "Bout" or "List" of mediation; the "larger Glory" is synecdochic for the new circumference Presence of God mediated to the "less" circuit world by

Christ the marriageable Lamb of Rev 19:7-9—"just sufficient Ring" synecdochic for the Lamb and the eternal betrothal He offers to His Sealed and Crowned Elect, Emily Elizabeth)

       l.8   "just": Ac 3:14 ("the Holy One and the Just"); Ac 7:52; 22:14; Ro 3:26; Rev 15:3 ("just and true are thy ways, thou King of saints")

       l.8   "sufficient": IICo 12:9 ("My grace is sufficient for thee: for my strength is made perfect in weakness"); Joh 14:8-11; IICo 3:5; 9:8

       l.8   "Ring": Rev 22:3 ("the throne of God and of the Lamb")

867   Escaping backward to perceive

       ll.1-8   "Escaping...Divine": Mt 14:22-33 (the poet may have had in mind Simon Peter's circumstance as a universal one instructing in the ways of God to man)

868   They ask but our Delight-

       l.1   "Delight": Ca 2:3; 7:6 ("delight" is in the presence of the beloved)

       l.3   "grant": Rev 3:21; 19:8 (the "grant" is again associated with the presence of the beloved)

       l.3   "Countenance": Ca 2:14 ("O my dove...let me see thy countenance...thy countenance is comely")

869   Because the Bee may blameless hum

       ll.2,8,12 "Thee," "Thou": see note, lines eight, sixteen, P537 (the Canticles pronouns are directed at the Divine beloved)

       ll.4-5   "Because...Maid": Ps 123:1-2 ("Unto thee lift up mine eyes, O thou that dwellest in the heavens...as the eyes of a maiden...so our eyes wait upon the Lord our God"); for the fear of God's face, Ex 33:20

       ll.8-11 "When...Furze": ICo 15:42-55 the metamorphoses are emblematic of resurrection)

       l.12   "I...Thee": Rev 4:10 ("worship him that liveth for ever and ever"); Rev 14:7 ("worship him that made heaven, and earth"); Rev 15:4 ("all nations shall come and worship before thee"); Rev 19:10; 22:9 ("worship God")

871   The Sun and Moon must make their haste-

ll.1-4   "The...burned": Rev 21:23 ("And the city had no need of the sun, neither of the moon, to shine in it: for the glory of God did lighten it, and the Lamb is the light thereof"); Rev 22:5 ("And there shall be no night there; and they need no candle, neither light of the sun; for the Lord God giveth them light: and they shall reign for ever and ever")

ll.5-8   "Eye...Worms": Rev 1:14; 2:18 ("the Son of God, who hath his eyes like unto a flame of fire")

ll.9-10   "Oh...Eye": ICo 13:12 ("For now we see through a glass, darkly; but then face to face: now I know in part; but then shall I know even as also I am known"); Rev 3:17-18 ("thou art wretched, and miserable, and poor, and blind, and naked: I counsel thee to...anoint thine eyes with eyesalve, that thou mayest see")

l.11   "That...Day": Rev 21:23-25; 22:5 (the eternal "Day" of the New Jerusalem; "Day" also may be a metonym for the glory of "His Countenance," and hence of the beatific vision)

ll.12-13 "The...Thee": Rev 22:5 ("they need no candle, neither light of the sun; for the Lord God giveth them light"; the KJV uses the candle image figuratively: "The spirit of man is the candle of the Lord," Pr 20:27; see also Job 29:3; Ps 18:28; Mt 5:15)

873   Ribbons of the Year-

l.8   "Maker's Girl": Ge 1-2; Job 36:3; Ps 95:6; Isa 45:11 (the "Maker" is the Creator God whose deputy is here a personified nature flinging off the "Brocade" of the seasons as a "Girl" her "faded Bead" or "Wrinkled Pearl")

874   The wont frown always- some sweet Day

l.1   "sweet": Ca 2:3, 14; 5:513, 16; 7:9
l.1   "Day": Ca 3:11 ("the day of his espousals,...the day of the gladness of his heart")

Comment: See *Poems*, II, 649-650 and Franklin, II, 1057.

875   I stepped from Plank to Plank

l.8   "Some...Experience": Ro 5:3-4 ("we glory in tribulations also: knowing that tribulationm worketh patience; And patience, experience; and experience, hope")

876   It was a Grave, yet bore no Stone

ll.1-3   "Grave...Consciousness": Ro 7:24; IICo 5:4; Php 3:21 (circuit world consciousness as the body prison)
l.4   "Human Soul": Ge 2:7
l.6   "If...born": Joh 3:6 ("That which is born of the flesh is flesh; and that which is born of the Spirit is spirit")
l.9   "Resurrection": ICo 15:21, 42
Comment: See *Poems*, II, 650-651 and Franklin, II, 931, 1160.

877   Each Scar I'll keep for Him

l.1   "Scar": Isa 53:5; Zec 13:6; Joh 20:25, 27 (an identification with the Passion Christ)
ll.2-4   "Instead...one": Rev 21:11 ("Having the glory of God: and her light was like unto a stone most precious, even like a jasper stone, clear as crystal"; in addition to an identification with the Bride, the poet may here identify with Christ as the "Gem," Isa 28:16)
l.5   "bore": Isa 53:4 ("Surely he hath borne our griefs, and carried our sorrows: yet we did esteem him stricken, smitten of God, and afflicted")
l.7   "His...more": Heb 5:7-8 ("Who in the days of his flesh, when he had offered up prayers and supplications with strong crying and tears unto him that was able to save him from death, and was heard in that he feared; Though he were a Son, yet learned he obedience by the things which he suffered")

881   I've none to tell me to but Thee

ll.1,2,8,10,13 "Thee," "Thou": see note, lines eight, sixteen, P537
ll.1-2   "I've...nobody": Ca 5:6
l.5   "sweet": Ca 2:3, 14; 5:5, 13, 16; 7:9

l.5 "Face": Ca 2:14; 5:15
l.10 "Woulds't...seek": Ca 2:14; 3:1-2; 5:6, 15; 6:1
l.12 "lips": Ca 4:3, 11; 5:13; 7:9
ll.10-13 "just say...Thee": Ca 5:8 (the Canticles imagery and the topoi of profane love are used in P881 as "typic" of the yearning for the Divine Beloved)

882 A Shade upon the mind there passes

l.3 "Sun": Ps 84:11; 89:36; Mal 4:2; Lu 1:78; IIPe 1:19; Rev 1:16; 2:28; 21:23; 22:5, 16
l.5 "That...notice": Mt 13:15 ("For this people's heart is waxed gross, and their ears are dull of hearing, and their eyes they have closed"; see also Isa 6:9-10; Ac 28:26-27)
ll.6-7 "God...away": Job 1:21 ("Naked came I out of my mother's womb, and naked shall I return thither: the Lord gave, and the Lord hath taken away; blessed be the name of the Lord")
l.8 "Loved": Ca 2:9-17; 5-7; Rev 19:7-9; 22:4 (loss of the "Loved," of the face and presence of the sun, is typic with regard to the beloved, profane and Divine)

883 The Poets light but Lamps-

l.4 "vital Light": Ge 1:3-5; Joh 1:4-9 (the poet identifies with the "Light" of Divine Creation)

885 Our little Kinsmen- after Rain

ll.9-12 "As...enlarged": Mt 6:26-27 ("Behold the fowls of the air: for they sow not, neither do they reap, nor gather into barns; yet your heavenly Father feedeth them. Are ye not much better than they? Which of you by taking thought can add one cubit unto his stature?")

886 These tested Our Horizon-

l.1 "These...Horizon": Ge 5:24; 28; 32; IIKi 2:11; Eze 1, passim; IICo 12:1-6 ("These" may refer to any number of Biblical characters who pushed against or crossed circumference: Enoch, Elijah, Moses, Jacob, Ezekiel, St. Paul, Christ; also relevant may be the summary of that "cloud of witnesses," Heb 11-12; of course, the provenance may be non-Biblical, a simple reference to lost loved ones)

888   When I have seen the Sun emerge

ll.1-2   "When...House": Ps 19:4-6 ("a tabernacle for the sun...a bridegroom coming out of his chamber...as a strong man to run a race. His going forth is from the end of heaven, and his circuit unto the ends of it: and there is nothing hid from the heat thereof": one of the poems equating the Sun-Son-Bridegroom, for which see also Mal 4:2; Lu 1:78; IIPe 1:19; Rev 1:16; 2:28; 21:23; 22:5, 16)

889   Crisis is a Hair

l.1   "Crisis": IICo 5:11 ("Crisis" is the "terror of the Lord"—the uncertainty whether we wake or sleep, live or die, are clothed or unclothed, bodied or bodiless)
l.15   "Eternity": Isa 57:15

890   From Us She wandered now a Year,

ll.1,4   "wandered," "Wilderness": Jos 14:10 ("the children of Israel wandered in the wilderness")
l.2   "tarrying": Mt 25:5; Heb 10:37 (the verb has apocalyptic resonance)
l.4   "Etherial Zone": Rev 21-22 (Heaven)
l.5   "No...lived": Ex 33:20 ("And he said, Thou canst not see my face: for there shall no man see me, and live"); Isa 64:4; ICo 2:9 ("Eye hath not seen, nor ear heard, neither have entered into the heart of man, the things which God hath prepared for them that love him"); IJo 4:12 ("No man hath seen God at any time")
l.8   "Mystery": ICo 15:51 ("Behold, I shew you a mystery; We shall not all sleep, but we shall all be changed")
Comment: See Poems, II, 656-657.

891   To my quick ear the Leaves- conferred-

l.5   "presumed...hide": Ge 3:8 ("Adam and his wife hid themselves"); Ge 3:10

893 Drab Habitation of Whom?

l.1 "Habitation": Ps 71:3; 91:9 (a KJV word for the dwelling place of God; "In whom ye also are builded together for an habitation of God through the Spirit," Eph 2:22)

l.2 "Tabernacle": Ex 25-40 (the Old Testament tabernacle was the sanctuary or house of God, in Ex 26:1 and Heb 9:2-3 the tabernacle specifying the holy of holies only—the place of the presence of God; St. Paul uses "tabernacle" to refer to the body as abode of the spirit: "For we know that if our earthly house of this tabernacle were dissolved, we have a building of God, an house not made with hands, eternal in the heavens," IICo5:1)

l.2 "Tomb": Mt 27:60 (the cocoon in P893 is a metonym for Ned and the questions are rhetorical—the poem a Hitchcockian emblematic expression of faith in the cocoon as "Porch of Gnome," the grave as platform for resurrection, ICo 15:50-55)

Comment: See *Poems*, II, 659.

894 Of Consciousness, her awful Mate

l.4 "Behind...God": Pr 15:3 ("The eyes of the Lord are in every place, beholding the evil and the good")

l.7 "triple Lenses": IJo 5:7-8 (the reference may be to the Trinity)

895 A Cloud withdrew from the Sky

ll.1-4 "A...me": ICo 15:40-41 ("There are also celestial bodies, and bodies terrestrial: but the glory of the celestial is one, and the glory of the terrestrial is another. There is one glory of the sun, and another glory of the moon, and another glory of the stars: for one star differeth from another star in glory")

ll.9-12 "Never...now": Ge 3:24; Rev 21:12 (cherubims guarding re-entry to Eden or the angels at the twelve gates of the New Jerusalem; the poet uses the analogy of familiarity with the gatekeepers of Heaven's bourne in order to chastise her own epistemological complacency)

Comment: See *Poems*, II, 659-660 and Franklin, II, 1118.

897 How fortunate the Grave-

l.1   "Grave": Ho 13:14; ICo 15:54-55

l.2   "Prizes...obtain": ICo 9:24 ("Know ye not that they which run in a race run all, but one receiveth the prize? So run, that ye may obtain"); Php 3:14

ll.3-4 "Successful...Suitor": ICo 15:26 ("The last enemy that shall be destroyed is death")

l.4   "not in vain": ICo 15:58 ("ye know that your labour is not in vain in the Lord"); Php 2:16 ("that I may rejoice in the day of Christ, that I have not run in vain, neither laboured in vain")

899   Herein a Blossom lies-

ll.1-4 "Herein...Rind": ICo 15:35-55

l.2   "Sepulchre": Mt 28:1

l.3   "overcome...Bee": IJo 5:4 ("For whatsoever is born of God overcometh the world"); Rev 2:7 ("To him that overcometh will I give to eat of the tree of life, which is in the midst of the paradise of God"); Rev 2:11 ("He that overcometh shall not be hurt of the second death"); Rev 2:17 ("To him that overcometh will I give to eat of the hidden manna"); Rev 21:7 ("He that overcometh shall inherit all things")

Comment: P899 uses the "Blossom" within its calyx as a metaphor for the soul within the body in the circuit world. To burst the bounds of the calyx ("Cross it") is to overcome that for which the "Bee" is synecdochic. To "Remain" is a collapse within the unaesthetic calyx, within the fleshly crypt of the circuit world. P899, then, seems to be a Hitchcockian, emblematic nature poem of religio-aesthetic provenance: first, the "Blossom" is the soul passing beyond the circuit world via the "Sepulchre"; second, the "Blossom" is the Beautiful created by pain, suffering, and violent rupture in the process of the transmutation of the natural. To be Philistine is here no less catastrophic than to fail as one of the Elect.

900   What did They do since I saw Them?

l.13   "the Just": Ac 3:14; 7:52; 22:14 (a title for Christ)

l.14   "And...Reward": ITi 2:6 ("Who gave himself a ransom for all"); Heb 10:12 ("But this man, after he had offered one sacrifice for sins for ever, sat down on the right hand of God")

Comment: See *Poems*, II, 662 and Franklin, II, 1115.

901   Sweet, to have had them lost

l.1   "Sweet": Ca 2:3, 14; 5:5, 13, 16; 7:9 (the Canticles word used in association with the profane beloved)

l.2   "news": Pr 25:25 ("As cold waters to a thirsty soul, so is good news from a far country")

l.2   "saved": Eph 2:8; Rev 21:24 (the word is chosen for the hyperbole in its reverse effect)

l.5   "Shall...Hand": Ac 7:56 ("the Son of man standing on the right hand of God"; the phrasing has apocalyptic echoes suggesting usurpation of the prerogatives of the Deity for which see also Mt 20:23; 22:44; 25:33-34; 26:64; Ac 2:25, 33-34; Ro 8:34; Col 3:1; Heb 1:3)

l.6   "Most precious": Rev 21:11

Comment: See *Poems*, II, 662-663 and Franklin, II, 1192.

902   The first Day that I was a Life

l.1   "Life": Joh 11:25 ("I am the resurrection, and the life: he that believeth on me, though he were dead, yet shall he live"; the poet may here speak of rebirth although the language of the poem remains general—see also Joh 3:3-8; 10:10; Ro 6:4)

l.8   "full": Eph 3:19; 4:13

ll.13-14 " 'Which'...say": Eph 1:4 ("According as he hath chosen us in him before the foundation of the world, that we should be holy and without blame before him in love")

l.15   " 'Which'...'They'": Jos 24:15 ("choose you this day whom ye will serve")

Comment: See *Poems*, II, 663-664.

903   I hide myself within my flower,

ll.3-4   "You...loneliness/angels...rest": Heb 13:2 ("Be not forgetful to entertain strangers: for thereby some have entertained angels unawares")

Comment: See *Poems*, II, 664-665 and Franklin, I, 46; II, 984.

906   The Admirations- and Contempts- of time-

ll.1012   "Light...Infinite": Joh 1:1-9; IJo 1:5

907   Till Death- is narrow Loving-

l.1   "Till Death": Ge 3:19 (the words are part of the "Solemnization of Holy Matrimony," *Book of Common Prayer*)

ll.2-3   "The...privilege": Ca 4:9 ("Thou hast ravished my heart")

l.5   "But...you": Ro 5:8 (the love of Christ expressed in His death "procures" the "Destitution")

l.6   "Destitution": Heb 11:37 (the deprivation of the faithful who would imitate Christ)

ll.8-9   "Thenceforward...perfect": Ro 8:29 ("For whom he did foreknow, he also did predestinate to be conformed to the image of his Son, that he might be the firstborn among many brethren"); IICo 3:18 ("But we all, with open face beholding as in a glass the glory of the Lord, are changed into the same image from glory to glory, even as by the Spirit of the Lord"); Eph 4:13; IJo 3:2

ll.10-12 "Yourself...somewhat": Php 3:7-14

908   'Tis Sunrise- Little Maid- Hast Thou

l.1   "Sunrise": Isa 60:3; Rev 21:24

ll.1,6,10,11,14 "Thou," "thee": see note, lines eight, sixteen, P537 (the Canticles pronouns are spoken with plaintive intimacy by the Divine Beloved)

ll.1,5,9 "Little," "little": IJo 2:1, 12-13, 18, 28; 3:7, 18; 4:4; 5:21

l.2   "Day": Rev 6:17; 16:14 (the "great day of God Almighty")

l.4   "Retrieve...industry": Joh 9:4 ("the night cometh, when no man can work")

ll.5-6   " 'Tis...yet": Mr 13:34-36 ("For the Son of man is as a man taking a far journey...and commanded the porter to watch. Watch ye therefore: for ye know not when the master of the house cometh, at even, or at midnight, or at the cockcrowing, or in the morning: Lest coming suddenly he find ye sleeping"); Mt 25:1-13 (this parable contains the sleeping motif and the advent of the Bridegroom)

l.7   "Lily": Ca 2:1-2, 16; 4:5; 5:13; 6:2-3; 7:2 (the flower associated with the profane beloved and here along with the "Bee" typic of the Bride and Bridegroom, Rev 19:7-9; 21)

ll.9-10   "My...thee": ITh 5:2 ("the day of the Lord so cometh as a thief in the night"; IIPe 3:10; for other figurative uses of "Night": Lu 12:20; 17:34; Joh 9:4; 11:10)

l.11   "Morning": Rev 2:28; 28:16 (the Bridegroom is the star of the morning, thus symbolizing apocalyptic hope)

l.13   "Sweet": Ca 2:3, 14; 5:5, 13, 16; 7:9

Comment: See *Poems*, II, 667.

910   Experience is the Angled Road

l.7   "Choose": Eph 1:4 ("According as he hath chosen us in him before the foundation of the world")

l.8   "Preappointed": Ac 17:26, 31; ICo 4:9; Ga 4:2; Heb 1:2; 3:2; IPe 2:8 (the predestinarian echoes are ironic; "That no man should be moved by these afflictions: for yourselves know that we are appointed thereunto," ITh 3:3)

Comment: See *Poems*, II, 668-669 and Franklin, II, 1033.

911   Too little way the House must lie

l.1   "House": IICo 5:1 ("For we know that if our earthly house of this tabernacle were dissolved, we have a building of God, an house not made with hands, eternal in the heavens")

l.4   "white inhabitant": Rev 2:17; 3:4-5; 6:11; 7:9, 13-14; 19:8 (apocalyptic white is used as a displacement suggesting the destiny of the soul)

l.5   "narrow...between": Mt 7:14 ("Because strait is the gate, and narrow is the way, which leadeth unto life")

ll.7-8   "Each...once": Heb 9:27 ("And as it is appointed unto men once to die, but after this the judgment")

912   Peace is a fiction of our Faith-

l.1   "Peace...Fiction": Joh 14:27; 20:19, 21, 26 (Christ speaks of leaving His peace with His disciples; St. Paul speaks of peace as a fruit of the Spirit, Ga 5:22, and of Christ as "our peace," Eph 2:14; the poet speaks of peace as a fiction—a word empty of presence—since at the heart of "Faith" is that absence spoken of in the next three lines)

914   I cannot be ashamed

l.1   "ashamed"; IITi 2:15 ("Study to shew thyself approved unto God, a workman that needeth not to be ashamed")

l.2   "cannot see": IJo 4:12 ("No man hath seen God at any time")

l.7   "Hight...high": Ge 14:18 (the "most high God" is phrasing used throughout the Old Testament, often shortened to simply "most High," Ps 9:2 or "Highest," Ps 18:13, and in the New Testament "most high God," Mr 5:7, "most high," Ac 7:48, and "Highest," Lu 1:32, 35; 6:35, are repeated)

l.10   "Services": Ro 12:1 ("I beseech you therefore, brethren, by the mercies of God, that ye present your bodies a living sacrifice, holy, acceptable unto God, which is your reasonable service"); see also Ro 9:4; Php 2:17; Heb 9:6, 9

l.10   "Snow": Ps 51:7; Isa 1:18; Mt 28:3; Rev 1:14 (snow is associated with death, the purgatorial suffering of the circuit world, and with the white of the apocalyptic especially the virginal firstfruits, Rev 14:1-5, and the Bride, Rev 19:7-9, but also all who walk in white, Rev 3:4-5)

915   Faith- is the Pierless Bridge

ll.1-4   "Faith...eye": Heb 11:1, 3("Now faith is the substance of things hoped for, the evidence of things not seen...Through faith we understand that the worlds were framed by the word of God, so that things which are seen were not made of things which do appear")

ll.5-8   "It...Vail": Eph 6:13-16 ("Wherefore take unto you the whole armour of God,...Above all, taking the shield of faith"); Heb 4:14-16 ("Seeing then that we have a great high priest...Let us therefore come boldly unto the throne of grace"); Heb 6:19-20 ("Which hope we have as an anchor of the soul, both sure and stedfast, and which entereth into that within the veil; Whether the forerunner is for us entered, even Jesus, made an high priest for ever after the order of Melchisedec"); Heb 10:19 ("Having therefore, brethren, boldness to enter into the holiest by the blood of Jesus, By a new and living way, which he hath consecrated for us, through the veil, that is to say, his flesh; ...Let us draw near with a true heart in full assurance of faith")

ll.10,12 "Bridge," "Necessity": Heb 7:12; 8:3; 9:16 (Christ is the "Bridge" and "Necessity" whose death is testator of that new testament "behind the Vail")

Comment: See *Poems*, II, 670-671.

916   His Feet are shod with Gauze-

l.1   "His...Gauze": Eph 6:15 ("And your feet shod with the preparation of the gospel of peace")

l.2   "His...Gold": Eph 6:17; Rev 14:14

l.3   "His...Onyx": Eph 6:14; Rev 21:19

l.4   "With...inlaid": Rev 21:20

ll.5-6   "His...Tune": Rev 5:9; 14:3; 15:3 (an apocalyptic bee whose only work is to sing the songs of Moses and the Lamb); Rev 14:13 ("they may rest from their labours")

l.8   "Noon": Rev 21:25 (the eternal day of the New Jerusalem); see note, line one, P533

Comment: St. Paul's Christian Soldier and the Gem chapter of Revelation metaphorically underpin this apostrophe to the "Bee" whose apocalyptic adornment and song in instinctive enjoyment of "Noon" typify for the poet the pleasures of Paradise. See *Poems*, II, 671 and Franklin, II, 1196.

917   Love- is anterior to Life-

l.1   "Love...Life": Ge 1:26-27; 2:7 (before the foundation of the world God has chosen Christ through Whom the world was created, Joh 1:1-14); IJo 4:9 ("In this was manifested the love of God toward us, because that God sent his only begotten Son into the world, that me might live through him"); Rev 1:8, 11; 21:6; 22:13 (Christ, "Love," is the Alpha and Omega, the beginning and the ending, the first and the last)

l.2   "Posterior...Death": Joh 3:16; ICo 15; Rev 1:8, 11; 2:7; 21:6; 22:13

l.3   "Initial...Creation": Joh 1:1-3 ("In the beginning was the Word, and the Word was with God, and the Word was God. The same was in the beginning with God. All things were made by him; and without him was not any thing made that was made"; the typographical imagery of the poem suggests play here upon the initial "L":"Love," "Life," "Light"—for which see Joh 1:4-9; in addition, the initial Creative Word is the first letter of the Greek alphabet, Alpha, Rev 1:8, 11; 21:6; 22:13)

l.4   "The...Earth": Joh 3:17 ("For God sent not his Son into the world to condemn the world; but that the world through him might be saved"; Christ is the advocate of "Earth" and "Earth" raised to a power—exponent as mathematical/typographical image—the second Adam raising the earthy to the heavenly, the natural to the spiritual, ICo 15:42-49; Christ as Alpha and Omega is also King of "Earth": "And from Jesus Christ, who is the faithful witness, and the first begotten of the dead, and the prince of the kings of the earth," Rev 1:5)

918   Only a Shrine, but Mine-

l.3   "Madonna": Mt 1:18; Lu 1:27
l.5   "Thou...Wo": Isa 53:3-4; Mt 26-27
l.8   "The...heal": Isa 53:5 (the Messianic verses from Isaiah on the Passion explain lines four to eight, especially "next to it" which remains opaque until placed side-by-side with Isa 53:5)
l.10   "if...Will": Mt 26:39, 42 (Christ in Gethsemane prays that the "cup" of the Father's will might pass: O my Father, if it be possible, let this cup pass from me: nevertheless not as I will, but as thou wilt")
l.12   "Thou...thee": Mt 6:8
Comment: The virginal "Nun," bound to that "Shrine" of intercession to which all the "Feet" of the circuit world come, prays for a healing perhaps related to her anchoritic life. See *Poems*, II, 672 and Franklin, II, 1197.

919   If I can stop one Heart from breaking

ll.1-4 "If...Pain": Mt 10:42 ("And whosoever shall give to drink unto one of these little ones a cup of cold water only in the name of a disciple, verily I say unto you, he shall in no wise lose his reward")
ll.2,8 "I...Vain": ICo 15:58 ("Therefore, my beloved brethren, be ye stedfast, unmoveable, always abounding in the work of the Lord, forasmuch as ye know that your labour is not in vain in the

Lord"); Php 2:16 ("Holding forth the word of life; that I may rejoice in the day of Christ, that I have not run in vain, neither laboured in vain"); see also Ga 2:2; 4:11; ITh 2:1; 3:5

920   We can but follow to the Sun-

l.2   "As...down": Ec 1:5 ("The sun also ariseth, and the sun goeth down, and hasteth to his place where he arose")
l.5   "Dust": Ge 2:7; 3:19; Ps 103:14 ("All go unto one place; all are of the dust, and all turn to dust again," Ec 3:20)
l.6   "Earthen": IICo 4:7 ("But we have this treasure in earthen vessels")
l.6   "Door": Job 38:17 ("Have the gates of death been opened unto thee? or hast thou seen the doors of the shadow of death?")
Comment: See *Poems*, II, 673 and Franklin, II, 1030.

921   If it had no pencil

l.3   "sweet": Ca 2:3, 14; 5:5, 13, 16; 7:9
l.4   "thee": see note, lines eight, sixteen, P537
Comment: See *Poems*, II, 673 and Leyda, II, 80.

922   Those who have been in the Grave the longest-

l.6   "White": Rev 3:4-5, 18; 6:11; 7:9, 13-14; 19:8 (death is here associated with apocalyptic white)
l.7   "Once...achieve": Heb 9:27 ("And it is appointed unto men once to die, but after this the judgment")

924   Love- is that Later Thing than Death-

ll.1-2   "Love...Life": see notes, lines one-four, P917
l.5   "Tastes Death": Heb 2:9 ("But we see Jesus, who was made a little lower than the angels for the suffering of death, crowned with glory and honour; that he by the grace of God should taste death for every man")
l.5   "first": Rev 1:5 ("And from Jesus Christ...the first begotten of the dead")

l.5   "sting": ICo 15:55 ("O death, where is thy sting? O grave, where is thy victory!")

l.5   "Death...first": Ge 3:19 (the first death which is part of the curse of Adam and Eve)

l.6   "Second": ICo 15:47 ("the second man is the Lord from heaven"); Rev 2:11; 20:6, 14; 21:8 (the second death, eternal damnation)

l.7   "little interval": Joh 16:16 ("A little while, and ye shall not see me: and again, a little while and ye shall see me, because I go to the Father")

l.8   "Deposits...God": Col 3:1, 3 ("If ye then be risen with Christ, seek those things which are above, where Christ sitteth on the right hand of God...For ye are dead, and your life is hid with Christ in God")

l.10   "Beloved": Mt 3:17

l.10   "Charge": Ps 91:11; Mt 4:6

ll.9-12   "Then...Large": Ro 8:34 ("Who is he that condemneth? It is Christ that died, yea rather, that is risen again, who is even at the right hand of God, who also maketh intercession for us"); Heb 7:25 ("Wherefore he is able to save them to the uttermost that come unto God by him, seeing he ever liveth to make intercession for them"); Heb 9:24 ("For Christ is not entered into the holy places made with hands, which are figures of the true; but into heaven itself, now to appear in the presence of God for us")

l.12   "smaller/lesser": Ge 1:16 (the "lesser light" and the "Large," Christ and God)

Comment: See *Poems*, II, 674-675.

925   Struck, was I, nor yet by Lightning-

l.7   "Sportsman's Peradventure": Ge 18:24, 28-32 (Abraham's pleading for the leniency of God is here part of P925's ironic depiction of an arbitrary force: Lightning, Enemy, Sportsman, Bandit)

l.8   "mine Enemy": Job 16:9; 27:7; Ps 7:4; 13:2; 41:11 (the phrasing is frequent in the KJV where it is used for the adversaries of God—of course, here used with irony)

l.16   "afraid": Ge 3:10 ("I was afraid"; another ironic echo, the poet choosing the paradisiacal "Orchard" as setting for her repudiation of original sin in pleading her own ineffectuality and innocence)

l.17 "Most...me": Job 13:15 ("Though he slay me, yet will I trust in him: but I will maintain mine own ways before him")

l.20 "Sun": Ps 84:11; 89:36; Mal 4:2; Lu 1:78; IIPe 1:19; Rev 1:16; 2:28; 21:23; 22:5, 16 (the recognition at nature's "Setting" by the beloved—"My beloved is mine, I am his," Ca 2:16—[who is here the Sun-Son] is typic of the beatific vision)

ll.23-24 "Till...eyes": Rev 22:4 ("And they shall see his face"; the poet combines the beatific vision with the idea of an eternal dawn, possession of the "morning star," Rev 2:28; 22:16, the Sun-Son-Bridegroom)

Comment: See *Poems*, II, 675-676 and Franklin, II, 1024-1025.

929 How far is it to Heaven?

ll.1-2 "How...way": Mt 25:33-34 ("And he shall set the sheep on his right hand, but the goats on the left. Then shall the King say unto them on his right hand, Come, ye blessed of my Father, inherit the kingdom prepared for you from the foundation of the world")

ll.5-7 "How...hand": Mt 25:41 ("Then shall he say also unto them on the left hand, Depart from me, ye cursed, into everlasting fire, prepared for the devil and his angels")

Comment: See *Poems*, II, 678.

930 There is a June when Corn is cut

l.7 "Vermillion": see note, line one, P15

l.9 "Two...exist": Ec 3:1-2 ("To every thing there is a season, and a time to every purpose under the heaven: A time to be born, and a time to die; a time to plant, and a time to pluck up that which is planted")

l.10 "The...Just": Lu 14:14 ("And thou shalt he blessed; for they cannot recompense thee: for thou shalt be recompensed at the resurrection of the just"); Heb 12:22-23 ("But ye are come unto mount Sion, and unto the city of the living God, the heavenly Jerusalem, and to an innumerable company of angels, To the general assembly and church of the firstborn, which are written in heaven, and to God the

Judge of all, and to the spirits of just men made perfect"); Isa 45:21; Ac 3:14; 7:52; 22:14 (Christ, the Just, reigns in the eternal summer of Heaven, Rev 22:1-5: "And he shewed me a pure river of water of life, clear as crystal, proceeding out of the throne of God, and of the Lamb...the tree of life, which bare twelve manner of fruits, and yielded her fruit every month...And there shall be no more curse...the Lord God giveth them light: and they shall reign for ever and ever")

l.16   "The...prefer": Jude 25 ("To the only wise God our Saviour, be glory and majesty, dominion and power"; the poet wrote to Susan Dickinson: "That is why I prefer the Power—for Power is Glory, when it likes, and Dominion, too-", *Letters*, II, 432)

Comment: See *Poems*, II, 678-679; Franklin, II, 1130-1131; Leyda, II, 89; and *Letters*, II, 432.

934   That is solemn we have ended

l.7   "better": Heb 11:16 ("But now they desire a better country, that is, an heavenly: wherefore God is not ashamed to be called their God: for he hath prepared for them a city")

l.8   "Still...explained": ICo 13:12; IJo 3:2

Comment: See *Poems*, II, 680-681.

936   This Dust, and it's Feature-

l.1   "Dust": Ge 2:7; 3:19; Ps 103:14

l.1   "Feature": ICo 15:45, 47 (a metonym for the "first Adam" and the "image of the earthy")

l.3   "second Future": ICo 15:45-51 (the "last Adam" or the "Lord from heaven," the "image of the heavenly" guaranteeing resurrection triumph over the second death, Rev 2:11; 20:6, 14; 21:8)

l.4   "Cease...identify": IICo 3:18 ("But we all, with open face beholding as in a glass the glory of the Lord, are changed into the same image from glory to glory, even as by the Spirit of the Lord"); IJo 3:2 ("Beloved, now are we the sons of God, and it doth not yet appear what we shall be: but we know that, when he shall appear, we shall be like him; for we shall see him as he is")

l.9   "This world": Ro 12:2; ICo 7:31; Ga 1:4; Eph 6:12; Tit 2:12

l.9   "species/Fashions": ICo 7:31 ("for the fashion of this world passeth away") l.11 "absorbed Attention's": Rev 22:4 ("And they shall see his face; and his name shall be in their foreheads")

Comment: See Poems, II, 681-682.

939 What I see not, I better see-

1.1 "What...see": Mt 13:13-14 ("Therefore speak I to them in parables: because they seeing see not; and hearing they hear not, neither do they understand. And in them is fulfilled the prophecy of Esaias, which saith, By hearing ye shall hear, and shall not understand; and seeing ye shall see, and shall not perceive")

1.2 "Through Faith": Heb 11:1, 3 ("Now faith is the substance of things hoped for, the evidence of things not seen...Through faith we understand that the worlds were framed by the word of God, so that things which are seen were not made of things which do appear")

ll.6-8 "I...beloved": Ca 1:16; 2:8, 14-16; 5:15-16

1.9 "arise": Ca 2:13 ("Arise, my love, my fair one, and come away")

ll.10,12 "Thee," "Thy": see note, lines eight, sixteen, P537

1.11 "Till...interrupt": Ca 2:17; 4:6 ("Until the day break, and the shadows flee away"; daybreak interrupts enjoyment of the continuous presence of the beloved)

1.12 "And...perfectness": Ca 1:15-16; 4:1, 7; 7:6 ("Behold, thou art fair, my beloved")

Comment: See *Poems*, II, 683.

940 On that dear Frame the Years had worn

1.1 "Frame": Ps 1-3:14 ("For he knoweth our frame; he remembereth that we are dust")

1.3 "Light": Joh 1:7-9 (the poet plays upon the word "Light" as suggestive of her birth in her family home and her spiritual enlightenment or rebirth unto a "House" not made with hands, IICo 5:1-2)

1.4 "The...Us": Joh 1:7 ("The same came for a witness, to bear witness of the Light, that all men through him might believe"; as John the Baptist was to Christ so apparently a spiritual midwife, perhaps a surrogate mother, was to the poet) l.5   "Precious": IPe 2:4-7 (the "spiritual house" built of precious "lively stones" connects with the "Gem" chapter, Rev 21:11, 19)

l.5   "conceiveless": Isa 64:4; ICo 2:9

l.5   "fair": Ca 1:8, 15-16; 2:10, 13; 4:1, 7, 10; 5:9; 6:1, 10; 7:6

941   The Lady feeds Her little Bird

ll.5-6   "The...afar": Lu 16:19-26 (the words "crumbs," "afar," and "gulf" appear in the account of the beggar Lazarus and the rich man; the parable is frequently echoed when as here is used the beggar persona)

943   A Coffin- is a small Domain,

l.3   "Paradise": Lu 23:43; IICo 12:4; Rev 2:7

l.5   "Grave": ICo 15:55 ("O death, where is thy sting? O grave, where is thy victory?")

l.6   "Yet...Sun": Rev 21:23; 22:5 (the sun is absent from Paradise)

ll.7-8   "And...upon": Ge 1:10, 20

ll.11-12 "Circumference...End": Lu 1:33 ("and of his kingdom there shall be no end": see also Isa 45:17; Eph 3:21; "Circumference" may here be the Alpha and Omega, the beginning and the end, Rev 1:8; 21:6; 22:13)

Comment: See *Poems*, II, 685.

944   I learned- at least- what Home could be-

l.3   "Covenant": Ge 2:18-25 (the marriage covenant; there may be some irony in the poet's assumption of the reader's knowledge of Old Testament blood sacrifice and the Passion of Christ involved in the old and new un-"pretty" covenants)

l.6   "pattern": Heb 8:5; 9:23 (the "pretty ways of Covenant" of marriage are shadows of heavenly things; the "patterns of things in the heavens" are instantiated by that unity of Christ and the Church, husband and wife, in the tradition of the allegorization of the profane love of Canticles and its continuation by St. Paul, Eph 4-5;

thus, profane love and earthly marriage are part of the "Way," typic of marriage to the Lamb, Rev 19:7-9)

l.9   "Garden": Ca 4:12, 16; 5:1; Isa 65:17-25; Ge 2-3; Eze 28:13; 31:8-9; Rev 22:1-5 (letters to recently married friends suggest that the poet viewed marriage as a recapturing of a prelapsarian unity, innocence, and presence, a Paradise or "Garden")

l.31   "Where...be": Rev 21:23; 22:5 (the eternal is the place of the day or bright and morning star, IIPe 1:19; Rev 22:16, but the poet is afflicted by the sense of the potential unmeaning of the apocalyptic, i.e., that "Dawn" is not preceded by nights of "diviner care," that there is a radical disjunction between profane longing and apocalyptic consummation making "pretty ways" wishful thinking)

Comment: See Poems, II, 685-686.

945   This is a Blossom of the Brain-

l.2   "small": Mt 13:32 ("Which indeed is the least of all seeds")

l.2   "italic Seed": Joh 1:1-5 (the words of her poems, drawing from the idea of the Incarnate Word; the metaphor of the fructified seed echoes the parables of the Sower and Mustard Seed, Mt 13; see also its sexual basis in the covenant promises extending back to the Creation of Adam and Eve, Ge 1:27-28—promises spiritualized in Romans chapters four and nine, the third chapter of Galatians, and the eleventh chapter of Hebrews; in religio-aesthetic terms her poems are analogous to the abiding Word: "Being born again, not of corruptible seed, but of incorruptible, by the word of God, which liveth and abideth for ever," IPe 1:23)

ll.3-4   "Lodged...fructified": Ro 8; ICo 15:35-55; IPe 1-2 (again the model for "Design" and fructification by the "Spirit" is the Incarnate Word: "For Christ...being put to death in the flesh, but quickened by the Spirit," IPe 3:18)

ll.5-8   "Sky...unknown": Joh 3:8 ("The wind bloweth where it listeth, and thou hearest the sound thereof, but canst not tell whence it cometh, and whither it goeth: so is every one that is born of the Spirit")

ll.9-11   "When...spot": Mt 13:44-46 ("Again, the kingdom of heaven is like unto treasure hid in a field; the which when a man hath found, he hideth, and for joy thereof goeth and selleth all that he hath, and buyeth that field. Again, the kingdom of heaven is like unto a merchant man, seeking goodly pearls: Who, when he had found one pearl of great price, went and sold all that he had, and bought it"); Lu 15:4-7

Comment: The religio-aesthetic of P945 is an incarnational one. Just as the Incarnate Word is fructified by the Spirit in the believers so also the words of the poet are disseminated on the wind and cherished by those capable of responding. To lose such an Incarnation is to lose redemption-resurrection hope—the death of God with the loss of the "Flower of our Lord." "If Christ be not raised," ICo 15:17, is equivalent in P945 to "if poets be not disseminators of 'italic Seeds' and 'Flowers of the Soul'."

951   As Frost is best conceived

l.1   "Frost": Job 37:10; 38:29 ("By the breath of God frost is given")

ll.5-8   "If...countenance": Ge 3:17-19

ll.9-10   "Cannot...stain": Eph 5:27 (a church without spot, "crease," "stain," or wrinkle is a pure bride)

Comment: Unlike the dew of God's favor, the "Frost" is the face of His disfavor. Interestingly, Dickinson rewrites the story of the Fall by suggesting that the "Frost" blackens and wilts the personified face of the landscape beyond correction or counteraction; the "Garden" is "Gash[ed]" and "put in twain," the "countenance" "wilted," "crease[d]," and "stain[ed]," wrinkled and spotted, but by the "force" of "Frost" arbitrarily imposing its "Affliction." The fact that the unworthy face ("wilted countenance") originates in a Fall whose circumstances are riddling, impenetrably opaque, does not lessen its effects of division nor erase its associations with loss of spousal favor and Edenic innocence and union. See *Poems*, II, 690-691 and Franklin, II, 1045.

954   The Chemical conviction

ll.1-3   "The...Disaster": IIPe 3:10-11 (see Sewall, 345-346, for the discussion of Professor Hitchcock that is the scientific and Biblical background of P954; nevertheless, the "Disaster" is not just the cosmic one of elements melting with fervent heat but the more personal one of loss of faith regarding the fate of dead loved ones)

l.4   "My...Trust": Heb 11:1, 3 (scientific "conviction" has "fractured" Biblical faith since the metamorphosis involved in the conservation of energy may not be equivalent to that "change" in the resurrection spoken of by St. Paul, ICo 15:51-52, a change carrying conviction regarding "Faces" in the hereafter, ICo 13:12)

ll.5-6   "The...see": ICo 13:12; IJo 3:2 (perhaps an ironic gibe at the notion that the scientific theory—that matter is not really destroyed but metamorphosed—can be translated into conviction regarding the duration of personality)

l.7   "Creatures": Ro 8:19-23 (the "Finished Creatures" are those who have finished the course, IITi 4:7, and who now bear the "image of the heavenly," ICo 15:49, having been conformed to the image of Christ, IICo 3:18; IJo 3:2)

Comment: From cosmic, impersonal laws of thermo—dynamics and the phase theory of matter, Henry Adams garnered some solace; Dickinson insists on the domestication of the "Chemical conviction"—that it give some degree of hope that relationships of personal affection will continue in Eternity.

957   As One does Sickness over

ll.5-6   "As...Twig": De 32:35

l.7   "Perdition": Rev 17:8, 11 (eternal damnation or spiritual destruction, often conflated with the location, hell or the "bottomless pit")

l.10   "suffering": Mt 27:19; Mr 8:31; Lu 8:32; 24:26; Ac 17:3; 26:23; IICo 1:5 (the identification is with the Passion Christ)

l.12   "evidence": Heb 11:1 (faith is an imaginative rehearsal, a piquancy-of-the-pit exercise utilizing the dialectic of P67)

Comment: The "Soul," finding its identity obscured by "blessed Health," "rewalks" the route of the Passion, of "Sickness" and "suffering," in order to re-focus "Identity." That such a "faint Rehearsal" should be necessary—that the topography of "Sinners in the Hands of an Angry God" in stanza two should be re-traversed in order to make calling and election sure—may suggest that P957 had a preparationist function for the speaker. To know existence is to know the "Precipice" above "Perdition"—"scrutiny of Chances" perhaps the discipline of Hell. See *Poems*, II, 693-694 and Franklin, II, 1051.

959   A loss of something ever felt I-

ll.1-8   "A...out": Ge 3:23-24 (paradigmatic expulsion-loss-separation-disaffiliation)

l.12   "Delinquent Palaces": Ge 2-3; Eze 28:13-14; 31:8-9, 16; 47:1-12; Rev 2:7; 22:1-5 (Eden or Paradise)

l.16   "Kingdom...Heaven": Mt 3:2; 4:17; 5:3, 10, 19-20; 7:21; 8:11 (here a metonym for the apocalyptic in contrast to an idealized past sought through memory)

Comment: In P348, Nature is a Gulliver and the speaker a xenophobic Lilliputian, or, to switch to an Emersonian metaphor, an opaque rather than transparent eyeball—consciousness of bodily existence in the circuit world is an awareness of division and loss, of separation from nature. In P313, life in the body is "Life's penurious Round"—being left shipwrecked on the "Reefs in Old Gethsemane." Ensconced in "homelier time," the speaker of P313 attempts to comprehend "Heaven"—the ideal state of both past and future. Both P313 and P348 help in understanding the loss of Edenic unity in a past beyond recollection and how this Eden might be conflated with Heaven—as seemed to be the case when the poet spoke of Paradise (in P959 the "Delinquent Palaces"). Deracinated, adrift, bereft are the speakers of these poems—their experiences riddling and unsettling. P959 offers the philosophic mind as a consolation in stanza three, but as in Wordsworth's "Immortality Ode," the loss incurred in the move toward a characteristic self-consciousness and recollection in adulthood is unrelieved—the "glory and the dream" become "loss of something."

961   Wert Thou but ill- that I might show thee

ll.1,5,7,9,13,17,19 "Thou," "Thee": see note, lines eight, sixteen, P537

l.19   "Sweet": Ca 2:3, 14; 5:5, 13, 16; 7:9

l.20   "For...Love": Ca 1:2-4; 8:6-7

Comment: See *Poems*, II, 696. P961 is a "Putative"(see notes, lines fourteen to nineteen, P179), that is a poem that by its role playing, by its "faint Rehearsals," hopes to somehow obligate or placate the absent, ideal audience—at once an expression both of hope, desire, and devotion. Placed necessarily in the subjunctive, P961 presents the beloved as Patient, Stranger, Defendant, and Tenant/Groom to whom unstinting "Service" would be shown.

962   **Midsummer, was it, when They died-**

l.7   "Widen...Perfectness": ICo 13:10 ("But when that which is perfect is come, then that which is in part shall be done away"); IJo 3:2

963   **A nearness to Tremendousness-**

ll.1,3   "Tremendousness," "Boundlessness": Ge 1:1, passim (God whose center is everywhere and circumference nowhere)
l.2   "Agony": Lu 22:44
ll.3,6   "Affliction": Isa 53:1-9; 63:9
l.4   "Laws": Ex 20
Comment: A Passion poem in which "Agony" and "Affliction" become the new covenant connecting the self with the "new circumference," with "Illocality." The old of the "Laws" leaves one at ease in the circuit world, a "quiet Suburb." Better "Affliction" with "nearness to Tremendousness," better awash in "Immensity," than contentment with the secondary and tertiary—measurable "Acres" and "Laws." See *Poems*, II, 697 and Franklin, II, 980.

964   **"Unto Me?" I do not know you-**

l.1   "Unto Me?": Mt 7:21-22; 25:31-46 (the pivotal two words in the context of interrogations are found in Mt 7:21 and 25:40)
l.1   "I...you": Mt 7:23 ("And then will I profess unto them, I never knew you: depart from me, ye that work iniquity")
l.2   "Where...House?": Mt 7:24-27 (wise and foolish houses may be intended or perhaps something not linked directly to line one, e.g., Joh 14:2-3 or IICo 5:1)
l.3   "Judea": Mt 2:1
l.4   "Paradise": Lu 23:43; Rev 2:7
l.7   "Arms":De 33:27; Job 40:9; Ps 77:15; 89:10; Isa 40:10-11; 52:10; 63:5; Joh 12:38 (synecdochic of God's omnipotence)
l.7   "sufficient": IICo 3:5; 12:9
l.8   "Omnipotence": Rev 19:6 ("for the Lord God omnipotent reigneth")
l.9   "I...spotted": Nu 19:2; 28:3, 9, 11; 9:17, 26 (references to unblemished, Old Testament, sacrificial animals are

relevant since Christ is the "Pardon" "without spot," Heb 9:14; IPe 1:19)

l.9   "spotted": Eph 5:27; Jas 1:27; IIPe 2:13; 3:14; Jude 23 (spots suggest sins)

l.9   "Pardon": Isa 55:7 ("Let the wicked forsake his way, and the unrighteous man his thoughts: and let him return unto the Lord, and he will have mercy upon him; and to our God, for he will abundantly pardon")

ll.10-11 "Least...Chiefest": Mt 5:19; 11:11; 20:22; Mr 10:44; Lu 22:26 ("And whosoever of you will be the chiefest, shall be servant of all," Mr 10:44)

l.12   "Occupy...House/Breast": Joh 14:2-3; Rev 19:7-9; 21-22 (two other possibilities: first, Jesus might invite His interlocutor into the "bosom of the Father," Joh 1:18; second, there here may be a reference to "Abraham's bosom," Lu 16:22-23); Mt 25:21, 23 ("enter thou into the joy of thy lord"); Rev 22:14 ("enter in through the gates into the city")

965   Denial- is the only fact

ll.1-2   "Denial...Denied": Ge 2:16-17; 3:1-3 (Adam and Eve were denied the fruit of the tree of the knowledge of good and evil)

l.3   "Whose...significance": Ge 3:6, 12-13 (the "Will" is a "numb significance" before temptation)

l.4   "The...died": Ge 2:17 ("in the day that thou eatest thereof thou shalt surely die")

ll.5-6   "And...Beam": Ge 3:17-18 (a reference to the Fall's effects upon nature)

l.7   "What...was": Ge 3:5, 7 ("For God doth know that in the day ye eat thereof, then your eyes shall be opened, and ye shall be as gods, knowing good and evil...And the eyes of them both were opened, and they knew that they were naked")

l.8   "The...Home": Ge 3:23-24 (the price of "Wisdom" is expulsion from the garden, "Our Home"; wisdom, the "spoiler" of the original "Home," is little "Comfort" since its function is to expose with clarity the essence of postlapsarian life as "Denial")

Comment: See Poems, II, 698 and Franklin, II, 982.

966   All forgot for recollecting

ll.1-2   "All...One": Php 3:13-14 ("Brethren, I count not
myself to have apprehended: but this one thing I do, forgetting those
things which are behind, and reaching forth unto those things which
are before, I press toward the mark for the prize of the high calling of
God in Christ Jesus")

ll.3-4   "All...Accompanying": Mr 1:16-18 (Simon and
Andrew forsake all to follow Christ as disciples); Lu 14:33 ("So
likewise, whosoever he be of you that forsaketh not all that he hath, he
cannot be my disciple")

ll.5-10   "Grace...small": Mt 19:27-29 ("Then answered Peter
and said unto him, Behold, we have forsaken all, and followed thee;
what shall we have therefore?...And every one that hath forsaken
houses, or brethren, or sisters, or father, or mother, or wife, or
children, or lands, for my name's sake, shall receive an hundredfold,
and shall inherit everlasting life")

l.6   "accounted": Lu 20:35

ll.15-16 "Prove": Ro 12:2

l.15   "Sweet": Ca 2:3, 14; 5:5, 13, 16; 7:9

l.16   "Thee": see note, lines eight, sixteen, P537

Comment: See *Poems*, II, 699 and Franklin, II, 983-984.

968   Fitter to see Him, I may be

ll.1-2   "Fitter...Me": Isa 40:3; 64:4; Mt 3:3; 22:1-14; 25:1-
13; Mr 1:3; Lu 3:4; IITi 2:21 (the preparationist motif)

l.1   "Him": Rev 19:7-9 (the Bridegroom)

l.4   "bestow": ICo 15:10; IICo 1:11; IJo 3:1

l.5   "To...Earth": Ca 1:8; 5:9; 6:1 ("O thou fairest among
women")

l.6   "Waiting...worth": Isa 64:4 ("For since the
beginning of the world men have not heard, nor perceived by the ear,
neither hath the eye seen, O God, beside thee, what he hath prepared
for him that waiteth for him")

ll.7-8   "I...chosen/common-then": Mt 20:16; 22:14; Mr
13:20; Ro 4:6; Eph 1:4; Jas 2:23; IIPe 1:10; 2:4; Rev 7:14 (the
language regarding her calling and election glances at imputed
righteousness[Ro 4] and common grace[Ro 1:19-20])

l.9   "Time...Gaze": ICo 13:12 ("For now we see through
a glass, darkly; but then face to face: now I know in part; but then

shall I know even as also I am known"); Rev 22:4 ("And they shall see his face; and his name shall be in their foreheads")

l.11   "The...face": Ro 8:29; ICo 13:12; 15:49; IICo 3:18; IJo 3:2; Rev 22:4 (the "face" conformed to His image)

ll.12-13 "Grace...One Day": Joh 1:14-17; Ac 15:11; Ro 1:3-6; IICo 8:9 ("One Day" refers to the Ascension [Mr 16:19; Lu 24:51; Ac 1:9; Heb 4:14-15])

l.15   "grow": Eph 2:21; 4:15; IPe 2:2; IIPe 3:18

l.15   "new": IICo 5:17; Eph 4:24

ll.16-17 "That...Door": Rev 3:20 ("Behold, I stand at the door, and knock: if any man hear my voice, and open the door, I will come in to him, and will sup with him, and he with me")

l.18   "go no more": Ps 23:6; Heb 13:14; Rev 3:12

l.19   "change": ICo 15:51-52; IICo 3:18; Php 3:21

l.19   "fair": Ca 1:8, 15-16; 2:10, 13; 4:1, 7, 10; 5:9; 6:1, 10; 7:6

l.21   "Love": Rev 19:7-9 ("Love" is the Divine Beloved whose type has an unspotted bride, Ca 4:7, and whose Bride is variously Israel, Jerusalem, the church, or the Bride of Revelation: Isa 61:10; 62:3-5; Eze 16:10-14; Mal 3:17; Eph 5:25-27; Rev 19:7-9; 21; 22:17; the poet adopts this figuration in her contention that she is adorned in "Love," the imputed righteousness of the wedding garment, e.g., Mt 22:11-12)

l.21   "array": Rev 19:8 ("And to her was granted that she should be arrayed in fine linen, clean and white: for the fine linen is the righteousness of saints")

l.22   "I...sight": Eze 16:14 ("it was perfect through my comeliness, which I had put upon thee"); Col 1:22 ("to present you holy and unblameable and unreproveable in his sight"); Rev 14:4-5 ("These were redeemed from among men, being the firstfruits unto God and to the Lamb. And in their mouth was found no guile: for they are without fault before the throne of God"); see also Eph 1:4; 5:27; Col 1:28; Jude 24; Rev 21

l.25   "sweet": Ca 2:3, 14; 5:5, 13, 16; 7:9

l.25   "I...Vain": Php 2:16 ("Holding forth the word of life; that I may rejoice in the day of Christ, that I have not run in vain, neither laboured in vain")

l.26   "But...loss": Php 3:7 ("But what things were gain to me, those I counted loss for Christ") l.26 "obtain": ICo 9:24-25 ("So run, that ye may obtain...Now they do it to obtain a corruptible crown; but we an incorruptible")

l.27 "reward": Ro 4:4-5 ("Now to him that worketh is the reward not reckoned of grace, but of debt. But to him that worketh not, but believeth on him that justifieth the ungodly, his faith is counted for righteousness")

ll.27-28 "Beauty": Eze 16:14

Comment: Much of the lexicon of P968 can be related to Canticles: "delight," "beauty," "fair," "love," "eyes," "sweet," and "countenance" (Ca 1:2, 9, 15-16; 2:3-4, 10, 13-14; 4:1, 7, 9-10; 6:4-5; 5:5, 12-13, 15-16; 7:6; 8:4, 6, 10). Such profane love figuration combines with that of the apocalyptic, Bride of Christ variety in a poem expressing not only concern about circuit world calling and election but New Jerusalem recognition and identity. See *Poems*, II, 700-701 and Franklin, II,. 991-993.

970   Color- Caste- Denomination-

l.5   "All...forgotten": Ec 3:20 ("All go unto one place; all are of the dust, and all turn to dust again")

ll.9-14 "If...well": ICo 15:42-44, 53-55 (stanza three contains a Hitchcockian emblem of the resurrection: "Chrysalis" — "Butterfly")

Comment: See *Poems*, II, 702.

971   Robbed by Death- but that was easy-

l.7   "Glory": Isa 66:11; ICo 15:43; IICo 3:18; 4:17; IPe 1:7-8; 5:4; Jude 24; Rev 21:11, 23

l.8   "Beloved": Ca 1:14, 16; 2:3, 8-10, 16-17; 4:16; 5:1-2, 4-6, 8-10, 16; 6:1-3; 7:9, 11, 13; 8:5, 14

972   Unfulfilled to Observation-

ll.1-2   "Unfulfilled...Eye": Ec 1:8 ("All things are full of labour; man cannot utter it: the eye is not satisfied with seeing, nor the ear filled with hearing"; to observation the diurnal round leads to an extinction of the sun, while to "Faith" there is here a revelation: the diurnal round as typic of "New Horizons" beyond nature)

l.3   "Faith": Heb 11:1 ("Now faith is the substance of things hoped for the evidence of things not seen")
Comment: See *Poems*, II, 703 and Franklin, II, 998.

973   'Twas awkward, but it fitted me-

ll.2-3   "An...Steadfastness": ICo 7:37 ("Nevertheless he that standeth stedfast in his heart, having no necessity, but hath power over his own will, and hath so decreed in his heart that he will keep his virgin, doeth well")
Comment: See *Poems*, II, 704.

975   The Mountain sat upon the Plain

l.7   "Grandfather of Days": Da 7:9; ("the Ancient of days did sit whose garment was white as snow")
l.8   "Of...Ancestor": Ge 1:2-5 (God as Creator of "Dawn")

976   Death is a Dialogue between

l.2   "Spirit": ICo 15:45-46 (St. Paul distinguishes between the soul, *nephesh*, Ge 2:7, and the spirit, *pneuma*, which is incorruptible)
l.2   "Dust": Ge 2:7; 3:14, 19; Ps 103:14
l.3   " 'Dissolve' ": IICo 5:1 ("For we know that if our earthly house of this tabernacle were dissolved, we have a building of God, an house not made with hands, eternal in the heavens")
l.4   " 'Trust' ": IICo 1:9-10 ("But we had the sentence of death in ourselves, that we should not trust in ourselves, but in God which raiseth the dead: Who delivered us from so great a death, and doth deliver: in whom we trust that he will yet deliver us")
l.5   "Ground": Ge 2:7, 9; 3:17, 19, 23
l.8   "Clay": Job 19:4; 10:9; 13:12; 33:6; Isa 64:8; Ro 9:21 (a synecdoche for the body)

977   Besides this May

l.3   "Another": Rev 22:1-3

l.4   "fair": Ca 1:8, 15-16; 2:10, 13; 4:1, 7, 10; 5:9; 6:1, 10; 7:6

l.6   "know Him": ICo 13:9, 12 ("For we know in part, and we prophesy in part...now I know in part; but them shall I know even as also I am known")

l.7   "Sweet": Ca 2:3, 14; 5:5, 13, 16; 7:9

l.8   "Nature": Rev 22:2-3 (a "Nature" freed from its curse, Ge 3:17)

l.9   "Saints": Rev 5:8; 7; 8:3-4; 11:18; 14:1-5, 12; 15:3; 19:8; 21:7, 24, 26-27

l.10   "May": see above, lines three and eight

Comment: See *Poems*, II, 706.

978   It bloomed and dropt, a Single Noon-

ll.2,17   "Flower," "single...Earth": Ca 2:1 ("I am the rose of Sharon, and the lily of the valleys")

l.2   "Red": see note, line one, P15

l.7   "To...disappeared": Ca 3:1 ("I sought him, but I found him not"; P978 uses the Canticles topos of unrequited or lost love)

l.19   "Great Nature's Face": Rev 22:4 (the potentially infinite offerings of "Nature" via intermittent epiphanic awareness is typic of the beatific vision, of enjoyment face-to-face of the presence of the beloved)

Comment: P978 uses imagery from nature and profane love to speak of the religio-aesthetic. To burn with passionate, Paterian intensity in response to the Beautiful is the aesthetic equivalent of responding to the hour of salvation(Isa 49:8; IICo 6:2), the rose here being the ideally-circumferential, substitute face of the Bridegroom. See *Poems*, II, 706-707 and Franklin, II, 1027-1028.

980   Purple- is fashionable twice-

l.1   "Purple": see note, line one, P15 ("Purple" suggests that Presence in nature at spring, but it is also a regal color suggesting accession to higher status: Jg 8:26; Ca 3:10; 7:5; Mr 15:17; Lu 16:19; Joh 19:2)

ll.3-4   "And...Emperor": Rev 1:5-6 ("And from Jesus Christ, who is the faithful witness...And hath made us kings and priests unto God and his Father")

982   No Other can reduce

l.2   "mortal": ICo 15:53-54

ll.3-8   "Like...Estimate": Ps 103:14 ("For he knoweth our frame; he remembereth that we are dust")

ll.3,6   "Nought": Ge 2:7; 3:19; Job 4:19; 34:15; Ps 103:14; 104:29 (there may here be a glance at *ex nihilo* creation, Job 26:7 and, not in the present KJV, II Maccabees 7:28: "I beseech you, my child, to look at the heaven and the earth and see everything that is in them, and recognize that God did not make them out of things that existed. Thus also mankind comes into being")

l.8   "Jehovah's": Ps 83:18; Isa 26:4

No Other can reduce Our (1863 version)

l.9   "exalt": IPe 5:6

l.10   "Mortal": ICo 15:53-54

l.12   "from hence": Rev 14:13

l.14   "Creator's House": Joh 14:2 ("In my Father's house are many mansions: if it were not so, I would have told you. I go to prepare a place for you")

l.15   "Eternity": Isa 57:15; Rev 4:9-10; 5:13-14; 10:6; 11:15; 15:7; 22:5

Comment: See *Poems*, II, 708-710 and Franklin, II, 871, 1226.

984   'Tis Anguish grander than Delight

l.2   "Resurrection": ICo 15:12-55; Php 3:10-11; Heb 6:2; 11:35; Rev 20:5-6

l.2   "Pain": Ac 2:24 ("Whom God hath raised up, having loosed the pains of death")

l.3   "smitten": Isa 53:4 ("Surely he hath borne our griefs, and carried our sorrows: yet we did esteem him stricken, smitten of God, and afflicted")

l.5   "Graves": ICo 15:55

l.6 "When...go": Lu 24:12; Joh 20:5-7 ("Cerements" suggests the linen burial clothing of Christ and is here synecdochic of the body and circuit world circumscription)

ll.7-8 "And...Two": ITh 4:16-17 ("For the Lord himself shall descend from heaven with a shout, with the voice of the archangel, and with the trump of God: and the dead in Christ shall rise first: Then we which are alive and remain shall be caught up together with them in the clouds, to meet the Lord in the air: and so shall we ever be with the Lord")

l.7 "Creatures": IICo 5:17; Jas 1:18; Rev 14:4

l.7 "clad": IICo 5:1-5

l.7 "Miracle": ICo 15:51 ("Behold, I shew you a mystery; We shall not all sleep, but we shall all be changed"); ICo 15:54-57 (see these verses for the variant "Victory")

l.8 "Two and Two": Ge 7:9, 15

Comment: See *Poems*, II, 710-711 and Franklin, II, 1222.

985 The Missing All, prevented Me

ll.1-2 "prevented...Things": Mt 16:26 ("For what is a man profited, if he shall gain the whole world, and lose his own soul? or what shall a man give in exchange for his soul?"); see also Mt 10:42; 13:3-23, 31-32, 46; 17:20; 18:2-14; 19:13-14, 30; 20:16; 25:40, 45; Lu 9:48 (repudiation of "All," of the eudaemonistic philosophy of the world, is based upon the paradoxes at the heart of the Gospel—if you would save your life, you must lose it, Mt 16:25-26; if you would be filled, you must hunger, Mt 5:6; Dickinson takes her Lilliputian philosophy from Christ's Kingdom preachments—a seed, a grain, a pearl, a child—and the Beatitudes, Mt 5:3-12)

Comment: See *Poems*, II, 711 and Franklin, II, 1210.

986 A narrow Fellow in the Grass

ll.23-24 "Without...Bone": Ge 3:1-4, 13-17 (the snake is associated with the curse upon nature and man's alienation from it; "And I will put enmity between thee and the woman," Ge 3:15— "Bone" here perhaps synecdochic of woman, Ge 2:23, or finitude, Ge 3:19)

Comment: See *Poems*, II, 711-714 and Franklin, II, 1137-1139.

988   The Definition of Beauty is

l.1   "Beauty": Ps 27:4; 48:2; 50:2; 90:17; Ca 6:4; Isa 33:17; Rev 21 ("Beauty" is used of the beloved—profane or Divine, Zion or New Jerusalem—an absent Paradise whose longed-for presence is the essence of the poet's religio-aesthetic; Heaven and "Melody"—see the variant phrasing in P797 and *Poems*, II, 715—may be thought of as synonymous: Rev 5:9; 14:3; 15:3)

l.4   "Since...one": Rev 5:9; 14:3; 15:3; 19:7-9; 21-22 (Heaven as song, the Beloved, and/or the New Jerusalem)

Comment: See *Poems*, II, 715 and Franklin, II, 1090.

990   Not all die early, dying young-

l.5   "Hoary Boy": Le 19:32; Pr 16:31 (a Biblical oxymoron)

l.6   "statured": Eph 4:13

l.7   "Junior...Fourscore": Ps 90:10 (another Biblical oxymoron)

Comment: See *Poems*, II, 716-717 and Franklin, II, 1072. The poem was enclosed in a letter to Dr. Holland, Leyda, II, 104, suggesting that the "Act"of line seven may be synonymous with the Paulinian run, strive, or work: Ro 15:20; ICo 9:24-25; 15:58; 16:10; Ga 2:2; Php 1:6, 27; 2:12, 16; Col 1:10; IITi 2:5, 21.

992   The Dust behind I strove to join

l.1   "Dust": Ge 2:7; 3:19 (synecdochic of the body, its mortality and circuit world limitations)

l.2   "Disk": Ro 8:29; ICo 15:49; IICo 3:18; IJo 3:2 (the disk image suggests the "new circumference" world of achieved identity, the image of the heavenly or the ideally circumferential face enjoying presence and vision, Rev 22:4)

Comment: P992 when compared with other poems dealing with identity—e.g., P351, P576, P859, and P937—suggests similar struggle to forge cosmos out of the chaos of the material image and the attendant sense of futility with regard to its failure to coalesce into uniform "Sequence" and "Sound."

994   **Partake as doth the Bee**

l.1   "Partake": Heb 3:1, 14; 12:8-10; IIPe 1:4 (the poet's "Bee" partakes spiritually not carnally, Ro 15:27)

l.3   "Rose": Ca 2:1 (the beloved, beautiful, ideally circumferential, is to be possessed at a distance—the spiritualization of the physical represented by bee and flower)

Comment: See *Poems*, II, 719; Franklin, II, 1208; and Leyda, II, 87.

996   **We'll pass without the parting**

ll.1-4   "We'll...where": Ge 31:49 ("The Lord watch between me and thee, when we are absent one from another")

Comment: See *Poems*, II, 720; Franklin, II, 1205; and Leyda, II, 121.

997   **Crumbling is not an instant's Act**

l.6   "Dust": Ge 3:14; Isa 65:25; Mic 7:17 (dust is associated with the serpent; dust, worm, and rust are all associated with decay: Ge 3:19; Job 7:5; 19:26; 21:26; Ps 103:14; 104:29; Mt 6:19-20; Jas 5:3)

l.8   "Rust": Mt 6:19-2-

l.9   "Ruin...work": IPe 5:8

998   **Best Things dwell out of Sight**

l.1   "Best...Sight": Ac 17:24; ICo 2:9; 13:12; IICo 5:7; ITi 6:16; Heb 11:1; IJo 4:12

l.2   "Pearl": Rev 21:21

l.2   "the Just": Lu 14:14; Ac 3:14; 7:52; 22:14; 24:15; Heb 12:23

l.5   "Wind": Joh 3:8

ll.5,6   "Capsule": Ro 7:24; IICo 5:4; Php 3:21 (the body prison)

999   **Superfluous were the Sun**

l.1   "Sun": Ge 1:15-16; Mal 4:2; Lu 1:78; IIPe 1:19; Rev 1:16; 2:28; 21:23; 22:5, 16 (the Sun-Son is here the creative Word, Joh 1:1-14)

1.2   "When...dead": Ge 1:4, 10, 12, 18, 21, 25, 31 (the Creation refrain—"and God saw that it was good"—points to a past "When" now dead, P999 insisting that the "Fame" of the Word, its essence, is neither a "When" or "Where")

ll.3-4   "Day...said": Ge 1:3, 5-6, 8-9, 11, 13-14, 19-20, 23-24, 26, 28-29, 31; 2:2-4, 18 (the Creation is partitioned into days upon which God speaks—"And God said," "And God called")

ll.5-8   "That...'Where' ": Heb 11:1, 3 (the "Faith" is in the Word that is Light and Love but not "When" and "Where," a Word whose essence is spiritual, not bound finally by time and place)

1.9   "dateless Fame": Joh 17:24; Heb 1:10; 4:3; IPe 1:20 (the atemporal Word is the basis for her religio-aesthetic faith, for the plenitude upon which her "Periods" rest although "Periods may lie" suggests the limitation and ambiguity of such an enterprise)

1001   The Stimulus, beyond the Grave

1.1   "Grave": ICo 15:55
1.2   "His...see": Rev 19:7-9; 22:4
Comment: See *Poems*, II, 723 and Franklin, II, 1215.

1002   Aurora is the effort

1.1   "Aurora...effort": Lu 1:78 ("Aurora" is emblematic of the Deity, the "dayspring from on high")
1.2   "Of...Face": Rev 22:4 ("Aurora" is nature's mediation of the Divine, here typic of the beatific vision)

1004   There is no Silence in the Earth- so silent

1.1   "There...World": Hab 2:20 ("But the Lord is in his holy temple: let all the earth keep silence before him")
Comment: P1004 insists that there is no silence like that before "Nature," God's speech (Ge 1) or "haunted House." But to break the silence would be to "haunt the World" for Art is the house which tries to be haunted.

1005   Bind me- I still can sing-

l.4   "Slay": Job 13:15 ("Though he slay me, yet will I trust in him: but I will maintain mine own ways before him")

l.5   "Paradise": Lu 23:43; Rev 2:7; 21-22

l.6   "thine": Ca 8:6

1006   The first We knew of Him was Death-

ll.1-4   "The...been": Ro 5:14-19; 6:3-10; ICo 15:21-22, 45; IICo 5:14-17; Php 3:10

l.2   "second": ICo 15:47; Heb 9:28; 10:9 (the second Adam, the Christ of the resurrection and ascension, Mt 28; Ac 1-2)

l.2   "Renown": Isa 11:1; Eze 34:29

l.3   "Except": ICo 15:36 ("that which thou sowest is not quickened, except it die")

l.3   "first": Rev 1:5 (Christ as the "first begotten of the dead")

l.3   "justified": Isa 45:25; Ro 3:24-25; 4:5; 5:1-2, 8-11; 8:30

ll.3-4   "Except...been": Joh 12:23-24 ("And Jesus answered them, saying, The hour is come, that the Son of man should be glorified. Verily, verily, I say unto you, Except a corn of wheat fall into the ground and die, it abideth alone: but if it die, it bringeth forth much fruit")

1010   Up Life's Hill with my little Bundle

l.6   "Spotless...blame": Ca 4:7; Eph 1:4; 5:27; IIPe 3:14; Rev 14:1-5; 19:7-9

l.7   "Heart...accepted": ICo 7:37

l.8   "Homelessness...Home": Mr 10:29-30 ("And Jesus answered and said, Verily I say unto you, There is no man that hath left house, or brethren, or sisters, or father, or mother, or wife, or children, or lands, for my sake, and the gospel's, But he shall receive an hundredfold now in this time, houses, and brethren, and sisters, and mothers, and children, and lands, with persecutions; and in the world to come eternal life")

1012   Which is best? Heaven-

l.2   "Heaven": Rev 4; 19-22

l.4   "esteem": Heb 11:26 ("Esteeming the reproach of Christ greater riches than the treasures in Egypt: for he had respect unto the recompence of the reward")

l.7   "yield": Heb 12:11

l.9   "choose": He 11:25 (another key echo of the "Faith" chapter of Hebrews)

1013   Too scanty 'twas to die for you,

l.1   "Too...you": Joh 15:13 (love of the Divine Beloved demands a death-in-life—P1013 responding ironically to Biblical admonition and paradox)

l.2   "The...that": compare with P444 and P1554 (the Spartans at Thermopylae would have to die only once for Law or State)

ll.3,6   "living": Ro 12:1 ("I beseech you therefore, brethren, by the mercies of God, that ye present your bodies a living sacrifice, holy, acceptable unto God, which is your reasonable service")

l.3   "Sweet": Ca 2:3, 14; 5:5, 13, 16 (the Canticles word of endearment here used ironically)

l.3   "costlier": Lu 14:26-28

ll.5-8   "The...dead": IICo 4:7-18

ll.5,7   "Dying": ICo 15:31 ("I protest by your rejoicing which I have in Christ Jesus our Lord, I die daily"); IICo 4:10-11 ("Always bearing about in the body the dying of the Lord Jesus, that the life also of Jesus might be made manifest in our body. For we which live are always delivered unto death for Jesus' sake, that the life of Jesus might be made manifest in our mortal flesh")

ll.7-8   "without...dead": IICo 6:9

1014   Did We abolish Frost

l.1   "abolish": IITi 1:10 (the abolition of "Frost" would parallel that of the abolition of death: the twin curses)

l.1   "Frost": Ge 3:18-19 (the "Blonde Assassin" is the principle of death in fallen nature)

l.2   "The...cease": Rev 10:6; 21:23; 22:1-5 (a ceaseless "Summer" is Paradise regained)

1016   The Hills in Purple syllables

l.1   "Purple": see note, line one, P15

1017   To die- without the Dying

ll.1-2   "To...Life": see notes, lines one, three, and five to seven, P1013

l.2   "Life": Rev 2:7, 10; 21:6, 27; 22:1-2, 14, 17 (the crown, tree, book, and water of life are all elsewhere, matters of apocalyptic hope)

ll.3-4   "This...Belief": Mt 9:28; Mr 5:36; Lu 8:50; Joh 9:35 (examples of the yoking of "Belief" and "Miracle")

1018   Who saw no Sunrise cannot say

ll.1-2   "Who...be": Rev 1:16 ("his countenance was as the sun shineth")

l.5   "Light": Joh 1:4-9; IJo 1:5

l.6   "Afflicted...Day": IICo 4:17-18 ("For our light affliction, which is but for a moment, worketh for us a far more exceeding and eternal weight of glory; While we look not at the things which are seen, but at the things which are not seen: for the things which are not seen are temporal; but the things which are not seen are eternal"); Heb 10:32-33

l.7   "Blindness": ICo 13:12

l.7   "beheld": Joh 1:14 ("And the Word was made flesh, and dwelt among us, (and we beheld his glory, the glory as of the only begotten of the Father,) full of grace and truth"); IICo 3:18

l.8   "And...Eye": Isa 6:9; Eze 12:2; Mt 13:14-15; Mr 4:12; Lu 8:10; Joh 12:40; Ac 28:26-27; Ro 11:8; IICo 3:14-15; Heb 5:11

1019   My Season's furthest Flower-

l.1   "Flower": Ca 2:12; 5:13

l.2   "tenderer": Ca 2:13, 15; 7:12

ll.3-4   "Because...Friend": Ru 2:1-2

l.4   "Friend": Ca 5:16

1020   Trudging to Eden, looking backward,

l.1   "Eden": Ge 2-3; Eze 28:13-14; 31:8-9, 16; 47:1-12; Rev 21-22 (Eden seems here synonymous with Heaven or Paradise; David Copperfield would be symbolic of man unparadised—a dispossessed, homeless outcast)

Comment: See *Poems*, II, 729.

1021   Far from Love the Heavenly Father

l.1   "Love": IJo 4:8 ("God is love")

l.1   "Heavenly Father": Mt 6:14, 26, 32

l.2   "Leads": Ps 23:2-3; Mt 6:13 (the verb is chosen for ironic reverberations)

l.2   "Chosen": Mt 20:16; 22:14; Mr 13:20; Joh 13:18; 15:16, 19; ICo 1:27-28; Eph 1:4; IITh 2:13; Jas 2:5; IPe 2:9; Rev 17:14

l.2   "Child": Mt 5:9, 45; 9:15; 13:38; 18:2-6; 19:13-14; Joh 12:36; 13:33; Ro 8:16-17; 9:7-11; Ga 3:7, 26; 4:28-31; Eph 1:5; 5:8; IPe 1:14; IJo 4:4 (the "Child" of God, of the light, promise, or kingdom)

l.3   "Realm...Briar": Jg 8:7, 16; Isa 5:6; 7:23-25; 32:13; 55:13 (briers are associated with the wilderness and with uncultivated, useless places contrasting with the vineyard of God); Mt 13:7 (in the parable of the sower, the "Realm if Briar" or thorns would be a valueless place); Mt 27:29; Mr 15:17; Joh 19:2, 5 (briers or thorns would suggest the Passion)

l.4   "Meadow mild": Ps 23:2 ("He maketh me to lie down in green pastures: he leadeth me beside the still waters"); Ge 2-3; Eze 28:13; Rev 22:1-3

l.5   "Dragon": Isa 27:1; 35:7; Mal 1:3; Rev 20:2

l.6   "Hand": Joh 10:28-29

l.6   "Friend": Jas 2:23

l.7   "Guides": Ps 31:3; 48:14; 78:52; Isa 49:10; 58:11; Joh 16:13 (again the verb is chosen for its ironic effect; see also the use of "leadeth," Ps 23:2-3)

l.7   "Little One": Mt 10:42; 18:6, 10, 14

1.7 "predestined": Eph 1:5 ("Having predestinated us unto the adoption of children by Jesus Christ to himself, according to the good pleasure of his will")

1.8 "Land": Ge 12:1; De 32:49; Heb 11:9 (an ironic use of the land of promise—the "Native Land" is neither Eden, promised land, nor New Jerusalem)

1022 I knew that I had gained

ll.1-5 "I...unrelieved": Php 3:7-14

ll.7-8 "Another...Continent": IICo 3:18; 4:7-11

1024 So large my Will

1.8 "Who...all": Isa 40:10; Mt 16:27; Ro 2:6; 14:12; ICo 3:8; Rev 20:12; 22:12

1.12 "Immortality": Ro 2:7; ICo 15:53-54; ITi 6:16

1027 My Heart upon a little Plate

ll.1-2 "My...delight": Mt 14:6-11

1028 'Twas my one Glory-

ll.1-4 " 'Twas...Thee": Isa 61:10; 62:3-5; Rev 19:7-9 (a reminder to the Bridegroom of her bridal status)

1.3 "Remembered": Lu 23:42 (see also P217 and P1180)

1.4 "Thee": see note, lines eight, sixteen, 537

1029 Nor Mountain hinder Me

ll.1-4 "Nor...Cordillera": Ro 8:37-39

1030 That Such have died enable us

ll.1-3 "That...lived": Heb 12:1-2

1.4 "Immortality": ICo 15:53-54; ITi 6:16

1031 Fate slew Him, but He did not drop-

ll.1-7   "Fate...Her": Isa 53; Mt 26-28; ICo 15 (the Passion and Resurrection pattern described in generalized, *Acts and Monuments* language)

l.1   "slew": Ac 2:23; 5:30, 36; 10:39; 13:28; Rev 5:12; 13:8

l.5   "stung": ICo 15:55-56

l,8   "Acknowledged...Man": Joh 19:5 ("Behold the man!")

1032   Who is the East?

ll.2,3,6,7 "Yellow," "Purple": see note, line one, P15

1033   Said Death to Passion

l.1   "Death": Ge 3:19; Job 21:26

ll.1,3,5 "Passion": Mt 26-27; Ac 1:3

ll.5-6   "Bore...East": ICo 15:50-55 (via the Passion, death becomes emblematic not of a West or sunset as terminus but an emblem of a transition or passage from circuit world to new circumference)

l.6   "East": Mr 16:2; Lu 1:78-79 (the "East" is associated with the sunrise and Resurrection)

l.7   "Sun": Ps 84:11; 89:36; Mal 4:2; Lu 1:78; IIPe 1:19; Rev 1:16; 2:28; 21:23; 22:5, 16 (the Sun-Son)

ll.8-9   "Resituated...done": ICo 15:55 (death is here "resituated" because transvalued in terms of ICo 15, becoming a sunset "typic" of everlasting life)

1036   Satisfaction- is the Agent

ll.3-4   "Want...Infinity": Mt 5:6 ("Blessed are they which do hunger"; for desire as the circuit world calculus see also, e.g., P67)

1037   Here, where the Daisies fit my Head

l.6   "Flower": Job 14:2; Ps 103:15; Isa 40:6-8; IPe 1:24

l.7   "Enemy": ICo 15:26

ll.9-10   "Nor...become": Ro 38-39

ll.11-12 "A...Home": ICo 15:38, 42-55

1038 Her little Parasol to lift

l.5 "Summer further": Rev 22:1-3
l.5 "wear": Isa 61:10; Eze 16:10; ICo 15:53-55; IICo 5:2-4; Rev 3:5, 18; 19:8 (the response of the morning glory to the sun is typic of her imitation of the Sun-Son, IICo 3:18, the glory of the eternal morning or summer, the bright and morning star, Rev 2:28; 22:16; for the eternal summer what is worn is spoken of in bridal or Paulinian-resurrection figuration)
l.6 "Nature's Drawer": ICo 15:35-55 (the earth, the body, and/or the grave in the language of Corinthians)
l.7 "Present": IICo 11:2; Eph 5:27; Col 1:22, 28; Jude 24
l.8 "blemishes": Eph 5:27 ("That he might present it to himself a glorious church, not having spot, or wrinkle, or any such thing; but that it should be holy and without blemish"); IPe 1:18-23; Jude 24
Comment: See *Poems*, II, 736.

1039 I heard, as if I had no Ear

l.2 "Word": Joh 1:1
l.3 "Life": Joh 1:4
ll.4-6 "And...Thing": Mt 13:16 ("But blessed are your eyes, for they see: and your ears, for they hear")
l.7 "Light": Joh 1:4-9
ll.10-12 "My...in": ICo 15:35-38, 42-44
l.13 "Spirit": Ec 12:7; ICo 15:45
l.13 "Dust": Ge 2:7; 3:19; Ps 103:14; Ec 12:7
l.14 "Eternity": Isa 57:15; Rev 10:6
Comment: See *Poems*, II, 736-737; *Letters*, II, 480-482; and Leyda, II, 157-158.

1040 Not so the infinite Relations- Below

l.1 "Not...Relations": Rev 22:3
ll.1-2 "Below...forfeit": Ge 3 (numerous poems deal with the postlapsarian "Division" which occurs, paradoxically enough, with

"Adhesion" to home or beloved or nature in the circuit world—see e.g., P313, P348, P951, P959, P965, P1013, P1017, and P1021)

l.2   "On High": Ps 93:4; 113:5; Hab 2:9; Lu 1:78; Eph 4:8; Heb 1:3 (KJV phrasing for God's dwelling place)

l.3   "Affliction": Isa 53:4, 7; 63:9; Col 1:24

l.3   "Wo": Isa 53:3-4

l.4   "A...knew": Rev 21:4 ("And God shall wipe away all tears from their eyes; and there shall be no more death, neither sorrow, nor crying, neither shall there be any more pain: for the former things are passed away")

1041   Somewhat, to hope for,

l.1   "hope": Ro 8:24 ("For we are saved by hope")

l.4   "suffer": Ro 8:17-20

1042   Spring comes on the World-

l.3   "thou": see note, lines eight, sixteen, P537

l.3   "come": Ca 2:8-14; 4:16; 5:1; 7:11-13 (the advent of the beloved)

1043   Lest this be Heaven indeed

l.4   "Heaven": Rev 4; 19-22

1044   A Sickness of this World it most occasions

ll.3,8   "for Condition," "For Deity": Heb 11:16

1045   Nature rare uses Yellow

ll.1,4,5,6 "Yellow," "Blue," "Scarlet": see note, line one, P15

1047   The Opening and the Close

l.5   "Seed": ICo 15:38

l.8   "In...decayed": ICo 15:36 ("Thou fool, that which thou sowest is not quickened, except it die")

1048 **Reportless Subjects, to the Quick**

ll.1,5 "Reportless": Heb 11:39

l.1 "Quick": Isa 11:3 ("And shall make him of quick understanding in the fear of the Lord: and he shall not judge after the sight of his eyes, neither reprove after the hearing of his ears"); Joh 5:21; 6:63; Ro 8:11

ll.5-6 "Ear...stimulus": Mt 13:9 ("Who hath ears to hear, let him hear")

ll.7-8 "But...fabulous": ICo 1:23-24; 2:7-16

1052 **I never saw a Moor-**

l.5 "I...God": Ge 18:29 ("And he spake unto him yet again"); Ge 35:15 ("And Jacob called the name of the place where God spake with him, Bethel"); Ex 19:19 ("And when the voice of the trumpet sounded long, and waxed louder and louder, Moses spake, and God answered him by a voice")

l.6 "Nor...Heaven": IIKi 2:21 ("And it came to pass, as they still went on, and talked, behold, there appeared a chariot of fire, and horses of fire, and parted them parted them both asunder; and Elijah went up by a whirlwind into heaven"); IICo 12:2 ("I knew a man in Christ above fourteen years ago, (whether in the body, I cannot tell; or whether out of the body, I cannot tell: God knoweth;) such an one caught up to the third heaven")

ll.7-8 "Yet...given": Joh 20:29 ("blessed are they that have not seen, and yet have believed"); ICo 2:9; IICo 4:18; ITi 6:16; Heb 11:1 ("Now faith is the substance of things hoped for, the evidence of things not seen")

Comment: See *Poems*, II, 742.

1052 **It was a quiet way-**

l.1 "way": Mt 7:14; Joh 14:6

l.2 "He...his": Ca 2:16; 6:3; 7:10

ll.3-4 "I...Eyes": Ca 4:9

l.5 "on/high": see note, line two, P1040

l.7 "Chariots": IIKi 2:11

l.8 "Wheels": Eze 1:15-21

l.14 "The...new": Rev 21:1, 5

l.17   "No...us": Rev 22:2

ll.18-20 "It...Dawn": Rev 22:5 ("And there shall be no night there; and they need no candle, neither light of the sun; for the Lord God giveth them light: and they shall reign for ever and ever"); Rev 22:16

Comment: Using Canticles and apocalyptic figuration, P1053 recounts an ascent to the New Jerusalem as the Bride of Christ. See *Poems*, II, 743-744 and Franklin, I, 569-570.

1054   Not to discover weakness is

ll.1-23   "Not...strength": IICo 12:9-10 ("And he said unto me, My grace is sufficient for thee: for my strength is made perfect in weakness. Most gladly therefore will I rather glory in my infirmities, that the power of Christ may rest upon me. Therefore I take pleasure in infirmities...for when I am weak, then am I strong"); "strength" is not simply the "Artifice" of the seemingly self-contained, self-controlled life but also the "Mystery" in the paradox of efficacious grace)

Comment: P1054 describes the paradoxes of an elect "Consciousness" with regard to the sources of strength and faith. See *Poems*, II, 744 and Franklin, II, 1224.

1055   The Soul should always stand ajar

l.1   "The...ajar": Isa 40:3; Mt 22:1-14; 25:1-13

ll.2-8   "That...more": Rev 3:20 ("Behold, I stand at the door, and knock: if any man hear my voice, and open the door, I will come in to him, and will sup with him, and he with me")

Comment: P1055 is a preparationist poem using traditional apocalyptic figuration. See *Poems*, II, 745 and Franklin, II, 1231.

1056   There is a Zone whose even Years

ll.1-8   "There...Noon": Rev 21-22 (the vision of P1056 is one of the New Jerusalem especially the paradisiacal verses of Rev 22:1-5)

l.3   "Sun...Noon": Rev 21:23; 22:5 (the Lord God or Lamb gives light in Heaven, a "Sun" replacing the sun and moon of Ge 1:14-16)

l.4 "perfect Seasons": Rev 22:2

l.8 "Consciousness...Noon": Rev 22:4 ("Consciousness" at its apogee would be the beatific vision in which the Elect know even as known and the final resolution of identity with the name of the Lamb upon the forehead)

Comment: P1056 describes the New Jerusalem as the temperate "Zone" of Eternity—eternal "Summer" and "Noon." See *Poems*, II, 745 and Franklin, II, 1233.

1058 Bloom- is Result- to meet a Flower

l.1 "Bloom...Result": Eph 5:27; Rev 19:8 (the "Result" is in religio-aesthetic terms the perfected life and poem presented as firstfruits to the Lamb/Bride-groom appearing in the guise of "Great Nature" and the "Meridian" in P1058)

ll.6-8 "So...Meridian": ICo 15 (the mystery of metamorphosis, of "Bud" to "Bloom"—suggested by the "Butterfly," an emblem of the resurrection, and the "Meridian," the zenith of that celestial sphere circling the earth and symbolic of Christ)

ll.9-11 "Bud," "Dew," "Heat": Isa 18:4-5 (for "Dew" see also note, line twenty one, P122)

ll.13-14 "Great...Day": Rev 19:7-9 (Christ, the Bridegroom, awaits "Her," the perfected Bride)

Comment: The imagery of nature becomes bridal imagery with apocalyptic overtones in P1058.

1059 Sang from the Heart, Sire,

ll.4-6 "Red," "Cochineal," "Vermillion": Mt 26:28; Lu 22:44; Joh 19:34 (associations with the Passion of Christ)

l.16 "Hallowed name": Mt 6:9

1060 Air has no Residence, no Neighbor,

l.1 "Air": Ge 2:7; Joh 3:8

l.5 "Pillow": Ge 28:11, 18

l.6 "Essential...Inn": Ge 2:7; Joh 6:63 ("It is the spirit that quickeneth")

l.7 "Later...Light": Ec 12:2-3 (figuratively speaking, the life of the spirit extends beyond the darkness of death) l.8   "Till...persuading/conveying Mine": Ec 12:7

Comment: P1060 uses the air-wind-breath-Spirit associations
metaphorically to hint at intimations of immortality.

1062   He scanned it- staggered-

l.1   "staggered": Job 12:25 ("The grope in the dark
without light, and he maketh them to stagger like a drunken man")

ll.1,6   "He...staggered," "Groped...there": Ps 107:26-27
("They mount to the heaven, they go down again to the depths: their
soul is melted because of trouble. They reel to and fro, and stagger like
a drunken man, and are at their wits' end"; compare P1062 with P249
in the context of Ps 107:23-30)

ll.5-7   "His...Himself": De 28:28-29 ("The Lord shall smite
thee with madness, and blindness, and astonishment of heart: And
thou shalt grope at noonday, as the blind gropeth in darkness, and
thou shalt not prosper in thy ways: and thou shalt be only oppressed
and spoiled evermore, and no man shall save thee"); Isa 59:10 ("We
grope for the wall like the blind, and we grope as if we had no eyes:
we stumble at noonday as in the night; we are in desolate places as
dead men")

1063   Ashes denote that Fire was-

l.1   "Ashes": Ge 18:27; Job 30:19

l.3   "Creature's": Ge 1:20-24; 2:19; Ro 1:25; 8:19-21;
Rev 5:13 (used with the specific force of living creatures as products of
God's creation)

ll.5-8   "Fire...Carbonates": Mal 3:2 ("But who may abide
the day of his coming? and who shall stand when he appeareth? for he
is like a refiner's fire, and like fullers' soap"); Heb 12:29 ("For our
God is a consuming fire"; see also De 4:24; Isa 4:4; Mt 3:12—in the
chemical equivalent of the Passion, P1063 presents the circuit world as
the crucible for refinement by fire, the anti-climactic final lines
underscoring the fact that "what Carbonates" is disclosed to science,
the "Chemist," as consolidated "Ashes," the "Grayest Pile")

1065   Let down the Bars, Oh Death-

ll.1-8   "Let...told": Eze 34:12-14, 23-24; Joh 10:7-30

l.1   "Oh Death": ICo 15:55

l.2   "Flocks": Isa 40:11 ("He shall feed his flock like a shepherd: he shall gather the lambs with his arm, and carry them in his bosom, and shall gently lead those that are with young")

ll.5-6   "Thine": Heb 13:20 ("Jesus, that great shepherd of the sheep")

l.6   "Fold": Isa 65:10 ("And Sharon shall be a fold of flocks, and the valley of Achor a place for the herds to lie down in, for my people that have sought me")

ll.7-8   "Too...told": IPe 5:4 ("And when the chief Shepherd shall appear, ye shall receive a crown of glory that fadeth not away"; the underlying trope for P1065 has paradisiacal, apocalyptic reverberations: Ps 23:1; Isa 11:6; 65:25; Jer 31:10; 49:19; 50:44; Eze 37:22-25; Rev 5:6, 8, 12-13; 7:9-17; 14:1-4; 19:7-9; 21:22-23; 22:1-3)

1067   Except the smaller size

l.7   "The...Hesperides": Rev 22:1-5 (the eternal summer of the New Jerusalem, a time after "Indian Summer Noon" in which is achieved the ideally circumferential perfected life or "West Indian," Eph 4:12-13; Col 4:12; Heb 12:23)

Comment: See *Poems*, II, 751-752; Franklin, I, 609; and Leyda, II, 112.

1068   Further in Summer than the Birds

l.1   "Further...Birds": Ca 2:12 (the songs of birds are associated with the summer and the world of profane love, bodily desires—part of the pathos of the "Grass," synecdochic of the circuit world)

l.2   "Pathetic...Grass": Job 5:25; Ps 37:2; 72:6, 16; 90:5-6; 103:15-16; Isa 40:6-8; IPe 1:24 (fertility and fecundity are associated with the "Grass" as well as the evanescent, fugitive, ephemeral quality of sublunary existence)

l.4   "It's...Mass": Mt 26:26-30 (the Eucharist; a Requiem Mass may also be implied, especially since the poem emphasizes "Repose"—the language of the poem owing less to the KJV than to liturgy: "Ordinance," "Mass," "gradual," and "Canticle")

ll.6,13 "Grace": Ps 84:11; Zech 4:7; Joh 1:16-17; ICo 15:10; IICo 8:9; Rev 1:4; 22:21 ("Grace" is the unmerited favor of God)

l.9   "Noon": see note, line one, P533

l.11   "spectral Canticle": Ca 1:1 (relevant since in some respects P1068 is a displaced love song about an absent Lover—the light on the unfurrowed face of "Summer" and "Noon" typic of The Light; stanza three contains synaesthesia with its "spectral Canticle" an unsubstantial, ghostly light upon the late August landscape)

l.13   "Remit": Mt 26:28

l.14   "No...Glow": IJo 1:5 (the "Glow" does not differentiate into the "Furrow[ed]" face of God; the "Grace" here not remitted is that final allowance of entrance into God's presence and the beatific vision, Rev 22:4)

l.18(Norcross transcript) "At...here": Rev 22:5

Comment:P1068 poses problems in the reading of furthest "Summer" and highest "Noon." Is the "minor" celebration of an "unobtrusive Mass" an indication of a dirge for the dead—summer then being an anti-climax before death—or an indication of a Eucharistic sacrament that is the penultimate before true fulfillment? Are "Summer" and "Noon" pivots or platforms, points turning time and season downward or platforms symbolizing a saturation or fullness typic of something higher? Regardless, the focus of the poem is not upon the "Repose" at the end of stanza three but upon change, transition, metamorphosis—the transition when sense has been spiritualized to the full, when "Druidic Difference[s]" have been sensitively recorded, when the emblematic and sacramental maneuvers with nature's signs haunt art to saturation. See *Poems*, II, 752-755; *Letters*, II, 449; III, 768; and Leyda, II, 109, 307. "My Cricket," as the poet spoke of P1068, may glance at the fifth verse of the twelfth chapter of Ecclesiastes.

1069   Paradise is of the option

l.1   "Paradise": Lu 23:43; Rev 2:7; 21-22

l.2   "Whosoever will": Rev 22:17 ("And the Spirit and the bride say, Come. And let him that heareth say, Come. And let him that is athirst come. And whosoever will, let him take the water of life freely")

l.3   "Eden": Ge 2-3; Isa 51:3; Eze 28:13; 31:8-9, 16; 36:35; Joe 2:3

l.4   "Adam": Ge 2:19

l.4   "Repeal": Ge 3:23-24 (the Fall with its loss of the Garden of Eden)

Comment: See *Poems*, II, 756; *Letters*, II, 453-454; and Leyda, II, 114-115.

1070   To undertake is to achieve

l.7   "few": Mt 7:14; 20:16; 22:14; Lu 10:2; 13:23

l.8   "Sources/Natures": IIPe 1:4

Comment: See *Poems*, II, 756-757; *Letters*, II, 453-454; Franklin, II, 1206; and Leyda, II, 114-115.

1071   Perception of an object costs

ll.1-4   "Perception...Price":   Mt   5:1-12;   16:24-26 (perception like discipleship has at its heart the paradox that to possess is to lose, to lose is to gain; the price of perception is nothing less than everything since it entails a conscious awareness that beatitude is deprivation)

l.5   "Object Absolute...nought": Ge 1 (the created world is a Word ultimately spoken into existence and sustained by a continuing act of creative will; for the idea of ex nihilo creation, see II Maccabees 7:28; Heb 11:3)

l.6   "Perception...fair": Heb 11:3

ll.7-8   "And...far": ITi 6:16 (God alone is Being or Perfection, e.g., Mt 5:48)

l.8   "so far/so Heavenly far": Eph 4:10 ("He that descended is the same also that ascended up far above all heavens, that he might fill all things")

Comment: See *Poems*, II, 757-758 and Franklin, II, 1146. P1071 is about the Sovereign God of Creation and not about epistemological subtleties or involuted theories of Romantic imagination. "For in him we live, and move, and have our being" (Ac 17:28). Mediate, imperfect, and yet intimate, the consciousness that is "Perception" can play at "fair" as long as "Perfectness" is assumed; other less sanguine poems place consciousness on the plank over the solipsistic abyss.

1072   Title divine- is mine!

     ll.1-2   "Title...Wife": Rev 19:7-9; 21:2, 9; 22:17 (the Bride of Christ)

     l.3   "Degree": Lu 1:52 ("He hath put down the mighty from their seats, and exalted them of low degree"; the word from Mary's song here apparently used with irony)

     l.4   "Empress...Calvary": Mt 27:33; Lu 23:33 (hers is the cross without the crown)

     l.5   "Royal": IPe 2:9; Rev 1:6

     l.5   "Crown": Rev 2:10; 3:11; 4:4, 10; 19:12

     l.6   "Betrothed": Ho 2:19-20

     ll.8-9   "Garnet...Gold": Lu 22:44; Joh 19:34; Rev 21:18, 21 (the "Garnet" suggests the red of the Passion, which is the reality of "Wife"—"Gold" being associated with the idealized Bride of Revelation; the phrasing "Garnet to Garnet/Gold to Gold" echoes the *Book of Common Prayer*: "ashes to ashes, dust to dust"; the fatalistic, all-encompassing circularity of this language is also seen in the next two lines as well—part of the strategy of P1072 in viewing the circuit world betrothed as a "Bridalled" estate)

     l.12   " 'Husband'": Eph 5:33; Rev 21:2

     Comment: See *Poems*, II, 758-759; *Letters*, II, 394; and Leyda, II, 47.

1075   The Sky is low- the Clouds are mean.

     l.8   "Diadem": Job 29:14; Isa 28:5; Eze 21:26 (the cruel aspects of nature are evidenced when she is without her "Diadem"—here suggestive not only of queenly rule and power but of justice and righteousness as well)

     Comment: See *Poems*, II, 760-761; *Letters*, II, 455-456; and Leyda, II, 119.

1076   Just Once! Oh least Request!

     l.1   "Oh...Request": Job 6:8 ("Oh that I might have my request; and that God would grant me the thing that I long for!")

     ll.2,6   "Adamant," "Flint": Eze 3:9 (the KJV uses the language but not to describe the Deity)

l.3　　"Grace": see note, line six, P1068
l.8　　"Heaven": Mt 6:9
l.9　　"Sweet": Ca 2:3, 14; 5:5, 13, 16 (the Canticles word of endearment may here be used ironically)
Comment: See *Poems*, II, 761-762 and Franklin, I, 506.

1077　These are the Signs to Nature's Inns-

ll.3-4　"Whosoever...Bread": ICo 11:27 ("Wherefore whosoever shall eat this bread, and drink this cup of the Lord, unworthily, shall be guilty of the body and blood of the Lord")
l.11　　"Purple": see note, line one, P15

1079　The Sun went down- no Man looked on-

ll.1,5　"Sun": Ps 84:11; Mal 4:2; Lu 1:78; IIPe 1:19; Rev 1:16; 2:28; 21:23; 22:5, 16 (a displacement for the face of God)
ll.1,5　"no...on": IJo 4:12 ("No man hath seen God at any time")
l.3　　"Majesty": Heb 1:3; 8:1
ll.3,6-8　"The...alone," "The...Witness": Nu 35:30; De 17:6; 19:15; Mt 18:16; Joh 8:17; IICo 13:1; ITi 5:19; Heb 10:28 (the Bible has numerous instances of the requirement of two or three witnesses with firsthand knowledge)
l.8　　"Witness": ICo 15:15 (witness of sunrise typifies testimony to the resurrection)
l.8　　"Crown": Isa 28:5; Rev 14:14; 19:12

1080　When they come back- if Blossoms do-

ll.2-3　"I...again": Joh 3:3-8
ll.13-15　"One...Tomorrow": ICo 15:51-55; IJo 3:2
Comment: Somewhere between "Last Year" and "Tomorrow," "Blossoms," the zenith of "Art," create in the memory of the speaker "doubt," "fear," and "pang" whether "their last Experiment/Last Year" may not be final (instead of a last like that of the shoemaker, a pattern for infinite re-creation). A "Putative" [see note, lines fourteen to nineteen, P179; P851; and P961] is P1080 since just as the "Blossoms" of nature attract "His look" so also must her poems be "Blossoms" somehow attracting an absent, Ideal Face.

Failing that, "When once the Art is out" the rest is silence—the unmeaning of the apocalyptic. So nature, and its counterpart "Art," which tries to be haunted, must continue as "Experiment," as "typic" of that final Reality in which "Blossoms can be born again." See *Poems*, II, 763-764 and Franklin, II, 1251-1252.

1081   Superiority to Fate

l.8   "Paradise": Lu 23:43; Rev 2:7; 21-22

1086   What Twigs We held by-

l.14   "everlasting Light": Isa 60:19-20 ("The sun shall be no more thy light by day; neither for brightness shall the moon give light unto thee: but the Lord shall be unto thee an everlasting light, and thy God thy glory. Thy sun shall no more go down; neither shall thy moon withdraw itself: for the Lord shall be thine everlasting light, and the days of thy mourning shall be ended"); Zec 2:5; Rev 21:23; 22:5
ll.15-17 "The...are": IICo 4:18; Heb 11:3

1088   Ended, ere it begun-

ll.2-4   "Title...Story": Ps 90:9 (a reference to the story trope)

1090   I am afraid to own a Body-

l.1   "Body": Ge 2:7, 21-24; ICo 15:44
l.2   "Soul": Ge 2:7; ICo 15:45
ll.5-6   "Double...Heir": Ge 1-2 (the creature is the "unsuspecting" recipient of body and soul at God's creative "pleasure"; the ideas of primogeniture and entail are behind these lines and the next)
l.7   "Deathlessness": Ec 12:7; ICo 15:53-54

1091   The Well upon the Brook

ll.1-4   "The...Ground": Joh 4:10-14

1092   It was not Saint- it was too large-

ll.1-4   "It...spiritual": ICo 2:9-15

1093   Because 'twas Riches I could own,

ll.1-6   "Because...Air": Mt 6:19-21

1094   Themself are all I have-

1.1   "Themself...have": Le 23; Nu 28-29 (the presentation of the flowers echoes the KJV context of the firstfruits offering and spotless sacrifice)
1.2   "Myself...be": Ca 4:7; Eph 5:27
1.3   "Cheek": Ca 1:10; 5:13
1.4   "Ivory": Ca 5:14; 7:4
1.5   "Would...Me": Eph 1:4; Jas 1:18; IPe 1:18-21 (the poem conflates the sacrificial, bridal, and election figuration)
Comment: See *Poems*, II, 770-771.

1096   These Strangers, in a foreign World,

ll.1-4   "These...Refugee": Mt 25:31-46; Heb 13:2

1097   Dew- is the Freshet in the Grass-

1.1   "Dew": Ge 27:28; Ex 16:13-14; Ps 110:3; Ho 6:4; 13:3; Zec 8:12 (the dew is associated with God's Providence and also renewal and evanescence)
1.1   "Freshet...Grass": Isa 35:5-7 (in Emersonian terms P1097 insists that the kingdom flourishes with a new type of vision)

1.3   "turns...feet": IICo 4:18
1.4   "Artisan": Ec 12:1; Isa 40:28; Ro 1:25; IPe 4:19 (the Creator)
1.7   "Mistake...in": Heb 11:3
1.9   "Sign": Ge 1:14
1.11   "Obtain...Child": Lu 18:17 (the sacramental vision of "Nature's Show" would be permitted the "Child"; compare the final stanzas of P130)

Comment: See *Poems*, II, 771-772 and Franklin, II, 1145.

1098   Of the Heart that goes in, and closes the Door

l.1   "closes...Door": Mt 25:10
l.3   "Though...broke": Ec 12:6

1099   My Cocoon tightens- Colors teaze-

ll.1-8   "My...Sky": ICo 15:46-55
ll.9-12 "So...divine": ICo 13:12
Comment: Whitman's "Cradle" is here "Cocoon" and his clue, "death," is here metamorphosis. P1099 is a Hitchcockian emblematic poem of change: resurrection and ascent. However, P1099 may be primarily a theodicy—a poem justifying the circuit world as a place of metamorphosis, of search for the "clue divine." The pupa state dramatized in stanza one is anything but quiescent with its teasing "Colors," "feeling for the Air," and "dim capacity for Wings." The hoped for but as yet unachieved imago of stanza two is an object of faith not sight for the circuit world of stanza three is characterized by "baffle," "cipher," and "blunder"—a vale of soul making not of euphoric revelation.

1100   The last Night that She lived

ll.15-16 "A...infinite": Ex 20:5; 34:14; De 4:24; 5:9 (although the speaker's jealousy is not infinite, it is similar to the jealousy motivating the first two of the Ten Commandments in this respect: exclusivity; the speaker's jealous regard for the "Dying" one is exclusive, resenting as it were the continuing existence of "Others")
ll.22-23 "Then...Reed...Water": IKi 14:15
Comment: See *Poems*, II, 773-774 and Franklin, II, 1142-1144.

1101   Between the form of Life and Life

ll.1-2   "Between...big": Ro 2:20; IITi 3:5 (a Paulinian usage contrasting the form, semblance, or shape of knowledge or godliness with its genuine substance; P1101 adapts the distinction to that between authentic experience of the "extatic" and inert materiality or "Liquor in the Jug")

  l.8 "I...tried": see P214

1102 His Bill is clasped- his Eye forsook-

  ll.10-12 "Heaven...Tune": Rev 5:11-13

1103 The spry Arms of the Wind

  l.7 "without...Gate": Heb 13:12 ("Wherefore Jesus also, that he might sanctify the people with his own blood, suffered without the gate")
  ll.9-10 "To...Home": IICo 5:1

1105 Like Men and Women Shadows walk

  l.6 "quickened": Joh 6:63; Ro 8:11
  Comment: "Shadows" are Dickinsonian Brobdingnagians whose "Courtesy" is a conventional limit upon their perception. P1105 reverses the Emersonian natural-to-spiritual gambit, having the "transparent eyeballs" be rather myopic, "[un]quickened" exemplars; that the "Shadows" miss the Lilliputian spiritual "Boroughs/limits" may be an ironic twist of Dickinsonian humor—what should shadow or image the Divine glides by with courteous inattentiveness.

1107 The Bird did prance- the Bee did play-

  l.9 "Heavy laden": Isa 46:1; Mt 11:28
  Comment: See *Poems*, II, 779-780.

1108 A Diamond on the Hand

  l.4 "The...unknown": Rev 19:7-9; 21:2, 10-27 (the "Gem" may symbolize Bride of Christ status; the "Diamond," although mentioned in a reference to Eden, Eze 28:13, and in the Old Testament background to the Gem Chapter of Revelation, Ex 28:13-21; 39:8-14, is not mentioned in the twenty-first chapter of Revelation—the gem or jewel does, nevertheless, suggest bridal adornment and accession: Isa 61:10; Eze 16:12; Rev 21:2, 10-27)

1109   I fit for them-

l.4   "labor": Joh 6:27 ("Labour not for the meat which perisheth, but for that meat which endureth unto everlasting life, which the Son of man shall give unto you: for him hath God the Father sealed")
l.10   "The...Aim": Php 3:14 ("I press toward the mark for the prize of the high calling of God in Christ Jesus")
Comment: See *Poems*, II, 780-781.

1110   None who saw it ever told it

l.1   "None...it": Ge 3(Adam and Eve); Ge 18(Abraham); Ge 32:30(Jacob); Ex 33:11; Nu 14:14(Moses; all are examples of those who saw God's face but "[n]ever told it")
ll.2-4   " 'Tis...breath": Ex 33:20 ("Thou canst not see my face: for there shall no man see me, and live")
l.6   "Diamond": Mt 13:46; Rev 21:21
l.8   "serve": Ex 20:5; De 6:13; 10:20; Mt 4:10; Rev 22:3 (for the variant "seek" see Mt 13:45)
Comment: See *Poems*, II, 781. The rare gem of great value is the beatific vision (Rev 22:4).

1111   Some Wretched creature, savior take

l.1   "Wretched creature": Ro 7:24; 8:19-21
l.1   "savior": Lu 2:11
l.2   "Who...die": IICo 5:8
l.3   "sweet": Ca 2:3, 14; 5:5, 13, 16
l.3   "mercy's": Jas 5:11 ("Behold we count them happy which endure. Ye have heard of the patience of Job, and have seen the end of the Lord; that the Lord is very pitiful, and of tender mercy")
l.3   "sake": Mt 5:10-11; 10:22, 39; 16:25; Mr 8:35; 10:29; 13:1; Lu 9:24; 21:17; Joh 13:38; 15:21; Ac 9:16; Ro 8:36; ICo 4:10; Php 1:29; IPe 3:14; Rev 2:3 (the associations are consistently with loss, suffering, and death and the formula "my/thy/his name's sake")

l.4   "Another...me": Mr 14:35 (P1111 may follow the Gethsemane prayer of Christ with its request that this not be the final "Hour"—see also Joh 12:27)
Comment: See *Poems*, II, 782.

1112   That this should feel the need of Death

ll.7-8   "Not...He": Rev 11:18; 13:16; 19:5, 18; 20:12 ("great" and "small" are mentioned frequently and together)
Comment: See *Poems*, II, 782.

1113   There is a strength in proving that it can be bourne

l.6   "cedar Feet": IIKi 19:23; Isa 37:24; Eze 17:22; Am 2:9 (the cedars were noted for height)

1114   The largest Fire ever known

ll.1,5   "Consumes": De 4:24; Heb 12:29 (God is a "consuming fire," an idea used figuratively here of the sun, the "largest Fire ever known")
Comment: See *Poems*, II, 783-784 and Franklin, II, 1190.

1115   The murmuring of Bees, has ceased

l.7   "The...Book": Rev 1:1, passim (a reference to The Revelation of St. John the Divine, the last book of the Bible, its focus upon the eschatological being used here figuratively for the dying seasons of the year)
l.8   "Whose...June": Ge 1:1, passim (a reference to the first book of the Bible, Genesis, its focus upon God's Creation and man's beginnings being used here figuratively for the birth and growth seasons of the year)
l.9   "Creatures": Ge 1:20-21, 24; 2:19
Comment: See *Poems*, II, 784-785.

1116   There is another Loneliness

l.4   "circumstances of Lot": Ge 19; Lu 17:28-32; IIPe 2:7-8 (as righteous, Lot was an alien in Sodom and Gomorrah; also, Lot was without his wife)

l.6   "And...befall": Ec 3:19; Ac 20:22; Jas 1:25 (the diction and syntax here echo the KJV)

Comment: See *Poems*, II, 785-786.

1118   Exhiliration is the Breeze

l.1   "Exhiliration...Breeze": Rev 1:10 (the ecstasy here described is like St. John's being "in the Spirit"; for the cognate "extasy" see note, line fifteen, P783; note, lines five, eight, P1191; and note, line seven, P1468)

ll.2-4   "That...found": Ge 28:10-19; 32:24-32 (the two visionary experiences of Jacob may be most relevant, although a number of Biblical figures might serve: Moses, Elijah, Abraham, Isaiah, Jeremiah, St. Peter, and perhaps, especially, Ezekiel, Eze 3, and St. Paul, IICo 12:1-5)

l.8   "Enchanted Ground": Ge 28:17 ("How dreadful is this place! this is none other but the house of God, and this is the gate of heaven"); Ex 3:5; Ac 7:33 (the holy ground of theophanies)

1119   Paradise is that old mansion

l.1   "Paradise...mansion": Ge 2-3 (the Garden of Eden may be intended since Adam is mentioned; see also Eze 28:13-14; 31:8-9, 16; 47:1-12; Rev 2:7; 21-22; see also Joh 14:2: "In my Father's house are many mansions: if it were not so, I would have told you. I go to prepare a place for you")

ll.3-7   "Occupied...excesses": Ge 3:23-24; ICo 15:22, 45 (in Adam's Fall all participate thereby losing "Paradise")

1122   'Tis my first night beneath the Sun

l.1   "Sun": Mal 4:2; Lu 1:78; IIPe 1:19; Rev 1:16; 2:28; 21:23; 22:5, 16 (the Sun-Son or Heavenly Bridegroom)

l.7   "Delights": Ca 2:3; 7:6 (the "Delights" of the Heavenly Beloved are heights, anticipations, and distances)

1123   A great Hope fell

l.1   "Hope": e.g., Ro 8:24-25 (a favorite Paulinian word expressive of fundamental faith; the nautical metaphor for the mind is carried through three of the four stanzas; St. Paul does at least once use shipwreck in a relevantly figurative way, ITi 1:19)

l.5   "Witness": Rev 1:5; 3:14 (Christ then is not the faithful and true "Witness" to the mind in "Ruin" but appears later in the poem in another guise at the speaker's death)

l.10   "wound": Mt 26-27 (synecdochic for the Passion, which has become the "Ruin" and "wreck" of the mind—the whole of "Life" entering the "wide wound")

l.16   "tender Carpenter": Mt 13:55; Mr 6:3 (perhaps a somewhat sentimental reference to Jesus; nevertheless, the variant—"sovreign/unsuspecting Carpenters"—roughens the finality of the last lines)

Comment: See *Poems*, II, 788-789.

1124   Had we known the Ton she bore

ll.1-4   "Had...error": Isa 53:3-4; Mt 11:28-30 (perhaps P1124 contains the beginnings of another Passion poem)

Comment: See *Poems*, II, 789-790.

1125   Oh Sumptuous moment

l.5   "abundance": IICo 12:7

Comment: See Poems, II, 790. P1125 offers a vision of that "moment" of metamorphosis when all becomes abundance and fullness, a transvaluation of the circuit world's "famish" and "Gallows" sub specie aeternitatis—as in P1382, it is "joy unspeakable and full of glory"(IPe 1:8).

1126   Shall I take thee, the Poet said

l.1   "Shall...said": see "The Form of Solemnization of Matrimony," *Book of Common Prayer*

l.4   "Till...tried": Ps 19; Rev 19:11-13 (the perfect Word of God before which man is "speechless," Mt 22:12)

ll.8-11 "There...nomination": IICo 9:15; 12:4; IPe 1:8 ("Philology" falters before the inexpressible; the "Vision" is not amenable to "nomination," does not traffic in the legal world of the "propounded word")

l.12   "The...reveal": Ge 3:24 (cherubim guard the Tree of Life in the Garden of Eden); Ex 25; IKi 6; IICh 5 (cherubim adorn the Ark of the Covenant); Eze 10; 11:22 (cherubim are associated with the visions of Ezekiel); IISa 22:11; Ps 18:10 (ridden by Yahweh, they are associated with theophanies, revelations of God's glory)

Comment: See *Poems*, II, 790-791. Perhaps P1126 is about the limits of language and poetry since the worlds of court and lexicon cannot yield that "portion of the Vision" that is beyond. Marriage to such a "Vision" comes "unsummoned," choose is replaced by chosen.

1129   Tell all the Truth but tell it slant-

l.1   "Truth": Isa 60; Joh 1; 3; 14:6; I Jo 1; Rev 21-22 (the Incarnate Word is Truth and Light; the Old Testament associates God with truth and light, e.g., Ps 19; 43:3)

l.3   "Too...Delight": Ex 34:33-35; IICo 3:13-14 (Moses vailed his face so that the reflected glory of the light of God's presence would not blind the people; such a face-to-face encounter in the presence of God may have been closer to the notion of "Truth" here than anything propositional; the Psalmist repeatedly refers to the "light of God's countenance," which contains the implicit apocalyptic hope that the diurnal round will eventually cease in the ideal presence of God, Rev 21-22; the "infirm Delight" is the product of the "unfurnished eyes" of the circuit world, ICo 13:12)

ll.7-8   "The...blind": Ex 33:20; 34:33-35; Ac 13:11; IICo 3:13-14; ITi 6:16; IJo 4:12 (direct "Truth" blinds the darkened eyes of the circuit world)

1131   The Merchant of the Picturesque

l.1   "The...Picturesque": Ge 1-2 (the God of Creation)

ll.3-4   "But...calls": see P130 where the same doubleness is associated with the skeptical adult bees v. the innocent, believing birds: " Permit a child to join."

ll.5-6   "To...courtesy": Mt 18:3-4; 19:14; Mr 10:14-15; Lu 10:21; 18:16-17 ("I thank thee, O Father, Lord of heaven and earth, because thou hast hid these things from the wise and prudent, and hast revealed them unto babes," Mt 11:25) l.8   "artless currency": see, e.g., P130 where the sacramental vision, the innocent, spontaneous, unself-consciously worshipful approach to nature of the "Child," is the "artless" obeisance that the "Merchant" rewards with intimacy and certainty

l.9   "Counterfeits": e.g., Mt 6:30; 8:26; 14:31; 16:8; 17:20; Heb 3:19; 4:6, 11 (any adult lacking faith is a "Counterfeit")

Comment: See *Poems*, II, 793-794.

1132   The smouldering embers blush-

ll.1-2   "The...Coal": Ca 8:6-7

l.3   "Hast...nights": Ca 3:1

l.8   "Prometheus...knew/It...true": Joh 1:9 (a personal application of the KJV ("true Light")

Comment: See *Poems*, II, 794.

1133   The Snow that never drifts-

l.13   "spice/fair/sweet": Ca 1:8, 15-16; 2:3, 10, 13-14; 4:1, 7, 10, 14, 16; 5:1, 5, 9, 13, 16; 6:1-2, 10; 7:6, 9; 8:2, 14 (words from the Canticles lexicon)

Comment: See *Poems*, II, 795.

1134   The Wind took up the Northern Things

l.5   "The...Earth": Eze 37:9; Da 7:2; 8:8; 11:4; Zec 2:6; Rev 7:1

l.9   "Chambers": Job 9:9; Ps 19:5; 104:3, 13

Comment: See *Poems*, II, 795-796.

1135   Too cold is this

l.4   "Agate": Rev 21:19

ll.6-9   "How...Asterisk": ICo 15:35-55 (St. Paul speaks of God's giving "to every seed his own body," ICo 15:38—the "bare grain" of verse thirty-seven being literally the "Kernel"; the "Asterisk" suggests the apotheosized beloved—the star imagery in St. Paul, ICo 15:40-41, perhaps echoing glorified angelic bodies of the Old Testament, e.g., Job 38:7, and also KJV descriptions of Christ, Nu 24:17; Mt 2:2; IIPe 1:19; Rev 2:28; 22:16)

Comment: See *Poems*, II, 796-797. P1135 contains a self-consciously self-referential graphic convention—"an Asterisk"—perhaps to indicate that which has been lifted (symbolic of spiritual ascent) and that which is ideally circumferential.

1136   The Frost of Death was on the Pane-

    ll.2,5   "Flower": IPe 1:24
    l.4   "Mortality": IICo 5:4
    l.12   "Snake": Ge 3 (the serpent is associated with "Death")
    l.18   "hated Life": Ec 2:17
Comment: See *Poems*, II, 797-798.

1138   A Spider sewed at Night

    l.6   "Himself...inform": Ex 3:14; Rev 19:12 (the self-containment of the Divine is stressed in the Artist-Spider, P1275; P605 suggests ex nihilo creation by the Spider, such a use being consistent with that of Swift and Arnold—II Maccabees 7:28; Heb 11:3)
    l.7   "Immortality": ICo 15:53-54
    l.9   "Was Physiognomy": ICo 13:12 (the inward-turned, self-contained, self-referential artistic activity of the Spider is the spinning out from within of a web typic in its "Arc" of that ideally circumferential world of the beatific vision, Rev 22:4; whether weaving a wheel-shaped "Ruff" to set off the face of the "Dame" or a "Shroud" to encircle as a winding sheet the spirit, the Artist-Spider has as "Strategy" nothing less than the creation of a face ["Physiognomy"] for that anticipated event)
Comment: See *Poems*, II, 800. P1138 should be compared with other identity poems such as P351 in which there are difficulties with the coalescence of the physical image and P482 in which the function of the idealized face in her psychic economy is apparent. P451 suggests that what is within "It's picture publishes-precise" upon the "Arterial Canvas" of the face, "Duke" or "Dwarf" according to the "Central Mood" of the self. P458 is a much less sanguine view of the implications for such a mirror-solipsism view of identity.

1139   Her sovreign People

ll.1-4   "Her...fallible": Mt 6:28-30

Comment: See *Poems*, II, 800 and *Letters*, II, 465. "Nature" is here characterized with traits of the Deity: sovereignty, omniscience, and infallibility.

1142   The Props assist the House

l.1   "Props": Heb 6:1-6 (the call to perfection means that the "Props" and "Scaffolds" are foundational)

l.1   "House": ICo 3:9-17; IICo 5:1-2; Eph 2:20-22; Col 2:7; 4:12; Heb 3:1-6; IPe 1; 2:5-6 (the individual as God's dwelling, temple, or habitation runs throughout the Bible—e.g., the tabernacle of the Old Testament is replaced by the "temple not made with hands," Heb 8-9, the tabernacle within, Rev 21:3)

ll.6,8   "recollect," "retrospect": Php 3:13

l.7   "Augur/Scaffold": ICo 3:11

l.7   "Carpenter": Mt 13:55; Mr 6:3

l.9   "Hath...Life": Mt 5:48 ("Therefore leaving the principles of the doctrine of Christ, let us go on unto perfection; not laying again the foundation of repentance from dead works," Heb 6:1; "that ye may stand perfect and complete," Col 4:12)

l.10   "A...Nail": Joh 20:25; Col 2:14 (that the "retrospect" of the "perfected Life" is that of suffering is suggested by the Passion "Nail" and by the "Plank" of P875)

l.12   "Affirming...Soul": IPe 1:9

Comment: See *Poems*, II, 801-802 and Franklin, II, 855.

1144   Ourselves we do inter with sweet derision

l.1   "sweet": Ca 2:3, 14; 5:5, 13, 16; 7:9 (the language here is deliberately oxymoronic given the subject)

l.1   "derision"; Lu 23:35 (the echo may be of that mockery surrounding the Crucifixion)

l.2   "channel": ICo 15:55 (death is the "channel" of the "dust" linking "life's penurious round" with the "new circumference"; if the "channel" is the self-entombment of a celibate reclusiveness, then it is "typic" of death since a death-in-life, a giving up of hope for having "Paradise constantly" as had the married Samuel Bowles)

l.2   "dust": Ge 2:7; 3:19 (synecdochic for the body and its finitude; see also "earth to earth, ashes to ashes, dust to dust" in the "Burial of the Dead," *Book of Common Prayer*)

l.3   "balm": Jer 8:22 (traditionally, Jesus is the "Balm in Gilead"; the usage here is ironic since the solace from the "religion" described in line four is hardly "balm")

l.4   "That...believes": Mt 14:31; 21:21; Mr 9:24; Joh 10:24; 3:36; 6:47; 11:25-26; Ac 25:20; Heb 11:6

Comment: See *Poems*, II, 803; *Letters*, II, 574; and Leyda, II, 276. Withdrawal from life is in some respects symbolic of its inconclusiveness—the seesaw of doubt and belief, neither validating nor invalidating. Nevertheless, and paradoxically, such self-entombment, death-in-life is "typic" of that death which gives with emphatic finality the proof or disproof. P1144 is difficult to decode since sent to Samuel Bowles with a note expressing envy of his enjoyment of earthly "Paradise" and perhaps rationalizing or justifying reclusiveness.

1145   In thy long Paradise of Light

l.1   "In...Light": Rev 22:5 ("And there shall be no night there; and they need no candle, neither light of the sun; for the Lord God giveth them light: and they shall reign for ever and ever")

l.2   "No...be": Rev 10:6

l.3   "long for": Rev 7:16 ("They shall hunger no more, neither thirst any more"; the paradoxical play upon "long" as duration or desire adds complexity to P1145 since it obliquely questions her philosophy-of-deprivation theodicy)

l.3   "Earthly": ICo 15:47-49; IICo 5:1; Php 3:19

l.4   "mortal": ICo 15:53-54; IICo 4:11

l.4   "Company": Heb 12:22

Comment: The problematic repetition of "long" suggests that circuit world consciousness continues to be conditioned by duration and desire: that which it supposedly rejects out of hand. P1145 may present a negative theology of paradise with the poet emptying it of positive content much like a Pseudo-Dionysius speaking of God in metaphors of light.

1146   When Etna basks and purrs

l.3   "Garnet Tooth": Ex 24:17; Isa 29:6; 30:27, 30 (the face of God as a devouring fire imagery connecting Etna with the pit, Rev 9:1-2; 20:1-3, 14-15; 21:8)

1147   After a hundred years

l.2   "Nobody...Place": Job 7:10 ("He shall return no more to his home, neither shall his place know him any more")
l.3   "Agony...there": Lu 22:44
l.12   "Dropped...memory": Ec 9:5 ("For the living know that they shall die: but the dead know not anything, neither have they any more a reward; for the memory of them is forgotten")

1149   I noticed People disappeared

l.2   "When...child": ICo 13:11
l.5   "Now know I": ICo 13:12
Comment: The speaker of P1149—like the dubiously superior adults of Blake's *Songs of Innocence and Experience*—presumes a "Fact" gained by a simple semantic shuffle: "died" replaces "disappeared."

1151   Soul, take thy risk

l.1   "risk/chance": ICo 15:37 ("And that which thou sowest, thou sowest not that body that shall be, but bare grain, it may chance of wheat, or of some other grain")
l.2   "Death": ICo 15:36 ("Thou fool, that which thou sowest is not quickened, except it die")
Comment: See *Poems*, II, 806.

1152   Tell as a Marksman- were forgotten

ll.19-21 "That...Faith": Heb 11:1, 17-19 (for "Faith," see also Mt 21:21)
l.22   "Mercy/Power": IISa 22:33; Ps 27:1; Isa 12:2
l.22   "Almighty": Ge 17:1; 35:11; Rev 21:22
ll.22-25 "begging/asking...meant": Mt 21:22 ("And all things, whatsoever ye shall ask in prayer, believing, ye shall receive")

Comment: See *Poems*, II, 807-808. The Biblical parallels would include Abraham and Isaac (Ge 22) and God the Father and Son. Tell would be added to those who acted by "Faith" listed in the eleventh chapter of Hebrews.

1153   Through what transports of Patience

l.1   "Patience": Ro 5:3-4; 15:5; Col 1:11; ITi 6:11; IITi 3:10; Tit 2:2 (one of the virtues recurring in Paulinian admonitions here used with "transports" in a deliberately oxymoronic way for ironic effect)

l.2   "Bliss": Rev 2:7; 21-22 (the Paradise achieved is "stolid," the oxymoronic language again used ironically with regard to the ataractic "Blank" in the absence of the desired)

ll.3,7   "thee," "Thy": see note, lines eight, sixteen, P537 (the pronouns suggest the beloved)

l.4   "Attest/remit...this": Mt 26:28; Joh 20:23; Ac 2:38 (remit, remitted, and remission are always used in the context of forgiveness of past sins; here the speaker desires both a certification of past, individual Passion, and its removal)

ll.5-6   "By...this": IITi 4:7 (the oxymoronic "bleak exultation" is another indication that the speaker views ironically this Pyrrhic spiritual victory)

l.7   "Thy...dying": Mt 27 (death is here viewed as a male prerogative; the speaker wishes to substitute a comparatively insignificant, "Abbreviate[d]" death for that presence which has not been granted as a reward for "Patience")

Comment: See *Poems*, II, 808. Although P1153 may be a poem of profane love—a complaint of isolation, loneliness, and suffering in the absence of the beloved—it might also be read as a Bride of Christ poem, a metonymic displacement for that presence not granted until the New Jerusalem (Rev 19, 21-22), of which dying becomes a diminutive abbreviation.

1154   A full fed Rose on meals of Tint

l.1   "Rose": Ca 2:1 ("typic" of Christ)

l.4   "Mortality": ICo 15:53-54; IICo 5:4

l.5   "The...fair": Ca 1:15-16; 2:10, 13; 4:1, 7; 7:6; Mt 26-28; IJo 3:16

l.6   "Itself...before": Mt 21:9
ll.6-7   "Itself...sake": Php 2:6-8
l.8   "To...more": Isa 53:3-5

Comment: See *Poems*, II, 808. Death is the mother of beauty—"Each bright Mortality/The Forfeit is of Creature fair." In order to be given as the perfect token of affection, the "full fed Rose" must be harvested, the certain "Forfeit" of its evanescent beauty. The sacrifice of this ideally circumferential embodiment of beauty and love "for our unknown sake" is described in language suggesting that the "Rose" is the Rose of Sharon, the Lily of the Valley, the "bright and morning star"(Rev 22:16).

1155   Distance- is not the Realm of Fox

ll.1-4   "Distance...Beloved": Ca 3:1-2; 5:6-8; 6:1, 13; Ro 8:38-39; Eph 3:14-19 (the essence of "Distance" is that it physically separates from the "Beloved")

Comment: See *Poems*, II, 809. Distance is, paradoxically, the essence in the circuit world of the "fulness of God" whose profane counterpart is attraction to the "Beloved." "Distance" is not territory ("Realm of Fox") nor movement through space and time ("Relay of Bird"), but rather "Distance is" oxymoronically "Until" culmination of the self in the "Beloved" causes the collapse of time and space, of all antinomies, into Presence. P1155, then, is an apocalyptic poem in local dress.

1156   Lest any doubt that we are glad that they were born
         Today

ll.1-2   "they...noble Holiday": Mt 1:16; 2:1-6; Lu 2:11-14 (the birthday of Sue fell within a week of Christmas)
l.3   "Without...Immortality": ICo 15:53-54; IITi 1:10 (the equation of the two gifts is a testimony to the place of Sue in the poet's life, a blasphemous hyperbole guaranteed to draw the attention of her sister-in-law)

Comment: See *Poems*, II, 809 and *Letters*, II, 484.

1158   Best Witchcraft is Geometry

ll.1-4   "Best...mankind": Da 1-5 (Daniel, "cunning in knowledge and understanding science," would be an excellent example of the extraordinary individual for whom "Witchcraft" would be an ordinary science)

Comment: See *Poems*, II, 810 and *Letters*, II, 478-479.

1159   Great Streets of silence led away

ll.7-8   "But...exhaled": Rev 10:6 ("And sware by him that liveth for ever and ever, who created heaven, and the things that therein are, and the earth, and the things that therein are, and the sea, and the things which are therein, that there should be time no longer")

Comment: See *Poems*, II, 810-811; *Letters*, II, 470; and Leyda, II, 147.

1160   He is alive, this morning-

l.1   "morning": Ca 6:10

ll.1-2   "He...alive": Ca 2:8-13; 3:6, 11; 4:16; 5:1-2 (the advent or awakening of the beloved; there may also be here a hint of the resurrected heavenly beloved: Mt 28:6; Rev 1:18; 2:8)

ll.1-7   "He...regale": Ca 2; 4:11; 5:1 (the response of the landscape to the beloved is part of the hyperbole of profane love)

l.2   "awake": Ca 4:16

l.6   "Amber": see note, line one, P15 (the color would be associated with the presence of the beloved)

ll.7-8   "Me...dumb": Ca 5:2 (since the Canticles figuration is here typic of the heavenly, P1160 may indirectly express apocalyptic anxieties, Rev 3:20)

Comment: See *Poems*, II, 811; *Letters*, II, 472; and Leyda, II, 172.

1161   Trust adjusts her "Peradventure"

l.1-2   "Trust...you": Ge 18:24, 28-32; 31:31; 32:30; 38:11; 42:4; Ex 32:30 (perhaps the most famous "Peradventure" is the series in which Abraham expostulates with God regarding Sodom; nevertheless, the "Peradventure" of P1161 may be from II Kings 2:16, although again suggesting an imagined result that may or may not be contrary to fact—had she sought an Elijah only to be left with an

Elisha? Or, is the example of the mysterious Elijah used to underscore the fleeting unreality, the unsatisfactory ephemerality of any presence in the circuit world? Regardless, P1161 intertwines possible and actual, imagined and real, with a complexity not lessened by the sentences surrounding it in the letter to Higginson, *Letters*, II, 478-480; Leyda, II, 154)

Comment: See *Poems*, II, 811-812.

1162   The Life we have is very great.

l.1   "The...great": Ga 2:20 ("I am crucified with Christ: nevertheless I live; yet not I, but Christ liveth in me: and the life which I now live in the flesh I live by the faith of the Son of God, who loved me, and gave himself for me")

ll.2-4   "The...Infinity": IJo 3:2 ("Beloved, now are we the sons of God, and it doth not yet appear what we shall be: but we know that, when he shall appear, we shall be like him; for we shall see him as he is")

ll.5-6   "But...shown": Da 7:13-14, 27 ("I saw in the night visions, and, behold, one like the Son of man came with the clouds of heaven, and came to the Ancient of days, and they brought him near before him. And there was given him dominion, and glory, and a kingdom, that all people, nations, and languages, should serve him: his dominion is an everlasting dominion, which shall not pass away, and his kingdom that which shall not be destroyed...And the kingdom and dominion, and the greatness of the kingdom under the whole heaven, shall be given to the people of the saints of the most High, whose kingdom is an everlasting kingdom, and all dominions shall serve and obey him"); Rev 1:6-7

Comment: P1162 should be read in the context of an early October, 1870, letter to Mrs. Holland. See *Poems*, II, 812; *Letters*, II, 482-483; Leyda, II, 155; and also the discussion in Sewall, 613.

1163   God made no act without a cause

ll.1-4   "God...blame": Ge 15; De 5; 29-30; Jos 24:1-13; Ro 8:28-30; 9:11; Eph 1:11; 3:11; Php 3:12-13 (the ideas of the covenant and of election assume a purpose and plan not comprehended in toto by the individual but assumed as matters of faith)

l.1   "God...cause": Ps 19: Joh 1:1 (although strictly speaking not cosmological arguments, these two Biblical references assume an orderliness and design in God's creation—the Logos instantiating in the world God's creative and redemptive purposes)

l.2   "No...aim": De 6:5; 10:12; 30:11, 14; Mt 22:37

ll.3-4   "Our...blame": De 29-30; ICo 13:12; Php 3:12-13 ("Yet the Lord hath not given you an heart to perceive, and eyes to see, and ears to hear, unto this day," De 29:4; "O the depth of the riches both of the wisdom and knowledge of God! how unsearchable are his judgments, and his ways past finding out!" Ro 11:33; the Bible repeatedly stresses the faulty, limited nature of human knowledge)

Comment: "Act," "cause," "inference," and "premises" are from the lexicon of logic and philosophy, making the Biblical provenance difficult to pinpoint. The rhetorical strategy of P1163 seems to be to use cosmic import for consolatory purposes. See *Letters*, II, 484-485 and Leyda, II, 160-161.

1165   Contained in this short Life

l.1   "short Life": Ps 89:47

ll.7-8   "Whose...infinity": Rev 21:1

The least finished draft:

l.3   "friend": Pr 18:24

l.4   "Omnipotence": Rev 19:6

l.7   "Come unto me": Mt 11:28

l.8   "Firmaments": Ge 1:6-8, 14-20

ll.9-10   "The...dazzled": IICo 12:1-4

Comment: "Magical extents" are Wordsworthian "spots of time" or intimations of immortality "Unmanifest/Unwitnessed to the sense"(Mt 16:17) and yet intermittently revealed within the circuit world. See the two rough draft copies plus variants, *Poems*, II, 813-814.

1166   Of Paul and Silas it is said

ll.1-4   "Of...instead": Ac 5:17-28; 16:19-40 (the account in Acts 5 involves Peter at Jerusalem and goes with lines three and four of the poem; the account in Acts 16 involves Paul and Silas at Philippi and goes with the first two lines—the latter containing an oblique proscription of suicide, Ac 16:27-28) l.7   "The...optional": Ro 7:24; IICo 5:4; Php 3:21 (the "staple" as the body prison)

l.8   "Immortal": ICo 15:53-54

Comment: "Prison," whether in Jerusalem or Philippi, becomes in P1166 metaphorical for that "Security" offered the individual by the mundane, pedestrian, and commonplace; by such, the inviolable, untrammeled "Mind" cannot be bound. See *Poems*, II, 814-815 and Franklin, II, 1265.

1167   Alone and in a Circumstance

l.3   "spider": Job 8:14 (the inconsequential fragility of the spider's web is relevant here since it is a metaphor for creations of the imagination; see P605, P1138, P1275, and P1423)

ll.5,9   "Home," "late abode": ICo 3:16 (the speaker suffers dispossession of "abode"—here a metaphor for imagination and its stolen reveries, "Larceny of time and mind")

ll.14-16 "The...Heir": Eph 2:2 (the "inmates of the Air" are subtle, not to be confused with the realm of "Tax," "Title," "Law," and "Statute," and akin to the "baseless fabric of this vision," the creations of thin air by Prospero in *The Tempest*; the circumstance about which the speaker is uncommunicative is this being taken captive by imaginative creations)

ll.23-27 "offense...By spider": Ex 20:3-4

ll.27-28 "forbid...specify": Ge 44:17; Jos 22:29; 24:16; ISa 12:23; 24:6; 26:11; Job 27:5; Ga 6:14 (frequently used phrasing here revealing the unwillingness of the speaker to state the nature of the "offense nor here nor there")

Comment: P1167 is a sophisticated, oblique confession of succumbing to an idolatrous dispossession via the imaginative creations of another artist. See the discussion by Johnson, *Poems*, II, 816.

1169   Lest they should come- is all my fear

l.2   "sweet": Ca 2:3, 14; 5:5, 13, 16

1170   Nature affects to be sedate

ll.1-8   "Nature...turned": Heb 11:3

Comment: See *Poems*, II, 817.

1171   On the World you colored

ll.2-3   "rose," "Vermilion": see note, line one, P15 (the color is associated with the presence of the beloved)

ll.8,11   "Misery," "Midnight's...Pattern": Ge 3:19 (called the "Mighty Funeral-/Of All" in P660, here used to speak of loss of the beloved)

l.8   "fair": Ca 1:8, 15-16; 2:10, 13; 4:1, 7, 10; 5:9; 6:1, 10; 7:6

l.12   "Goods of Day": Ge 1:4, 10, 12, 18, 21, 25, 31 (the Creation refrain following each "Day" of God's creative activity: "it was good"; the prelapsarian, Edenic quality of P1171 turns after the word "Misery" in line eight)

Comment: See *Poems*, II, 818.

1172   The Clouds their Backs together laid

ll.1-8   "The...comes": Ps 29

ll.3-5   "The...stuff": Job 28:26; 38:25; 39:19-21

l.4   "played/skipped": Ps 114:4, 6

ll.6-8   "How...comes": Job 14:13

l.8   "missile/vengeance": De 32:35; Ps 94:1; Heb 10:30

Comment: For the variant "skipped" in line four, Johnson suggests Psalms 114:4 as source and points out that the poet underlined "played" as if to emphasize her choice (*Poems*, II, 818-819).

1173   The Lightning is a yellow Fork

l.1   "Lightning": Mt 24:27 (associated metaphorically with the Second Coming); Mt 28:3 (used to describe the countenance of the angel of the Lord who announces the Resurrection); Rev 4:5; 8:5; 11:19; 16:18 (apocalyptic overtones; the Son of man in the first chapter of Revelation is described in terms from the Book of Daniel, e.g., Da 10:6)

l.2   "Tables": Ps 23:5; 78:19; Lu 22:30; ICo 10:21 (the "Table" is associated with intimate communion with God, the direct experience of His Presence; to the Eucharistic associations, as well as those of refuge, comfort, and security, should be added the notion of familial acceptance as the equivalent in P1173 of the comprehension of the Divine revelation)

1.3   "fingers": Ps 8:3

1.5   "mansions": Joh 14:2 ("In my Father's house are many mansions: if it were not so, I would have told you. I go to prepare a place for you")

ll.5-7   "never...Dark": ICo 13:12

Comment: The "Dark" of P1173 is the Deus absonditus—the God whose "Lightning" both reveals and conceals to the human "ignorance" of the circuit world. Not even the "fingers" are revealed, just the "Cutlery." The "Lightning" is the leviathan of Job, the White Whale of *Moby Dick*:

> Canst thou draw out leviathan with an hook?
> or his tongue with a cord which thou lettest
> down? Canst thou put an hook into his nose
> or bore his jaw through with a thorn? ...
> Who hath prevented me, that, I should repay
> him? whatsoever is under the whole heaven is
> mine. I will not conceal his parts, nor his
> power, nor his comely proportion. Who can
> discover the face of his garments? or who
> can come to him with his double bridle? Who
> can open the doors of his face? his teeth
> are terrible round about (Job 41:1-2, 11-14).

As the whale is a mask for Ahab so the "Lightning" is for the speaker—God does not reveal His face! His ways are past finding out—the "Apparatus of the Dark."

1174   There's the Battle of Burgoyne-

1.3   "Man and Beast": Ge 6:7; Ex 9:25; 12:12; Nu 3:13; 8:17; Ps 36:6; 135:8; Jer 21:6; 32:43; 36:29; Zep 1:3

1.5   "Sunset...majestic": Ps 104:1-24

1.6   "solemn War": Eph 6:12 (the martial metaphor appears in verses eleven to eighteen; other verses suggestive of an inner "War" or conflict: Ro 7:22-24; ICo 9:25-27; ITi 6:12; IITi 4:7; the apocalyptic overtones may suggest a cosmic war, e.g., Rev 19:11-21)

Comment: P1174 is a Hitchcockian emblematic nature poem in which the "Battle" of darkness with light eventuating in "Sunset" suggests a more serious "solemn War" of the forces of good and evil. The Psalmist's straightforward relish of the "majestic" does not "comprehend" this deeper significance evident to a "chastened stare."

1175   We like a Hairbreadth 'scape

ll.1-8   "We...divine": De 32:35; Job 31:23; Lu 12:5; IICo 5:10-11; Heb 10:31; Jude 23

Comment: See *Poems*, II, 820. P1175 is a pleasures-of-the-abyss poem—a relishing of the afterglow, the divine "Resonance" that "tingles in the Mind."

1176   We never know how high we are

l.2   "Till...rise": Eph 4:12-15

ll.3-8   "And...King": Nu 13:32 (the timorous scouts exaggerated the stature of the inhabitants of the promised land, thereby rationalizing inaction in the face of an impossibly "Heroic" endeavor, an endeavor "normal" to Caleb and Joshua)

ll.4,7   "statures," "Cubits": Mt 6:27 ("Which of you by taking thought can add one cubit unto his stature?")

Comment: See *Poems*, II, 820. P1176 yields the insight that recited "Heroism" is not simply the obverse of Lilliputian pusillanimity. Similarly, in P405 "Hope" and "Desire" would "intrude upon" the scant "Cubits" of claustrophobic "Suffering."

Chapter 3

References and Notes on Poems 1178 - 1775
[1870 - 1886]

1178   My God- He sees thee-

ll.1-8   "My...him": Ps 19:1-6 ("The heavens declare the glory of God; and the firmament sheweth his handywork. Day unto day uttereth speech, and night unto night sheweth knowledge. There is no speech nor language, where their voice is not heard. Their line is gone out through all the earth, and their words to the end of the world. In them hath he set a tabernacle for the sun, Which is as a bridegroom coming out of his chamber, and rejoiceth as a strong man to run a race. His going forth is from the end of the heaven, and his circuit unto the ends of it: and there is nothing hid from the heat thereof")

l.1   "My...thee": Ge 1:3-4, 14-18

l.3   "Gold": see note, line one, P15

ll.3-6   "Fling...feet": Ps 96:11-12; 98:7-8

l.8   "Oh...right": Mal 4:2; Lu 1:78; Joh 1:1-18; Eph 5:14; IIPe 1:19; Rev 2:28 (the "Second" is the Sun-Son, the second member of the Trinity, as well as being a measure of time; "Second" is also related to the Biblical background of the last line)

l.9   "In...him": ICo 9:24 ("one receiveth the prize"—a piece of Biblical wit since the Sun-Son is doomed from the foundation of the world to be "Second," e.g., Joh 17:24, and the "Sun" is doomed to perish, Rev 21:23-24; 22:5)

Comment: See *Poems*, III, 822. The best "Shine" of the Sun-Son is the most perfect circuit world face enjoying as a "Second's right" God's inspection ("He sees thee") and presence in the "long Race."

1179   Of so divine a Loss

ll.1-2   "Of...Gain": Php 3:7 ("But what things were gain to me, those I counted loss for Christ")

Comment: See *Poems*, III, 822-823; *Letters*, II, 489-490; and Leyda, II, 178-179.

1180   "Remember me" implored the Thief!"

ll.1-4   "Remember...guaranty": Lu 23:39-43 ("And he said unto Jesus, Lord, remember me when thou comest into thy kingdom. And Jesus said unto him, Verily I say unto thee, to day shalt thou be with me in paradise," Lu 23:42-43)

l.5   "That...remain": Mt 8:8; Joh 1:1; 17:14, 20-21; Ro 9:9; IPe 1:23-25

l.5   "fair": Ca 1:8, 15-16; 2:10, 13; 4:1, 7, 10; 5:9; 6:1, 10; 7:9

l.6   "Delight": Ca 2:3; 7:6

l.6   "Dust": Ge 2:7; 3:19; Ps 103:14

l.9   "Of all": ICo 15:19

l.9   "hope": Ro 8:20-25

ll.9-10   "Of...stands": Ge-Rev (the "Affadavit" may be a synecdoche for the Word of God, the sworn testimonies of many; perhaps the lines refer specifically to this recorded incident of Christ and the two thieves, Lu 23:39-45)

l.11   "That...fear": Lu 23:41

l.12   "Friends": Jas 2:23 (a classic case of imputed righteousness)

Comment: See *Poems*, III, 823. "Hospitality," Ro 12:3; ITi 3:2; Tit 1:8; IPe 4:9; "Courtesy," IPe 3:8; and "Trust," IICo 1:9-10; ITi 4:10; 6:17—the latter perhaps deliberately ambiguous—are in dynamic tension with the poem's legal lexicon.

1181   When I hoped I feared-

ll.1-2   "When...dared": Ro 8:24-25; Heb 11:1

ll.3-4   "Everywhere...remain": Eph 5:27

l.5   "Spectre...harm": ICo 15:55; IPe 3:13-14

l.6   "Serpent...charm": Ge 3:1-5, 13; IICo 11:3; Rev 12:9

ll.7-8   "He...him": IICo 1:5-7; 12:9-10; 13:4; Php 3:10; Heb 2:9-10; IPe 2:19-24; 4:1, 12-19 (the prototypical "King of Harm" or "Prince of Harm," who has "carried captivity captive," Eph 4:8, is Christ Himself in His Passion, Mt 26-27; the speaker embraces salvation by suffering, justification by fear in a manner similar to that expressed in P313)

Comment: See *Poems*, III, 824; Franklin, I, 595; *Letters*, II, 491-492; and Leyda, II, 181. Sewall sees the provenance of P1181, appropriately, as *The Imitation of Christ* (Sewall, 693).

1183   Step lightly on this narrow spot-

l.4   "Emerald": Rev 21:20
l.4   "Seams enclose": ICo 15:35-55 (for the calyx image see P339)

Comment: See *Poems*, III, 826; Franklin, II, 1311; *Letters*, II, 491-492; and Leyda, II, 181.

1184   The Days that we can spare

l.1   "The...spare": Ge 18:24, 26; Ps 39:13; Jon 4:11; Ro 8:32; IIPe 2:4 (arrogation of Divine prerogative is here ironic)
l.7   "We...Time": Rev 10:6
ll.7-8   "without...him": Job 9:11; Isa 40:12-28; 45:15; 55:8-9; Ro 11:13 (the Deus absconditus resists circuit world "Economy" and "Arithmetic")

Comment: See *Poems*, III, 826-827; Franklin, II, 1317; *Letters*, II, 491-492; and Leyda, II, 181.

1185   A little Dog that wags his tail

l.3   "Of such": Mt 19:14
l.16   "Beseech": e.g., Ex 33:18 (the choice of "Beseech" over "Adjure" is in the direction of the most frequently used in the KJV)

Comment: See *Poems*, III, 827-828 and Franklin, II, 1325-1326.

1186   Too few the mornings be,

ll.3-7   "No...away": Lu 2:7 (in Bethlehem, there was "no lodging" for Joseph and Mary at the time of Christ's birth)

Comment: See *Poems*, III, 829; *Letters*, II, 488; and Leyda, II, 176. Using the inhospitableness shown Joseph and Mary at the birth of the Incarnate God as a metaphor, P1186 bemoans a similar lack of receptivity to evanescent intimations of immortality.

1187   Oh Shadow on the Grass,

1.1   "Shadow": Col 2:17; Heb 8:5 (the "Shadow" as a "Step," an image of heavenly things)

ll.3-4   "Go...Heart": Ca 1:8, 11, 15-16; 2:10, 13; 3:2-4, 11; 4:7, 9-10; 5:2, 9; 6:1, 6, 10; 7:6, 8, 11; 8:6 (in addition, "shadows" in Canticles are portents of a new day, Ca 2:17; 4:6; see P1126 for the use of "nomination," along with the language of marriage, to suggest that "Vision" is not a verbal fabrication—revelation is not "unto nomination,"; again, the cognate "designate" is used in a poem on the insubstantiality of the spirit, a "limitless Hyperbole," "Hypothesis" of the "Air")

1.6   "While...guess/dress": Mt 22:11-14 (see P325 in which the "White Gown" is associated with the "Victors designate," the "Saved"; the dress would be Taylor's evangelical robe of righteousness and the wear of the Bride of Christ, Rev 19:7-9)

1.8   "Oh...Face": Ro 8:29-30; 9:11; 11:5; ITh 1:4; IIPe 1:10

Comment: See *Poems*, III, 829-830. P1187 should be compared with P968 for similarities in theme and image. P130 also uses the key word "consecrate" to suggest participation in a sacramental vision of nature; the dubiety of the natural revelation in P1187 contrasts.

1188   'Twas fighting for his Life he was-

ll.1-8   " 'Twas...Interior": Ge 32:24-30 (Jacob who fought for his "Life" as a matter of destiny and identity, his name changed to Israel"; ICo 9:24-26; IICo 10:3-5; Eph 6:10-18; ITi 1:18; 6:11-12; IITi 4:7 (St. Paul frequently uses martial imagery and metaphor; the advice of the angel Michael to Adam in the final two books of *Paradise Lost* may have influenced the stress on life as a "Campaign inscrutable/Of the Interior")

l.5   "It...once": Heb 9:27

1189   The Voice that stands for Floods to me

l.1   "Voice": Ca 2:8, 12, 14; 5:2; 8:13

l.1   "Floods": e.g., Isa 44:3 (a KJV word for rain)

l.3   "Face": Ca 2:14; 5:15; 6:10

l.5   "Substance": Ca 8:7; Heb 10:34; 11:1

l.6   "Sum": Heb 8:1 (the profane beloved is also the "Sum": Ca 5:9; 6:9; 8:7)

l.8   "Poverty": Mt 5:3; Lu 6:20; IICo 8:2, 9; Jas 2:5

Comment: The profane love topoi are used to praise the "Sum" (Heb 8:1), The Beloved (Rev 19:7-9).

1191   The pungent atom in the Air

l.4   "Relinquished...Estate": Ge 3 (loss of summer parallels loss of paradise)

l.5   "For...Delight": see P1353 ("The last of Summer is Delight" comparable to "walk[ing] within the Vail" "without a Knock"—the transition of the seasons granting an epiphany, an experience of Presence)

l.7   "As...Dominion": Ge 1:26; Ps 145:13; Da 4:34; 6:26; 7:13-14; Rev 1:6 ("Limit" is synecdochic of that "dominion" granted the first man, Adam, and, by extension, all mankind; "Dominion" is synecdochic of God's omnipotence as Creator)

l.8   "Or...Extasy": see, e.g., P184 (P184 suggests that a world without such epiphanic awareness as granted by seasonal transitions in P1191 would be one "With Holy Ghosts in Cages!" and "A Diagram—of Rapture!"—the inanimate, cold world bemoaned by Wordsworth, a world of scientific analysis alone and godless materialism); for other poems using "extasy" see P125, P165, P392, P551, P653, and P783.

Comment: Indubitable pungency of summer-autumn air forces an admission of loss, but the second stanza insists that "we" are just as "positive" that the seasonal transition suggests "Delight" as "Limit" is of "Dominion" and "Dams" are of "Extasy."

1192   An honest Tear

ll.1-8   "Air...decays": Joh 11:35 (see also Lu 6:21; 7:38, 44)

1194   Somehow myself survived the Night

l.3   "That...suffice": Rev 7; 21:24 (the Sealed Elect are the "Saved"; see also P325, P539, P590, P640, P901, P1347, and P1502)

ll.5-6   "Henceforth...led": De 32:35; IICo 5:11; Heb 10:31; IIPe 1:10; Jude 23 (to live life daily as that of a criminal whose sentence of death has been commuted is to know the "terror of God," to be one uncertain of election in the hands of a "living God")

l.7   "Morning Chance": ICo 15 (the resurrection of the "Dead"); Rev 6:17; 16:14 (the "great day of God Almighty," the Judgment)

Comment: The "Day" of line two is the "Yellow eye" of the "Canon's face" (P590) with "Judgment interven[ing]"; the "living place" of line five is the plank in "I stepped from Plank to Plank" (P875).

1195   What we see we know somewhat

ll.1-2   "What...little": ICo 13:12; Heb 11:3
ll.3-4   "What...fickle": Ro 7:15
l.5   "Lands...Locks": Ge 3; Ro 6:23 ("Locks," a synecdoche for sin and death)
l.6   "Granted...pick'em": ICo 15 (triumph over death in the resurrection)
ll.7-8   "Transport's...Adam": Ge 3 (loss of Eden, transport to the penal colony of the circuit world, would be a "doubtful Dividend," the paradoxical Fortunate Fall, *O Felix Culpa*, if the wish of the preceding lines were granted; see Adam in *Paradise Lost*, XII, 469-478 and Ro 5:20)

Comment: See *Poems*, III, 832-833. P1195 describes the postlapsarian conditions of the circuit world.

1196   To make Routine a Stimulus

1.4 "Specific Grace": Ps 84:11; Joh 1:17; Ac 15:11; Eph 2:5, 8; IPe 3:7 (grace is the unmerited favor of God, here, paradoxically, the specific "Capacity to Terminate," death)

1.5 "Arrow": De 32:23; Job 6:4; Ps 64:7; 91:5; Isa 5:28 (the arrow is often associated with destruction, judgment, and death)

Comment: See *Poems*, III, 833 and Franklin, II, 1328. Adding piquancy to "Routine" is death, a goad toward significance and beauty.

1197 I should not dare to be so sad

1.2 "So...again": e.g., Ex 16:35 (the years of wandering in the wilderness by the Israelites recorded from Exodus to Deuteronomy in the Pentateuch are here used metaphorically for years the speaker spent pursuing an unrealized goal)

1.3 "Load": Ex 6:4; 16; 19-20; 23-24; 32-34; Le 26:9; De 5:2; 9:9; 26:16; Jg 2:1 (selected references to God's covenant with the Israelites including the promise of Canaan, Ex 23:30-31; here the promised land is a metaphor for the unnamed and cherished ideal, goal, or beloved that had been the source of the speaker's sadness "so many Years")

ll.6-7 "And...side": Nu 13:31-33 (the spies who gave the false report to the Israelites regarding the giants in the promised land)

1.8 "Begin...now": Nu 14:1-4 (the speaker identifies with the "congregation" of the Israelites who wish to return to Egypt fearing death at the hands of the giants; P112, P168, and P597 suggest the poet knew well the fate of Moses, Nu 33:50-56; De 32:48-52)

Comment: See *Poems*, III, 833-834 and Franklin, II, 1321. P1197 expresses nostalgia for an unrealized ideal or lost beloved that had once been the object of a quest comparable to the covenant-sanctioned one of the Israelites for the promised land. Chary of the risks of renewed pursuit and aware of Divine disfavor ("The Superhuman...withdraws"), the speaker perishes (Pr 29:18a).

1200 Because my Brook is fluent

ll.3-6 "Because...flee": Ge 1:2 (the "Brook" is here the "Sea" suggestive of the primordial chaos, the formless "void" or "deep," the "waters" over which the shaping Spirit moves; in a number of places the Bible suggests God's control: Job 26:12; 28:11;

38:8, 16; 41:31; Ps 78:16, 20; 89:9; the Brook-Sea may be a metaphor for the inner self responsible for poetic creativity but not always under control)

l.7   "where": Rev 21-22 (the New Jerusalem)
l.7   "the Strong": Ps 24:8; 89:8; Rev 18:8
l.8   "Is...Sea": Rev 21:1 ("And I saw a new heaven and new earth: for the first heaven and the first earth were passed away; and there was no more sea")

1201   So I pull my Stockings off

l.4   " 'Ought to' ": Ge 34:7; Le 4:2, 27; Mt 23:23; Ac 5:29; ITh 4:1; IJo 3:16; 4:11 (a frequently repeated Biblical admonition; the penciled variant, "or'ter," suggests an impish, Twainian spirit of the boy persona toward rules)
ll.5-6   "Went...didn't": Ex 33:19; Ro 9:15-18
l.7   "Moses...used": Nu 20:12; 27:12-14; 33:50-56; De 1:35-40; 3:23-27; 32:48-52 (Moses was not allowed to enter the promised land, though given a view of it from Mt. Nebo before his death; for poems on Moses see P112, P168, P597, and P1733, P168, and P597 relating directly to the theme of P1201)
l.8   "Ananias wasn't": Ac 5:1-11 (the story of Ananias and Sapphira who sold a possession but kept back "part of the price of the land"; being accused of lying to God, Ananias "fell down, and gave up the ghost")
Comment: See *Poems*, III, 835 and Franklin, II, 1335.

1202   The Frost was never seen-

l.1   "The...seen": Job 37:10; Ps 147:16
l.15   "Of...Inn": ICh 29:15; Ps 39:12; 119:19; Heb 11:13; IPe 2:11
l.16   "Of...Air": De 29:29; Job 15:8 (the fourth stanza expresses the mysterium tremendum)
ll.17-18 "To...prefer": Ac 8:27-40 (Philip "analyze[s]" a portion of Isaiah [Isa 53:7-8] for the Ethiopian eunuch; Johnson suggests that the relevant passage regarding Philip is from the Gospel of John—see Joh 14:8-9 and Poems, III, 836)
Comment: P1202 reveals the difficulties of a theodicy within a fallen universe (Ge 3) in which the "blonde Assassin" (P1624) of an

"Approving God" strikes unseen: "The Garden gets the only shot/That never could be traced." "Nature, red in tooth and claw" leaves the speaker nonplussed before the "Unproved" and "Unknown"; the theodicy problem is not amenable to analysis and inference. "Faith bleats to understand"(P313).

1203   The Past is such a curious Creature

      l.6   "I...fly": Mr 9:25

1204   Whatever it is- she has tried it-

      l.1   "What...it": ICo 15
      l.2   "Awful...Love": IJo   4:8,   16   (the   oxymoronic language is used because the beloved has been lost to God through death)
      l.3   "Is...chastising": De 8:5; Ps 94:12; Pr 13:24; ICo 11:32; Heb 12:5-11; Rev 3:19
      l.4   "Dove": Ca 1:15; 2:14; 4:1; 5:2; 6:9
      l.5   "petition": Ps 20:5; IJo 5:15
      ll.7-8   "When...away": ICo 2:9
      l.10   "thy...House": Joh 14:2; IICo 5:1; Rev 4; 21-22
      l.11   "Transgression": e.g., IJo 3:4 (a piece of Biblical wit suggesting that being allowed to think of circuit world friends is a "Transgression" in Heaven against the "Awful Father"; see the Lord's Prayer, Mt 6:9-13, and the verses immediately following: "For if ye forgive men their trespasses, your Heavenly Father will also forgive you: But if ye forgive not men their trespasses, neither will your Father forgive your trespasses," Mt 6:14-15)
      Comment: See *Poems*, III, 837-838.

1205   Immortal is an ample word

      l.1   "Immortal...word": ICo 15:53-54
      l.5   "Heaven above": Rev 4; 21-22
      l.7   "Hand": Ge 3:6, 19, 22 (the agency of the Fall which brings death); e.g., Ps 102:25 (synecdochic of God's creative power)
      Comment: See *Poems*, III, 838; *Letters*, II, 494; and Leyda, II, 184.

1206   The Show is not the Show

l.2   "they...go": Ps 22:29; Ps 107:23
l.4   "Neighbor": Heb 8:11
Comment: See *Poems*, III, 838-839 and *Letters*, II, 500-501.

1207   He preached upon "Breadth" till it argued him narrow-

ll.1-2   "He...define": Mt 7:13-14
ll.3-4   "And...Sign": Mt 12:38-39; 16:1-4; Joh 8:32; 14:6
(Jesus, who refused the Sadducees and Pharisees their "Sign," was the "Truth"; the humor is in the contrast between Jesus who "never flaunted a Sign" and the long-winded preacher)
l.5   "Simplicity...presence": ICo 1:29; IICo 1:12; 11:3
l.7   "innocent Jesus": Mt 27:4, 24
l.8   "enabled/discerning": Mt 16:3 (another indication that the poet found the preacher pharisaical)
Comment: See *Poems*, III, 839-840; *Letters*, II, 500-501; and Leyda, II, 195-196. P1207 is one of a number of examples that prove that Dickinson often used the Bible to indulge her American humor vein.

1208   Our own possessions- though our own-

ll.1-4   "Our...Possibility": Mt 19:16-30 (see especially verses 22 and 26)
Comment: P1208 is a variation upon the philosophy of deprivation—the paradoxes of the Beatitudes (Mt 5:1-12); the sanction for "hoard[ing]" treasures in heaven (Mt 6:19-20); the assurance that "Dimensions/Of Possibility" guarantee that the last shall be first (Mt 19:30). The repetition of line one reinforces the obvious hyperbole no less jocoserious than the message of "Success is counted sweetest" (P67). See *Poems*, III, 840; *Letters*, II, 500-501; and Leyda, II, 195-196.

1209   To disappear enhances

l.4   "Immortality": ICo 15:53-54
ll.13-20 "Of...Delight": Ge 2:17; 3:3
l.17   "Fruit": Ca 2:3; 4:13, 16; 6:11; 7:13; 8:11-12

1.20   "Delight": Ca 2:3; 7:6

Comment: Prohibition and distance enhance, "Never" gives to the worthless "Honor," and "Death" is the mother of what "Excellence" and "Delight" are yielded within the "extatic limit" of the circuit world. P1209 is a death-is-the-mother-of-beauty poem. See *Poems*, III, 841-843; Franklin, II, 1329-1330; *Letters*, II, 500-501; and Leyda, II, 195-196.

1210   The Sea said "Come" to the Brook-

ll.1-8   "The...Me": Pr 18:4 (the brook's proverbial association with wisdom here with subtle modulations used to privilege Lilliputian status)

Comment: See *Poems*, III, 843-844; Franklin, II, 1342; *Letters*, II, 500-501; and Leyda, II, 195-196. P1207-P1210 were among poems sent in part or in toto to Higginson; for the additional complexities this adds to their context, see Sewall, 532-576.

1211   A Sparrow took a Slice of Twig

l.1   "A...Twig": Ps 84:1-4; Mt 6:25-33 (the "Sparrow" eschews worms for a "Twig"; embodying the paradoxical Beatitudes philosophy of "Frugality," Mt 5:6, the "Sparrow" is "Invigorated" by an "empty Plate")

ll.5-8   "Invigorated...away": Ge 1:20; Ps 19:1; 150:1

Comment: See *Poems*, III, 844-845. As "Epicure of Firmaments," the diminutive "Sparrow" qualifies as a Hitchcockian emblem of spiritual ascent. Proceeding by indirection, P1211 emphasizes assurance of providential design and election. One variant for lines seven-eight reads: "As speculations flee/By no Conclusion hindered." Perhaps the mystical "Sparrow" of P1211 shares a Paulinian anti-intellectualism: Col 2:8; ITi 1:6; 6:20; IITi 2:16; 3:7; Tit 1:10; IPe 1:18.

1212   A word is dead

ll.1-6   "A...day": Ge 1; Joh 1:1-3; Heb 4:12; IPe 1:25; Rev 19:13 (Biblical precedents for the potency of the written and spoken word)

Comment: See *Poems*, III, 845-846; *Letters*, II, 496; and Leyda, II, 187.

1213   We like March

l.2(1872), and l.1(1878) "Purple": see note, line one, P15 and note, line fourteen, P756
l.10(1872), and l.9(1878) "News...others": Lu 1:11-38 (March as the "Annunciation" month of all the seasons)
l.12(1872), and l.11(1878) "Blue": see note, line one, P15 and note, line fourteen, P756
Comment: See Poems, III, 846-847. Along with dawn, sunset, and noon, March is one of those pivotal, transitional times during which occur epiphanies, insights, intimations, and revelations via the natural world, suggesting a "new circumference" beyond. Numerous poems combine mention of March with the "Blue Bird," renewal with death: P736, P812, P828, P844, P1177, P1320, P1395, P1404, P1690, and P1764.

1215   I bet with every Wind that blew

l.1   "every Wind": Eph 4:14 ("That we henceforth be no more children, tossed to and fro, and carried about with every wind of doctrine, by the sleight of men, and cunning craftiness, whereby they lie in wait to deceive")
l.4   "And...Balloon": ITi 1:19 ("some having put away concerning faith have made shipwreck")

1216   A Deed knocks first at Thought

l.1   "A...Thought": Jas 1:17-25; IJo 3:8
l.7   "ear of God": Ps 5:1; 17:1, 6; 31:2; 39:12; 55:1; 80:1; 84:8; 86:1, 6; 143:1; Isa 37:17; Da 9:18
l.8   "It's...audible": Ro 2:6 ("Who will render to every man according to his deeds"); see also Mt 16:27; ICo 3:8; IICo 5:10; Rev 2:23; 20:12; 22:12

1217   Fortitude incarnate

l.7   "Hoary": Job 41:32b ("one would think the deep to be hoary")

l.8   "Sea/Deep": Ge 1:2 (the variant "Evil" for "Hoary" in line seven may be related to the variant "Deep" here since the primordial chaos might connote a preexistent, evil matter devoid of Spirit)

l.9   "Edifice/Architect": Ge 1:1, 10

l.12   "Better...Tombs": Job 21:32 (the tomb as man's natural end)

Comment: See *Poems*, III, 848-849.

1219   Now I knew I lost her-

l.20   "Idolatry": Ex 20:1-5; Le 26:1 (the hyperbole is Biblical: the "Penury" is as if one were to toil for the restoration of the worship of idols—a pre-Old Covenant practice; the object of such immoderate attachment may have been Sue Dickinson)

Comment: See *Poems*, III, 849-850 and Franklin, II, 1339-1341.

1220   Of Nature I shall have enough

ll.1-4   "Of...Familiarities": ICo 15:42-44 (the cessation of "Nature" upon being "sown in dishonor" among the flowers will allow her to enjoy with abandonment the "Bumble bee's/Familiarities"—a piece of Biblical wit perhaps accompanying a gift of flowers)

1221   Some we see no more, Tenements of Wonder

l.1   "Some...more": Job 7:8

ll.7-10 "Grapples...Tomb": ICO 15:50-55 (the "Sublime Theme" is that of immortality, which is as able as the "Dust" used by God at man's creation, Ge 2:7, to "equip" the tenants of "Wonder" with "feature[s]"—the "change" spoken of by St. Paul—and to "enlist" the grave in its victory)

l.8   "Dust": Ge 2:7; 3:19; Ps 103:14 (see ll.8-9 of P515)

1222   The Riddle we can guess

ll.1-4   "The...surprise": Jg 14:12-18

Comment: See *Poems*, III, 851; *Letters*, II, 480-482; and Leyda, II, 157.

1223   Who goes to dine must take his Feast

ll.1-4   "Who...within": Mt 22:11-14; 26:17-30; Rev 3:20 (Eucharistic and preparationist motifs)

ll.5-8   "For...worthier": Heb 8:5; 9:23-24 (the patterns of heavenly things shadowed by "ignoble Services"); Eph 4:15-16; Col 2:17-19 (the head-and-body metaphor here becomes the "Mind" and "ignoble Services"); Ro 12:1-2; ICo 2:16; IICo 3:18; Php 2:5; Heb 8:10 (the renewed, transformed "Mind," a gift bestowed from God and therefore instantiating in the individual the "patterns of things in the heavens")

Comment: See *Poems*, III, 851-852.

1224   Like Trains of Cars on Tracks of Plush

l.5   "sweet": Ca 2:3, 14; 5:5, 13, 16
Comment: See *Poems*, III, 852.

1225   It's Hour with itself

l.1   "It's...itself": Mt 26:40; Mr 14:67 (Gethsemane as the paradigm for the "Soul"—a place of "Subterranean Freight" and "Terror" and "Cellars"—and the Passion as that for self-understanding)

l.7   "Place": Ge 2:7 (the soul created by God)
l.8   "Is...still": Ps 46:10; Zec 2:13

1227   My Triumph lasted till the Drums

ll.1-3   "Triumph," "Dead," "Victory": ICo 15:54-55; IICo 2:14 (language from St. Paul underscores the speaker's return from "Triumph" to a sense of circuit world isolation, loss, and separation)

ll.5-6   "To...Conclusion": Rev 2:10; 3:11; 4:4, 10; 7; 22:4 (the seal, the crown, and the name of the Lamb upon the forehead signify the translated, transfigured, "finished Faces" of celestial, as contrasted with circuit world, identity)

l.7 "And...Glory": ICo 15:43 (perhaps the "Glory" is of those who have experienced the resurrection and are separated from the speaker); Rev 21-22 (perhaps "Glory" refers to God as the light of the New Jerusalem, thereby being synecdochic of Heaven for the speaker); ("Glory," as embodied in the person of Christ, IICo 4:4, and now experienced by "They" as Presence, is available only piecemeal to the speaker in the circuit world, IICo 3:18, and thus may be a source of frustration)

Comment: Continuing to exist, however "chastened" by Paulinian consolations, the speaker, stealthily slipping by the graves, meditates on the insincerity of circuit world "contrition" almost as if her own envy and sorrow were responsible and in complicity with a world of "Drums," "tyrannies," and "Bayonets." That "This World is not Conclusion" (P501) may console momentarily only to remind that absence of final "Retrospect" is the pit of circuit world consciousness.

1228 So much of Heaven has gone from Earth

ll.3-4 "If...given": Ro 1:7; ICo 1:2; 6:2-3; ITh 3:13; IPe 2:9; Jude 14 (the saints are the children of the covenant or "Affidavit" who have preceded the speaker in death)

l.5 "The...Mole": Jude 3 (perhaps the beloveds "gone from Earth" to "Heaven" are thought of as analogous to the earliest Christian believers)

l.9 "Too...Belief": Heb 11:1-3
Comment: See *Poems*, III, 854-855.

1229 Because He loves Her

ll.1-2 "Because...fair": Ca 1:15; 4:1 ("Behold, thou art fair my love")

ll.3-4 "What...wear": Ca 5:9 ("What is thy beloved more than another beloved, O thou fairest among women? what is thy beloved more than another beloved, that thou dost so charge us?")

l.11 " 'Tis...sufficiency": Rev 19:1 (the "Glory" of the beloved Bridegroom); see also note, line seven, P1227

l.12 "trying/running": Ca 1:4; 3:1-4; ICo 9:24-26; Php 2:16; IITi 4:7; Heb 12:1 (the final two lines contain a bold spiritualization of sense)

Comment: The "He" of P1229 may be spouse, lover/ admirer, public/critic, and/or Heavenly Bridegroom. The "Her" may be Helen Hunt, Sue Dickinson, the Shulamite, another competing female artist or adored beloved, and/or the Bride of Christ. The second stanza in particular suggests a competing artist whose created fair "Face" has been successfully accepted ("her magic pace/...we so far behind")—an outstripping that must be propitiated as "Forests" do by genuflections before the "Wind" and as the speaker does by the adulatory P1229. Thus, love and notice of the "He" in the poem are associated with acceptance of a fair "Face," perhaps suggestive of acceptable natural beauty or artistic production, but also possibly a sign of election, of being chosen in a spiritual sense (Mt 22:14; Ro 8:29-31; IIPe 1:10). The third stanza pushes the profane love topoi with their Canticles imagery toward the apocalyptic overtones of the Bride of Christ (Rev 19:7-19; 22:4). See *Poems*, III, 855-856 and *Letters*, II, 480-482.

1230   It came at last but prompter Death

l.4   "Peace": Isa 9:6; Heb 7:2 (the echo may be deliberately ironic)
l.7   "Gate": Job 38:17; Ps 9:13; Isa 38:10

1231   Somewhere upon the general Earth

l.4   "consecrated": Ex 28:3, 41; 30:29-30; Le 8:10-12; 16:32; Nu 6:11-12; ICh 29:5; IICh 13:9; Eze 43:26; Heb 7:28; 10:20 (a KJV word suggesting a making sacred by separation or setting apart; for use of the word see also P130, P1187, P1261, and P1555)
l.5   "Indifferent Seasons": Rev 22:2
l.8   "Immortality": ICo 15:53-54; IITi 1:10
l.9   "just...prove": Ro 1:17; 12:2; IICo 13:5; Ga 3:11; 6:4; ITh 5:21; Heb 10:38; 12:23 (also, to prove to be as Christ, the Just One, Ac 7:52; 22:14)
l.11   "God...Width": Ge 21:33; Ps 90:2; Isa 9:6; 40:28 (the everlasting God Whose kingdom is for ever and ever, Rev 22:5)
l.12   "Eternity": Isa 57:15
Comment: The "Magic" that "consecrated" the poet must have been an religio-aesthetic experience of love and beauty with transubstantial and sacramental powers to imaginatively transform the profane experiences of her circuit world. Stanza two in particular

reads like a Keatsian complaint regarding separation from a world of imagination—a world of "Indifferent Seasons" that elsewhere she associates with that of the sacramental vision of the child (P130).

1232   The Clover's simple Fame

ll.2-4   "Remembered...notability": Ex 32:4; Ro 1:23 (the "enameled Realms" are those of idolatry, which the poet wishes to skirt in considering "Fame"; the divergent role of the "Cow" here adds Biblical wit to the first lines of P1232)

ll.5-6   "Renown...degrades/profanes...Flower/power":   Ex 20:1-5 (to avoid profanation, beauty must remain unself-conscious)

ll.7-8   "The...compromised it's power/forfeited the Dower": Ge 19:26; Lu 17:32-33 (to look behind suggests attachment to what has been sacrificed or lost for beauty)

Comment: See *Poems*, III, 857-858. In P1232, the design giving significance to "Clover" and "Daisy" becomes emblematic of the place of "simple Fame" within the speaker's artistic credo.

1233   Had I not seen the Sun

l.1   "Sun": Ps 84:11; 89:36; Mal 4:2; Lu 1:78; IIPe 1:19; Rev 2:28

l.3   "Light": Joh 1:4-9; IJo 1:5

ll.3-4   "Wilderness...made": Ex 14-Jos (the "Wilderness" would entail all the wanderings of the Israelites before the entry into the promised land recorded in the Book of Joshua; the provenance of the oppositions here, though personally applied, are Biblical: light-dark, wandering-arrival, promise-fulfillment, blindness-sight)

Comment: With the Form of the Good as the Sun/Son and the Cave as the "Wilderness," P1233 contains an updating in Biblical terms of Plato's myth of the cave.

1234   If my Bark sink

l.2   " 'Tis...sea": Rev 4:6; 15:2; 22:1

l.3   "Mortality's...Floor": IICo 5:4

l.4   "Immortality": ICo 15:53-54

Comment: See *Poems*, III, 858-859.

1235   Like Rain it sounded till it curved

ll.2-3   "Wind...walked": Ps 104:3

l.7   "A...heard": Eze 1:24

ll.11-14 "It...stirred": Ge 7:11; Ps 46:2-3

l.15   "Then...away": IIKi 2:11

l.16   "Upon...Cloud": Eze 1; 10; Da 7:9, 13 (the vision of Daniel of the Ancient of days and Son of man contains the cloud and wheel, and similar imagery is also found in Ezekiel but not in the ascension account of Elijah)

Comment: See *Poems*, III, 859 and Leyda, II, 214.

1236   Like Time's insidious wrinkle

l.2   "On...Face": Ca 4:7

l.3   "Grace": see note, line six, P1068 ("Grace" here is figured as the "garment" of imputed righteousness, Mt 22:11; see also, e.g., Ro 4:6; IICo 5:21; Php 3:9)

l.4   "Though...crease": Eph 5:27

l.5   "The...comely": Job 37:10

Comment: See *Poems*, III, 859-860. That beauty should be without spot, prime without aging, the garment without wrinkle are the irreconcilables of the circuit world of "Time" and "Frost"—a world whose corrosive effects make the speaker "clutch the Grace" while resenting the concomitant dependency, limitation, and imperfection. With an ironic sense of order within disorder, P1236 ends with the oxymoronic "comely Frost" disheveling with impunity.

1237   My Heart ran so to thee

l.1   "My...thee": Ca 3:11; 4:9; 5:2; 8:6; Mt 5:8

l.6   "achieve/espouse": Rev 19:7-9

l.6   "thy Face": Rev 22:4

l.7   "Grace": see note, line six, P1068 (there is here a sense of competition with "He" to whom has been given a special favor, advantage, or grace—the "He" being "My Heart")

l.13   "But...him": Mr 10:35-45 (James and John wish a preeminent reward with Christ in Heaven; a similar envy, "Greed," and not "malignity," motivates the speaker in the love triangle of P1237)

l.14   "my Premium": Rev 19:7-9; 22:4 (the reward is Presence, the beatific vision, and marriage to the Bridegroom, the Lamb)

l.15   "Bethleem": Mic 5:2; Mt 2:1-6 (Bethlehem, as the birthplace of Jesus Christ, the Bridegroom, is perhaps meant here to suggest the New Jerusalem, Rev 19-22)

Comment: See *Poems*, III, 860-861. The love triangle of P1237 is the Bridegroom, "My Heart," and the speaker. Election as Bride of Christ has apparently caused this division of sensibility, her "Heart" already "Basking in Bethleem" and she, "affronted," remaining in the circuit world with protestations of "the Greed of him-/Boasting my Premium." A Bride of Christ poem, P1237 is an elegant lover's complaint, reminiscent of such metaphysical poems as Marvell's "Definition of Love," which exploits as well the traditional tensions of the love triangle found in Shakespeare's sonnets.

1238   Power is a familiar growth

l.1   "Power...growth": Ge 3:5-7 (among other things, "Power" is associated with pain, will, wisdom, imagination, and metamorphosis in the poetry; paradoxically, bane and blessing, curse and comfort, "Pain" is "growth"—the inescapable condition of the postlapsarian circuit world; see especially P1335, P1474, and P1670 for poems associating power with loss of innocence, dream, and paradise as well as an insouciant finitude—"a power of Butterfly must be," as P1099 states)

l.3   "bland Abyss": Job 33:18, 24, 28, 30; Ps 30:3, 9; 55:3; Eze 32:23-25; Rev 9:1-2; 20:1-3 (the "Abyss" is the pit)

l.6   "clay": Job 10:9; 33:6; Isa 45:9 (closely associated with the idea of the body as mortal dust, Ge 2:7; 3:19)

Comment: See *Poems*, III, 861. "Power" is the inescapable "familiar growth," necessitated by the circuit world, to be escaped by "chance" at death. Thus, P1238 seems to be a pleasures-of-the-Abyss poem with its vision of life as a "Plank" (P875) or "Crisis" (P889) in which certainty or disproof comes only with the "final glance" (De 32:35; IICo 5:11).

1239   Risk is the Hair that holds the Tun

l.11   "Persuasive...Perdition": ITi 6:9; Rev 17:8, 11

Comment: See *Poems*, III, 861-862.

1240   The Beggar at the Door for Fame

ll.1-2   "The...supplied": Lu 16:19-21
l.3   "But...thing": Joh 6:31-35, 47-58
l.4   "Disclosed...denied": Mt 5:6
Comment: See *Poems*, III, 862. The poet here fuses Biblical ideas regarding "Bread" with her own philosophy of depravation and denial perhaps to reconcile herself to her obscurity. Nevertheless, the lofty idealism of P1240 parallels that of Christ in His response to Satan when first tempted in the wilderness: "Man shall not live by bread alone, but by every word that proceedeth out of the mouth of God" (Mt 4:4).

1241   The Lilac is an ancient shrub

ll.3,8   "Firmamental Lilac," "Flower of Occident": Ge 1:16
l.7   "To...Tough": Joh 20:24-29 (see P555 and P861)
ll.12-16 "The...Analysis": Heb 11:1, 3 (above "synthesis" is the "Flora unimpeachable," like Thoreau's eternized trees, Dante's rose, or the tree of life [Rev 22:2], grasped not by "Time's Analysis" but imagination)
l.17   "Eye...possibly": ICo 2:9 ("Eye hath not seen, nor ear heard, neither have entered into the heart of man, the things which God hath prepared for them that love him")
l.18   "Be...Blind": Ro 1:20 (perhaps the "Blind" are not those who fail of discernment at the level of common grace since even the "Scientist of Faith" "detain[s]/profane[s]" "Revelation" by his "theses"; the "Blind" then may be those who fail to achieve imaginative vision—who "baffle at the Hint" and "cipher at the Sign" without "at last...tak[ing] the clue divine," P1099)
l.19   "Revelation": Book of Revelation (although general and special revelations may be intended, it may be more appropriate to read "Revelation" as synecdochic of the type of apocalyptic vision embodied in the Bible's climactic book—a Hitchcockian, emblematic vision of Creation as "Flora unimpeachable/To Time's Analysis")
Comment: See *Poems*, III, 862-863.

I saw Eternity the other night
Like a great ring of pure and endless light.

> All calm, as it was bright;
> And round beneath it, Time in hours, days, years,
> Driv'n by the spheres
> Like a vast shadow mov'd, in which the world
> And all her train were hurled.

So wrote Henry Vaughan in his "Silex Scintillans. The World." In similar fashion, yet showing the influence of nineteenth-century botany, P1241 presents a "Firmamental Lilac" that is the poet's vision of Eternity. Although perhaps far-fetched, it is true that the lilac as a member of the olive family world connect with the Passion (Mt 26-27, especially Mt 26:30-56) and Ascension of Christ (Lu 24:51; Ac 1:9; Ro 8:34; Eph 4:8; IPe 3:22). See also Zec 4:3; Rev 11:4.

1242   To flee from memory

    ll.2-3   "Had...fly": Ps 55:6

1243   Safe Despair it is that raves-

    l.2   "Agony...frugal": Lu 22:44
    l.6   "Trouble": Joh 12:27 ("Now is my soul troubled; and what shall I say? Father, save me from this hour: but for this cause came I unto this hour")
    l.7   "Love...one": IJo 4:8 (presumably P1243 concerns the undramatic, private life of "Agony," of the "Soul" that cannot be "Garrisoned" from "Trouble"; the exemplar for such a life would be Christ whose "Love" included the Passion, Mt 26-27, as well as triumphant death-resurrection, Mt 28; the poem may be an oblique criticism of sentimental notions of "Love" and "Dying" as well as flamboyant and unrealistic protestations of "Despair")
    l.8   "Nor...double": Heb 9:27 ("And as it is appointed unto men once to die, but after this the judgment")
    Comment: See *Poems*, III, 864.

1244   The Butterfly's Assumption Gown

    l.1   "Assumption": Mr 16:19; Lu 24:51; Ac 1:2, 9; Ro 8:34 (the Ascension of Christ); Ge 5:24 (the translation of Enoch); IIKi 2:11 (the translation of Elijah); Mt 17:3; Mr 9:4; Lu 9:33; Rev 11:3 (the inferred "Assumption" of Moses)

1.1   "Gown": Mt 22:11-12; Rev 19:8 (the "Gown" of imputed righteousness worn by the Bride of Christ)

1.2   "Chrysoprase": Rev 21:20

1.4   "How...descend": Ro 12:16; Eph 4:9-10 (as a Hitchcockian emblem of resurrection and ascent, the "Butterfly" condescends in going among the "Buttercups")

Comment: See Poems, III, 864-865. In P1244, and intimations-epiphany poem, the Assumption Butterfly's "Gown" deigns to grant the New Englanders a revelation of heavenly "Apartments" (the "Gown" a metaphor for the afternoon sunlight as the variant third line suggests).

1245   The Suburbs of a Secret

1.1   "The...Secret": Pr 25:9 ("discover not a secret to another")

1246   The Butterfly in honored Dust

1.1   "honored Dust": Ge 3:19 (as an emblem of the resurrection, the "Butterfly" dies an "honored" yet final death); ICo 15:43 ("It is sown in dishonour; it is raised in glory: it is sown in weakness; it is raised in power")

1.3   "Catacomb": ICo 15:50-55 (the "Fly" is cheated of its carrion by the resurrection)

1.4   "chastened": Ps 6:1; 38:1; 94:12; 118:18; ICo 11:32; Heb 12:5-8; Rev 3:19 (a KJV term consistently used for the solicitous disciplining of His followers by God and here an integral part of the Biblical wit)

Comment: See *Poems*, III, 865-866.

1247   To pile like Thunder to it's close

1.1   "To...close": IISa 22:14; Job 26:14; 28:26; 37:4-5; 38:25; Ps 18:13; 77:18; 104:7 ("Hast thou an arm like God? or canst thou thunder with a voice like him?" Job 40:9)

1.3   "While...hid": Ge 3:8, 10; Rev 6:14-17

1.5   "Or...come": Ge 1; Joh 1:1-14; IJo 4:8 (God as Love and creative Word, therefore "coeval") l.7   "Experience...consume": Ex 32:10, 12; 33:3, 5; Nu 16:21, 45; De 4:24; Ca 8:6-7; Heb 12:29 ("For our God is a consuming fire")

l.8   "For...live": Ex 33:20 ("Thou canst not see my face: for there shall no man see me, and live")

Comment: To be consumed by the climactic grandeur and beauty of the beatific vision (Rev 22:4) "would be Poetry." Love and creative speech/language, whose higher case, eternal instantiation is God, become approachable (not, however, provable) in the circuit world by the approximations of metaphors (e.g., crumbling "Thunder") that become higher case "Poetry" in the apocalyptic Presence of Revelation—a Presence paradoxically enough whose "Experience" would "consume" all metaphor by making language irrelevant. "For None see God and" continue the use of analogy.

1249   The Stars are old, that stood for me-

l.2   "The...worn": Ge 3:19 (as "typic" of sunset, the "West" connotes death)

l.3   "Yet...Gold": Ca 6:10 (as "typic" of sunrise, "Gold" suggests the beloved)

ll.3-4   "Yet...earn": Ca 1:10-11; 3:10; 5:11, 14-15; Rev 1:12-13, 20; 2:1; 3:18; 4:4; 5:8; 8:3; 14:14; 21:15, 18, 21 (the provenance of "Gold" would include the profane love of Canticles and the apocalyptic glory of Revelation)

ll.7-8   "But...slain": Isa 25:8; ICo 15:50-55

Comment: See *Poems*, III, 867; *Letters*, II, 517-520; and Leyda, II, 215. The apparent frustration of "Victory" by the defeat of desire's attainment paradoxically becomes its fulfillment ("vanquished her with my defeat") since it occasions celebrating song (as had the flight of the poet in provoking the bird's melody, *Letters*, II, 518). Thus, P1249 becomes a metonymic displacement for Presence (Rev 21-22) since it delineates the occasions and limits of song. The theme of the poem is best summarized in the letter to Higginson in which the final four lines are printed: "Death obtains the Rose, but the news of Dying goes no further than the Breeze. The Ear is the last Face" (*Letters*, II, 518).

1250   White as an Indian Pipe

l.3   "Fabulous...Noon": Jos 10:12-13

1251   Silence is all we dread

l.1   "Silence...dread": Ps 28:1; 35:22; 83:1; 94:17
l.2   "There's...Voice": Rev 1:10-15; 21:3-5
l.4   "Himself...face": Ex 33:20, 23; Rev 22:4 (P1251 expresses dread regarding the potential unmeaning of the apocalyptic—dread that the face-to-face contact with the Infinite once enjoyed by the Old Testament patriarchs is forever lost in "Silence")

Comment: See *Poems*, III, 868; *Letters*, II, 512-513; and Leyda, II, 205-206.

1253   Had this one Day not been,

l.1   "Had...been": Ca 3:11
l.3   "smitten": Nu 14:42; De 28:7; Jg 20:32; ISa 4:3; Isa 53:4 (a frequent KJV past participial form of which the poet seemed fond; see P165; P984; P1253; and for the alternate, P609; P1046; frequent associations with violent aggression would have given the word additional force used in more personal, psychological ways, such as the "Bands of smitten Face" in the apocalyptic vision of P984)
l.5   "Lest...less": Ca 1:2-4; 2:4; 8:6-7
l.7   "stricken": Isa 53:4 (another past participial form; see P1368; P1600; P1757; the alternate is used frequently as well, e.g., P799, but the flavor is less that of the KJV; Isa 53:4 contains both "smitten" and "stricken," suggesting that the verbs are part of a Passion-Crucifixion lexicon used in connection with profane love; see especially P165)

Comment: This "Day" of "espousal" in Canticles terminology is "typic" of marriage to the Bridegroom (Rev 19:7-9).

1254   Elijah's Wagon knew no thill

ll.1-8   "Elijah's...inscrutable": IIKi 2:11-12 ("And it came to pass, as they still went on, and talked, that, behold, there appeared a chariot of fire, and horses of fire, and parted them both asunder; and Elijah went up by a whirlwind into heaven. And Elisha saw it, and he cried, My father, my father, the chariot of Israel, and the horsemen thereof. And he saw him no more: and he took hold of his own clothes, and rent them in two pieces")

Comment: See *Poems*, III, 869-870. The "feats inscrutable" of Elijah refer to passage beyond the circuit world to Heaven bypassing death. See P800 and P1235.

1255   Longing is like the Seed

ll.1-4   "Longing...found": Ro 9; Ga 3:29; (her religio-aesthetic "Longing" is the promise of the "Seed"; P1255 is a "children of promise" poem about God's elect, Ro 8:29-30; IPe 1:23; IJo 3:9)

ll.5-6   "The...unknown": Mt 13:18-43

l.7   "What...achieved": IIPe 1:1-10

l.8   "Sun": Ps 84:11; 89:36; Mal 4:2; Lu 1:78; IIPe 1:19; Rev 2:28 (the "Seed's" seeing the "Sun" is a metonymic displacement for apocalyptic Presence, Rev 19, 21-22)

Comment: See *Poems*, III, 870-871; *Letters*, II, 511-512; and Leyda, II, 222.

1256   Not any higher stands the Grave

ll.1-2   "Not...Men": Job 3:13-19

l.4   "Than...Ten": Ps 90:10

l.7   "Propitiate...Democrat": Ge 3:19 ("propitiation," used three times in the KJV—Ro 3:25; IJo 2:2; 4:10—always refers to Christ's redemption of the sins of mankind; here the word purposely underscores the irrevocable inauspiciousness of death, the futility of seeking for benevolence in the leveling "Democrat")

Comment: See *Poems*, III, 871-872; *Letters*, II, 511-512; and Leyda, II, 222.

1257   Dominion lasts until obtained-

l.1   "Dominion...obtained": IPe 5:11; Jude 25; Rev 1:6 ("Thy kingdom is an everlasting kingdom, and thy dominion endureth throughout all generations," Ps 145:13)

ll.4-5   "Eternally," "everlasting": Ge 21:33; De 33:27; Ps 41:13; 90:2; 93:2; 145:13; Isa 9:6; 60:15, 19-20; Jer 10:10; Da 4:3; 7:14; Hab 1:12; Joh 3:15; 17:2-3; Ro 1:20; 2:7; 6:23; 16:26; ITi 1:17;

IIPe 1:11 (words used for the eternity of God, His kingdom and covenant, and here used for contrast with "Brides of permanence")

1.5   "Lips": Ca 4:3, 11; 5:13; 7:9 (the "Lips" are leaves of grass, here perhaps synecdochic of any ephemeral circuit world beauty or beloved)

1.6   "Dew": Ge 27:28, 39; Ex 16:13-14; Ca 5:2; Ho 14:5; Zec 8:12 (traditionally associated with God's blessing and, by extension, with the favor of the beloved)

1.7   "Brides"; Isa 61:10; 62:3-5; Rev 19:7-9; 21:2, 9; 22:17 (the "Brides" are the leaves of grass known only to the bridegroom "Dew")

Comment: Like Keats's "bride of quietness," the "Lips/Known only to the Dew" are, paradoxically, the only "Brides of permanence" wedded to the circuit world—a world whose circumscription contrasts with the "permanence," "Dominion," "Possession," "everlasting[ness]," and eternity of the "new circumference" or Heaven-New Jerusalem. See *Poems*, III, 872; *Letters*, II, 511-512; and Leyda, II, 222.

1258   Who were "the Father and the Son"

ll.1,9,11 " 'Father...Son' ": Lu 10:22; Joh 1:18; 3:35; 14:9-13; IJo 2:22; 5:7; IIJo 9 ("All things are delivered unto me of my Father: and no man knoweth the Son, but the Father; neither knoweth any man the Father, save the Son, and he to whomsoever the Son will reveal him," Mt 11:27)

1.21   "Heaven": Rev 21-22
Comment: See *Poems*, III, 872-873.

1259   A Wind that rose

1.1   "A...rose": Ps 135:7; 147:18; Am 4:13
1.19   "Invisible": Col 1:15; ITi 1:17
Comment: An epiphany-intimations poem, P1259 offers a "Wind" whose "heavenly hurt" restores "Arctic Confidence/To the Invisible." See *Poems*, III, 874-875; *Letters*, II, 517-521; and Leyda, II, 212, 215. The poet writes in L407: "Your Note was like the Wind. The Bible chooses that you know to define the Spirit"(*Letters*, II, 520). This would suggest specific reference to Pentecost, the second chapter

of Acts, at which time the Spirit manifests itself as "a rushing mighty wind"(Ac 2:2).

1260   Because that you are going

l.17   "The...been": ITi 4:8b
l.19   "Paradise": Ge 2-3; Eze 28:13-14; 31:8-9, 16; 47:1-12; Rev 2:7; 22:1-5
l.21   "The...me": ITi 4:8b
l.22   "A...plain": Rev 21-22 (even her favorite "Gems" will not be sufficient absent the beloved)
l.23   "Redeemer": Job 19:25; Isa 49:7; 59:20 (the title for Jesus Christ as Saviour of mankind)
l.23   "Unless...Face": ICo 13:12; Rev 22:4
ll.8,25 "Immortality": ICo 15:54-54
ll.29-30 "Of...reprehend": Rev 1:18; 20:13-14 (the keys of Heaven and Hell are held by the Alpha and Omega; the poet here deals in apocalyptic hyperbole to accentuate the importance of the beloved, suggesting she would yield her "Right" of final destiny in a substitutionary manner for a commutation of "His Face" for the "less priceless" one—a blasphemous suggestion that the beatific vision [Rev 22:4] become a reunion of profane lovers)
l.33   "If...admits": IJo 4:8 ("He that loveth not knoweth not God; for God is love")
l.35   "Because...God": Ex 20:5; 34:14; De 4:24; 5:9; 6:15; Jos 24:19 ("Thou shalt not bow down thyself to them, nor serve them: for I the Lord thy God am a jealous God, visiting the iniquity upon the children unto the third and fourth generation of them that hate me," Ex 20:5)
l.37   "If...him": Mt 19:26; Mr 10:27; Lu 18:27 ("But Jesus beheld them, and said unto them, with men all this is impossible; but with God all things are possible," Mt 19:26)
ll.39-40 "He...Gods": Ex 20:3-5 (the poet begrudges God His commandment versus idolatry, which she believes He will rescind in giving to her in Heaven the "confiscated God," her profane beloved)
Comment: See *Poems*, III, 875-878.

1261   A Word dropped careless on a Page

l.1   "Word": Joh 1:1, 14; IJo 5:7; Rev 19:13

l.3   "folded": Heb 1:12

l.3   "perpetual": Jer 51:39, 57

l.4   "Maker": Job 36:3; Ps 95:6; Pr 22:2; Isa 17:7; 45:9, 11; 54:5; Hos 8:14; Heb 11:10 (a term for the God of Creation)

Comment: See *Poems*, III, 878; *Letters*, II, 499; and Leyda, II, 196.

1262   I cannot see my soul but know 'tis there

l.1   "I...there": Ps 16:2; 42:5, 11; 43:5; 86:4; 103:1-2; 146:1 (the Psalms repeatedly use the "soul" as separate from the speaker)

ll.2-3   "Nor...dwell": see note, line one, P674 and note, line one, P1142

l.4   "But...well": Rev 3:20 (the "confiding guest" is the Lamb-Bridegroom who must be honored by the "raiment," Rev 3:5, 18)

ll.5-10 "What...feast":   Mt   22:1-14;   Rev   19:7-9 (preparationist lines suggesting Edward Taylor's "robe of evangelical righteousness" must be worn by the guest of the soul as preparatory for the "sudden feast"; "adequately dressed" and "perpetual drest" are those saints "arrayed in fine linen, clean and white...the fine linen...the righteousness of saints," Rev 19:8)

Comment: See *Letters*, II, 501-502 and Leyda, II, 196-197.

1263   There is no Frigate like a Book

ll.3,7   "Coursers," "Chariot": IIKi 2:11

Comment: See *Poems*, III, 879; *Letters*, II, 514-515; and Leyda, II, 207.

1264   This is the place they hoped before,

l.1   "hoped": Heb 11:1 ("Now faith is the substance of things hoped for, the evidence of things not seen")

l.2   "hoping": Ro 8:24-25 ("For we are saved by hope: but hope that is seen is not hope: for what a man seeth, why doth he yet hope for? But if we hope for what we see not, then do we with patience wait for it")

ll.5-6   "Too...balm": see note, line ten, P1142

Comment: See *Letters*, II, 507 and Leyda, II, 200-201.

1265   The most triumphant Bird I ever knew or met

l.1   "The...met": pattern and thought parallel P783
where the "triumphant Bird" of P1265 achieves an "independent
Extasy" comparable to "intimate Delight"; other "bird" poems of
relevance: P321, P575, P613, P774, P783, P861, P1046, P1084,
P1279, P1395, P1530, P1574, P1585, P1630, P1634, P1723, P1761,
and P1764
l.3   "Dominion": IPe 4:11; 5:11; Jude 25: Rev 1:6 (the
song of the bird is an apocalyptic adumbration)
l.6   "intimate Delight": IPe 1:8
l.9   "Does...fit!": Rev 5:9-13; 14:2-7; 15:3-8 (the
"Glory" fitting the song is a heavenly one; the song adumbrates the
Song of Moses and the Lamb, the song of eternity, of worshipful praise
directed toward that "Glory" at the center of the New Jerusalem; see
also note, line seven, P1227)
Comment: See *Poems*, III, 881-882; *Letters*, II, 504-505, 507-
508; and Leyda, II, 201. The epiphany of P1265 is a "delicious
Accident," the Shechinah "Glory" of God manifesting itself for a
moment in birdsong—a song "for nothing scrutable" since a revelation
from beyond the circuit world or "transitive Estate." The experience in
toto is a harbinger of the beatific vision (Rev 22:4).

1269   I worked for chaff and earning Wheat

l.1   "I...Wheat": Ps 1:4; 35:5; Isa 5:24; 41:15; Jer 23:38;
Mt 3:12; 13:24-30; Lu 3:17 ("chaff," as refuse, is associated with the
ungodly and wicked; the edible "Wheat" is associated with the godly
and elect; the speaker "worked" under the old covenant of law and
works and piqued upon receiving the unmerited favor of God after
having struck a bargain, thinking all the while in Old Testament terms
that "to him that soweth righteousness shall be a sure reward," Pr
11:18b, and that "there shall be no reward to the evil man; the candle
of the wicked shall be put out," Pr 24:20; nevertheless, "by grace are
ye saved through faith; and that not of yourselves: it is the gift of God:
not of works, lest any man should boast," said St. Paul, Eph 2:8-9; Ga
2:16)

1.2   "Was...betrayed": Mt 20:1-16 (the Parable of the Labourers dramatizes the circuit world calculus in conflict with God's generosity, the laborers there grousing as the speaker here expresses a sense of betrayal)

1.3   "What...arbitrate": Mt 13:24-30 ("Fields," synecdochic for God's creation, "arbitrate" because they comprise the arena of grace; the eschatological burden of the Parable of the Tares would suggest that no individual in the circuit world has the "right" to root up the tares, to separate sheep from goats, to establish any merely sublunary standard of good and bad)

1.4   "In...ratified?": Ge 6:18; 9:8 (God's covenant with Noah); Ge 15:7; 17:2 (with Abraham); Ge 17:19; 26:3 (with Isaac); Ge 28:13; Ex 2:24; 6:4 (with Jacob); Ex 6:4; 19-20; 24; 34:27 (with Moses and the Israelites); the old covenant, codified in the Commandments and reinforced by the priestly system, appeals to the speaker's sense of clear guidelines and reciprocal obligations

1.5   "I...Chaff": Mt 26; Joh 6:31-35, 48-58 (at the Last Supper, the "Wheat" becomes part of the Eucharistic elements: "Jesus took bread, and blessed it, and brake it, and gave it to the disciples, and said, Take eat; this is my body," Mt 26:26; as the anti-type of the manna, Jesus is the "Wheat," the "Bread of Life," Joh 6:48; only the elect, the beneficiaries of imputed righteousness, may "taste" the "Wheat," as the Parable of the Marriage Supper of the Lamb suggests, Mt 22:1-14; Lu 14:16-24)

1.6   "And...friend": Mt 6:11 (the Lord's Prayer gives thanks for "Wheat," "our daily bread"); Jer 31:31; Mal 3:1; Lu 1:68-80; Ro 11:27; Ga 3:17; Heb 8:6-8; 9:15 (the "ample friend" may be Christ who has ratified the new covenant of grace and faith)

1270   Is Heaven a Physician?

1.1   "Is...Physician?": Rev 21-22 (although "Heaven" is the New Jerusalem, it is here perhaps synecdochic of the broader plan of redemption, God's revelation as manifested to and puzzled over by the speaker); Mt 9:12; Mr 2:17; Lu 4:23; 5:31 (Christ's self-identification as the Great Physician); Mt 8:5-15; Mr 2:3-12; 5:25-34; Lu 6:17-19; 13:11-13; 14:2-4; Joh 4:46-53 (a number of Christ's healings from which may be inferred His role as Great Physician)

1.2   "They...heal": Isa 53:5; Mt 10:1, 8; Mr 3:2, 15; Lu 5:7; Joh 4:47; IPe 2:24 (the medical lexicon of P1270 is used figuratively to speak of the efficacy and operation of God's grace in the circuit world)

ll.5-6   "Is...owe": Mt 6:12 (the Lord's Prayer in part reads, "And forgive us our debts, as we forgive our debtors"); Mt 6:20 ("But lay up for yourselves treasures in heaven, where neither moth nor rust doth corrupt, and where thieves do not break through nor steal"); Mt 18:23-35 (the kingdom of heaven as debts owed); Mt 19:21; Lu 12:33; 18:22; ITi 6:19; IPe 1:4

ll.7-8   "But...to": Joh 17:1-26 (the prayer of the Great High Priest reveals that "before the foundation of the world" God's plan had existed, the speaker not being a "Party" to the "negotiation")

1273   That sacred Closet when you sweep-

l.1   "That...sweep": Mt 6:6
l.9   "August...Domain": Ge 3:19 (the supercession of the present by "Memory" suggests the loss of Paradise)

1274   The Bone that has no Marrow,

l.1   "The...Marrow": Ge 2:23; Joh 3:1-6; ICo 15:45-55; IICo 5:1-6, 14-17 ("Bone" is here synecdochic of: 1. Eve, made from bone; 2. St. Paul's new creature or new creation in Christ; 3. St. Paul's resurrected, changed, incorruptible spiritual body)

ll.9-10   "But...obtain?": ICo 15:45-55 ("finished Creatures" are the resurrected saints, those who have experienced what Donne termed in "The Second Anniversary" the soul's "third birth"; "finished" has distinctive Paulinian echoes, Ac 20:24; IITi 4:7)

l.11   "Old...Phantom": Joh 3:1-6 (the "Phantom" of Nicodemus is the enigma of metamorphosis, rebirth in an incorruptible spiritual body since "flesh and blood cannot inherit the kingdom," ICo 15:50)

Comment: P1274 seems to deal with questions raised by St. Paul: "But some man will say, How are the dead raised up? and with what body do they come?" ICo 15:35).

1275   The Spider as an Artist

l.7   "Neglected...Genius": Ge 1; Joh 1:1 (the "Spider," in diminutive form attractive to the poet, copies in its cobwebs the creation of cosmos out of chaos by the Creator God; see notes, lines six and nine, P1138 and note, line three, P1167)

1277   While we were fearing it, it came-

l.4   "fair": Ca 1:15-16; 2:10, 13; 4:1, 7, 10; 6:10; 7:6
l.9   "The...Utmost": Rev 3:4-5, 18; 6:11; 7:9, 13-14; 19:7-9 ("Utmost," imaged as the robe of righteousness, is synecdochic of "new circumference" consciousness)
l.10   "The...new": Rev 6:17; 16:14; 22:5
Comment: See *Poems*, III, 887-888. "Fitting" for the circuit world is a consciousness characterized by an anticipation in fear, dismay, and despair since it fits or prepares the individual for that resurrection morning "Fitting" in the fine, clean, white linen of the saints. The metaphor of habiliments allows the poet to speak obliquely of the change of consciousness necessitated by His Presence (Rev 22:4) —"Here."

1278   The Mountains stood in Haze-

l.12   "Was...Invisible": Col 1:15; ITi 1:17; Heb 11:27
Comment: In P1278 the "Twilight" speaks in the language of silent feeling its steeple message of ascent, an intimation coming, paradoxically enough, just before the transition from sunset to darkness. The curtain of darkness falls with the poem's muted ending leaving a "neighborly" feeling of the beyond. P1278 should be contrasted in this regard to P258.

1279   The Way to know the Bobolink

ll.1-4   "The...inferred": see note, line one, P1265
l.11   "Transport": see note, line six, P122; note, line fifteen, P783; and see also P1191 and P1468
ll.9-12   "Of...Apostasy": Heb 10:1, 16 (the "Bobolink" is a heterodox, antinomian bird in his "Sentiments")
ll.13-14 "Extrinsic...Joy": IPe 1:8 (the autotelic "Joy" of the "Bobolink" is "typic" of a higher, religio-aesthetic "joy unspeakable")
l.22   "The...gone": Da 2:47; ITi 6:15; Rev 17:14; 19:16 (the imitation of the Biblical phrasing is a deliberate hyperbole underscoring the potent magic of the "Sorcerer" now departed)

1280   The harm of Years is on him-

l.1   "The...him": Ge 3:15, 19 (Satan and Death)
l.2   "The...Time": Ge 3:14, 19
l.3   "Depose...Fashion": ICo 7:31; 15
l.4   "And...room": Ro 6:9; Eph 1:21; IPe 4:11; 5:11; Jude 25; Rev 1:6 ("Dominion" is synecdochic for Jesus Christ, the Lamb, the Alpha and Omega)
l.5   "Forget...Forces": Isa 14:12-19; Rev 12; 16; 20 (Lucifer is the morning star whose glory has decayed having fallen from Heaven; Lucifer or Satan and his "Forces" are spoken of in Revelation)
ll.6-8   "least Vitality/Beside Vitality": IITi 1:10 ("But is now made manifest by the appearing of our Saviour Jesus Christ, who hath abolished death, and hath brought life and immortality to light through the gospel")

Comment: P1280 is a highly elliptical treatment of Satan as the embodiment of the principle of death in time and over whom/which Eve, the New Eve, and Christ triumph. Perhaps the imperatives are intended to demythologize—to strip away the glamour from the "Pageant"—the "Glory of Decay"—Milton presents through his dramatization of Satan in *Paradise Lost*.

1282   Art thou the thing I wanted?

ll.1-8   "Art...God": Isa 45:15 (the speaker becomes like the self-subsistent Deus absconditus after repudiating the oral hunger associated with the profane beloved and circuit world desire; associations of longing for the profane beloved with orality echo Canticles 1:7-8; 2:3, 16; 4:5; 6:2-3)

Comment: See *Poems*, III, 891-892. Tinged perhaps with the acerbity of making virtue of necessity, P1282 utilizes the gustatory metaphor of the "Palate" in stating a Joycean religio-aesthetic ideal of the artist as "Like God," apart from his work, beyond "minor" desire, "paring his fingernails."

1283   Could Hope inspect her Basis

ll.1-4   "Could...none": Ro 8:24-25 ("For we are saved by hope: but hope that is seen is not hope: for what a man seeth, why doth he yet hope for? But if we hope for that we see not, then do we with patience wait for it"); Heb 11:1 ("Now faith is the substance of things hoped for, the evidence of things not seen")

Comment: See *Poems*, III, 892.

1284   Had we our senses

l.6   "Blind": Isa 35:5; ICo 13:12 (blindness is a temporary palliative, a circuit world expedient justifying God's "Earth" to man, P1284 being a theodicy of sorts)

Comment: See *Poems*, III, 892-893.

1286   I thought that nature was enough

ll.1-6   "I...Divine": Ge 1:1-27 ("nature," "Human nature," and "Divine" recapitulate the steps in the Creation account)

Comment: See *Poems*, III, 893-894.

1287   In this short life

l.1   "In...Life": Ps 89:47a ("Remember how short my time is")

1288   Lain in Nature- so suffice us

ll.1-4   "Lain...Seed": ICo 15:35-55 (the "Pod" or body is sown in corruption; the "Seed" or soul/spiritual body is sown in incorruption)

l.5   "Maddest...created": Isa 14:12-20 (only God has power over death, Rev 1:18)

1289   Left in immortal Youth

ll.1-8   "Left...Day": Ge 19:23-25 ("The sun was risen upon the earth when Lot entered into Zoar. Then the Lord rained upon Sodom and upon Gomorrah brimstone and fire from the Lord out of heaven; And he overthrew those cities, and all the plain, and all the inhabitants of the cities, and that which grew upon the ground")

ll.3-4   "Retrospection/Peradventure," "Again": Ge 18:23-33
Comment: See *Poems*, III, 895.

1290   The most pathetic thing I do

l.8   "Goliah": ISa 17:4
Comment: P1290 has that Blakean quality heightening the
pathos of the "make believe" game played by the child-Lilliputian
persona whose naivete is revealed in innocent chiding of the cosmic
Brobdingnagian, the Goliath-God. The poem poses obliquely the
question whether the Deus absconditus can be heartbroken after all.
The reference by the speaker to Goliath is intentionally self-
deprecatory but unintentionally hardly flattering since the giant of
Gath cast defiant taunts upon the Israelites (ISa 17:8-10) and
blasphemous imprecations upon David (ISa 17:43) for whom, as a
Lilliputian-youth, Goliath had only disdain (ISa 17:42). See P540.

1291   Until the Desert knows

l.7   "Utmost": Mt 12:42; Lu 11:31 (the KJV word for
extremity, here used as hyperbole)
Comment: See *Poems*, III, 896.

1293   The things we thought that we should do

ll.1-4   "The...begun": Ro 7:18-19
ll.5,9   "The...seek," "Heaven": Heb 11:14, 16 ("For they
that say such things declare plainly that they seek a country...But now
they desire a better country, that is, an heavenly: wherefore God is not
ashamed to be called their God: for he hath prepared for them a city")
l.6   "run": ICo 9:24 ("So run, that ye may obtain"); ICo
9:26; Ga 2:2; Php 2:16; Heb 12:1
l.8   "Son": Rev 1:13; 2:18; 14:14
l.10   "When...done": Php 3:13-14; IITi 4:7
Comment: See *Poems*, III, 897-898; *Letters*, II, 553-554; and
Leyda, II, 251-252.

1294   Of Life to own

ll.2-3   "From...reservoir": Joh 4:10, 13-14; 7:37-38; 14:6

Comment: See *Letters*, II, 525 and Leyda, II, 221-222, the latter printing the Higginson poem, "Decoration."

1295   Two Lengths has every Day-

l.4   "Hope": Ro 8:24-25; Tit 1:2; 2:13; 3:7; Heb 6:18-19; 11:1

l.5   "Eternity": Isa 57:15

l.6   "Velocity...Pause": Mt 25:46

l.10   "On...Chart": Rev 5:1 (the book of doom for the unrighteous); Rev 13:8; 17:8; 21:27 (the Lamb's Book of Life containing the names of the righteous); Rev 20:12-15 (the book of life containing an enumeration of the deeds of the dead; the earlier draft version of lines seven and eight of the poem would suggest that this is the "Chart" of doom the poet has in mind)

Comment: See *Poems*, III, 898-899.

1296   Death's Waylaying not the sharpest

l.7   "Cluster": Ca 1:14; 7:7-8

Comment: See *Poems*, III, 899-900; *Letters*, II, 521; and Leyda, II, 216-217.

1297   Go slow, my soul, to feed thyself

l.1   "Go...thyself": Ca 1:7; 2:16; 3:1-4; 6:2-3

l.2   "Upon...approach": Ca 2:8-13; 4:16

ll.1,3,5,7 "Go": Ca 1:8; 3:2, 11; 7:11

l.4   "Prevail...Coach": Ca 1:9; 3:9; 6:12

ll.5-6   "Go...amiss": Ca 4:9; 6:5; 7:4; 8:10

ll.7-8   "Go...Kiss": Ca 1:2; 2:4, 10, 16-17; 4:9-11; 5:1; 6:3; 7:10 (if "Cupid taught Jehovah" to the "untutored mind" of the poet, then the outrageousness of the wit here may be partially explained)

l.7   "boldly": Eph 3:12; Php 1:20; Heb 4:16; 10:19; IJo 4:17

l.7   "price": ICo 6:20; 7:23

l.8   "Redemption": Eph 1:7, 14; Heb 9:12, 15

Comment: If, as Johnson has suggested, P1297 was "inspired by the coming of spring" (*Poems*, III, 900), then the poem characterizes the seasonal change in the Canticles imagery of the advent of the beloved. "Rare approach," "Competing Death," "final eye," "paid'st his price," and "Redemption" suggest a reading of this experience as "typic" of anticipation of the Bridegroom (Rev 19:7-9) and the beatific vision (Rev 22:4). Lines five and six should be compared with similar concerns expressed at greater length in P968. See *Poems*, III, 900; *Letters*, II, 523; and Leyda, II, 218-219.

1298   The Mushroom is the Elf of Plants-

l.8   "And...Tare": Mt 13:24-43 (darnel is a weedy grass here surreptitiously springing up with the "Grass"; the tares, as false grain, link with the reference to Judas Iscariot)
l.5   "As...always": Mt 25:5; 26:38; Lu 24:49 (to "tarry always" is to be neither root nor fruit, grass or flower)
l.19   "Apostate/Iscariot": Mt 10:4; 26:14
Comment: See *Poems*, III, 901-904; *Letters*, II, 525; Leyda, II, 222; and Richard Wilbur's "Children of Darkness."

1299   Delight's Despair at setting

ll.1-2   "Delight's," "Delight": Ca 2:3; 7:6
l.8   "Sun": Ps 84:11; 89:36; Mal 4:2; Lu 1:78; IIPe 1:19; Rev 2:28; 22:16

1300   From his slim Palace in the Dust

l.1   "Dust": Ge 3:19
l.3   "exody"; Ex 12-14; the Book of Exodus (the word for the Biblical deliverance from Egypt and departure is here perhaps chosen to avoid euphemism)
l.4   "That...him": Ec 3:19
Comment: Johnson identifies Edward Dickinson as the subject of P1300 (*Poems*, III, 905). See Sewall, 71.

1301   I cannot want it more

l.8   "He...obtains": ICo 9:24; Heb 6:15

1302   I think that the Root of the Wind is Water-

ll.1-8   "I...Atmosphere": Joh 3:8; IJo 5:5-8
ll.3-4   "Were...keep": Ge 1:6-10
Comment: P1302 is a relation by indirection using traditional imagery of "Wind" and "Water" to speak of a "maritime conviction" (the Spirit and the "Water" "beareth witness").

1303   Not One by Heaven defrauded stay-

l.1   "Not One": Mt 10:29-31; 18:10-14
l.3   "restitutes": Ac 3:21
l.3   "sweet": Ca 2:3, 14; 5:5, 13, 16

1304   Not with a Club, the Heart is broken

ll.13-16 "Shame...your's": Ge 3:7-11 (the fourth stanza suggests the conclusion of *Paradise Lost*)

1305   Recollect the Face of me

ll.1-8   "Recollect...Chivalry": Lu 23:39-43 ("And he [one of the malefactors] said unto Jesus, Lord, remember me when thou comest into thy kingdom. And Jesus said unto him, Verily I say unto thee, To day shalt thou be with me in paradise")
Comment: See also P1180 for another treatment of the two thieves and Christ at the Crucifixion. Unlike the silent and distant Deus absconditus, Christ the Courtier was as approachable as one of her affectionate friends.

1307   That short- potential stir

l.2   "That...once": Heb 9:27 ("And as it is appointed unto men once to die, but after this the judgment")
l.7   "Beggar": Lu 16:20, 22

1308   The Day she goes

l.1   "Day": Ec 12:3
l.3   "Existence...width": Job 14:5, 14, 16; 31:4; Ps 39:4; 90:12

1309   The Infinite a sudden Guest

ll.1-2   "The...be": Mt 24:42-44; Mk 13:32-37; ITh 5:2; IIPe 3:10; Rev 3:3, 20; 16:15

l.1   "sudden": Mr 13:36 ("Lest coming suddenly he find you sleeping"); ITh 5:3 ("For when they shall say, Peace and safety; then sudden destruction cometh upon them, as travail upon a woman with child and they shall not escape")

ll.3-4   "But...away": Joh 14:16-26; 15:26-27; 16:7-16 (the Biblical wit and paradox of P1309 turns on the fact that the Comforter, the Holy Spirit, remains after the departure of Christ—thus God cannot "stupendous come" if God has "never went away"; also, see the final words of Jesus in the first Gospel: "Teaching them to observe all things whatsoever I have commanded you: and, lo, I am with you alway, even unto the end of the world," Mt 28:20)

1310 The Notice that is called the Spring

l.3   "Hoary": Le 19:32; IKi 2:6, 9; Isa 46:4 (the poet favors the KJV word for old age associated here and elsewhere with death, winter, and an ascetic, stoical endurance—the "Hemlock" mood of P525; see also P216, P990, P1130, P1217, and P1316)

l.4   "And...Chair": Mt 19:28; Lu 22:30; Rev 3:21; 20:4 (the advent of spring is "typic" of an apocalyptic promise)

l.7   "longest Day": Rev 21:23-25; 22:5

1311   This dirty- little- Heart

ll.1-4   "This...shrine": Ps 51:10 ("Create in me a clean heart, O God; and renew a right spirit within me"); see also Ps 24:4; 73:1; for other poems using "freckled" to suggest a sullied and unworthy heart see P401, P1094, and P1737)

l.5   "But...fair": Ca 1:15-16; 2:10, 13; 4:1, 7, 10; 6:10; 7:6

ll.6-7   "To...Soul": Rev 2:23 ("I am he which searcheth the reins and hearts: and I will give unto every one of you according to your works"); see also Ca 1:7; 2:14; 3:1-4 (the profane beloved is "typic" of the Divine; from among numerous poems using "Visage" or "face" see also P409, P464, P552, P663, P968, and P1187; the "finished face" of the "eligibly fair" Bride here contrasts with the "knees" of the final line, a synecdoche for the body, Ps 109:24; Heb 12:12)

1312   To break so vast a Heart

ll.1-4   "To...Blast": Ps 80:10; 92:12; 104:16; Ca 5:15; Eze 17:23 (references to the cedars of Lebanon both literal and figurative abound in the Old Testament, being noted for excellence and beauty, age and strength; the destruction of cedars was usually associated with God's wrath directed against the enemies of the Israelites, Isa 37:24; Zec 11:2; Johnson suggests that the subject of P1312 may have been Edward Dickinson—see *Poems*, III, 909-910; the Biblical personage who fits P1312 is Job whose character might be described as a "Cedar straight" and whose sufferings seemed an "undeserved Blast")

1313   Warm in her Hand these accents lie

ll.1-4   "Warm...wear": Ro 5:11-21 (the free gift of the book is spoken of in terms of the vicarious atonement requiring the Passion renunciation of separation on the part of the speaker)

1314 When a Lover is a Beggar

ll.7-8   "Bread...obloquy": Ex 16:14; De 8:3 (manna was provided by God to the children of Israel in the wilderness); Nu 11:6 (the children of Israel complained); Joh 6:31-58 (Christ is the "Bread of Heaven")

Comment: The Biblical wit of the poem turns on the point that the "Bread of Heaven," paradoxically enough, resents the bestowal of "What [is] begged" since complacent possession leads to the hubris of "Owner[ship]."

1315   Which is the best- the Moon or the Crescent?

l.6   "Shudder...attain": Php 3:11-14
l.8   "He...born": Job 14:1 ("Prism" is synecdochic for the body or the circuit world)

1316   Winter is good- his Hoar Delights

l.1   "Hoar": see note, line three, P1310

1317   Abraham to kill him

ll.1-2   "Abraham...prevail": Ge 22 (the story of Abraham and Isaac also fascinated the writer of Hebrews as an example of faith, Heb 11:17-19)

l.2   "distinctly told": Ge 22:2 ("And he said, Take now thy son, thine only son Isaac, whom thou lovest, and get thee into the land of Mariah; and offer him there for a burnt offering upon one of the mountains which I will tell thee of")

Comment: See *Poems*, III, 911-912. P1317 suggests that Abraham followed the etiquette of obedience. Mixing the lexicons of manners and morals is a discordia concors used elsewhere (e.g., P401). "Tyranny" and "Mastiff" as appellations for the Deity at least equal in vitriol the "Burglar" and "Banker" of P49.

1318   Frigid and sweet her parting Face-

l.1   "Frigid...Face": Ca 1:10; 2:14; 4:1-4; 5:9-16 (the absent "Face" of the lover yields "Riches" and "Realm," robbing the speaker of her complacent identifications with "Penury and Home"; the poem may perhaps be read as a metonymic displacement for presence of a Divine Beloved, Rev 19; 21-22)

1319   How News must feel when travelling

ll.9-12   "What...remain": Ro 14:11 ("For it is written, As I live saith the Lord, every knee shall bow to me, and every tongue confess to God"); see also Isa 45:23; ICo 13:12; Php 2:10-11

1320   Dear March- Come in-

l.16   "Purple": see note, line one, P15 and note, lines two-three, P716

1321   Elizabeth told Essex

l.3   "clemency...Deity": IICo 1:3; Eph 2:4; Jas 5:11 (the mercy of the Deity is a KJV commonplace)

l.4   "However...survive": Ps 100:5
l.5   "secondary succor": Mt 5:7; 6:12, 14; Mr 11:25; Lu
6:36; Jas 2:13 (the KJV idea of mercy extended to the merciful; there
may here be an echo of IICo 6:2)

1322   Floss wont save you from an Abyss

l.1   "Floss": Job 8:14; Isa 59:5 (the proverbial vanity,
insecurity, and insubstantiality associated with the spider's web)
l.1   "Abyss": see note, line three, P1238
ll.5-6   "But...Well": Ge 24:17-20; Ex 2:16; Joh 4:4-14
(since the "Floss" cannot be ruled, the "Rope" will be a necessity for
drawing water for the "Trough")
l.8   "Prices   reasonable":   Mt   13:44-46   (the
understatement echoes the Biblical hyperbole)
Comment: See *Poems*, III, 914.

1323   I never hear that one is dead

l.2   "Without...Life": Ec 9:11
l.6   "abyss": see note, line three, P1238
ll.14-15 "lonely...Consciousness": Mt 26:36-45 (the agonized
Passion "Consciousness" was the paradigm for life as awareness of
extinction)
Comment: See *Poems*, III, 915.

1325   Knock with tremor-

l.1   "Knock...tremor": Rev 3:20
l.2   "These...Caesars": Mt 22:17-22; Lu 20:22-25; Mk
12:14-17; Joh 19:15 (those who are lovers of mammon or temporal
power and glory or those who were guilty of complicity in the
crucifixion)
l.4   "Flee": ITi 6:11
l.6   "These...summons": Mt 16:24-27
l.8   "rend you": Mt 7:6 ("Give not that which is holy
unto the dogs, neither cast ye your pearls before swine, lest they
trample them under their feet, and turn and rend you")
l.9   "What...show": Joh 6:30
Comment: See *Poems*, III, 916-917.

1326   Our little secrets slink away-

ll.1-3   "Our...years": Mt 13:35; Joh 1:1-4; 17:24; IPe 1:20; Rev 13:8 (the coeternal Word; the reference may be to the secret of Jesus as Messiah for which see Mt 11; Mr 8:27-30; Lu 7:19-28; 10:21-24)

l.7   "sweet": Ca 2:3, 14; 5:5, 13, 16; 7:9

1329   Whether they have forgotten

l.5   "Miseries...conjecture": Ec 8:6-7

l.7   "Iron": Rev 2:27; 12:5; 19:15 (the apocalyptic metal associated with God's rule and judgment)

l.8   "Hardened": Ro 9:18

l.8   "I know": Rev 2:2, 9, 13, 19; 3:1, 8, 15

Comment: See *Poems*, III, 918-919.

1330   Without a smile- Without a Throe

l.2   "Assemblies": Ex 12:6; Le 23:36; Nu 29:35; De 9:10; 10:4; Eze 44:24 (a day of holy meeting, communal worship, and of God's dealings with His people, including the revelation of His law; "Assemblies" may then be a type of which the ideal presence in Revelation is the anti-type)

Comment: Summer is the God who never becomes the intimate, affectionate "Friend," whose Presence entrances but remains "Unknown" even though the meetings have been many, the poet obliquely suggesting that in contrast transitional weather is epiphanic.

1331   Wonder- is not precisely Knowing

l.8   "Gnat": Mt 23:24

1333   A little Madness in the Spring

l.5   "Apocalypse": Rev 1, passim (the last book of the New Testament, Revelation or The Apocalypse, St. John the Divine's vision of Heaven and last things; the variant "Apocalypse" suggests that the poet thought of "Spring" perhaps as emblematic of the resurrection and life hereafter or at least as an occasion for a nature-induced epiphany aided by a "little Madness")

    l.5   "whole/fair/bright/sweet": Ge 2:6; Ca 1:15-16; 2:3, 10, 13-14; 4:1, 7, 10; 5:5, 13-14, 16; 6:10; 7:6 (among others, the variants dropped in favor of "whole" were the Canticles adjectives; the choice heightens the contrast between a modest, appreciative, restrained, and responsive vision and the gargantuan possessive one of the "Clown"—a similarly "Incautious" vision is criticized in P327; for the variant "quick," see Ac 10:42; IITi 4:1; IPe 4:5—God being the One "who quickeneth all things," ITi 6:13)

    Comment: See *Poems*, III, 921-922.

1334 How soft this Prison is

    l.2   "sweet": Ca 2:3, 14; 5:5, 13, 16; 7:9
    ll.3-4   "No...repose": Ge 3:19; Rev 1:18; 17:14; 19:16 (the Deity has invented death and is "King" thereof)
    l.8   "Incarceration-Home": Job 17:13; Ec 12:5
    Comment: See *Poems*, III, 922-923; *Letters*, II, 537-538; and Leyda, II, 231-232.

1335   Let me not mar that perfect Dream

    l.4   "come again": Joh 14:2-3
    l.5   "Not...know": Mt 24:36
    l.5   "Power": Mt 24:30; 28:18; Ro 1:4; Rev 4:11; 5:12-13; 12:10; 19:1 (the Bridegroom)
    ll.6-8   "The...Paradise": Ge 2-3 (the "Garment of Surprise" in part refers to the prelapsarian nakedness of Eve while still "At Home" in the Garden of Eden)
    l.6   "Garment": Mt 22:11-12; Rev 3:4 ("Behold, I come as a thief. Blessed is he that watcheth, and keepeth his garments, lest he walk naked, and they see his shame," Rev 16:15)
    Comment: See *Poems*, III, 923.

1336   Nature assigns the Sun-

    l.1   "Nature...Sun": Ge 1:14-18

ll.1-4   "Nature...Astrology": Ge 1 (the poem follows the order of creation in Genesis, first "Nature" then "Human nature"—see P1286)

Comment: See *Letters*, II, 541-542 (Johnson identifies the source of "Friend" as Ps 116:12) and Leyda, II, 239.

1337   Upon a Lilac Sea

l.1   "Lilac": Ca 2:16; 6:3

l.5   "The...fling": Ca 2:8-13 (the advent of the beloved with spring)

l.6   "To...Balm": Ge 37:25; Ca 1:13-14; 4:14; 5:13; 7:13 ("Balm" is synecdochic for the delights of the beloved—the "Dooms" being pleasurable, Edenic ones)

Comment: See the discussion in Sewall, 580; *Poems*, III, 924; *Letters*, II, 544; and Leyda, II, 237-238.

1338   What tenements of clover

ll.1-8   "What...guess": Ps 84
Comment: See *Poems*, III, 924-925.

1339   A Bee his burnished Carriage

ll.1,4   "Carriage": Ca 1:9; 3:9; 6:12

ll.2,5   "Rose": Ca 2:1

ll.1-12   "A...humility": Ca 2:16; 4:5; 6:2-3 ("I am my beloved's, and my beloved is mine: he feedeth among the lilies," Ca 6:3); Rev 7:17

Comment: See *Poems*, III, 925-926 and *Letters*, II, 545-546. The sentence introductory to P1339 in the letters echoes the Wisdom books ("Sweet" and "Shadow of Death": Job 3:5; 10:21-22; 24:17; Ps 23:4; 44:19; Ca 2:3, 14; 5:5, 13, 16).

1340   A Rat surrendered here

l.4   "Ignominy's": Pr 18:3

1341   Unto the Whole- how add?

l. 1   "Whole": Ge 1-2; Ro 8:22 (the "Whole" of sublunary creation)

1.2   " 'All' ": Ge 1:26, 29; 2:1-3, 20; 3:17, 20 (frequently repeated to suggest the completeness of creation); Job 34:15 (suggestive of the finite limitation of "all flesh"); Ec 1-5; 9 (frequently used by Koheleth to express pessimism about the vanity of "All"—see especially Ec 3:19-20)

1.3   "Utmost": Ge 49:26; Lu 11:31 (Biblical "utmost" suggests outermost boundary)

1.4   "Balm": Jer 8:22; 46:11 (by figurative extension, Christ is the Balm of Gilead, the guarantor of the "further Realm," a release from the anguish of the circuit world)

1342   "Was not" was all the Statement.

l. 1   " 'Was not'...Statement": Ge 5:24 ("And Enoch walked with God: and he was not; for God took him"); *Poems*, III, 927 (identified by Johnson)

1.7   "Because...mention": Ge 5:24 (the Biblical wit derives from the label "Philology"—love of the word—given to the terse explanation of Enoch's disappearance)

Comment: The translation of Enoch and Elijah, which allowed both to circumvent death while escaping the circuit world, fascinated the poet. See P800, P1235, and P1254 and also *Poems*, III, 927 and *Letters*, I, 178.

1343   A single Clover Plank

l. 1   "Plank/Spar": the even more melodramatic "Spar" is used symbolically in other poems—P201, P510, and P879

ll.1,9   "Plank": see note, lines one and four, P875 and note, line ten, P1142 (the situation of the speaker in P875 is similar to the plight of the "Bee" in P1343)

ll.5-6   "Firmament": Ge 1:6-8, 14-20; Ps 19:1 (the "open firmament" is for Dickinson's bees, birds, and butterflies—all creatures of ascent, Ge 1:20; "below" is the created sky and "above" is Heaven)

1.7   "Billows": Ps 42:7; Jon 2:3 (the nautical imagery with the "Firmament" as "Boat" may also be seen in P798)

1.7   "Circumference": see note, line five, P798

l.10   "Responsible...nought": Mt 6:28-30; Lu 12:27-28
l.16   " 'Alas' ": Jg 6:22; Joe 1:15 (an exclamation of pain)
Comment: See *Poems*, III, 927-928.

1344   Not any more to be lacked-

ll.1-2   "Not...known": Job 7:1-10; Ec 9:5-6 ("He shall
return no more to his house, neither shall his place know him any
more," Job 7:10)
l.9   "Of...it": Php 3:14
ll.13-16 "Some...Monotony": Lu 9:62
Comment: See *Poems*, III, 928-929. From the circuit world
point of view, P1344 is a meditation upon a point beyond life and
circumference at which the inconsequence of existence within
"Nature" becomes evident. The "it" of stanza three may be a dead
beloved or perhaps a religio-aesthetic ideal only to be realized in the
"new circumference" beyond. The poet suggests that those who have
"solaced," "rescinded," or "plated" have succumbed to Thoreau's "life
without principle."

1346   As Summer into Autumn slips

l.4   "We...away": Ca 1:6; 6:10 (for the sun as the
Bridegroom: Nu 24:17; Mal 4:2; IIPe 1:19; Rev 1:16; 2:28; 21:23;
22:5, 16)
l.7   "Of...lovely": Ca 5:16
l.8   "The...loved": Ca 1:7; 3:1-4 (the Canticles imagery
underpins the personification of the seasons as the beloved)
Comment: See *Poems*, III, 929-930; *Letters*, II, 529-530; and
Leyda, II, 229-230.

1347   Escape is such a thankful Word

l.1   "Escape...Word": Lu 21:36; ICo 10:13; Heb 2:3;
12:25; IIPe 1:4; 2:18, 20
l.5   "Escape...Basket": Ex 2:1-10; IICo 11:33 (two
famous Biblical escapes via basket—those by Moses and St.
Paul—may here be adapted, that of St. Paul more nearly fitting the
metaphor of stanza two)

l.9   " 'Tis...savior": Php 3:20; ITi 4:10; IITi 1:10; Tit 1:4; 3:4-6; IIPe 2:20 ("savior," a title for Christ)

l.10   "It...saved": Mt 10:22; Ro 5:9-10; ICo 1:18; IICo 2:15; Rev 21:24 (the "saved" or elect)

l.11   "And...Head": see note, lines three-four, P1539 (the echo is of the "Now I lay me" prayer in *The New England Primer*)

Comment: See *Poems*, III, 931.

1348   Lift it- with the Feathers

ll.1-2   "Lift...fly": Isa 40:31

ll.3-4   "Launch...sea": Ge 1:6-8 (the firmament, here "typic" of Heaven; the nautical metaphor for flight into the empyrean "among Circumference" is used in P798 and for "rowing" in "Paradise" in P249; see also P328)

ll.5-6   "Advocate...Eyes": De 33:26; Ps 24:7-9; 121:1; 123:1; Isa 45:8; 51:6; Jer 3:2; Joh 4:35 (the admonition or exhortation to lift up the "lower Eyes" to the fields, hills, or heavens appears repeatedly in the KJV; "Azure" may also fittingly be connected with the veil of the tabernacle and temple—see note, line one, P15)

l.8   "Paradise"; Lu 23:43; IICo 12:4; Rev 2:7 (like St. John the Divine, the speaker feels an "obligation" to share a higher, paradisiacal vision)

Comment: See *Poems*, III, 931-932.

1349   I'd rather recollect a setting

l.2   "sun": Nu 24:17; Mal 4:2; IIPe 1:19; Rev 1:16; 2:28; 21:23; 22:5, 16

Comment: See *Poems*, III, 932.

1351   You cannot take itself

l.2   "Human/living soul": Ge 2:7

ll.3-6   "That...behold": Ex 24:10; Isa 49:6; ITi 6:16; IJo 1:5 (God is Light and lives in Light; the Light lighting every man in the world is Christ, Joh 1:9; the "indestructible estate" for "any Human soul" is analogous to the condition of God: "Who only hath immortality, dwelling in the light which no man can approach unto,"

ITi 6:16; the children of light are the elect, IPe 2:9, who reign with God in Heaven, Rev 1:6; 22:5)

Comment: See *Poems*, III, 933.

1353 The last of Summer is Delight

l.3 "Ectasy's...Review": see note, line fifteen, P783 and note, lines five and eight, P1191

l.5 "nameless": Ge 32:29

l.6 "celestial Mail": Ex 19-20; 34 (perhaps a reference to a direct communication from God such as the giving of the Ten Commandments); Ex 28 (perhaps the reference is to the garments of Aaron that allowed entrance into the holy of holies)

ll.7-8 "Audacious...Vail": see note, lines five-eight, P915 (the Biblical reference suggests the boldness of entering the holy of holies into God's Presence without mediation or protective covering, a high priestly function, Ex 30:10; Nu 18:7; see also note, line one, P15)

Comment: See *Poems*, III, 934-935; *Letters*, II, 546-547; and Leyda, II, 243.

1355 The Mind lives on the Heart

ll.3-4 "If...fat": Mt 6:22 ("The light of the body is the eye: if therefore thine eye be single, thy whole body shall be full of light")

ll.4-5 (variant) "fat," "lean": Nu 13:20; Isa 10:16; 17:4

ll.5-6 (variant) "But...pine": Mt 6:23 ("But if thine eye be evil, thy whole body shall be full of darkness")

ll.7-8 (variant) "Throw/cast...Bone": Mt 7:6 ("Give not that which is holy unto the dogs, neither cast ye your pearls before swine, lest they trample them under their feet, and turn again and rend you"); Mt 15:26-27

Comment: See *Poems*, III, 936-937; Franklin, II, 1375; *Letters*, II, 546-547; and Leyda, II, 243.

1357 "Faithful to the end" Amended

ll.1-8 " 'Faithful'...Emolument/Yourself": Rev 2:10b (the change is not, perhaps, the textual emendation—"death" becoming "end"—but rather the deletion of the "Heavenly clause," the "base Proviso" that would reduce piety to moralism)

l.1   " 'Faithful'...Amended": Mt 24:13 ("But he that shall endure unto the end, the same shall be saved"); Rev 2:10b ("be then faithful unto death, and I will give thee a crown of life")

l.5   " 'Crowns'...Prizes": Jas 1:12 ("Blessed is the man that endureth temptation: for when he is tried, he shall receive the crown of life, which the Lord hath promised to them that love him"); Rev 2:10

l.7   "solely/Majesty": Heb 1:3; 8:1

l.7(version II) "fair": Ca 1:15-16; 2:10, 13; 4:1, 7, 10; 6:10; 7:6 (the Canticles word underscores the inaptness of "servile Prizes" in matters of faith, love, and beauty)

l.8(version II) "Yourself": Rev 1:11-20 (the speaker boldly suggests that the Son of Man, the Alpha and Omega, try on such a crown so crassly offered)

Comment: See *Poems*, III, 938-939; *Letters*, II, 546-547, 552; and Leyda, II, 243.

1358   The Treason of an accent

l.2(version I) "Ecstasy": see note, line fifteen, P783 and notes, lines five and eight, P1191

ll.1-2(version II) "Joy": IPe 1:8

l.3(version II) "rapture": see note, line seven, P1468

l.4(version II) "Sanctity...be": IJo 3:2-3; Rev 22:4 (the introduction to the Higginson version reads: "There is so much that is tenderly profane in even the sacredest Human Life—that perhaps it is instinct and not design, that dissuades us from it," *Letters*, II, 547)

Comment: That intuitive awareness of divine things is an unspeakable "Joy" or "Ecstasy" resisting transfer or recovery via linguistic means is apparently the theme of P1358. See *Poems*, III, 939; *Letters*, II, 547-548; and Leyda, II, 243-244.

1359   The long sigh of the Frog

ll.7-8   "inordinate...release": Ro 7:24; IICo 5:8

Comment: Traditional associations of the frog are with birth, the physical, and uncleanness (Rev 16:13). See *Poems*, II, 940; *Letters*, II, 553-554; and Leyda, II, 251-252.

1360 I sued the News- yet feared- the News

1.2   "Realm": IICo 5:2 ("Realm" is here heaven)

1.3   "The...was": IICo 5:1 ("For we know that if our earthly house of this tabernacle were dissolved, we have a building of God, an house not made with hands, eternal in the heavens"); see also note, line one, P725 and note, line one, P1142

1.4   "Thrown...me": Ps 118:19-20; Isa 22:22; 26:2; Rev 3:7-8; 21:27; 22:14

Comment: The "News" is perhaps that given to Nicodemus: "That which is born of the flesh is flesh; and that which is born of the Spirit is spirit" (Joh 3:6). See *Letters*, II, 552-553 for both P1360 and its connection to Nicodemus, spiritual rebirth, and the promise of the kingdom. See *Poems*, III, 940; *Letters*, II, 552-553; and Leyda, II, 249.

1361   The Flake the Wind exasperate

ll.1-2   "The...lie": Joh 3:8

Comment: See *Letters*, II, 560-561 where the poet paraphrases IICo 4:18 before quoting P1361. Both the letter and P1361 may be oblique, gentle rebukes of the conventional complacencies stemming from design arguments. See also Leyda, II, 255-256.

1362   Of their peculiar light

ll.1-4   "Of...by": Nu 24:17; Ca 6:10; Mal 4:2; IIPe 1:19; Rev 1:16; 2:28; 21:23; 22:5, 16 (associations are with the Sun/ Bridegroom and of the beloved with the sun and morning—two of the beloveds would be Mrs. Higginson and Mr. Dickinson)

Comment: See *Poems*, III, 941; *Letters*, II, 558-559; III, 919; and Leyda, II, 256.

1363   Summer laid her simple Hat

1.8   "The...Awe": Rev 22:4 (in P1733 "awe" is associated with that "very physiognomy" seen by Moses, thereby suggesting the face and presence of God; in P1620 "awe" is an affective ache for "Circumference" that "Bride of Awe"; in P1400 a "neighbor from another world" remains an "awe"-inspiring, ghostly presence mirrored in the "abyss's face" of the well; see also P575)

Comment: See *Poems*, III, 941-942; *Letters*, II,. 566-567; and Leyda, II, 259-260.

1364   How know it from a Summer's Day?

l.7   "Admonition": Heb 8:5 (the "Admonition" regards whether Indian summer suggests a "shadow of heavenly things")
Comment: See *Poems*, III, 943; *Letters*, II, 562-563; and Leyda, II, 258.

1365   Take all away-

l.3   "Is...Immortality": ICo 15:53-54
Comment: The language of P1365 may also echo some of the last words of the KJV, Rev 22:19. See *Poems*, III, 843-944; *Letters*, II, 551-552; and Leyda, II, 246.

1366   Brother of Ingots- Ah Peru-

l.1   "Ingots/Ophir": IKi 9:28; 10:11; ICh 29:4; IICh 8:18; 9:10; Job 22:24; 28:16; Ps 45:9; Isa 13:12 (noted for its gold, ivory, and silver, Ophir would have suggested both incalculable opulence and an exotic, faraway land; version three of P1366, relating to the death of Elihu Root, may make oblique reference to the length and dangers of the voyage to Ophir—see IKi 22:48)
Comment: See *Poems*, III, 944; *Letters*, II, 632; III, 682; and Leyda, II, 334.

1367   "Tomorrow"- whose location

ll.1-4   " 'Tomorrow'...leaves": Mt 6:34; Lu 12:16-21 (the parable of the rich man underscores the fact of the presentness of all time; "Tomorrow" consciousness is that "hallucination" tenaciously held by natural man in the circuit world; the radical contingency of all humanly experienced time is also emphasized—Jas 4:13-15—a time contingent upon the will of God)
ll.5-6   "Tomorrow...tare": Mt 13:24-30, 37-43 (the parable of the tares points to the apocalyptic burden of present time, suggesting that the owned finalities are those of the "Retriever" and not of the "Wise")

Comment: See *Letters*, II, 574-575 and Leyda, II, 266.

1368 Love's stricken "why"

l.1 " 'why' ": Mt 27:46 (see also P313)
Comment: See *Poems*, III, 945; *Letters*, II, 556; and Leyda, II, 252-253.

1369 Trusty as the stars

l.1 "Trusty...stars": Ge 1:16-18 (the simile refers to nature)
ll.3-4 "lit...home": Ge 1-2 ("Genesis' new home" may be the creation or, more specifically, the firmament)
Comment: See *Letters*, II, 568 and Leyda, II, 262.

1370 Gathered into the Earth,

ll.1,3 "Gathered": Rev 14:19
l.2 "And...story": Ps 90:9
l.4 "Glory": Mt 25:31; Lu 24:26; Jude 24; Rev 21:11, 23 (the presence of God)
l.5 "Awe": see note, line eight, P1363

1371 How fits his Umber Coat

l.2 "The...Nut": Mt 6:28-30 (the metaphor of God as the Weaver who spins and the Tailor who clothes underpins the first two stanzas)
l.3 "without a seam": Joh 19:23
l.4 "Raiment": Mt 6:28; Joh 19:24
l.5 "Who...Cloth": Job 38-42 (the question form echoes Job)
l.12 "undone": Isa 6:3-5 (Isaiah's vision of the glory of the "whole earth")

1372 The Sun is one- and on the Tare

l.1   "Sun": Nu 24:17; Ps 84:11; 89:36; Mal 4:2; IIPe 1:19; Rev 1:16; 2:28; 21:23; 22:5, 16 (the Sun/ Bridegroom, also Judge of great and small, Ac 10:42; IITi 4:1, 8; Rev 11:18; 20:12)

ll.1-4   "Tare...all": Mt 13:24-30, 37-43 (the apocalyptic overtones of judgment link P1371 to P1367; P1372, with its emblematic quality, may be profitably compared and contrasted with the Wadsworth sermon in Leyda, II, 261-262.

1373   The worthlessness of Earthly things

l.1   "Earthly things": Php 3:19

l.4   "Synods/Zion": Ps 9:11; 76:2; 137:3; Isa 60:14; Ro 11:26; Heb 12:22; Rev 14:1 (from the city of David to the New Jerusalem, Zion is the dwelling of God and His chosen people; here "Zion" is used metaphorically for one of the strands of nature's song—a song of inordinate delight)

l.4   "inordinate": Eze 23:11; Col 3:5

Comment: See *Poems*, III, 947. P1373 is aimed at senti-mental, anthropomorphic fictions straitjacketing "Nature." The "Ditty" of a "Nature" profligate in creative abundance beyond merely human fancies of design or proportion is a song of hardheaded realism. Nevertheless, the song of Zion is part of the medley of "Nature," but one whose "inordinate" suggests the incautious and uncontrolled.

1374   A Saucer holds a Cup

ll.5-6   "Table...King": ISa 20:29; IISa 9:7, 10-13; IKi 2:7; 4:27; 10:5 (the tables of David, Saul, and Solomon noted for abundance)

Comment: See *Poems*, III, 947-948.

1375   Death warrants are supposed to be

l.1   "Death warrants": Mr 15:13-14; Joh 19:6

l.4   "Idol's": Ex 20:4; Le 26:1

l.6   "Crucifix": Mt 27:35

Comment: See *Poems*, III, 948.

1376   Dreams are the subtle Dower

l.1   "Dreams...Dower": Ge 28:11-22; Ge 46:2-4 (Jacob's two experiences would suggest that dreams communicated God's messages—intimations from beyond the circuit world)

l.4   "Purple": see note, line one, P15 (the speaker is flung out of the holy of holies into the mundane light of common day)

Comment: See *Poems*, III, 949.

1377   Forbidden Fruit a flavor has

l.1   "Forbidden Fruit": Ge 2:16-17; 3:1-3, 11, 17 ("But of the tree of the knowledge of good and evil, thou shalt not eat of it: for in the day that thou eatest thereof thou shalt surely die," Ge 2:17)

l.2   "lawful Orchards": Ge 1:30; 2:9, 16-17 (prelapsarian Eden)

Comment: See *Poems*, III, 949.

1378   His Heart was darker than the starless night

ll.1-4   "His...dawn": Isa 14:12

Comment: Johnson describes the poem as rough and unfinished in *Poems*, III, 950. Lucifer as subject would account for much of the verbal play of P1378 as is, specifically the moral and astronomical lexicons.

1380   How much the present moment means

l.1   "present moment": Ro 8:18, 38; ICo 3:22; IICo 5:8-9; Ga 1:4; IITi 4:10; Heb 12:11 (the present as evil and as a potential idol saturates St. Paul's thinking, which finds in the Demas's mentality the exclusion of eternity and the reduction of all time to one dimension—as is also the case here with the poet's "Fop," "Carp," and "Atheist")

l.5   "Moment's...Rim": Job 21:13; 34:20; Lu 4:5

l.6   "commuted Feet": De 32:35 (the image is an Edwardsian one of walking in imminent danger of the pit)

ll.7-8   "The...inundate": Rev 1:15; 14:2; 16:3-5; 19:6 (the imagery of the inundating waters is apocalyptic, suggesting imminent judgment)

Comment: See *Poems*, III, 941, 951; *Letters*, III, 919; and Leyda, II, 256.

1381   I suppose the time will come

ll.1-4   "I...booming": Ca 2:12-13

1382   In many and reportless places

ll.1-4   "In...Deity": IPe 1:8
l.7   "sumptuous Destitution": Mt 5:6 (the paradoxical beatitude of Christ's preachments—the last first, the poor rich, the lost found, the hungry filled)
Comment: See *Poems*, III, 952.

1384   Praise it- 'tis dead-

l.1   "Praise...dead": Ec 4:2 ("Wherefore I praised the dead which are already dead more than the living which are yet alive")
l.6   "alabaster": Rev 2:17; 3:4-5, 18; 4:4; 6:11; 7:9, 13-14; 15:6; 19:8, 14; 20:11 (the Revelation color connects P1384 with the silent world of the "meek members of the Resurrection" in P216)
l.7   "Dust": Ge 3:19; Ps 103:14
Comment: See *Poems*, III, 953-954.

1385   "Secrets" is a daily word

ll.1-12   " "Secrets"...Sepulchre": Ec 12:14; Ro 2:16
Comment: Johnson notes that on the verso Dickinson wrote: "Let me go for the Day breaketh"(*Poems*, III, 954; Ge 32:26). Jacob will not allow the angel to go until he receives a new name, Israel, a clarification of his identity to go along with the divine blessing. It is tempting, though perhaps mere speculation, to read P1385 within the Genesis context, making the inference that the poem concerns matters of personal destiny.

1386   Summer- we all have seen-

ll.1-4   "Summer...loved": Joh 4:48; 6:30, 36, 40; 20:8, 29; IPe 1:8; IJo 4:16 (the progression of "seen," "believed," "loved" is a

KJV one usually applied in the relationship to God; here "Summer" is the unconcerned, distant object of adoration created by God—Ge 1:14; Ps 74:17—for the purpose of endowing embryonic ecstasies in such seeing and believing lovers as the speaker)

Comment: See *Poems*. III, 954-955.

1387   The Butterfly's Numidain Gown

l.2   "With...on": Eze 1:7b

Comment: See *Poems*, III, 956. For the associations of the butterfly with "Ecstasy" and "Immortality" see P1244, P1434, P1521, P1627, and P1685.

1388   Those Cattle smaller than a Bee

l.5   "Of blameless": Mt 6:26; Lu 12:24

l.13   "Of...calling": IIPe 1:10

l.14   "judge": Mt 7:1; Ac 10:42; IITi 4:1; Heb 12:23; Rev 11:18; 19:11; 20:12-13

l.16   "justify": Ac 13:39; Ro 3:24-30; 5:16-18; 8:30; Ga 2:16-17; 3:8, 24; Tit 3:7

l.16   "scourge": Isa 10:26; Mt 10:17; Ac 22:24-25; Heb 11:36; 12:6

Comment: See *Poems*, III, 956-957. The use of the lexicon of election, justification, and judgment for these Lilliputian "Cattle" reinforces the humor and hyperbole of P1388, while obliquely reminding that "Nature" is not in a congenial and convenient way amenable to human categories.

1390   These held their Wick above the West-

l.1   "These...West": Mt 25:7 ("Wick" is here synecdochic of soul and the "West" of that "Cottage" that is the body and bodily death)

ll.2-3   "Till...it": Ex 26:1, 31, 36; 27:16; 28:5-8, 15, 33; 35:6, 23, 25, 35;36:35;38:18, 23;Eze 1:4, 27;8:2 ("Red," as one of the colors of the vail, and "Amber" are both associated with vision and epiphany)

l.8   "Did...no": Php 1:23-24

Comment: In the context of *Letters*, II, 569, P1390 may be read as associating the year's "last flower" with human death as terminus—only the sunset promising renewal at dawn. In the context of *Letters*, II, 572, P1390 may be read autobiographically as concerned with the inevitable waning of literary prowess and fame with Tennyson and Browning as examples. In the context of *Letters*, II, 606, P1390 may be read as revelatory of the poet's double-mindedness about the soul's passing beyond the circuit world—the recent deaths of Edward Dickinson and Samuel Bowles as frame of reference. In this regard, a later letter to young Samuel Bowles regarding his father's "immortality" is also relevant (*Letters*, III, 667-668). In the context of *Letters*, III, 814-815, P1390 may be read as a Hitchcockian emblematic poem with sunset as the transition time giving rise to a generalized meditation on the soul's destiny. See also *Poems*, III, 957-958 and *Leyda*, II, 264, 288.

1392   Hope is a strange invention

l.1   "Hope...invention": Ro 4:18; 5:1-5; 8:20, 24-25; 15:13; ICo 13:13; 15:19-20; Heb 6:18-19; IPe 1:3, 21 (the confident expectation or trust is in the "electric Adjunct" not nature)

Comment: See *Letters*, II, 579-580 where the second stanza only is printed, two words altered, and the antecedent shifted from "Hope" to "Nature" creating a much different meaning of the final lines—a meaning reminiscent of P214's inebriation with "Nature." Nevertheless, as printed in the variorum, P1392 is a Paulinian faith poem—"Hope" a Christian basic frequently combined by St. Paul with faith. See also *Poems*, III, 959-960 and *Leyda*, II, 270.

1393   Lay this Laurel on the One

l.2   "Too...Renown": Ge 6:4
l.4   "Him...chasten": Ps 94:12; Heb 12:6; Rev 3:19
l.4   "it...He": Joh 19:5

Comment: See the discussion in *Poems*, III, 960-962; *Letters*, II, 583; and *Leyda*, II, 274.

1394   Whose Pink career may have a close

ll.1-2   "Whose...knows": IPe 1:24

ll.3-4   "To...meet": Mt 6:27-32
Comment: See *Letters*, II, 583 and Leyda, II, 274.

1395   After all Birds have been investigated and laid aside-

l.2   "Blue": see note, line eight, P703 (since in the bluebird-March poem P1213 purple and blue are associated, see also note, line one, P15 and note, line three, P716)

l.4   "ostensible Vicissitude": Heb 11:3

l.5   "March": see note, line ten, P1213

Comment: The "Blue-Bird" apparently is the poet's New England-acclimated, Keatsian nightingale—see P1465 and P1530 and the discussion in *Poems*, III, 963-965. See also *Letters*, II, 588 and Leyda, II, 278.

1396   She laid her docile Crescent down

l.1   "She...down": Mt 11:29-30; Ga 6:5 (the "Crescent" may be her cross or burden or perhaps a synecdoche for the body)

l.7   "Constancy": Rev 2:10 (the deceased "She" is that "Constancy" rewarded by the crown implied by the incomplete "Crescent" of the first line)

l.8   "Before...flew": Rev 10:6 (the "Shaft" or arrow of time is the circuit world "emblem" of "Constancy"; the Biblical with of stanza two turns upon the speaker's self-conscious awareness that only a time whose trajectory is in the final analysis as incomplete as the "docile Crescent" can give temporary and ironic significance to "News" and "stolid trust")

Comment: See the discussion of the text in *Poems*, III, 965-966. See also *Letters*, II, 588 and Leyda, II, 278.

1397   It sounded as if the Streets were running

ll.1-2   "It...still": Rev 1:15; 4:5; 6:1;8:5;10:3-4; 11:19; 14:2;16:18; 19:6 (the sound of waters, thunder, and lightnings is apocalyptic)

l.3   "Eclipse...Window": Rev 6:12; 9:2; 21:23; 22:5 (although "Eclipse" may refer to the apocalyptic status of sun and moon, it may simply be synecdochic for darkness)

l.4   "And...feel": see note, line eight, P1363

l.5   "By...Covert": Rev 6:15
l.6   "To...these": Rev 10:6
l.7   "Opal/Bluest/Beryl": Ex 28:20; Ca 5:14; Eze 28:13; Da 10:6; Rev 21:20; see also note, line eight, P703

Comment: There would be Biblical precedent for treating the gale or storm as a divine revelation (Ex 19:16-22; Ps 18:7-15; Hab 3:3-16). See *Poems*, III, 967-968; *Letters*, II, 588; and Leyda, II, 278.

1398   I have no Life but this-

l.5   "Earths...come": Rev 21:1
ll.1-8   "I...you": Ps 73:23-28 (since the poet wrote having in memory a Psalm to God, other possibilities might be as follows: Ps 26; 27; 46; 48; 84; 91; 103; 139; the language of the poem also echoes Ro 8:38-39)

Comment: See the discussion in Sewall, 510-511; *Poems*, III, 968-969; *Letters*, II, 589-590; and Leyda, II, 278.

1399   Perhaps they do not go so far

ll.3-4   "lapse...clothes": ICo 15:53
l.5   "It...certainly": ICo 13:12

Comment: See *Poems*, III, 969-970; *Letters*, II, 590; and Leyda, II, 253.

1400   What mystery pervades a well!

ll.1-4   "What...jar": Ge 16:14; 29:2; Nu 21:17-20; Pr 5:15; 10:11; Ca 4:15; Joh 4:6-14 (associations of the well and its water/mirror with the magical and spiritual are not necessarily Biblical, although a number of figurative usages and connections of the well with God's gifts are germane for P1400; so also is the Canticles metaphor of the beloved as a well of living waters)
ll.5-6   "Whose...glass": Ex 33:20-23
ll.7-8   "Like...face": Ge 1:2; ICo 13:12 (see note, line three, P1238; the "deep" as the abyss or primordial chaos relates the "lid of glass" to the "floorless" sea; for other relevant uses of "abyss" see P291, P546, and P599)
l.12   "At...me": see note, line eight, P1363
l.14   "The...sea": Ge 1:2

ll.19-20 "Have...ghost": see *Letters*, II, 554

ll.23-24 "That...get": Joh 14:9; ICo 13:9-12

Comment: P1400 works on several levels, suggesting that the "lid of glass" within the well is perhaps the face of Susan, nature, or God. See *Poems*, III, 970-972; *Letters*, II, 598; and Leyda, II, 285.

1401   To own a Susan of my own

l.3   "Whatever...forfeit": Rev 21-22 (an awareness that whatever Heaven is, it will be forfeited by the idolatry expressed in the poem)

l.3   "forfeit": Ex 20:3-6

l.3   "Lord": Ge 2:4-Rev 22:21 (the title used thousands of times in the KJV for God and Jesus Christ and here suggesting that P1401 is a prayer of sorts)

Comment: Although apparently a jeu d'esprit, a mock prayer with comic hyperbole, P1401 may have had the more serious rhetorical intent of placating the poet's sister-in-law. See *Letters*, II, 598-599.

1402   To the stanch Dust

l.1   "To...Dust": Ge 2:7; 3:19;Job 7:21; 10:9; 17:16; 20:11; 21:26; 30:19; 34:15; 42:6; Ps 22:15, 29;103:14; 104:29

l.2   "We...thee": *Book of Common Prayer*, "Burial of the Dead. At the Grave" reads: "Unto Almighty God we commend the soul of our brother departed, and we commit his body to the ground; earth to earth, ashes to ashes, dust to dust; ..."

l.3   "Tongue/guile": Ps 22:15; 32:2; Rev 14:5

l.6   "Sanctity/firmament...enforce/salute": Ge 1:6-8; Ps 19:1; 150:1; Eze 1:22-26; 10:1; Da 12:3 (apart from and in addition to the apocalyptic resonance, the contrast of the responsive firmament to that in the final lines of P216 is of note)

Comment: See *Poems*, III, 972-973.

1403   My Maker- let me be

l.1   "My Maker": Job 4:17; 35:10; 36:3; Ps 95:6; Pr 22:2; Isa 45:9, 11;51:13;Heb 11:10

l.2   "Enamored...thee": Ca 1:2-4; 2:2-4; 4:1, 7, 10;6:4; 7:6;8:6 (the variant readings for line two suggest the greater distance

needed from Sue in order to avoid missing the "more" of line four—
perhaps in reference to loss of Heaven for reasons of idolatry)

　　l.4　　"more": IICo 4:17
　　Comment: See *Poems*, III, 973.

1404　March is the Month of Expectation

　　l.1　　"March...Expectation": Ca 2:11-13
　　l.2　　"The...know": ICo 13:9-12
　　l.3　　"Persons/transports/Treasures...prognostication": see
note, line fifteen, P783 and notes, lines five and eight, P1191
　　l.6　　"But...Joy": IPe 1:8
　　ll.7-8　　"first...Boy": Rev 19:6-9
　　Comment: A passage-transition poem in which nature yields
her epiphany ("transports" and "prognostication"), P1404 pushes
toward personification ("Persons"-"We"-"Boy") while obliquely
hinting ("Month of Expectation" and "Betrothal") at the Canticles-
Bride of Christ significance of this experience of March. See *Poems*,
III, 974-975.

1405　Bees are Black, with Gilt Surcingles

　　l.5　　"Fuzz...contingent": Ac 13:48; IPe 1:20 (their
function as "Marrows of the Hill" is here treated with the mock gravity
of the Biblical "ordained" and the philosophical necessary-contingent
contrast, suggesting that "Fuzz" has an adaptation in nature as well as
in poetic comic rhyme)
　　Comment: See *Poems*, III, 975; *Letters*, II, 549, 581-582; and
Leyda, II, 271.

1406　No Passenger was known to flee-

　　ll.1-4　　"No...again": Ec 9:5
　　Comment: See *Poems*, III, 976 and Leyda, II, 266.

1407　A Field of Stubble, lying sere

　　l.1　　"Stubble": Isa 47:14; Joe 2:5; Zep 2:2; Mal 4:1; Mt
3:12; Lu 3:17; (Biblical chaff or stubble is associated with the
apocalyptic and time's passage)

l.6 "Alms": Mt 6:1-4; Lu 11:41; 12:33; Ac 9:36 (the only hint of that sacramental language so evident in two other well-known Indian summer poems, P130 and P1068)

Comment: See *Poems*, III, 976-977; *Letters*, II, 577; III, 919; and Leyda, II, 268-269.

1408   The Fact that Earth is Heaven-

ll.1-2 "Heaven": Ps 115:3; 123:1; Isa 6:1; 66:1; Mt 6:9; Ac 7:49; Heb 8:1; Rev 21:1 (the place where God dwells, the object of that apocalyptic hope here treated with irony and paradox)

ll.5-6 "Not...us": ICo 15:47-49

l.8 "To...place": Rev 3:10; 6:10; 11:10; 12:12;13:6, 8, 14; 14:6; 17:8 ("dwell in heaven" and "dwell on earth" are frequently used in Revelation)

Comment: Addressed to her brother, P1408 presents earth as paradise (Ge 2-3; Eze 28:13-14;31:8-9, 16;47:1-12; Rev 2:7; 21-22), a notion frequently repeated in congratulatory letters to her married friends. See *Poems*, III, 977-978.

1409   Could mortal lip divine

l.1 "mortal": Ro 6:12; ICo 15:53; IICo 4:11 (this Paulinian word contrasts effectively with the matter of the discarded second stanza in the semifinal draft)

l.1 "divine": Ge 44:15; Pr 16:10

ll.2-3 "undeveloped...syllable": Joh 1:1

l.7(rough draft) "Tabernacles...Minds": Ex 40; Ps 46:4; Joh 1:14; IICo 5:1-8; Heb 9:11; Rev 21:3 (the mind as tabernacle suggests the presence of God—a presence that is the "undeveloped Freight" of language)

l.8(rough draft) "Truth": Joh 14:6

Comment: See *Poems*, III, 978-979. In miniature, P1409 gives the philosophy of language displacements of a mind acutely aware of the tenuous, slippery, and fragile in that lexicon incommensurate with the weighty "Truth" of "Unknown Zones."

1410   I shall not murmur if at last

ll.1-4 "I...so": ICo 13:12

ll.1-3(rough draft) "We...stain": Ex 33:20-23; Rev 22:4

Comment: "He has hid his rare life/From our gross eyes," the poet writes in P338. As His creatures were God's dream estate, so also were Emily Dickinson's friends to her—friends to be imagined or verbally contacted at that distance guaranteeing stainless "Adoration," worship without diminution. So P1410 is part of the theodicy of her poetry—an oblique defense of the Hidden, which in the suspension of the world of dream-imagination is at least potentially real. Thus, the protocols of Dickinson's friendships were not unrelated to the agonies and ecstasies felt in the "little circuit" because of the distances imposed by the faceless Deus absconditus. See the discussion in Johnson, 53-54; *Poems*, III, 979-980; and Leyda, II, 272.

1411   Of Paradise' existence

l.1   "Of...existence": Ge 2-3; Eze 28:13-14; 31:8-9, 16; 47:1-12; Lu 23:43; IICo 12:4; Rev 2:7; 21-22

ll.5-6   "Bisecting Messenger": Ge 3:19 (death as that which separates from earthly paradise and life); Joh 1:1 (the Incarnate Word bisecting heaven and earth, life and death); ICo 15:22, 45-47 (the Lord bisects Adam)

1412   Shame is the shawl of Pink

l.1   "Shame...Pink": Ge 3:7-11 (the Fall makes Adam and Eve aware of their "Shame," which is then covered by "aprons"); Job 8:22; Ps 35:26; 109:29; 132:18 (to be "clothed with shame" is a frequent KJV figurative usage)

ll.1,4   "Shawl," "Veil": Ge 24:65; Ru 3:15; Ca 5:7 (the "shawl" may suggest the eligibility of the beloved and therefore may anticipate the dress of the Bride of Christ in Revelation); Ex 34:33-35 (the shawl or veil enshrouds the glory of God radiating from Moses' face); Ex 26:32-33; 30:6; 39:34; Le 24:3; IICh 3:14 (the shawl may suggest the veil of the temple); Heb 10:20 (the veil is the flesh)

l.1   "Pink": Ex 26:31 (scarlet is the color of the veil); Lu 22:44; Heb 6:6; 12:2 (the color of Christ's bodily "Shame" in His Passion and Crucifixion)

l.3   "infesting Eyes": the "no other way" of P327 and the "gross eyes" of P338 l.8 "Shame...divine": Ge 3 (self-conscious awareness of shame is distinctively human); Lu 22:44; Heb 6:6; 12:2 (the "tint divine" because associated with Christ's Passion and Crucifixion); Rev 3:18; 16:15 ("Shame" impels the elect to secure the necessary white raiment worn in Heaven)

1413   Sweet Skepticism of the Heart-

l.1 "Sweet...Heart": Ca 2:3, 14; 3:11; 4:9; 5:2, 5, 13, 16; 7:9;8:6 (the "Balm" of "Sweet Skepticism" is treated as the beloved in the oxymoronic lexicon of Ca 8:6)
l.3 "Balm": Ge 37:25;Ca 1:13-14; 4:14; 5:13; 7:13; Jer 8:22; 46:11 (see also note, line three, P1144; note, line six, P1337; and note, line four, P1341)
l.5 "Truth": Joh 14:6
l.7 "delicious": Ca 2:3
ll.7-8 "Compared...Fear": see P135, P148, and P167 (here "transport" and the Gethsemane of the little circuit's Passion are treated in terms of her philosophy of deprivation); P256 and P1000 ("transport" may be associated with an adumbration of the beatific vision—a glimpse of the "Savior's face" or of the "easy Guest"); P984 ("transport" may be associated with the resurrection, ICo 15); P313 (the idea of justification by "Fear")

1414   Unworthy of her Breast

l.1 "Unworthy...Breast": Ca 1:13; 4:5; 7:3, 7-8; 8:1, 8, 10 (a figurative usage signifying acceptance by the idealized mother, the New Eve, into the New Jerusalem)
l.2 "scathing test": Rev 12:17
l.4 "By...light": Rev 12:1
l.5 "How...white": Rev 19:8 (the white dress of the speaker is "counterfeit" when compared with the raiment of the New Eve)
Comment: Using figurative language, P1414 speaks of the ideal New Jerusalem much as Heaven is spoken of as Abraham's bosom in the Gospel of Luke (Lu 16:22).

1415   A wild Blue sky abreast of Winds

l.3   "Door": Ps 78:23

Comment: P1415 owes a general indebtedness perhaps to personification found in the Psalms (e.g., Ps 19). The "arrogant campaign" of the "upper friends" is that very freedom of nature from the pathetic fallacy so evident in P1415's attempt to collapse the distance between perceiver and perceived.

1416   Crisis is sweet and yet the Heart

l.1   "Crisis": ICo 15 (see also note, line one, P889; metaphorically, "Crisis" in P1416 is the full flower of the "Rose" before its being "surrendered," "rescinded," or "Expended" and thus it may symbolize death or a zenith-apogee crossover point—the juncture of the "little circuit" and the "new circumference")

l.1   "sweet...Heart": Ca 2:3, 14; 3:11; 4:9; 5:2, 5, 13, 16; 8:6 ("Crisis" is treated as the beloved's yielding "Dowers of Prospective" on this "little circuit" "hither side" of the budding "proudest Rose")

l.7   "transport/rapture": see note, lines seven-eight, P1413

Comment: The ambience of the unfinished P1416 is that of the second chapter of Canticles. The preference of the ideally circumferential "proudest Rose" for the "transport of the Bud" is emblematic (the "Hour of her Bud" echoes phrasing of the KJV used for the last hours of Christ—Mt 26:40, 45, 55; 27:45-46; Joh 12:23, 27; 13:1; 16:21, 32; 17:1). Like the "Sweet Skepticism" of P1414, "Crisis" is a sweet lover from the organic point of view of the circuit world. See *Poems*, III, 982-983.

1417   How Human Nature dotes

ll.1-6   "How...know": ICo 13:12

ll.11-12 "Where...anywhere": Ec 11:5; Joh 3:8; 13:36; 16:5 (the "Redoubtablest" question regards the final destiny of the speaker)

l.13   "Creation...this": Ge 1-2; Rev 3:14; 4:11 (the "Creation" beyond the circuit world would be an apocalyptic guaranteed by the creative Word)

Comment: See *Poems*, III, 983. Like the "Sweet Skepticism" of P1413 and the "Crisis" of P1416, the "Prospective" of P1417 befriends a "Human Nature" that sees through a glass darkly and knows only in part in this circuit world. Paradoxically enough, in P1417 "meaning" is the unfinished story, the unanswered question allowing the speaker to stave off the potential unmeaning of the apocalyptic.

1418   How lonesome the Wind must feel Nights-

ll.1-12 "How...Tall": Ge 1:1-2; 8:1; IIKi 2:11, 16; Job 38:1; 40:6; Ps 135:7; 147:18; Pr 30:4; Jer 10:13; 14:6; 22:22; Eze 1:4; 8:3; 11:1; 37:9; Hos 13:15; Am 4:13; Joh 3:8; Ac 2:2-4 (the wind is associated with manifestations of the Spirit in, for example, God's Creation in Genesis, the theophanies in Job and Acts, and in the translation of Elijah in II Kings; figurative usages abound in the KJV but apparently no such extended personification as P1418)

ll.9-11 "How...Espousing": Ex 10:19; Job 19:12; Ps 27:3; 34:7; 50:10; Ca 3:11; Jer 2:2; Ac 2:2; Rev 6:13 (the word choice echoes the KJV)

l.12   "Temple": Ps 11:4; Hab 2:20; Rev 7:15; 16:1, 17; 21:22 (the habitation of God)

Comment: See *Poems*, III, 984.

1419   It was a quiet seeming Day-

l.4   "accidental Red": Ex 26:31-36; 35:6, 23, 25, 35; 36:35 (the veil, the appurtenances of the tabernacle, and the priestly garb all contained scarlet; the associations of the veil with the holy of holies and thus with God's Presence is directly relevant since the sunset transition occasions an epiphany)

ll.7-11 "But...Cloud": Rev 6:12-17 (in P1419 the language for sunset and departing light is that of cataclysm in the cosmos, the apocalyptic day of the Lord or of God's wrath)

l.10   "Awe": see note, line eight, P1363

ll.11-12 "As...Cloud": Joe 2:10, 31; 3:15; Mt 24:29; Ac 2:19-21; Rev 6:12 (one of the apocalyptic phenomena was the moon's turning to blood; the poet apparently rejected the phenomenon of the lightning, Mt 24:27; see *Poems*, III, 985)

Comment: See *Poems*, III, 984-985 and *Letters*, II, 598.

1420   One Joy of so much anguish

l.1   "Joy": IPe 1:8

l.1(variant) "Sound": ICo 15:52

l.2   "Sweet": Ca 2:3, 14; 5:5, 13, 16

l.4   "iniquity": Ex 20:5 (the suggestion is of idolatrous attraction)

l.5   "Birds": Ca 2:12 (associated with the advent of the beloved)

l.6(variant) "Red": see note, line one, P15

l.6(variant) "shouts": ITh 4:16

l.6   "Quick": Joh 6:63; ICo 15:45 (the word may reinforce the spiritual, "typic" dimension of the experience)

l.6   "Day": Ca 3:11; Mt 24:36; Ac 1:7; ITh 5:2; IIPe 3:10 (the associations may be with the beloved and with the apocalyptic)

l.7   "ravished": Ca 4:9

ll.11-12 "When...Immediately": ICo 15:50-55 ("Death's Immediately" is that change in "a moment in the twinkling of an eye" when "this corruptible must put on incorruption")

l.11   "When...sunder": Heb 4:12 ("For the word of God is quick, and powerful, and sharper than any two-edged sword, piercing even to the dividing asunder of soul and spirit")

Comment: See *Poems*, III, 985-986. The landscape of P1420 pushes toward the Hitchcockian with its emblematic "Quick of Day" and "Dirks of Melody"—predawn intimations of the Beyond bringing the poet ravishing, unspeakable "Joy."

1421   Such are the inlets of the mind-

l.3   "eminence/Table Land": Jos 13:15-21; Isa 40:4; Zec 14:10-11 (the "Table Land" or plain has apocalyptic overtones suggesting the New Jerusalem)

l.4   "immortality": ICo 15:53-54

Comment: See *Poems*, III, 986.

1422   Summer has two Beginnings-

ll.1,2,3 "Beginnings," "Beginning": Rev 1:8; 21:6; 22:13

l.6   "Grace": Joh 1:14-17; Ro 5; Rev 1:4; 22:21 (the unmerited favor of God is here the Indian summer "Beginning" of October, emblematic of rebirth to a higher life)

ll.7-8   "As...Face": Ex 33:2-23; Rev 22:4 (the "going" "Face" of "Summer" is a "finer" one since it adumbrates the beatific vision of ideal face-to-face Presence; see the discarded lines of P1410, *Poems*, III, 979)

ll.9,10,11 "forever," "Forever,": Rev 1:6; 4:9-10; 5:13-14; 7:12; 10:6; 11:15; 15:7; 22:5 (the language of beginnings as initiations of an atemporal "Forever" beyond the green "Riot" of a recurrent "Summer"—the circuit world's "Forever is deciduous"—is taken from Revelation)

l.12   "Except...die": ICo 15:50-55

Comment: P1422 should be compared with other Indian summer poems: P130, P1068, and P1407.

1423   The fairest Home I ever knew

l.1   "fairest": Ca 1:8; 5:945 6:1

l.1   "Home": Job 8:14 (the insubstantiality of the web is at the heart of its beauty); see also P725 and note, line one, P1142 (the dwelling of the beloved spun from within by the "spider")

l.4   "spider": see notes, lines six and nine, P1138

l.4   "Flower": Ca 2:1, 16; 4:5; 5:13; 6:2-3; 7:2

l.5   "mechlin...Floss": Rev 19:8 (the clothing of the "Parties" anticipates Revelation)

Comment: See *Poems*, III, 987; *Letters*, II, 597; and Leyda, II, 284. In P1423, the artist-spider creates a "fairest Home" upon the ideally circumferential "Flower," here perhaps symbolic of that estate comprised of her circuit world friends.

1424   The Gentian has a parched Corolla-

l.1   "The...Corolla": Job 14:2; Ps 103:15; Isa 28:1, 4; IPe 1:24 (flowers are frequently the bases of figurative usages)

l.2   "azure": see note, line one, P15 and note, line eight, P703

ll.3-4   " 'Tis...Beatified": Rev 22:4 (the "Corolla" of the flower "Beatified" becomes the seal, crown, and face of Revelation)

ll.16-17 "Fidelity...o'er": IITi 4:7 (the "Truth" taught by the "Gentian" transcends its own conditions, synecdochically "Creation")

Comment: See *Poems*, III, 987-988. The poet's fringed gentian, among other things, is St. Paul who finishes the course steadfastly keeping the faith (the poet rejects four alternatives before choosing one of St. Paul's favorite words in the thirteenth line—"Abundant"). As an Hitchcockian nature poem, P1424 presents the gentian as emblematic of "Fidelity," its ideally circumferential "Fringed career" adumbrating the new circumference world of seal and crown (Rev 22:4).

1425   The inundation of the Spring

l.1   "The...Spring": Job 5:10; Ps 65:9-10; Ho 6:3 (in resurrection "Spring," the theophanic flooding sweeps the body away leaving the soul in a shoreless "Water"—the Melvillian landsman weened by terror from "aught Peninsular")
l.4   "But...whole": Joh 4:6-14; Rev 21:6; 22:1-2, 17 (the complete whole of the "Water"-soul contrasts with the incomplete "Peninsula"-body)
ll.5-8   "In...Peninsula": Joh 3:5-6
Comment: See *Poems*, III, 988-989. The "Mind without corporeal friend" or "Water whole" learns from the theophany of "Spring" to become "acclimated" to a world beyond "little circuit," "Peninsular" desires.

1426   The pretty Rain from those sweet Eaves

ll.1-2   "sweet...Eyes": Ca 1:15; 2:3, 14; 4:1, 9; 5:5, 12-13, 16; 6:5; 7:4; 8:10
ll.3-4   "Took...Surprise": Ca 3:11; 4:9; 8:6
l.8   "Was...Crown": Ca 3:11; Rev 2:10; 4:4 (the ideally circumferential tear is the crown of the beloved)
Comment: The conventional iconography of the weeping widow (e.g., Job 27:15; Rev 18:7) may be behind P1426.

1427 To earn it by disdaining it

ll.1-4   "To...thee": Mt 5:3-12 (the paradoxical Beatitudes philosophy of destitution as a higher plenitude is behind this treatment of temporal "Fame")
l.8   "Honor": Joh 5:44; IITi 2:20

1428   Water makes many Beds

ll.1-8 "Water...comes": Joh 3:5-8 ("Water," synecdochic of those white elect born of the spirit, has as habitation an "awful chamber" and "undulating Rooms" unconfined by space and time— "end" or "clock"—and lacking the certain reference point of an "Axis"; thus, P1428 treats with greater detachment and equanimity issues at the heart of the Master letters, issues dealt with in a modernist way by Stevens's Ulysses in "The Presence of an External Master of Knowledge")

Comment: See Poems, III, 990.

1429   We shun because we prize her Face

ll.1-3 "We...stain": Ex 33:20-23; Rev 22:4 (see the discussion of these lines in P1410)

Comment: See *Poems*, III, 979-980, 991 and Leyda, II, 272.

1430   Who never wanted- maddest Joy

ll.1-3 "Who...Abstemiousness": Mt 5:6 (the Beatitudes philosophy of hunger as paradoxically a "Banquet"; the "maddest Joy" is the product of circuit world deferral, IPe 1:18)

l.4 "Defaces...Wine": Mt 26 (perhaps the "Banquet of Abstemiousness" replaces the Communion, adumbrating Rev 19:7-9)

ll.5-8 "Within...soul": Php 3:7-14 (the second stanza restates the philosophy of "Abstemiousness" in terms of St. Paul and Browning's "Andrea del Sarto")

Comment: See *Poems*, III, 991.

1431   With Pinions of Disdain

ll.1-4 "With...Ornithology": Ps 11:1; 55:6; 90:10; Isa 40:31

l.1 "Disdain": Ro 7:24; IICo 5:4; Php 3:21 (presumably a "Disdain" of the body prison)

l.5 "sordid Flesh": ICo 15:39, 50

l.7 "electric gale": see note, line fifteen, P783; notes, lines five and eight, P1191; note, lines seven-eight, P1413 (the experience is variously spoken of as delight, joy, transport, and ecstasy—an experience involving exultation and heightened, epiphanic awareness)

      l.8   "The...soul": ICo 15:42-44 (the "electric gale" instructs the poet insofar as is possible in that mysterious change in the twinkling of an eye spoken of by St. Paul—"body is a soul," an experience "typic" of the Resurrection)

      ll.10-12 "How...immortality": ICo 15:50-55

      Comment: See *Poems*, III, 992.

1432   Spurn the temerity-

      l.2   "Rashness...Calvary": Lu 23:33
      l.3   "Gay...Gethsemane": Mt 26:36

      Comment: See *Poems*, III, 992-993; *Letters*, II, 638-639; and Leyda, II, 300. The Biblical allusions add to the bold hyperbole of P1432.

1433   How brittle are the Piers

      l.2   "On...tread": Heb 11:1
      ll.5-6   "It...him": Heb 11:3
      l.7   "He...Son": Joh 3:17; 17:3, 18-25
      ll.7-8   "He...firm": Heb 12:2 (the associations of "Plank" with the cross—Mt 27:32, 40, 42—may make these lines bittersweet, thereby connecting P1433 with such other "Plank" poems as P280, P875, P1142, and P1264; a "Plank" is an overcrowded and incomplete "Bridge," hardly a complacent symbol for "Faith")

      Comment: See *Poems*, III, 993-994; *Letters*, II, 610-611; and Leyda, II, 293.

1434   Go not too near a House of Rose-

      l.1   "Go...Rose": Ca 2:1 (the ideally circumferential "Rose," the beloved, yields its joy only in the space of insecurity—a distance without possession)

      l.6   "Ecstasy": see note, line fifteen, P783; notes, lines five and eight, P1191; note, line seven, P1413; and note, line seven, P1431

      l.8   "Joy's...quality": IPe 1:8

Comment: In P1434 neither proximity nor possession nor for that matter striving itself should violate God's ordained "insecurity"— a certain uncertainty perhaps comparable to that "certain Mystery" G.M. Hopkins spoke of as God. The "Go not" of P1434 is a directive revealing of the poet and should be contrasted with more assertive approaches (Frost's "Directive," for example) and the more "masculine" tradition she inherited of the Apostolic Commission (Mr 16:15). The "insecurity" of line seven should be compared with the "sweet Skepticism" of P1413, the "Crisis" of P1416, and the "Banquet of Abstemiousness" of P1430. See *Letters*, II, 614, especially for the Biblical context of the letter to Mrs. Tuckerman (Joh 3:6: "That which is born of the flesh is flesh; and that which is born of the Spirit is spirit").

1435   Not that he goes- we love him more

l.1   "Not...more": Joh 16:5
l.3   "Beyond...frontier": Rev 21-22 (the reference to the "Gem" chapter in the letter to Mrs. Bowles suggests that P1435 relates to the last chapters of Revelation)
l.4   "moved": Ge 1:2
l.4   "made": Ge 1:7, 16, 25-26, 31; 2:2-4, 9, 18, 22; 3:1 (the wording of line four suggesting the Creator God reveals the poet's view of Samuel Bowles—he was a divine, creative influence who "led us while he stayed")
Comment: See *Poems*, III, 994-995; *Letters*, II, 601-602; and Leyda, II, 287-288.

1436   Than Heaven more remote,

l.2   "Heaven...root": Rev 5:5; 22:16
l.3   "But...seed": ICo 15:38, 42-44 (perhaps these lines on the "root" and "seed" owe something to St. Paul's discussion of the seed of the corruptible body, which must be planted in death; Jesus' preachments frequently use husbandry metaphors, such as the vine and branches, the sower planting seed, or the grain of mustard seed, with apocalyptic overtones; however, the "fitted seed" here seems to refer to specific lost beloveds who have "flown indeed," who are distanced, deaf, and silent)
l.10   "They...praise": Ps 115:17

ll.14-16 "But...too": ICo 15:50-55

1437   A Dew sufficed itself-

l.1   "Dew": Ex 16:13-15; Nu 11:9; Jg 6:37-40; Job 38:28; Ca 5:2; Ho 14:5; Zec 8:12 (the Biblical associations of the "Dew" are of a special providential design and purpose and of the importance of the individual in such a relationship with the heavens; in P1437, the "Dew" is the ideally circumferential as experienced evanescently in nature, the substitute face of God, and a persona representing those blind to the radical incommensurability of human consciousness with the external world, an obliquity presented in somewhat different guise in P290; see also, note, line one, P513)

l.8   "Physiognomy": see P1138, P1499, and P1733 (the suggestion is that the face-to-face relationship with the "Dew" has been lost)

l.15   "By...instability": see note, lines seven-eight, P1413 and note, line six, P1434 (the supports of the "transparent eyeball" are as wobbly and insubstantial as Cranch had depicted; P1437 is every bit as devestating a caricature with its mawkish hyperbole—"awful Tragedy"—and its subtle imputation that, scrutinized, Emersonian correspondences crumble into "Hope's Necrology")

Comment: See *Poems*, III, 995-998 and Franklin, II, 1357-1358.

1438   Behold this little Bane-

ll.1-8   "Behold...found": Ca 5:7-8; 8:6-7

l.7   "Paradise": Ge 2-3; Eze 28:13-14; 31:8-9, 16; 47:1-12; Lu 23:43; IICo 12:4; Rev 2:7; 21-22

1439   How ruthless are the gentle

l.3   "God...Lamb": Joh 1:29, 36; IPe 1:19; Rev 5:6, 8, 12-13; 12:1; 19:7-9; 21:22-23; 22:1(Jesus Christ, the Lamb, has the "gentle" and "kind" traits of the Godhead, here treated oxymoronically); Mt 3:13-17 (perhaps the "contract" is the baptism of Jesus broken in Gethsemane, Mt 26:36-46, and at the Crucifixion, Mt 27)

1.4　　　"To...Wind": Ac 2:2 (God puts in office, after the contract with the Lamb is broken, the Holy Spirit; in the Gospel of John, the Holy Spirit is termed the Comforter, Joh 14:16, 26; 15:26; nevertheless, the poet was aware of the evanescence and intermittence of corroboration from this "Wind" of the Godhead, Joh 3:8; a rational theodicy might insist upon a Shepherd "to qualify" as replacement for the absent "Lamb" but the oxymoronic faces of God are not amenable to such focusing by conventional and convenient human categories)

1440　　The healed Heart shows it's shallow scar

1.4　　　"Are...torn": Mt 27:35; Joh 19:23 (the Biblical echo reinforces the idea of the circuit world as the Passion in P1440)

1441　　These Fevered Days- to take them to the Forest

1.2　　　"Where...crawl": Ge 3:8; Ps 23:2
1.3　　　"And...stillness": Ps 121:5

1442　　To mend each tattered Faith

ll.1-8　　"To...before": Isa 61:10; Mt 6:28-30; IICo 5:2-7; Heb 11:1 (the metaphor of clothing and its associations with "Faith" may anticipate the white raiment worn by the elect in the New Jerusalem, Rev 3:5, 18; 7:9; 19:7-9)

1443　　A chilly Peace infests the Grass

1.4　　　"shadows": Job 14:2; Ps 109:23 (the phrase "shadow of death" appears frequently in the KJV, e.g., Ps 23:4)
1.7　　　"But...here": Job 7:9; Ps 6:5; Ec 9:10
Comment: See *Poems*, III, 1000 and *Letters*, III, 925.

1444　　A little Snow was here and there

1.4　　　"Decade...Decade": Ec 1:5
1.6　　　"Impregnable...Rose": Ca 2:1 (the beloved as the ideally circumferential rose)
Comment: See *Poems*, III, 1001 and Leyda, II, 300.

1445   Death is the supple Suitor

l.1   "Death...Suitor": ICo 15:54-55 (as "supple Suitor" "Death" is both the first Adam and the last, ICo 15:45-47, a profane lover as in Canticles and the Bridegroom of Rev 19, both needed since "flesh and blood cannot inherit the kingdom," or in terms of P1445, be married to the Bridegroom)

l.2   "wins...last": ICo 15:26, 55-57 (the poet echoes "at last" twice in P1445—"last" being used four times in her favorite chapter of I Corinthians—to underscore the final defeat of death and to connect this with the "last Adam" and "last trump")

l.7   "But...Bugles": Zec 9:14; Mt 24:31; ICo 15:52; ITh 4:16

l.8   "bisected Coach": ICo 15 (the "bisected Coach" is the coffin that awaits the resurrection of the body, that change in the twinkling of an eye from terrestrial to celestial, flesh and blood to spirit, natural to spiritual, corruptible to incorruptible, mortal to immortal, first Adam to last Adam)

l.10   "Troth unknown": Rev 19:7-9

l.11   "Kinsmen/Kindred": Rev 1:7; 5:9; 7:9; 11:9; 13:7; 14:6

l.12   "throngs": Rev 7:9; 19:6

l.12   "Down/Porcelain": Rev 3:4-5, 18; 7:9, 13-14; 19:8 (the white raiment of the New Jerusalem)

Comment: See *Poems*, III, 1001-1002. P1445 should be compared and contrasted with the earlier P712.

1446   His Mind like Fabrics of the East

l.1   "His...East": Ex 26:31; 36:35 (assuming the "Fabrics" might have been of Tyrian purple, one association would be with revelation, God's presence); Jg 8:26; Ca 3:10; Rev 17:4 (Tyrian purple would have been associated with the regal); Mr 15:17, 20; Joh 19:2, 5 (the same rich "Fabrics of the East" would be associated directly with Christ, presumably the subject of P1446)

l.4   "An...Purchaser": Mt 10:1-15 (the purchasers may have been the disciples; P401 uses textile imagery and refers also to the disciples)

l.5   "For...Gold": Mt 10:9; IPe 1:7

ll.6-8 "More...was": Mt 10:38-39; 13:44-46

Comment: See *Poems*, III, 1002. It is here assumed that P1446 deals with Christ, but P1623 would suggest that a poem like P1446 might have as subject Bowles, Wadsworth, or others.

1448   How soft a Caterpillar steps-

l.1   "Caterpillar": IKi 8:37; Ps 78:46; Isa 33:4; Joe 1:4; 2:25 (the Biblical caterpillar is associated with spoliation and destruction; P1448 uses this larva of the butterfly as a Hitchcockian emblem of resurrection)

l.6   "terrestrial": ICo 15:40 (the poet draws attention to a Biblical background relevant to all her circuit-world-creature poems: "All flesh is not the same flesh: but there is one kind of flesh of men, another flesh of beasts, another of fishes, and another of birds," ICo 15:39; the tactile imagery and synecdochic "Hand" are reminders of the "flesh")

ll.7-8   "career/circuit/mission...me": ICo 15 (the poem ends with an apparent anticlimactic understatement that is actually a rhetorical question for the pupa-larva-imago is a "career-circuit" whose "mission" is to remind her of spiritual matters of ultimate identity and destiny; for "circuit" see note, line four, P313)

Comment: See *Poems*, III, 1003.

1449   I thought the Train would never come-

ll.1-12   "I...atone": Ca 2

1450   The Road was lit with Moon and star-

l.4   "Hill": see note, line one, P722

ll.5-6   "To...Terrene": Ge 28:10-17 (P1450 may owe some debt to Jacob's vision at Bethel; other possibilities of influence: IIKi 1-2; Mt 17; IICo 12:1-5; Rev 9)

Comment: See *Poems*, III, 1004.

1451   Whoever disenchants

ll.1-8   "Whoever...are": Ge 3:1-6 (the "serpent was more subtil than any beast of the field," the arch disenchanter who insinuates that "Things are not what they are;" nevertheless, the poem's unsettling generality of reference and its suggestion that "guileless" and "graphic" are lost in that universal lie of disabused adulthood, the "Treason/Perjury" of the self-conscious "Caviler," may indicate that P1451 is a subtle, oblique theodicy—a complaint against the impossibility of the reenchantment of the postlapsarian world; see, e.g., P348)

Comment: See *Poems*, III, 1004-1005.

1452   Your thoughts dont have words every day

ll.1-3   "Your...sips": Joh 1:1 (the "single," "signal," and "esoteric" qualities of words may perhaps suggest The Word)

ll.4-5   "Of...seems": Mt 26:26-29 (the poet likens words to the "communion/sacramental Wine")

l.6   "So...be": Joh 1:16-17; ICo 14:9 (the variants for "easy" are nine in number, including "fully," "free," "bounteous," and "gracious"—an indication that the poet considered these words as God's unmerited favor or, as the word Eucharist itself means, God's good grace)

l.7   "You...price": Mt 27:6, 9; ICo 6:20

l.8   "Nor...infrequency/divinity": Joh 1:1 (the variant "divinity" again attributes the source of words to the Incarnation; the variant "Stint" suggests limit, restriction, scant supply, that very frugality and destitution comprising the obverse of the circuit world experience of God's grace)

Comment: See *Poems*, III, 1005.

1453   A Counterfeit- a Plated Person-

l.6   "How...Lie": Rev 22:15

Comment: See *Poems*, III, 1006; *Letters*, II, 640; and Leyda, II, 313.

1454   Those not live yet

l.2   "Who...again": Job 14:14 (the question of Job was relevant to this Easter poem sent to her sister-in-law: "If a man die, shall he live again?")

l.3   "Again...twice": Joh 3:1-8 (those of Nicodemus's consciousness think literally—"not live yet"—unaware that for "every one born of the Spirit" all is unity and connection, this circuit world hyphenated by the sea of death to that of the new circumference; another of the poet's favorites repeats "Again," IPe 1:3, 23)

l.7   "Death...Sea": ICo 15 (St. Paul here changes death as period into death as hyphen)

l.8   "Deep...Schedule": Rev 1:6, 18; 4:9-10; 5:13-14; 7:12; 10:6; 11:15; 22:5

l.9   "Of...be": Rev 1:16; 2:28; 22:5, 16 (perhaps the "Disk" refers to God or the Son as a star or sun in the New Jerusalem); Rev 22:4 (perhaps the "Disk" is the ideally circumferential face of God or the "Disk" comprised of the poet experiencing the beatific vision face-to-face); Rev 2:10; 3:11; 4:4, 10; 7:3-8; 9:4 (perhaps less likely is that the "Disk" represents the seal and crown of the elect)

ll.10-11 "Costumeless...he": Joh 4:24; Rev 22:17 (the last lines of the poem remind that God is a Spirit to be experienced accordingly; St. John the Divine wrote Dickinson's favorite Bible book while "in the Spirit" and among its final verses is one in which the "Spirit and the bride say, Come")

1455   Opinion is a flitting thing,

l.2   "But...Sun": Ps 100:5; 117:2; Joh 14:6; IJo 5:6-7 (God as Truth is "oldest"); Rev 21:23; 22:5 (the sun is outlasted since it is absent from the New Jerusalem)

Comment: See *Letters*, II, 651-652 and Leyda, II, 316. It is possible that the poem is using the first two persons of the Trinity for purposes of wit—"Truth" as the Father and "Sun" as the Son-Bridegroom (Nu 24:17; Mal 4:2; IIPe 1:19; Rev 2:28; 22:16)

1456   So gay a Flower

ll.1-2   "So...Mind": Mt 6:28-29; Lu 12:27

1459   Belshazzar had a Letter-

ll.1-8   "Belshazzar...Wall": Da 5:5, 25-28 (the story of Belshazzar's defiant feast is told in the fifth chapter of Daniel giving in detail the interpretation of the one "Letter" written by "Belshazzar's Correspondent," God, and recorded in "that immortal Copy" or the Bible; the unusually high moral dudgeon of P1459 and P1453, perhaps reminiscent of Whittier's "Ichabod," suggests that the poet felt strongly regarding the Lothrop case)

1.8   "On...Wall": Da 5:5, 27; Rev 6:5

Comment: See *Poems*, III, 1006, 1008-1009 and Letters, II, 640.

1460   His Cheek is his Biographer-

1.2   "As...blush": Jer 6:15; 8:12

1.3   "Perdition": Joh 17:12; Rev 17:8, 11

1.4   "sins in peace": Ge 15:15; 26:29; 28:21;Ex 4:18; Jg 18:6; ISa 1:17; 20:42; 25:35; 29:7; IISa 15:9;IIKi 5:19; Mt 5:34; Lu 7:50; 8:48; Ac 16:36 (suggesting pardon, reconciliation, covenant, vow, pledge, forgiveness, or healing, the wording "Go in peace" appears frequently in the KJV; line four is a piece of Biblical wit aimed at a nephew's venial sin of pie love—a piece of which conflating "Go in peace" with Jesus' "go, and sin no more," Joh 8:11)

Comment: See *Poems*, III, 1009.

1461   "Heavenly Father"- take to thee

1.1   " 'Heavenly Father' ": Mt 6:14, 26, 32; 15:13; 18:35; Lu 11:13 (the poet may also have in mind the opening words of the Lord's Prayer, Mt 6:9)

ll.2-3   "The...Hand": Ge 1:27; 2:7 ("supreme iniquity," synecdochic for Adam fashioned by God from the dust; the first three lines of the poem are somewhat ambiguous and may mean that God must take responsibility for his supreme creation's "iniquity" or that God is the "supreme iniquity" in Whose image Adam has been created; imagistically, God's glowing, shining "Hand" contrasts, perhaps ironically, with the dust of mankind)

1.4   "In...contraband": Ge 3:1-21 (the reference is to the Fall of Adam)

1.5   "Though...us": Ge 3:9-13 (God's lack of "trust" is evidenced by four questions)

1.6   " 'We...Dust' ": Ps 103:14 (the actual phrasing is from the Psalmist with an echo of Ge 3:19)

ll.7-8   "We...Duplicity": Mt 6:9-13 (these final lines read much like a sardonic inversion of the Lord's Prayer)

Comment: See *Poems*, III, 1009-1010.

1462   We knew not that we were to live-

l.3   "Our...is": Eph 6:14
ll.4-6   "We...off": ICo 15:53-54; IICo 5:1-4
ll.7-8   "By...Life": IITi 1:10
Comment: P1462 should be contrasted with verses ten through eighteen of Ephesians, the sixth chapter, for the poet here, in contrast, conveys a potent sense of the illusoriness of this body prison or, as she told Maria Whitney, "we are each unknown to ourself and each other." PF70, *Letters*, III, 922-923, suggests that P1462 may be directly indebted to IICo 1:9. See *Poems*, III, 1010; *Letters*, II, 627-628, 634; III, 922-923; and Leyda, II, 307.

1463   A Route of Evanescence

l.2   "Wheel": Eze 1:15-21; 10:2-19
l.3   "Emerald": Rev 21:19-20
l.4   "Cochineal": Ex 26:31 (scarlet is associated with the veil over the holy of holies)
l.5   "Bush": Ex 3:2-4; De 33:16; Mr 12:26;Ac 7:30, 35 (associated with theophanies)
l.6   "Head": Ca 2:6; 5:2, 11; 7:5; 8:3
l.8   "An...Ride": Ps 139:9
Comment: From the Psalmist to St. John the Divine, flight is a metaphor for release and ascent in a spiritual sense. In addition, the creation of a wind rustling the "Bush" and the suggestions of communications from far-off, exotic places and the sunrise are obliquely if not directly Biblical. Thus P1463 may perhaps be read as an epiphany poem. See *Poems*, III, 1010-1013; *Letters*, II, 639-640; III, 655, 681, 740-741, 769-770; and Leyda, II, 329-330, 333-334, 379, 396.

1464   One thing of it we borrow

l.1   "it": e.g., Ex 17:14; Rev 1:11; 5 ("it," referring to Higginson's book, *Short Studies of American Authors*, is synecdochic for the lexicon, language in general, or her art; this self-referentiality reveals an ambivalence toward the fleshly incarnations of literature about which she has avarice of the emotions, to steal Joyce's terminology)

l.3   "Sorrow": Isa 53:3-4
l.4   "Sweetness": Ca 2:3, 14; 5:5, 13, 16
l.5   "covet": Ex 20:17
l.7   "Avarice": Ex 20:17
l.8   "Dross": Ps 119:119; Isa 1:22, 25 ("dross" is associated with the impurities of sin—to traffic in literature necessitates the taint from its fleshly incarnations, "Booty" and "Sorrow," or to use the language from Lowell's "After the Burial,": "splendid conjectures" and "sweet despair")

Comment: P1464 obliquely celebrates the glory and despair of the poet's own art, its "Sweetness" and "Anguish," while richly mingling the Biblical lexicons of the Passion, of Canticles, and of the Decalogue (covetousness explicit and idolatry implicit). See *Poems*, III, 1013; *Letters*, II, 649-650; and Leyda, II, 315.

1465   Before you thought of Spring

l.8   "Indigo": Ex 26:31-33; see also note, line one, P15; note, line eight, P703; and note, lines two-three, P716 (the instantiation of the spiritual is suggested by the "Inspiriting habiliments" of the bluebird; for blue as one of the colors of the veil and its associations with God's presence, see the preceding notes)
l.9   "With...Song": Ca 2:11-12 (spring, birds, and song are associated with the beloved)
l.16   "seraphic": Isa 6:2, 6 (another indication that the bird's color and song are associated with God's presence)

Comment: Associated with the skies and a "suddenness" blessed by God, the bluebird is a harbinger of spring and rebirth. Apparently an epiphany poem, P1465 presents a New England solitary singer relishing its autotelic art. See *Poems*, III, 1014-1015; *Letters*, II, 639-640; and Leyda, II, 311.

1466   One of the ones that Midas touched

ll.1-2   "One...all": Job 23:10; Isa 13:12; La 4:1-2 (used frequently in a figurative manner, gold is a Biblical standard of purity and worth; it is also the color of Revelation, e.g., 3:18; 4:4;21:18, 21;

the name and song of the bird imply the ideally circumferential—"O" is used in the higher case six times; see also note, line one, P15)

      l.3   "Prodigal": Lu 15:11-32

      l.13   "Jesuit": Mt 1:1, 16

      ll.13-16 "The...wants": Ca 1:13-14; 2:3; 3:6; 4:6, 12-15; 5:1, 10-14; 6:2-3; 7:12-13; 8:12-14 (the beloved is a perfume, an apple tree, a garden, an orchard or vineyard; the song of the bird is associated with the recapturing of such a paradise)

      l.24   "With...Peace": Isa 9:6; Joh 1:29, 36; Heb 7:2; Rev 5:6, 12; 7:9-17; 14:1-4; 19:7-9 (the speaker is a swain who hears in the song of the Lamb and Peace a prelapsarian promise)

      ll.27-28 "lost...Tree": Ge 3:6

      Comment: See *Poems*, III, 1015-1017; *Letters*, II, 639-640; and Leyda, II, 329.

1467   A little overflowing word

      l.1   "A...word": Joh 1:1 (the poem is apparently self-consciously about words)

      ll.4-5   "Though...decay": Mt 24:35 ("Heaven and earth shall pass away, but my words shall not pass away")

1468   A winged spark doth soar about-

      ll.1-4   "A...sere": Eze 1:4-14 (the general provenance of the poem is that of visionary experience, the language perhaps suggesting Ezekiel; fire is often associated with theophanies in the Bible, e.g., Ex 3:2;13:21; 19:18;IKi 18:38; Job 1:16;Ac 7:30;apocalyptic fire and flame repeatedly appear, along with lightning, in Revelation, e.g., 1:14; 2:18; 19:12)

      l.7   "Rapture": Ge 5:24; IIKi 2:11(Enoch and Elijah were raptured); Da 12; Mr 13;ICo 15:20-28;Rev 7 ("Rapture" may refer to a belief that the elect will be taken from the earth before a period of future suffering; also, "Rapture" suggests a heightened, mystical awareness of divine things, or what the poet elsewhere terms "Extasy"—see note, line fifteen, P783 and notes, lines five and eight, P1191)

      Comment: See *Poems*, III, 1017.

1469   If wrecked upon the Shoal of Thought

1.1   "If...Thought": Mt 26:36-46 (the "Reefs in Old Gethsemane" of P313 may suggest the equation of "Thought" with disastrous suffering)

1.2   "Sea": Ge 1:2 (the depths of "Thought" are associated with the primordial chaos, allowing the poet here to express metaphysical diffidence)

1.4   "Simplicity": IICo 11:3

Comment: See *Poems*, III, 1018.

1470   The Sweets of Pillage, can be known

ll.1-4   "The...Grief": Lu 23:39-43 (the inadvertent pillaging of heaven by the thief on the cross must have piqued the poet's sense of the paradoxes of the divine mercy; Beckett insisted that *Waiting for Godot* dealt with Augustine's conclusion from the example of the two malefactors: neither despair nor presumption is warranted by an inscrutable divine mercy)

1471   Their Barricade against the Sky

ll.4-5   "Their...March": Ex 14:9-10, 13

1.11   "The...Scar": Isa 53:5 (the second stanza of the poem raises questions regarding the deeper indication or cause behind the advance of the seasons and the "Massacre of Air;" the poet dismisses a sacramental reading: these are not wounds to be commemorated by a holy day but simply the "Holidays of War")

Comment: See *Poems*, III, 1018-1019.

1472   To see the Summer Sky

ll.1-3   "To...flee": Ps 19:1-5

1473   We talked with each other about each other

1.7   "Arks...us": Ge 6-9 (herein is given the story of Noah and his ark)

1.8   "Ararats": Ge 8:4 (in the seventh month the ark of Noah comes to rest upon the mountains of Ararat)

Comment: P1473 employs the Noah story metaphorically in dealing with communion and separation in an awkwardly silent tete-a-tete. On the other hand, if for the "Palsied" of line five is substituted the variant "sentenced," then P1473 may be a more general meditation upon the oppressive and distracting burden of time for those condemned to the circuit world, thus heightening the dubeity of Time's compassionate offer of "Reprieve." Much depends on whether the "We" are Noahs or his condemned contemporaries, a matter of certainty of election. See *Poems*, III, 1019-1020.

1474   Estranged from Beauty- none can be-

l.2   "For...Infinity": ICo 15:53-54 (the poet yokes immortality to the idea of "Beauty")

ll.3-4   "And...creased/leased": Ge 2:7; ICo 15:50-55 (man, created a living soul in God's image, has no "power to be finite" because of this immortal "Identity"; the variant line four—"When Fate incorporated us"—reinforces P1474's idea that "Beauty" is the essence of God's creative nature, a nature participated in by the author)

Comment: See *Poems*, III, 1020.

1475   Fame is the one that does not stay-

l.4   "Ascend incessantly": Job 29:3; Ps 18:28 (Fame is figuratively viewed as the candle of God's favor allowed to shine after the death of the poet; "Fame" is much like the promised land for Moses—see P597 and P1201 and compare with P1006)

ll.6-8   "Lightning," "Electrical," "Flame": Ex 3:2; Eze 1:13-14; Da 7:9; 10:6; Mt 24:27; 28:3; Rev 1:14; 2:18; 4:5; 8:5; 11:19; 16:18; 19:12, 20; 20:9 (the poet uses here the apocalyptic-visionary lexicon to describe the manifestations of Fame)

Comment: See *Poems*, III, 1021.

1476   His voice decrepit was with Joy-

l.1   "His...Joy": Ca 2:8, 14; 5:2; 8:13 (the voice of the beloved is associated with the anticipations and joys of profane love; elements of this "livid interview" anticipate Rev 3:20; 19:7-9; and 22:4—but not without trepidation regarding the potential unmeaning of the apocalyptic)

l.3   "How...be": Ca 1:2-4, 9, 15; 2:2, 4-5, 7, 10, 13;3:5, 10; 4:1, 7, 10: 5:2, 8: 6:4; 7:6, 12; 8:4-7

l.4   "To...Lips": Ca 4:3, 11; 5:13; 7:9

l.6   "Delight": Ca 2:3; 7:6

l.7   "Terror": Ca 6:4, 10; 8:6

l.8   "This...interview": Ca 1, passim (the poet uses the topoi of profane love in P1476 to express ambivalence regarding apocalyptic hopes)

Comment: See *Poems*, III, 1021-1022.

1477   How destitute is he

ll.1-4   "How...Sum": Mt 6:19-21; 25:18

l.5   "When...Pence": Mr 12:41-44

ll.6-8   "Will...India": Pr 5:15-19; Ca 8:7

Comment: See *Poems*, III, 1022 for a discussion of the worksheet draft.

1478   Look back on Time, with kindly eyes-

ll.1-4   "Look...West": Ge 1:14-18 ("Time" is here the circuit world diurnal round of rising and setting sun, the "West" synecdochic of its circumscription by death; the inadequate, feeble "Time" and "trembling sun" of P1478 imply, by their very limitations, Biblical consolations, e.g., Isa 60:19-20; see also Ps 84:11; 89:36; Mal 4:2; Lu 1:78; ICo 15; IIPe 1:19; Rev 2:28; 10:6)

Comment: See *Poems*, III, 1023.

1479   The Devil- had he fidelity

ll.1-8   "The...divine": Isa 14:12-15 (the "Devil" is guilty of perfidy among the angels in heaven and is cast out [Lu 10:18]; hence, the opportunity to be "thoroughly divine" was lost)

l.3   "Because...ability": Ge 3 (his cunning shown at the Fall); IICo 11:3, 14; Eph 2:2; 6:11; ITi 3:6; IPe 5:8; IJo 2:13; 3:8 (his pride, deceit, and subtlety are emphasized again and again in the New Testament)

l.4   "But...mend": Rev 9:1-11; 12:9; 20:2-10 (that the "Devil" is incorrigible is suggested by his fate in the Book of Revelation)

Comment: That the poet would conceive of the "Devil" as potentially a "best friend" (Pr 18:24; Jas 2:23) whose "Perfidy" is a virtue needing only to be resigned for all to be well is a piece of outrageous Biblical wit. See Sewall, ;5 and *Poems*, III, 1023.

1480   The fascinating chill that music leaves

ll.3-4   "Ecstasy's," "Rapture's": see note, line fifteen, P783; notes, lines five and eight, P1191; and note, line seven, P1468

l.3   "impediment": Ro 7:24; IICo 5:4; Php 3:21 (the "natural body" of St. Paul is that "impediment," that "soil" into which music comes as an "estranging creature" with intimations of immortality; perhaps the perfection of art has about it an aura of pristine, prelapsarian purity and innocence, a garden of the ideally circumferential in contrast to the Garden of the Creator with its dissonant Fall)

ll.4-5   " 'Tis...soil": ICo 15 (the organic metaphor here may be indebted to St. Paul's discussion of the resurrection; the use of soil as a metaphor indicating human types may also be found in the parable of the sower, Mt 13:18-23)

l.6   "creature": Ge 1:20-24; 2:19 (the Genesis Creation word for the products of God's creative activity; the poet is self-consciously and perhaps defiantly choosing such a lexicon to praise the "fine" and "upper wooing" creations of circuit world art; "creature" and "Creator" appear in one of St. Paul's most emphatic pro-nouncements against idolatry, Ro 1:25)

l.8   "Creator": Ge 1-3; Ec 12:1; Isa 40:28; Ro 1:25;IPe 4:19

Comment: See *Poems*, III, 1023-1024.

1481   The way Hope builds his House

l.1   "Hope": Ro 4 (the promise to Abraham is not through the law but rather faith—"Who against hope believed in hope"); Ro 5; 8:18-25 (St. Paul in discussing "Hope" contrasts it with the "Laws" of the final line of P1481; the law may be the Penteteuch, the whole of the Old Testament, or the "Book of the Covenant" with its old dispensation of works, Ex 20-23; in P1481 the "Laws" are metaphorically connected with a circuit world tabernacle of rafters and ledges); ICo 15:19; Heb 11:1

l.1   "House": ICo 3:16-17; 6:19; IICo 5:1-4; Eph 2:21-22; Rev 21:3 (the individual as temple, tabernacle, house, or habitation is a frequent KJV metaphor); see note, line one, P674; and note, line one, P1142 (P1481 apparently speaks of the "house not made with hands eternal in the heavens," IICo 5:1)

ll.5-6   "Abode...superficies": Heb 11:3 (on the level of "Laws," the apparent is taken as "supreme," the appearances of "sill," "Rafter," and "Ledges" the poet terms "superficies")

Comment: See *Poems*, III, 1024. Compare P1481 with P1142. To some degree P1481 flaunts the power of imagination to construct "Pinnacle" houses of greater durability than those "smit" and "mortised" ones that the poet may have associated with a more prosaic construction metaphor, Mt 7:24-27.

1482   'Tis whiter than an Indian Pipe-

l.1   "whiter": Rev 1:14; 2:17; 3:4-5, 18; 4:4; 6:2, 11; 7:9, 13-14; 19:8, 11, 14; 20:11 (the apocalyptic color of Revelation)

ll.3-6   "No...there": Joh 4:24

ll.7-8   "A...Air": Ge 2:7; ICo 15:; (breath or "Air" is here associated with the "spirit"); Joh 3:5-9 (the poet may have had in mind the nonplussed Nicodemus)

ll.9-10 "This...be": IJo 3:2 ("Beloved, now are we the sons of God, and it doth not yet appear what we shall be: but we know that, when he shall appear, we shall be like him; for we shall see him as he is")

l.11   " 'Tis...Hypothesis": ICo 15:50-55; Php 3:13

Comment: See *Poems*, III, 1024-1025. P1482 deals with the question of the nature and destiny of the spirit (ICo 15:350). The meditation is permeated by dread of the potential unmeaning of the apocalyptic.

1483   The Robin is a Gabriel

l.1   "The...Gabriel": Da 8:16-26; 9:20-27; Lu 1:11-21, 26-38; Rev 8:2 (Gabriel is a messenger associated with revelation, with portentous announcements, and with apocalyptic hope because of his presence before God in Revelation; see note, line fourteen, P725)

l.4   "Transport's": see note, lines seven-eight, P1413 and also P1279 and P1723; "Transport" is apparently an experience (a foretaste as it were) of the Presence of God through song and much like her "Extasy" for which see note, line fifteen, P783 and notes, lines five and eight, P1191

Comment: Having a sturdy integrity, entertaining only "Perspicacity," and "Cajoling Consternation/By Ditties to the Enemy," the "Robin" may be Emily Dickinson herself. The worksheet draft of P1483 describes the "Robin" as a "Troubadour" rather than a "Gabriel," a substitution suggesting that for her the provenance of song was not simply of the secular, circuit world; the draft also suggests that the "Fugitive" of line thirteen may be an oblique reference to the poet's concern for fame. See *Poems*, III, 1025-1026 and Leyda, II, 320-321.

1484   We shall find the Cube of the Rainbow.

ll.1-2   "We...doubt": Ge 9:13-16 (the "Rainbow" is synecdochic of an older dispensation whose transparent simplicity is amenable to mathematical exactitude; such directness is used for purposes of contrast in P1484)

l.3   "But...conjecture": IJo 4:8; Rev 19:7-9 (the "Arc," synecdochic of that newer dispensation, is the product of a "Lover" whose conjectures elude finality and closure, remaining an enigma for the poet; the choice of the geometric "Arc" may imply the completion of the circle, the ideally circumferential consummation of love as the Bride of Christ, but the "Arc" is as well the shape of the incomplete crescent associated with the sublunary, circuit world of nature—see P1315, P1339, P1605, and P1673)

Comment: See *Letters*, III, 655-656, a letter to Mrs. Edward Tuckerman in which the poet writes: "Had it been a Mastiff that guarded Eden, we should have feared him less than we do the Angel—." See also *Poems*, III, 1026 and Leyda, II, 317.

1485   Love is done when Love's begun,

ll.1-5   "Love...Day": Ro 8:35-39 (the "Boon" of "Truth," here unstated, is that the fickle and fleeting love of Ovidian treatments is not the only one)

Comment: See *Poems*, III, 1026.

1486   Her spirit rose to such a hight

ll.1-6   "Her...her": Ex 33:20-23; 34:29-35; IICo 3:7 (like Moses in God's presence, Sue has fed upon "awe" until her countenance reflects the glory or light of God—see Ps 4:6; ITi 6:16; Rev 1:16)

Comment: See *Poems*, III, 1027.

1487   The Savior must have been

1.1   "The...been": Lu 2:11; Joh 4:42; Ac 5:31

1.3   "To...day": Mt 1:18; 2:1 (Christmas)

1.4   "little Fellowmen": Mt 19:14; Lu 18:16-17;ITi 4:10 (the phrasing "little children" appears repeatedly in the First Epistle of John, e.g., IJo 2:1, 12-13, 28; 4:4)

1.5   "The...Bethlehem": Mt 2:1, 5-6, 8, 16

1.7   "Was leveled": Mt 26-28 (the suffering, death, and resurrection of Christ levels the road by triumphing over that extinction otherwise implicit in every birth)

Comment: See *Poems*, III, 1027-1028; *Letters*, III, 681-682 (a letter revealing the poet's appreciation of "Children" given the densely paradoxical implications of the context); and Leyda, II, 334.

1488   Birthday of but a single pang

Comment: Pang, affliction, and doom comprise the lexicon (here used for aging) of the Passion, Mt 26-27. See *Poems*, III, 1028.

1489   A Dimple in the Tomb

1.1   "Tomb": Job 21:32

ll.2-3   "Makes...Home": ICo 15:55

Comment: See *Poems*, III, 1028-1029; *Letters*, III, 660-661; and Leyda, II, 322.

1490   The Face in evanescence lain

ll.1-8   "The...divine": ICo 15; Rev 2:10; 7; 22:4 (the face "lain" in death becomes a "Flower" or actualized seed, that spiritual body of incorruption and immortality spoken of by St. Paul and that sealed and crowned, ideally circumferential "Face" of the elect prepared for the beatific vision)

Comment: See *Poems*, III, 1029-1030; *Letters*, III, 657; and Leyda, II, 319.

1491   The Road to Paradise is plain

ll.1,7   "Paradise": Ge 2-3; Eze 28:13-14; 31:8-9, 16; 47:1-12; IICo 12:4; Rev 2:7; 21-22

ll.1-6   "The...preferred": Mt 7:13-14 ("Enter ye in at the strait gate...Because strait is the gate, and narrow is the way, which leadeth unto life, and few there be that find it")

l.9   "But...things": ICo 2:9; 15:50-55; IJo 3:2 (the energies of P1491 are channeled against complacency regarding the smiling beauties and predictabilities of a conventional Heaven)

l.10   "Mines...Wings": Mt 6:19-20

Comment: That P1491 was enclosed in a letter to Mrs. Holland may to some degree account for its daring, anti-Philistine agnosticism regarding "Paradise"—its treatment of the "Road" exposing the distance of Victorian sensibility from New Testament austerities. See *Poems*, III, 1030; *Letters*, III, 666-667; and Leyda, II, 325-326.

1492   "And with what body do they come?"

l.1   " 'And...come' ": ICo 15:35 ("But some man will say, How are the dead raised up? and with what body do they come?")

ll.3-4   "What...House": Mt 24:36, 42-44, 50; 25:13; Rev 3:20 ("Door," "Hour," and "House" appear in these verses of apocalyptic imagery)

l.4   "Illuminate...House!": ICo 15:44, 49 (although the poem is supposedly elegiac in giving solace to Perez Dickinson Cowan, it becomes an occasion for personal reassurance regarding the recognizable bodily form of lost beloveds in the hereafter)

l.7   "Paul": Ac 9:11; 13:9 (Saul of Tarsus, later St. Paul, the author of the fifteenth chapter of I Corinthians, perhaps the poet's favorite chapter in the KJV)

ll.7-8   "Paul...Bethlehem": Ac 9 (on the Damascus road, Paul is converted when confronted by Jesus, "the Man that knew the News;" the "News" is here the Gospel itself, Isa 52:7; Mt 1:21-23;

4:23; as an apostle, St. Paul was called to preach this "News," so beautifully expressed for the poet in ICo 15; line eight of P1492 is synecdochic of St. Paul's rebirth with all that is implied therein)

Comment: See *Poems*, III, 1031; *Letters*, III, 678-679; and Leyda, II, 332-333.

1493   Could that sweet Darkness where they dwell

l.1   "Could...dwell": Job 10:21-22
l.2   "Be...us": ICo 15:51
l.3   "loveliness": Ca 5:16

Comment: P1493 has much the same provenance as P1492, but the point of view and tone much differ. See *Poems*, III, 1031-1032; *Letters*, III, 661-662; and Leyda, II, 323 for the context suggesting that P1493 is elegiac with regard to Samuel Bowles.

1494   The competitions of the sky

l.1   "The...sky": Ge 1 (God's creation does not suffer the corrosion of circuit world productions; see P290)

Comment: The poet writes to Louise and Frances Norcross: "Did the 'stars differ' from each other in anything but 'glory,'" there would be often envy" (*Letters*, III, 677). As Johnson points out (Letters, III, 678), the echo is of ICo 15:41: "There is one glory of the sun, and another glory of the moon, and another glory of the stars: for one star differeth from another star in glory." See *Poems*, III, 1032 and Leyda, II, 331.

1495   The Thrill came slowly like a Boon for

l.1   "The...Boon/Light": Joh 1:8-9; 8:12; 9:5; IJo 1:5; Rev 19:7-9; 21:23-24; 22:5 ("Thrill," "sumptuous," "Rapture," and "ravished" comprise a carnal-profane lexicon used in describing an experience of the divine "Boon," perhaps as Bride of Christ)

ll.3-5   "It's...missed": Ge 6-9 (the "Flood" is used as a metaphor not only for its connotations regarding physical passion but also for its suggestions that she, like Noah, has experienced "sumptuous" favor while avoiding "desolation")

l.6   "Rapture": see note, line seven, P1468 (such "Thrill" and "Rapture" as P1495 describes must be experienced beyond the circuit world in a "changed" body)

l.6   "changed...Dress": ICo 15:51-52; Rev 3:4-5, 18; 19:7-9 (the spiritual body has such dress as do the elect, the white raiment of the Bride of Christ)

l.7   "And...Change": Joh 11:25 (Christ, the Bridegroom, is the "resurrection and the life" and thus the guarantor of that "change" spoken of by St. Paul as the resurrection, ICo 15:51-52; the poet stands then in the presence of the "Change" or of Christ Himself, Rev 19:7-9)

l.8   "ravished": Ca 4:9

l.8   "In...Holiness": Rev 19:7-9 (the language is that of mystical union with the Bridegroom who is "Holiness," e.g., Rev 3:7; 4:8; 15:4)

Comment: See Sewall, 661-662, for a consideration of P1495 in the context of the poet's relationship with Judge Lord. See also *Poems*, III, 1032.

1496   All that I do

ll.1-3   "All...mind": Rev 20:12

ll.4-6   "I...behind": Job 34:21; Ps 139 (there is here an unsettling blurring of the line between solicitude and surveillance from such an "enamored mind")

ll.7-9   "Not...preside": Mt 10:29

ll.10-11 "What...Bride": Rev 19:7-9 (the final lines are not a flat, rhetorical question since the portrait of "omnipresence" in P1496 as "review[ing]," "pushing," "l[ying] in wait," and "presiding" is hardly flattering and the variant "impending" for line eleven interjects an added suggestion of menace; ostensibly a Bride of Christ poem, P1496 may express fears regarding the apocalyptic)

Comment: See *Poems*, III, 1033.

1497   Facts by our side are never sudden

ll.9-13   "Adieu...I'": ICo 15 (P1497 has a provenance similar to that of P1495 but in marked contrast expresses agnosticism regarding any "resumption" after being summoned by the "Adieu" of death, the "portentous Neighbor")

Comment: See *Poems*, III, 1033-1034.

1498   Glass was the Street- in tinsel Peril

l.7   "It...italic": Joh 1:1; Rev 1:8, 11

Comment: In a poem apparently about the phenomenon of observing boys and sleds from the window, Emily Dickinson draws attention to the self-conscious artistry of her recorded experience—words made meaningful by the Word. In addition to the self-referential sense of play in the use of "italic" (the Alpha and Omega, the all-encompassing Word, alone yielding intelligibleness), there is the witty mimicry of the "shod vibrations"—in fact, such a self-conscious manipulation of type as trope turns P1498 into an extended metaphor for the way a poem means. See *Poems*, III, 1034.

1499   How firm Eternity must look

l.1   "Eternity": Isa 57:15 (here "Eternity" is apparently synecdochic of the ideally circumferential "Face" of God)

l.2   "To...me/thee": Ge 3:19; Job 4:19; Ec 3:20 (the finitude of man is metaphorically dust in contrast to the hard rock that is "Eternity")

ll.3-4   "The...Identity": De 32:4, 15, 18, 30-31; IISa 23:3; Ps 18:2, 31, 46; 28:1; 42:9; 94:22 (God is spoken of metaphorically as the rock); ICo 10:4 (St. Paul speaks of Christ as the "Rock")

l.3   "Adamant": Ge 2-3; Ro 5:14; ICo 15:22, ; (the "Estate" of "Eternity" may be "Adamant," the poet deliberately calling attention to the wordplay by use of the higher case)

ll.5-6   "How...Physiognomy": Ro 8:29; IICo 3:18; Php 3:21; Rev 22:4 (propaedeutic to the beatific vision is the process whereby the "insecure" are conformed to the ideally circumferential "Physiognomy" of God)

ll.7-8   "To...thee": Col 3:3-4 (the "crumbling" and "insecure" identity only finds coherence through being "concealed/intrenched/inlaid" in Christ, the Mediator whose elect, sealed, and crowned with the name upon their foreheads are then prepared for the ideal presence, the beatific vision, Rev 22:4)

l.7   "cohere/present/propound": Ex 33:20 (the variant, "present," suggests the meaning that "no man shall see God and live"); IJo 2:1; Rev 1:5; 3:14 (the variant, "propound," suggests Christ's mediatorial function as advocate and witness)

Comment: See *Poems*, III, 1034-1035. In P1499, Christ's is the ideal face translated by the heart P253), the achieved "Identity" that superimposes its circumferentiality upon the "crumbling" and "insecure" face of the poet (see, for example, P351 for a poem dealing with the terrors of identity diffusion).

1500   It came his turn to beg-

ll.1-2   "It...life": Lu 12:22-23; 16:19-22
l.3   "Is...Alms": Lu 12:33
l.4   "Penury": Lu 21:4
l.7   "snake": Ge 3

Comment: P1500 deals with the Lazarus aspect of the psyche ("Penury in Chief")—that awareness of the disabused that the life begged is paradoxically an absolute penury. P1500 dramatizes an "I" regnant with an ironic body prison (Ro 7:24; IICo 5:4; Php 3:21) awareness—an awareness that circuit world largesse ("Alms") is never more than an ambiguous "reprieve." Its "reprieve" must be surreptitious for fear that the attractions once laid to rest (synecdochically spoken of as Garden of Eden sins, the "snake" of her thoughts) may again come to the fore. The rich KJV reverberations of the poem's lexicon—"life," "beg," "Alms," and "Penury"—reinforce its essential paradoxes. See *Poems*, III, 1035.

1501   It's little Ether Hood

ll.1-3   "It's...supple": Isa 3:23 (this "Hood" is apparently thought of as a heavenly, white diadem—see Rev 1:14; 2:10; 3:4-5; 4:4, 10; 7; 19:8 for the apocalyptic color and crown)
l.4   "sagacious God": Ro 16:27; ITi 1:17; Jude 25
ll.5-7   "Till...Drama": ICo 15:38 (the "Drama" in the broadcasting of the dandelion seeds may have been seen as "typic" of resurrection hope; there may be in line six a sidelong glance at ex nihilo creation, Ge 1:1; Ro 4:17; Heb 11:3)

1502   I saw the wind within her

ll.1-2[scrap1 recto] "I...me": Joh 3:8

l.4[scrap1 recto] "Humility": Php 2:8

l.14[scrap1 recto] "Redemption": Lu 21:28; Eph 1:7; Col 1:14; Heb 9:12

l.3[scrap 1 verso] "The...remembrance": Ps 6:5

ll.3-4[scrap1 verso] "saved," l.1[scrap 2] "saved": Rev 21:24

ll.10-11[scrap1 verso] "timid Bulwark": IISa 22:2; Ps 18:2; 31:3; 71:3; 91:2; 144:2; Jer 16:9

l.13[scrap1 verso] "Universe...needy": Ps 72:4, 12-13

ll.1-2[scrap3] "Beggar": Lu 16:20-21

l.3[scrap 3] "But...succor": IICo 6:2

l.7[scrap 3] "Not...own": Eph 2:4-10

Comment: See *Poems*, III, 1036-1037 where the very rough and unfinished state of the poem is apparent. P1502 seems to be an observation of a "little maid," a Gibraltar as it were, deficient in humility but sufficient in works (the circuit world lexicon suggesting this: "buy," "bought," "competing Days," "assistance," "pay," "price," and "own") who is seen by the speaker as a "precious Beggar" just as "needy" as the rest of the "Universe," one in need of faith and humility.

1503   More than the Grave is closed to me-

ll.1,2,3 "Grave": ICo 15:55

l.2   "Eternity": Isa 57:15; Rev 1:6; 5:13; 7:12; 15:7; 22:5

ll.4-6   "It...appears": Job 8:9

Comment: See *Poems*, III, 1037-1038. P1503 conveys a sense of the unreal, illusory nature of the circuit world while at the same time expressing dismay that the "Grave" and "Eternity" are not palpable realities.

1504   Of whom so dear

ll.1-2   "Of...hear": Ca 1:3; 2:14; 8:13

1505   She could not live upon the Past

l.2   "The...her": IICo 5:8 (again, P1505 expresses a strong sense of bodily life as illusion)

l.3   "sweet": Ca 2:3, 14; 5:5, 13, 16 (death treated as the Canticles beloved)

l.3   "last": ICo 15:26 (death itself)
Comment: See *Poems*, III, 1038-1039.

1506   Summer is shorter than any one-

l.3   "Seventy Years": Ps 90:10
l.5   "Sorrow": Ge 3:16-19
l.7   "Delight": Ca 2:3; 7:6 (the Canticles word apparently links up with the metaphorical values of "Summer" to contrast with "Sorrow," the word directly connected with circuit world limitation and death)
Comment: See *Poems*, III, 1039.

1508   You cannot make Remembrance grow

l.7   "Cedar": Ps 92:12 (the strength of the cedar was proverbial; see note, lines one to four, P1312)
ll.7-8   "Feet...shod": Eph 6:15 (the language only is here echoed although the "armour" spoken of by St. Paul may have suggested the word "Adamant" to the poet)
ll.9-11   "Nor...anew": Job 14:7-9 (the verbal echoes here seem more than coincidental)
Comment: See *Poems*, III, 1040.

1509   Mine Enemy is growing old-

l.1   "Mine Enemy": ISa 19:17; IKi 21:20; Job 16:9; 27:7; Ps 7:4; 13:2, 4; 41:11; Mic 7:8, 10 (for the variant, "My Foe," see Ps 27:2;30:1)
l.4   "avenge": Isa 1:24
Comment: Johnson notes that on the verso of a copy of the poem was written: "With love, for Supper—if deferred it will fade like Ice Cream" (*Poems*, III, 1041; *Letters*, III, 920). The experience of love as a banquet would have been familiar to the poet in profane (Ca 2:4) and sacred (Rev 19:7-9) forms. P1509, titled by the poet "Cupid's Sermon," may be an oblique approach to the psychological dynamic behind love since it explicitly states the obverse one behind "Revenge" and "Hate." The apprehension expressed by the poet to Higginson, "lest one of them [four poems were enclosed] you might think profane," may apply especially to P1509 (Leyda, II, 333-334)—

apprehension perhaps about how her philosophy of deprivation would be received in such a form and within such a context ("Hymns to a Charity").

1510   How happy is the little Stone

ll.1-4   "How...fears": Mt 6:27-33 (these verses deal with providential design and the issue, important for P1510, of stature; P333 expresses a somewhat similar desire to identify with an insentient order free of the "Exigencies" of adult striving; the diminutive "little" echoes an identification with emphases in Christ's teachings, Mt 18; Mk 10:14-15; the "Stone" is mentioned in the Creation account, Ge 1-2, and of course has apocalyptic reverberations for the poet perhaps not relevant to P1510, Rev 2:17; 21)

l.7   "Sun": Mal 4:2; Lu 1:78; Rev 2:28 (here and in the added quatrain the poet identifies with the Sun-Son)

ll.9-10   "Fulfilling...simplicity": IPe 2:4-10 (the lines fuse the Leibnizian idea of a chain of being, a preconcerted harmony in Creation, Ge 1-2 and P290, with the Calvinistic idea of foreordination, Ro 8:29-30; Eph 1:5, 11; IPe 1:2)

ll.11-12 "Obtaining...Realm": Php 4:11 (the doctrine of estates or stations is treated subversively in this added quatrain—the poet finding in the potential of the transcendently worthwhile genius her answer to Mrs. Jackson, Niles, and Higginson)

ll.13-14 " 'Twas...Tomb": Mt 28; IPe 1:20 (foreordained from the foundations of the world by the Father, Christ is the chief corner "Stone," the embodiment and exemplification to believers of the meaning of predestined election; the poet flies in the face of such placid orthodoxy by treating the Resurrection as a feat of Emersonian individualism—a daring hyperbole guaranteed to shock Higginson; better an "Extent" earned by genius than a "Heaven" automatically imputed on the shaky basis of a "surly Technicality," or so the poet implies in a fair copy sent to her sister-in-law; as P303 demonstrates, the poet was very much aware of the complexities involved in choosing vs. being chosen, "Careers/And Exigencies" vs. "absolute Decree[s]," and thus gives in P1510 no simple, straightforward set of identifications to be read apart from the dense rhetorical context outlined by Johnson and recorded in the correspondence)

Comment: See *Poems*, III, 1042-1043; *Letters*, III, 697, 722-723, 725-726, 738-739; and Leyda, II, 367.

1512   **All things swept sole away**

ll.1-2   "All...immensity": IICo 5:17
Comment: See *Letters*, III, 716 and Leyda, II, 348-349.

1514   **An Antiquated Tree**

l.1   "An...Tree": Mt 27:32, 40, 42; IPe 2:24
ll.5-6   "Coat...Oblivion's": Jude 13
l.7   "Remotest Consulate": Rev 9:1-2, 11; 11:7; 17:8;
20:1, 3 (perhaps the "bottomless pit" is intended, those Plutonian
shores associated with Poe's "Crow"; see also Mt 89:12; Jude 6, 13;
Rev 16:10)
Comment: The poem appears in a letter to Mrs. Holland in
which the poet speaks of the crow as " 'in his own Body on the Tree',"
Johnson identifying the Scriptural allusion (IPe 2:24). Somewhat
apologetically, the poet adds: "Could you condone the profanity/"
(*Letters*, III, 690). The first appearance ("prima facie") of the crow in
a leafless tree of early spring is treated profanely in terms of the
Crucifixion. "They love," the poet goes on to tell Mrs. Holland, "such
outlawed Trees" (*Letters*, III, 689). The Scripture reference here is
either to the Cross (Mt 27:32, 40, 42; IPe 2:24) or to that withered,
leafless tree cursed by Jesus (Mt 21:19). The inversion of Christian
pieties associated with Easter—i.e., a spring poem focused on the
"Crow" whose antique, venerable blackness suggests the past, death,
and the pit—is at the heart of the Biblical wit here, a wit used
somewhat gingerly with an interlocutor such as Mrs. Holland. See
Poems, III, 1044-10;, *Letters*, III, 689-690; and Leyda, II, 3;-346.

1515   **The Things that never can come back, are several-**

l.3   "Joys": Ac 20:24; Ro 5:11; 14:17; 15:13; Ga 5:22;
Php 4:1; Heb 12:2; IPe 1:8; IJo 1:4; Jude 24 (joy, one of St. Paul's
favorite terms, appears in numerous other places in the KJV,
suggesting a calm confidence or blessed assurance of spiritual realities
beyond the circuit world)
l.9   " 'Here'...'Heres' ": Mt 24:23; 28:6; Heb 13:14
(there are a number of "Heres" in the Old Testament, e.g., Ex 3:4,

associated with theophanies and a number in the New Testament associated with circuit world limitation and apocalyptic hope)

ll.11-13 "Spirit...Land": Joh 3:8 (the consolation offered Mrs. Holland is based upon the idea that the "Native Land" of the "Spirit" is locationless, a "Land" of which circuit world "Heres" are only "typic," that is, as seen by "Compound Vision")

Comment: See *Poems*, III, 10;-1046; *Letters*, III, 714-715; and Leyda, II, 359. Though not mentioned, Nicodemus may be the link between P1515's stress on irrecoverable "Childhood" and the need for a "typic" imagination as the basis for circuit world consolation (see P140, P1274, and the third chapter of the Gospel of John).

1517   How much of Source escapes with thee-

l.1   "How...thee": Mt 1:18-25; Joh 1:1; Heb 12:2; Rev 1:8; 3:14 (the Christmas occasion and the Christlikeness of the departed Dr. Holland suggest that the "Source" is Jesus Christ)

l.2   "How...be": Rev 4

Comment: See *Poems*, III, 1047; *Letters*, III, 721-722; and Leyda, II, 359.

1518   Not seeing, still we know-

ll.1-4   "Not...caress": Ca 2:14; 3:3; 6:13 (to look upon the beloved is the ideal in the topoi of profane love here used metaphorically to speak of her anxieties and trepidations regarding the presence of the Beloved—a presence according to the KJV not seen by circuit world eyes,ICo 2:9; 13:12; IICo 4:18; ITi 6:16; Heb 11:1; IPe 1:18)

l.5   "And...away": Ge 3:10 (the fear of Adam in the Garden); Ex 3:6 (the fear of Moses before God); Rev 1:17 (the fear of St. John the Divine before the Alpha and Omega)

l.6   "Seraphic fear": Isa 6:2, 6 (the seraphim who enjoy the Lord's eternal Presence suggest for the poet her fears regarding any such celestial tete-a-tete)

ll.7-8   "Is...'dare' ": Ge 3:5 ("Eden's innuendo" is the insinuation by the serpent that taking the "dare" will lead to godlike, open-eyed awareness—an awareness in that presence that at once attracts and terrifies the poet; nothing less is suggested by her fearfulness regarding an audience with her dear friend Mrs. Tuckerman—better to "guess," "hide," and "half caress")

Comment: P1518 is apparently a metonymic displacement for that ideal presence experienced only in the beatific vision (Rev 22:4). See *Letters*, III, 720-721 and Leyda, II, 358.

1519   The Dandelion's pallid tube

l.7   "The...Suns": Mal 4:2; Lu 1:78; IIPe 1:19;Rev 2:28
l.8   "sepulture": Mt 27:60-66; 28:1-8 (synecdochic for the "Winter" now past with the advent of spring)
Comment: See *Letters*, III, 719 and Leyda, II, 357.

1520   The stem of a departed Flower

l.3   "The...Court": Rev 21:19
Comment: See *Letters*, III, 686-687 and Leyda, II, 343.

1521   The Butterfly upon the Sky,

l.6   "And...believe": Rev 3:12; 4:1; 19-21 (Heaven)
ll.7-8   "So...grieve": Ps 55:6 (among other things, the "Butterfly" is associated with spring, the Resurrection, and the Assumption—that "Dower[of other] latitudes"; see P18, P64, P129, P137, P173, P257, P328, P354, P496, P533, P970, P1099, P1244, P1246, P1526, and P1627)
Comment: See *Letters*, III, 704-705 and Leyda, II, 326.

1522   His little Hearse like Figure

ll.4-5   "The...Morals": Ec 1:14; 2:11; 8:14; 9:1-2 (apparently the "Religion" of the "Bumble Bee," the Weberian, Puritan work ethic of "Industry and Morals" confirming election, is here treated as "vanity"—such circuit world assiduity and shrewdness perhaps actually futile within the eternal scheme of things and misleadingly doctrinaire as instruction for any idle, first-flower-of-spring, "delusive Lilac")
l.6   "righteous thing": Rev 22:11 ("righteous" in the copy to Gilbert reads "founded," Ps 89:11; Am 9:6)
l.7   "Perdition": Rev 17:8

Comment: The poet added lines at the conclusion of the poem—lines contrasting Edwards with Jesus. "All liars shall have their part" (Rev 21:8); "And let him that is athirst come" (Rev 22:17). Given the context, P1522 is a lament from the point of view of "The Bumble Bee's Religion" but a song of apocalyptic hope when obliquely related to the words of Jesus. See *Poems*, III, 1049-1050; *Letters*, III, 701; and Leyda, II, 325.

1523   We never know we go when we are going-

l.2   "We...Door": Job 38:17; Ps 9:13 (shutting the door as a metaphor for passing beyond the circuit world; see also Mt 25:10)

Comment: See *Poems*, III, 1050; *Letters*, III, 691-692; and Leyda, II, 347.

1525   He lived the Life of Ambush

l.2   "And...Dusk": Job 3:5, 9; 10:21-22

l.4   "Asterisk": ICo 15:40-41, 47; IIPe 1:19; Rev 2:28; 22:16 (the "Lord from heaven," the "bright and morning star," is the guarantor of Samuel Bowles's apotheosis, his "subtle Name" replaced by that of the "dayspring from on high," Lu 1:78; Rev 22:4)

ll.5-6   "confident...Impregnable": IICo 5:4-8

ll.7-8   "Immortality...star": ICo 15:53-54; IITi 1:10; Rev 2:28; 22:16

Comment: See *Poems*, III, 1051-1052; *Letters*, III, 839; and Leyda, II, 363, 373. The "Asterisk," suggesting the omission of the bodily and accession to the celestial, joins the seal and crown as objects of the poet's apocalyptic longings for the ideally circumferential.

1526   His oriental heresies

l.3   "And...Air": Ps 72:19; 115:15; 121:2; 124:8; 134:3; Lu 10:21; Ac 17:24 ("Earth and Air" echoes the Biblically formulaic "heaven and earth" associated with the God of Creation, thus implying that the "gay apostasy" and "oriental heresies" of the bee may involve idolatry, Ex 20:3-4; Ro 1:25)

ll.9-10(worksheet draft) "peace...revelry": Php 4:7

l.16(worksheet draft) "He...attain": Php 3:11-14 (the glances at the Paulinian lexicon add Biblical wit to the Ulysses-like memories and longings of this sybaritic "Bee")

Comment: See *Poems*, III, 1052-1053; *Letters*, III, 718; and Leyda, II, 358.

1527   Oh give it Motion- deck it sweet

l.1   "give it Motion": Ge 1:20; 2:7 (the breath of life and motion are linked with man as a living soul)

l.1   "sweet": Ca 2:3, 14; 5:5, 13, 16

l.3   "Upon...words": Ca 7:9

l.4   "Affiance": Ca 1, passim (the poem uses the profane love topoi to speak of the union of "Motion" with "Dust")

l.5   "Pink stranger": ICo 15:39, 50

l.5   "Dust": Ge 2:7; 3:19; Ps 103:14

Comment: P1527 may be a plaintive cry to God in the face of separation through death, an apostrophe to the imagination stymied in the face of death, or perhaps a dramatization of unsuccessful renunciations of circuit world attractions.

1528   The Moon upon her fluent Route

ll.1-4   "The...God":Ge 1:14-18; Ps 8:1, 3; 19:1; 136:9; 150:1 (in the context of the design argument, "Substantiate," "Aims," and "Know" achieve positional ironies, reminding with subtle indirection of the futility of even such a mutation as this of the pathetic fallacy)

l.5   "Astral Ones": ICo 15:40-49

l.5(variant) "Heaven 'to come' ": Rev 1:4, 8; 4:8 (the phrasing appears elsewhere and seems linked with "Heaven": ITi 4:8; Col 2:17; Heb 2:5; 6:5; 9:11; 10:1; 13:14)

ll.6-7   "The...Know": ICo 13:12 (the finitude of the circuit world entails that incomplete knowledge whose complement necessitates a heavenly amnesia, a bittersweet anodyne for the poet who suffers distances from lost beloveds)

Comment: See *Poems*, III, 1053-1054; *Letters*, III, 731; and Leyda, II, 371.

1529   'Tis Seasons since the Dimpled War

l.8   "Pink Redoubt": ICo 15:39, 50 (see also note, line five, P1527; the "Dimpled War" of Cupid takes place within the circuit world associated with the flesh)

Comment: The wit of P1529 may to some extent depend upon familiarity with the Paulinian military metaphors regarding not "War" against "flesh and blood" (here profane love and its attractions) but against "principalities and powers" (Ro 8:36-39; ICo 9:26; IICo 7:5; Eph 6:10-18; ITi 6:12; IITi 4:7).

1530   A Pang is more conspicuous in Spring

ll.1-3   "A...Minds": Ca 2:12 (spring and the singing of the birds are associated with the presence of the beloved)

l.6   "Blue": see note, line one, P15; note, line eight, P703; and note, lines two-three, P716 (as one of the colors of the veil, "Blue" is associated with ideal presence)

l.7   "Resurrection": ICo 15:42-55

ll.7-8   "Resurrection...Stone": Mr 16:4;Lu 24:2; Joh 20:1 (apparently "Stone" is here synecdochic for that burden of anguish occasioned by absence, loss, and/or separation—an anguish demarcating the limits and seasons of the imagination)

l.6(worksheet) "slain": Rev 6:9

l.7(worksheet) "write": Rev 21:5 (the poet is aware that her words do not "make all things new")

Comment: See *Poems*, III, 1055-1056.

1531   Above Oblivion's Tide there is a Pier

l.1   "Above...Pier": Ps 107:30 (the apparent Victorian conventionality of a haven of rest is quickly dispelled by depiction of a spare and austere meeting with a "Fame" whose service grants only a cold "well done" for transcending the "Balms" of a Philistine hedonistic calculus; P1531 creates an apocalyptic in which the poet retains her face while substituting her own religio-aesthetic philosophy of deprivation for the very face of God)

l.2   " 'Few' ": Mt 7:14; Rev 3:4

l.3   "Balms": Jer 8:22 (the Balm in Gilead would be associated with Christ and, therefore, with more conventional hopes for the comforts secured by the Lamb or Bridegroom in Heaven)

l.7   "Enough...died": Rev 7; 14:1

Comment: P1531 is certainly proof that at least in certain moods there was no failure of nerve with regard to the poet's belief in an elect destiny for the "Few" with a commitment to the imagination. See *Poems*, III, 1056-1057.

1532   From all the Jails the Boys and Girls

l.2   "Ecstitically leap": see note, line fifteen, P783 and note, lines five and eight, P1191 (presumably P1532 concerns the release of children from worlds of school and work—a metaphor for an unself-conscious, ecstatic release almost paradisiacal in its dimensions)

l.3   "Beloved": Ca 1:14, 16;2:3, 8-10, 16-17;4:16;5:1-2, 4-6, 8-10, 16; 6:1-3; 7:9-11; 8:5, 14

l.7   "lie in wait": Ex 21:13; De 19:11; Jos 8:4, 13; Jg 9:25;16:9, 12; Ps 10:9; 59:3; 71:10; La 4:19; Mic 7:2; Lu 11:54; Ac 20:3, 19; 23:16, 21; Eph 4:14 (words suggesting the turpitude associated with the adult world of ambush, war, and spiritual deception; this KJV phrasing underscores the unsuspecting, Blakean innocence of the children)

l.8   "Foe/Sweet/Bud/Dew": Ca 2:3, 14; 5:2, 5, 13, 16; 6:11; 7:12

Comment: Canticles imagery surrounds this Edenic vision of children as embodiments of prelapsarian homo ludens. P1532 may in its unique way be every bit as much an "Afternoon" epiphany poem as the more famous P258. See *Poems*, III, 1057.

1533   On that specific Pillow

ll.4-5   "whether...or": ITh 5:10 (St. Paul frequently uses this construction)

l.6   "situations/comprehension new": ICo 13:12; Rev 22:4

ll.7-8   "The...do": Php 3:13-14

Comment: See *Poems*, III, 1057-1058.

1534   Society for me my misery

ll.1-2   "Society...Thee": Joh 15:18-19 (what her religio-aesthetic election produced may be the subject of P1534)

1535   The Life that tied too tight escapes

l.5   "living Grass": Ge 1:11-12; Rev 7:17 (the attractions for the escaped horse are paradisiacal)
l.6   "sees/spies": Nu 13:1-20 (the poem may glance at the promised land idea as a basis for the metaphor of escape—"Rein" and "Bridles" synecdochic of that bondage of an older dispensation)
l.7(variant) "Barns": Mt 6:26 ("Barns" are synecdochic of that world of "tied" consciousness)
Comment: See *Poems*, III, 1058.

1536   There comes a warning like a spy

l.3   "stealing...stealth": IISa 19:3
l.4   "is away/passed away": Rev 10:6; 21:1 (there may here be a very muted apocalypticism)
Comment: See *Poems*, III, 1059.

1537   Candor- my tepid friend-

l.1   "Candor": ICo 13:6
l.2   "Come...me": e.g., Lu 11:16 (apparently line two is an imperative rebuking Sue for taunting her, perhaps with some bit of adult, pharisaical, casuistical reasoning)
l.3   "Myrrhs...Mind": Mt 2:11 (the oblique reference to the Magi becomes synecdochic of all involuted, adult consciousness)
l.4   "iniquity": ICo 13:6
Comment: In the relevant letter to Sue, Emily Dickinson prefaces P1537 by saying: "How inspiriting to the clandestine Mind those words of Scripture, 'We thank thee that thou hast hid these things'" (*Letters*, III, 790-791). The Scriptural quotation and allusion to the "clandestine Mind" suggest verses from Luke (Lu 10:21 and Lu 10:23-24, respectively; Johnson identifies the quotation in the *Letters*, III, 790-791, as Mt 11:25).

1538   Follow wise Orion

l.1   "Follow...Orion": Job 9:9; 38:31; Am 5:8 (the poem apparently uses Orion as suggestive of God's omnipotence dwarfing the "Unobtrusive Blossom" of the worksheet draft)

ll.2-3(worksheet) "Catch...it": Job 38:28; Ho 13:3

Comment: The words with which the poet prefaced her poem—"A 'Pear' to the Wise is sufficient"—suggest that P1538 may have been intended as a reproof (Pr 25:11-12; *Letters*, III, 734). See *Poems*, III, 1059-1060.

1539   Now I lay thee down to Sleep-

l.1   "Now...Sleep": Ps 4:8
l.2   "I...keep": Ps 25:20
l.2   "Dust": Ge 2:7; 3:19
ll.3-4   "live," "Soul": Ge 2:7 (the Biblical wit of the poem turns on the imputation of soullessness to Sue; the pronominal switches and the parodic substitutions of "Dust," "live," and "make" for the anticipated *New England Primer* readings may not be totally absent acerbity, although the tone is difficult to ascertain)

Comment: See *Poems*, III, 1060.

1540   As imperceptibly as Grief

l.1   "Grief": Isa 53:3; Mt 26-27 (the Passion word is used to describe experience of circuit world evanescence)

l.2   "Summer lapsed": Ge 3 (as a lapse from grace, the loss of summer is the loss of presence, of that ease of reassurance found in the warm weather chapters of Thoreau's *Walden*)

l.11   "harrowing Grace": see notes, lines six and fourteen and "Comment," P1068 (the oxymoronic quality of this "Grace" reveals its paradoxical doubleness: beneficent epiphany of the beautiful, synecdochic of immortality, and yet vexing reminder as well of circuit world circumscription; for another relevant use of "harrowing" see P673)

l.12   "Guest...gone": see note, line four, P1262 (the "Guest" is "Summer" as a divine presence now at one with the "Beautiful"); see also P1055 and P1309 for the guest trope

l.14   "without a Wing": Ps 18:10; 104:3 (the contrast is instructive since "Our Summer" is now possessed by a poem, the "Beautiful" or such immortality as is glimpsed from the circuit world)

l.16(variant) "homogeneous Gown": Rev 3:5, 18 (perhaps associated with the "Guest" of the same chapter and an additional means of speaking metaphorically of divine presence)

ll.22-24(variant) "Cricket...Floor": Ec 12:5

Comment: See *Poems*, III, 1060-1063; *Letters*, II, ;3-;4; Leyda, II, 114-115; and Franklin, II, 1069-1071.

1541   No matter where the Saints abide,

l.1   "No...abide": Rev 15:3; 19:8

l.2   "Circuit": Isa 40:22; Job 22:14; Ps 19:6 (the "Circuit" as the abode of God in the heavens)

l.3   "Firmament": Ge 1:8 (the "Firmament" as the Heaven of the Creation account; perhaps the "Saints" are to be seen as apotheosized "stars of heaven," Ge 26:4; Ex 32:13; De 1:10; 10:22; 28:62; ICh 27:23; Ne 9:23; in Daniel 12:3 the Elect shine as the brightness of the firmament; the ideally circumferential state of the apotheosized "Saints" is apparently envied by the poet)

l.4   "Star": Rev 2:28; 22:1

Comment: See *Poems*, III, 1063-1064.

1542   Come show thy Durham Breast

l.1   "Come": Ca 2:10, 13; 4:8; 7:11

l.1   "Breast": Ca 1:13; 4:5; 7:3, 7-8; 8:1, 8, 10

l.2   "loves thee": Ca 1:3-4, 9; 4:7; 6:1; 7:12-13

l.3   "Delicious Robin": Ca 2:3, 16; 4:5, 16; 5:1; 6:2-3

l.5   "At...Tree": Ca 2:3, 13; 7:7-8; 8:5

ll.6-7   "Do...minute": Ca 3:11; 4:8-12

ll.10-12   "For...ensuing": Ca 2:17; 4:6; 5:6; 6:1 (the language and imagery of Canticles suggest the topoi of profane love)

Comment: See *Poems*, III, 1064 and, for the context of P1542, see *Letters*, III, 738-739 and Leyda, II, 375.

1543   Obtaining but our own Extent

ll.1-2   "Obtaining...Realm": Php 4:11 (see also note, lines eleven-twelve, P1510)

ll.3-4   " 'Twas...Tomb": Mt 28; IPe 1:20 (see also note, lines thirteen-fourteen, P1510)

Comment: See P1510; Sewall, 585-586; Poems, III, 1042-1043, 1064-1065; Letters, III, 697, 722-723, 725-726, 738-739, 744-745; and Leyda, II, 367, 381-382. Within the context of the letter to James Clark, P1543 redirects its attention (with the change of "our" to "his") to the deceased Wadsworth. The latter becomes a Passion figure, a "Man of sorrow" (Isa 53:3-4), whose "personal Expanse" the minister "carried with himself"—an explicit identification of Rev. Wadsworth with the resurrected Christ.

1544   Who has not found the Heaven- below-

ll.1-2   "Heaven...above": Rev 4; 21-22
ll.3-4   "Angels...remove": Rev 1:1, passim (angels are mentioned approximately seventy-five times in the Book of Revelation; the poet may have had in mind a certain type of consciousness such as Jacob's epiphanic awareness of divine presences at Bethel, Ge 28:12, 17)
ll.1-4   "Who...remove": Heb 12:22-24 (the poet may have had in mind such an experience had by the Elect of "Heaven-below")
Comment: See *Letters*, III, 787 and Leyda, II, 285.

1545   The Bible is an antique Volume-

ll.1-3   "Bible...Holy Spectres": IPe 1:21 ("For the prophecy came not in old time by the will of man: but holy men of God spake as they were moved by the Holy Ghost")
l.4   "Bethlehem": Mt 2:1
l.5   "Eden": Ge 2-3 (the variant line five—"Genesis - Bethlehem's Ancestor"—may be an attempt at typological linkage, Ge 3:15 with Mt 1:21-25; 2:1)
l.6   "Satan...Brigadier": Rev 20:7-8 (Satan as military leader)
l.7   "Judas...Defaulter": Mt 10:4; 26:14; Joh 13:3, 26; 14:22 (Judas Iscariot, the traitor who betrayed Christ)
l.8   "David...Troubadour": IISa 23:1-2 (the "Spirit of the Lord" spoke through David's psalms, and yet Dickinson labels him the singer of courtly love—perhaps to be connected with her admission that "Cupid taught Jehovah to many an untutored Mind"; in the KJV many Psalms are attributed to David; for David as Orpheus see, e.g., Smart's "On the Goodness of the Supreme Being")

l.9   "Sin...Precipice": Mt 4:5-8 (the temptations of Christ took place on a "high mountain" and "pinnacle of the temple," "distinguished Precipice[s]"; also, the poet may here refer to hell or the bottomless pit, Isa 14:15; Rev 9:1-2; 20:1-3)

l.10   "Others...resist": Jas 4:7

ll.11-12 "Boys...'lost' " Joh 3:15-18; IICo 4:3-4

l.13   "Tale": Ge-Rev ("Tale" is synecdochic of the Bible itself and all its stories)

l.13   "warbling Teller": Ps 1, passim (the poet views the Orphic David of the Psalms or the Solomon of Canticles as model singers of a Bible as song or poetry, the variants for "warbling" suggesting a number of its salient features: "thrilling" or dramatic with leading characters, plot, rises and falls; "hearty," "bonnie," "breathless," "spacious," "ardent," "friendly," "winning," and "mellow" or Emersonian in its openness and buoyancy; "typic" and "tropic" or figuratively rich and suggestive in its language, that is the Bible as poetry in the Arnoldian sense)

l.14   "All": IIPe 3:9

ll.15-16 "Orpheus'...condemn": Joh 3:17-18 (to captivate and thereby save the imagination is Orpheus's aim as was George Herbert's to "make a bait of pleasure" through his verse; the universalism of the poem is marked especially in its final four lines and variants)

Comment: See *Poems*, III, 1065-1067 and *Letters*, III, 732.

1546   Sweet Pirate of the heart,

l.1   "Sweet": Ca 2:3, 14; 5:5, 13, 16

l.1   "heart": Ca 4:9

l.3   "wrecketh": Ca 4:9 (the nautical lexicon's substitute for the KJV "ravished")

l.4   "spice's": Ca 4:10, 14, 16; 5:1, 13; 6:2; 8:14

l.5   "Attar's": Ca 1:13; 3:6; 4:6, 14; 5:1, 5, 13

Comment: The nautical metaphor of P1546 is enriched by the language and situation of the fourth chapter of Canticles. See *Letters*, III, 723 and Leyda, II, 360. The "ebbing voice" of the Tuckerman boys may be an additional link to Canticles (Ca 2:8, 14; 5:2).

1547   Hope is a subtle Glutton-

l.1   "Hope...Glutton": ICo 15:19-20 (circuit world fleshly mindedness succumbs to "Hope" as an ignis fatuus—"Hope" inverted and inward turned becomes oral fears of death)

l.2   "He...Fair": IPe 5:8

l.3   "inspected closely": Ro 8:6; IJo 3:3 (from the perspective of spiritual-mindedness)

l.4   "Abstinence": Ro 8:24-25; Heb 11:1-3; IPe 1:3-9 (the spiritual-minded awareness of "Hope" as "Abstinence" P1547 translates metaphorically into the oral austerity of the Elect whose otherworldliness allows enjoyment of a halcyon banquet "typic" of the Marriage Supper of the Lamb)

ll.5-8   "His...remain": Rev 7:16-17; 19:7-9

l.6   "One": ITi 1:1 (the equation of Jesus with "Hope"; see also note, line one, P1392)

1548   Meeting by Accident,

l.4   "An...divine": IJo 4:6 (the Biblical wit turns upon the multiple meanings of "divine")

1549   My Wars are laid away in Books-

l.1   "Wars": Ro 7:23; IICo 10:3-5; ITi 1:18-19; IITi 2:3-5; 4:7-8; Jas 4:1-2; IPe 2:11

l.3   "Foe": ICo 15:21, 26, 54-55; Rev 6:8

l.9   "sweet": Ca 2:3, 14; 5:5, 13, 16 (perhaps used, along with the "Chums" of the next line, for ironic and oxymoronic effect, clashing as it does with the metaphors from Paulinian combativeness)

l.10   "By...away": Heb 12:1

l.11   "Since...ten": Ps 90:10

Comment: See *Poems*, III, 1068-1069.

1550   The pattern of the sun

l.1   "pattern": Ro 8:29; ICo 15:49; IICo 3:18; Php 3:21; ITi 1:16; IJo 3:2-3 (the poem apparently deals with whether "we shall also bear the image of the heavenly," ICo 15:49; line two suggests that the "pattern" is sui generis, inimitable)

l.1   "sun": Mal 4:2; Rev 1:16; 2:28; 22:16

l.3   "sheen": Joh 1:4-9; IJo 1:5; Rev 21:23-24

l.3   "Disk": Rev 22:4-5 (the ideally circumferential face achieved by the Sun-Son, apparently to be perceived analogically but not finally imitated or possessed; P1550 may then be one of a number of poems on the theme of the potential unmeaning of the apocalyptic)

1551   Those- dying then,

ll.1-3   "Those...Hand": Ps 16:8-11 (those in Biblical times had an assurance, as did the Psalmist, of a place at "God's Right Hand"; the Elect, the sheep, are placed on "God's Right Hand" at the last judgment, Mt 25:31-36; Christ's exaltation to "God's Right Hand" was the guarantee for the believing Elect of a similar destiny, and thus Psalm 110 was frequently echoed in the New Testament: Mt 22:44; 26:64; Mk 12:36; 16:19; Lu 22:69; Ac 2:25, 33-35; 7:55-56; Heb 1:3, 13; 8:1; 10:12; 12:2; Ro 8:34; Eph 1:20; Col 3:1; other KJV associations with "Right Hand" perhaps relevant to P1551 would be God's Creation, Isa 48:13; blessing, Rev 1:16-17; deliverance, Ps 80:15-19; Isa 41:10, 13; power, Ex 15:6-12; De 33:2; Ps 16:8; 44:3; 48:10; 77:10; 98:1; 118:15-16; 139:10; Isa 41:10, 13; also not to be overlooked is the association in Canticles of the embrace of the beloved with the "Right Hand," Ca 2:6; 8:3)
l.4   "That...now": Nu 11:23; Ps 74:11; Isa 50:2; 59:1; La 2:3 (the KJV equivalent of amputation is the shortened or withdrawn "Hand" of God, here suggestive of loss of power and presence)
l.6   "Belief": Ro 4:24; 6:8-11; Eph 1:19-20; 1Th 4:14; 1Ti 1:16 ("Belief" in P1551 is specifically that in the resurrection and its concomitant, eternal life; P1551 is intensely personal, and incisively clinical, and not an expression of some fuzzy-minded weltschmerz over nineteenth-century loss of faith)
ll.8-9   "Better...all": Pr 15:16-17; 16:8, 19; 17:1; 19:1; 25:7; 28:6; Ec 4:6, 13; 5:5; 6:9; 7:1-3, 5, 8; 9:16 (the "better—than" construction is derived from the bittersweet and oxymoronic wisdom sayings of the KJV)

1552   Within thy Grave!

l.1   "Within...Grave": Mt 28:1-8; 1Co 15:54-55
l.2   "Oh...flight": Lu 24:51; Ac 1:9-11; 2:31-36 (the "flight" may refer to the resurrected and exalted Christ)
l.3   "Thou...mankind": Lu 2:9-11; Joh 1:1-14

1.4 "To...night": Joh 14:2-3, 27

Comment: Although P1552 apparently refers to the Resurrection and Ascension of Christ, that advent and loss may be paradigmatic, i.e., a hyperbole fittingly underscoring the poet's own sense of loss regarding a deceased beloved.

1553 Bliss is the plaything of the child-

1.1 "Bliss...child": Mt 19:14 ("Suffer little children, and forbid them not, to come unto me: for of such is the kingdom of heaven")

1.3 "The...Girl": Ge 2-3 (the "natural piety" of the Garden that the poet believed to some extent was recaptured at marriage)

1.4 "Rebuke...can": ICo 13:11 ("When I was a child, I spake as a child, I understood as a child, I thought as a child: but when I became a man, I put away childish things")

Comment: "The Child is father of the Man" is the "secret" of P1553, a poem pleading for the "natural piety" of Wordsworth's "My Heart Leaps Up When I Behold" versus the stern "Rebuke" of St. Paul and other adults of "Real Life" ilk. See *Poems*, III, 1070.

1554 "Go tell it"- What a Message-

11.1,3 "Message," "endearment": IJo 1:5-7; 3:11 (the "Message" of "endearment" contrasts to that of the Spartans)

1.3 "murmur": Ex 16:7-9; Nu 14:27, 36; 16:11, 41; 17:5, 10 (the KJV word for disruptive dissension and complaint here in stark contrast to uncompromising obedience; the poet's audience would also have been aware of the "evil report" from false spies of the promised land, Nu 13:32—a "Message" reflecting "murmur" as well as timorousness)

1.5 "Lure": Ho 2:14

1.7 "sweet": Ca 2:3, 14; 5:5, 13, 16

1.8 "give...Kiss": Ca 1:2; 7:12; 8:1, 6-7 (to some extent the wit of the poem is achieved by the juxtaposition of Spartan austerities with the longings according to "Nature" of Canticles)

Comment: See *Poems*, III, 1071.

1555 I groped for him before I knew

ll.1-2   "I...need": Ca 3:1-2; Mt 5:6 (through the spiritualization of sense, the profane "nameless need" for any circuit world bounty foreshadows the later hunger for the consecrated "Bread of Life")

l.3   "chaff": Ps 35:5; Jer 23:28; Da 2:35; Mt 3:12 (the KJV word for the refuse that does not nourish)

l.4   "foreshadowed Food": Mt 26:26 (the Eucharistic bread); Joh 6:31-35, 48-58 (Jesus as "the only Food"; for another poem on circuit world life as "typic" of a higher hunger see P579; the "foreshadowed Food" may also suggest apocalyptic promises of Revelation: the cessation of hunger, Rev 7:16, and the Marriage Supper of the Lamb, Rev 19:7-9)

l.4(variant) "unsullied": Heb 9:13-14

l.5   "taste": Ca 2:3; Ps 34:8; Heb 6:4-5; IPe 2:3

l.5   "spurn and sneer": Lu 6:25 (the attendant dangers for those who do not embrace the Beatitudes philosophy of deprivation)

l.6   "Though...suppose": Col 2:17; Heb 8:5 (that is when the "nameless need" is viewed in "typic" fashion as an image or shadow of divine things)

l.7   "consecrated": Ex 29:31-32; Le 8:28, 31;Heb 10:20 (for the association of the word with the Eucharist, see P130)

l.8   "The...grows": Joh 6:31-35, 48-58

Comment: See *Poems*, III, 1071.

1556   Image of Light, Adieu-

l.1   "Image": Col 2:17; Heb 8:5; 10:1 (P1556 says "Adieu" to that created light "typic" of the Light)

l.1   "Light": Joh 1:4-9; 8:12; 9:5; 12:35-36; IJo 1:5-7; Rev 21:23-24; 22:5 (God the Father and Son are "Light," Christ spoken of as the "image of the invisible God," Col 1:15, who dwells in that "light which no man can approach unto," ITi 6:16)

ll.2-3   "Thanks...short": see P258; Ge 28:10-17; 32:24-30 (interviews of Jacob with God or His emissaries); Ex 3-4; 19; 24:15-18; 34; Nu 20:6-13 (interviews of Moses with God; the "interview" could be any and all attenuated substitutes experienced by the poet in the circuit world: the diurnal round, the Bible, and intimations of immortality, for example, from a certain slant of light; for all their apparent flippancy of tone in a poem apostrophizing light, these lines are tinged with bitterness regarding an absent ideal presence once enjoyed by patriarchs but now inaccessible in a present made of words, metaphors based upon corruptible images)

Comment: See *Poems*, III, 1072.

1557   Lives he in any other world

l.1   "Lives he": Ro 6:23; ICo 15:50-55

l.1   "other world": Ro 12:2; ICo 5:10; 7:31; Ga 1:4 (the "other world" of Heaven is constantly implied by St. Paul)

l.2   "My...reply": Heb 11:1

ll.3-4   "Before...me": ICo 15:51-55 (perhaps the promised "all" of resurrection is no longer so "distinct" as to transmute St. Paul's rhetorical questions into imperatives)

Comment: See *Poems*, III, 1072.

1558   Of Death I try to think like this-

l.1   "Death": ICo 15:54-55

l.2   "Well": ICo 15:55 (the grave, here a sealike "Brook"; the "Well" has positive KJV associations: with corroborations of the Covenant and evidences of God's power over the waters, be they brooks or seas, Ex 15:1-6; Nu 21:14-18; De 2:18, 29; and with metaphors for the beloved, Ca 4:15, and for the promise of everlasting life, Joh 4:14)

l.3   "Likeness...Brook": Nu 33; 35; De 3-4; Jos 3-4 (Jordan, as the barrier to the inheritance of the promise, is perhaps that Well-Brook-Death, a terminus a quo not ad quem)

l.4   "slay us": Ex 5:21; ISa 5:10-11 (KJV idiom)

l.5   "But...Dismay": see P313 (circuit world "reefs" or "brooks" endear the shores beyond—an expression of the poet's theodicy of paradox and oxymoron, a fear to justify, a dismay to sweeten, a decay to welcome)

l.6   "sweetness": Ca 2:3, 14; 5:5, 13, 16; 7:9

l.7   "Flower": Ca 2:12; 5:13

l.7   "Hesperian": Ge 2-3; Eze 28:13-14; 31:8-9, 16; 47:1-12; IIEsdras 7:36; Rev 19; 21-22 (the equivalent in Greek mythology to the poet's paradise; the story of the daughters of Hesperus who guarded the golden apples in the Isles of the Blest with the aid of a dragon may explain a number of things in P1558: the menace of line four, the Heraclean "Zest" of line six, the "decoying" of the sun, which was part of the mythological explanation of sunset, and the intrepid "Child['s]" play with its all-or-nothing outcome)

    ll.11-12 "Sea," "roaring": ICh 16:32; Ps 96:11; 98:7; Isa 5:30; 51:15; Jer 31:35; 51:55; Lu 21:25 (a frequent KJV pairing)

    l.13   "Purple": see note, line one, P15; note, line eight, P703; and note, line three, P716 ("Purple" is the regal color, Jg 8:26; Joh 19:2; Rev 17:4; and the color associated with the beloved, Ca 3:10; 7:5)

    l.13   "Flower": Ca 2:12; 5:13 ("Flower" may here be the Hesperian golden apples, the fruit of Eden, Ge 3:2-6; the Canticles imagery allows P1558 to use the profane love topoi in speaking of death as a recapturing of a childlike, prelapsarian innocence that is at the same time an embrace of the beloved)

    Comment: See *Poems*, III, 1072-1073; Leyda, I, 355; and P98, P122, P313, P503, P1067, and P1400.

1559   Tried always and Condemned by thee

    l.1   "Tried": Job 23:10; Ps 7:9; 12:6; 66:10; Da 12:10; Zec 13:9; Heb 11:17; Rev 3:18 ("tried" has a metallurgical as well as juridical provenance, thereby suggesting the refinement achieved beyond death—a bodiless purity requisite for "earn[ing] the look" of ideal presence)

    l.1   "Condemned": Rev 11:18; 14:7; 15:4; 16:7; 18:8, 10; 19:2, 11; 20:4, 12-13 (the beloved is presented as possessing the grace-giving powers of the Deity—only the Deity may try, judge, condemn, and reprieve/deliver)

    l.2   "Permit/allow/bestow": ICo 15:10; 16:7; IICo 1:11; 8:1; ITh 2:4; Heb 6:3; IJo 3:1 KJV language associated with the grace-giving powers of the Deity)

    ll.2-3   "Permit," "earn": Eph 2:8-9 (a further KJV paradox in P1559 is that of "permit"/ "earn," grace/ works)

    l.3   "earn the look": Ca 1:6; 2:9; 4:8-9; 6:10-13; ICo 13:12; IICo 3:18; Rev 22:4 (the look of the beloved and the beatific vision, the one lost, the other gained, presumably, at death—a set of relationships here deliberately inverted to exaggerate her desire to extend circuit world presence with the beloved beyond death) ll.3-4   "dying," "live": IICo 4:10; 6:9 (the KJV background of her paradoxical wit is the Paulinian conjunction of dying and living, since receipt of the grace of God as the "knowledge of the glory of God in the *face* of Jesus Christ," IICo 4:6)

Comment: See *Poems*, III, 1073 and Sewall, 662-663.

1560   To be forgot by thee

l.11   "Worthy to be": IISa 22:4; Ps 18:3; Lu 15:19, 21; Ro 8:18

l.12   "low"(variant): Lu 1:52

l.12   "meek"(variant): Ps 37:11; Mt 5:5 ("low" and "meek" would suggest the compensation of destitution, an emphasis out of keeping with the praise of being forgotten in P1560; nevertheless, the lines addressed to Helen Hunt Jackson may draw attention to the flowers and, obliquely, to the conditions of beauty, thus suggesting that a simple, straightforward, and self-deprecatory eulogizing of the poetess may have been only the apparent theme of P1560)

Comment: See *Poems*, III, 1074-1075; *Letters*, III, 772; and Leyda, II, 396.

1561   No Brigadier throughout the Year

l.5   "Pursuing...us": Job 30:15

l.11   "Heaven looked upon": Job 28:24; Ps 14:2; 33:13; 53:2; 80:14; 102:19; Isa 63:15

l.14   "sky": Ge 1:6-20; De 33:26; Job 37:18; (synecdochic of God, its Creator)

ll.17-18 "The...Evergreens": Mt 8:20

ll.19-20 "His...things": Le 11:13-20; De 14:11-20 (the vague, ethereal diet of the "Jay" may partially qualify it as Biblically clean)

l.22   "Future": Rev 19:17

l.23   "Immortality": ITi 1:17 (synecdochic of God Who decides the destiny of the "Jay"); ICo 15:50-55 (the future life in Heaven)

l.24   "Neighbor": Mt 5:43; 19:19; 22:39; Lu 10:27-36 (the capstone of the poet's hyperbolical personification of the "Jay" is this glance at the Golden Rule and Thoreau-like special pleading for its eternal destiny)

Comment: Some "Dispute" congenial to the poet's theriophilic bent may lurk behind P1561. Biblically, the animals have no soul granted immortality by God (De 12:23). See *Poems*, III, 1074-1076; *Letters*, III, 769-770; and Leyda, II, 396.

1562   Her Losses made our Gains ashamed-

l.1   "Her...ashamed": Php 3:7-8 (the language of loss and gain is Paulinian, as in P968, but see also, Mt 16:26)

l.2   "Life's...Pack": Mt 10:38; 16:24; 27:32 (life as a cross); Job 1:21 (the elemental destitution of circuit world existence); Ro 7:24; IICo 5:4; Php 3:21 (perhaps synecdochic of the body prison; nevertheless, the apiarian metaphor underpinning P1562 suggests that "empty Pack" is George Eliot as bee, as the conveyor, but not ultimate repository, of honey)

ll.3-4   "As...Back": Mt 2:2, 9; 24:27; Ac 12:4 (George Eliot displayed a self-validating courage in the face of unbelief, as confident that her circuit world discipline would lead to apotheosis as if confirmed by more conventional, external, cosmic signs)

ll.5-6   "Life's...knows": Mt 11:28-30

l.7   "Honey": Ge 43:11; De 8:8 (circuit world sustenance); Ex 3:8, 17 (the food of the promised land); Isa 7:14-15 (the food of Christ); Ca 4:11; 5:1 (associated with the beloved; the bee-Eliot is the sweetness-and-light, aesthetic-world equivalent of the Biblical Christ)

l.8   "sweeter": Ps 19:10; 119:103; Ca 2:3, 14;5:5, 13, 16 (honey, the Biblical standard of sweetness and further associations with the beloved)

Comment: See Sewall, 586-587; *Poems*, III, 1076-1077; *Letters*, III, 769-770; and Leyda, II, 396.

1563   By homely gift and hindered Words

ll.4-5   " 'Nothing'...World": Ge 1:1; Isa 40:12-28; Ro 4:17; Heb 11:3 (ex nihilo creation may be here given an individual application suggesting that poetry is all because of life's enforced reticences; "Words," "force," and "World" may suggest a connection with the first chapter of the Gospel of John)

Comment: See *Poems*, III, 1077. Ex nihilo creation is discussed in II Maccabees 7:28.

1564   **Pass to thy Rendezvous of Light,**

l.1   "Rendezvous": ITh 4:17
l.1   "Light": Joh 1:4-9; ITi 6:16; IJo 1:5 (God is Light and dwells in light); Rev 21:23-24; 22:5 (the Lord God is the light of the New Jerusalem or Heaven; thus, "Light" is here synecdochic of Heaven)
l.2   "Pangless": Rev 21:4 (Gilbert has "leaped" beyond pain and death)
l.3   "Mystery": ICo 15:51 (St. Paul discusses how this mortal puts on immortality); Rev 10:7 (the "mystery of God" known to Gilbert but experienced by the poet in the space-time of the circuit world); see also, note, line three, P1558 (Jordan, as the barrier to the promised land, Nu 33:51; 35:10; De 3:25; Jos 1-7, might be "typic" of the metaphorical stream of death through which the poet "ford[s]," and the river's associations with Elijah's ascension may also be relevant, IIKi 2)
Comment: See *Poems*, III, 1078; *Letters*, III, 799, 863-864; and Leyda, II, 408-409.

1565   **Some Arrows slay but whom they strike-**

ll.1-2   "Some...him": IISa 18:9-17 (the poet may have had in mind the death of the beloved Absalom)
ll.3-4   "Who...Tomb": Mt 27:59-60; Joh 20:1-10 (the lines may deliberately hint at the resurrection of Christ)
Comment: See *Poems*, III, 1078; *Letters*, III, 842-843; and Leyda, II, 423.

1567   **The Heart has many Doors-**

l.1   "The...Doors": see note, line one, P674 and note, line one, P1142 (the KJV metaphor of the individual as habitation or dwelling)
l.1   "Heart": Ca 4:9; 5:2; 8:6
l.1   "Doors": Ca 8:9 (the beloved as a door; see also, Rev 3:20)
l.2   "I...knock": Ca 5:2; Rev 3:20 (an open door would grant the presence of the beloved)

l.3	"sweet": Ca 2:3, 14; 5:5, 13, 16

l.3	" 'Come in' ": Ca 2:10, 13; 4:8; 5:1; 7:11; Rev 3:20 ("Behold, I stand at the door, and knock: if any man hear my voice, and open the door, I will come in to him, and will sup with him, and he with me")

l.6	"Repast": Rev 19:7-9

l.7	"That...exists": see P338

l.8	"Supremacy": Rev 19:6 (synecdochic of the Lord God who reigns at the Supper of the Lamb; P1567 is a metonymic displacement for ideal presence)

Comment: See *Poems*, III, 1079; *Letters*, III, 798-800; and Leyda, II, 408-410.

### 1568	To see her is a Picture-

l.1	"To...Picture": Ca 4

l.2	"To...Tune": Ca 1:1; 2:8, 14

l.3	"To...Intemperance": Ca 4:9; 5:8; 8:6-7

l.6	"To...Friend": Ca 5:16

ll.7-8	"A...Hand": Mal 4:2; Lu1:78; 2:7 (in the context of motherhood, P1568 may view Mrs. Holland as the Virgin Mary as well as the beloved); Ca 6:10 (the beloved as the sun)

ll.6-7(variant) "Is...Redemption...receive": Ro 3:24; Eph 1:7 14; Col 1:14; Heb 9:12, 15 (the unorthodox comparison adds to the string of hyperboles; for the association of "melody" with the idyllic, Isa 51:3; Rev 15:3)

Comment: See *Poems*, III,. 1080-1081; *Letters*, III, 760-761; and Leyda, II, 391.

### 1569	The Clock strikes one that just struck two-

l.1	"The...two": Ge 2:23-24; Mt 19:5; Eph 5:31 (all of Ephesians chapter five is relevant but especially verses twenty-two to thirty-three in which is discussed the "great mystery" of marriage joining man and wife as one as Christ is joined with the church; the poet viewed marriage as the means of recapturing prelapsarian Eden)

l.2	"schism...Sum": Ge 3 (perhaps a reference to the Fall, a "schism" in God's math or "Sum") l.3 "Vagabond/Sorcerer...Genesis": Ge 2-3 (Eve, the disreputable tramp of Genesis who becomes a "Sorcerer" controlling future events through marriage and offspring, Ge 3:15)

l.4   "Has...Pendulum": Ge 2-3 (the "Pendulum," which before ineluctably struck in its oppositions of man and woman, life and death, now has been magically "wrecked" by the "Vagabond/Sorcerer" who reverses its physical principles of momentum and force of gravity, thereby overcoming the effects of the Fall and, at least to the poet's mind, recapturing a prelapsarian paradise; specifically, the "Pendulum" is synecdochic of time, with its concomitant Fall and promised death, and it is this time that the "Vagabond/Sorcerer" wrecks by bruising the head of the serpent through marriage and the promised Second Adam, ICo 15)

Comment: See *Poems*, III, 1981-1082; *Letters*, III, 762-763, 824-825; and Leyda, II, 392. The wit of P1569 is both Biblical and scientific, a wit heightened by the dramatic actions of the "Vagabond" against an order embodied in "Clock," "Sum," "Genesis," and "Pendulum"—division and damage achieving a higher order, Blakean fashion.

1570   Forever honored be the Tree

l.4   "Gabriels": see note, line fourteen, P725 and note, line one, P1483

l.7   "Angels...way": Ge 18:1-10; 19:1-22; 32:24-30; Jos 5:13-15; Jg 13:1-23 (the relevant angels are those registering in "Nature's Book" by taking human form; "Robins," celestial visitants unaware from beyond the circuit world, occasion this lull-in-a-storm epiphanic awareness or Wordsworthian "spot of time" much as slanted light on a specific afternoon does elsewhere, P258)

Comment: See *Poems*, III, 1082-1083; *Letters*, III, 765-767, 915-916; and Leyda, II, 395-396.

1571   How slow the Wind-

ll.1-2   "Wind," "sea": Ge 8:1; Job 38; Rev 7:1; 21:1 (from Genesis to Revelation, the wind and sea are at the beck and call of God; see, for example, Mr 4:41)

l.3   "Feathers": Ps 91:4 (synecdochic of God, especially as manifested in a solicitous presence; "Feathers" contrasts with the

"Sweet Foot" of the letter to Mrs. Tuckerman—"Sweet Foot" synecdochic of the attentive and responsive presence of the beloved, Ca 5:3; 7:1)

      Comment: See *Poems*, III, 1083-1084 and *Letters*, III, 781.

1573   To the bright east she flies,

      l.1   "bright east": Ge 2:8; Eze 47:1-12 (associations of "east" with Eden and paradise); Mal 4:2; Mt 24:27; Lu 1:78; IIPe 1:19; Rev 2:28; 7:2; 22:16 (apocalyptic associations of the sunrise and resurrection with Christ and the New Jerusalem or Heaven)

      l.2   "Paradise": Ge 2-3; Eze 28:13-14; 31:8-9, 16; 47:1-12; Rev 2:7; 21-22

      l.2   "Brothers," "Paradise": Rev 1:1, passim (the winged, angelic hosts of Heaven)

      l.4   "wings": ICo 15:35-55 (synecdochic of Mrs. Dickinson's resurrected celestial, spiritual body); Mal 4:2 (figuratively suggestive of the Kingdom of Heaven)

      ll.9-11   "We...strays": IICo 4:16-18

      l.12   "Homeless...home": IICo 5:6

      Comment: See *Poems*, III, 1084; *Letters*, III, 770-771; and Leyda, II, 394-395.

1574   No ladder needs the bird but skies

      l.1   "ladder": Ge 28:12

      ll.3-4   "Nor...sings": Isa 6:2-6; 37:16; Rev 4 (presumably the cherubim and seraphim sing willingly their praise to God; the "leader's grim baton" and the innocent song of childhood seem Blakean as in "Holy Thursday," "A Cradle Song," "Nurse's Song," and others from Blake's *Songs of Innocence and Experience*)

      ll.6-7   "As...moiety": Mt 19:14 ("Suffer little children, and forbid them not, to come unto me: for of such is the kingdom of heaven)

      l.8   "cherubim": Ge 3:24; Ex 25:18-22; Ps 18:10; 80:1; Isa 37:16; Eze 10; Heb 9:5 (cherubim are winged angels; for example, in Exodus they spread their wings on the ark above the mercy seat where God manifests His presence; elsewhere, cherubim surround the throne of God)

Comment: In P1574, the bird-child-cherub enjoys the beatitude that is the kingdom of heaven or that "moiety" that is an equal share of God's presence. The "Him" of line six apparently refers to the child under Maria Whitney's care. In euphoric language reminiscent of Wordsworth, Emerson, and Alcott on childhood, the poet wrote her friend:

> I can easily imagine your fondness
> for the little life so mysteriously
> committed to your care. The bird that
> asks our crumb has a plaintive distinction.
> I rejoice that it was possible for you to be
> with it, for I think the early spiritual
> influences about a child are more hallowing
> than we know. The angel begins in the
> morning in every human life. How small the
> furniture of bliss! How scant the heavenly
> fabric! (*Letters*, III, 777)

See *Poems*, III, 1085, 1093-1094; *Letters*, III, 776-777; and Leyda, II, 398.

1575   The Bat is dun, with wrinkled Wings-

l.1   "Bat": Le 11:19; De 14:18; Isa 2:20 (Biblically an abomination, the creature taxes the poet's ingenuity in finding it a niche as one of the Creator's "Eccentricities")

l.9   "Firmament": Ge 1:6-8, 14-17, 20; Ps 19:1; 150:1 (a word evocative of the issue of design; stanza three has some of the inscrutable complexity of Blake's "The Tyger" and Job 38-41, making stanza four somewhat anticlimactic)

l.13   "Creator": Ge 1:1-31; Ec 12:1; Isa 40:28

l.14   "Ascribe...praise": Ps 150:1; Rev 4:11

Comment: See *Poems*, III, 1085-1086. Not circular or circumferential (a condition of incompletion elsewhere treated tragically, P1396 and P1605) is the eccentric "Bat" (the poet?) who, as a "fallow Article," is a flying joint connecting two "Umbrella[s] quaintly halved," singing and writing what is indecipherable, a creature of unreconciled yet accepted contradictions—"dun" and "fallow" versus "Air" and "Firmament."

1576   The Spirit lasts- but in what mode-

l.1   "The...mode": ICo 15:35 ("But some man will say, How are the dead raised up? and with what body do they come?")

ll.2-3,9 "Body," "Spirit," "Flesh": ICo 15:35-55 (the language of P1576 is that of St. Paul's discussion of the resurrection)

ll.2-9   "Below...Flesh": Ro 8

ll.10-11 "Like...live": Ge 1:2

l.13   "know-now": ICo 13:12 (the poet agonizes over the continuity from circuit to new circumference existence)

l.17   "Adamant": Ps 28:1; 35:22; 83:1 (synecdochic of God as silent and hidden, the Deus absconditus)

l.21   "Rumor's Gate": a synecdoche for the Holy Bible itself whose revelation will not now yield the poet extra-circuit world knowledge of Gilbert or Rev. Wadsworth

l.22   "Mind...sown": ICo 15:42-44

l.23   "Prognostic's Push": IIPe 1:21 (the poet suggests the limitations of post-revelation, post-prophecy circuit world consciousness; see P1545)

Comment: See *Poems*, III, 1086-1087; *Letters*, III, 801-802; and Leyda, II, 410-411.

1577   Morning is due to all-

l.1   "Morning": Ca 6:10

l.2   "Night": Ca 1:13; 3:1, 8; 5:2

l.4   "Auroral light": Rev 21:23-24; 22:5 (the Platonizing idealization of married love pushes P1577 away from the profane toward the paradisiacal light of the New Jerusalem)

Comment: References to Genesis 3 and Revelation 21 are found in the letter to Samuel Bowles the younger. See *Poems*, III, 1087; *Letters*, III, 796; and Leyda, II, 406.

1578   Blossoms will run away,

l.1   "Blossoms...away": Isa 40:8; IPe 1:24

l.3   "Memory": Mt 6:24 (a synecdoche for God versus the circuit world mammon of "Blossoms" and "Cakes," a piece of Biblical wit in a note to Nellie Sweetser, which makes clear the context by quoting Jos 24:15)

Comment: See *Letters*, III, 785 and Leyda, II, 404.

1579   **It would not know if it were spurned,**

ll.5-6   "aspire," "despair": Lu 23:39-43 (presumption and despair are the two poles for those uncertain of election, the paradigmatic case being the two thieves on the Cross—see P1180; the very real sense of unworthiness and fear of rejection do not diminish the wit of the final lines with their "Cavalier" who might dare to enter and "perish there")
Comment: See *Poems*, III, 1088.

1580   **We shun it ere it comes,**

l.2   "Joy": Mt 25:21, 23; Joh 17:13; Ro 5:11; 14:17; 15:13; Heb 12:2; IJo 12; Jude 24 (joy is so consistently associated with presence that it surely must point to that ideal presence of the beatific vision, Rev 22:4, about which the poet expresses the ambivalence of approach-avoidance, "shun" and "sue" or "beguile," the very rhythms of the song of songs, Canticles)
l.7   "Old...Heaven": Ca 5:2; Rev 3:20; 19:7-9; 22:4
l.8   "Like...thee": Rev 3:20; 19:7-9 ("thee" is the Lamb, the Bridegroom; specifically, the "dismay" is an apprehension that the longed-for presence will disappoint, that the ideal presence begins and ends with the words produced by the imagination)
Comment: See *Poems*, III, 1088; *Letters*, III, 758; and Leyda, II, 386-387.

1581   **The farthest Thunder that I heard**

ll.1,5   "Thunder," "Lightning": Ex 9:23; 19:16; 20:18; ISa 7:10; IISa 22:14-15; Job 28:26; 37:4-5; 38:25, 35; Ps 18:13; 29:3; 77:18; 104:7; Isa 29:6; Eze 1:13-14; Da 10:6; Mt 24:27; 28:3; Rev 4:5; 6:1; 8:5; 11:19; 14:2; 16:18; 19:6 (theophanies and visions are spoken of in terms of thunder and lightning, such frequent figurative expressions for God's manifestations being too numerous to list)
ll.5-6   "The...myself": Ac 9:3-7 (there is here perhaps a parallel with the Damascus road experience of Saul of Tarsus, a life-changing "Lightning" not witnessed by his companions; these lines—lines six, eleven, twelve, fifteen, and sixteen—suggest the exclusivity

of this experience as perhaps a type of election, Eph 5:13; IPe 2:9; IIPe 1:10)

ll.7-8   "But...Life": Mt 13:45-46; 16:26

l.10   "Happy/ransomed": Isa 35:10; Mt 20:28; ITi 2:6

ll.9-12   "Indebtedness...Electricity": ICo 2:7-16 (the poet may be speaking of a higher illumination beyond the natural or "Oxygen" of the circuit world)

l.13   "It...Days": Ge 1:3 (the line suggests the primacy of light as a manifestation of God in love and life; God as the "Father of lights," Jas 1:17, is the giver of all gifts: life, love, pleasure, order, knowledge, salvation, and eternal life)

ll.14-15 "And...concomitant": Ps 34:5; Ec 8:1; Mt 5:14-16 (receivers of the "Light" become givers as well, not a sentimentalization but an elegant Dantean, Augustinian vision of all "clamor bright" enveloped by Light-Love)

l.16   "waylaying Light": Ac 9:3 (the "Light" that sidetracked yet converted St. Paul, giving him an "Explanation" for "Life's reverberation"); Joh 1:1-9; 8:12; IJo 1:5 (God and the Word-Logos are "Light:); Joh 14:6 (Jesus is the "Light" laying the "way" through illumination)

ll.17-20 "The...found": Eph 5 (the poet is a child of lightning, a Bride of Christ who has found life's "Explanation" in a bodiless theophany, a quiet "Thought" whose significance is conveyed in the imagery traditional for divine revelation, light, Ac 22:6, 9; IITi 1:10; Heb 6:4; 10:32; the traditional associations of light with God's countenance should not be overlooked since the Lightning-Electricity of P1581 anticipates the beatific vision, Nu 6:25-26; Ps 4:6; 44:3; 80:7; 89:15; 90:8; Rev 1:16; 21:23; 22:4-5)

Comment: See *Poems*, III, 1089-1091; *Letters*, III, 831, 840-841; and Leyda, II, 430-431.

1582   Where Roses would not dare to go,

l.1   "Where...go":Ca2:1 (even the ideally circumferential rose might be a reproach to the presence of the beloved)

l.2   "What...way": Ca 3:11; 4:9; 5:2; 8:6

l.3   "Crimson": 2Ch 3:14 (associated with presence)

ll.3-4   "Scouts...Enemy": Nu 13; Eze 20:5-6 (the same dynamic of wish for confirmation of being the chosen and fear of rejection may have as background the timorous Israelites before the promised land)

Comment: See *Poems*, III, 1091.

1583 Witchcraft was hung, in History,

l.1 "Witchcraft...History": Ex 22:18; De 18:10-12; ISa 15:23 (witchcraft as an excoriated sin, a sign of rebellion)

l.3 "Witchcraft": IICh (witchcraft in perhaps a more positive sense as enchantment; but see also its associations with idolatry, Mic 5:12-13; Ga 5:20)

1584 Expanse cannot be lost-

ll.1-3 "Expanse...Deity": Ps 19; 90 (the "Promise" of the "Deity" as law or "Decree" rather than light and love is the consolation provided her sister-in-law by the poet who was reassured by the thought that God cannot discontinue Himself)

l.4 "His...Infinity": Ge 21:33; De 33:27; Ps 41:13; 90:2; 93:2; 106:48; 1;:13; Isa 9:6; Hab 1:12; IIPe 1:11; Rev 1:6; 4:9-10; 5:13-14; 7:12; 11:15; 15:7; 22:5

l.5 "Whose...tight": see note, line twenty-one, P1576

l.6 "Before...sown": see note, line twenty-two, P1576

ll.7-8 "Not...thereon": see note, line twenty-three, P1576

l.9 "The...opened": Mr 10:30; Lu 18:30; Rev 11:15 (the "World" is Heaven); Rev 4:1; 19:11 (the door opened in Heaven by Gilbert and followed by the poet in imagination may owe something to the vision of St. John the Divine in Revelation)

ll.10-12 "Shuts...thee": Joh 13:36

l.14 "Tracts of Sheen": Rev 21:23-24; 22:5 (perhaps a reference to the eternal light of the New Jerusalem)

ll.15-16 "Tent," "Troops": Ec 11:7; ICo 15 (synecdochic of mortal and immortal, corruptible and incorruptible, natural body and spiritual body)

Comment: See *Poems*, III, 1086-1087, 1091-1092, 1094-1095; *Letters*, III, 800-801; and Leyda, II, 408-409.

1585 The Bird her punctual music brings

l.1   "Bird...music": see P783 (the "punctual music" is itself a species of grace, the incarnation of a heavenly "Beauty")

l.3   "Human Heart": De 30:14; Ps 27:8; 34:18; Ac 1:24; IICo 1:22; 3:3; 4:6; Eph 3:17 (the heart mediates the divine influence through song; Biblically the heart is the seat of individuation—emotional, intellectual, and spiritual—and in P1585 perhaps shorthand for the spiritual self)

l.4   "Heavenly": ICo 15:48-49; Eph 1:3; Heb 8:5; 9:23 (the "punctual music" is associated with the celestial new circumference beyond the circuit world)

l.4   "Grace": Ps 84:11; Joh 1:16; ICo 15:10 (the unmerited favor of God; see note, line six, P1068; the poet may have in mind the etymology of the word, which suggests the singing of praise)

ll.5-6   "What...take": Ge 3:19 (in heterodox fashion the poet transvalues the Adamic curse into the "thrilling toil" of the creation of "Beauty")

l.7   "But...Rest": Ge 2:2-3 ("Work" and "Rest" are the rhythms of the Divine Creation of Genesis; "electric" echoes perhaps such treatments of "lightning" as P1581)

l.8   "Magic": see note, line three, P1583

Comment: The experience of birdsong occasions outrageously heterodox assertions by this maker whose "Beauty" and "Magic" are grace enabling, besting the God of Genesis who rests on the seventh day and collapsing the invidious, Philistine work-avocation dichotomy in true Emersonian fashion.

1586   To her derided Home

l.1   "To...Home": Ec 12:5 ("Also when they shall be afraid of that which is high, and fears shall be in the way, and the almond tree shall flourish, and the grasshopper shall be a burden, and desire shall fail: because man goeth to his long home, and the mourners go about the streets")

ll.2-6   "Weed...flower": Job 14:2; Isa 40:6-8; Mt 6:28; IPe 1:24 (the "Weed of Summer" and "fameless flower" is, first, the lowly child-weed identified with nature, devoid of self-conscious anxiety about the burden of the grasshopper or the failure of desire; this is the "Weed" also as suggestive of the ephemeral inconsequence of the circuit world flesh); Ca 2:1, 16; 4:5; 5:13; 6:2-3; 7:2 (second, "Weed" or "flower" is perhaps the beloved, especially the white lily with its apocalyptic, Bride of Christ overtones)

l.8   "Lady...Bower": Ca 4:12, 15; 5:1; 6:11;7:6-13;8:13-14 (the transition via death is from the garden or bower directly to the "Bliss" or Heaven of the next line)

l.9   "Bliss": Rev 19:7-9; 21-22 (Heaven with its promised Marriage Supper of the Lamb and ideal presence)

ll.10-11 "Jesus...moiety": Mt 11:28-29 (these verses may also account for the "meek and lowly" language used to describe the "fameless flower"; see also note, lines three-four and six-seven and "Comment," P1574—the flight and song of the bird of the earlier poem are the "Codes" that in P1586 become the anxiety-free death and sweeping/ wafting of the "Weed" to Heaven; see also Mt 25:31-40, especially the thirty-fourth verse)

l.12   "That...Seraphim": Isa 6:1-8 (the "Seraphim," above God's throne in the famous vision by Isaiah of the Lord in the year that King Uzziah died, are suggestive of the eternal enjoyment of ideal presence; see also note, line eight and "Comment," P1574)

Comment: The variants—"Dandelion," "Leontodon," and "Buttercup"—reinforce the flower imagery of the poem and, as circumferential, may be substitute faces preparatory for the beatific vision (Rev 22:4). See *Poems*, III, 1093-1094.

1587   He ate and drank the precious Words-

l.1   "ate...drank": Mt 26:26-29; Joh 6:48-58 (the language suggests the Eucharist); Joh 4:7-15; 6:48; ICo 3:1-2; Heb 5:12-14; 6:5; IPe 2:2-3 (oral imagery used figuratively to suggest nourishment of the "Spirit")

l.1   "Words": Joh 1:1 (Christ as the Logos, the Divine Expression; the reference may be to the KJV itself)

l.2   "His...robust": Eph 3:16-19; 4:13-16; IPe 2:2; IIPe 3:18

ll.2-3   "Spirit," "poor": Mt 5:3

l.4   "Nor...Dust": Ps 103:14 ("For he knoweth our frame; he remembereth that we are dust")

l.6   "Bequest of Wings": Joh 6:54; ICo 15 (synecdochic for the resurrection and promised eternal life—"Wings" being associated with cherubim, seraphim, the angelic hosts, and the prophetic visions of such as Ezekiel and Daniel)

l.7   "Was...Liberty": Rev 1:11, passim (the vision of St. John the Divine *is* his book, just as the words written in the Lamb's Book of Life from the foundation of the world *are* the only true life—a world imagined in words by a "loosened spirit," Revelation in a sense becoming a metaphor for the KJV and how to read it, just as love *is* a song or poem using Canticles as the guiding metaphor)

Comment: Canticles contains numerous references to love as feeding and to the beloved as nourishment. See *Letters*, III, 741 and Leyda, II, 378.

1588   This Me- that walks and works- must die,

l.1   "This...die": Ge 2:17; 3:19; Heb 9:27

ll.3-4   "Adversity...prosperity": Ec 7:14

ll.5-7   "The...push": see notes, lines twenty-one, twenty-two, and twenty-three, P1576; see also P1584

Comment: See *Poems*, III, 1094-1095.

1589   Cosmopolites without a plea

l.2   "Alight": Mt 5:14-16; Joh 1:1-9 (presumably the elect literati are the "Cosmopolites" whose "dappled Journey" is a Plotinian flight of the "Alone to the Alone," a movement from the circuit world prison to "Theology," or the instantiation of visions of "Paradise" in the word—apparently the poet is holding a book in her hands; compare P1587, which also utilizes a religio-aesthetic vocabulary)

l.3   "Paradise": Ge 2-3; Eze 28:13-14; 31:8-9, 16; 47:1-12; Rev 21-22

l.4   "Hand": Ge 3:22 (synecdochic for that agency involved in Fall, "Knock," and "Theology")

l.6   "compensation fair": Ge 3:15 (the "compensation fair" would be the prelapsarian, paradisiacal, light-bearing creations of the "Cosmopolites; also, "fair" is a Canticles word frequently used for the beloved, Ca 1:8, 15-16; 2:10, 13; 4:1, 7, 10; 5:9; 6:1, 10; 7:6)

l.7   "Knock...opened": Mt 7:7-8; Lu 11:9-10 (other perhaps not irrelevant knockings would be Ca 5:2; Rev 3:20, suggesting that such a "Theology" of importunity is related to the "Prognostic's push" of P1576, P1584, and P1588)

Comment: See *Poems*, III, 1095-1096;*Letters*, III, 743; and Leyda, II, 379-380.

1590   Not at Home to Callers

l.2   "Naked": Job 1:21; Ec 5:15
l.2   "Tree": Ac 5:30; 10:39
l.3   "Bonnet...April": Ca 2:12-13 (the renewal of presence)
Comment: See *Poems*, III, 1096 and Leyda, II, 394.

1591   The Bobolink is gone- the Rowdy of the Meadow-

l.3   "Presbyterian": ITi 4:14 (perhaps chosen for suggestions of the dour and sober)
l.4   "overflowing Day": Ge 2:2 (perhaps synecdochic of that Creative plenitude of which P1591 is the paean)
l.5   "Sabbath": Ex 16:23-29; 20:8-11
l.6   "Heaven," "Earth": Ge 1:1-8
l.6   "all the saints": Ps 31:23; 34:9; 148:14; Zec 14:5; Ro 16:15; IICo 1:1; 13:13; Eph 1:15; Php 1:1; 4:22; Rev 8:3; 15:3; 20:9
l.7   "shouted...pray": Ps 35:27; 65:13; 132:9, 16; Job 38:7
l.8   "his maker": Job 35:10; 36:3; Ps 95:6; Isa 45:11 (God, the Maker of Heaven and Earth, Ge 1-2)
ll.8-9   "Decalogue": Ex 20:1-17 (the Ten Commandments; the "Bobolink" and his swaggering epigone are apparently Emersonian antinomians as inebriated and disruptive as the "little Tippler" of P214)
ll.11-12 "When...way": Ps 30:8-10; 31:9, 22; 86:5-6
l.13   "unanointed": Ex 28:41; 29:7, 36; 30:26-30; Le 6:13; 8:10-12; 21:10 (rejection of ritualistic consecration is part of the antinomianism that "overturned the Decalogue")
Comment: See *Poems*, III, 1096-1097.

1592   The Lassitudes of Contemplation

ll.5-6   "Dreams...fair": Ge 28:11-22; 32:24-30; 46:1-4 (dreams consolidating the "mettle" of Jacob); ISa 3 (another Biblical dream "consolidat[ing] in action," this time the calling of Samuel); Da

2 (dreams of Nebuchadnezzar and Daniel; numerous Biblical dreams would have given the poet precedent for interpreting "Lassitudes of Contemplations," "spirits still vacation," and "Dreams" as occasions for epiphanic awareness, for communication outside the pale of the mundane, circuit world—"Lassitudes of Contemplation" thereby joining other heightened-receptivity hiatuses such as Indian summer, noon, and dawn)

Comment: See *Poems*, III, 1097-1098.

1593   There came a Wind like a Bugle-

l.1   "Wind": Rev 4:5; 6:1, 13; 8:5, 7-8; 9:17-18; 120:3-4; 11:5, 19; 12:15-16; 13:13; 14:2, 10; 15:2; 16:8, 18, 21; 19:6, 20;20:9-10, 14-15;21:8 (apocalyptic storms; see also note, line one, P824)

l.1   "Bugle": Da 8; Rev 8-9 (an oblique reference to Gabriel, who is associated with the Day of Judgment)

l.2   "Grass": Rev 8:7;9:4 (also associated with the limited circuit world, Ps 103:15; IPe 1:24)

l.3   "Green Chill": Rev 21:20

l.5   "We...Doors": Rev 6:16

l.6   "Emerald": Rev 21:19

l.6   "Ghost": Ac 2:2-4 (a connection with the "Wind" of line one)

l.7   "Doom's...Moccasin": Mt 24:27; Rev 4:5; 8:5; 11:19; 16:18 (apocalyptic associations with lightning)

l.9   "Trees": Rev 7:3; 8:7; 9:4

l.11   "rivers": Rev 8:10; 16:4

l.12   "looked," "lived": Rev 4:1; 6:8; 14:1;15:5;20:4-5

l.12   "that Day": Rev 6:17; 16:14 ("that great Day of God Almighty")

l.14   "tidings": Da 11:44-;

ll.15-17 "How...World": Ec 1:4-7 (the poem returns to philosophical aphorism echoing Koheleth)

Comment: See *Poems*, III, 1098.

1594   Immured in Heaven!

l.1   "Heaven": Rev 4:1-2; 19-21

l.2   "Cell": Rev 21 (Heaven is a high-walled city; St. John the Divine refers to a door in Heaven suggesting a building or room, e.g., Rev 3:8, 20; 4:1; associations of the beloved with a habitation or enclosed space are numerous in Canticles: 1:17; 2:4, 14; 3:4; 4:12, 16; 5:1-2; 6:2; 8:2, 9-13)

l.3 "Bondage": Ca 5; 8:6-7

l.4 "sweetest": Ca 2:3, 14;5:5, 13, 16; 7:9 (the beloved of Canticles, Gilbert, or the Bridegroom of Revelation may be the "sweetest of the Universe")

l.5 "ravished": Ca 4:9; Rev 19:7-9 (in Revelation the Heavenly City is the bride adorned for the Bridegroom or Lamb; thus, Gilbert's being immured in Heaven is envisioned using the marriage-"Bondage" trope, the "Cell" as Heavenly City-Bride; see Rev 21:2, 9; 22:17)

Comment: See *Poems*, III, 1099 and *Letters*, III, 927, the fragment suggesting that the Canticles imagery of P1594 should be spiritualized.

1595   Declaiming Waters none may dread-

ll.1-4 "Declaiming...full": Pr5:15; 18:4-7; 20:5 (the language of line two echoes Ps 23:2; the proverbial wisdom underpinning the poem has as one source Shakespeare's *Henry VI;* for "Waters" within the individual see also, Joh 4:14; the letter in which P1595 was sent to Sue contains the Banquet-Beggar trope, Lu 16:19-31, perhaps linking line two of the poem with Ps 23:5)

Comment: See *Poems*, III, 1099; *Letters*, III, 829; and Leyda, II, 439.

1596   Few, yet enough,

l.1 "Few...enough": Mt 7:14 ("Because strait is the gate, and narrow is the way, which leadeth unto life, and few there be that find it")

l.2 "Enough...One": Mt 18:19-20 (perhaps a witty hyperbole upon these verses since P1596 was sent to Sue)

l.3 "etherial throng": Rev 7:4 (the sealed and crowned Elect)

l.4 "each one": Rev 6:11

l.5 "stealthily": Lu 8:17; Ro 2:16 (the Biblical wit turns on the view of God as the revealer of secrets, e.g., Da 2:47; Mt 6:4-6, and the play upon belonging by "right" not righteousness—an outrageous process of self-election perhaps intended so deliberately for Sue's benefit)

Comment: See *Poems*, III, 1099.

1597   'Tis not the swaying frame we miss,

l.1   "frame": Ps 103:14 ("For he knoweth our frame; he remembereth that we are dust")

l.2   "steadfast Heart": ICo 7:37

ll.4-5   "Love...Oar": Ca 8:6-7 (see also Isa 33:21-22 since the "Love" of Judge Lord saves, is the "electric Oar" that bears "through the Tomb"—an unorthodox rejection of Christ as the Resurrection, Joh 11:25)

l.6   "That...Tomb": Mt 27:60; 28; ICo 15:54-55 (the "Love" of Judge Lord's "steadfast Heart" becomes the guarantor of immortality, the poet not consoled by such heterodox sentiments she knows presumptuous)

Comment: See *Poems*, III, 1100 and Leyda, II, 419-420.

1598   Who is it seeks my Pillow Nights-

l.2   "inspecting face": Rev 6:16; 20:11

l.3   " 'Did'...ask": Mt 25:40, 45

l.5   "Martial Hand": Mt 25:33-34, 41; Rev 1:16-17

l.7   " 'All'...what": Rev 21:8b ("all liars, shall have their part in the lake which burneth with fire and brimstone: which is the second death")

l.8   "Phosphorus": Rev 19:20; 20:10, 14-15; 21:8 (perhaps the poet's version of the "darkness visible" of Milton's hell)

Comment: See *Poems*, III, 1100-1101.

1599   Though the great Waters sleep,

l.1   "great Waters": Ps 32:6; 77:19; 104:25; 107:23 (synecdochic of God's creation in the individual, such as Judge Lord or Samuel Bowles, and in the cosmos itself)

l.1   "sleep": Rev 21:1

l.2   "Deep": Ge 1:2 (the primordial chaos or abyss shaped into cosmos by the Spirit; the argument of P1599 is a favorite one used to reassure herself regarding lost beloveds—i.e., God cannot discontinue Himself, that is, what He creates he cannot uncreate)

l.4   "No...God": Nu 23:19; Mal 3:6; Ro 11:29; Jas 1:17 (part of the ingenuity of P1599 is its treatment of the immutable Creator using the lexicon of recent geological controversy; see Sewall, 346)

l.5   "Ignited...Abode": Ge 1-2 (the cosmos as the created "Abode" of God may be intended as well as the individual, Ge 2:7; for the individual as habitation see note, line one, P674 and note, line one, P1142)

l.6   "To...out": Ps 102:25-28;; Isa 51:6; Heb 1:10-12; IIPe 3:7-10; Rev 20:9-11; 21:1 (the threatened cataclysmic extinction of the cosmos)

Comment: See *Poems*, III, 1101-1102; *Letters*, III, 828-829, 898; and Leyda, II, 429, 448.

1601   Of God we ask one favor,

ll.1-2   "Of...forgiven": Mt 6:12, 14 (perhaps the legal lexicon of the poem connects with the Lord's Prayer, which asks forgiveness for trespasses and debts)

l.3   "For...know": Ps 19:12-14 (if the poet has in mind these words of the Psalmist, then she does generalize them as the rule in the circuit world and this with no little recrimination; nevertheless, P1601 may simply reject a sense of sin for an ironic stress on a Divine omniscience difficult if not impossible of corroboration, Job 26:6; 34:21-22; Joh 2:24-25)

l.4   "Crime": Ge 3:6-7 (the Fall, the original, hidden "Crime")

ll.5-6   "Immured...Prison": Ro 7:24; IICo 5:4; Php 3:21 (the circuit world as the body prison); Eze 8:12; Heb 11:3 (the circuit world as a "magic Prison" of appearance and illusion); Isa 42:5-16 (metaphorically speaking, anticipation of Bride of Christ status makes the "whole of Life" a "magic Prison")

ll.7-8   "We...Heaven": Mt 5:3-12 (an oblique gibe at her own Beatitudes-based philosophy of deprivation, which stresses "Happiness" beyond the circuit world with its joy tainted by misgiving, guilt, and fear, P313)

Comment: The two published drafts of letters to Helen Hunt Jackson in which P1601 appears make clear that the poem is a surrogate prayer, the poet in the letter expressing solicitude for the soul of her friend. See *Letters*, III, 866-869. The unpardonable "Happiness" of P1601 is apparently her affection for an appreciative, fellow poet. See also *Poems*, III, 1102 and Leyda, II, 447-448. How unconfining for her art was the matrix of the correspondence is nowhere better evidenced than in the brilliant breadth of reference in P1601.

1602   Pursuing you in your transitions,

l.1   "transitions": ICo 15:51

l.2   "Motes": Mt 7:3-5 (this echo allows the poet to connect P1602 with the reference to the "waylaying Light" which introduces the poem in L937; for "waylaying Light" see note, line sixteen, P1581; the "Light" affects the "Prism" just as in "other Myths" the "Light" has "taken Captivity Captive"[L937 and Eph 4:8], has triumphed over death thus assuring eternal life)

l.3   "other Myths": ICo 15; Eph 4 (the "other Myths" would include St. Paul's discussion of change from corruption to incorruption, mortal to immortal, which have their circuit world analogues in Helen Hunt Jackson's "transitions" for "Crutch to Cane to Wings" spoken of in L937)

ll.4-6   "Your...play": ICo 15 (as the alembic of the imagination, the "Prism" is transition, is metamorphosis, is the assurance of "change" in the Paulinian sense—the hope of immortality given in intimations only, not held; the "Prism" as metaphor for the self suggests its radical displacement, absence, and deferral in the circuit world of pursuit and play—a "Prism" whose "requisition" is the hoped-for apotheosis; thus, P1602 is a muted, elegiac poem in which Dickinson prays that Helen Hunt Jackson's destiny will be the eternal light, ideal presence [Rev 19:7-9; 22:4-5] which she herself sought)

Comment: See *Poems*, III, 1103; *Letters*, III, 840-841; and Leyda, II, 429-430.

1603   The going from a world we know

ll.1-2   "The...still": Mr 10:30; Ga 1:4 (examples from the preachments of Jesus and St. Paul suggesting the two worlds, present and to come; Dickinson's two-world, eschatological consciousness differs, with its optative mood hiding isolation and anxiety behind a child persona and ending with what is only grammatically a yes-no question)

        l.2   "wonder": Rev 12:1, 3; 17:6, 8

        l.6   "unknown": Ac 17:23 (the Deus absconditus, the hidden God)

        l.7   "secret compensate": ICo 13:12; Rev 19:7-9; 22:4 (the poet may have in mind such specific compensations as the Marriage Supper of the Lamb and the beatific vision; P1603 emphasizes the "unknown," not the God of revelation but of secrets, De 29:29; Job 15:8; Da 2:22, 28-29; Ro 16:25; ICo 2:7; 4:5)

        Comment: See *Poems*, III, 1103-1104; *Letters*, III, 826-827; and Leyda, II, 426.

1604   We send the Wave to find the Wave-

        ll.3-4   "The...return": Ge 8:8-12 (the dove "Messenger" returned twice to Noah, once with an olive leaf, but on the third flight the dove did not return since the "fountain of the great deep" had abated; using the KJV as the basis for the wit of P1604, the poet equates the "Deluge" with the continued flow of her correspondence with the Norcross cousins—their epistolary inspiration apparently the "fountains of the great deep" whose damming is not a human prerogative, Job 38:8-11; Ps 33:7; Pr 8:29)

        l.7   "The...gone": Rev 21:1 ("And I saw a new heaven and a new earth: for the first heaven and the first earth were passed away; and there was no more sea")

        Comment: See *Poems*, III, 1104-1105; *Letters*, III, 838; and Leyda, II, 424.

1605   Each that we lose takes part of us;

        ll.1-2   "Each...abides": ICo 13:10 (implying the ideally circumferential, the "crescent" implies the fragmentary, partial nature of the circuit world)

        ll.3-4   "Which...tides": Rev 21:23 (inverting the circuit world scheme underscores the apocalyptic consequence of the loss of Judge Lord; for lovers as astronomical bodies see Ca 6:10)

        Comment: See *Poems*, III, 1105; *Letters*, III, 817-818; and Leyda, II, 419.

1606   Quite empty, quite at rest,

       l.5   "rumored Springs": Isa 12:3; Joh 4:14; 7:38; Rev 21:6; 22:1 (perhaps a reference to the destiny of Judge Lord; the beloved is spoken of as a spring, Ca 4:12)

       l.8   "Crumbless," "homeless": Mt 15:27; Mr 7:28; Lu 16:21 (the poet underscores the radical nature of her dispossession with the label "Crumbless"—she once again stands a "beggar/Before the door of God"); Lu 9:58 (the "homeless" of line eight connects with the locked "Nest" of line two)

       Comment: See *Poems*, III, 1106; *Letters*, III, 815-817; and Leyda, II, 420-421.

1607 Within that little Hive

       l.2   "Such...lay": Ca 4:11; 5:1
       Comment: See *Letters*, III, 815-817 and Leyda, II, 420-421.

1608   The ecstasy to guess

       l.1   "ecstasy": see note, line fifteen, P783 and notes, lines five and eight, P1191 (the first line of P1608 stresses the partiality and inadequacy of circuit-world knowing, ICo 13:12; Php 3:13)

       l.2   "bliss": IPe 1:8 ("bliss" may be synecdochic for Heaven, as well as being a reference to the psychological state of heavenly rapture or joy)

       l.3   "grace": Ro 3:24; Eph 2:8-9 (the wit of P1608 turns on the faith-works antithesis—"works" the common coin of purchase and receipt, question and answer, and mundane talk, rather than the unmerited gift of the Deus absconditus, inexplicable but guessed at by "ecstasy")

       Comment: See *Poems*, III, 1106-1107 and *Letters*, III, 878.

1609   Sunset that screens, reveals-

       l.1   "Sunset...reveals": Mt 10:26; IPe 1:5, 12-13; Rev 1:1 (as one of the poet's transition times, "Sunset" excites hopes and fears associated with the apocalyptic—the poet heroically attempting to transmute its screening darkness into promise)

l.3   "Amethyst": Rev 21:20 (the purple color suggests the veil and its concomitant promise of God's presence—see note, line one, P15; note, line eight, P703; and note, lines two-three, P716; nevertheless, the use of "screens," "menaces," and "Moats" in P1609 suggests anxiety regarding the potential unmeaning of the apocalyptic)

l.4   "Moats": see P313 (the "Reefs" of stanza four)

l.4   "Mystery": ICo 15:51 (the "Mystery" would include sleep, death, resurrection, and Heaven, for all of which the "Sunset" is not unambiguously "typic")

1610   Morning that comes but once,

ll.1-2   "Morning...twice": Ca 6:10 (the beloved is associated with the morning); Lu 1:78; Rev 2:28; 22:16 (Christ, the Bridegroom is also associated with the morning; the apocalyptic associations of the poem reinforce the suggestion, however, that morning is death purchased by "Life")

l.3   "Dawns": Mt 28:1; IIPe 1:19 (further associations of Christ with the dawn)

l.3   "single Morn": Rev 16:14 (perhaps the "great day of God Almighty" since "Two Dawns" defy circuit-world possibility)

l.4   "Make...price": Ec 9:11-12

1611   Their dappled importunity

l.1   "dappled": Ca 4:7; Jer 13:23; Eph 5:27 (apparently the poet identifies with the "dappled" adder's tooth, expressing a sense of unworthiness and fear of rejection)

l.1   "importunity": Lu 11:8-9

l.4   "Bliss": Rev 4; 21-22 (Heaven; the poet suggests to Mrs. Todd that Heaven does not stand on ceremony nor should she; perhaps P1611 is an oblique request that Heaven mollify her fears by embracing an "Etiquette" of gentility like the one of P712)

Comment: See Leyda, II, 450. The context of Mrs. Todd's diary suggests a reading of P1611 tied to the occasion of a gift of adder's tooth.

1612   The Auctioneer of Parting

1.1   "Auctioneer...Parting": Ac 20:28; ICo 6:20; 7:23;
Eph 1:14; IIPe 2:1 (the outrageous heterodoxy of P1612 turns topsy-
turvy at least two accepted KJV notions—the first being that we have
been bought with a price, not sold something); Ro 5:15-21; 6:23; IICo
9:15; Eph 2:8-9; 3:7; 4:7; Heb 6:4; Jas 1:17; IPe 4:10 (second is the
KJV view of grace as the unmerited, free gift of God unto salvation
and eternal life; the "Auctioneer" of P1612 is God the Father who uses
the Crucifixion of His Son to reiterate His message—"gone"—a
message of despair, dispossession, uprootedness, and ultimately death,
the Cross the gavel of doom's finality rather than the central Christian
symbol of triumph over sin and death, e.g., ICo 1:17-18; Ga 6:14; in
P1612 the "single human Heart" is that of Jesus Christ and the poet's
the second, "Two," depending on the completeness of the
identification; Jesus is here auctioned—He does not "give his life a
ransom for many," Mt 20:28; Mr 10:45; ITi 2:6)
1.3   "Shouts...Crucifix": Mr 15:34 (the expression of
abandonment from the lips of Christ corroborates the "Going, going,
gone" of the Deus absconditus "Auctioneer"; see a similar use of
language in the second stanza of P313 and compare P1612 with P553)
1.4   "And...down": Isa 22:22-25; Mt 27:35; Joh 20:25
(the action here suggests crucifixion; "down" echoes Mt 27:39-43)
1.5   "Wilderness": Ex 14-15; Nu 1; 10-13; 20-25; 33 (the
wilderness of the exodus, here used metaphorically to reinforce
P1612's characterization of the "Heart" isolated and orphaned in the
circuit world)
            Comment: See Leyda, II, 451.

1613   Not Sickness stains the Brave,

ll.1-4   "Not...Heart": Ro 8:35-39 (the syntax, the anaphora,
and some of the wording are certainly Paulinian, especially the basis
for line three in verse thirty-eight: "nor things present, nor things to
come")
1.2   "Dart": Eph 6:16 (for the association of ideas here
connecting with the military metaphor, see *Letters*, III, 592; III, 826;
and P1554)
1.4   "Heart": Ca 4:9
            Comment: The hyperbole and wit of P1613 depend on the
poet's inversion of St. Paul's stress on the impossibility of separation
from the "love of God which is in Christ Jesus our Lord," the poet

suggesting that the "Brave" are "stain[ed]" by separation from the beloved. The separation motif is also found in Canticles (Ca 3:1-3; 5:6-7; 6:1, 13). See *Letters*, III, 826 and Leyda, II, 425-426.

1614   Parting with Thee reluctantly,

l.1   "Thee": Ca 1:3-4, 9, 11; 4:7; 6:1, 13; 7:5, 12-13; 8:1-2

l.1   "Parting...reluctantly": Ca 3:1-3; 5:6-7; 6:1, 13 (the "parting" idea recurs in Canticles)

l.3   "Heart": Ca 3:11; 4:9; 5:2; 8:6

l.3   "Foreigner": Ca 6:13 (the poet may think of herself as the Shulamite, this reference linking to the direct one, in L946, to Adam and Eve, Ge 3:10)

l.4   "Remembers": Ca 1:4

Comment: See *Poems*, III, 1108; *Letters*, III, 846-847; and Leyda, II, 436.

1615   Oh what a Grace is this,

ll.1-5   "Oh...Proceed": IITi 1:1-12 (L953 speaks of a gift, apparently of flowers, which to the poet's mind becomes emblematic of "Beauty," "Boundlessness," "Gift," and "Immortality"; Johnson identifies verse twelve as a possible source, the other verses, however, containing language echoed in the letter and poem)

ll.1-2   "Grace," "Peace": IICo 1:2; ITi 6:21; IPe 1:2; IIPe 1:2; Rev 1:4 (the words are frequently found together)

l.1   "Grace": ICo 15:53-54; ITi 6:16; IITi 1:10 (the antecedent of "Grace" may be the word "Immortality" in L953; "Grace" may also be beauty itself and the beloved as a flower, emblematic in the circuit world of "Boundlessness" and "Immortality" beyond, Ca 2:1; 6:4; Ps 50:2; 90:17; "Grace" and "Peace" become familiar to the poet through the "atmospheric acquaintance" of beauty, are transmuted into song via synesthesia in the last line of P1615)

l.4   "Without...Proceed": Rev 22:1-5

Comment: See *Letters*, III, 851-852 and Leyda, II, 436-437.

1616   Who abdicated Ambush

ll.1-8   "Who...Star": see notes and "Comment," P1525

Comment: P1616 uses a typographical convention meta-phorically to suggest the apotheosis of the beloved in much the same manner as P1638 (the "Asterisk" perhaps "italic of both Worlds," L968). See also P1135 and P1647; *Poems*, III, 1109; *Letters*, III, 839; and Leyda, II, 373.

1617   To try to speak, and miss the way

l.3   "Is...poverty": Ca 2:3, 14; 5:5, 13, 16; 7:12; 8:7 (P1617 is apparently in response to a gift from Mrs. Tuckerman—a gift unmerited, a reminder of circuit-world poverty of "Soul")

ll.4-6   "The...conceal": Isa 61:10; Rev 3:5; 7:9; 19:7-9; 21:2 (the metaphor of being acceptably clothed connects the religio-aesthetic concerns of the poem, occasioned by the gift from the beloved with its Canticles provenance)

ll.7-8   "Mutineer...Soul": Ge 2:7; 3:6-7

Comment: See *Poems*, III, 1109-1110 and Leyda, II, 415.

1618   There are two Mays

l.1   "There...Mays": Ge 3:2; Joh 3:4 (the "may" and "can" are associated with "Fall" and rebirth, death and eternal life; the "two Mays" are also the sweet bay and arbutus whose Revelation white flowers provoke this elegant, apocalyptic meditation, L1037)

l.2   "Must": Joh 3:7

l.3   "Shall": Ge 3:4-5; Joh 3:12

l.4   "I will": Ge 3:15-19; Joh 3:14-17 (P1618 seems to parallel the verbs from the third chapters of Genesis and John; with specific reference to line four, for other possibilities see Ca 6:1, 13; Mt 26:39-42; Rev 2:10, 17; 3:12, 20; 21:6-9; 22:17)

Comment: See *Poems*, III, 1110-1111 and *Letters*, III, 899.

1619   Not knowing when the Dawn will come,

l.1   "Not...come": Mt 24:36

l.1   "Dawn": Mt 24:27; 28:1; Mr 16:2; Lu 1:78-79; IIPe 1:19; Rev 2:28; 22:16

l.2   "I...Door": Rev 3:20

Comment: See *Poems*, III, 1111; *Letters*, III, 903-904; and Leyda, II, 465. The context of the letter makes clear the element of apocalyptic anticipation in P1619.

1620   Circumference thou Bride of Awe

l.1   "Circumference": Rev 2:10; 3:11; 7:2-8 (points to that ideal circumferentiality experienced only in Heaven, suggested by the seal and crown and concluded by marriage to "Awe")

l.1   "Bride of Awe": Ca 1, passim; Rev 19:7-9; 21:2, 9; 22:17 ("Circumference" is in possession of "Awe" as "Bride" in possession of Bridegroom, the "Possessing" of line two, however, syntactically ambiguous)

l.2   "thou shalt": Ex 20:3-5, 7-17 (P1620 is the poet's theodicy, an religio-aesthetic response in Platonic and Keatsian terms to issues raised in such poems as P313; therefore, she uses the emphatic quality of the Ten Commandments, flying in the face of one of their main proscriptions)

l.3   "Possessed": Ex 20:3-4, 17 (P1620 deliberately underscores possession, using the profane love topoi to explain the holy-youth artist's covetous quest for circuit-world beauty—a quest that ends, paradoxically, with the circumference-completeness of death; L898 underscores finitude—"Success is dust," Ge 3:19; Ps 103:14)

l.4   "covet thee": Ex 20:17 (also relevant, Ca 4:9; Rev 19:7-9)

Comment: See *Poems*, III, 1111-1112; *Letters*, III, 822, 918; and Leyda, II, 422.

1621   A Flower will not trouble her, it has so small a Foot,

l.1   "Flower": Job 14:2; Ps 1-3:15; Isa 40:6-8; IPe 1:24 (the KJV frequently associates the flower with circuit-world finitude; the recipient of the flower will not be troubled since the destinies of the organic and human orders differ)

l.2   "Lasts": Mt 19:30; 20:16; Mr 9:35; 10:31; Lu 13:30 (part of the wit of P1621 is the KJV first-last paradox since the "Flower" and its recipient are being compared with regard to duration, size, and ranking in the Chain of Being; to the lexicon of the cobbler and botanist is added that of manners—the nineteenth-century vanity regarding the beauty of the small "Foot" and "Boot"—and of apocalyptic, Isa 44:6; 48:12; Rev 1:11, 17; 22:13)

Comment: Even a cursory reading of the OED definition for "Foot,"Last," and "Boot" suggests the multiple resonances and wit of the poet even in such a jeu d'esprit as P1621.

1622   A Sloop of Amber slips away

l.1   "Amber": Eze 1:4, 27; 8:2

l.3   "Purple": see note, line one, P15; note, line eight, P703; and note, line three, P716

l.4   "Ecstasy": see note, line fifteen, P783 and notes, lines five and eight, P1191.

Comment: Using the visionary colors of amber and purple, P1622 treats the transition time of sunset as occasion for epiphany. See *Poems*, III, 1113 and *Letters*, III, 921.

1623   A World made penniless by that departure

l.1   "World": Ps 90:2; Heb 1:2; 11:3

l.2   "minor fabrics": Ge 1:1, 8; 2:1, 4

l.3(variant) "Firmaments": Ge 1:6-8

l.3   "But...spirit": Pr 18:14

l.4(variant) "Heaven," "skies," "suns": Ge 1:1-8, 14-20

l.4   "The...Dregs": Ps 75:8 (inverted as part of the poem's hyperbole)

Comment: The poet uses the language of Genesis ("Gods," "Heavens," "Firmaments," and "Stars") as part of her hyperbole describing her inconsolable grief, her circuit-world penury after the loss of Judge Lord. See *Poems*, III, 1113-1114.

1624   Apparently with no surprise

ll.1-8   "Apparently...God": Mt 6:28-32 (devoid of self-conscious anxiety about a world of surprise, accident, and death, a "happy Flower" thrives in nature, but the poet wonders whether such can be the source of consolatory analogies regarding providence for her; the vulnerability of the flower is frequently connected with that of man in the KJV, Job 14:2; Ps 103:15; Isa 40:6; IPe 1:24)

l.3   "Frost": Job 37:10; 38:29; Ps 147:16 (the KJV suggests that the "Frost" is an instrumentality of God—"the breath of God," paradoxically enough)

l.8   "Approving God": Ge 1:4, 10, 12, 18, 21, 25, 31 (God approves His created world as "good" repeatedly in the first chapter of Genesis)

Comment: See *Poems*, III, 1114-1115.

1625   Back from the cordial Grave I drag thee

l.1   "cordial Grave": ICo 15:54-55

l.2   "He...Hand": Ca 2:6; 5:4; 8:3

l.3   "arm": Ca 8:6 (apparently P1625 personifies death as a lover competing from the "cordial Grave" either for the soul of the poet or for that of a friend beloved by her)

Comment: A line deleted from PF 112 speaks of the "mower" and "scythe," part of the traditional depiction of death with apocalyptic overtones (Rev 14:14-20). See *Poems*, III, 1115 and *Letters*, III, 928. Perhaps P1625 should be contrasted with P712 as revelatory of the poet's hesitations about the threatening opacity of the beyond.

1626   No Life can pompless pass away-

ll.2-4   "The...here": Rev 19:5; 20:12

l.5   "mystery": ICo 15:51

l.6   "hospitable Pall": Rev 3:5, 18; 7:9; 19:8

ll.7-8   "A...all": Mt 7:13-14 (perhaps the poet's wry humor shows in her view of death's democratic generosity)

Comment: See *Poems*, III, 1115-1116.

1627   The pedigree of Honey

ll.1,3   "pedigree," "lineage": Nu 1:18; Mt 3:9; Lu 2:4 (synecdoches for a Pharisaic and Sadducean legalism inimical to the ecstatic experience of "Bee" and "Butterfly")

l.3   "Ecstasy": see note, line fifteen, P783 and notes, lines five and eight, P1191.

Comment: See *Poems*, III, 1116-1117.

1628   A Drunkard cannot meet a Cork

l.5   "Remembrance": Lu 22:19 (the Eucharist word connects this spring experience with similar ones in other poems, such as P130 and P214)

l.8(variant) "Has...spring": Joh 8:52 (the variant suggests that "spring" in line eight refers to resurrection, ICo 15)

Comment: See *Poems*, III, 1117.

1629   Arrows enamored of his Heart-

l.3   "And...Balms": Ps 69:20-21; Mt 27:34, 48; Joh 19:28-30 (Judge Lord is being characterized in Christ-like terms, her "Salem," Heb 7:1-2, 17, 21-22)

l.4   "disdained...there": Lu 23:34

Comment: See *Poems*, III, 1118 and *Letters*, III, 918.

1630   As from the earth the light Balloon

l.1   "earth": ICo 15:47

l.1   "light/fair": Ca 1:15-16; 2:10, 13; 4:1, 7, 10; 6:10; 7:6

l.2   "Asks...release": Ro 7:24; IICo 5:4; Php 3:21 (release from the body prison)

l.3   "Ascension...was": Ec 12:7

l.4   "Residence/rapture": see note, line seven, P1468

l.5   "spirit": Ec 12:7; ICo 15:45

l.5   "Dust": Ge 2:7; 3:19; Ps 103:14; Ec 12:7

ll.8-9   "As...song": see, among others, P653, P783, P861, P1420, P1465, P1466, P1578, and P1585 (the song of the bird is often associated with the spirit, with ecstasy, and with release from temporal limitation; P1630 indicates again the poet's sense of dispossession, of circuit-world song as inescapable displacement [her "Competeless Show," P290], of true song as only possible in "Residence" or Yeats' Byzantium or the New Jerusalem, the song of Moses and the Lamb, Rev 15:3)

Comment: See *Poems*, III, 1118-1119.

1631   Oh Future! thou secreted peace

l.1   "Future": Rev 6:17; 16:14; 20:4 (the great day of God Almighty, the day of judgment)

l.1   "secreted peace": Rev 2:7 (paradise)

l.2   "subterranean wo": Rev 9:1-2, 11; 20:1-3 (the bottomless pit)

l.3   "Is...grace": Isa 40:3; Mt 3:3; Mr 1:3; Lu 3:4; Joh 1:23 (in the KJV, the way of the Lord, Bringer of grace, is always straight)

l.4   "That...thee": Heb 9:27

l.5   "course": Ac 20:24; IITi 4:7

l.5(variant) "lines": Job 38:5; Ps 16:6; 19:4; Isa 28:17

l.7   "sacred Prey": Mt 25:32

l.8   "Advancing...Dew": Rev 4-6; 13-17; 19 (apocalyptic imagery of the devouring beast would hardly be flattering as applied to the "Future" in P1631, the poet perhaps venting her anxiety regarding such treatment of ignorant innocence)

Comment: Apostrophizing the "Future," the poet asks an extended rhetorical question similar in import to that of Poe in "The Raven": "Is there no balm in Gilead," Jer 8:22. Location and direction become metaphors for the unavoidable, ineluctable, and inevitable Apocalyptic, although allowing the poet some latitude for irony—irony directed at the vanity of her own wishes and at the ghoulish opacity of the "Future." See *Poems*, III, 1119.

1632   So give me back to Death-

l.1   "So...Death": Mt 22:30; ICo 15:54-55 (P1632 is spoken to Christ, the giver of resurrection triumph over death—a resurrection triumph that, paradoxically enough, has deprived her of reunion in "Death" and the "Grave" with Judge Lord)

l.2   "The...feared": Mt 10:28

ll.2,4-5,7-8 "Death," "Life," "Grave," "Hell," "Heaven": ICo 15:54-55; Rev 1:18; 2:7, 10; 3:5; 6:8; 20:12-15; 21:1-10, 27; 22:1-2, 14-19 (Resurrection and Apocalyptic comprise the lexicon of P1632, first, giving cosmic import to her heterodox rejection of "Death" as resurrection life and its acceptance as condition for reunion with the beloved and, second, allowing her the hyperbole in suggesting the immeasurableness of her "Grave," her death-in-life, the extremes of *all* imagined hells and *all* imagined heavens)

Comment: See Leyda, II, 419.

1633   Still own thee- still thou art

l.4   "Grave": ICo 15:54-55

l.8   "recallless sea": Rev 21:1 (perhaps synecdochic of death in general, especially in its aspect of irreversible separation from the living; P1599, another elegiac poem dealing with Judge Lord, makes reference to the "great Waters"—see notes, lines one and two, P1599; "reportless," "recallless," and the "question" and "answer" of lines five and six reveal the poet's concern with deathbed professions—a searching for corroboration of faith, a curiosity regarding glimpses of passage beyond the circuit world, that she expressed in letters upon the deaths of Samuel Bowles, Reverend Wadsworth, Judge Lord, and others)

Comment: See *Poems*, III, 1120. The poet chose the more prosaic "answer" in the sixth line instead of the variant, "tidings," a word with profound, positive KJV connotations, Isa 40:9; 52:7; Lu 1:19; 2:10.

1634   Talk not to me of Summer Trees

l.3   "Tabernacle": Ps 61:4; Heb 9:11; Rev 21:3

l.4   "Of...kind": IICo 5:1

l.5   "winds": Joh 3:8

l.5   "noon": Job 11:17 (the sun at zenith was a special time for Dickinson, suggesting perhaps the absolute pellucidity of pure vision, the transition time from ante to post meridiem in which the circuit world at full light becomes "typic" of eternity)

l.7   "Bugles": ICo 15:52; ITh 4:16; Rev 8:2, 6, 13

l.7   "call...least": Mt 25:40-46; Rev 11:18; 19:5; 20:12

ll.6,8   "Homes," "Realms": Rev 21-22 (Heaven)

l.8(variant) "unreported": Nu 13:30-33 (the reported promised land)

Comment: An intimations of immortality poem, P1634 uses apocalyptic figuration in elegantly making the Emersonian and Miltonic case for the mind as "its own place," an "Etherial Home." See *Poems*, III, 1120-1121.

1636   The Sun in reining to the West

l.5   "Amethyst": Rev 21:20 (for the purple color see also note, line one, P15; note, line eight, P703; and note, line three, P716; sunset, along with, for example, noon, dawn, and Indian summer, is a transition time of epiphany—here the homely image of the cart turning homeward suggesting reassurance, the domesticating of the apocalyptic with the reference to "Whiffletree" in a manner anticipating Frost)

1637   Is it too late to touch you, Dear?

ll.3-4   "Love...too": ICo 15:40, 48 (the with involving three types of "Love" may owe a debt to St. Paul)
l.5(?)   "I...charge": Ps 91:11-12; Mt 4:6; Lu 4:10-11 (Johnson has not included this line as part of P1637 although including the similarly separated line one)
Comment: See *Poems*, III, 1122; *Letters*, III, 865-866; and Leyda, II, 444.

1638   Go thy great way!

l.1   "Go...way": Lu 24:50-51 (L967 makes clear the associations of Lord's passing with the Ascension)
ll.2,4   "Stars": Nu 24:17; Mt 2:2; ICo 15:41; IIPe 1:19; Rev 2:28; 22:16 (the identification of Judge Lord with Christ is here not explicit but the stars are directly related to the celestial, to the resurrection, and to the apotheosis of the beloved; see L967 for a direct reference to her favorite Resurrection chapter as introduction to P1638)
ll.4,5   "Asterisks," "point": see note, lines one to eight and "Comment," P1616 (the "point" is a period at the extremity of the circuit world standing for death; "Asterisks" are exploded points whose centerlessness now suggests Judge Lord's disembodied state, his apotheosis)
Comment: See *Poems*, III, 1123; *Letters*, III, 860-861, 863; and Leyda, II, 443-444. The reference to "Caller" in L967 is apparently apocalyptic, Rev 3:20.

1639   A Letter is a joy of Earth-

l.1   "joy": Ps 16:11; 21:6; ICo 13:12; IPe 1:8; IJo 3:2; Rev 22:4 (the "joy" imitated by a "Letter" is that of ideal presence, of the beatific vision, the language of letter and poem a displacement for such; the poem is in the second paragraph of L963 in which the poet refers to those of the "sacred Past," such as James Clark and Reverend Wadsworth, who now enjoy, perhaps, an "untiring *Anno Domini*," adding her desire from them of "but one assenting word")

Comment: See *Poems*, III, 1123; *Letters*, III, 854-855, 857; and Leyda, II, 440-441. Leyda reads "assuring" for "assenting."

1640   Take all away from me, but leave me Ecstasy,

l.1   "Ecstasy": see note, line fifteen, P783 and notes, lines five and eight, P1191 (in P1365 the only thing left is "Immortality")

ll.1-5   "Take...poverty": Mt 5:3-12; 16:26; Rev 3:17-18 (P1640 may owe its orientation to riches and poverty to KJV paradoxes regarding the circuit world—paradoxes such as those in the Beatitudes)

Comment: See *Poems*, III, 1123-1124; *Letters*, III, 854-855, 866-867, 888-889; and Leyda, II, 440, 447-448.

1641   Betrothal to Righteousness might be

l.1   "Betrothed...be": Isa 61:10; 62:5; Rev 19:7-9; 21:2-3, 9; 22:17 (marriage to the Lamb)

l.2   "Ecstasy": see note, line fifteen, P783 and notes, lines five and eight, P1191

l.3   "Pinks": Rev 2:17; 3:4-5, 18; 7:9; 19:8 (white is the New Jerusalem color, the color of the "new circumference," which contrasts with the "Pinks" of circuit-world "Nature"; see Ca 4:3)

Comment: See *Letters*, III, 877.

1642   "Red Sea," indeed! Talk not to me

l.1   " 'Red Sea' ": Ex 15:4, 22 (in chapters three through fifteen of Exodus, the story of Moses, Pharaoh, and the Israelites—the story of the exodus—is told; nevertheless, the poet probably has in mind New Testament references to the parting of the Red Sea and destruction of the Egyptians as wonders, signs, and miracles, Ac 7:36; Heb 11:29)

l.2 "purple": see note, line one, P15; note, line eight, P703; and note, line three, P716 ("purple" is the color of revelation and vision, of presence within the vail; "purple" perhaps also refers to Pharoah's anger, his hardened heart as it is referred to numerous times in these chapters)

l.3 "Pharaoh": Ex 3:10-15:9

l.4 "Would...thro": Ex 14:23-28; 15:4, 19 (the "Columns" of Pharaoh are inundated by the waters of the Red Sea)

l.5 "Guileless": Ex 8:8, 29; 9:28; 10:8, 11, 24, 28; 12:31 (a reference to Pharaoh's guile in breaking repeatedly his promises to the Israelites; yet Pharaoh is "Guileless" of the greater miracle, "such Glory fine," expressed in the sunset—the less fine wonders the crudely direct plagues visited upon the Egyptians)

l.8 "Is...divine": e.g., Ex 10:1-2 (the plagues are intended as signs to Pharaoh of the superiority of God to his magicians, Ex 7:22; 8:7, 18-19; in contrast, the subtlety of the sunset is such that the "Line" between circuit-world "Marine" and "new circumference" "divine" cannot be ascertained by the inquiring "Eye")

1643   Extol thee- could I- Then I will

l.1 "Extol": Ps 30:1; 145:1

l.3 "fair," "fairest": Ca 1:8, 15-16; 2:10, 13; 4:1, 7, 10; 5:9; 6:1, 10; 7:6

l.4 "sweetest": Ca 2:3, 14; 5:5, 13, 16

ll.5-8 "Perceiving...immortality": ICo 15:40-55 (P1643 is apparently an unfinished eulogy perhaps occasioned by viewing a picture of a departed beloved, the Canticles language pushing beyond to resurrection hope with the participatory "Partaking," Heb 3:14; IIPe 1:4; line two, P1651)

Comment: See *Poems*, III, 1125 and *Letters*, III, 878.

1644   Some one prepared this mighty show

l.1 "Some...show": Ge 1-2 (the God of Creation)

l.3 "The nations": Mt 24:7; Rev 2:26

l.3 "the Days": Ge 3:14

l.7   "Ethiopian": Ge 2:13 (a reference to paradise; see also Eze 28:13-14; 31:8-9, 16; 47:1-12; Rev 2:7; 21-22)

Comment: See *Poems*, III, 1125-1126; *Letters*, III, 874; and Leyda, II, 450.

1646   Why should we hurry- why indeed

l.1   "Why...indeed": Mt 6:25-34 (P1646 in its rough form responds to this admonition from Jesus to not be anxious—the poet's answer being that the burden of apocalyptic consciousness is inescapable and, furthermore, it does not eventuate in "bland" certainty)

l.4   "immortality": ICo 15:53-54
l.6   "that...begun": Php 1:6
l.7   "though...lie": Heb 4:11; Rev 14:13
l.8   "A...uncertainty": ICo 9:26
l.9   "Besets...sight": IICo 5:7
l.10   "This...night": Joh 9:4; ITh 5:2-6; IIPe 3:10

Comment: See *Poems*, III, 1126-1127 and *Letters*, III, 878.

1647   Of Glory not a Beam is left

l.1   "Glory": Joh 1:14 (the manifestation of presence through circuit-world beauty by the poet, Helen Hunt Jackson—the poet elsewhere viewing the "perfected Life" in terms of an architectural metaphor, P1142); see also note, line seven, P1227

l.2   "Eternal House": IICo 5:1 ("For we know that if our earthly house of this tabernacle were dissolved, we have a building of God, an house not made with hands, eternal in the heavens")

l.3   "Asterisk": see note, lines four-five, P1638
l.4   "Stars": see note, lines two-four, P1638

Comment: See *Poems*, III, 1127; *Letters*, III, 904-905; and Leyda, II, 460. The sentence introducing P1647 in the letter to Colonel Higginson, a sentence repeated from an earlier draft, surely connects the poem with the Paulinian resurrection chapter, ICo 15:51-55.

1648   The immortality she gave

ll.1-4   "The...love": ICo 15:51-55 ("immortality" and "Grave" are echoed directly from these verses as well as "Trumpet" and "Tomb" in the earlier draft introductory sentence to P1648, *Letters*, III, 905)

l.4 "The...love": Ca 8:6 ("for love is strong as death")

Comment: See *Poems*, III, 1128; *Letters*, III, 904-905; and Leyda, II, 460.

1649   A Cap of Lead across the sky

ll.3-4 "We...withdrawn": Mal 4:2; Mt 17:2; Rev 1:16 (the "mighty Face" is that of the sun but also of the hidden Deity, the Deus absconditus)

l.6 "noon": see P776 (as a time of transition, "noon" would be associated with heightened vision and epiphanic awareness)

l.6 "well": see notes, lines one-four and seven-eight and "Comment," P1400 (the "lid of glass" is nature as impenetrable mystery, the thunderstorm bringing an un-Emersonian, hellish chill to the poet)

l.8 "Hell": De 32:22; Job 11:8; Ps 55:15; Isa 14:9, 15; Eze 31:16-17; Mt 8:12; 11:23; 22:13; Jude 13; Rev 1:18; 9:1; 20:1-3 ("Hell" or the pit has associations with bottomless depths, everlasting darkness, and death)

1650   A lane of Yellow led the eye

l.2 "Purple": see note, line one, P15; note, line eight, P703; and note, line three, P716 (the sunset as "low summer of the West" offers a sense of presence "typic" of eternity belied only by "Bird" and "flower")

1651   A Word made Flesh is seldom

l.1 "A...seldom": Joh 1:14 ("And the Word was made flesh"); Joh 6:51-58

l.2 "And...partook": Mt 26:26 ("Take, eat, this is my body"); ICo 10:16-17

l.3 "Nor...reported": Joh 1:6-8; Rev 1:1, 9-11 (the "Word" is reported in the New Testament, the poet drawing an analogy with her own activity in writing P1651 as an religio-aesthetic report of the "Word" incarnate in poetry)

ll.4-8   "But...strength": Mt 26; Joh 6:31-58; Heb 6:4-5; Rev 2:17 (the underpinning language of the "Word" as "food" is Eucharistic)

ll.9-10   "A...die": Ge 1; 2:7 (God, as the Creator of universe and man, cannot according to the poet, discontinue Himself; just as He has breathed the indestructible "Spirit" into man so also does the poet breathe life into words; see P754)

ll.11-12 "Cohesive...He": IJo 5:7 (the Word and Spirit are one; the Word may "die" only if the "Spirit" may "expire," the latter word exposing the illogicality)

l.13   "Made...us": Joh 1:14 ("And the Word was made flesh, and dwelt among us")

ll.14-16 "Could...Philology": Joh 1; Php 2:6-8; Rev 19:13 (that the very "Word of God" by "consent" could condescend to Incarnation is the very "consent" of Being behind her own incarnational poetic; nevertheless, the liquour here tasted is one never brewed for "seldom," "tremblingly," and ecstatically is such "specific strength" taken from "Word made Flesh": her "loved" word love was finally love of the "Word," of the essential "Spirit" beyond the corporeal)

1652   Advance is Life's condition

l.1   "Advance...condition": Ac 20:24; ICo 9:24-26; Php 3:13-14; ITi 6:12; IITi 2:3-5; 4:7 (the ideas of life and death in P1652 are Paulinian—life viewed as "Advance," death not as "terminus" but "Relay")

l.2   "The...Relay": ICo 15:54-55

ll.3-4   "Supposed...so": ICo 15:26 (death as the hated enemy or "terminus")

l.5   "Tunnel": ICo 15:55 (the "Grave" as "Relay," as potential resurrection promise)

l.6   "Existence...wall": ICo 15:21, 26, 54-55 (the "wall" is death, that which separates the circuit world from the new circumference beyond; paradoxically enough, the final three lines of P1652 are a theodicy, her raison d'etre for the circuit world, a capitulation to its created conditions)

ll.7-8   "Is...all": see Tennyson's *In Memoriam* (" 'Tis better to have loved and lost/Than never to have loved at all")

1653   As we pass Houses musing slow-

l.1   "As...slow": see note, line one, P674 and note, line one, P1142 (the KJV considers the habitation of God as "Houses," or tabernacles built with hands, and as individuals, the tabernacle within)

1654   Beauty crowds me till I die

l.2   "Beauty...me": Ps 4:1; 6:2; 9:13; 25:16; 27:7; 30:10; 31:9; 51:1; 86:16 (a frequent expression of the Psalmist—"Have mercy upon me, O Lord"—may here be echoed)
l.4   "in...thee": Ac 4:19; 8:21; 10:31; Ro 3:20; IICo 4:2; Ga 3:11; ITh 1:3; ITi 2:3 ("in the sight of God" is phrasing frequently used; "Beauty" in P1654 is the circuit-world equivalent of God—to experience "Beauty" is to experience God's presence, to see His face, an experience "typic" of the beatific vision, Rev 22:4)
Comment: See *Poems*, III, 1130.

1655   Conferring with myself

l.2   "My...disappeared": Heb 13:2 (see also P1202, lines fifteen-sixteen)

1657   Eden is that old-fashioned House

l.1   "Eden...House": Ge 2:8, 10, 15; 3:23-24; Eze 28:13; 36:35 (the prelapsarian innocence enjoyed by Adam and Eve in Eden is not enjoyed by the "unfurnished eyes" of the circuit world until beyond death when, paradoxically, the very notion of a memory-obsessed circuit world of temporalized consciousness with its suspicion, doubt, and discovery has been rendered unintelligible and unidentifiable by the poet's dwelling in Heaven or the ideal presence of God; is P1657 a Blakean and Emersonian meditation on the failure of the fallen imagination to appreciate the paradise within and without or is it a witty and penetrating consideration of the incoherence of the paradisiacal idea itself when viewed from the circuit world's "every day" of drive and discovery, an incoherence not so much overcome but rendered simply irrelevant by the leisurely, "Unconscious," sauntering insouciance initiated by "the Day"—"Faith" apparently accepting but still "bleat[ing] to understand")

1658   Endanger it, and the Demand

l.6   "Fleet": Job 14:2 (see also Ge 3:19; Ps 103:14; synecdochic of circuit-world mortals whose imaginations fire hope, longing, and desire)

l.8   "Meat": Nu 11:13, 31-32 (the meat given the children of Israel, an example of objects of imaginative yearning; the poet wittily plays here upon the etymology of "Carnival," P1658 suggesting that the collapse of cultural products, imaginative illusions, to "Nature" would be a fundamental loss, the demand for what the poet elsewhere calls "Show" [such as the melodrama of the first two lines] endemic to the circuit world)

1659   Fame is a fickle food

l.10   "Men...die": Ge 2:17 ("But of the tree of knowledge of good and evil, thou shalt not eat of it: for in the day that thou eatest thereof thou shalt surely die")

1660   Glory is that bright tragic thing

ll.1-7   "Glory...oblivion": Isa 14:12-15 (Lucifer as the type of ephemeral glory)

l.3   "Dominion": IPe 4:11; 5:11; Jude 25; Rev 1:6

l.5   "That...Sun": Mal 4:2; Lu 1:78; IIPe 1:19; Rev 2:28; 22:16

1661   Guest am I to have

l.1   "Guest...have": Mt 22:1-14; Rev 3:20

l.2   "Light": Joh 1:4-9 ("Light" triumphs over the darkness of death)

l.7   "My fidelity": Rev 2:10

Comment: P1661 is a preparationist, Bride of Christ poem.

1662   He went by sleep that drowsy route

ll.1-2   "He...Inn": ICo 15:51-55

1663 **His mind of man, a secret makes**

ll.1-2 "His...start": Ro 11:33-34
ll.3-4 "He...part": Job 22:14; Isa 40:22
Comment: "Impregnable to inquest" is the Deus absconditus of P1663.

1664 **I did not reach Thee**

l.1 "I...Thee": Ca 1:3-4, 9, 11; 4:7; 6:1, 13; 7:5, 12-13; 8:1-2, 5 (the beloved sought by the "I" of P1664)
l.13 "Right hand": Ca 2:6; 8:3; Mt 20:21-23; Rev 1:17 (symbolic of the favor of the beloved)
ll.29-30 "We...new": Rev 1:14-15; 7; 19:6, 8; 21:5 (the language and imagery suggests the apocalyptic)
ll.33-34 "Now...Thee": ICo 13:12; Rev 22:4 (these lines express anxiety over the potential unmeaning of the apocalyptic, the failure to see the face of the beloved)
Comment: See *Poems*, III, 1134-1135.

1665 **I know of people in the Grave**

l.7 "My...Earth": IPe 1:2-10 (perhaps P1665 speaks of her sense of election)

1666 **I see thee clearer for the Grave**

l.1 "I...Grave": ICo 15:55 (a death-is-the-mother-of-beauty-and-knowledge poem, P1666 applies the logic of P67 to the notion of death as deprivation)
Comment: See *Poems*, II, 470 and III, 1136.

1667 **I watched her face to see which way**

l.7 "A...fail": Ec 12:5
l.8 "A...Frost": Job 14:2

1668 **If I could tell how glad I was**

ll.1-2 "glad": Ca 1:4; Rev 19:7 (inexpressible joy may suggest ecstasy or vision, IICo 12:4; IPe 1:8)

l.8 "Eternity": Isa 57:15; Rev 1:6; 4:9; 22:5

1669 In snow thou comest

l.1 "In...comest": Ec 6:4

ll.2,6 "shalt go": Job 16:22; 17:16; Ec 5:15-16

l.3 "sweet": Ca 2:3, 14; 5:5, 13, 16

l.4 "And...sound": Ca 2:12 (the sounds of the birds are associated with the advent of the beloved, the glances at Canticles heightening an irony overcome in the assurances of the second stanza)

l.5 "In...comest": Ge 3:16; Job 1:21; 14:1-2; Ec 6:4; 7:1

ll.7-8 "That...thee": Joh 3:5-8; 14:6 (the poet presents herself as the "way" and the "life," as the hope that men may "anew embark to live"—a heterodox and hyperbolical statement of her "Gift" or "letter" to the world, P441; P1706)

1670 In Winter in my Room

ll.1-39 "In...dream": Ge 3:1-7 (P1670 is a recapitulation of the temptation: the serpent—presumptuous, bold, insinuating, "ringed with power," inquisitive, accusatory, and "Secreted" in "Form" and "Pattern"—luring the "eyes" of the "I" out of fear of his pursuit, embodies deception, false metamorphosis, and unideal circumferentiality that the Gnostic in the poet rejects as nightmare)

l.2 "Worm": Job 25:6 (perhaps synecdochic of man in his physicality and finitude)

ll.16, 29-31 "In...him": Ge 3; IICo 11:14; Eph 6:11(the cunning, wily, protean nature of the serpent, his various manifestations here tied together by the "string" of attraction and desire)

l.27 "He...me": Ge 3; Job 1-2; Mt 4 (the preternatural acuteness of the serpent is repeatedly stressed in the KJV)

1671 Judgment is justest

l.1 "Judgment": IICo 5:10; IIPe 2:9; IJo 4:17; Jude 6, 15; Rev 14-20 (the Last Judgment)

1.1   "justest": Joh 5:30; Ac 3:14; 7:52; 22:14 (the wit of the poem involves the poet's insistence that "Judgment" admits of comparative and superlative just as there are safer and safest hues of color in stanza two—all with full awareness that the Just One admits of no degrees)

1.2   "Judged": Rev 20

1.3   "His...away": Ro 2:6; Rev 20:12-13

1.4   "Disk": ICo 13:12; Rev 22:4 (the "Disk" is the face of the "Judged," in P1671 composed of "sincerity" and "Honor"; the poem responds to the apocalyptic question: "But who may abide the day of his coming? and who shall stand when he appeareth?" Joe 2:11; Mal 3:2)

1.7   "posthumous Sun": Rev 21:23-24; 22:5 (the "posthumous Sun" is the giver of "Judgment")

1.8   "Not...endure": Rev 3:5, 18; 7:9; 19:8 (perhaps a reference to Revelation white)

1.9   "That...burn": Rev 1:14; 2:18; 19:12 ("His eyes were as a flame of fire"; the "Judgment" of God is associated with fire and burning, Isa 4:4; Mal 3:2; 4:1; Mt 3:10-12; Rev 17:16; 18:8-9, 18; 19:20; 20:9-15; 21:8)

1672   Lightly stepped a yellow star

ll.1-6   "Lightly...Hall": Ge 1:14-18; Ps 8; 19 (part of the wit of P1672 is its praise of the God of the created lights in the firmament using the vehicle of personification)

1.7   "Father...Heaven": Mt 6:9 (here the poet uses the terms of personal endearment of The Lord's Prayer, raising the question of why the "Father" is not personal rather than "punctual")

1.8   "You...punctual": Ps 90:4 (the anticlimactic view of the Creator God reduced to a philistine railroad conductor may suggest that P1672 is as much critique of vulgar theism as of the meretricious lures of pathetic fallacy)

1673   Nature can do no more

1.1   "Nature...more": ICo 15:19 (with un-Emersonian forthrightness, the poet takes the measure of "Nature")

ll.2-8   "She...opportunity": Ec 1:2-11 (a "Nature" that has run the gamut of her colors, whose only future is a predictably negative reimbursement of "Her crescent," is a "Nature" of repetition without release, an "imposing negative" comparable to that spoken of by Koheleth; see also St. Paul on the "terrestrial," "earthy," and "natural," ICo 15, P1673 an oblique argument for the necessity of a vision transcending mere "flesh and blood")

1674   Not any sunny tone

ll.1-5   "Not...home": Ec 12:3-7 ("human nature's home" is not the grave; this sentiment, as well as the translation of the KJV into her own idiom, suggests these verses of Ecclesiastes—darkness, "musick," "voice of the bird," and "home" appearing in the KJV)

l.4   "grave of Balm": Jer 8:22 (the "Balm" would suggest the understated modesty of nature but also the grave as a restorative; the "Balm" of Gilead was associated with death through embalming and may also be "typic" of Christ, *The* Balm of Gilead); ICo 15:54-55

ll.7-9   "Than...are": ICo 15:54-55 (a pretentious "Tomb," the poet suggests, stands the Biblical promise on its head, sending the message that death is terminus)

1675   Of this is Day composed

ll.1-2   "Of...noon": Ge 1:5, 8, 13, 19, 23, 31 (an adaptation of the refrain from the first chapter of Genesis)

ll.4-6   "And...deprive": Rev 19:7-9; 21-22 (the apocalyptic attracts and repels, the poet left finally in uncertainty about her bridal status)

l.7   "Glory": IITh 2:14; IITi 2:10; Heb 1:3; 2:9-10; Jas 2:1; IPe 1:11; 4:13; Jude 24-25; Rev 1:6; 4:11; 5:12-13; 19:1 (the Bridegroom, His Presence)

ll.7-8   "And...leave": Mt 5:3-12 (the poet is left with the penury and deprivation promised the circuit-world "poor in spirit"— the fasting of those left without the Bridegroom, Lu 5:34-35)

1676   Of Yellow was the outer Sky

l.3   "Till...slid": Ex 26:31 (the "Vermillion" of the "Sky" suggests the vail, P1676 a natural epiphany poem; see also note, line one, P15; note, line eight, P703; and note, line three, P716)

l.4   "Whose...shewn": Joh 19:23

1678   Peril as a Possession

ll.1-7   "Peril...Fire": De 32:35; Job 33:18, 24; Ps 28:1; 30:3; 40:2; Isa 38:18; Rev 20:1-3, 14-15 (perhaps P1678 is a piquancy-of-the-pit poem)

1679   Rather arid delight

l.2   "Contentment accrue": ITi 6:5-7 (the wit of the poem is in its clashing lexicons of "Ecstasy"—"delight," "joy," "Rapture"—and of profit-and-loss—"accrue," "Expense," "unpaid")

l.3   "Ecstasy": see note, line fifteen, P783 and notes, lines five and eight, P1191 ("abstemious" is oxymoronic and inappropriate when applied to the realm of Spirit)

l.5   "Rapture's": see note, line seven, P1468

l.7   "With...knocking": Rev 3:20

l.8   "Rent...unpaid": Ro 3:24; 5:11 (a deliberately outrageous reference to the Atonement, the discordia concors of P1679 intended to expose the ludicrousness of a philistine approach to spiritual matters)

1680   Sometimes with the Heart

ll.1-4   "Sometimes...all": Lu 10:27 ("Thou shalt love the Lord thy God with all thy *heart,* and with all thy *soul*, and with all thy *strength,* and with all thy mind; and thy neighbour as thyself"; see also Mt 22:37; Mr 12:30, the poet having followed the sequence in Luke)

l.3   "Scarcer once/Scarcely one": Ro 5:7-8
Comment: See *Poems*, III, 1142-1143.

1681   Speech is one symptom of Affection

ll.7-8   "Behold...seen": ICo 15:51 (the poet may refer to the Apostle Paul's discussion of the resurrection; Johnson suggests that the poet here refers to the Apostle Peter, IPe 1:8; for other possibilities see Mt 16:16-17; Joh 1:29-34; ICo 2:9; IICo 4:18; ITi 6:16; Heb 11:1)
Comment: See *Poems*, III, 1143.

1682   Summer begins to have the look

l.8   "everlasting hill": Ge 49:26; De 33:15; Hab 3:6

l.13   "All": Ge 2:1-3; Rev 4:11 (created nature, both "Conclusion" and "perennial," is that "enchanting Book" yielding "typic" significations—here that seasonal change reminds of a higher metamorphosis)

l.16   "Recalls...immortality": ICo 15:54-55

1684   The Blunder is in estimate

ll.1-8   "The...Eternity": IICo 4:16-18 (a Paulinian and Emersonian poem on the presence of Heaven while still in the circuit world, an "eternal weight of glory" poem)

1685   The butterfly obtains

l.1   "obtains": ICo 9:24b ("So run, that ye may obtain")

l.12   "For Immortality": ICo 15:54-55 (the butterfly as Hitchcockian emblem of the resurrection)

1686   The event was directly behind Him

l.1   "The...Him": Mt 27 (the obscurity of reference in P1686 makes it difficult to determine whether the crucifixion is intended)

l.2   "Robe": Mt 27:28, 31; Lu 23:11; Joh 19:2, 5

ll.7-8   "And...soul": Lu 23:46 (the reference may be to the triumph of the Resurrection, Mt 28; regardless of KJV provenance, P1686 suggests the illusory nature of act/event engaged in by circuit-world actors whose "loaded gun" precision leads inexorably to the result of the final lines—a nightmarish view of "event" as execution and perhaps also as immolation of the "Flesh")

1688   The Hills erect their Purple Heads

l.1   "Purple": see note, line one, P15

1689   The look of thee, what is it like

l.1   "The...like": Ex 33:20-23; ITi 6:16; IJo 4:12 (the poet asks what God looks like)

l.2   "Hast...Foot": e.g., Ex 3:20; Isa 66:1 (KJV references to "hand" and "Foot" are figurative, the poet's demand for anthropomorphic, anatomical signposts a part of P1689's comedy of identity)

l.3   "Mansion": Joh 14:2 (the suggestion that God's "Identity" may be a matter of His dwelling)

l.5   "realms": Da 4:3; Mt 6:10, 13; Rev 11:15

ll.6-8   "Hast...severe": Ex 20; Rev 20 (the poet has in mind the God of Law and Judgment, although the KJV contains abundant reference to the compassion, delight, and mercy of God)

l.12   "That...same": Ps 90:1-2; Mal 3:6; Jas 1:17 (the KJV at numerous points speaks of the immutability of God; nevertheless, in P1689 the poet has found God indeterminate, her demand for certification of such a final piece of wit)

1690   The ones that disappeared are back

l.3   "Precisely...heard": Ca 2:12 ("the voice of the turtle is heard")

1691 The overtakelessness of those

l.1   "overtakelessness": Am 9:13; ITh 5:4

l.2   "accomplished Death": Lu 9:31; 18:31; Joh 19:28; ICo 15:54-55

ll.3-4   "Majestic...Earth": ICo 15:40, 47

l.5   "soul": Ge 2:7; ICo 15:45

l.5   " 'Home' ": Ec 12:5; IICo 5:6

l.6   "flesh": ICo 15:50 (as with so many poems related to death, P1691's provenance is her favorite resurrection chapter)

1692   The right to perish might be tho't

ll.1-8   "The...scrutiny": Ro 14:7 ("For none of us liveth to himself, and no man dieth to himself")

1693   The Sun retired to a cloud

l.1   "Sun": Nu 24:17; Mal 4:2; IIPe 1:19; Rev 1:16; 2:28; 21:23; 22:5, 16 (for the Sun-Son-Bridegroom see among others notes, lines thirteen-sixteen and fourteen, P611; note, line one, P1122; note, line eight, P1255; note, line two, P1349; note, line two and Comment, P1455; note, line three, P1550; and note, line five, P1660)

l.4   "scarlet": see note, line one, P15

l.5   "forehead": Eze 9:4; 16:12; Rev 9:4; 14:1; 20:4; 22:4

l.7   "purple": see note, line one, P15

1697   They talk as slow as Legends grow

l.5   "Plots of Wit": Ge-Rev (the KJV itself, *the* "Plot" of *the* "Wit")

l.6   "Predestined": Ro 8:29-30; Eph 1:5, 11; IPe 1:2 (the reference to the Biblical idea of predestination conveys wittily the aura of pretentious solemnity)

1699   To do a magnanimous thing

l.6   "Notwithstanding...known": Mt 6:1-4

l.8   "Rapture": see note, line seven, P1468

1700   To tell the Beauty would decrease

ll.3-4   "There...sign": Rev 21:23-24; 22:5 (the light of the New Jerusalem is typified by the "Spell" experienced by the poet, an intimation of immortality)

l.7   "Rapture": see note, line seven, P1468

1701   To their apartment deep

ll.1-4   "To...God": Ca 1:4; Rev 3:20; 19:7-9; 21-22 (this Bride of Christ poem is spiced by the irreverently colloquial "Untumbled" describing God's "abode" and the excluded "ribaldry"— the foregrounded trisyllabics part of the strategy of wit)

Comment: The alterations of Mrs. Bianchi significantly bowdlerized the poem. See *Poems*, III, 1151-1152.

1702   T'was comfort in her Dying Room

l.6   "To...play": Zec 8:5

1704   Unto a broken heart

l.1   "Unto...heart": Lu 4:18
ll.3-4   "Without...too": Mt 17:12; 26-27 (the Passion Christ is the model in the poet's mind)
Comment: See *Poems*, III, 1153.

1706   When we have ceased to care

ll.2-4   "The...Heaven": Ca 8:7 (the "Gift" perhaps a circuit world affection; the experience recounted may be "typic" of that of the apocalyptic: the reward is given when all tears, desire, and hunger have ceased)
l.7   "look upon": Ca 1:6; 6:13

1708   Witchcraft has not a Pedigree

l.1   "Witchcraft": Ex 22:18; De 18:10; ISa 15:23; IIKi 9:22; IICh 33:6; Mic 5:12; Ga 5:20 (KJV associations of witchcraft with sin, rebellion, idolatry, and the rebellious woman are of interest but may be misleading for interpreting P1708; "Witchcraft" is here synecdochic of God's supernatural agency—an agency without "Pedigree"—in creating a living soul in Adam and Eve; "Witchcraft" is also synecdochic of the Paulinian "mystery" of the resurrection, which explains its relevance to "mourners" and deceased)
l.2   "Breath": Ge 2:7
ll.3-4   "And...death": ICo 15:50-55

1709   With sweetness unabated

l.2   "hour...come": Mr 14:41; Joh 12:23; 13:1; 17:1
l.9   "Purple": see note, line one, P15; note, line eight, P703; and note, line three, P716 (a gentle, nature epiphany poem in which heaven reviews the return home of autumn to "Nature" at one of the poet's "typic" transition times)

1710   A curious Cloud surprised the Sky,

ll.1-3   "Sky...sheet": Ps 104:2; Isa 40:22

ll.6,7,9   "statelier," "robes," "majesty": Job 40:10; Isa 22:21; Eze 7:20; 23:41; 26:16; Lu 15:22; 20:46; Joh 19:2; Rev 7:9, 13-14 (KJV language associated with regality)

1711   A face devoid of love or grace,

l.1   "A...grace": Joh 1:14 (the face of P1711 is the obverse of the idealized countenance of God)

1712   A Pit- but Heaven over it-

l.1   "Pit": Nu 16:30; Job 17:16; Rev 9:1-2; 20:1-3 (hades or hell; see also IISa 22:6; Job 26:6-7; Ps 18:5; 116:3; 139:8; Rev 1:18; 20:13-14; P1678; and note, line eight, P1649)

ll.1-2   "Heaven...abroad": Ge 1:1, 8; Rev 3:12; 4:1-2; 6:13-14; 20:1-3 (P1712 marries the "Pit" and "Heaven" with an intimacy suggesting that the "Bomb" held to the bosom is the poet's metaphor for her idea of the holy, the mysterium tremendum, the depth that is *all,* the apocalyptic that cannot be fathomed; for the concluding lines not in the variorum see Franklin, II, 555)

l.5   "To...slip": De 32:35; Ps 35:6; 73:2 (see the related use of "feet" in line eleven)

l.10   "The...thought": Ge 1:2 (the "deep," the abyss, the depth—perhaps the poet's equivalent of Poe's maelstrom)

ll.15-16 "Its...tomb": ICo 15:38-55

l.17   "Doom": Mt 23:14, 33; Mr 3:29; 16:16 (the sentence of damnation, the essence of the "Pit" traditionally, which is here embraced only to be transvalued by the poet—her bold, rhetorical question reinforced by the sound of sense, a "Circuit" in sound)

Comment: See *Poems*, III, 1156.

1716   Death is like the insect

l.1   "Death...insect": ICo 15:26

l.11   "Wring...it": ICo 15:50-55 (see also lines five-six, P1691)

l.12   " 'Tis...will": Job 17:14; 19:26; 21:26; 24:20; Isa 14:11 (traditional KJV associations of the worm with death; it is possible that the Deity's "will" is intended, Ge 3:19)

Comment: See *Poems*, III, 1158.

1717   Did life's penurious length

l.1   "Did...length": Ps 90:10

1718   Drowning is not so pitiful

ll.6-7   "To...company": Ec 9:4, 10
ll.8-10   "For...see": ICo 13:12; Rev 22:4 (the promised, after-death, face-to-face meeting with God)
Comment: See *Poems*, III, 1159 and *Letters*, III, 923.

1719   God is indeed a jealous God

l.1   "God...God": Ex 20:5 ("for I the Lord thy God am a jealous God")
ll.2-4   "He...play": Ex 20:3-4 (apparently friendships broke the first two Commandments; for other references to the jealousy of God see Ex 34:14; De 4:24; 5:9; 6:15)
Comment: See *Poems*, III, 1159-1160.

1720   Had I known that the first was the last

ll.1-3   "first...last," "last...first": Mt 20:16 ("So the last shall be first, and the first last: for many be called, but few chosen")
ll.4-5   "I...Cup": Mt 20:22-23; 26:39-42; Mr 10:38-39; 14:36; Lu 22:42; Joh 18:11 (a witty treatment in hindsight of her commitment to the Beatitudes philosophy of deprivation, Mt 5:3-12)

1721   He was my host- he was my guest,

l.1   "He...guest": Ca 2:4; 3:4; 4:8-16; 5; Rev 3:20 (a Bride of Christ poem)
Comment: See *Poems*, III, 1160.

1722   Her face was in a bed of hair,

ll.1-8   "Her...believes": Ca 4:1-5, 9-15; 5:9-16; 6:4-9; 7:1-9 (the description of the beloved)

Comment: See *Poems*, III, 1161.

1723   High from the earth I heard a bird;

l.17   "untoward transport": see note, line six, P122; note, line fifteen, P783; note, lines five and eight, P1191; and note, line seven, P1468

Comment: See *Poems*, III, 1161-1162.

1724   How dare the robins sing

l.3   "account": Mt 12:36; Ro 14:12; Heb 13:17; IPe 4:5 (here synecdochic of the afterlife)

ll.10-11 "To...immortality": ICo 15:53-54

ll.15-16 "Whose...overcome": ICo 15:35-55 (for St. Paul the resurrection changes the grave into a garden, which mystery is the basis for P1724's concluding metaphor on the transcendence of nature—a nature of robins, sun, and dew)

Comment: See *Poems*, III, 1162-1163.

1725   I took one Draught of Life-

ll.1-4   "I...said": Ca 8:6-7; Mt 16:24-26 (her absolute price paid for the "White Election")

ll.5-6   "weighed," "balanced": Da 5:27

l.5   "Dust": Ge 2:7; 3:19; Ps 103:14

l.8   "A...Heaven": Rev 19:7-9; 21:6; 22:1-2 (her own penury the result of the unintelligible frugality of God, the poet has in mind the contrasting oral munificence of Heaven, given the descriptions of the Marriage Supper of the Lamb and of the New Jerusalem)

1727   If ever the lid gets off my head

l.8   "soul": Ge 2:7; ICo 15:45 (conveying a state of inner disaffection and alienation, one in which the "head" is beleaguered by an unsponsored "brain," P1727 echoes in a different lexicon the situation of the stymied St. Paul, Ro 7:23-25)

1728   Is Immortality a bane

l.1   "Immortality": ICo 15:53-55

l.1   "bane": Ge 4:11 ("And now art thou cursed from the earth"; the Biblical wit of P1728 rests upon the etymology of "bane" in the word for death, bringing to mind the curse of Cain—the poet suggesting that the blessing-bane of "Immortality" creates of man a Cain: "a fugitive and vagabond shalt thou be in the earth," Ge 4:12)

1729   I've got an arrow here.

l.5   "Vanquished...know": Ca 4:9

1730   "Lethe" in my flower,

l.3   "In...orchards": Ge 2; Eze 28:13-14; 31:8-9, 16; 47:1-12; Rev 22:1-5 (a vision of prelapsarian Eden or paradise)

l.6   "As...beholds": Ge 3:5-7; Rev 3:18 (a Blakean and Emersonian recapturing of the pristine "Eye" yields a vision of the ideally circumferential rose)

1731   Love can do all but raise the Dead

l.1   "Love...all": ICo 13:7 ("Love" is housed in "flesh" and is not a "giant"—the latter the Paulinian claim from which P1731 wittily dissents)

l.4   "flesh/Dust": Ge 2:7, 21-24; 3:19; Ps 103:14; ICo 15:50

l.7   "Fleet": Job 14:2 (synecdochic of "Death")
Comment: See *Poems*, III, 1165.

1732   My life closed twice before its close;

l.1   "My...close": Mt 10:39; 16:25-26; Joh 3:3-8; 12:25 (any spiritual experience of renunciation and self-abnegation would here qualify as well as the simpler fact of physical withdrawal and the closing of an upstairs door; separations from lost beloveds experienced as emotional deaths in the circuit world would be possibilities)

l.3   "Immortality": ICo 15:50-55 (the "unveil" suggests St. Paul as well, ICo 13:12) l.3   "unveil": see note, line one, P15; note, line ten, P122; note, line four, P263; note, line twelve, P311; note, line thirteen, P398; note, line fourteen, P756; note, lines five-eight, P915; note, lines seven-eight, P1353; and note, lines one and four, P1412

l.4   "third event": Rev 19:7-9 (marriage to the Lamb as Bride of Christ); Rev 20:14; 21:8 (the "second death"); Rev 21-22 (the enjoyment of the New Jerusalem; a less palatable "third event," although one not ruled out by the poem, is the nihilistic, unmeaning of the apocalyptic)

ll.7-8   "Parting...hell": Mt 7:23; 25:32-33 (Jesus' view of the apocalyptic is as a "Parting" event—an event involving separation, departure, damnations, salvations; "part" is used repeatedly in Revelation, the poet's point that Heaven is a place of division, judgment, loss, and irrevocable separation of which she has had a circuit world foretaste; as in P1712, there is here an unsettling intimacy in the relation of heaven to hell, as if the one is in essence indistinguishable from the other)

Comment: See *Poems*, III, 1166.

1733   No man saw awe, nor to his house

l.1   "No...house": Ex 33:20-23; De 4:12; Joh 1:18; ITi 1:17; 6:16; IJo 4:12, 20 (the unapproachable Deus absconditus)

ll.3-4   "Though...been": Ge 1:26-27 ("human nature" made in the image of God)

l.5   "dread abode": Ge 3 (synecdochic of Adam and Eve who attempt to "flee" after the Fall)

ll.7-8   "A...vitality": Ge 3 (the Fall is described in terms of a "comprehension," verses six-seven, which has its proscription in verse twenty-two, the "Detained vitality" literally the curse of death)

l.9   "Returning...route": Ge 3:24 (the recapturing of the lost Eden, the return into the presence of "awe"; the "Returning" of the "Spirit" to God was spoken of in a favorite section of the KJV, Ec 12:7, but there was no map of this "different route" as there had been of the Fall; all that is left to the circuit world since the proscription of stanza two is the "Spirit" as breath, the "breathing" of the individual the "very physiognomy" of God in its present attenuated, delimited embodiment)

ll.10-11   "The...work": Ge 2:7; ICo 15:45

l.13   " 'Am'...wrote": Ex 3:2 (the language suggests the incident of the burning bush in which God calls Moses to lead His people out of Egypt; see also De 5:25-26; the KJV contains numerous references to God as a consuming fire, Ex 33:3, 5; De 4:24; 9:3; Heb 12:29)

l.14   " 'Yet...face' ": Ex 33:11 (similar phrasing also occurs in the incident at Peniel involving Jacob: "I have seen God face to face, and my life is preserved," Ge 32:30)

Comment: See *Letters*, III, 923,

1734   Oh, honey of an hour,

l.1   "Oh...hour": Ex 3:8, 17; 13:5; De 6:3; 11:9 (associations with the promised land, a romantic image of fulfillment); Ca 4:11; 5:1 (associations with the beloved)

l.5   "unfrequented flower": Ca 2:16; 4:5; 5:13; 7:2 (the reference given by Johnson may be directly relevant here—Isa 35:8)

Comment: See *Letters*, II, 617-618 and Leyda, II, 305-306.

1735   One crown that no one seeks

l.1   "One...seeks": Mt 27:29; Mr 15:17; Joh 19:2, 5 (the crown of thorns worn by Christ at the crucifixion, "typic" for the poet of the ideally circumferential crown of life, Rev 2:10; 3:11; 4:4)

l.5   "Pontius Pilate": Mr 15:1-14; Joh 19:1-5, 14-19 (in Judea, Pontius Pilate was procurator at the time of Christ's crucifixion, acting as judge in the proceedings)

l.7   "That...him": Joh 19:1-5, 14-19 (the Roman soldiers enacted a mock "coronation" of Christ as "King of the Jews," a title Pilate wrote for the cross upon which Christ was executed; the scarlet or purple robe—the accounts differ—placed upon Jesus at this mock "coronation" may connect with the colors of the vail repeatedly used by the poet in epiphany poems, Mt 27:28; Joh 19:2, 5)

Comment: See *Poems*, III, 1167-1168.

1736   Proud of my broken heart, since thou didst break it,

l.4   "passion": Ac 1:3

ll.5-6   "Thou...Nazarene": Mt 26:36-46 ("O my Father, if this cup may not pass away from me, except I drink it, thy will be done," Mt 26:42; "without compassion" refers to those disciples who slept in Gethsemane as Jesus prayed in "anguish"; Jesus of Nazareth was called a "Nazarene," Mt 2:23)

l.7   "pierce," "peerless puncture": Joh 19:34, 37; 20:25 (the "pierce tradition" refers to the wounds received by Christ from the nails and spear)

ll.7-8   "Thou...mine": Mt 27 (the poet has turned her own Passion, her own crucifixion as an imitation of Christ's, into a matter of pride and honor)

Comment: See *Poems*, III, 1168.

1737   Rearrange a "Wife's" affection!

l.3   "freckled Bosom": Jer 13:23 (see P401)

l.5   "Fastness": ICo 15:58; Col 2:5

l.6   "clay": Job 10:9 (synecdochic of mortality, finitude; the poet also wishes to stress "clay" to potter as wife to husband, Isa 45:9; 64:8; Jer 18:6; Ro 9:21)

l.7   "Seven years": Ge 29:18, 20, 27, 30 (seven was here a sign of commitment to fulfill a pledge—Jacob wishing to secure Rachel as his wife; the KJV uses seven repeatedly, its Old Testament etymology connected with "troth" or oath, a sacred "troth" being full or perfect when declared seven times, e.g., Ge 21:22-31)

l.12   "Anguish...anodyne": Mt 6:19-21 (see Sewall, 659)

l.13   "Burden...triumphant": Isa 53:4 (identification with the Christ of the Passion)

ll.14-15 "None...Sunset": Mt 27:29; Mr 15:17; Joh 19:2, 5 (the crown of thorns worn by Christ at the crucifixion)

l.16   "Then...on": Rev 2:10; 4:4, 10

l.19   "Weary Keeper": Ps 121:5

l.20   "Leads...thee": ICo 15:50-55

1739   Some say goodnight- at night-

l.6   "And...dawn": Ca 2:17; 4:6 (the presence of the beloved associated with the dawn; "dawn" is also associated in the poet's mind with the resurrection hope of the elect in that ideal presence beyond the circuit world, Mt 28:1; IIPe 1:19; Rev 19:7-9; 21-22)

l.7   "purple": Ca 3:10; 7:5 (see also, note, line one, P15)

1740 Sweet is the swamp with its secrets,

l.8 "And...goes": Ge 3:13 ("And the woman said, The serpent beguiled me, and I did eat"; the snake is associated with the postlapsarian adult world of swamps, secrets, and guile)

Comment: See *Poems*, III, 1170-1171.

1741 That it will never come again

ll.3-4 "Believing...exhilarate": ICo 13:7, 12; Php 3:13; Heb 11:1, 3; IPe 1:7-9 (the poet has in mind the idea of faith)

ll.5-6 "That...estate": ICo 15:51 (the "mystery" and "change" grasped by faith involves an "estate" removed from that of the circuit world—this asymmetry is the mother of beauty not faith, according to P1741)

1743 The grave my little cottage is,

ll.1-4 "The...tea": Rev 3:20 (P1743 is a Bride of Christ, preparationist poem; for the house-habitation see note, line one, P674 and note, line one, P1142)

l.7 "everlasting life": Joh 3:16, 36; 4:14; 5:24; 6:27, 40, 47; Ro 6:22

ll.7-8 "Till...society": Rev 19:7-9

Comment: See *Poems*, III, 1172.

1744 The joy that has no stem nor core,

ll.1-4 "The...show": IPe 1:8 ("Whom having not seen, ye love; in whom, though now ye see him not, yet believing, ye rejoice with joy unspeakable and full of glory")

l.2 "Nor...sow": ICo 15:37-38

ll.5-6 "By...preferred": ICo 10:3-4; Heb 6:4-5

l.8 "And...pod": ICo 15:44-45 (the "pod" is synecdochic of the "natural body"; the "pod" is "patented" by God with its "seed," Ge 2:7; ICo 15:45)

Comment: Line seven may be the poet's witty dismissal of the Half-way Covenant, ineffectual in matters of mystical "joy."

1746   The most important population

ll.3,7-8 "They...full": Rev 7:9-10; 21:24 (this depiction of the "minor Nation," P1068, enjoying the grace of nature is influenced by the vision by St. John the Divine of the "nations" praising the Lamb)

1748   The reticent volcano keeps

ll.5-6 "If...her": Ex 6:3; Ps 83:18; Isa 12:2; 26:4 ("Jehovah" is a name for God); Ge 1 (God as Creator spoke the world of nature into existence—the "tale" "told to her" indicated by the repetition of "And God said" in the first chapter of Genesis)
l.12 "Immortality": ICo 15:53-54
Comment: See *Poems*, III, 1174-1175.

1749   The waters chased him as he fled,

l.1   "waters": Ge 1:2; 6:17; 7:6
l.3   "billow": Ps 42:7; Jon 2:3
l.4   " 'Come' ": Mt 24:42-43; ITh 5:2; Rev 2:5; 3:3, 11, 20; 22:7, 12, 17, 20
l.5   " 'My...glass' ": Rev 4:6; 15:2; 21:18, 21
ll.6-7   " 'My...Year' ": Rev 7:16-17
l.8   "bliss": Lu 23:43; IICo 12:4; Rev 2:7; 21-22 (Paradise here attracts and repels, the ambiguous conclusion of P1749 suggesting the potential unmeaning of the apocalyptic)

1751   There comes an hour when begging stops,

l.2   "interceding": Ro 8:26; ITi 2:1 (intercession, a KJV word for prayer, suggests the interview here not granted)
l.3   "vain": Mt 6:7 (used with irony; see also Mt 21:22: "And all things whatsoever ye shall ask in prayer, believing, ye shall receive")
l.4   " 'Thou'...sword": Ex 20:1-17 ("Thou shalt not" prefaces the prohibitions of the Ten Commandments; the "Word of God" is spoken of as a two-edged "sword" in Heb 4:12; Rev 19:15)
l.6   " 'Disciple...again' ": Lu 11:1 (the term "disciples" is used in the Lukan version of The Lord's Prayer, followed by verses

encouraging importunity: "For every one that asketh receiveth; and he that seeketh findeth; and to him that knocketh it shall be opened," Lu 11:10—hence the irony of "call again")

1752 This docile one inter

l.7   "House...Death": Job 17:13
Comment: See *Poems*, III, 1176.

1753 Through those old Grounds of memory,

l.7   "statutes": Ex 20:3-17 (the Ten Commandments as a set of proscriptions not touching "longing")
l.14   "gold": see note, line one, P15 ("gold" is associated with the beloved and paradise: Ge 2:11-12; Ca 1:10-11; 3:10; 5:11, 14-15; Eze 16:13; 28:13; Rev 21:18, 21)
ll.15,16 "longing," "withheld": Ps 84:2, 11; 107:9 (P1753 inverts KJV promises dramatizing Moses on Nebo as paradigmatic of the human condition)

1754 To lose thee- sweeter than to gain

l.1   "To...gain": Mt 16:26 (adapted and applied for paradoxical effect; "sweeter" is used for a circuit world beloved, Ca 2:3, 14; 5:5, 13, 16; 7:9)
l.4   "dew": Ex 16:13-14 (synecdochic of providential blessing)
Comment: See *Poems*, III, 1177-1178.

1756 'Twas here my summer paused

ll.1-8 " 'Twas...Bride": Ca 2:8-13; Rev 19:7-9; 21:1-2, 9; 22:17 (the "Tropic Bride" is the profane beloved of summer; the presentation of her fate as Bride of Christ, with its associations of separation, winter, "manacle," and "sentence," is hardly flattering)

1757 Upon the gallows hung a wretch,

l.4   "nature's curtain": Ps 104:2; Isa 40:22
l.7   " 'Twas'...gasped": Lu 21:4

Comment: See *Poems*, III, 1179.

1758   Where every bird is bold to go

l.4   "Must...away": Rev 7:17; 21:4 (the birds and bees already enjoy the condition, lost for humans, of harmony with nature—see Isa 11:6; 65:25)

1760   Elysium is as far as to

l.1   "Elysium": Ge 2-3; Eze 28:13-14; 1:8-9, 16; 47:1-12; Rev 2:7; 21-22 (Paradise or Heaven)
l.8   "The...Door": Rev 3:20 (the poem gives the presence of a "Friend" apocalyptic proportions)
Comment: See Leyda, II, 376.

1762   Were nature mortal lady

ll.1,6   "nature": ICo 15:44-46
l.1   "mortal": ICo 15:53-54
l.4   "The...clime": ICo 15:51-52

1764   The saddest noise, the sweetest noise,

l.1   "sweetest": Ca 2:3, 14; 5:5, 13, 16
ll.2-3   "The...spring": Ca 2:12 (the Canticles echoes suggest ties to earthly beloveds)
ll.5-8   "Between...near": Joh 3:1-8; ICo 15:50-55 (the transition season becomes "typic" of rebirth or resurrection)

1765   That Love is all there is,

ll.1-2   "That...Love": Ca 8:6-7; ICo 13; IJo 4

1766   Those final Creatures,- who they are-

l.2   "faithful...close": Rev 2:10 ("be thou faithful unto death, and I will give thee a crown of life")

1767   Sweet hours perished here;

l.1   "Sweet": Ca 2:3, 14; 5:5, 13, 16; 7:9

1768   Lad of Athens, faithful be

l.3   "Mystery": ICo 15:51 (the two admonitions involve the Socratic "Know Thyself" and the Paulinian "Mystery" of the resurrection and immortality)

Comment: See *Poems*, III, 1183-1184; *Letters*, III, 796-797, 927; and Leyda, II, 338.

1769   The longest day that God appoints

l.1   "The...appoints": Rev 6:17; 16:14 (the "longest day" is the Judgment Day, the "great day of God Almighty"; nevertheless, and indeed a tribute to the poet's wit, the poem works on two levels, the "longest day" also referring to even the harshest diurnal round of circuit world suffering)

l.2   "Will...sun": Rev 21:23; 22:5 (the sun no longer exists in the New Jerusalem, but of course the sunset also marks the end of the day)

Comment: The KJV provenance of P1769 adds to its hyperbole, placing the circuit world troubles of the Norcross cousins sub specie aeternitatis and at the same time mollifying their grief. See *Poems*, III, 1184; *Letters*, III, 459; and Leyda, II, 128-129.

1770   Experiment escorts us last-

l.1   "Experiment": ICo 2:9; 13:12; Heb 11:1 (the poet's wry Lockean, Newtonian substitution for faith)

l.1   "last": ICo 15:52 (synecdochic of death and the mystery of the resurrection)

Comment: In the sentence leading into P1770, the poet quotes Christ's request in Gethsemane that the cup pass from Him (Mt 26:39) and words from the High Priestly Prayer of Christ, which to her "taste [of] interrogation": "Father, I will that they also, whom thou hast given me, be with me where I am; that they may behold my glory, which thou has given me: for thou lovedst me before the foundation of the world" (Joh 17:24). "Experiment" echoes such radical doubt (see

Letters, III, 481). See *Poems*, III, 1184; *Letters*, III, 480-482; and Leyda, II, 157-158.

1771   How fleet- how indiscreet an one-

l.4   "We...serve": Le 19:20 (scourging was a punishment for some sins); Ge 3-Rev 20 (from the expulsion of Adam and Eve from the Garden of Eden to the Last Judgment, God is presented in the KJV as a God of justice and judgment demanding perfect obedience under threat of everlasting punishment; God is here contrasted with that "joyful little Deity," the Roman god of erotic love, Cupid); Ex 20:3-4 (God as the jealous proscriber of idolatry)
Comment: See *Poems*, III, 1185 and *Letters*, III, 695.

1773   The Summer that we did not prize,

l.2   "Her...easy": Mt 6:19-21 (see Sewall, 659-660)
l.3   "Instructs...now": Pr 22:6 (see Sewall, 660)
Comment: See *Poems*, III, 1185-1186.

1775   The earth has many keys.

ll.5,6   "witness": Joh 8:18; Rev 1:5; 3:14 (in an analogous way, the "cricket" testifies to the essence of the circuit world—death)
l.7   "cricket": Ec 12:5

Appendix

Biographical Information on Selected Persons

Samuel Bowles (1826-1878), editor of the *Springfield Republican* in which a number of Dickinson's poems were published, was a frequent correspondent and close family friend.

Edward Dickinson (1803-1874), attorney and Massachusetts politician, was father of the poet and a major figure in the town of Amherst and Amherst College.

Emily Norcross Dickinson (1804-1882) was the invalid mother of the poet.

Lavinia Norcross Dickinson (1833-1899) was the only sister of the poet.

Susan Gilbert Dickinson (1830-1913) was the wife of the poet's brother and a significant correspondent and critic of the work shared with her.

William Austin Dickinson (1829-1895), like his father before him a lawyer and leader in Amherst College and in the town as well, was the poet's brother.

Thomas Wentworth Higginson (1823-1911), minister, literary man, and Civil War hero, was a correspondent with the poet at a formative time.

Edward Hitchcock (1793-1864) was a science professor at Amherst College whose approach to nature influenced the poet.

Josiah Gilbert Holland (1819-1881) and Elizabeth Holland (1823-1896) were two of the poet's closest friends. Josiah Holland was an editor who had studied medicine.

Helen Hunt Jackson (1830-1885), the daughter of an Amherst professor and a famous nineteenth century poet, corresponded with the poet encouraging her to publish.

Otis Phillips Lord (1812-1884), attorney, politician, and Massachusetts Supreme Court Justice, was a close family friend and a beloved intimate of the poet.

Donald Grant Mitchell (1822-1908), whose *Reveries of a Bachelor* (1850) and *Dream Life* (1851) depicted rural New England life, wrote under the pseudonym of Ik Marvel.

Louise Norcross (1842-1919) and Frances Lavinia Norcross (1847-1896) were the poet's cousins with whom she had close ties as indicated by the letters.

Charles Wadsworth (1814-1882) was one of the most prominent ministers of the century with whom the poet corresponded and for whom she apparently had great admiration.

ABOUT THE AUTHOR

Fordyce R. Bennett was born in Batavia, New York. He received his B.A. in English from Olivet Nazarene College and his M.A. and Ph.D. from the University of Illinois at Champaign, Illinois and then for the past twenty years at Mount Vernon Nazarene College, where he is presently Professor of English and Chair of the Division of Communication, Language, and Literature. He has published previously in the *American Transcendental Quarterly, Fitzgerald-Hemingway Annual, Thoreau Society Bulletin, Mark Twain Quarterly*, and *Studies in the American Renaissance*. He is married, with two daughters, and lives in Mount Vernon, Ohio.